Whistle Blowing

Also available:

SOWING THE WIND: *A Report for Ralph Nader's Center for Study of Responsive Law on Food Safety and the Chemical Harvest*, by Harrison Wellford

UNSAFE AT ANY SPEED: *The Designed-in Dangers of the American Automobile* (expanded and updated, 1972), by Ralph Nader

VANISHING AIR: *Ralph Nader's Study Group Report on Air Pollution*, by John C. Esposito

THE WATER LORDS: *Ralph Nader's Study Group Report on Industry and Environmental Crisis in Savannah, Georgia*, by James M. Fallows

WATER WASTELAND: *Ralph Nader's Study Group Report on Water Pollution*, by David Zwick with Marcy Benstock

WHAT TO DO WITH YOUR BAD CAR: *An Action Manual for Lemon Owners*, by Ralph Nader, Lowell Dodge, and Ralf Hotchkiss

THE WORKERS: *Portraits of Nine American Jobholders*, by Kenneth Lasson

WHISTLE BLOWING

*The Report of the Conference
on Professional Responsibility*

*edited by Ralph Nader,
Peter J. Petkas,
and Kate Blackwell*

Grossman Publishers
New York 1972

Publisher's Preface

On January 30, 1971, the Conference on Professional Responsibility, held in Washington, D.C., brought together some of the leading exponents of "whistle blowing"—the act of a man or woman who, believing that the public interest overrides the interest of the organization he serves, publicly "blows the whistle" if the organization is involved in corrupt, illegal, fraudulent, or harmful activity—and some of the individuals who in different circumstances have felt compelled to speak out against the activities of their organizations. The conference was organized by Ralph Nader and his associate Peter Petkas, and sponsored by the Clearinghouse for Professional Responsibility. (The conference program and a list of its participants can be found in Appendix A.) This book is the report of that conference.

The proceedings began with four keynote speeches, which became the first four chapters of this book. Ralph Nader, who delivered the first, has uncovered and exposed abuses of the public interest by business and governmental groups since the publication of *Unsafe at Any Speed* in 1965. His efforts, in automobile safety, meat and poultry inspection, environmental quality, and other areas, have often been aided by whistle blowers, whose information and assistance have sometimes been rendered anonymously, sometimes publicly. It was a General Motors engineer, in fact, who first called his attention to the hazards of the Corvair. In the publication of the reports of study groups he has sponsored, in the creation of student Public Interest Research Groups, and in the establishment of the Clearinghouse for Professional Responsibility, he has both continued and broadened what he calls "full-time citizenship."

Wisconsin's Senator William Proxmire, the second keynote speaker, has served in the Upper Chamber since 1957. He has earned a reputation for speaking his mind to the public and to his colleagues, and is well known as a friend of the ordinary taxpayer and an opponent of those who would squander the public purse for private or parochial gain. He is perhaps best known as the nemesis of the defense establishment; a deeply patriotic man, he has not let the saber rattlers and the flagwavers daunt him in his efforts to curtail unnecessary expenditures and inefficient defense programs. Whistle blowers have made his work more effective, and he hopes to sew protections for them into the fabric of our laws.

Robert Townsend, author of the bestseller *Up the Organization!*, is an inside expert on how corporations operate. He has served as a director of Dun and Bradstreet, as head of investment and international banking for the American Express Company, as president and chief executive officer of an international rent-a-car company that is still number two, and chairman of the executive committee of a magazine and college textbook publishing company. Townsend, fifty-one, is now retired: he says he doesn't want any more money and that there's no job, public or private, that he would accept under any circumstances. Whatever he does, he says, he does for two reasons: first, because he loves the United States and thinks its leaders, public and private, have "gotten it into this mess," from which he would like to help the people extricate themselves; and second, because he enjoys it. Townsend believes that whistle blowing may be the only way left to save the free enterprise system.

Professor Arthur S. Miller of the National Law Center, George Washington University, is a specialist on constitutional law. He has written a number of wide-ranging articles on subjects at the frontier of constitutional development in civil rights and individual liberties and the relationship of individual citizens to various power centers within our society. His 1959 monograph for the Center for the Study of Democratic Institutions, *Private Governments and the Constitution,* was a milestone in advanced thinking on the role of the corporation in our constitutional system. Professor

Miller believes that present law must be changed in a number of areas before whistle blowers will have adequate protection from unfair and arbitrary treatment.

These keynote speakers were followed to the podium by several whistle blowers. In short presentations they described the nature of their actions, the pressures that led them to act, and the retaliation most of them faced; they also suggested, on the basis of their experiences, ethical and tactical guidelines for would-be whistle blowers. Their presentations formed the basis for the second part of this book, which recounts their experiences. Parts III and IV also evolved out of the whistle blowers' suggestions, as well as from the discussions that followed at the conference and from further research into corporate, legal, and government attitudes toward whistle blowing.

Contents

IV. Strategies for Whistle Blowers

I

Keynotes on Whistle Blowing

An Anatomy of Whistle Blowing

Ralph Nader

Americans believe that they have set for themselves and for the rest of the world a high example of individual freedom. That example inevitably refers to the struggle by a minority of aggrieved citizens against the royal tyranny of King George III. Out of the struggle that established this nation some chains were struck off and royal fiats abolished. Americans became a nation with the conviction that arbitrary government action should not restrict the freedom of individuals to follow their own consciences.

Today arbitrary treatment of citizens by powerful institutions has assumed a new form, no less insidious than that which prevailed in an earlier time. The "organization" has emerged and spread its invisible chains. Within the structure of the organization there has taken place an erosion of both human values and the broader value of human beings as the possibility of dissent within the hierarchy has become so restricted that common candor requires uncommon courage. The large organization is lord and manor, and most of its employees have been desensitized much as were medieval peasants who never knew they were serfs. It is true that often the immediate physical deprivations are far fewer, but the price of this fragile shield has been the dulling of the senses and perceptions of new perils and pressures of a far more embracing consequence.

Some of these perils may be glimpsed when it is realized that our society now has the numbing capacity to destroy itself inadvertently by continuing the domestic chemical and biological warfare against its citizens and their environments. Our political economy has also developed an inverted genius that can combine an increase in the gross national product with an increase in the gross national misery. Increasingly, larger organizations—public and private—possess a Medea-like intensity to paralyze conscience, initiative, and proper concern for people outside the organization.

Until recently, all hopes for change in corporate and government behavior have been focused on external pressures on the organization, such as regulation, competition, litigation, and exposure to public opinion. There was little attention given to the simple truth that the adequacy of these external stimuli is very significantly dependent on the internal freedom of those within the organization.

Corporate employees are among the first to know about industrial dumping of mercury or fluoride sludge into waterways, defectively designed automobiles, or undisclosed adverse effects of prescription drugs and pesticides. They are the first to grasp the technical capabilities to prevent existing product or pollution hazards. But they are very often the last to speak out, much less to refuse to be recruited for acts of corporate or governmental negligence or predation. Staying silent in the face of a professional duty has direct impact on the level of consumer and environmental hazards. But this awareness has done little to upset the slavish adherence to "following company orders."

Silence in the face of abuses may also be evaluated in terms of the toll it takes on the individuals who in doing so subvert their own consciences. For example, the twenty-year collusion by the domestic automobile companies against development and marketing of exhaust control systems is a tragedy, among other things, for engineers who, minion-like, programmed the technical artifices of the industry's defiance. Settling the antitrust case brought by the Justice Department against such collusion did nothing to confront the question of subverted engineering integrity.

The key question is, at what point should an employee resolve that allegiance to society (e.g., the public safety) must supersede allegiance to the organization's policies (e.g., the corporate profit), and then act on that resolve by informing outsiders or legal authorities? It is a question that involves basic issues of individual freedom, concentration of power, and information flow to the public. These issues in turn involve daily choices such as the following:

To report or not to report:

1) defective vehicles in the process of being marketed to unsuspecting consumers;

2) vast waste of government funds by private contractors;

3) the industrial dumping of mercury in waterways;

4) the connection between companies and campaign contributions;

5) a pattern of discrimination by age, race, or sex in a labor union or company;

6) mishandling the operation of a workers' pension fund;

7) willful deception in advertising a worthless or harmful product;

8) the sale of putrid or adulterated meats, chemically camouflaged in supermarkets;

9) the use of government power for private, corporate, or industry gain;

10) the knowing nonenforcement of laws being seriously violated, such as pesticide laws;

11) rank corruption in an agency or company;

12) the suppression of serious occupational disease data.

It is clear that hundreds and often thousands of people are privy to such information but choose to remain silent within their organizations. Some are conscience-stricken in so doing and want guidance. Actually, the general responsibility is made clear for the professional by codes of ethics. These codes invariably etch the primary allegiance to the public interest, while the Code of Ethics for United States Government Service does the same: "Put loyalty to the highest moral principles and to country above loyalty to persons, party, or Government department." The difficulty rests in the judgment to be exercised by the individual and its implementation. Any potential whistle blower has to ask and try to answer a number of questions:

1) Is my knowledge of the matter complete and accurate?

2) What are the objectionable practices and what public interests do they harm?

3) How far should I and can I go inside the organization with my concern or objection?

4) Will I be violating any rules by contacting outside parties and, if so, is whistle blowing nevertheless justified?

5) Will I be violating any laws or ethical duties by *not* contacting external parties?

6) Once I have decided to act, what is the best way to blow the whistle—anonymously, overtly, by resignation prior to speaking out, or in some other way?

7) What will be likely responses from various sources—inside and outside the organization—to the whistle blowing action?

8) What is expected to be achieved by whistle-blowing in the particular situation?

In Part IV of this book we have developed a series of possible strategies with these questions in mind and in light of all the experiences presented in the intervening pages. But the decision to act and the answers to all of these questions are unique for every situation and for every individual. Presently, certitudes are the exception.

There is a great need to develop an ethic of whistle blowing which can be practically applied in many contexts, especially within corporate and governmental bureaucracies. For this to occur, people must be permitted to cultivate their own form of allegiance to their fellow citizens and exercise it without having their professional careers or employment opportunities destroyed. This new ethic will develop if employees have the right to due process within their organizations and if they have at least some of the rights—such as the right to speak freely—that now protect them from state power. In the past, as the balance of this book documents, whistle blowing has illuminated dark corners of our society, saved lives, prevented injuries and disease, and stopped corruption, economic waste, and material exploitation. Conversely, the absence of such professional and individual responsibility has perpetuated these conditions. In this context whistle blowing, if carefully defined and protected by law, can become another of those adaptive, self-implementing mechanisms which mark the relative difference between a free society that relies on free institutions and a closed society that depends on authoritarian institutions.

Indeed, the basic status of a citizen in a democracy underscores the themes implicit in a form of professional and individual responsibility that places responsibility to society over that to an illegal or negligent or unjust organizational policy or activity. These themes touch the right of free speech, the right to information, the citizen's right to participate in important public decisions, and the individual's obligation to avoid complicity in harmful, fraudulent, or corrupt activities. Obviously, as in the exercise of constitutional rights, abuses may occur. But this has long been considered an acceptable risk of free speech within very broad limits. Throughout this book, in the stories of whistle blowers and in the chapters advocating reform and spelling out strategies, we set out many of the risks and the necessary limitations on blowing the whistle in the public interest.

Still, the willingness and ability of insiders to blow the whistle is the last line of defense ordinary citizens have against the denial of their rights and the destruction of their interests by secretive and powerful institutions. As organizations penetrate deeper and deeper into the lives of people—from pollution to poverty to income erosion to privacy invasion—more of their rights and interests are adversely affected. This fact of contemporary life has generated an ever greater moral imperative for employees to be reasonably protected in upholding such rights regardless of their employers' policies. The corporation, the labor unions and professional societies to which its employees belong, the government in its capacity as employer, and the law must all change or be changed to make protection of the responsible whistle blower possible.

Each corporation should have a bill of rights for its employees and a system of internal appeals to guarantee these rights. As a condition of employment, workers at every level in the corporate hierarchy should have the right to express their reservations about the company's activities and policies, and their views should be accorded a fair hearing. They should have the right to "go public," and the corporation should expect them to do so when internal channels of communication are exhausted and the problem remains uncorrected.

Unions and professional societies should strengthen their ethical codes—and adopt such codes if they do not already have them. They should put teeth into mechanisms for implementing their codes and require that they be observed not only by members but also by organizations that employ their members. Unions should move beyond the traditional "bread and butter" issues, the societies should escape their preoccupation with abstract professionalism, and both should apply their significant potential power to protecting members who refuse to be automatons. Whistle blowers who belong to labor unions have fared only slightly better than their unorganized counterparts, except when public opinion and the whistle blower's fellow workers are sufficiently aroused. This is partly a result of the bureaucratized cooptation of many labor leaders by management and the suppression of rank and file dissent within the union or local.

Government employees should be treated like public servants if they are to be expected to behave like them. Today, civil service laws and regulations serve two primary functions, each the exact opposite of those intended by Congress. First, they tend to reward or at least shield incompetence and sloth. Second, they discourage creativity and diligence and undermine the professional and individual responsibility of those who serve. You might say that the speed of exit of a public servant is almost directly proportional to his commitment to serve the public. The Civil Service Commission itself is in need of major reform. Its clients are the personnel managers of the various agencies, not the individual employees. Like other regulatory agencies it has been captured by the very group whose conduct it was created to regulate. A new administrative court should be created and invested with all the employee protection functions now given to the commission. Civil servants should be guaranteed the right to bring agency dereliction to public attention as a last resort. And they should have the right to go to court to protect themselves from harassment and discharge for doing their duty. To reduce the high cost of pursuing their lawful remedies, employees who challenge agency action against them should continue to receive their pay until all of their appeals are exhausted, and they should be permitted to recover the costs of their appeals from the government if they ultimately win.

All areas of the law touching upon the employee-employer relationship should be reexamined with an eye to modifying substantially the old rule that an employer can discharge an employee for acts of conscience without regard to the damage done to the employee. Existing laws that regulate industry should be amended to include provisions protecting employees who cooperate with authorities. The concept of trade secrecy is now used by business and government alike to suppress information that the public has a substantial need to know. A sharp distinction must be drawn between individual privacy and corporate secrecy, and the law of trade secrecy is a good place to begin. The Freedom of Information Act, which purports to establish public access to all but the most sensitive information in the hands of the federal government, can become a toothless perversion because civil servants who release information in the spirit of the act are punished while those who suppress it are rewarded.

Whistle blowing is encouraged actively by some laws and government administrators to assist in law enforcement. Under the recently rediscovered Refuse Act of 1899, for example, anyone who reports a polluter is entitled to one-half of any fine collected—even if the person making the report is an employee of the polluting company. And corporations constantly probe government agencies to locate whistle blowers on their behalf. Consumers need routine mechanisms to encourage the increased flow of information that deals with health, safety, environmental hazards, corruption, and waste inside corporate and governmental institutions. Whistle blowing can show the need for such systemic affirmations of the public's right to know.

The Clearinghouse for Professional Responsibility, P. O. Box 486, Washington, D.C. 20044, will assist in the endeavor to establish such mechanisms and will suggest alternative actions to sincere persons considering blowing the whistle. Organization dissenters on matters of important public interest should feel free to contact the Clearinghouse with any information they believe will help citizens protect themselves from the depredations of large organizations.

The rise in public consciousness among the young and among minority groups has generated a sharper concept of duty among many citizens, recalling Alfred North Whitehead's dictum, "Duty arises from our potential control over the course of events." But loyalties do not end at the boundaries of an organization. "Just following orders" was an attitude that the United States military tribunals rejected in judging others after World War II at Nuremberg. And for those who set their behavior by the ethics of the great religions, with their universal golden rule, the right to appeal to a higher authority is the holiest of rights.

The whistle blowing ethic is not new; it simply has to begin flowering responsibly in new fields where its harvests will benefit people as citizens and consumers. Once developed and defended as recommended by the other participants in the Conference on Professional Responsibility and by the final chapters of this book, a most powerful lever for organizational responsibility and accountability will be available. The realistic tendency of such an internal check within General Motors or the Department of the Interior will be to assist traditional external checks to work more effectively in their statutory or market-defined missions in the public interest.

This book presents a detailed excursion through the pathways of courage and anguish that attend the exercise of professional and personal responsibility. We hope by this method to provide a context of case studies from which a broader view of the overall phenomenon of internal dissent within larger organization can develop. The focus is the range of conditions for whistle blowing and the possibilities for understanding and defending whistle blowers. However, the exercise of ethical whistle blowing requires a broader, enabling environment for it to be effective. There must be those who listen and those whose potential or realized power can utilize the information for advancing justice. Thus, as with any democratic institutions, other links are necessary to secure the objective changes beyond the mere exposure of the abuses. The courts, professional and citizen groups, the media, the Congress, and honorable segments throughout our society are part of this enabling environment. They must comprehend that the tyranny of organizations, with their excessive security against accountability, must be prevented from trammeling a fortified conscience within their midst. Organizational power must be insecure to some degree if it is to be more responsible. A greater freedom of individual conviction within the organization can provide the needed deterrent—the creative insecurity which generates a more suitable climate of responsiveness to the public interest and public rights.

2

The Whistle Blower as Civil Servant

William Proxmire

Revolution, as President Nixon has reminded us, is as American as apple pie—and as the State of the Union Address. But how can we tell whether we are having an authentic revolution or a phony one? An invasion is termed an incursion. Air support is labeled interdiction. Military assistance is called "Food for Peace." There are countless ways to corrupt the English language and public policy.

But Mr. Nixon's point is well taken. The people are becoming more and more resentful of the concentration of power and are demanding change. The federal government is increasingly the object of this resentment because political power has historically tended to drift towards Washington. In the past there were good reasons for some of this drift. The Great Depression of the thirties and World War II presented problems that could only be handled by a strong central government. The trend has gone so far, however, that today the central government is, in many ways, the problem.

In 1969 Secretary of the Treasury Joseph Barr predicted a taxpayers' revolt. Barr was not wrong. The taxpayer was fed up with high taxes, with the burdens of war, with an already ominous inflation, and with the fact, Barr revealed, that twenty-two persons with incomes over $1 million each in a single year paid no income tax at all.

Today, the war goes on and appears to be widening; the inflationary spirals are still not under control; and despite the pump-priming effects of a bloated military budget, the nation is faced with a serious recession.

Unemployment is at a nine-year high. And make no mistake: unemployment has not increased because of the "painful transition" towards peace. There has been no transition to a peacetime economy.

The military budget was at a wartime level in 1969, and it is at a wartime level today. Despite strenuous efforts within the Congress, military spending has gone down by only a few billion dollars. In 1969, defense spending was $81 billion. Today it is hovering at about $77 billion, and the President is requesting $80 billion in new obligational authority. By no stretch of the imagination can $80 billion be considered a peacetime military budget. The six percent unemployment problem that we face today is wartime unemployment.

The President has called for a new revolution. I join him. But let's make it meaningful. I call for a peaceful professional revolution against the massive buildup of political and economic power in the executive branch of government, and specifically in the Department of Defense.

By peaceful, I mean nonviolent. Violence is clearly no answer to the critical situation that is before us. We want to render the Pentagon accountable to the Congress and the public for its actions. We want to eliminate waste and inefficiency. We want to slice the fat out of the budget. We want to make it smaller and more manageable. We want a strong defense program. But we want to remove it from areas and activities for which it is not suited and in which it has improperly insinuated itself: civilian surveillance, propaganda, foreign policy–making and international commitments, the purchase of weapons. Violence would be counterproductive.

By professional revolution I mean a reversal of the passive and acquiescent role played by the professional and managerial class of federal officials and private citizens without whom the corruption of the public trust could not be carried out.

Blowing the whistle, or raising a hue and cry, or

living up to the ethical standards that are already embodied in various codes of conduct is part of the antidote to the poisonous abuse of power that is infecting our society.

The bureaucrat, no less than the corporate employee, has to decide whether his primary allegiance is to his country and to his personal integrity or to his employer.

Do we live in a true society in which responsibilities are shared and the general welfare is a common goal, or is it every man for himself and the devil take the hindmost? It is a truism that the professional man— and every citizen, for that matter—has a higher responsibility than his own well-being or the well-being of his employer. But it has become a commonplace, I am sorry to say, for this responsibility to be ignored.

One of the reasons for this is the high risk involved in being ethical. What a tragic commentary it is that the price of being ethical is the loss of one's job, reduction in status, and personal ruin. At the very least, one's career is liable to be nipped in the bud.

Ernie Fitzgerald's case is only one of several that have surfaced in recent years. Innumerable others have occurred. Admiral Rickover, as well as Fitzgerald, has told in congressional testimony of the bureaucratic genius for retaliation against the wayward official who seeks to do his duty. Men are cut off from responsibility, isolated, transferred, demoted, suspended, ordered to take psychiatric tests, and subjected to the inscrutable and devious tactics of the personnel department.

There are laws on the books intended to prevent such abuses of authority. There are civil service regulations and a Civil Service Commission intended to protect the individual employee.

The laws, the regulations, and the Civil Service Commission have proven to be worthless. The reason for this is that rules of proper behavior need to be enforced in order to be effective, and they are not.

And the reason for this is equally clear. The Civil Service Commission and the Justice Department and the Pentagon are all agencies of the executive branch of the federal government. Is it likely for one agency of the executive branch to impartially investigate the wrongdoing of another agency of the executive branch? Apparently not.

The FBI has recently provided a diabolical variation of this theme. Who in the federal government would dare to investigate the excesses of the most powerful investigative bureau of all? Who investigates the investigators? The answer is, no one, if we remain within the confines of the executive branch.

Neither is it possible for the legislative branch to take it upon itself to correct all of the individual irregularities with respect to the treatment of executive employees. There are simply too many. The Congress is already overwhelmed with the task of living up to its own constitutional responsibility for managing the public purse.

The solution, in my judgment, is to seek a remedy outside of the executive or the legislative branches. I believe that every federal employee should have the right to file a civil action in a federal court against the federal government for damages that result from the unjust actions of his former superiors. This legal right of action should extend to those immediate superiors, bureau chiefs, and agency heads responsible for unlawful dismissals or other punitive acts.

I intend to introduce legislation along these lines in the current session of Congress and I welcome suggestions from those present while the language is in the drafting stage.

What I hope to accomplish with this bill is creation of a safety net for federal employees threatened with loss of job without just cause. If an official speaks out against waste or corruption within government he ought not be subjected to the kind of harassment and reprisals that now take place. A man ought not be punished for committing truth before a congressional committee.

My second suggestion is directed at the private sector, and the sponsor of this conference, among others. The rise of the public interest law firm and the consumer advocate over the past several years has been phenomenal. Some of the most constructive and effective criticism of public policy and government programs has emanated from such groups. Environmental pollution, tax policy, business regulation, food and drug controls, among other activities, have not escaped the investigation of the public interest organizations.

However, one area of political activity has remained seemingly immune from scrutiny. This is the area of national defense.

As I indicated earlier, the extravagance of the Pentagon, its uncontrollability, and its virtual sovereignty in military and foreign affairs, is responsible for much of what is wrong with America today.

Two of the men being honored today were formerly in the Department of Defense. But where are the public interest groups and the advocates who would seek to penetrate the mysteries of the Pentagon, to disclose irregularities, to dramatize bad policies, and to reveal the ways in which the public interest is not being served?

The fact that the President is asking for a large increase in defense spending gives no cause for comfort or for relaxing the new vigil over this area of political activity.

Let me cite an example of the hidden and furtive nature of the defense budget and the need to shed more light on it. Military foreign assistance has been limping along at the mere sum of $500 million to $600 million per year, or at least everyone thought it was until recently.

The 1970 federal budget estimated that $545 million would be spent in 1970 and $625 million in 1971. My Subcommittee on Economy in Government investigated the program and came up with these interesting facts:

The federal government has been spending not several hundred million dollars for military assistance, but several billion dollars.

No one really knows the precise amount that we are spending. Estimates range between $3 billion and $4 billion. The Army has actually kept no record of the hundreds of millions of dollars in weapons and ammunition given away to Thailand and South Vietnam. It doesn't know.

Part of the reason for the official ignorance is that the program was fractured into several parts at the outset of the Vietnam War and at various other times. Presently, a number of agencies have responsibilities for military assistance, including the State Department, the Agency for International Development (AID), the Defense Department, the Army, the Navy, the Air Force, and the Department of Agriculture. Most of the money is funneled through the Pentagon, but no one seems to be in charge of all of it.

The Food for Peace Program has been used to generate local currencies in foreign countries for military purposes. It is true that this use of Food for Peace appears to be within the letter of the law; however, it has never been publicly identified as part of military assistance. The public and the Congress were not aware of it. The highest officials in the State Department and the Defense Department were not aware of it until recently. The federal budget document has been positively misleading, referring to it in the most humanistic terms as a program to combat hunger and malnutrition, promote economic growth in developing nations, and develop and expand export markets for United States commodities.

Much of the aid that goes to foreign military establishments is classified. The country-by-country breakdown of recipients is classified. When I asked the Defense Department why this information should be kept secret from the American public, I was told that it would be embarrassing to the nations who receive the aid. The Pentagon feels no shame in hiding from the taxpayer the true costs of foreign military assistance, but the country-by-country breakdown has to be kept a secret because it would be embarrassing to the foreign governments.

The Lockheed situation is another case in point. This giant aerospace firm has filed claims in excess of $1 billion against the Defense Department based on four of its military contracts. The contract prices of the programs involved amount to several billion dollars. The claims are for sums over and above the contract prices. The reason for the claims, simply stated, is that Lockheed is spending far more on the contracts than the government originally agreed to pay. The question is, who picks up the tab for the cost overruns, the contractor who entered into binding commitments with the government, or the taxpayer?

The Deputy Secretary of Defense has recently indicated his preference. Under the proposal recently made public, Lockheed would be let off the hook on all of its contracts and would be paid sums totaling somewhere between $600 million and $1.4 billion. Typically, the Pentagon's public statement on the proposed settlement was too vague for anyone to completely understand.

Lockheed, meanwhile, has rejected part of the government's offer and is now acting as if it wants to go to court. Of course, it is also demanding that the government continue to underwrite the incredible cost overruns it is incurring on the C-5A program until the matter is finally settled.

Naturally, this corporation has the right to demand anything it wants to demand. But is it necessary, is it even legal or proper, for the Pentagon to accede to all of its demands?

The effect of all this is that Congress and the public are being whipsawed between the spineless and corporate-oriented behavior of the Department of Defense and the arrogant and greedy posture of its largest contractor.

The problem of the defense budget, the many programs that are hidden within it, the mismanagement, the waste, the inefficiency, and the excesses that go on under the shibboleth of national security are getting worse, not better. The contract system alone, whereby some $30 billion is spent for weapons each year, badly needs to be overhauled. What kind of a relationship do we have when the government allows and encourages its contractors to evade their contractual responsibility, to overrun the costs, to degrade the technical performance standards, and to delay delivery? The challenges that remain for all of us today are clear.

The fact is that the defense program gets away with budgetary murder each year. And we need more than just courageous individuals like Ernie Fitzgerald, John McGee, and the others who have spoken out to blow the whistle. We need private groups on the outside who will lend their professional expertise to the subject of miltary affairs, who will remain free and independent of ties to the Department of Defense or its contractors, and who will become voices for reform.

3

The Whistle Blower as Entrepreneur

Robert Townsend

When Ralph Nader mentioned the Whistle Blowers Conference to me, something went "click." The time seems right to test America and see what she deserves.

Are you happy with America? Content to see her continue in the direction she's going?

If about one-third of Americans answer "No," then we are about where we were in 1775, when about one-third were pro-British, one-third didn't know, and one-third were somewhere between opposed and violently opposed to the state and trends of the country. But who is the enemy today? Who's causing this winter of our discontent? Russians? Chinese? Domestic Communists? Long-haired kids? Military juggernauts? Lack of leadership?

In my opinion, the enemy is organizations. Big organizations. They accumulate large amounts of money and power, and if they're private corporations they chase narrow antisocial goals in the name of the almighty dollar.

Who are we going to look to, to make these giant organizations honest—to make them stop destroying the quality of all our lives (including theirs and their employees') for their own private interests?

The government? Union Carbide has all the know-how in chemistry, the government practically none; General Motors all the know-how in automobiles, the government just what they're allowed to know. And those government officials that can't be snowed can be bought. The military juggernaut owns John Stennis, body and soul.

The law? Union Camp, Inc., dictated the laws which enabled it to turn the Savannah River into an open sewer.

Corporate leaders? No, but why not? In my judgment, there are two reasons. First, we have a double legal standard in this country. If you—Peter Petkas, citizen—walk across the hall and kill your neighbor, you will probably be severely punished under the criminal law. If you—Peter Petkas, president of the Allison Division of General Motors—release a known defective airplane engine which causes the death of thirty-eight people, you won't be punished at all. Your company may be fined $7500 under the civil code. This they will deduct from taxes as a normal business expense. So corporate murder costs two hundred dollars a head before taxes and a hundred dollars a head after taxes. Standard Oil of California drew a million-dollar fine— the biggest in corporate history. It amounts to what they take in, in revenues, in two hours. If you earned $168 a week, the equivalent for you would be a two-dollar fine. So there's work to be done to eliminate the double legal standard and let the punishment fit the crime.

The second reason we can't expect leadership from our corporate moguls is that at the moment of assuming command we unfit them for the job. What we should do is tell them to take off their coat, go out among their people and their customers, and find out at first hand what the problems and opportunities are. What we do is give them two more secretaries, a private limousine, a private helicopter, a private elevator, a private dining room, a big increase in pay, and outside directorships. The result is that Lee Iacocca is never heard from again by his own people.

America became great in engineering and production because of its entrepreneurs. It was great at taking the calculated risk. Recently we've seen lawyers and accountants become chief executives. These people are trained in the elimination of risks—they know how to play it safe. Anybody who has been there knows that nine times out of ten the safe way is the surest way to oblivion. Example: Here's what a few generations of nonleadership has done to our great steel industry. On January 26, 1971, in an article entitled, "Stumbling Steel," the *Wall Street Journal* reports that the industry is seeking federal help of several kinds, including (and I translate into the language of the spoiled child):

1) tighter restrictions on steel imports ("Mommy, that bully is stronger than I am—hit him");

2) relaxed antitrust attitudes on mergers ("Mommy, the naughty teacher won't let me cheat on my tests—and how can I pass if I can't cheat?");

3) more flexible enforcement of antipollution laws ("But Mommy, I want to break the neighbor's windows—if it's illegal, then change the law");

4) tax breaks ("Mommy, gimme some candy").

Unfortunately, this is typical of leadership in our giant organizations.

This is why we need whistle blowers.

Whistle blowing has a long, distinguished corporate tradition. Most companies today have an internal audit operation, which goes around to the various offices and branches and supposedly blows the whistle on wrongdoing. Most companies have certified public accountants (the financial equivalent of the family doctor) to give them an annual checkup. Unfortunately, both these operations wind up doing little more than counting the petty cash. Nobody audits the decision to build an SST.

Every respectable practice has to have a father figure, and I propose Dwight Eisenhower as the modern father of whistle blowing. In his farewell address he warned us to beware of the "military-industrial complex." In retrospect, we should have paid much more attention. He had been on the inside of the military, he was an intimate of the corporate leaders of his day, and he had seen the military-industrial complex at work from the Oval Office in the White House. If we had only listened.

(Note: I don't regard the military-industrial complex as a sinister conspiracy and I don't want to give that impression. I think if we gave Billy Graham $85 billion a year for a few years and then tried to take it away from him he might destroy America in his efforts to hang onto it.)

When do we blow the whistle, Mr. Townsend? I think the answer to that is easy. Let's go back to some principles on which most Americans can agree: "Thou shalt not kill" (Exodus 20:13). "Thou shalt not steal" (Exodus 20:15). Example: A television or dental x-ray machine is released to the public with dangerous radiation. An automobile or airplane engine is released with a dangerous defect. A union leader blocks a major safety device.

Stealing can be polluting the air or water. Hypothetical case: Union Carbide is polluting the water. State, federal, and local governments start spending money and energy to get them to stop. Union Carbide starts spending large sums of money, first to pretend they're not polluting, and when that fails to stall for time. This is all done by paid liars who are normally called the public relations department. Meanwhile, two years ago one of their own scientists solved this particular pollution problem by inventing a process which turns the waste into a harmless substance. But because it costs a few dollars and didn't produce a profit, he couldn't get anybody's attention. Let him blow the whistle, and we'll make his process available, not only to his own company but to others as well.

Stealing can be Xerox Corporation avoiding the expenditure of five dollars per copy machine on a device which would reduce noise. By this omission it forces each customer to spend hundreds of dollars to isolate the machine.

Stealing can be claiming in advertising something for your product that it doesn't have, or offering services that you know you can't deliver.

If whistle blowing is going to help America, each whistle blower should ask himself "What's in it for me?" before he blows the whistle. And only blow it if you're clean. There is so much injustice and frustration in unions and corporations that the Clearinghouse could be overwhelmed with private grudges.

Also, before you blow the whistle see if your case is as complete as you can make it. Suppose you were King Solomon considering the case: would you be able to verify it, are there the necessary names, dates, and facts to substantiate it? Do you have enough information so that you would be able to render a judgment?

One question which I'm sure has crossed your mind is, "Mr. Townsend, won't this whistle blowing increase costs, reduce profits? And therefore isn't it bad for the free enterprise system?" It seems to me that the answer is clear: whistle blowing may save the free enterprise system—but if our system in fact depends on unpunished lying, stealing, and murder, then who wants to save it?

My twenty years in organizations have given me great faith in individuals and absolutely no faith in large institutions. Because the leaders of large organizations are distracted and corrupted by luxuries and the trappings of corporate success, they have no time to consider fundamental values like honesty, truth, and justice. They have no time to listen to the voices of their own people who know what's right and what's wrong with their products and services. Not knowing what's wrong, the leaders speak to the public only with the forked tongues of their public relations department.

On three totally separate occasions I set out to build honest organizations in which the goals were known, there was no secrecy, and a real effort was made to see that everybody got what they deserved. In each case, the results were electrifying—in human energy, in fun, and in profits. The reason for this is plain— everybody else working for a big organization is so disgusted, frustrated, or bored that he can barely deliver twenty percent of his energy toward the corporate goal if it has any. People from coast to coast are sick of the nauseating phoniness, triviality, and waste of big organizations. Give them a chance to work for a company which fires the paid liars, deals openly, tells the truth—in short, a company they can be proud of—and maybe you've started to save the free enterprise system.

4

Whistle Blowing and the Law

Arthur S. Miller

These remarks emphasize two main themes about whistle blowing:

1) The law at present provides very little protection to the person who would blow the whistle; in fact, it is more likely to assess him with criminal or civil penalties.

2) The law should provide, in its institutions and principles, protection in certain instances.

The first of these is a statement of "what is" and the second of "what ought to be."

Whistle blowing is sometimes actively encouraged by the government. The tax evasion informer, for example, when he snitches on someone, gets a portion of the money recovered. The same applies in customs matters and in at least one congressional statute concerning pollution—the Refuse Act of 1899. Those who turn in polluters supposedly can get monetary rewards—that is, if the statute is ever enforced, which at least until 1969 it had not been.

So, too, with the administration of the criminal law. Those who are caught would be far fewer in number were it not for a systematic use of stool pigeons by the police. The police need the active help of the citizenry if laws are to be enforced: we all remember Kitty Genovese and the three dozen people who heard her cries for help and who did nothing. When government has its interests threatened, it does not hesitate to ask for assistance.

SANCTIONS AGAINST THE WHISTLE BLOWER

It is one thing when government seeks the assistance of citizen against citizen in the enforcement of law; it is quite another when some person within government or within one of the private governments of industry or labor considers that he has a duty higher than to his immediate employer and who, accordingly, says "Hold on, enough" loud and long. (He will have to be heard and his views publicized, as we will note shortly.) When the person within one of the organizations of our hierarchically structured, bureaucratically organized society disapproves some action taken by that organization, he immediately runs the risk of severe adverse sanctions.

And sometimes many people would agree that the whistle blower deserved heavy sanctions. General MacArthur was sacked by President Truman for publicly disagreeing with his Commander in Chief. Otto Otepka got the deep freeze for squealing to a congressional committee. One should not think that all whistle blowing runs in one direction—that of "humane liberalism" or something similar. Quite the contrary. It can reach the depth of the unlamented Senator Joseph McCarthy, who said that he blew the whistle on subversives in the State Department. (He was greatly aided and abetted by the mass media, which swallowed his fantasies whole without bothering to check on them.) Indeed, the whistle blower is not liked. We have invidious terms for him: he is a "fink" or a "stool pigeon," a "squealer" or an "informer," or he "rats" on his employer. The preeminent virtue is loyalty, and the principle is "your organization, love it or leave it."

But there are some—far too few as yet—whose whistle blowing truly reflects both a higher loyalty and the public good—men who, in the words of the code of ethics for federal government employees, believe that "any person in government service should put loyalty to the highest moral principles and to country above loyalty to person, party, or government department." So some lawyers in the Justice Department publicly dissent from the administration's civil rights policies; Ernest Fitzgerald puts his job on the line by drawing attention to cost overruns on the C-5A airplane; Tamplin and Gofman draw the ire of the Atomic Energy Commission for daring to question radiation health standards set by the AEC; and FBI agent Shaw found himself suddenly transferred to Montana for daring to write a letter in partial criticism of J. Edgar Hoover.

PUBLIC GOVERNMENT

The employee of public government who snitches can often expect to be fired, cast into some obscure limbo, or criminally punished. Those who are not protected by civil service regulations — including political appointees and persons whose services are contracted to the government by corporations and consulting firms— are particularly vulnerable. Unfortunately, this category, since it includes many scientists and others with a reputation for independent initiative, covers those most likely to blow the whistle and to do so effectively. Job security for these whistle blowers is not great, as Walter Hickel learned.

If he is wrapped in the security of civil service regulations, he may be less vulnerable, since he cannot be dismissed without cause and without the benefit of minimum procedural rights, in some cases including a full hearing. A full hearing is what those who have the whistle blown on them least want—whether that hearing be a formal, judicial-type hearing or an informal hearing from which may come documents and exhibits subject to public scrutiny. The clever administrator can usually avoid all this by simply abolishing the job of the whistle blower.

In short, government officials, despite civil service rules and regulations, are second-class citizens within their organizations, deprived of a full First Amendment right to speak—a sentiment given classic expression by Oliver Wendell Holmes when he said in 1892, "The petitioner may have a constitutional right to talk politics, but he has no constitutional right to be a policeman." Fortunately, however, there has been some movement away from this position by the courts. The Supreme

Court, for example, held in 1968 that a high-school teacher could not be fired simply because he criticized his school board in a letter to the editor of a local newspaper.

There are other second-class citizens in government. The soldier is one, even one of those poor unfortunates who manage to get drafted in a country which provides ample ways of avoiding the draft. If he wants to speak out or march against the Vietnam "war," he very likely will find himself in trouble with his commanders. The organization exacts a loyalty higher than to one's ideals or to the highest moral principles of the country. How far the military can go in suppressing dissent in the ranks is, however, an unanswered constitutional question—one that is very much in flux, one that could result in the Supreme Court's making a lot of law in the next few years.

PRIVATE GOVERNMENT

Government in this country should be viewed not only from the narrow perspective of the visible institutions of public governance—federal, state, and local —but also from the point of view that social groups (corporations and labor unions, for example) are a part of a web of "invisible" *private* government. This statement appears in a recent issue of *Industry Week*: "Power is taking a corporate form all over the world. That may be the real what's happening of today. Managers in the near future will be inheriting more and more of the traditional acts and roles of politicians. Power is being pushed into corporate hands. . . . Is management ready to lead? Power, problems, planning—the responsibility is clear, that the future is too important to be left to the politicians. It's also too important to be left to the technicians. The future is left up to the corporations, the manager is moving to the world stage center."

"We are at the edge of a new renaissance, a new business age," writes David Secunda, vice president of the American Management Association, "and the corporation is the rolling force. Business corporations will probably influence our lives more than the government will." So we are governed by two sets of government

—one visible and public, one invisible and private—
and industry spokesmen often candidly acknowledge
this. So should Congress and the courts.

Those who toil in the private bureaucracies face
problems at least as severe as those in public bureaucracies. Other than the universities, where academic
freedom prevails and professors are at least as secure
in their jobs as are federal judges in theirs, and possibly
in industries where strong collective bargaining agreements protect the employees, sanctions of being fired,
or being held civilly—or even criminally—liable for
blowing the whistle are possible, even probable. The
technical writer for the B. F. Goodrich Company who
was ordered to falsify a qualification report for the
A-7D aircraft had to resign in order to get the story
told (and the practice stopped). A high executive for
Bethlehem Steel who joined a local civil rights group
found himself summarily fired — not an example of
whistle blowing, to be sure, but illustrative of what can
happen to the poor drones in industry.

An employee owes loyalty to his organization under
the principles of law—contract or personal injury or
agency law. The technical word is that he is in a fiduciary relationship. To breach it, he might be enjoined
by a court or held liable in damages. Furthermore, if
he discloses "trade secrets," he might, under the laws
of some states, be punished criminally. Speaking generally, there is an obligation to keep a confidence if
the person knows it is a confidential matter.

Under federal law, the National Stolen Property Act
makes it a crime to steal anything *tangible* from an employer. This does not apply to intangibles, such as ideas,
but there are bills pending in Congress to make it do
so. Furthermore, it is a federal crime to peddle or sell
information for profit.

That's the picture, and it is a glum one. A secrecy
syndrome affects our public and private bureaucracies,
backed by the law. That veil of secrecy is pierced now
and then by the whistle blowers, either openly or cov-
ertly, and at times by enterprising investigative reporters who are able to sniff out shortcomings and wrong-
doings.

By and large, however, the media and also the professional organizations are essentially establishment-oriented institutions. The press will pounce on the bizarre but tends to leave untouched much that goes on. Vice President Agnew to the contrary, the media, even those located in the northeastern United States, are house organs for the status quo, quite content—with some notable exceptions—blandly and blindly to repeat governmental or industry propaganda or hide the derelictions of our organizational society. Muckraking is at least faintly distasteful. "If you can't say something good about the United States, keep your mouth shut": that is the prevailing principle.

WHAT SHOULD THE LAW BE?

That the law needs changing seems to be self-evident. For those who are willing to put principle above job security, to blow the whistle when the magnitude of the harm and the degree of public danger require it, legal protections are needed.

However, one should be very careful about extending the principle of whistle blowing unduly. Surely it can be carried too far. Surely, too, an employee owes his employer enough loyalty to try to work, first of all, within the organization to attempt to effect change. Only when his way is blocked there, and only when the matter involves something more than mere trivia, should he put the whistle to his lips and blast away. There are no clear boundaries to how one might discern his duty in such instances. Each person must decide for himself, often with little external guidance, when he should say, "Enough is enough."

But the law can give, both in principle and institutionally, some external boundaries. To do so will take a combination of legislative, administrative, and judicial action.

The courts first: Due process could be accorded the employee, not only of public government, but also of private government. Already the Supreme Court has applied the Constitution to private corporations in more than one case: a company town in Alabama; a shopping center; political parties. It would take only a slight extension of present law to make the Constitution's due process principle applicable to the corporations and labor unions. That would mean that an employee would have a constitutional right to be treated fairly.

On a less lofty judicial plane, courts could allow for damage suits for "spite firings," much as the law traditionally has given protection against "spite fences" erected by feuding neighbors.

Neither of these would overly hamper the employer. Only those actions considered reasonable—not motivated by malice or ill will or based on false information—would be protected.

All of that could be done without legislation. Congress could, both for government and for those industries that fall within the expansive definition of interstate commerce, enact a "code of fair dealings" for employees. Indeed, it has already done so in part —in the labor laws that permit the unions to flourish and that protect employees against unfair labor practices, and also in the Civil Rights Act of 1964, which protects one against discrimination because of race, creed, or sex. The protection of the union, for many, will be enough, especially in those industries where union leaders have not crawled into bed with the corporate managers.

What is needed, however, is a legislative prescription for fair dealings—both for those who work for the government and those who work in industry.

Much, too, can be done administratively—by the executive branch and by the agencies who ostensibly regulate industry. As long ago as 1942, the President unilaterally inserted a "nondiscrimination in employment" clause in all federal contracts. That it was not enforced merely shows how far we have to go to make government govern adequately. And the powers of the agencies seem to be broad and flexible enough to allow them to issue rules that would protect the whistle blowers when they should be protected—by, for example, requiring that if an employee tips off the agency about an illegal act by his employer, the employer could not take sanctions against him if the allegations were proved.

All of this is predicated on one assumption: that Congress and the agencies, and indeed the courts, have a real sustained interest in doing something meaningful. The opposite may well be the case—as the several studies by Nader's Raiders indicate and as others have documented. The corporate state, American style, has not yet moved to that degree of protection of human liberty that is so necessary.

Another point needs underscoring: it will do little good for someone to blow the whistle unless he is heard. And he cannot be heard unless someone listens. The way that this can be done is through the communications media, aided by crusading members of Congress. This suggests two causes of action:

1) The Freedom of Information Act, enacted by Congress a few years ago, should be given full enforcement in letter and in spirit. As matters now stand, that act is rather a meaningless charade, the government not acting much differently from the way it did before enactment.

2) Some means of entry, of access, to the media must be established. My colleague Jerome Barron has argued for a constitutional right of access to the media, in order to make the "marketplace of ideas" foundation of the First Amendment truly effective. The law may be moving in that direction, however glacially, but over the strenuous opposition of the media barons.

A response is needed as well. It does no good to be heard or listened to unless there's a meaningful response and consideration is given. We all know the attitude of frontier days in this country: "Let's give the man a fair trial and hang him." You can't give the whistle blower a fair hearing and then say goodbye. The outside citizen should have an expanded way of blowing the whistle, of getting into court, or getting hearings.

A word, in conclusion, about the professional responsibility of the government lawyer. Who is his client? Is it true that, as recently stated in the *American Bar Association Journal,* the person who writes the legal opinions for the Department of Justice is "the president's lawyer?" Is he merely a legal mechanic, confined to grinding out legal justifications for proposed policies? If so, then I suggest that the lawyer in government is no longer a professional—the same may be true for his counterpart in private law firms and also in the house counsel of the corporations—and that we are faced with one of two choices: (a) either make him a true professional, one who sees beyond the immediate interests of his client (surely that is true for the government attorney), or (b) let us all drop the nonsense that the lawyer is a professional and call him a legal lackey. There may be a middle ground there, but not much of one.

There is much room for imaginative work by the bar associations and other organizations of professional lawyers. Why don't the lawyers blow the whistle on biased or incompetent judges? Can we rely on the American Bar Association? We cannot. The ABA Screening Committee had adverse information regarding Judge Carswell and failed to disclose it to the Senate committee. We cannot rely on them.

Let me emphasize that there are important, unresolved problems concerning whistle blowing. But if a society is to be built on the human scale, if we are not all to be immersed forever as nameless and faceless cogs in public and private bureaucracies, then we had better get on with the job, create some law protecting the whistle blower in proper instances, and also give hard, sustained thought to the type of society we want. Whistle blowing helps in pointing out shortcomings, but it is of no help at all in saying what *should* be done. Let our whistle blowers be joined by some hardheaded thinkers and doers, by those who will conceptualize the good society we all want. If the quality of life is to be improved, both are necessary.

II

The Whistle Blowers

Introduction

Who are the whistle blowers? Why do they decide to speak out? How can they be most effective when they do? What can they expect after they take action?

Nine men and women, all prominent whistle blowers in different areas of public concern, posed these questions at the Conference on Professional Responsibility. All emphasized that there is no formula for whistle blowing. The "how" and "when" of speaking out as a critic of a government or corporate employer depend on the issue itself and how it may best be developed, the various sources of support, the available means of getting the message to the public, and the possible repercussions to the individual. Because these nine whistle blowers and two others who came to the forefront after the conference represent a wide range of circumstances, their experiences as they reported them and as documented elsewhere are described in detail in the following chapters.

William Stieglitz resigned because of professional differences with his government employer and then spoke out about what he considered inadequate auto safety standards. Fumio Matsuda left the Japanese auto industry to become a full-time critic and defender of motorists outside the industry. Ralph Stein and his colleague Christopher Pyle took a similar route when they left the Army and went on to make dramatic disclosure of secret military surveillance of civilians. Dr. A. Dale Console resigned his job with a drug company and pondered for two years how he might speak out before he delivered his indictment of the drug industry before a congressional committee.

The most vulnerable whistle blowers are often those who speak out from within their organizations—Edward Gregory at General Motors, Jacqueline Verrett in the Food and Drug Administration, Drs. John Gofman and Arthur Tamplin within the Atomic Energy Commission, Ernest Fitzgerald in the Defense Department, Charles Pettis of Brown and Root, and the workers at the Colt Firearms Division in Hartford, Connecticut. Gregory, Verrett, and the Colt workers have remained with their organizations without serious difficulty. Drs. Gofman and Tamplin, who publicly questioned AEC safety standards, have undergone enormous pressures, budget cuts, isolation, and personal recriminations that may yet result in forcing them out.

These individuals testify to the fact that whistle blowers may emerge in any profession or at any job level. They may be of vastly different temperaments, backgrounds, and skills. Among the conference participants, six were critics of the government agencies for which they worked, three had criticized their corporate employers—as had Pettis and the Colt men, three are scientists, three engineers, two students, and one an auto quality control inspector. Pettis is also an engineer, and the Colt workers are quality inspectors. The whistle blowers range in age from twenty-eight to sixty. Some were more successful than others in accomplishing what they set out to do, and some were better able than others to respond to the frustration and the harassment.

They share, however, to a remarkable degree, a common view of individual responsibility. None was content, when conflict arose, to relinquish his professional standards or his personal self-esteem. They pose a two-fold question: Can such integrity and candor survive and grow in our corporate and governmental hierarchies? And what will happen to the organizations and their purposes if men and women like these are totally suppressed?

5

A. Ernest Fitzgerald

If enough well-intentioned, tough, and skillful people take stands inside the Pentagon, the deterioration of stewardship can be slowed, at least temporarily.
—*Ernest Fitzgerald*

It was late in the morning and the hearings were drawing to a close. A few senators had already slipped from the committee room, though most of the press remained among their tangle of cameras and lights. Senator William Proxmire, chairman of the committee, paused a moment, then said, "I am going to ask something unusual, but I think it will be most helpful. It would save the time of the subcommittee and would perhaps save your time, too, Mr. Secretary and gentlemen. I would like to ask Mr. Fitzgerald to come forward and sit next to Mr. Schedler at the witness stand here."[1]

From somewhere in the back of the room a man left his seat and made his way to the witness table. There, flanked by two assistant secretaries, sat the Secretary of the Air Force, Robert C. Seamans, Jr. In comparison to the handsome, silver-haired Secretary, the man who quietly made a fourth at the table was hardly imposing. He was about five-foot-ten and slightly overweight. Ernie Fitzgerald was in fact a very average-looking man. Nonetheless, he was responsible for the fact that the Secretary of the Air Force had been sitting before a congressional committee since early that morning.

Just two weeks before the hearings, the four men at that witness table were, at least nominally, as the Air Force liked to say, "on the same team." Fitzgerald was

deputy for management systems in the Office of the
Assistant Secretary for Financial Management. His
specialty was cost control. One of the programs he
worked on was the C–5A, the giant cargo plane being
built for the Air Force by the Lockheed Aircraft Corporation. In November, 1968, Fitzgerald appeared
before Senator Proxmire's Joint Economic subcommittee and told them that the C–5A had a $2 billion
cost overrun, a fact revealed by Air Force analysts as
much as two years before but never reported by the
Pentagon. Proxmire's staff suspected the boondoggle;
Fitzgerald's testimony confirmed it. At that point, he
lost his status as a "team player." When the subcommittee convened a year later, the question was no
longer cost overruns but what happened to the man
who disclosed them.

"The Dismissal of A. Ernest Fitzgerald by the Department of Defense," the 216-page report that issued from
the hearings, is something of a classic in the annals of
whistle blowing. Rarely are such instances documented;
almost never so thoroughly. Describing the events that
led to his departure from the Pentagon, Fitzgerald
remarked, "The only thing that makes me unique at all
is that I have not gone away quietly, whereas most of
the others have."[2]

THE WHISTLE BLOWER

When he went to work for the Air Force in 1965,
Ernie Fitzgerald seemed cast from the same mold as
hundreds of other government employees. He was then
thirty-nine years old, was married, had three children
and a laconic drawl that came from Birmingham, Alabama. There was little in his background to indicate he
would not be a complying member of the Air Force
team. His boyhood in Birmingham featured the usual
hallmarks of Americana, the usual sandlot football
games and school days, as his mother told a reporter
later, when Fitzgerald's story was taken up by the
press. Later he acquired the common credentials for
adulthood: service with the Navy during World War II
and a degree in 1951 from the University of Alabama.
He married a classmate and went to work as an indus-

trial engineer for Hayes International, moving later to Kaiser Aluminum. Eventually he became a management consultant, founded his own consulting company, and developed a specialty in cost control. Among his clients were the Air Force and the Navy. "My business was reducing costs," he says, "and like any other consultant I had many difficulties from time to time, was thrown out of a place or two, but in general had good success in reducing costs, and in particular I enjoyed and had some success in reducing costs of weapons systems."[3]

His work was good enough for the Air Force to hire him in 1965 as deputy for management systems in the Office of the Assistant Secretary of the Air Force. He was high in the ranks of Pentagon personnel, a GS–17 classification, a job that drew thirty-one thousand dollars a year. He and his family settled in a comfortable house in a suburb of Washington. There was money, security, and long weekends if he wanted them.

Among the hundreds of people who arrive daily at the sprawling building on the south bank of the Potomac, who make their way from the appropriate parking lot to one of the numberless offices in the great warren, Fitzgerald was perhaps unique in the wall decoration he chose for his office. It was a framed copy of the Code of Ethics for United States Government Service, the code approved by the Eighty-fifth Congress. It begins:

"Any person in Government service should:

"Put loyalty to the highest moral principles and to country above loyalty to persons, party, or Government department." Later the code admonishes: "Expose corruption wherever discovered."

As a wall decoration the code was highly acceptable to the Pentagon, though it is probable that few people noticed it and even fewer considered that the man at the desk beneath it took seriously what it said.

Fitzgerald was a member of an elite group in the Air Force, reporting directly, as one of three deputies, to the Assistant Secretary of the Air Force for Financial Management. The chain of command went directly up to the Secretary of the Air Force and from there to the Secretary of Defense. He was assigned to cost control problems of the largest Air Force weapons systems, including the F–111, Minuteman, SCRAM, and the C–5A. In February, 1966, after six months at the job, he was assigned "Outstanding" performance ratings. Again the following year, in February, 1967, his work was rated "Outstanding."

By that time, he had already discovered overruns in the C–5A program. In January of 1966 he pointed out to his superiors that projected Lockheed overhead increases, if not offset by underruns elsewhere, would result in contract overruns. In late 1966 he reported overruns of one hundred percent and more in key activities in the Lockheed C–5A program. He was also presenting analyses and recommending corrective actions on the Minuteman program. There were as yet no signs that his work was not valued by the Pentagon. In fact, in 1967 Fitzgerald was nominated, though not selected, by the Air Force for two awards. He was one of five employees nominated for the Department of Defense Distinguished Civilian Service Award and one of twenty employees nominated for the Air Force Association's Citation of Honor.

In December of 1967, Fitzgerald wrote a letter to General J. W. O'Neill, commander of the Space and Missile Systems Organization. It was a long ten-page letter about the costs of the Minuteman program and its bluntness was to mortally offend some of the top men on the Air Force team. In criticizing the handling of the Minuteman program, Fitzgerald was in effect criticizing the entire top military establishment for failure to encourage economy in contracts with large corporations.

"In a commercial business situation," Fitzgerald wrote, "similar pressures [to justify more money] are usually countered by a combination of top management restraint and the built-in awareness that excessive costs mean disaster to the business and those dependent on it for livelihood. There are no comparable countervailing pressures in our situation. Indeed, the opposite is true; more costs and, hence, more funds mean increased personal security as long as the increases are tolerated. . . .

"If this situation could be reversed, that is, if managers could be convinced that success in their careers depended at least in part on their ability to achieve difficult cost goals without sacrifice of quality, schedule, or program content, most would view cost reduction and control practices as aids rather than annoyances."

He further pointed out that "in formulating a broad management improvement plan for Minuteman I believe you should consider the problem posed by the mass migration of Air Force officers into the management ranks of contractors with whom they have dealt."

The remark that really struck home, however, was the one noted by Secretary Seamans when he brought the letter before the Proxmire committee. It was Fitzgerald's observation that "I think the Minuteman program has suffered and is suffering from its own credibility gap. Some time back, lying was a way of life in the program. Financial figures were plucked from thin air, and deceptive technical information was presented as a matter of course. I believe this practice has done immeasurable harm to the program. A more serious and lasting effect is the example set for young officers and the damage done to the image of the Air Force.

"The solution to this problem is ultrasimple: Tell the truth, no matter how painful."

The Secretary introduced this paragraph as evidence that Fitzgerald had "hurt his relationship with people in the Air Force by the manner in which he carried out his job."[4]

Seamans responded: "I have yet to meet any responsible person in the military or in the civilian side of the Air Force that I can accuse of lying."[5]

By February, 1968, Fitzgerald's performance ratings had declined to "Satisfactory." In the meantime, he continued to build up a file of correspondence with the Office of the Secretary of Defense concerning procurement policies. On August 27, 1968, he wrote a lengthy letter on acquisition cost control to Colonel Henry M. Fletcher, Jr., director of procurement policy in the Office of the Secretary of Defense. In this letter Fitzgerald complained that economy recommendations from him and other cost analysts were being blocked and that analysts were subject to verbal abuse and other pressures when they persisted in making their recommendations.

"In addition to the Minuteman program," he wrote, "similar situations have arisen on several of our major programs, notably the F–111, including the Mk–1 avionics portion, and the C–5A. Vast cost growth has taken place, and analyses have identified avoidable correctable causes. Proposed corrective actions have been blocked by government management people."

Fitzgerald charged that "opponents of cost control proposals try to ignore the analyses or ridicule the analysts without coming to grips with the facts. . . .

"When consideration of the facts is forced, and the existence of avoidable waste is proven, the opponents make speeches alluding to our commitments to competitive free enterprise, fixed price contracts, and disengagement. They then attack the proponents of improvement measures in earnest. The analysts who prepared the cost figures on which improvement proposals are based receive special attention in these attacks and few survive. Government analysts are transferred, isolated, or motivated to seek other employment. Outside contractor analysts invariably are forced into other lines of work."

By the time Fitzgerald was invited to testify before the Joint Economic Subcommittee in the fall of 1968, the Air Force was well aware of his dissenting views on procurement practices. Exposing these practices to the public was not, he says, a "planned choice": his energies were directed within the organization, where "I still believe that the job can best be done."[6] He did not, however, consider withholding the unclassified information which was available to him and which the committee was seeking.

Up until then, Fitzgerald had been tolerated as a gadfly within the Air Force. But as a witness before a congressional committee, he apparently presented a different sort of threat to his superiors. In the weeks before the hearing, he encountered a number of pressures to prevent or perhaps weaken his testimony.

Before Fitzgerald told anyone about the invitation to testify, Robert C. Moot, the controller of the Department of Defense, called to ask him about the invitation. "I never learned for sure how Mr. Moot came to know about my invitation," he recalled. "I was told later, however, that all mail, even personal mail, with a congressional return address is routinely diverted, opened and read before it is delivered to the addressee."[7]

Fitzgerald relates that "Mr. Moot told me that the Assistant Secretary of Defense for Installations and Logistics was disturbed by the prospect of my testimony. He asked if I would turn the matter over to him, in effect assigning the invitation. I told Mr. Moot that my immediate superior, Mr. Nielsen, was out of town, and I could take no action without consulting him. Later, after it had been decided by the Secretary of Defense and the Air Force, over my objections I might add, that I would appear only as a backup witness, and that I would not prepare a statement, Mr. Nielsen and I met with Mr. Moot to discuss the matter.

"In summary, it appeared that the decision regarding my appearance was predicated on two assumptions. First, that I intended to present testimony which would 'leave blood on the floor.' Second, that Mr. Clifford, then Secretary of Defense, would not agree with my statement. Now there had been no discussion as to what I might say in my statement, so this seemed very strange indeed to me, the assumptions having been made without any discussion of my intent."[8]

Fitzgerald believed there were two reasons for the consternation over his testimony. There was the belief, which he learned later, that Senator Proxmire had seen the file of correspondence between Fitzgerald and the Office of the Secretary of Defense regarding procurement policy. Fitzgerald's contentions that inefficiency in procurement was so widespread as almost to constitute "national policy" might, the Air Force feared, raise annoying inquiries. The more specific fear was generated by the fact that the Joint Economic Committee staff had been looking into the C–5A. As Fitzgerald notes, "There appeared to be a desire at some quarters in the Pentagon to withhold the results of the Air Force analysis which pointed to the huge cost increases on the C–5A."[9] This was, he believes, the principal fear and the one that in fact materialized.

"When I was asked by Senator Proxmire to confirm his estimate of C–5A cost increases, I committed truth."[10]

From then on, Fitzgerald was treated as a pariah in the Air Force. He was immediately taken off major acquisition programs, and placed in unofficial "isolation," where he busied himself with cost problems of bowling alleys in Thailand. He was no longer invited to attend routine management meetings of which he had been a regular member. One of his two assistants was reassigned, and the remaining assistant was ordered not to report to him but to go directly to the military management deputies. The attitude of his colleagues underwent a marked change. "My quarantine from the major programs continued, accompanied by a degree of social ostracism," he told the committee. "Persistent rumors cropped up that I was to be fired."[11]

These rumors were given substance only twelve days after his testimony when Fitzgerald received notice that his career status had been revoked. He had been granted career status, as opposed to his original classification as consultant on a temporary basis, a month prior to the hearings. The first step toward his dismissal involved stripping him of any claims to his job. This tenure claim was removed with the explanation that his career status designation had been a "computer error."

Meanwhile, unknown to Fitzgerald, his superiors were carefully scrutinizing the possible ways for getting rid of him. The possibilities were outlined in a memorandum written on January 6, 1969, to Harold Brown, Secretary of the Air Force, by Brown's administrative assistant, John Lang. This memorandum was shown to Fitzgerald at the time by his superior, perhaps in the hope of encouraging him to resign. But he refused to give him a copy. Later both Fitzgerald and Senator Proxmire received copies of the memo from anonymous sources. Entitled "Background Information Relating to the Fitzgerald Case", the memo discussed three ways in which Fitzgerald might be removed from his job. The first was a simple "adverse action." Fitzgerald would be given notice that he was fired. He would, however, have full rights of appeal under normal administrative proceedings and would retain his job until that process was exhausted. The second method, "reduction in force," involved abolishing the job that Fitzgerald held. Because of his status as a special consultant rather than a member of the civil service, he would have no claim on another position. The memo pointed out that since Fitzgerald "is the only employee in his competitive level grouping and since he did not progress to this position from other lower grade positions, the net result is that he is in competition only with himself. He could neither 'bump' nor displace anyone."

Finally the memorandum noted: "There is a third possibility which could result in Mr. Fitzgerald's departure. This action is not recommended since it is rather underhanded and would probably not be approved by the Civil Service Commission, even though it is legally and procedurally possible. The Air Force could request conversion of this position to the career service, utilizing competitive procedures, and consider all the eligibles from the Executive Inventory and an outside search. Using this competitive procedure, Mr. Fitzgerald might or might not be selected. If not, displacement action would follow."[12]

None of these methods would have to be used, of course, if Fitzgerald left "voluntarily," and on several occasions the wisdom of this course was impressed on him.

On January 8, Fitzgerald was told by his superior, Mr. Thomas H. Nielsen, that as a result of his testimony and the ensuing publicity, "You have lost your usefulness. You work for me and you are not useful to me." Nielsen called him back later to explain that he was not fired and there was no intention to fire him. But a few days later, in a formal performance review, he was told by the same man, Mr. Nielsen, that he had no future in the Air Force. On February 6, he received a copy of a note which stated that Nielsen had requested Fitzgerald's counterparts in the Office of the Secretary of Defense to stop working with him on management systems control problems and to work instead with the

military staff in Air Force headquarters. On March 4,
he talked with Secretary Seamans who told him that
the staff didn't "like" him.

It wasn't until November 4, 1969, that Fitzgerald
received official notice that his old team preferred to
play without him. They had chosen method number
two of the Lang memorandum—"reduction in force"—
and abolished his job. Perhaps the Air Force enjoyed
the irony of dismissing the outspoken advocate of
economy by claiming "economy" reasons. The separation notice explained that the elimination of the position
was "necessitated by a reorganization under the current
Air Force retrenchment program." It noted that "there
is no appropriate available position in which you can
be placed at your present grade level or lower" and
advised him that "if you believe that this proposed
action violates your rights under Air Force reduction-in-
force regulations, you may submit a written request
for review under the appeal and grievance procedures.
. . ." On the same day, the Pentagon issued a press
release announcing that the "present Assistant Secretary,
Mr. Spencer J. Schedler, has been working on reorganiz-
ing plans for several months and with the Secretary's
approval has implemented the new organization of his
office in conjunction with the current reduction actions
in the Air Force."

The Air Force was adamant that the action was not
a "dismissal" or "firing" at all. During the hearings
when the old team was briefly reunited at the witness
table, Chairman Proxmire asked Secretary Seamans
with whom he consulted when he fired Fitzgerald. The
Secretary corrected the Chairman: "I did not decide
to fire Mr. Fitzgerald. I prefer to use the term, the
correct term, 'to abolish his job.' " There was a moment's silence. Then someone in the audience guffawed.
The staff began to laugh, the press laughed, even the
members of the committee laughed. Senator Proxmire
commented later, "In my almost thirteen years in the
Senate, I remember no occasion in which a witness was
so obviously embarrassed by his own statement."[13]

Unfortunately, losing a job is not a laughing matter
for the one who loses it; nor is it always the worst that
happens. More damaging in some respects is what

Fitzgerald calls the "personal denigration" that may be used to bring about a departure or justify a dismissal. "This aspect of my experiences of the last year is most distasteful for me to talk about," he says. "At the same time I think it is important to bring it out, since I have observed . . . that personal attacks and discrediting innuendo are frequently directed against economy advocates in the defense acquisitions business. I am certainly not unique in this regard."[14]

The most serious were accusations that Fitzgerald leaked confidential documents to members of Congress. In the days following Fitzgerald's dismissal, Spencer J. Schedler, Assistant Secretary for Financial Management, frequented the offices of a number of congressmen to explain why Fitzgerald was departing the Pentagon. The gist of his explanation was that Fitzgerald was not a "team player" and that he had violated security regulations.[15] In hearings before the Armed Services Committee on May 7, 1969, Secretary Seamans made the statement: "It is very interesting that in testimony in front of a number of committees, documents kept appearing, some of which are confidential, that were obtained from Mr. Fitzgerald."[16]

When Fitzgerald tried to talk with the Secretary about the charge, he was denied an audience. He was also denied his request to see copies of the confidential documents he was alleged to have leaked. Even for such a damaging charge he found there were no remedies provided within the civil service. Without the backing of Senator Proxmire and Congressman William Moorhead, the charges, though provably false, might have stood unchallenged. However, when Proxmire and Moorhead pressed Secretary Seamans during the hearings, he retracted the charge, or claimed that his statement had been misinterpreted: "I will say categorically now that Mr. Fitzgerald has not to my knowledge violated national security, and if this has been interpreted in this way, I would say that I am very sorry that this has been the case."[17]

Fitzgerald also discovered that during attempts to get rid of him the Air Force had run a special investigation, now filed away in the Pentagon. He had no way of gaining access to this file nor, it appeared, did a congressional committee. When the Proxmire committee asked for the file, Secretary Seamans denied there had been an investigation. Under pressure he finally agreed to hand over a "sanitized" version of the Fitzgerald file, purged of the names of all informants, who were referred to as T–1, T–2 and so on. From this purged version and from his associate who had been questioned during the investigation, Fitzgerald learned that the Air Force had first tried to establish "moral lapses" but had given that up. Then they tried to establish a conflict of interest by seeking information to show that Fitzgerald had retained an interest in his old management consulting firm while working for the Air Force. They did find clear evidence to exonerate him of this charge, but this information was omitted from the file when it was shown to Senator Proxmire and Congressman Moorhead. All that remained were the charges of anonymous "T's," chief among them the evidence that Fitzgerald was a "penny pincher" because he drove an "old Rambler."

There is an ironic footnote to the "special investigation" episode. These secret files are excluded from the provisions of the Freedom of Information Act which provides that information in "investigatory files" is exempt. However, in its efforts to deny that there had been an investigation, the Air Force theoretically lost its claim to an exemption under the act. Its recourse, however, was effective: it simply refused to produce the file.

CONCLUSION

As he points out, Fitzgerald came through his whistle blowing experience with more help than most people can expect. Immediately after his dismissal, he became a consultant to the Joint Economic Committee, a job which still consumes about half of his time. The publicity that surrounded the episode put him in demand as a speaker; in the following year he made some forty-four speeches around the country. But his career has unquestionably been affected. He is trying to build up an industrial management consulting firm like the one he left when he went to work for the Air Force. He is getting some small clients, but the big companies, where his special cost accounting skills would be most useful, aren't coming to him. Although his former firm handled major companies and supported twelve employees, Fitzgerald is now working alone. "It is not unrewarding," he says, "but as a practical matter, until the attitude of business changes, I won't be getting the kind of work I had before."

At the same time, he is challenging his dismissal by the Air Force and trying to establish precedents that might help future critics of government employers. One potential remedy is the federal statute that forbids anyone to intimidate or impede a witness in a federal departmental or congressional inquiry. Senator Proxmire attempted to enforce this statute by calling on the United States Justice Department to investigate the legality of Fitzgerald's dismissal. No investigation has ever been undertaken. "It is true," Fitzgerald points out, "that civil servants and military personnel appear well protected by statutes providing tough penalties for retaliation against government witnesses before congressional committees. But who's going to enforce them? Would John Mitchell put Melvin Laird in jail? Congress itself would help, but those members who have the power to protect witnesses have not been willing to do so when money for big military contractors is threatened."[18]

The second possible remedy is the Civil Service Commission, where Fitzgerald has filed a grievance asking for reinstatement and back pay. He is contending that he was fired for personal reasons, not for the stated reason of a "reduction in force." He filed his appeal immediately after he was dismissed on January 6, 1970. His first hearing before the commission was not held until May 4, 1971. "We have to exhaust all administrative remedies before we can file charges in court," Fitzgerald commented as the proceedings dragged on. "Instead, those 'remedies' are exhausting us."

At the May 4 hearing, the commission refused Fitzgerald's request for open hearings and conducted six days of closed sessions in May and June. Fitzgerald decided to challenge the commission's closed-hearings policy and went to the American Civil Liberties Union for help. Two ACLU attorneys, William L. Sollee and John Bodner, Jr., both of Washington, D.C., filed suit for him in federal district court contesting the commission ruling.

The first court decision came on June 25, 1971, when Judge William Bryant ruled that no further Civil Service Commission hearings could be held in closed session. On August 20, 1971, the Justice Department served notice that it would appeal the district court order, but by October, Justice lawyers had still not filed an actual brief. Charging stalling tactics, Fitzgerald's attorneys went back to district court in October and argued that the Civil Service Commission was ignoring Judge Bryant's order for open hearings. Bryant noted in the hearing that he had assumed his earlier order would assure open sessions. But he agreed to hear government arguments for holding off open sessions. Those arguments were made on October 22 with the government seeking a further postponement until the case was heard by the United States Court of Appeals. Bryant ruled that Fitzgerald would suffer from further delay of the open hearings because witnesses might be lost and memories dulled. However, he agreed to postpone implementing his order until both sides filed formal motions.[19]

In an order received by Fitzgerald's lawyers on November 22, the United States Court of Appeals set aside Judge Bryant's open hearing order until the appeals court could hear the case.[20] No date was set for those hearings.

This means that when the case is finally heard before the Civil Service Commission, key witnesses may be out of reach. The commission does not have the subpoena power to bring back witnesses once they leave the government.

Soon after his dismissal, Fitzgerald sought support from the professional society he has belonged to since he helped form the student chapter at his college, the American Institute of Industrial Engineers. When he asked the institute to investigate the professional and ethical questions involved in his dismissal, the American Institute of Industrial Engineers suddenly decided it was not a "professional" society; it was a "technical"

organization. Thus it absolved itself of dealing with
ethical questions. Fitzgerald was not altogether surprised. He believes that the ability of professional
groups to deal with such questions is undermined by
their practice of allowing "sustaining" or "corporate"
members. Large military contractors are contributing
members of his own society, for example.

Until the remedies for the public whistle blower are
strengthened, conscientious employees may want to
consider alternative avenues of reform, Fitzgerald suggests. "I still believe some good work can be done
internal to the bureaucracies, especially if you are
analytical and keep good notes. If enough well-intentioned, tough, and skillful people take stands inside
the Pentagon, the deterioration of stewardship can be
slowed, at least temporarily.

"Then, of course, you can always become a 'secret
patriot.' Senator Proxmire, Congressman Moorhead, I,
and other military economy advocates frequently receive
unclassified horror stories from outraged military men
and Pentagon civilians who do not wish to be identified.
This is a safe and prudent way to surface information
the public should have anyway. I believe our secret
patriots are making indirect but worthwhile contributions to the education of the taxpaying public. This,
in turn, will have a wholesome cumulative effect."[21]

Fitzgerald has not regretted his own decision to
speak out, though he is not particularly optimistic about
his effect on the military establishment. "I would like
to be able to say that even though the experience was
costly to me my old organization had learned their
lesson, taken the pledge, and had instituted reforms to
improve their stewardship. Unhappily, this is not the
case. The Air Force, and the whole Pentagon for that
matter, are more wasteful, secretive and deceptive than
before. . . .

"One of the points of my testimony which really
infuriated the Pentagon's leaders was the well-supported
charge that contracts with large firms are typically
modified to accommodate the financial needs and technical abilities of the favored giants, and that the Pentagon takes a dive, or throws the game, in negotiations
with big contractors who might be hurt if their con-

tracts were enforced. Now, mostly because of the Lock-heed debacle, this practice is out in the open. But to my knowledge, no Administration official is taking a strict constructionist view of contract law and enforce-ment in this case."[22]

Fitzgerald is now writing a book, tentatively titled *The High Priests of Waste*, in which he hopes to go further in telling the public about the underlying prob-lems of defense procurement policies. The fight is not over, so far as he is concerned. There is, he believes, "still an opportunity to capture benefits from the dis-closures I and many others have made."[23]

6

Dr. John W. Gofman and Dr. Arthur R. Tamplin

Where the future of the human species is at stake, be very sure your voice is loud enough and incisive enough to be heard and heard well. —*John W. Gofman*

Few members of the public had heard the names of John W. Gofman or Arthur R. Tamplin before the fall of 1969. They were two of hundreds of scientists laboring in laboratories and universities across the country, scientists whose names are rarely identified with the technology that their labors help produce. But twice that fall, in October and again in November, the names of Gofman and Tamplin made their way into the press, along with their startling estimates that sixteen thousand more people would contract cancer or leukemia every year if the United States population were exposed to the dose of radiation from nuclear power plants presently allowed by the Atomic Energy Commission. The two scientists expressed serious concern. They said they were sure the Atomic Energy Commission shared their concern and asked the AEC to increase the margin of safety by lowering the permissible radiation dose.

One wire service and a West Coast newspaper picked up their story. Drs. Gofman and Tamplin were, after all, AEC men themselves. Both had worked at the AEC-funded Lawrence Radiation Laboratory at Livermore, California, since 1963. Dr. Gofman was an associate director of the laboratory in charge of the Bio-Medical Research Division. He was an eminent scientist whose research on heart disease in the nineteen-fifties led to major advances in the field and was widely recognized by his peers. Dr. Tamplin was a group leader in the division, heading a project to develop an information system for assessing the effects of low-dose radiation. Their information, or so it seemed to those in the press who were interested, came from a respectable source and was, at least, worth reporting.

Even more importantly, after nearly two decades of research, the country was beginning to move ahead with the actual construction of nuclear power plants. No longer visionary shadows on the horizon, operating nuclear reactors were already—or would shortly be— near neighbors of millions of Americans. It was practically certain that the utilities, on the advice of the federal government, were planning to depend heavily on atomic energy. Already, drawing boards indicated one hundred nuclear power stations in the immediate future and five hundred before the year 2000. It was also becoming clear that the reactors would be located, not in isolated places as once thought, but next door to large population centers.[1]

The public was dimly, somewhat uncomfortably aware of questions of safety, centering around the possibility of accidents and the leakage of radiation into the environment. At the time of the Gofman-Tamplin statement, the public knew much more about the clean, cheap, safe electrical power it could expect from the "friendly atom" and about peaceful "nuclear explosives" for recovery of resources such as gas, oil, and metals. The Atomic Energy Commission had diligently kept the citizens informed about the benefits of atomic energy. Talk about safety, on the other hand, was generally clothed in scientific jargon the man on the street found difficult to understand. So far as the laymen could tell, the scientists seemed to be saying there was no way of answering all of the questions short of putting up the reactors.

Questions of safety were deferred to three organizations that promulgated standards to protect workers and the public from the hazards of radiation: the National Council on Radiation Protection, the International Commission on Radiological Protection, and the Federal Radiation Council. The first two groups were private organizations established in the late twenties, and for the next two or three decades were undisputed authorities for the setting of radiation standards. In 1959, aroused by public fears over fallout from nuclear weapons, the federal government established the Federal Radiation Council as a public authority to set more "official" guidelines. The standards established by these three groups were remarkably similar, as were their membership.[2] Few people raised questions about the standards they authorized, though within professional circles some scientists were alluding to doubts. In early 1969, for example, Dr. Brian MacMahon, a prominent Harvard epidemiologist, was writing in a medical journal: "It must be admitted that we still do not have most of the data that would be required for an informed judgment on the maximum limits of exposure advisable for individuals or populations."[3] This might have troubled the average citizen had he heard the statement, which he did not. It might have made him somewhat doubtful about putting the atom to work for him.

A few people were being more specific. In December, 1968, Professor Barry Commoner was talking most specifically about thyroid cancer. He told a meeting of the American Association for the Advancement of Science that radioactive iodine 131 released from nuclear power plants settled in the thyroid gland of animals and human beings. His studies indicated that human beings were subjected to serious risk. "A biologist cannot be satisfied with the statement that the radioactive pollutants released by a given nuclear power plant meet design specifications and government standards," he said. "He must ask, what radiation is released; how does it move through the web of life; what risks to the integrity of life does it involve; and what are their ultimate costs?"

Commoner pointed to the acknowledgment of the Federal Radiation Council that there is a human cost associated with the acceptance of its guidelines for radiation emissions: that "any radiation exposure involves some risk." "If we develop the industry without a full appreciation of what it really costs us," he warned, "we may find—at some future time when we become aware of the full price—that we are unwilling to pay the bill. If that should happen, the development of nuclear power and the nation's reliance on it will come to be regarded as a tragic and costly mistake."[4]

Dr. Linus Pauling had also warned as early as 1958 that radiation damage to human beings from development of nuclear power and other peaceful uses of atomic energy might be costly. But except for a rare voice like this, few cautionary words were reaching the ear of the public, and even fewer warnings of demonstrable dangers.

It was therefore strange to hear talk about risks, specific risks based on specific data, coming from AEC scientists like Gofman and Tamplin, and the public's attention was aroused. The interested citizen could not help but take notice of figures like sixteen thousand extra cancers and cases of leukemia a year. He could not help but follow the reasoning that safety standards that allowed the risk were perhaps no safety standards at all. He was compelled to wonder whether the Atomic Energy Commission and the eminent scientists cared as much for his safety as for their technology. The data supporting the arguments were, perhaps, beyond his ken; but he became interested to know why those data were wrong, if indeed they were wrong. He had, for perhaps the first time, a figure and a focus: sixteen thousand cancers and the AEC standards. For perhaps the first time, a clear route of action was proposed: tighten the standards. These are some of the points it is important to remember when reviewing the case of Drs. Gofman and Tamplin who, among many critics of the Atomic Eneregy Commission, have raised the biggest storm and in some ways made the strongest comment on what it takes to be an effective whistle blower.

The argument was formally launched on October 29, 1969, in a completely correct setting, a nuclear science symposium of the Institute of Electrical and Electronic Engineers. Speaking by invitation, Drs. Gofman and Tamplin presented a paper that outlined their estimates of sixteen thousand extra cancers and cases of leukemia. A review of the data led them, they said, "to have grave concern over a burgeoning program for the use of nuclear power for electricity and for other purposes, with an *allowable* dose to the population-at-large of 0.17 Rads [units of radiation] of total body exposure to ionizing radiation per year. A valid scientific justification for this 'allowable' dose has never been presented, other than the general indication that the risk to the population so exposed is *believed* to be small compared with the benefits to be derived from the orderly development of atomic energy for peaceful purposes."[5]

One month later, they presented the same estimates to Senator Edmund Muskie's Subcommittee on Air and Water Pollution. On both occasions, they emphasized that they were not opposing peaceful uses of the atom and that they sought to work with the Atomic Energy Commission to devise adequate protective measures to encourage that development. They told the Muskie subcommittee, "We should like to emphasize here and now, lest the words be twisted, that the population has *not* received anywhere near 0.17 Rads per year from atomic energy activities thus far. Nevertheless, the industry is only now getting going and the 0.17 Rads per year *is* on the Federal Statute books as *allowable*."

Citing experts who said the dosage is not now and is not expected to be as high as 0.17 Rads per year, the two scientists urged, "Let us immediately codify this into law so that no one can possibly be confused by a high allowable figure and concomitant statement that we will stay well below that figure. Industry urgently needs a real standard that will hold up over time, since a *later* revision downward can lead to excruciatingly costly retrofits to a developed industrial application. It is far better to lower the guidelines now and do our engineering design accordingly. We believe engineering talent can direct its effort to essentially absolute containment of radioactivity at every step in any useful atomic energy development. If we are fortunate enough later to find that some unknown effect operates to protect against the hazards we have demonstrated here, it will be easy enough to raise the guidelines for radiation exposure *then*. In this way we can avoid irreversible injury to our environment and to a whole generation of humans *while* we find out the true facts."[6]

The two scientists had not come suddenly to their position. At Lawrence Radiation Laboratory they were charged with assessing radiation effects. For a number of years they had been concerned about the lack of hard data to assess those effects while the country moved full steam ahead to make them a reality. In 1964, Dr. Gofman told a Plowshare symposium that "data requisite to provide a groundwork for a reasonable set of radiation standards for man are inadequate." At that time, there was little human data on the effects of low-dose radiation, although animal experiments already indicated that the risk might well be higher than generally assumed. Between 1964 and 1969 more human data became available, provided by the survivors of Hiroshima and Nagasaki, by Britishers treated for a form of spinal arthritis by x-rays, by children in the United States who were irradiated in infancy in the neck as treatment to reduce the thymus and who later developed cancer or leukemia, by tubercular patients radiated by fluoroscopy in the course of treatment, by infants irradiated *in utero* incidental to diagnostic x-ray studies in the mother. Direct human data became available down to extremely low total doses from the work of Stewart and Kneale, who found a doubling of the future incidence of cancer plus leukemia for one-third of a Rad delivered during the first thirteen weeks of pregnancy.[7] Gofman and Tamplin extrapolated from this data in order to estimate the effects of the radiation emissions allowed by the federal radiation standards.

Dr. Gofman was to say later, "Certainly I must admit I shared in the ecologically stupid view that standards for human radiation exposure required *human* data. I am appalled by my earlier failure to understand sound public health principles."[8] Even without the human data, he should have realized this, he says. All that was *known* implied risk; safety lay only in the *unknown*— in the hope that there was a threshold below which radiation did not harm the human body, the hope that exposure to radiation over a long period of time produced less serious results than exposure to the same amount of radiation all at once. The question was whether to count on the possibilities rather than the risks. It was an experiment so large they concluded it was unacceptable. Beyond it, they glimpsed the possibility of inadvertent genocide.

In addition, they now had data that showed approximately what the risk would be if the population were exposed to the allowable dose. Having found that, what were they to do with it?

Dr. Tamplin began to include some of that data in a handbook he was developing for the Atomic Energy Commission. AEC spokesmen were later to repudiate the handbook, but before the issue was public it brought no response from the organization. In fact, their principal adversary in the AEC admitted later he had not even read the handbook before Gofman and Tamplin became controversial.[9] If he had, the Atomic Energy Commission might have been prepared for what was to come.

The event that launched the public debate was precipitated, ironically, by the AEC. In the spring of 1969, the AEC asked Dr. Tamplin to prepare a refutation of Dr. Ernest Sternglass, who had written that fallout radiation had caused four hundred thousand infant and fetal deaths in the United States. A member of the faculty of the medical school of the University of Pittsburgh, Dr. Sternglass published these estimates in the *Bulletin of Atomic Scientists* and later in *Esquire*, where the public had a fair shot at it. The AEC was enraged. They strongly and with some justification believed that Dr. Sternglass was wrong, and they picked Tamplin to clear up the matter. Accordingly, Dr. Tamplin wrote a paper for *Environment* refuting Dr. Sternglass but adding his own estimates that fallout might have caused four thousand infant deaths. This was not quite what the Atomic Energy Commission had in mind. In August, 1969, Dr. Tamplin received a telephone call from Dr. John Totter, head of the AEC Division of Biology and Medicine. Dr. Totter wanted Dr. Tamplin to publish his paper *without* his own estimates of deaths. It was a stormy conversation, followed up by a letter from Dr. Totter that repeated, in presumably more delicate language, what he had requested by telephone. (The letter was later widely circulated by the AEC.) He was careful to point out that "our interest should in no way imply that we are attempting to dictate to you what you can and cannot publish." He went on to say, "We are concerned that when numbers are arrived at, particularly any estimation of mortality risk, the seriousness of the subject makes it vital that the greatest care be used in determining these numbers and in assuring that the test truly reflects the uncertainties inherent in their determination. I think in this we all share a mutual concern for accuracy and wise interpretation of the available facts." He still wanted a refutation of Dr. Sternglass for a "fuller understanding of radiation effects," but wanted it separated from any other estimates of infant deaths. He emphasized that a refutation was "particularly worthwhile since Dr. Sternglass has chosen to conduct his debate in the public media and popular magazines."[10]

Dr. Tamplin refused. He and Dr. Gofman, who was present during the conversation, felt that their estimates of infant deaths were accurate and that it would be misleading *not* to include them in the article. Otherwise, they believed, the impression would be that fallout was not believed to have caused infant deaths or at least that there were no other estimates of such deaths. Their response to the conversation with Dr. Totter, the "infamous telephone call" as they call it, was one of immense indignation. It was the beginning of a confrontation that was to consume more of their time and energy than they could have imagined at that moment. And it was, in many ways, a paradigm of the larger debate to follow. Dr. Totter did not refute Tamplin's estimates; neither did the Atomic Energy Commission succeed in refuting the estimates Gofman and Tamplin presented later. Dr. Roger Batzel, who succeeded Gofman in 1969 as head of the biomedical division at Lawrence Radiation Laboratory, said in an interview tape-recorded for the *Atlantic*: "As far as the scientific information is concerned, we have no, at least, I have no fundamental differences about their scientific conclusions." What Gofman and Tamplin were fighting was a political, not a scientific battle, a profound reluctance on the part of most of the AEC to release any risk statistics, or talk publicly about any risks, however well founded, involved in development of atomic energy.

The following fall they made public their estimates of the cancer and leukemia cases that would be caused if the population were exposed to the allowable dose of radiation under AEC standards. They expected their data to be examined and, if possible, refuted. Demonstrating that sixteen thousand extra deaths *would* occur is different from demonstrating that 2 billion extra dollars *have been* spent. Ernest Fitzgerald could point to facts and figures that were tangible, the nuts and bolts, as it were, of a very real aircraft. Gofman and Tamplin had no bodies to present. They had the data that proved to them what *would* happen and said that it ought to be averted. The Atomic Energy Commission immediately challenged them, not by arguing that the estimates were wrong but arguing that the standard-setting organizations believed the risk was "acceptable" and, further, that the population had not been and would not be exposed to the allowable dose.[11] The issue was taken up by the Joint Committee on Atomic Energy in hearings that ran to three volumes. Drs. Gofman and Tamplin submitted further reports; so did the AEC. Far from retreating from their position, in January, 1970, Gofman and Tamplin said their review of the data now led them to estimate thirty-two thousand extra cancers and cases of leukemia a year and between fifteen thousand and 1.5 million additional deaths from genetically determined diseases. They continued to call for lowering the allowable dose from 0.17 Rads per year to 0.017 Rads per year.

By now the one wire service and lone West Coast newspaper that had reported their first speech were being joined by the major television networks, the major newspapers, radio networks, and magazines. Editors were assigning reporters to long-term analyses of the question of radiation safety, and most of them were quoting Gofman and Tamplin. They were turning up on podiums across the country. A good number were professional meetings like those of the Institute of Electrical and Electronic Engineers, the American Association for the Advancement of Science, the Center for the Study of Democratic Institutions, and the Amer-

ican Cancer Society. They went before Congress with
twenty-one reports for the Joint Committee on Atomic
Energy. They spoke to environmentalists at the Congressional Teach-In in April, 1970, and at the University of Minnesota, and in Oregon. They spoke at
the New York City Council hearings on reactor siting
and before the Santa Cruz board of supervisors. In
attempting to trace their activity, the Atomic Energy
Commission staff found twenty press interviews between
October, 1969, and July, 1970. There were probably
more. In November, 1970, they published a book called
"Population Control" Through Nuclear Pollution (Chicago: Nelson-Hall). The AEC staff also reported that
Lawrence Radiation Laboratory set up a special printing arrangement for the Gofman-Tamplin reports,
reproducing twenty-seven thousand copies of their
twenty-one reports at laboratory expense.

But if the directors of the laboratory were generous in
printing their reports, they were doing other things at
the behest of the AEC officials in Washington that
seemed designed to quietly ease Gofman and Tamplin
out of the AEC. Having launched the public debate in
the committee rooms in Washington and in the press,
Gofman and Tamplin were soon fighting to keep their
jobs on the West Coast. In December, 1969, a month
after the Muskie Subcommittee hearings, Dr. Tamplin
was informed that seven of the scientists in his group
of eleven were being "reassigned." A few months later,
two of the remaining three scientists were also reassigned
to "higher priority work on radioecology."[12] It then
became the laboratory's judgment that, having only one
assistant, Dr. Tamplin no longer required a full-time
secretary. He was left as a leader of a "group" of one.

The "reassignments" were subsequently explained by
AEC officials as a reallocation of resources reflected in
a general budget reduction in the Bio-Medical Research Division. Gofman and Tamplin estimate that, of
Lawrence Radiation Laboratory's budget reduction of
three hundred thousand dollars in 1970, approximately
sixty percent of the total cut was taken from Dr. Tamplin's program. They also claim that the reductions and
reassignments so restricted his work that for all in-
tents and purposes he had no program left.

The laboratory's directors than told Dr. Tamplin they would no longer pay his travel expenses when he was invited to speak on his work. They also proceeded to dock his pay when he was away from the laboratory on speaking engagements, even at such notable forums as a meeting of the American Cancer Society in March, 1970. (This meeting took place on a weekend. Dr. Roger Batzel, head of the bio-medical division, was so zealous that he docked Tamplin's pay for Saturday and Sunday. He later refunded the weekend pay.) The subsequent explanation for these measures was that there is a budgetary difference between a trip to deliver a "scientific" paper and a trip to deliver a "technical" paper, the first being worthy of remuneration and the second, not. Dr. Tamplin's speeches were considered "technical" papers.

The most direct attempt at censorship came when the laboratory directors deleted certain portions—the "opinion" portions—of a paper Dr. Tamplin prepared for delivery before the American Association for the Advancement of Science in December, 1969.

Dr. Gofman's work on the effects of low-dose radiation on chromosomes also received a budget cut, from $320,000 to $270,000 for 1970. At the same time, Dr. Totter, head of the AEC Division of Biology and Medicine, was telling newsmen that Dr. Gofman's work was "worthless." He told a *Chicago Sun-Times* reporter that his staff had been urging him since 1966 to "cut out" Gofman and Tamplin. He did not mention that in 1966 Gofman's chromosome work had hardly begun, almost no laboratory funds had been spent on it, and an assessment could hardly have been made. He told the same reporter that Tamplin's information system was "unreliable."[13]

Gofman and Tamplin protested vigorously both their functional restrictions and what they considered personal attacks on their integrity as professionals by AEC staff members. Only a few weeks after their appearance before the Muskie subcommittee, Dr. Gofman wrote AEC Chairman Glenn T. Seaborg—an old scientific colleague—the first of a series of "Dear Glenn" letters, appealing to the AEC Chairman to stop the "harassment by your staff of our efforts to determine and present the truth concerning the hazards of ionizing radiation for man." In January he contacted AEC Commissioner Theos Thompson to ask for "constructive cooperation" and requested that AEC staff refrain from "name-calling, character assassination," and attacks on his and Dr. Tamplin's "scientific integrity and ability."

In June, 1970, after Tamplin received the second of his staff reductions and after Dr. Totter had disparaged them openly to the press, Gofman and Tamplin decided they would not be "cut out" quietly. Like many other professionals, they had little job security and no channels for challenging any cutback in their projects. They were not civil service employees, but employees of the Univeristy of California, which runs the Lawrence Radiation Laboratory on an independent contract with the AEC. They began to contact people outside the AEC: Senator Edmund Muskie, Senator Mike Gravel, Congressman Chet Holifield, Ralph Nader, and members of the press. On July 6, 1970, Ralph Nader wrote Senator Muskie asking him to look into the Gofman-Tamplin case. Nader said the Atomic Energy Commission was trying to "render them voiceless." At the same time, Thomas O'Toole was reporting to readers of the *Washington Post* that Drs. Gofman and Tamplin feared they were being squeezed out. On July 7, Congressman Holifield, chairman of the Joint Committee on Atomic Energy, issued a press release asking the AEC to prepare "a complete and detailed account of this matter." The same day, the AEC issued a press release denying any persecution. On July 21, the AEC delivered to Congressman Holifield and Senator Muskie its "Staff Report on the Gofman-Tamplin Allegations of Censorship and Reprisal by the AEC and the Lawrence Radiation Laboratory." (The report exonerated the AEC and LRL from "motivations" to silence or get rid of Gofman and Tamplin. Every adverse action was carefully explained as a budgetary consideration or laboratory policy.) On July 29, Drs. Gofman and Tamplin wrote Congressman Holifield and AEC Chairman Seaborg that the report was "a shallow, glib, obviously false effort by AEC staff to whitewash one of the greatest scandals in American science." They asked for public hearings. Predictably, Congressman Holifield, a long-time antagonist of atomic energy safety advocates, has not granted this request.

On August 5, Senator Muskie asked the American Association for the Advancement of Science to conduct an independent investigation. Dr. Seaborg promptly wrote Dr. Gofman that the AEC would do nothing until the AAAS review was completed; until then, the budget cuts would stand. On October 17–18, 1970, the AAAS board met and decided to consider the case at its next meeting in December. In December, the AAAS decided to establish a committee to look into cases of alleged scientific repression. By March, 1971, the members of the committee had not yet been announced and Gofman and Tamplin had received no word about an inquiry.

On March 18, Senator Gravel wrote Dr. Athelstan Spilhaus of the AAAS:

> Three months have passed since the AAAS Board of Directors asked its new Committee on Scientific Freedom and Responsibility to look into the Gofman-Tamplin case. Seven months have passed since Senator Muskie first asked the AAAS for its participation. Nine months have passed since Dr. Gofman was threatened with dismissal from the Lawrence Radiation Lab. More than a year has passed since the Lab made its first moves with regard to Dr. Tamplin, who has been without his research team for nine months. . . .
>
> The purpose of this letter is to ascertain what the AAAS is now doing about the Gofman-Tamplin case, why it is not public, and why the action is taking so long. Delay carries a message of its own. Perhaps Congress should look into the problem.

Dr. William Bevan, executive officer of the AAAS, replied on March 23. He said that the board was still seeking "distinguished citizens" to serve as members of the committee.

"It is the Board's view that the Committee, to be fully effective, must be composed of outstanding persons recognized by both the scientific community and the public at large to be of unimpeachable integrity and impartiality. The persons sought by the Board are without exception persons with a great many commitments already, and recruitment does not proceed as rapidly as all of us would like. However, the process has almost been completed. The charge to the Committee is to prepare general policy in this matter of both alleged abridgments of scientific freedom and failure of scientific responsibility and to recommend procedures for the review of such charges. Several cases await the review of the Committee."

Dr. Bevan added, "It is important, perhaps, to point out that the AAAS has not received from either Dr. Gofman or Dr. Tamplin a request to examine the circumstances of their case."

An AAAS staff member told one of the authors of this book that the association did not plan to investigate the case unless Gofman and Tamplin requested it. The new committee would work only on establishing procedures for handling problems of scientific freedom. By midsummer, 1971, the committee had been appointed but did not plan to meet until the fall.[14] By May, 1972, the committee was still considering procedures to recommend to the AAAS and its affiliated societies to handle such cases.

At this writing, Gofman and Tamplin are still at the lab, but barely. Tamplin is working virtually alone except for the assistance of one scientist, Dr. Donald Geesaman, who agrees with his estimates of cancer and leukemia risk. Dr. Gofman's chromosome project funds finally have been cut out. In the fall of 1969, Dr. Totter, already on record as believing Gofman's work to be "worthless" and that the AEC should stop supporting it, ordered a review of the work. Gofman protested to Dr. Seaborg, saying he did not object to a review but to its being conducted by a man already opposed to his work. The review proceeded. A five-man review committee was appointed, composed of three scientists who were sympathetic to Dr. Gofman and two who were not. The committee performed a mathematical miracle and produced seven opinions: three in favor of continuing his cancer-chromosome work and four opposed. The two "extra" opinions presumably were supplied by the Atomic Energy Commission when it reported the findings of the review committee. Dr. Gofman plans to leave Lawrence in January, 1973, after completing several reports on his work. Meanwhile he is searching for independent fundings.

What has proceeded from the Gofman-Tamplin whistle blowing, surely one of the loudest, more persistent examples of blowing the whistle today? Certainly more people are thinking about nuclear safety than ever before. Proponents of present safety standards have not been able to appease their critics, largely because Gofman and Tamplin simply won't be quiet. In the third of three articles on issues raised by Gofman and Tamplin, *Science* magazine (February, 1971) noted that the "sharp national debate over nuclear safety seems likely to continue despite the National Council on Radiation Protection's efforts to lay the matter to rest." The writer credited "the exchange between Gofman and the NCRP" with serving "to focus attention on the important question of how radiation protection standards are set."[15]

Since Gofman and Tamplin first questioned the standards and the method of setting them, the Atomic Energy Commission has been divested of its sole authority for standard setting. Under a law passed by Congress, the Federal Radiation Council has been abolished and its functions transferred to the Environmental Protection Agency. EPA now sets "generally applicable" standards for radiation exposure of human beings, to be implemented by the AEC. In January, 1970, two months after their initial testimony, the then Secretary of Health, Education, and Welfare Robert Finch ordered a complete review of all radiation standards, the first in a decade. (That review took nearly a year to get off the ground.)

Finally in June, 1971, the AEC proposed stricter radiation standards for nuclear power plants, which spokesmen said would reduce the permissible dose of radiation for the public one hundred times.[16] Under this proposal, radiation dosage would be limited to about one percent of the present permissible dose. The rule-making procedures to implement these standards were getting under way by January, 1972.

More scientists are beginning to speak out against the existing standards and to offer estimates of damage even more serious than those presented by Gofman and Tamplin. NCRP spokesmen still claim that "ninety-five percent of the experts" are in disagreement with the Gofman-Tamplin risk estimates.[17] This may be explained by the fact that most of the experts are members of the National Council on Radiation Protection or the International Commission on Radiological Protection, the groups that are responsible for setting standards. It is still the scientists outside the nuclear organization itself who are most vocal as its critics. Dr. Joshua Lederberg of Stanford University, a Nobel Prize-winning geneticist who calls government "the most dangerous genetic engineer," estimates a ten-percent increase in all genetically related diseases under present standards (compared to a five- to ten-percent increase estimated by Gofman and Tamplin). Lederberg says that average exposure to the "allowable" dose of radiation can ultimately result in an added burden of medical and health care costs due to genetically determined diseases of $10 billion annually.[18]

Dr. Linus Pauling, also a Nobel scientist, estimates ninety-six thousand extra cancers a year under existing standards. He calls for lowering the allowable dose "immediately."[19]

In hearings before the Senate Subcommittee on Air and Water Pollution, August 4, 1970, an AEC health physicist, Dr. Karl Z. Morgan, noted his agreement with the Gofman-Tamplin argument, although he did not talk about specific risk estimates.

"I believe present evidence points to the fact that most, if not all, types and forms of chronic radiation-induced damage relate more or less to the accumulated dose, and there is no justification for one to assume the existence of a threshold below which these forms of damage would not result. This, I believe, has been the principal force of the argument presented by Gofman and Tamplin. To this, I agree and lend my strongest support. In this statement, I might say I am supporting also the expressed positions of ICRP (International Commission on Radiological Protection) and NCRP (National Council on Radiation Protection), as well as the Federal Radiation Council. I hope this is or will be made the expressed opinion of the Atomic Energy Commission."

In fact, members of the standard-setting groups have acknowledged that their standards do include risks. Egan O'Connor, assistant to Senator Mike Gravel and specialist in nuclear energy problems, points out that a committee of the National Academy of Sciences endorsed the presently permissible dose while admitting that the price might be a quarter of a million "defective children" if the parents of the present generation were exposed to it.[20]

Question: Even if the population isn't receiving the permissible dose, why are standards permissible that admit the consequences? AEC Commissioner Theos J. Thompson, in an article entitled "Response to Gofman and Tamplin: The AEC Position," wrote: "For the record, the AEC fully concurs with the standards-setting philosophy that all radiation is potentially dangerous and that radiation should always be kept as low as *practicable*" (emphasis added). Question: who is to decide what is "practicable" and what are the implications for public safety versus technological progress?[21]

For the first time these assumptions are being questioned loudly, publicly, and on a broad scale. What are the risks? What is an "acceptable" risk? What are the benefits? Is any risk "acceptable" when it means a technologically avoidable increase in death, disease, and mutation? Who decides?

A growing number of people are also asking whether new institutions are required to offset the promotional bias of government and industry in the development of new technology. Gofman and Tamplin are among those calling for a system of "adversary assessment" of technology that will represent the public interest.

"What is needed is a group of competent scientists who would criticize any new application of science or expansion of technology. . . . It must seem that we are suggesting an end to technological progress. Quite the contrary, we are only suggesting that technology should no longer be an end unto itself, but it should be the means by which society meets its ends."[22]

There are those who believe that Gofman and Tamplin have also had a negative impact on the nuclear

safety debate. This is true among those who agree with
their risk estimates and give them much of the credit
for recent changes in safety standards. These observers
say that Gofman and Tamplin's zeal, their impassioned
rhetoric and their personal attacks on members of the
AEC establishment have clouded the issues and alien-
ated scientists who agree with their basic propositions.
Even further, some proponents of better nuclear safeguards fear that the two scientists have discouraged
other incipient whistle blowers in the AEC.

Gofman has complained that his critics "only attack
my style, my emotion, my sanity, my loyalty, my
public forums, my motives. Everything except the
issue."[23] Some would reply that Gofman particularly
has invited these attacks and contributed to the highly
charged nature of the debate. As a whistle blower, Gofman is a brash, impatient, outspoken, passionate man.
It is easy to overlook the kernel of his argument and
react only to his style. He tends to sweep away objections, even when they come from people who agree
with him on the basic issues, and to launch broadsides
against the entire nuclear establishment that puts sympathetic colleagues on the defensive.

Gofman and Tamplin have raised almost as many
questions about the role of the whistle blower as about
the safety of nuclear energy. Other scientists may have
been reluctant to criticize AEC policies for fear of
being labeled with such terms as "irresponsible,"
"alarmist," "extremist," and other epithets that have
clung to Gofman and Tamplin.[24] Gofman and Tamplin
have tended to stamp the image of the whistle blower
with their own fervor and an emotionalism highly suspect in the scientific community.

H. J. Dunster, of the United Kingdom Atomic Energy
Association, raised this objection to the Gofman-Tamplin book, *"Population Control" Through Nuclear Pollution*:

"The danger of this book is that it may discourage
us from trying to increase the involvement of science
in society. This increase can and must be achieved.
Fortunately, there is no need to copy the methods used
in this book. Some scientists and others may share the
authors' doubts about the Plowshare programme or

about the feasibility of nuclear warfare, without having to adopt their debating methods or their literary style."[25]

By fighting so vociferously, Gofman and Tamplin may have lost some of their credibility in the scientific community and frightened some who might have followed a less impassioned lead. On the other hand, would they have been successful? Or would another approach have led to oblivion for the whistle blowers—and for the issues they raised?

Gofman and Tamplin were in an extremely vulnerable position: as professionals they had little job protection of any kind. Like a great number of scientists, they were dependent on grant contracts that carried no guarantees and could be dropped at any time.

Further, when they decided to speak they knew they had no significant support within their scientific constituency and certainly none of any size in the AEC bureaucracy. Had they quietly presented their criticism to the AEC and their peers, they would probably have found themselves quietly eased out of their jobs.

Thus there was a functional objective in their impassioned plea to the lay public. Their simple cataclysmic examples and value-laden language cut through scientific and bureaucratic jargon and became a mechanism to reach the mass media and gain political and popular support. Through the media, they reached legislators, environmentalists, and the public. When they could not be discharged from their jobs without publicity, discharge became less likely.

In addition, as their challenge became stronger, the response from their opponents grew proportionately. The more data they presented and the more often they spoke publicly against the AEC safety standards, the harder their opponents tried to silence or discredit them. The only choice was to submit, be quiet and take the consequences, or renew their challenge in ever stronger terms, which in turn brought forth stronger attacks. In light of this challenge-response phenomenon and their lack of any but public support, Gofman and Tamplin's success may be due to the very course they took.

There is no question but that Gofman and Tamplin's championship of the cause of nuclear safety has helped

to improve safeguards for the public. They are instructive whistle blowers, both with regard to the vulnerability of the professional who speaks out and the
requirements for being heard. Others might have acted
differently in the same role. But Gofman and Tamplin
followed their own view of the public critic: "Where
the future of the human species is at stake, be very sure
your voice is loud enough and incisive enough to be
heard and heard well."[26]

7

Edward Gregory

I'd catch the brass when they came through the plant and tell them about it.   *—Edward Gregory*

In 1969, General Motors announced what was up to that time the largest automobile recall in history. Involved were 2.4 million Chevrolets recalled to repair faulty exhaust systems that allowed carbon monoxide to enter the passenger compartments. Behind the unprecedented recall, which is said to have cost over $100 million, was a safety inspector who had been warning General Motors for three years that the defect existed. When the company persisted in ignoring his reports, the inspector informed outside critics of the auto industry. His information played a major role in the eventual call-back of Chevrolets from the 1965 to the 1969 models.

The interesting part of the story is that Edward Gregory is still inspecting automobiles for General Motors and still blowing the whistle when he has to. The latter is inevitable, one concludes after meeting Gregory. He is probably as incapable of keeping silent about a rear quarter panel he knows is inadequately welded as he would be if another man called him a liar. To Gregory, the two are equally personal affronts. What is remarkable is that he has pitted his kind of old-fashioned code of behavior against a corporate ethic that says an individual's sense of duty must yield if it conflicts with company demands, and he has survived. He has also achieved some success with his suggestions for safety and quality improvements, though not nearly as much as he would like. He has done it by following routine channels established by the company itself and by holding management strictly to its own rules. When these channels fail and the company ignores its own procedures for improvement, he goes elsewhere for help.

Gregory is the first to say that life as a whistle blower is not always pleasant. "As a result of the 'stink' I caused, I have been ridiculed and downgraded by company officials who look upon me as a thorn in their side, not only because of [the exhaust problem] but because I am constantly on the outlook for safety defects and poor quality on the line. At one time, they threatened to fire me, stating that I was costing the company too much money with my suggestions."[1]

But Gregory has not lost his job and in some ways is more effective than before. There are several reasons, not the least of which is Gregory's readiness to fight to the hilt any harassment by supervisors. Also, he has an unblemished record of being right when he brings up a safety issue. Even more important has been the backing of his union and the support of an outside public interest organization. Because he is able to count on some measure of job security, Ed Gregory is not a one-time but a full-time whistle blower. As he puts it, "Safety to the driving-riding public is foremost in my mind so I have continued my 'minority campaign' to give the American motorist what he should be getting without us 'thorns.' "[2]

It was 1953 when Gregory went to work as a quality inspector in the huge General Motors complex in St. Louis. He moved to St. Louis from Hannibal, Missouri, where he had lived since he was ten. Except for service in Italy and Africa during World War II, which earned him three combat wounds, a Bronze Star, and Purple Heart citations, his life had centered around Hannibal and nearby Ellsberry, Missouri, where he was born. In Hannibal he worked as a railroad brakeman, shuttle car driver for a limestone mine, and employee of United States Steel's Atlas Portland Cement Company. He was thirty-five when he moved with his wife and two daughters to St. Louis.

In the Fisher Body plant where Gregory went to work,

the bodies of Chevrolets are made, painted, and trimmed, complete with doors, seats, windshield wipers, and seat belts. In the final process, the bodies are lowered over the engines and sent to another plant, where extras are added. Quality inspectors are stationed at certain points along the assembly lines to check the parts as they are installed on the cars. It is not an easy job, and sometimes the pressure of meeting a production deadline is severe. The work must be done quickly and often under the eyes of a harried foreman, who carries the responsibility of meeting the production quota.

Gregory advanced in the ranks of inspectors until by 1966 he held what he considers the "best," or most crucial, inspection position. This position is "buy-out" (sometimes referred to as "the hold"), where the final product is inspected before it is moved out of the plant.

General Motors employees are encouraged to make suggestions to the company that will improve production. Ostensibly, these suggestions cover a broad range. As outlined on the special form printed for employee suggestions, they include "labor savings, material savings, safety improvement, housekeeping improvement, quality improvement, and reduced scrap or repairs." But the emphasis in the "Rules of the General Motors Suggestion Plan" is clearly on savings to the company, and most employees understand the "suggestion plan" to mean ideas that will cut company costs. For example, an employee may be awarded several thousand dollars for making a suggestion that will delete two or three jobs.

Suggestions are reviewed by a suggestion committee composed of management representatives of major departments. The suggestion form says that every idea submitted will be "systematically investigated for merit" with the final decision on adoption left to the committee.

The incentive to make money-saving suggestions is most explicit in the awards section of the rules. Awards are based on the savings that result when "the benefits are measurable." Where there are no measurable savings resulting from an adopted suggestion, the amount of the award is left up to the committee. The maximum of any award is ten thousand dollars.

There is no award specified for suggestions that cost
the company money. (Any mention of "expensive"
suggestions is avoided on the form.) Nonetheless,
safety and quality improvement are specifically included.
Conceivably, suggestions in these areas could mean
adding employees or materials, thus increasing the
company's production costs. Technically, at least, employees are invited to make suggestions along these
lines and the company obligates itself to investigate the
suggestions. Gregory was to put General Motors and
its suggestion plan to its own test when he submitted a
suggestion that would have immediately added eight
employees to each shift at Fisher Body.

Gregory's first major safety suggestion was a by-
product of his avocation as a rock collector. One day
in 1966 when he and a friend returned from a rock
hunting expedition in the friend's 1965 Chevrolet,
Gregory noticed that the trunk of the car was filled
with quarry dust. Another man might have failed to
notice the dust or simply let it go, but this was Gregory's
field. He knew that dust should not have gotten into
the trunk if the car was properly sealed. Further, he
knew that if dust was entering the trunk, deadly carbon
monoxide could be seeping in as well, and from there
entering the passenger compartment. He investigated
and found that the quarter panels on the rear of the car
were not properly sealed, and he traced the problem
to poor welding. He immediately reported the problem
to his superiors at the Fisher Body plant and, following
the company's rules, submitted a suggestion: the defect
should be corrected on all models currently in production, and older models should be recalled for repair
when it was determined which models had the welding
problem. This was not, obviously, a money-saving
suggestion. But it seemed clear to Gregory that the
problem was a real one and was potentially very serious.

When he reported the defective quarter panels to his
superiors at Fisher Body he got nowhere. He demonstrated the defect on automobiles at the plant. They said
it wasn't a problem because no complaints of leaking
carbon monoxide had been reported in the field. He
found cars in the field with the defect. Still came the
answer: no complaints from dealers or customers.

Gregory refused to drop the matter. "I'd catch the brass when they came through the plant and tell them about it," he says. Such behavior became embarrassing to his supervisors. Over his vehement protests he was moved off "buy-out" to a part of the plant where "I couldn't make waves with an outboard motor." He was assigned to the "ink" section, making side mark-ups, far from where he could act as a daily watchdog over the suspect quarter panels.

This move did not succeed in silencing Gregory, however. He immediately filed a grievance with the union over his transfer and filed a second "suggestion" on how to correct the hazardous Chevrolet quarter panels. The second complaint was also turned down by the suggestion committee and a supervisor gave Gregory to understand that he had better let the matter go if he knew what was good for him. He did not. He was still finding the problem on cars whose exhaust systems had been damaged. He kept telling his superiors that if they acted now they could actually save money because, he was confident, the defect would have to be corrected sooner or later. He still speaks with incredulity over his company's obtuseness in refusing to seek out and correct a potentially expensive, not to mention hazardous, problem.

The union, Local 25 of the United Auto Workers, was backing Gregory in his grievance suit over his job transfer. The union position was that under the contract Gregory was entitled to his old job on "buy-out." Union officials said they agreed with him on the safety issue, too, but they claimed that the union had no control over the product that went out of the plant. They said the contract gave the union no authority to demand that an inspector not be forced to "buy" defective vehicles. Gregory set to work—and is still working —to strengthen the union position on the safety issue.

Finding the company intractable and the union apparently powerless to help him, Gregory began to consider other ways to move the company. The routine channels had obviously failed. The "suggestion plan" was a dead end so far as this case was concerned. He himself had been shifted to a position in the plant where he could not easily point out the defect on current models. All internal routes seemed tightly blocked. Several months after he first discovered the problem, Gregory read that a Senate committee was holding hearings on proposed safety standards for automobiles. Testifying at that moment in Washington were his own boss, James Roche, chairman of the board of General Motors, and a leading critic of the auto industry, Ralph Nader. Convinced that he needed help to get the defect corrected, Gregory was perfectly prepared to look for it where help seemed likely. The question of loyalty to his company never occurred to him. He had used the prescribed channels and gotten nowhere. People were in danger. He decided to contact Nader. He went to the phone and called the Senate committee room where the hearings were in progress. "I told the woman who answered who I was and what I wanted. I told her to get Nader." The woman was unable to provide Nader instantly, as Gregory would have liked, but she got the message through and a few hours later Nader called back. After talking with him, Nader began to check out the complaint.

Several weeks later Gregory got another call from Nader asking permission to use the information in a speech he was to make in New York. Gregory agreed. A couple of days after that, he was working overtime on the night shift. He and some of the foremen were "standing around talking about fishing and waiting for one of the lines to finish. I knew them all real well. One of the foremen and I used to fly together. Then somebody comes up and they all draw away from me into a huddle. They look over at me and they're suddenly cold toward me. I tell the foreman I've got to go call my wife. He says OK so I go call her and she says it's all over the radio and TV. The next day the white shirts from Detroit are down. None of them says a word to me. But it is obvious what's going on."[3]

More time passed. It was now well into 1967, which meant that the poor sealing on the quarter panels would not be corrected on the 1968 model Chevrolets. In spite of the fact that the whistle had been blown on General Motors and the problem made public by Nader, the company still showed no signs of action. Gregory was still filing complaints whenever he found another of the defective parts. On the advice of the union he had his third "suggestion" notarized. He recalls that this caused a flurry of concern among members of the suggestion committee. According to the instructions on the suggestion form, the committee was obliged to investigate any suggestion made by an employee. Gregory believes that the committee never investigated his complaints about the quarter panels and therefore failed to live up to its part of the bargain implied on the suggestion form. What angered him was that whether or not he was right on the issue, which he did not doubt, the company was failing to follow standards it had set for itself and its employees. No one contradicted his discoveries; they simply ignored them. These were factors that Gregory felt justified his decision to make the matter public.

For two years, Gregory kept up his badgering until events occurred that the company could not ignore. On July 11, 1968, a truck driver heading east on U.S. Route 40 about seventy-five miles from Salt Lake City noticed a 1968 Chevrolet Impala parked on the side of the road. Later that day, making his return run on the same road, he saw that the car was still there. He reported it to authorities in Salt Lake City, and a policeman rode out to investigate. He found the bodies of three people and two dogs inside the car. The dead were Charles L. Hunt, a Navy chief petty officer from Alameda, California, his wife, and a niece, Susan Koehler. The Hunts had been returning to California from a visit with relatives in Grand City, Missouri, and were taking Susan with them. Medical examinations showed they had died from asphyxiation by carbon monoxide. Chevrolet engineers traced the leak to a damaged exhaust system.

Within three days tragedy struck again. On July 14, a 1966 Chevrolet ran into another car when it stopped for a red light on a street in Baton Rouge, Louisiana. It was a minor accident, but two occupants of the Chevrolet were found unconscious and one woman was dead. It was found that Mrs. John Dunaway died from carbon monoxide poisoning, which had overcome, though not fatally, her husband and mother-in-law. The leak was traced to a tail pipe that had rusted through.

The "field reports" whose absence the company had long touted were at last coming in. Chevrolet engineers subsequently found twenty-eight other cases in which exhaust emissions were claimed to be entering the cars. Several of the passengers were temporarily overcome or reported such complaints as headaches and eye irritations.[4]

The recall announcement came on February 26, 1969, three years after Gregory first alerted the company to the problem—three years and at least four known deaths. General Motors said it was recalling 2.4 million Chevrolets made between 1965 and 1969 to fix the faulty sealing on the quarter panels that allowed seepage of carbon monoxide into the cars under certain conditions. At the same time, the company recalled 2.5 million 1968 and 1969 vehicles suspected of having a carburetor part that could break and jam the throttle in an open position. It was a massive, unprecedented recall that according to Gregory's estimates cost General Motors $100 million, with another $10 million in postage to notify automobile owners. Even so, only approximately 2.5 million vehicles of the 4.9 million autos involved in the recall campaign were eventually corrected. As is true with most recalls, many cars never made their way to dealers for correction, often because owners could not be located or failed to heed the recall.

In announcing the recall, General Motors spokesmen emphasized that only thirty cases had been reported in which exhaust fumes entered the cars and that certain conditions, including a wornout exhaust pipe, must exist before it could happen. "The whole affair," said GM's statement, "is like calling in the haystack to find the needle."[5] But others, such as Dr. William Haddon, Jr., former director of the National Highway Safety Bureau, differed. "If there are thirty cases where carbon monoxide is suspected, the actual number probably is considerably higher," Haddon said in a statement urging police officers to be more thorough in investigating cases where cars run off the road.[6] Too often, he said, these cases are routinely written off as "reckless driving" or "heart attack" and the possibility of a defect in the automobile is never considered. Carbon monoxide, it should be remembered, is odorless, colorless, and tasteless, thus making it difficult for motorists to detect.

Gregory had previously been a nuisance to the company; now he was an embarrassment and potential threat. In the face of his earlier warnings, General Motors clearly stood to be accused of negligence. Had it not been for his warnings many months earlier, and the fact that he had made them public through Nader, the recall would not have been so damaging to the company's image nor so potentially costly in terms of possible damage suits.

The company refused to admit negligence in a series of careful denials. Company spokesmen brought out the old allegation that Gregory's original proposal was rejected because there were no field reports of the problem. Then they insisted that the problem was not what Gregory reported anyway: it was not due to the way the metal panels were sealed, they said, but to plugs dropping out of the inside panels. When Nader made public Gregory's transfer to an innocuous inspection job, the company denied vigorously that it had tried to silence or intimidate him.

There was no way, however, for General Motors to avoid admitting that its method of fixing the recalled Chevrolets involved a sealing process similar to that originally proposed by Gregory. The company chose a novel course out of the predicament. Without admitting it should have heeded his earlier warnings, General Motors awarded Gregory ten thousand dollars, the maximum under its suggestion plan.

Gregory's career as a whistle blowing automobile inspector was by no means ended by success. In some respects, it was only begun. He has become an unofficial ombudsman at the Fisher Body plant for employees who find safety problems but are afraid to report them. His publicity during the recall affair has brought him calls and letters from unhappy Chevrolet owners throughout the country. Friends and neighbors in St. Louis frequently consult him about the service they get from local dealers. All the complaints he faithfully passes on to the company. If nothing is done about them, he funnels the information to public-interest groups concerned with auto safety. At last count, Gregory had submitted fifteen suggestions for improvement to Fisher Body's suggestion committee; one safety suggestion and two quality suggestions have been adopted.

An example of his reports is a suggestion submitted on June 22, 1970:

"I suggest that you use pop rivets on lower quarter panels extension. . . . When they repair it with a torch it burns out seal and also paint off the finished job. You shouldn't use heat on this quarter panel any place. I have got you stopped using brass in stress points. You should hang up a spot weld gun at Chevrolet and the two main holes at Fisher Body. One at the west end hole and at Chevrolet door at Fisher Body side. This is unsafe practice."[7]

Information from dealers and Chevrolet owners led to Gregory's reports that taillights on the 1969 Chevrolets were corroding and the springs rusting out. He reported faulty turn signals. Gregory spends hours of his spare time working over the cars of people who come to him with problems. Frequently these cases stimulate a report to the company, such as the following:

"I have reports that the 1969 and 1970 General Motors ball joints have to be replaced at around 30,000 miles. Poor design or quality in the joints should be checked. Also I have a tie rod off a 1965 Chevrolet Impala with 60,000 miles on it where the right wheel joint is out and the $50 tire was ruined. No grease fittings in the tie rod were found and we couldn't buy a General Motors tie rod with grease fittings but we did find a Moog that had fittings and he [the car owner] bought it. I would not own a car if it did not have grease fittings. They could go out at any time."[8]

He is also concerned about the safety of employees working for General Motors and has submitted six suggestions concerning a fire hazard in the body shop:

"At bay M–16 there is an overhead motor speed reducer. Paper and rags accumulate on the motor base which is a fire hazard. The last fire which resulted from this condition was Monday night, January 18, 1971. This is not only a fire hazard but a safety hazard to employees because in the fire Monday I suffered smoke inhalation and had to be sent to the nurse and then home for the balance of the shift. The nurse said that this was a personal sickness and my doctor stated that it was a direct result of the fire. The safety engineer, Jimmy Venson, was contacted and he stated that he had been overruled on taking steps to correct this situation."[9]

A suggestion filed simultaneously noted:

"On Wednesday, January 20, 1971, a second serious fire took place at M–16 bay when a trash bin caught on fire setting the sprinkler system off. The fire was ignited by sparks from the spot welder. The same situation prevailed Saturday night. The whole shop is in a dirty condition and is only cleaned up when 'company' arrives. It should be kept clean at all times for the safety of plant personnel."[10]

Gregory is tolerant, though somewhat disgusted, with his fellow employees' reluctance to report hazards. "They're scared," he says. "They tell me, you go ahead and send this [suggestion] in. They'll listen to you and you got Nader. But don't sign my name to it."

But if Gregory is an example, the role of the in-plant whistle blower could become less precarious. The worst he suffered—something he resented and fought vigorously—was his transfer off "buy-out" during the quarter panel controversy. No reduction in salary was involved and the work on the new job was no more difficult. "Buy-out" is simply where the most important safety inspections are made and that is where Gregory wants and feels he deserves to be. The grievance he filed in 1968 was in its third stage of arbitration, before a third-party referee, when Gregory was finally re-assigned to his old inspection post, beginning with the 1972 model year.

Only once has he been directly threatened with dismissal. In November, 1969, Gregory testified at a trial in Marshall, Texas, involving the defective quarter panel on a 1968 Chevrolet Impala. He was away from work for two days. When he returned, he was refused his pay for the absence and further found that his line foreman was preparing to fire him. "He said he already had the papers drawn up," Gregory recalls. "I blew up." He immediately called his committeeman (the

union representative who deals with members' grievances), and the firing attempt, which was apparently
never endorsed by higher company officials, got no
further. But the committeeman and the union refused
to fight for Gregory's lost pay, even though his absence
from work had been in obedience to a court order.
Gregory was irate. He marched to the telephone and
called UAW president Leonard Woodcock in Detroit.
The next day Gregory got his back pay.

Gregory is also critical of some General Motors
dealers, many of whom, he says, could not care less
about the customer after he buys a car. A man who
read about Gregory in the newspaper came to see him
when the engine on his 1970 Chevrolet blew up with
only twenty-eight thousand miles on the car. He had
left the car with a dealer, and when Gregory got there
"they had taken the engine completely apart. Then
they told the customer that the trouble was just carbon
on the engine. They told him they didn't put on any
new parts. And they charged him $324." Gregory was
incensed. He wrote four letters to the dealer and the
local General Motors zone office demanding restitution.
The dealer and zone officials agreed to meet with the
customer, who insisted on bringing Gregory along. The
company refused to meet with Gregory, and an official
told him, he says, "Stay out of this. You're an employee
and you're not to get involved."

From Gregory's point of view, he should be very
much involved and he is acting in the company's interests when he is. "They lost four sales on that deal," he
says, referring to the treatment of the customer whose
engine blew. Shortly after, the man bought new cars for
three members of his family and traded in his old
Chevrolet. None of the cars he purchased were made
by General Motors. (Gregory himself owns two Chevrolets.) What Gregory resents and believes is detrimental to the company is "a lack of responsibility of
the dealer and the zone office to the customer. The little
dealers are best. I've worked with them and I know.
They've got to give the customer service to make a
living. The volume dealers don't care."[11]

There have been other kinds of pressures to keep
Gregory from playing his chosen role. In May of 1970,

he says he was offered a supervisor's job. He didn't take it because he believed it was an effort to remove him from the line, where he can more easily detect defects. Sometime later, a company official, whom Gregory declined to name, asked whether he could talk to him. "I said, sure, you can talk to me. Anybody can talk to me about anything. Then he said that if I played my cards right I could get anything I wanted out of the company, including a lot more money. I said, 'yeah? That's good to know,' and let it drop."

Somehow, the feeling that the world is too big, the corporation too large, and the individual powerless never caught hold of Ed Gregory. An item in the newspaper that offends his sense of justice can set him off on a new campaign. Recently he read that seven people had died in Iowa from carbon monoxide poisoning. Gregory did some work and concluded that a stricter automobile inspection system could have prevented the problem. He is now trying to get his union to help him campaign for a national inspection law that would prevent such fatalities.

The ten thousand dollars he got from General Motors helped to finance his most recent campaign. Gregory used twenty-seven hundred dollars of his award money to buy an eighteen-foot Monarch Bell with which he patrols the polluted areas of the Mississippi River, fifteen miles from his home. Gregory is an avid fisherman, and originally the boat was meant to serve that purpose. But the fishing gear has not been unpacked for a year now. Gregory is too busy with his camera.

With an Instamatic and a Polaroid 350, Gregory has photographed the Mississippi from St. Louis to Hannibal, photographed it where old refrigerators and washing machines tumble into the river from the makeshift dump of an appliance company, where hopper cars have been cleaned of old bone meal and cement that now clog the river and its banks, where a glass company has disposed of its wornout molds and oily rags, where sludge has accumulated at the perimeters of a steel company, and where piles of brown foam ride the river's waves. Gregory takes care with his photography, and the color pictures are usually clear enough for the newspapers in Hannibal and St. Louis to print. Gregory also sends copies to the local office of the United States Army Corps of Engineers.

In four cases, Gregory has followed the photographs with formal charges against the polluters under an 1899 law that forbids discharging into waterways without a permit. Three of his complaints filed with the Corps of Engineers, involving a railroad company, a steel company, and a glass company, resulted in large-scale cleanups and stopped further dumping.

Gregory spent sixty-five hours in his boat last year and never dropped a line into the water. He regrets the temporary loss of his fishing, but not enough to interrupt his pollution campaign, which started after a fish kill a few years ago. Gregory went out to the river that day, smelled the rotting fish, and scooped up a handful of dirty suds on the surface. He remembered that "when I was a kid I used to go fishing with an old man. When I was thirsty he'd tell me to lean over the boat and take a drink. Now you couldn't pay me a thousand dollars to take a drink out of that river." He decided to do what he could, to blow the whistle on the people who had done that to the river.

Compared to some whistle blowers, Gregory is fortunate. His union has provided him a measure of job security, and Nader's organization gave him the means of getting his information to the public. He has had his share of unpleasantness as a result of whistle blowing, but he has not had to forfeit his family's income or his career for a single act. He has been able to continue as a "thorn" to prod his company toward being responsible for public safety, and he has preserved his integrity as an inspector. Many fellow employees who were shocked when he made the Chevrolet exhaust problem public now admire the way he has risked the company's wrath. Gregory's advice to other automobile inspectors is "Do not buy [defective] MVSS (Motor Vehicle Safety Standard) automobiles regardless of who orders you to do it."[12] He is thinking of the times when a harried supervisor rushing to meet a deadline tells an inspector to "buy," or approve, a part that ought to be corrected. He is thinking of inspectors who "buy" a defective automobile for fear of costing the company money.

As for blowing the whistle, Gregory says, "A guy shouldn't do it unless he has evaluated the problems and sees what will happen. He shouldn't blow the whistle until he has used all the routes within the company. Then if they don't move, blow it."[13]

8

Dr. Jacqueline Verrett

Given the same circumstances, having adequate data in hand, if the occasion arose I would not hesitate to discuss them openly.   —*Jacqueline Verrett*

For fifteen years scientific writing contained doubts about use of the artificial sweetener cyclamate. Yet it was not until a scientist in the Food and Drug Administration told the public through a television interview about her research on cyclamates that the first government ban on the chemical was announced October 18, 1969.

It did not occur to Dr. Jacqueline Verrett to refuse when a reporter asked her for an interview. "I saw no reason not to discuss the matter with the media," she recalls. She had been reporting her research to FDA officials for a year and a half. Other findings that cyclamates might be harmful to human beings had been circulated in the scientific community and had gotten into the press. So she hardly considered her interview as whistle blowing. But in fact it turned out to be. The public attention she aroused succeeded in moving FDA officials to act where internal reports and scientific journals had not.

Dr. Verrett received censure rather than credit from her superiors in the Department of Health, Education and Welfare. But she is still in her FDA laboratory injecting food additives into chicken eggs. She has even received a promotion in the meantime. And she says readily she would do the same thing again. She is not the only whistle blower to have survived the displeasure of superiors—in fact, to have outlasted them. But

Jacqueline Verrett remains one of the most visible and refreshing examples of candor in the federal government today, firmly convinced of the scientist's responsibility to communicate with the public.

Dr. Verrett went to work for the Food and Drug Administration in 1958 after completing her doctoral work in biochemistry at Fordham University. She was assigned to the division of pharmacology and toxicology and worked on a program surveying foods for radioactive fallout, work related to her doctoral research. When the radiation surveillance program was dissolved not long after her arrival, she was transferred to a small program just being initiated by FDA using the chicken embryo to investigate the toxic effects of materials involved in the food-processing industry. The program was new but the method of testing was not. Dr. Verrett explains that "since the time of Aristotle, the developing avian embryo has been thoroughly investigated, and modern-day nutritionists and toxicologists have used it to study the effects of countless materials."[1] FDA was beginning an attempt to study all the materials under its jurisdiction that Americans were consuming along with their food, and decided to apply the chick embryo technique to the investigation.

In the course of her work, Dr. Verrett began to find disturbing effects in the chick embryos injected with cyclamate. Soon she became convinced that her research showed a firm relationship between the chemical and deformities that developed in the embryos. On March 7, 1968, she reported these findings to a high-level FDA science seminar. It was at a time when concern about the safety of artificial sweeteners was growing, even within FDA, and the seminar had been convened for the express purpose of drawing together research efforts on these chemicals. In her 1968 year-end report, Dr. Verrett again reported her research findings to her FDA supervisors, but received no reaction. The FDA did not acknowledge her work and continued to give its official blessing to cyclamates. In April, 1969, a superior of Dr. Verrett's, concerned about the agency's failure to consider her results seriously, carried two deformed chicken embryos to the office of FDA Commissioner Herbert Ley. Dr. Ley

remained unmoved by the sight of such deformities as
wings growing out of the wrong part of the body, a leg
rotated in the socket, and extreme curvature of the
spine.[2] Again in her 1969 midyear report, Dr. Verrett
informed her superiors of the evidence against cyclamates. Still the sweetener remained, undisturbed, on the
FDA Generally Regarded As Safe (GRAS) list. Cyclamate manufacturers continued to assert that "the
American housewife need have no hesitancy about
using artificial sweeteners in the preparation of foods
and beverages."[3]

Warnings about cyclamates were not confined to Dr.
Verrett's neglected reports to the Food and Drug Administration. On November 15, 1968, *Medical World
News* reported that another FDA scientist, Dr. Marvin
Legator, cell biology research chief, had found that
rats injected with cyclamate showed dangerous genetic
effects. Dr. Legator was also trying to get the FDA to
consider his findings. In one memo to Commissioner
Ley he urged, "The use of cyclamates should be immediately curtailed, pending the outcome of additional
studies."[4]

Thus, Dr. Verrett hardly considered her research a
secret when a member of the press approached her
about it. Hers and other studies had been discussed in
scientific groups outside the FDA, although they had
not been published. They had also received mention in
the press, including a newspaper column on cyclamate
research by Jean Carper which reported both Dr. Verrett's and Dr. Legator's findings. It was this column
that led NBC's Paul Friedman to ask Dr. Verrett for
an interview.

Another reason that Dr. Verrett was not particularly
surprised or concerned about the interview was that
working in the FDA laboratory was hardly like working
behind closed doors. Indeed, FDA liked to encourage
publicity—at least certain kinds of publicity. She recalls that "during these years our laboratory operations
have been used in FDA films and other consumer-
oriented material to illustrate some of the new research
methods that FDA uses in their efforts to assure the
safety of commodities under their control. Additionally,
research reports of our studies presented at national

scientific meetings have on several occasions been singled out by, and reported in, the lay press. Our laboratory is a tour stop for visitors, and the major networks as well as other groups have filmed our operations. And of course visits by scientists from this country and many foreign countries have been numerous. For several years, the FDA had been using our laboratory as a showcase, and publicity about our activities was certainly not unusual, whether initiated by FDA or the press."[5]

For these reasons, the request for an interview by NBC-TV in late September, 1969, "did not strike me as unusual. Nor did I expect, although I probably should have, the furor it would cause in HEW."

But furor there was. When Dr. Verrett routinely notified her superiors of the prospective television interview, within minutes her office was full of a dozen people who tried to persuade her that "presentation of these studies in the news media might lead to 'undue public concern.' . . . While I could not control the nature of the interview or what would be revealed, I indicated that I felt that these findings could be presented in a manner which would not cause public panic."

There was also a recent event that made her superiors' "obvious reluctance to have this material discussed on television" even more incomprehensible and was, she says, "the overriding factor in my decision to proceed with the interview." The previous summer, Dr. Verrett had produced a preliminary study of another suspect additive, monosodium glutamate (MSG). It was a "totally inconclusive preliminary experiment" using only 180 eggs. Although the test did not find any harmful results, she emphasized to her superiors that it was in no way conclusive and in fact "gave no information whatsoever on the safety of MSG." Nonetheless, Commissioner Ley immediately presented Dr. Verrett's study to a congressional committee and hailed it as an "exquisite, sensitive, new toxicological approach." His implications were that MSG was thoroughly safe so far as FDA was concerned. At the same time, Commissioner Ley refused to utter a word about Dr. Verrett's cyclamate data, which used about thirteen

thousand eggs and established a definite causal relationship between the chemical and embryo deformities.
"It was clear to me," she says, "that as long as the
method [chick embryo research] could be paraded before the public as one of FDA's new techniques without
indicating any particular chemical, publicity was not
only acceptable but sought after. But when it raised
serious questions about the safety of a chemical, as in
the cyclamate study, then discussion should be restricted
to my scientific peers who could evaluate it but still
keep it closed to public view."[7]

The alarm in Dr. Verrett's office before the interview
spread to the commissioner's office after it was aired
on October 1, 1969. Commissioner Ley insisted that it
was the first he had heard of her research, despite her
four internal reports over the prior eighteen months.
He then asked the National Academy of Sciences/Na-
tional Research Council to review Dr. Verrett's work
as well as the research of Dr. Legator, which had been
mentioned in the NBC film. As for Dr. Verrett, "in the
following two weeks I was put under 'house arrest,' all
communication with the press was barred, and I was
told to confine my activities to the preparation of the
cyclamate data for presentation to the Academy."[8] She
was not even allowed to answer her office telephone.

Coincidentally, the same week the academy was
meeting to consider the FDA studies, the manufacturer
of cyclamate, Abbott Laboratories, reported that it had
found bladder cancer in rats that were fed cyclamate.
Shortly afterwards, on October 18, the then Secretary
of Health, Education, and Welfare, Robert Finch,
apologetically announced a ban on cyclamates; he chose
to ignore the FDA studies and referred only to the
manufacturer's findings of rat cancer. At the press conference Secretary Finch made his reluctance clear: "I
have acted under the provisions of law because . . . I
am required to do so." It was, he said, the rat cancer
findings, also unpublished, that "forced" the agency to
remove cyclamates from the GRAS list.[9] The results
of Dr. Verrett's and Dr. Legator's research "were
deemed by the Academy as not relevant to the human
consumption of cyclamate," she recalls.

But FDA officials went further than denying that her

research had in any way affected their decision. At the press conference announcing the ban, they criticized "the subject doctor" for speaking out of turn, for making unwarranted claims, being overzealous and "unethical." Asked whether he was happy with FDA handling of the issue, Secretary Finch said, "By and large, yes. I was unhappy and expressed my unhappiness about the subject doctor in the Food and Drug Administration who chose in the case of the eggs to go directly to the media without having consulted with their superior and with the office. That is not a procedure I approve and certainly they did not act in a very ethical way."[10] Surgeon General Jesse Steinfeld added his word of censure: "These experiments must be communicated, but the problem is that people to whom they should be communicated are other scientists working in the field who do have the ability to interpret them and relate them to other ongoing research. I think it unfortunate to publish them in general media along with interpretations which at this moment certainly are far from justified."[11]

Secretary Finch's charges were patently false, since Dr. Verrett had not sought the television interview and had cleared it with her superiors, to whom she had been reporting her data for eighteen months.

Dr. Verrett also firmly rejects Dr. Steinfeld's charge that she should have first published the material in a scientific journal, where it could be evaluated by her scientific peers. "This is usually a very lengthy and frustrating process," she says. "It usually takes several months to clear a scientific paper within FDA, and there is further a one or two year lag before it appears in print. Had I followed that route, my findings would probably not be in print as yet, and would remain unknown to this day.

"Further, from past experience, our publications have not yet elicited any constructive criticism or actual repetition of the work which in any sense negates or refutes the findings of prior investigations. The point of relevance of chick embryo data to humans is a valid one; however, we have serious limitations in our ability to relate animal data directly to humans no matter what the test species. All of this was, in any case, beside the point because the same observations of the effects of cyclamate on chick embryos had been made and published by research workers in Italy a year prior to my television appearance. This goes to show that the prerequisite of publication in scientific journals is no assurance of gaining the attention of other qualified scientists, government officials, or the public. In fact, publication in scientific journals is in many cases a most decent form of burial."[12]

Dr. Verrett has survived the storm she precipitated. In the wake of the cyclamate publicity, the Food and Drug Administration underwent a complete reorganization. But the chick embryo research has neither been curtailed nor expanded. "Strangest of all," Dr. Verrett says, "seven months later I received the first promotion I had had in seven years."

There may be several reasons for her survival, among them the pressure on the Food and Drug Administration to step up its testing of additives and Dr. Verrett's undiminished reputation for excellence in working with the chick embryo method. There is also little pressure the agency could apply short of firing, because her laboratory work does not depend on the cooperation of a great many associates and is too important at this point to curtail through the familiar method of cutting off funds.

Dr. Verrett says she does not regret the episode in any way and would not hesitate to do it again if the occasion arose. If anything, the cyclamate affair simply confirmed her view of the responsibility of scientists and of public servants, a view that led her to become and remain one of the most successful whistle blowers in the federal bureaucracy.

"It has been my observation over the years that data that are negative, and frequently of inferior quality, are readily accepted by FDA officials in support of the safety of chemicals. However, data indicating an adverse effect in any animal system must be subjected to endless repetition, confirmation, and critical review, often while the questionable chemical remains in the marketplace. This apparent double standard is certainly not in the consumer interest, and merely serves to support existing FDA policy and maintain the economic interests of the proponents of its use. Hence, given the same circumstances, having adequate data in hand, if the occasion arose I would not hesitate to discuss them openly, even though they might be in conflict with current FDA policy that had been developed in the absence of this new information."[13]

Whistle blowing involves responsibilities and rules to which Dr. Verrett gives articulate testimony. "In similar situations," she says, "there should be no reason for reticence in discussing scientific information openly. I feel that scientists are obliged to present their information in a manner that is readily understandable to the public, but being cautious to keep it in proper perspective so that it is not unnecessarily alarming. I also feel that it is the duty of the press not to sensationalize such information, distorting its meaning and significance. There was no exaggeration in the reporting of the cyclamate data by the press.

"Finally, I feel that officials are remiss if they downgrade the significance of findings, however difficult they may be to interpret, and then issue placating but meaningless statements to reassure the public, as was done by HEW officials in the case of cyclamate. They frequently stated that the rat cancer data were not applicable to humans, and further ridiculed the federal law requiring the cyclamate removal, when in fact this law is the only real protection we have."[14]

Dr. Verrett's experience illustrates that whistle blowing may involve the *translation* of information to the public in an understandable fashion and making it generally accessible. She disclosed nothing new in her television interview, unless making esoteric reports buried in even more esoteric journals understandable constitutes disclosure. In candidly answering the questions put to her, she fulfilled a fundamental obligation of a professional in our society: the duty to communicate the meaning of one's work to the public.

9

William Stieglitz

The standards were, in my opinion, a hoax on the American public, creating an illusion of improved safety which did not, in fact, exist. I could not be a party to this.
                                   —William Stieglitz

William Stieglitz received his copy of the first federal safety standards for automobiles along with the rest of the public on February 1, 1967. This was unusual because Stieglitz himself had been in charge of drawing up the standards as consultant to the Undersecretary of Commerce for Transportation. But ten days before the standards were issued he was abruptly assigned to other duties. When he saw them again in final form they were vastly different from those he had proposed.

Stieglitz took the regulations to his Washington hotel room and began to study them. It was approximately 5 P.M. At midnight he wrote out his resignation. That resignation, which Stieglitz personally handed to his superior the next morning, did more than any other single act to focus public attention on the deficiencies of the federal auto safety standards. As word of his departure carried to the press, newsmen rushed for an explanation. Stieglitz told them that he could not "in good conscience continue to serve."[1]

The next day press reports on the new standards featured Stieglitz's resignation prominently along with his comments on the failure of his former agency to follow sound safety policy. The *New York Times* commented in its typically restrained language that "Mr. Stieglitz's resignation adds another dimension to the furor that has grown since the twenty safety standards were issued. Heretofore, the criticism of the regulations came from outside the agency."[2] To the press and the public, the act of resigning was a powerful criticism in its own right. There were other critics, but Stieglitz's credentials as a long-time safety expert and above all as the man formerly in charge of the standards gave weight and substance to the criticism.

Stieglitz had not anticipated the publicity that attended his exit from the National Highway Safety Bureau. He had prepared no public statement and credits the press with being the real whistle blowers. "My only actions were to resign from a position that I found totally untenable on the basis of my professional convictions, and in reply to questions asked me by members of the press, to state the reasons for my resignation. The whistle blowing was done by the press in their coverage of my resignation and the reasons therefore, and by my professional peers who supported my actions."[3]

But if Stieglitz had not planned it, the effect was the same. Nor was his experience so different from others who have acted in accord with their standards of professional integrity and, in so doing, have exposed the failure of their organizations to achieve those standards. Stieglitz had no new information to divulge, but he exposed something equally serious: the refusal of the National Traffic Safety Agency to heed the advice and urging of one of its own chief experts. He also made public an example of professional responsibility that was to challenge and encourage other engineers. Finally, he became the focus, however inadvertently, of the criticism of the first auto safety standards.

If Stieglitz was surprised at the attention his resignation commanded, it may have been in part because it was a natural—he says "inevitable"—thing for him to do. For over thirty years he had worked in aviation safety and more recently had developed an expertise in automotive safety. Thirty years earlier he had promoted the idea that design errors lie behind many driver errors that lead to crashes. Throughout his career in private industry, where he has spent most of his life, and in the private consulting business he built later, he was concerned with designing vehicles that were "crashworthy," that protected, as far as possible, the occupants in crashes.

In February, 1971, Charles O. Miller, director of the Bureau of Aviation Safety of the National Transportation Safety Board, writing in the MIT *Technology Review*, pointed to Stieglitz as a pioneer safety advocate, one of the earliest to point out the design challenge to professional engineers. "In 1948," Miller wrote, "William Stieglitz, who is still quite active in automotive as well as aviation safety, gave the landmark paper in what today has become known as system-safety engineering. 'Safety,' he said 'must be designed and built into airplanes just as are performance, stability, and structural integrity. . . . A safety group must be just as important a part of a manufacturer's organization as stress, aerodynamics, weights, and so forth.' "[4]

Born in 1911 in Chicago, Illinois, Stieglitz studied electrical engineering for two years at Swarthmore College and graduated from MIT in 1932 with a bachelor of science degree in aeronautical engineering. He went to work in the aircraft industry as a specialist in aerodynamics and flight testing and was soon deeply involved in safety problems. While chief of the Fleet Wings division of Kaiser Aircraft, he lectured on aviation safety at Princeton in 1941–42. In 1944 he went with Republic Aviation, where he spent the next twenty years as a design engineer.

In 1946 Stieglitz organized a design safety group at Republic, the first such group to be formed as an integral part of the industry. In 1950, on loan from Republic, he worked with the Air Force on accident prevention and flight safety research. From 1950 to 1955 he was a member of the subcommittee on aircraft fire prevention for the National Advisory Commission for Aeronautics, the predecessor of NASA. During 1952–55 he was also a member of the NACA committee on aircraft operation problems.

Meanwhile, he was broadening his field to include automotive safety engineering, applying to automobiles the same ideas on "crashworthiness" he applied to aircraft design. In 1959 he testified before the House Subcommittee on Interstate and Foreign Commerce, chaired by Representative Kenneth Roberts, which was then holding the first congressional hearings to consider automobile safety. He submitted a paper on crash-worthiness written in 1950. The paper was addressed to aircraft but, as he was to show, applied equally to automobiles. For example, he cited aircraft crashes in which "many of these fatalities could have been prevented by stronger safety belts and seats."[5] He said the same design factors pertained to the automobile— to dashboard design, access of controls to the driver, and shiny chrome and high gloss paint that can blind the driver.

"Quite frankly, from personal observation of automobiles," he told the subcommittee, "it is my conviction that the interiors of these cars are designed, not from the standpoint of effective human utilization, but . . . from the standpoint of appearance and style. I think unquestionably there are a large number of needless accidents resulting from improper consideration of the human being in design."[6]

By the time Dr. William Haddon, head of the new federal traffic safety agency, persuaded him to become his chief engineering consultant, Stieglitz had built a reputation as one of the foremost safety experts in the country.

In the fall of 1964, Stieglitz resigned as manager of Republic's design safety and reliability division to set up a private consulting practice on aviation and automotive safety in Huntington, New York. Two years later, he was contacted by Dr. William Haddon, who had been appointed to head the new National Traffic Safety Agency. Dr. Haddon came to New York and asked Stieglitz to accept a consulting position and take charge of drafting the standards. Stieglitz was not enthusiastic. In a subsequent meeting with Haddon and Alan Boyd, then Undersecretary of Commerce for Transportation, he suggested several people he considered better qualified for the post. Haddon and Boyd objected to all of them. They wanted Stieglitz.

Stieglitz's reluctance was partly based on the fact that the job involved certain personal sacrifices. "It meant abandoning the consulting practice which I had spent two years building up, and a way of life that I enjoy."[7] But there were more serious misgivings.

"In the discussion prior to my accepting the position, I called attention to my earlier testimony before committees of both the Senate and the House of Representatives on the then pending traffic safety bills. One of the measures being considered involved merely extending to all vehicles the standards of the General Services Administration for automobiles purchased by the federal government. I had opposed this vigorously in my testimony, stating that in my judgment these standards were inadequate. I therefore told Dr. Haddon and Undersecretary Boyd that I could not and would not be a party to issuing these same standards as the initial federal motor vehicle safety standards. I was assured that whether or not this were done would be my responsibility."[8]

Stieglitz had indeed made his position absolutely clear during hearings before the Senate Commerce Committee and the House Committee on Interstate and Foreign Commerce in March and April of 1966. He criticized the General Services Administration standards as "woefully and totally inadequate to provide the level of safety that they are intended to provide." He then attacked the bill that would apply these standards to 1968 cars driven by the public, standards "which, on the industry's recommendation, are written around what they had in the 1965 cars." If that were done, he said, "we have improved nothing. We have applied a label, we have spread some whitewash, we have said, now it is safe. But we have not changed a thing. We cannot get safety this way, gentlemen. We cannot protect people by just giving a blessing to what already exists, and which we know hurts people or kills people. There is no reason we cannot write these standards."[9]

Haddon and Boyd still wanted Stieglitz, wanted him to write the standards. Finally, having been assured, to some extent at least, that the standards would be his responsibility, Stieglitz agreed. "I felt obliged to accept. Had I refused the position and then found the standards to be inadequate in my engineering judgment, I could only blame myself for not having tried."[10]

Stieglitz directed the first two phases of the initial safety standard–setting process, the preparation of the advance notice requesting suggestions for standards, and of the proposed standards published in the Notice of Proposed Rule Making. But already a fundamental difference was developing between Stieglitz and his superiors at the agency. The industry's strong argument was that the proposed safety features, as Stieglitz and his staff drafted them, could not be developed for the 1968 models. They wanted standards to reflect what they had already planned. Henry Ford threatened that the proposed standards would close down the industry, and House minority leader Gerald Ford demanded an explanation. Stieglitz was willing to acknowledge that the industry needed time to institute some of the new features. But he argued that the standards themselves should require building at least some crashworthiness performance into vehicles in which forty-eight thousand people were dying yearly and millions were being injured.

During the last phase of preparing the final standards, Stieglitz found the ground slipping from under him. Others in the agency were leaning toward industry's argument of what was "practical." They were demanding what he considered serious weakening of the standards. He objected strenuously. Finally, ten days before the final standards were issued, he was assigned to other duties and not consulted again.

When he read the standards in his hotel room on the night of February 1, he found that of the initial twenty-three standards, three—relating to tires, wheel rims, and headrests—were dropped on the grounds that more technical data were needed. Of the twenty standards issued, all were reworded, most were softened, and six were substantially compromised and scheduled for future rulemaking. The date for most to go into effect was moved forward four months.[11]

"They offered no advance in safety but were basically a rubber stamp of what would have been done in most 1968 automobiles without standards," he says. "From this point of view, they were, in my opinion, a hoax on the American public, creating an illusion of improved safety which did not, in fact, exist. I could not be a party to this. Under the circumstances I had no alternative to resigning. It was not an agonizing decision."[12]

When their differences became public, Haddon explained that Stieglitz's recommendations were "preposterously impossible."[13] In hearings before the Senate Commerce Committee in March, 1967, Stieglitz explained his position and stressed the problem of lead-time. "In my opinion, what should have been done on many of these standards was not to weaken the standards but to change the effective date to provide a legitimate lead-time requirement of industry. . . . I am perfectly willing to say that some of the proposed standards could not possibly have been met for 1968 automobiles. I didn't think they could be when I proposed them. But I felt that things had to start moving forward, and this lead-time block had to be broken."[14]

Rather than abandon the provisions which had value but truly could not be incorporated in the short time available between issuance of the standards and the new car production beginning in July, 1967, Stieglitz argued that two-part standards should be issued, with the first step applicable to 1968 vehicles and the second step applicable to 1969 vehicles. In this manner, the agency would not be merely endorsing existing industry practice from year to year but rather would be assuring orderly priority for safety advances. As had already been documented in the 1966 hearings leading up to the passage of the safety legislation, without mandatory requirements there is little priority or urgency in the auto companies to build safety features into motor vehicles.

Stieglitz documented his skepticism about industry arguments for lead-time. He cited as an example the Chrysler request for twenty-five to seventy-nine weeks to change their brake hoses to a type using a different reinforcing braid in order to comply with the proposed standard. Chrysler said it would require one engineer and one mechanic two weeks to work out the front wheel brake hose installation (even this Stieglitz stated was excessive). Further, to accommodate the various Chrysler models there would have to be eleven different installations, or a total of twenty-two weeks (two weeks for each of the eleven installations). Stieglitz chided Chrysler for implying that in all its corporate divisions there was only one engineer and one mechanic capable of routing a brake hose.

Stieglitz also criticized the agency for unnecessarily bowing to industry pressure. He cited as an example the proposed motor vehicle safety standard 101, "Control Location and Identification." As proposed, the controls listed had to be within the operational reach of a fifth-percentile adult female driver restrained by an upper torso restraint with enough slack to permit "a five-inch movement of her chest." The standard as finally issued required controls to be within the reach of "a person," with a "reasonable degree of slack" in the upper torso restraint.

As Stieglitz pointed out, the final standard contained numerous loopholes. The seat position was not defined, thus allowing compliance with the seat in the most forward position (even if the subject could not drive the car in such a position). The manufacturer could interpret "reasonable degree of slack" very broadly, even if the amount of slack made the restraint virtually ineffective. But most important, the "person" in the standard could be a six-foot, five-inch male with extra long arms. The standard was clearly meaningless.

The agency, according to Stieglitz, deleted the reference to fifth-percentile female because it claimed it did not have sufficient data on arm reach. Stieglitz cited a study providing data on the measurements of Air Force female pilots and flight nurses obtained in 1946. The agency rejected this information as nonrepresentative of the public. Stieglitz also cited a 1961 Society of Automotive Engineers publication, "Human Body Size and Passenger Vehicle Design," by Ross McFarland and Howard Stoudt of the Harvard School of Public Health. The authors said their data were approximations of the general driving population interpolated from several studies (including the 1946 Air Force information) and that: "Although the adjusted and weighted values in Table 1 are tentative, we believe they do, for most practical human engineering purposes, approximate sufficiently closely the true body measurements of this group to enable them to be used with confidence."

The agency refused to base its standard on these careful approximations. This difference in the arm reach of fifth-percentile Air Force flight nurses and the estimate by McFarland and Stoudt is two-tenths of an inch. The arm reach of a tall man—who would qualify as a "person" in the agency's standard—is many times greater than these values. Stieglitz concluded: "Thus in order to avoid a possible discrepancy of a fraction of an inch, the standard permits controls to be nine or ten inches beyond that of even a tall woman. I do not believe that the standard as written can be claimed to contribute appreciably to safety."

Stieglitz assesses the influence of his action on the agency as "negligible." "Many standards that I have objected to in February of 1967 are still basically in effect and have yet to be revised to a point where they are meaningful." But he does see one major change. "In one respect I do find the bureau acting in consonance with what I then argued for; that is, establishing standards on a basis of safety requirements and setting an effective date that allows adequate lead-time rather than weakening the standards to endorse what would be immediately achievable. I cannot say that this was the result of my influence, although it does represent a position I had taken before my resignation."[15]

The response from many fellow engineers has given Stieglitz tremendous personal satisfaction, however, and he credits his peers with helping him blow the whistle. He cites in particular the support of Frederic Salinger, an engineer in Seattle, Washington, and the Washington Society of Professional Engineers which, in response to a motion by Mr. Salinger, passed and forwarded to Senator Magnuson a resolution supporting Stieglitz's position and urging Senate committee hearings into the circumstances. "Judging from letters and comments I have received," he says, "it may be that my actions gave encouragement to other engineers who also feel strongly about their professional responsibility."[16]

Stieglitz has worked actively to encourage safety

committees in industrial plants, like the one he started at Republic Aviation in 1946. He has also encouraged physicians with special knowledge in treating crash victims to support safety measures. In an editorial written for the *Medical Tribune* on June 23, 1965, Stieglitz urged physicians to support the then pending bills to create a federal auto safety agency and set federal standards. "It is essential that the legislation be supported by all those interested in automobile safety," he wrote, "but especially by those with professional knowledge in crash injury and accident prevention."[17]

His experience has not been without some hardship. "From a personal standpoint it unquestionably was expensive economically," he says. "I had not only to start over, but was faced with the attitude of some clients expressed as 'You walked out on us once. Can we be sure you won't do it again?' Against this, of course, were new clients who had heard of me through the publicity attending my resignation, and who had approved of my stand. Nevertheless, it took considerable time to rebuild the practice to the level it had reached prior to my going to Washington."[18]

When asked whether he would take the same action again, Stieglitz responded that "there is no question in my mind that under similar circumstances I would do the same thing, and I sincerely believe that in the same situation I would do it in the same way. I wish to stress the words 'the same situation.' No two cases are ever the same, and I think that the manner in which one performs an action of this type must depend on the particular circumstances."[19]

To others who find themselves in similar situations, Stieglitz says, "There is no question that there are probably economic penalties which in some situations may be prohibitive. One's responsibilty for supporting a family may be so great that blowing the whistle publicly is impossible. Further, there is the pressure exerted by retirement plans, for one's investment in such a plan could make resignation almost impossible. This would be particularly true for older men.

"None of these factors, however, should inhibit a man from privately calling the situation about which he is concerned to the attention of someone who can act, and will protect his source of information. The cost of violating one's sense of professional integrity must be weighted against possible economic loss, in determining one's course of action. Peace of mind is intangible, but very important."[20]

10

Fumio Matsuda

I believed that the best policy for the company was to inform users about defects in their automobiles and to repair the defects.   *—Fumio Matsuda*

In 1957, Fumio Matsuda got the job in the Japanese auto industry he had been looking for since he finished industrial college nearly a decade before. He went to work for Nissan Motor Corporation as a service engineer. Eleven years later he quit to become one of Japan's most vocal critics of the industry's safety performance.

With his fledgling Japan Automobile Users Union, Matsuda has raised a ground-roots protest movement rarely seen in that country, much less in the giant automobile industry. Six court cases are now pending in the Japanese judicial system involving automobile defects on which Matsuda blew the whistle. Japanese citizens are able to buy for a small cost a magazine in which Matsuda meticulously details for them how much yen they are paying for poor servicing and shoddy parts and points out hazardous features of cars the Users Union has tested. Some of the defects are those he discovered while he worked for Nissan and tried to get the company to correct. He is far more effective, he has found, now that he is working on the outside. But the information he gathered during his years inside the industry gives him unique documentation and he was able to set up a network of industry employees and dealers to feed him additional facts.

In January of 1971, Ralph Nader met Matsuda during a speaking tour in Japan. Through interviews with

Matsuda, his staff, newsmen, consumer advocates, and others, Nader's associates were able to bring back the story of the Japan Automobile Users Union and of a unique whistle blower. Matsuda's experience closely parallels that of whistle blowers like Ed Gregory, the General Motors quality inspector. In Japan, he represents the most persistent technical criticism yet to challenge the auto industry in that country.

Fumio Matsuda was born in 1924 in the small town of Katsuyama, in Fukui Prefecture in northeast Japan, bordering the Japan Sea. His family had lived in Katsuyama for four hundred years and had been leading citizens of the town. Three generations before Matsuda, the family gave the town a mountain which they owned and assured Katsuyama of a large forest area unusual in most villages in Japan.[1] Matsuda was often told this story when he was a child and says that the example of social concern made a great impression on him.

The family's prosperity dwindled, and by the time Matsuda was born the family was no longer prosperous. Matsuda's father owned a small market that sold rice and kitchenware. Although Matsuda was the eldest son, his father released him from the traditional obligation of carrying on the family business (the second son is now running the market) and at age nineteen he entered an industrial college, Kogyo Senmore Gukao, in the town of Nikone. He studied engineering, his interests being mainly in design, although his career plans were vague. He graduated after three years, spent one year as an assistant at the school, and another studying economics. In 1948 he began to look for work. In Japan's postwar collapse he could not find a job in industry and finally became an examiner in the engineering office of the Self-Defense Department in Tokyo. During the first year he worked primarily on purchasing specifications for the internal combustion engine, and so began a lifelong preoccupation with the automobile. His aim was to become a design engineer in the automobile industry, an aim he was to fulfill in a highly unorthodox manner twenty years later.

During the time he worked as a civil service employee, Matsuda briefly moonlighted as an inspector of automobiles and trucks at the American maintenance depot. "I wanted to see it, [the depot] so I applied for a night job," he says. The double duty was wearing, so he soon quit the job at the depot. Finally, dissatisfied with his civil service job and unable to break into the infant auto industry, he joined the Japanese Self-Defense Force in 1949 as an inspector of vehicles. He was promoted to lieutenant, then to captain. Switching to the Air Force, he became an instructor at a technical school teaching service and maintenance of vehicles.

In 1957 he achieved his goal of entering private industry by getting a job as a service engineer with Nissan Motors. His first choice was design, but because he had no experience in the field he was assigned to the service department—a personnel decision that was to prove costly for the Japanese automobile giant. His duties included writing a technical manual for dealers and users, receiving complaints from dealers and users, and servicing automobile parts.

His concern with safety grew gradually. His first major discovery was that many consumer complaints could be traced to faulty design or to inferior material in parts. Subsidiary companies manufactured parts for Nissan and they were inspected by "lot tests." Matsuda realized that there was a difference in the quality of the items that composed the lots. Other defects occurred in the process of assembling the parts.

His list of discoveries grew longer. A transmission gear lacked the proper strength. A rear axle shaft broke because of a defect in design. A bad dust cover for the ball joint of the steering linkage tie rod allowed dust to get inside and wore out the ball joint quickly. "I began to find defects in all of the parts," he says, "in suspension, brakes, steering, everything."

At least twice a month in meetings with designers, Matsuda talked about these defects. He pointed out, for example, that inadequate coating on a brake tube allowed the tube to become rusted and cause crashes. These were the kind of defects, he says, that would only be found by service engineers, the people who heard the consumers' complaints.

The difference between Matsuda and his superiors

soon hinged on the extent to which the company was willing to inform customers of defects. He found that the policy was never to let them know—except in special cases when the user himself spotted the defects and the manufacturer allowed the service department to repair them. In cases where there were complaints of defects and a crash occurred, the policy was to "recall" the defective vehicles by secretly requiring repair when the consumers brought their cars for the regular two-year inspection required in Japan. This was accomplished by collusion with the Japanese government. One of several flaws Matsuda saw in this system was that not all cars made their way to the inspections. The rest continued with the unacknowledged defects.

The picture Matsuda began to see unfolding was one in which the automobile user was generally ignorant of serious defects and, even when he was aware of them, was unable to call the manufacturer to account and receive free repair or compensation for injuries in auto crashes. "After the car had crashed, no one could see the original defect and even if the owner knew about the defect, he was unable to prove it without assistance."

The next realization was that the service engineer was the best—or even the only—person equipped to aid the auto consumer. But he found little support among his fellow service engineers. "Their attitude was not to do anything that would jeopardize the company," he says.

As a service engineer, Matsuda did not belong to any automotive engineering societies. The employee union was "so close to the company" that he found no support from its ranks.

The pressure to act became intense as Matsuda saw drivers being held responsible for crashes that he believed stemmed from defects. Drivers were judged guilty of negligence that he knew was not theirs. His colleagues repeated the phrase "do nothing that will hurt the company." But Matsuda was evolving the theory that the best he could do for the company was to urge practices and policies that would win the trust of auto consumers. "I believed that the best policy for the company was to inform users about defects and repair the defects," he says.

Five years after he began working for Nissan, Matsuda suggested that the company publish a list of a thousand defects which he had documented. At that time, secret repairing of serious defects was costing Nissan some 1–2 billion yen a month. Publication of the defects could cost the company two or three times as much money. The company rejected his suggestion.

Next Matsuda suggested that the company recall all cars of a model that had been involved in an accident when a defect was recognized. His immediate boss rejected the suggestion; Matsuda went to his superiors, which infuriated his own supervisor. Again and again he went over his own superior to higher officials in the company until the relationship between him and his supervisor became strained. The supervisor began making damaging reports about Matsuda to the main office, falsely charging him with accepting bribes from dealers and leaking information to the press.

At the same time Matsuda was involved in a fight with the employee labor union, which he had charged with corruption. Specifically, he charged union leaders with spending union money on personal entertainment. He was also frustrated because the union failed to support his reform efforts.

Finally, discouraged by his attempts to help the automobile consumer within the company and by his rapidly deteriorating relationship with his superiors, he resigned in August, 1968.

He was now free to do what he wanted to do: to give automobile owners all the information they needed about defects. He developed a plan for an organization through which he could become an effective critic of the industry. But he knew that he faced tremendous difficulties. For over a year he did nothing but study auto design, earning a living by writing articles for magazines and newspapers and doing consulting work. Most of his acquaintances, even those who supported his ideas, believed then that his project would fail and he would never "beat the manufacturers." His family was skeptical and his wife complained as he began to spend more and more time in the one-room office he rented in Tokyo. Some publishers refused to print his articles, but reporters began coming to him for assistance and gradually he began getting his ideas into the public media.

During this time, he formed an important alliance with Masataka Itoh, a top reporter for the prestigious newspaper *Asahi Shimbum* in Tokyo. In June, 1969, Itoh broke a story that caused a furor in Japan. He reported that Japanese auto makers were recalling defective automobiles in the United States under the United States safety law requirements, but were not recalling the same autos sold in Japan, which had no recall law. After substantial newspaper publicity and public hearings in the Diet, a voluntary recall system was instituted for Japanese owners by the companies. Itoh followed this story with other reports on the Japanese auto industry, often using tips from Matsuda whose reliability he came to respect. Itoh in turn helped Matsuda with plans for his auto users union and became an invaluable source of support.

Matsuda was looking for people to back his new organization with financial support as well. The man who provided a large part of it was Haruo Abe, a Tokyo lawyer. In November, 1969, Abe asked Matsuda's help on a suit involving a Honda N–360, a case that became front-page news in the Japanese press. Abe was representing the family of a victim, who believed it was the car, not the driver, that caused the crash. But the lawyer needed the testimony of an expert. At first Matsuda turned down Abe's request on the ground that the job was too big for him to handle alone. But the family of the victim called him and he yielded, primarily because he realized they had nowhere else to turn. For forty days he investigated the minicar, refusing pay, and came up with evidence that the early model Honda N–360 had a serious stability defect that caused it to go out of control when the car is fully loaded (with the maximum of four passengers) and the car is decelerating. Through some of his contacts, he says he found that Honda durability tests themselves indicated a problem. He brought these tests to the attention of police investigators, and the family of the victim sought to press criminal charges of homicide against the president of Honda. As a consequence, the Ministry of Transport ran a series of tests on the vehicle, some new information was published in the press, and a police investigation was undertaken. Apparently, however, the prosecutor has declined to bring charges against the company or the president.

Another consequence of the Honda case was backing from Abe for Matsuda's automobile users union. Largely through Abe's influence, sixteen "founders" contributed 20 million yen (fifty-five thousand dollars) to found the Japan Automobile Users Union, officially organized on April 20, 1970. The names of the founders have been kept secret for fear of retribution by the powerful automobile industry, but Matsuda says they include several high-ranking members of the judicial system.[2] By the spring of 1971, ten thousand members were paying a monthly membership fee of 300 yen, or ten dollars a year, for which they received the monthly JAUU magazine. The magazine is also sold on the newsstands. Matsuda had assembled a staff of twenty. Three assistants and a secretary were working with him in the small office; the others, mostly volunteers, worked in research institutes during the day and came into the office at night. At that time, the union was able to act on about sixty percent of the complaints it received. The office was getting eighty to one hundred visits a week from auto owners, two to three hundred letters and around two hundred phone calls.

An essential part of the union's effectiveness has been Matsuda's network of contacts inside the auto industry, with salesmen and dealers, customers and service engineers. This network is carefully guarded, and Matsuda contacts them secretly. Professors in five universities work for him regularly without pay, he says, doing research and tests and writing articles for the magazine and feeding him information.

From his informants Matsuda has obtained lists of defects still kept by auto companies and given to dealers who make secret repairs, that is, repairs the customers pay for when they have their cars inspected without knowing that the defects existed when they bought the cars. Matsuda has charged that most auto defects are still handled secretly in Japan. He has also directed lawyers and police investigators to sources of information within the companies of which they were previously unaware, for example, manufacturer drawings and durability tests and receipts at servicing plants for repair fees.

Whenever Matsuda has made a new discovery he has approached the auto manufacturer first. If the manufacturer is unresponsive, the union has taken its case to the press. The result has been, says Matsuda, that every manufacturer except one has begun to respond to his requests for repair and redesign. His biggest weapon is their fear of publicity. Finally, the union looks for legal aid to help victims sue manufacturers. There are now six major pending law suits brought by public prosecutors which were instigated largely by the Users Union on behalf of crash victims. The union is cooperating in ten other auto liability cases.

Matsuda is working for the auto user from another angle: the expense of auto parts. In his magazine he informs consumers of the original price of the parts—which he obtains from informants—and then tells them what profit goes to the manufacturer and dealer. Recently, the union began to sell a new type of engine oil and antifreeze to its members at one-third to one-half the market price. A cooperating university researcher developed the products. The union keeps three percent to cover handling expenses but makes no profit.

Matsuda's organization has been harassed a good deal, which is one reason for his care in keeping secret the names of his informants. The office has been broken into once but no records were taken because Matsuda was sleeping there that night. When the organization was beginning, members of his staff received telephone calls from anonymous callers who accused one or another staff member of being a spy for one or more manufacturers. Staff members' families and neighbors received phone calls telling them that the union was subversive and would fail. He has managed to work out most of these staff problems.

In the fall of 1971, pressures against the Users Union took a new and more formidable turn. On November 2, Matsuda and Abe were arrested by the district prosecutor in Tokyo on charges brought by Honda. Honda claimed that their efforts to reach cash settle-

ments with the company in behalf of the victims of
Honda N–360 crashes constituted extortion. The prosecutor, in behalf of the company, charged that the
amounts they sought ($5 million for two hundred vic-
tims and their families) were too high; that Matsuda
and Abe "threatened" Honda with publicity and court
action; and that they refused to release the names of
all the victims they represented. Matsuda and Abe
were jailed for twenty-five days before they were released on bail set at approximately fifteen thousand
dollars each. Denying the charges, they plan a vigorous legal defense and offense. The prospect, at this
writing, according to observers in Japan, is for lengthy
court proceedings that could stretch over a ten-year
period and could seriously impair, if not destroy, the
work of the union.

Thus, at this time, the future of the Japan Automobile Users Union and of Fumio Matsuda is highly uncertain. So too, are the implications of the case for the
consumer movement in Japan. When we talked with
him, Matsuda said he saw himself as "a test case for
other whistle blowers in Japan." He hoped that his
experience, successes by his organization, and a mounting constituency for auto safety and consumer rights
would encourage other Japanese citizens to follow his
example. How effective he was may be measured by
the response of the Honda Company in its recent efforts
to suppress him and his organization. On trial now with
Matsuda is the right of citizens to use those tools available to corporations—negotiation, court action, and
exposure of abuses—to strengthen consumer safety
and corporate responsibility.

11

A. Dale Console

I reached a point where I could no longer live with myself.
                                        —Dale Console

In 1960, Dr. A. Dale Console, a former medical director at E. R. Squibb and Sons, gave the public and Congress their first detailed view of the way drug companies increase sales through exploitation of physicians and manipulation of improper prescription of drugs. In testimony before the Kefauver hearings on drug price competition, he described the "inroads the [drug] industry has made into the entire structure of medicine and medical care."[1]

"Unfortunately drugs are not always prescribed wisely," he told the committee, "and while the physician and patient among others must share the responsibility for this with the pharmaceutical industry, it is the industry that carefully nurtures and encourages the practice. . . .

"The pharmaceutical industry is unique in that it can make exploitation appear a noble purpose. It is the organized, carefully planned, and skillful execution of this exploitation which constitutes one of the costs of drugs, which must be measured not only in dollars but in terms of the inroads the industry has made into the entire structure of medicine and medical care. With the enormous resources at its command, it has usurped the place of the medical educator and has successfully substituted propaganda for education."[2]

Dr. Console went on to indict the industry—not Squibb alone—for promotional techniques that included:

1) a "barrage of irrelevant facts [the physician] has neither the time, the inclination, nor frequently the expert knowledge to examine critically,"[3]

2) the hard-sell tactics of detail men who follow the maxim "If you can't convince them, confuse them,"[4] and

3) the testimonials that "are used not only to give apparent substance to the advertising and promotion of relatively worthless products, but also to extend the indications of effective drugs beyond the range of their real utility."[5]

He was equally severe in his criticism of physicians and their organizations for the "unhealthy" and "in many ways corrupt" relationship with the drug companies they allowed and sometimes welcomed, frequently associated with the large grants and gifts the industry makes available to physicians.

It was a dramatic indictment, the more so because it came from the "inside," from someone who had been close to the drug industry as few critics had been before. For six and a half years, Dr. Console had worked as a drug company doctor, having resigned four years before the Kefauver hearings. Both then and in 1969, when he testified before Senator Gaylord Nelson's Monopoly Subcommittee of the Select Committee on Small Business, he gave the public a rare and vivid portrait of the individual who is forced to sacrifice his scruples to the will of the organization. His testimony was both a severe criticism of the industry and a comment on the manipulation of corporate employees to serve corporate aims.

As an example, Dr. Console described the company doctor's function of "reviewing" and "approving" advertising copy:

"Drug companies boast that *all* advertising copy is reviewed or approved by the medical staff. Most [ads] require 'approval' since review is pointless if the doctor has no voice in determining what is and what is not acceptable. This poses problems for the doctor. In the first place, *all* advertising copy makes a mountain of paper, some of which is difficult to digest. Overall, the task is dull and boring. In addition, the doctor who does not approve the majority of copy that reaches his desk is not likely to keep his job. Yet over and over again he is faced with advertising that is obviously misleading and which he cannot approve in good conscience. The dilemma is best resolved by a bizarre process of reasoning. . . .

"The doctor who reviews advertising copy must learn to ask himself not whether the advertisement is misleading, but rather whether it can pass. . . . Under [certain] conditions the advertisement can be defended against any attempt to prove it false or misleading. The doctor who wishes to keep his job in the drug industry will find it mandatory to use this kind of reasoning. In desperate situations what can pass can be stretched to almost infinite limits. The determining factors are the mental and verbal facility of the doctor or lawyer who must defend it."[6]

The list of what a drug company doctor must learn if he is to advance in the industry became so long, so personally and professionally obnoxious, that Console finally had enough.

He had found that the drug company doctor "must learn the many ways to deceive the Food and Drug Administration and, failing in this, to seduce, manipulate, or threaten the physician assigned to the New Drug Application into approving it even if it is incomplete.

"He must learn that anything that helps to sell a drug is valid even if it is supported by the crudest testimonial, while anything that decreases sales must be suppressed, distorted, and rejected because it is not absolutely conclusive proof.

"He must learn to word a warning statement so it will appear to be an inducement to use the drug rather than a warning of the dangers inherent in its use.

"He must learn, when a drug has been found too dangerous for use in this country, he can approve its use in other countries where the laws are less stringent and people have less protection. He must learn, when a drug has been found useless on one side of the Rio Grande, it can be sold as a panacea on the other side and that he is expected to approve the claims made for it.

"He will find himself squeezed between businessmen

who will sell anything and justify it on the basis that
doctors ask for it and doctors who demand products
they have been taught to want through the advertising
and promotion schemes contrived by businessmen. If
he can absorb all this, and more, and still maintain any
sensibilities he will learn the true meaning of loneliness
and alienation.

"During my tenure as medical director I learned
the meaning of loneliness and alienation. I reached a
point where I could no longer live with myself. I had
compromised to the point where my back was against
a wall and I had to choose between resigning myself
to total capitulation or resigning as medical director.
I chose the latter course."[7]

Dr. Console resigned from his position at Squibb
in June, 1957. The next two years he spent on a
psychiatric fellowship paid for by Squibb. When his
relationship with the company was completely severed
in 1959, and he began practicing psychiatry in Princeton, New Jersey, Console considered writing a book
about the industry. His intention was not to pillory
his former employer. On the contrary, he has defended
Squibb as one of the "more ethical" pharmaceutical
firms, and he destroyed the records in his private file
when he resigned, records which might have been used
as proof of specific abuses concerning specific drugs
had Dr. Console chosen that route. He decided instead
to offer "a distillate of my experience and the opinions
I have formed as a result of that experience."[8]

But he was concerned about the possibility of a
libel suit if he wrote the book. He was confident such
a suit would not be successful, but it would mean
heavy financial costs for him. Then the invitation to
testify before the Kefauver committee offered him the
platform he sought. It was an opportunity for whistle
blowing that was certain to attract public attention and
assured him immunity from "legal" harassment by the
industry.

The fifty pages of testimony he subsequently produced for several congressional committees provided
a strong witness for the need to strengthen government
control over the testing and marketing of drugs. His
evidence undermined notions that the industry was

successfully policing itself or that physicians were providing a viable check to abuses. As a physician himself, Console was a unique critic of his own profession's willingness to turn over "postgraduate medical education" to the drug industry.[9] He reminded them that "we are still human in spite of being physicians. As humans, we are vulnerable to all forms of flattery, cajolery, and blandishments, subtle or otherwise." He then demonstrated how "the drug industry has learned to manipulate this vulnerability with techniques whose sophistication approaches perfection."[10]

Reflecting later on what motivated him to become a whistle blower, Console said, "While I am convinced that I am motivated by a deep sense of moral indignation, I am equally motivated by a deep personal feeling of resentment. The roots of that resentment run deep, and my contribution was an incredible degree of idealism and unrealistic expectations that set me up as a patsy for disillusionment and disappointment.

"I grew up with the concept that medicine is a noble profession. I spent some fourteen years, or one-quarter of my present life span, cloistered in an ivory tower. For four years I was a medical student. Eight years were spent in postdoctoral (or residency) training, and the remaining years I was a member of the faculty of the medical college. Throughout these years I was exposed to all the very best that medicine has to offer.

"I had been exposed to, and was appalled by, shabby practices I had observed when I served as a substitute intern in small hospitals during medical school vacations. These were brief stints and after each of them I returned to the cloistered life in the ivory tower. Naively I came to believe that the totality of my personal experience was a true and accurate representation of the reality of medical practice."[11]

What he discovered when he entered the drug industry was far different. He concluded that "in today's practice of medicine one of the simplest professional tasks a physician is required to perform is the writing of a prescription. Since it is simple and uncomplicated, many physicians would like to reduce the practice of medicine to the practice of writing prescriptions. . . . Since a drug company's profit is dependent on the number of prescriptions written for its products, its advertising and promotion practices carefully nurture the concept that the prescription pad is omnipotent. The end result is what I once labeled a *folie à deux*. The physician and the drug company each serves his own purposes. Both of them dance but the patient pays the piper."[12]

Console also observed the transition of Squibb, indeed of the entire drug industry, from a "family corporation" to the "modern corporation," huge, largely anonymous, concerned with profits and an ever-increasing market rather than with consumer interests. "When I joined it, twenty years ago, Squibb was still a family corporation, management was still guided by the philosophy and the policies of the company's founder, and the medical director was a physician's physician. In time, ownership of the company changed hands, management changed, and most important the entire drug industry changed. Having written some fifty pages of testimony on the nature, meaning, and consequences of those changes, I now find myself in the position of trying to say it all in one sentence. I heard the sentence frequently spoken by a vice-president who offered it as fatherly advice and as an unsubtle threat: 'It's easy to find a lawyer who will tell you that you can't do something; the trick is to find one who will show you how you can do it, even if he costs more.' To me this single sentence always has been, and still is, the epitome of shabbiness and all of its ramifications."[13]

To counter the new corporation's focusing of enormous resources on narrow interests, Console is convinced that people within the organization must speak out. "We could make no greater mistake than to be lulled into a sense of false security by believing that some disembodied force called the government will act like a beneficent big brother and make certain that the special interests will not predominate. If the general welfare is to be protected, it will be protected by the actions of people, not the government, and the actions of people are one of the primary concerns of this Whistle Blowers Conference."[14]

His view of whistle blowing (a term Console himself prefers not to use) is that it should ideally be a lifetime affair, carried on in the private as well as the public sphere. In addition to his public statements, he has criticized the medical profession through private correspondence for serving the interests of the drug industry and has tried to institute change through internal channels. Recently, for example, he wrote the editor of a state medical journal criticizing the journal's practice of blatantly endorsing the products of drug companies that bought advertisements. This journal scattered through its pages boxed notices urging its readers to "Patronize Our Advertisers. They Merit Your Support." Even worse, he found one issue to contain the notice: "Not everyone can advertise in this JOURNAL. When you see an advertisement here you know that the company or the service has been stamped 'approved.' As you read our advertising pages, you get a compact little course on what's new. And if you tell the company that you saw his notice in these pages you remind him that this is a happy medium for his services or his company. These pages deserve your consideration."

Console protested that "stamped as 'approved'" suggested the society or journal had actually tested the products. It was at least an unjustified endorsement of products based solely on the willingness of companies to purchase advertising space in the publication, he said. The medical society reviewed the practice, and it has since been discontinued.

Console has also made a study of the difference between claims made for drugs marketed in Italy, where restrictions on advertising and labeling are few, and claims for the same drugs in the United States. The comparison shows, he says, that "any notion of the morality of the drug industry is a hollow mockery." Drug companies blatantly omit warnings to physicians and consumers in markets where regulations do not require them, even though their products must carry such warnings by law elsewhere. His study was prepared for a congressional inquiry into drug company practices abroad.

Though he analyzed his own motivation to speak out, Console refused to do the same for the hundreds who fail to do so. "We are faced with the knotty problem of why a small handful of people do act while the vast majority remain passive even though its vital interests are at stake. A partial answer to this question is found in the simple fact that only a small handful of the people are ever exposed to a naked view of the operations, techniques, and methods used by the special interest groups. This is, at best, a partial answer since it is also obvious that only a small percentage of those who do gain access to this restricted information elect to 'speak out' while the majority elects to 'go along with it.' "15

One reason may be that there is not always a way out of the organization, such as Console found when he entered psychiatry as a private practitioner. For the drug company doctor who remains in the industry, there is little protection. What recourse does he have against losing his job if he refuses to "approve" a worthless drug or a misleading advertisement? The answer is, none. Console makes the point that policing of the industry cannot be done entirely through government regulation. Professional watchdogs within the organization, acting on a daily basis, have a far greater opportunity to assure that the public is not harmed and physicians are not gulled by unsafe drugs. But until the medical profession provides protection for the conscientious drug company doctor, he may, like Console, find his "back against a wall" with the untenable choice of "resigning himself to total capitulation" or resigning as medical director.

12

Christopher Pyle
and Ralph Stein

What is important is that the story be told, that those who can effect change learn the truth, and that the telling of the story be legitimated. —Ralph Stein

Few whistle blowers have given more thought to how to speak out effectively than Christopher Pyle and Ralph Stein, who disclosed in early 1970 the Army's deep involvement in the surveillance of civilians. Their disclosure led to widespread public indignation, two court challenges of the practice, over fifty congressional inquiries, a congressional hearing, and finally an announcement by Defense Secretary Melvin Laird of limited curbs. But it took far more than a simple announcement to get that far, and Pyle and Stein are still working for a meaningful resolution to the constitutional questions they have raised.

Both former Army intelligence officers, Pyle and Stein left military service convinced that the data collected on the personal lives of thousands of citizens had no bearing on the military's legitimate responsibility for national security. They were acutely disturbed by the huge computerized data bank being assembled at Fort Holabird, Maryland, and its implications for the exercise of guaranteed freedoms.

At the same time, they knew that the military establishment had formidable resources to fend off criticism and to weather a storm unscathed—and unchanged. There was probably no other organization so fortified against outside criticism. A single disclosure might shock the public momentarily and move a few congressmen to demand explanations. But would it lead to fundamental reform or even to a close scrutiny of the surveillance practice by the institutions with the power to correct it, the Congress and the courts? Pyle and Stein thought not. Success, they were convinced, depended first on presenting an irrefutable case of carefully documented facts that suggested the magnitude of the problem. They needed to bolster their own first-hand knowledge with that of other former and present intelligence officers. It depended, too, on their ability to touch the levers of political power in the right way and at the right time. Finally, it depended on mobilizing people within the military establishment to enforce such curbs as might be imposed by blowing the whistle if they were ignored.

It was a bold experiment, as much a test of the political system as of the Army's right to probe the private lives of law-abiding citizens. They were also determined that it should be an example of responsible dissent. Pyle and Stein were not, and did not want to appear as, antimilitary or opposed to military intelligence. At one point, in fact, Stein was so attracted by intelligence work that he applied for a job in the Army's civilian career program. Pyle insists, "We are friendly critics in the best sense of the term."

For two years, as a captain in Army Intelligence, Pyle taught at the intelligence school at Fort Holabird, central Army Intelligence headquarters. His course, an elective, was on constitutional law, and it was usually crowded. The fare served up in the mandatory courses tended to be too dry for many of the young officers, and they liked Pyle as well as his course. One day one of his students asked Pyle whether he knew about the intelligence files kept in a building not far away from the classroom where he was teaching. Pyle did not. The student told him about the surveillance program, about the data bank, and about the infiltration of Army intelligence agents into groups the Army wanted to watch. Pyle was astounded. Through his students, he began to put together the whole picture of the CONUS (Continental US) intelligence program. Former stu-

dents, now agents in the field, gave him more information as he considered making the program known to
the public.

The picture as he began to see it was that after the
1967 summer urban riots the Army greatly increased
its coverage of civilian activities and enormously, without any real direction, expanded the guidelines as to
collecton of information. Stein later described the result: "In several central locations and in many local
offices the Army maintained . . . files on individuals
and organizations engaged in left wing, right wing,
racial, and antiwar activities. While the names of
many of the individuals would perhaps be well known,
the great majority of those whose lives and activities
are recorded in Army files can truly be described as
anonymous Americans who did no more than exercise
the rights guaranteed them under the First Amendment."[1]

Army special agents infiltrated antiwar groups, lived
with black Americans in Resurrection City, penetrated
college groups, monitored campus activity, photographed and videotaped dissenters and "compiled dossiers and published reports too numerous to be itemized
in a brief statement."[2]

The Army itself was later to tell a congressional
committee that it had dossiers on 25 million American
"personalities," including persons loosely described as
"considered to constitute a threat to security and
defense" as well as such public figures as Senator
Adlai Stevenson. The data bank contained files on
760,000 organizations and incidents and processed
12,000 requests for information a day.[3]

Pyle had enough of this information soon after he
left the Army to write an article outlining the program and giving a number of startling particulars.
This article, published in the *Washington Monthly* of
January, 1970, was the first the public—and many
civilians in the Pentagon—knew about the Army's
domestic spying activities. The article pointed out that
CONUS intelligence far exceeded—in large part had
nothing to do with—the Army's needs in preparing for
plots.

Stein commented later that "most of the information

collected in no way improves upon or positively adds to the Army's ability to perform its assigned civil disturbance function. All of this activity has been accomplished without statutory authority and in contravention of our long tradition of keeping the military apart from civilian affairs." Further, their investigations showed, it was accomplished without the knowledge of the civilian authorities who traditionally direct the military and were placed in the uncomfortable position of "learning about the Army's intrusive presence in civilian affairs from newspapermen and former intelligence agents."[4]

As Pyle had expected, the Army high command lowered a blanket of secrecy over its intelligence activities after his article appeared. The Pentagon's Office of Public Information refused comment, and agents were forbidden to discuss the program with newsmen. Army General Counsel Robert E. Jordan III suspended all replies to congressional inquiries, and the Army did not even acknowledge their receipt.

Criticism was so great, however, that by the end of the month the Army issued the first in a "series of partial admissions." As Pyle reported in a second article in the *Washington Monthly* (August, 1970), the Army confirmed the existence of a nationwide intelligence apparatus but included the false assurances that it collected political intelligence only "in connection with Army civil disturbance responsibilities" and did not include "individual biographies or personality data."[5] The Army acknowledged that it published an identification list of "persons who have been active in past civil disturbances activity" but failed to mention that the list also included detailed descriptions of people and organizations never involved in civil disturbances.[6]

The denials failed to settle the storm, and congressmen continued to demand full explanations. The leader of the critics, Senator Sam Ervin, chairman of the Senate Subcommittee on Constitutional Rights, said in a Senate speech on February 2, 1970, that "the Army has no business operating data banks for the surveillance of private citizens; nor do they have any business in domestic politics."[7]

Meanwhile, the civilian hierarchy in the Pentagon was also trying to find out what was going on in the CONUS program and launched its own investigation. In mid-February, Pyle reported, General Counsel Jordan went to Fort Holabird and "watched as the computer bank on dissidents disgorged a lengthy printout on Mrs. Martin Luther King."[8]

On February 25, Jordan sent an identical letter to more than thirty congressmen which included the brief confession: "There have been some activities which have been undertaken in the civil disturbance field which, on review, have been determined to be beyond the Army's mission requirements."[9] He assured them that the data bank and the published identification list had been ordered destroyed.

Jordan's promise placated some congressional critics, though not all, and it definitely did not satisfy Pyle, who by now was working with another former agent also concerned about the CONUS intelligence program. Ralph Stein became concerned about the "over-broad scope of military intelligence activity" while working as an analyst at the Counterintelligence Analysis Branch, specializing in left-wing activities. "Along with several other analysts," he says, "I attempted to present briefings and write reports which forced the listener or reader to focus on the Army's legitimate concerns with regard to civil disturbances, rather than on political matters and on the personal lives, thoughts, and associations of American citizens. Frequent discussions with my associates, both on and off duty, convinced me that public disclosure would be necessary to curb the rapidly expanding activities of military intelligence."[10]

When he left the Army, Stein was planning to write an article himself when Pyle's piece appeared in the *Washington Monthly*. He contacted Pyle, and the two decided to work together to keep the issue before the public and Congress.

They were immediately concerned with the fact that the Army's bland assurances were actually no assurances at all. Their investigations of the total intelligence apparatus proved them right. The promise to destroy the computerized data bank at Fort Holabird and the identification list failed to mention over 375 copies of a two-volume, loose-leaf "encyclopedia on dissent," containing descriptions of hundreds of organizations and individuals; a computer-indexed microfilm archive of intelligence reports and documents; a computerized data bank at the Continental Army Command headquarters in Fort Monroe, Virginia; noncomputerized regional data banks at each stateside Army command and at many military installations; and noncomputerized files at most of the Intelligence Command's three hundred stateside intelligence group offices.[11]

These facts were also brought to public attention, and criticism began again. Senator Ervin was clearly dissatisfied with the Army's assurances. Now Pyle and Stein began an intensive information-gathering effort, contacting military personnel, students, businessmen, and professionals across the country. They also decided to make their information "available where it would do the most good, specifically to Senator Ervin's Subcommittee on Constitutional Rights and to the American Civil Liberties Union."

Both men were in school in New York City, where Pyle was a doctoral candidate in political science at Columbia University and Stein was enrolled at the New School for Social Research. The decision to undertake the kind of whistle blowing that was required was not easy. As Stein recalls, there was a moral decision in the first place and, second, practical and personal considerations:

"The decision to reveal information gathered by intelligence methods and sometimes subject to security classification was not an easy one for moral and legal reasons. The decision to actively investigate the Army and travel about the nation soliciting the help of others was even more troublesome. A question of divided loyalties pressed urgently on my conscience. It was necessary for me not only to reflect on my subjective feelings, but to study at great length the issue involved from a legal and historical perspective. I arrived at the, for me, inescapable conclusion that the Army's domestic intelligence activities were proscribed by the First Amendment and by the weight of almost 195 years of American tradition and history and that to reveal the activities of the Army's Intelligence Branch was the only moral course.

"I would like to say that I have encountered no personal problems in carrying out my convictions, but, as I early discovered, dissent causes many to be fearful of consequences. My wife, while always helpful and strongly supportive, was nonetheless apprehensive and probably she still is today to some extent. Friends and relatives called to warn about the danger of being rejected for future employment, sometimes citing examples of which they claimed to have personal knowledge. Far more distressing, however, were the warnings of those who cautioned against speaking out because of indefinable, inhibiting dangers which these people felt precluded one from taking a controversial position with regard to the government.

"This demonstrated inhibition, this chilling effect on First Amendment rights, caused to no small degree by the latitude and indiscretion of both military and government surveillance, convinced me, as no other factor did, of the urgency of airing this issue and securing remedies, both legislative and judicial."[12]

Their coast-to-coast investigation of the Army uncovered numbers of former intelligence agents and military personnel who were willing to help, either by speaking out publicly or by giving their information anonymously.

The report that most alarmed the politicians, including the President, was former agent John M. O'Brien's letter to Senator Ervin in December, 1970, reporting that the Army had spied on and collected information about Senator Adlai Stevenson during 1969 and 1970, when he was Illinois state treasurer. O'Brien's letter, which outlined Army spying on some eight hundred civilians and activist organizations, laid the groundwork for hearings that Ervin's subcommittee held in February, 1971.[13]

At those hearings, other former agents stepped forward. Laurence F. Lane told the committee of an incident in which 119 demonstrators outside a gate at Fort Carson, Colorado, included no less than 53 undercover agents from all services. Intelligence gathered by agents, whether reliable or not, Lane said, was forwarded to Fort Holabird, where it went into the computers and then out again to other commands as substantiated facts.[14]

Oliver A. Pierce, another former Fort Carson agent, told of being ordered to infiltrate a young-adult project sponsored by the Pike's Peak Council of Churches that operated a recreation center for emotionally disturbed young people. He was ordered to see if its leader was influencing local GIs. After six months, Pierce said, he reported no influence but was kept on the job. He also reported that the Army sent an informant to the 1968 SDS (Students for a Democratic Society) National Convention in Boulder and sent five agents to monitor an antiwar vigil in the chapel of Colorado State College.[15]

Shortly after the hearings were concluded, Secretary Laird issued a directive limiting the military's surveillance activities and placing authority for such activities in the hands of designated civilians. Members of the subcommittee, however, still saw a need for controlling legislation. Pyle is now helping the subcommittee staff draft the legislation.

Pyle and Stein have also assisted the American Civil Liberties Union in litigation aimed at bringing about a judicial review of the constitutional questions raised by military surveillance of civilians. Stein testified in a Chicago case, *ACLU* v. *Westmoreland*, which is now on appeal. The ACLU has also filed a suit in the District of Columbia. But the difficulty of getting key documents as court evidence, before they disappear in the labyrinth of the military establishment, is an impediment in the suits. The District of Columbia District Court refused an ACLU motion to confiscate certain documents; the delay in appeals procedures will make it difficult for the ACLU to keep its evidence up to date.

Having started the machinery for reform, Pyle, Stein, and their associates have found that even the smallest success requires painstaking research and digging for facts. Above all, it requires the help of others who know the situation on the inside. "There is a pressing need," Stein says, "for more military intelligence personnel, both active duty and former, to step

forward and publicly relate their experiences where
surveillance and record keeping of civilians is involved.

"In some areas of the country and under some
personal circumstances this may not be easy, as I have
discovered even among my closest friends, and I respect the many people who have aided our investigation after receiving our promise of anonymity. What
is important is that the story be told, that those who
can effect change learn the truth, and that the telling
of the story be legitimated.

"All the promises of the civilian authorities cannot
safeguard us if the individuals who must take part in
the actual conduct of intelligence operations do not
remain alert to the dangers inherent in domestic intelligence and retain a sense of higher loyalty to the
nation and the American people. In this age of technology and with all the ills of bureaucratic accretion,
we cannot be protected from a full-scale resumption
of this surveillance activity in the future if the citizen–
special agent and the junior officer and career civilian
remain aloof to the problem or are fearful of exposing
abuse because of possible consequences."[16]

13

Charles Pettis

You've got to stand up against pressures on that kind of thing to live with yourself. **—Charles Pettis**

In February, 1966, Charles Pettis went to Peru as resident engineer on a $47 million project to build a road across the Andes. It was a huge undertaking, financed in the main by United States assistance, with $12 million authorized by the Agency for International Development (AID) and $23 million by the Export-Import Bank. Pettis worked for Brown and Root Overseas, Inc., an international engineering firm and subsidiary of the Brown and Root worldwide construction company, which had been hired by the Peruvian government to oversee the project. The contractor was another international construction company, Morrison-Knudsen. As resident engineer, Pettis was charged with making sure the project met contract specifications and protecting the interests of his firm's client, the Peruvian government.

It wasn't long before he began to be seriously disturbed by the engineering design which called for cutting channels up to three hundred feet deep through the mountains, with sheer cliffs on the sides of the road. The Andes are well known for their instability and frequent slides. Yet Pettis found that the design team had taken inadequate geological borings to determine where slides might occur. Other problems began to develop, and Pettis concluded that the road designs needed drastic overhauling. He also estimated that large contract overruns would occur, for which the Peruvian government would have to pay, if he went along with the plans. Despite his misgivings, Morrison-Knudsen, the contractor, proceeded with construction.

Pettis's fears were realized almost immediately when the road project sustained a number of serious slides, in which thirty-one men were killed. The first direct confrontation between Pettis and Morrison-Knudsen came when the contractor demanded that the monthly payroll be amended to include charges for slide removal. Pettis refused. He told the company that the extra charges were not included in the contract and that in his judgment the Peruvian government should not have to pay them.

His own company, Brown and Root, supported him at first, but in February, 1968, their attitude began to change. There was a high-level meeting that month, at which Morrison-Knudsen began to put pressure on Brown and Root. The Morrison-Knudsen representative said his company had bid the job low because of prior associations with Brown and Root. They hoped that their fellow corporation would not do anything to impair their happy working relationship in other parts of the world by being stubborn in Peru. The implications were not lost on Brown and Root. Morrison-Knudsen wanted a break and they got it. Pettis was incensed and told his employers he "wouldn't be a party to such a thing."

Brown and Root nevertheless ordered him to boost the payroll as Morrison-Knudsen demanded. When Pettis continued to refuse, he was replaced by another engineer, B. W. Donelson, who proved exceptionally pliable. Not only did Donelson order extra payments to the contractor, he apparently decided that he would obtain some extra business for himself as well. According to Pettis, he persuaded Morrison-Knudsen to give him a subcontract to feed the workers and by cutting food costs gleaned a substantial profit. His allegations were subsequently confirmed by investigators from the General Accounting Office.

Pettis, meanwhile, was under enormous pressure to bail out Brown and Root by assuring the Peruvian government that everything was proceeding properly on the project. He refused to do so and Peru stopped

payment on the road. Frantic, Brown and Root offered Pettis his pick of jobs anywhere in Latin America
if he would cooperate. At the same time, other subtle
pressures were applied. The American consul in Lima
gave him a temporary passport and tried to pass it
off as a bureaucratic error. Contractors' children threw
eggs at his children and refused to associate with them.
More and more isolated, without any support but his
own convictions, Pettis stuck to his position. In December, 1968, he was fired.

The next few years were a full dose of what of-
fending a corporate employer can mean. Pettis got
job offer after job offer but in every case, after he
gave a prospective employer his past job references,
the offer was canceled. The obvious explanation was
that Brown and Root were giving him an "unreliable"
label. He contacted the American Society of Civil
Engineers but was unable then to get any action in
his behalf.

Pettis and his family moved to Spain, where they
made plans to build a school. Meanwhile, he was ex-
ploring the possibility of a breach-of-contract suit.
When he asked his lawyer to contact Brown and Root,
the lawyer wrote Pettis that the company's position
"seems to be that your first duty was to the Brown
and Root 'team' rather than to the Peruvian government, and that by your action you violated this duty."
Pettis vehemently disagreed, as he had all along, maintaining that his professional duty was to the client
whose interests he was hired to protect.

In January, 1971, Pettis's lawyer came to Washington
to attend the Conference on Professional Responsibility. The next day he talked to an attorney in the
Public Interest Research Group about legal remedies
available to people like Pettis who are fired for taking
an unpopular stand in the course of duty.

A month later, Pettis himself came to the United
States. He went to see Martin Lobell, a member of
Senator William Proxmire's staff, who was helping
Proxmire look into contract policies of international
construction companies, particularly those with large
contracts in Vietnam, which included Brown and
Root and Morrison-Knudsen. Lobell got Pettis an

appointment at the General Accounting Office, the agency of Congress charged with keeping an eye on spending by the executive branch, which made a preliminary inquiry into the circumstances of his dismissal. In March, Senator Proxmire made a formal request for a major investigation by the GAO.

On December 25, 1971, Senator Proxmire released the GAO report, which confirmed Pettis's charges of fraud, improper construction, unauthorized payments, and use of inexperienced employees and improper equipment.[1] The GAO also criticized the Agency for International Development and the Export-Import Bank for failing to supervise the project properly. "The U.S. Mission in Peru and AID/Washington were aware of many of the project's problems by early 1967," the GAO said, "but did not take substantive action until the end of 1968."

Among Pettis's charges which the GAO substantiated were:

—"The consultant's [Brown and Root Overseas, Inc.] design for the Tarapoto road was deficient because, among other things, no core borings had been made to determine subsurface conditions."

—"The consultant's regional engineer had ordered the contractor [Morrison-Knudsen, Inc.] to perform work totaling almost $1 million without having authority to do so from the Government of Peru or the U.S. Mission."

—"The consultant's design had not called for proper placement of drainage pipes under the roadway."

—"During the early stages of the project, the contractor did not have employees experienced in road construction."

—"A fellow consultant employee had improperly used contract funds derived from food payments for personal expenses and had charged the Peru contract for material and labor used to construct a private house for himself." (The GAO report included a picture of the house with the caption: "Pictured above during its construction in 1968, the consult-

ant employee's house was the only luxurious residence in Tarapoto."[2])
—"The consultant changed its position [after
meeting with the contractor] and authorized payment to the contractor for slide removal," which
would have added $2.2 million to the cost of the
project, without the approval of Peru or AID.

The GAO did not find documentation for Pettis's
assertion that he had been blackballed in the construction industry, but added the following concluding paragraph:

"The question of whether Mr. Pettis has been blackballed cannot be established as any such action would,
by definition, be informal and not necessarily documented. We could not find any overt action to blackball
Mr. Pettis. The fact remains, however, that he has applied for thirty-one jobs since 1969 and has been un-
successful in obtaining employment in the engineer-
construction field."[3]

Since February, 1970, neither Brown and Root Overseas, Inc., nor Morrison-Knudsen has worked on the
project, which has been taken over by Peru. The government of Peru has filed a court suit against the
two firms, which includes charges of poor workman-
ship, fraud, and collusion.

Pettis is still living in Spain and is still unemployed.
The GAO report, as well as the support of William H.
Wisely, former executive director of the American Society of Civil Engineers, who made his own inquiries
and has interceded on Pettis's behalf with prospective
employers, may change his heretofore bleak employment prospects. Meanwhile he is suing Brown & Root
both for what he considers its breach of his contract
and for recovery of funds due the United States. He
is also writing a book about his experiences—in which
several publishers have expressed a keen interest.

Of his action, Pettis has said, "You've got to stand
up against pressures on that kind of thing to live with
yourself. You sure won't make much money that way
—I mean what the hell did I have to gain out of this?
—but you have to do it."[4]

14

The Colt Workers

"Professional responsibility" as the term is used in this book really means "individual" responsibility. Edward Gregory, the Fisher Body Plant inspector who appeared at the Conference on Professional Responsibility, is not a professional in the ordinary sense—he is not a doctor or a lawyer or an engineer. Seven employees of the Colt Firearms Company at West Hartford, Connecticut, who publicly revealed massive fraud and deception in the testing of Colt M–16 rifles bound for Vietnam, are not "professionals" in that sense either. Yet their revelations represent an expression of personal responsibility for the quality and consequences of their work that "professionals" rarely equal, but which is part of what "professionalism" is all about.

On November 1, 1971, the Connecticut Citizens Action Group (CCAG) released a report[1] charging that Colt was engaged in a systematic program of subverting government inspection procedures for the M–16 rifle. The report, which called for a congressional investigation and an investigation by the Justice Department for possible violation of federal criminal law, was based on extensive interviews with Colt employees. Seven employees later submitted affidavits affirming the truth of the charges to Congressman Les Aspin of the House Armed Services Committee and to Connecticut Senator Abraham Ribicoff.

The Colt workers and the CCAG report maintained that Colt management ordered its employees to tamper with endurance tests and interchangeability-of-parts tests—the successful completion of which is necessary before the Army may accept any particular shipment of rifles. Colt also ordered employees to repair weapons that failed an accuracy test by bending the barrel "either by straining the muzzle between the mounting beams or by striking the flash suppressor against the floor."[2] As the CCAG report expressed it, "It is difficult to conjure up a more amazing image than the picture of a worker in a modern factory grasping the world's most sophisticated rifle by the butt and 'whacking' its flash suppressor on the target range floor."

Both the endurance test and the interchangeability-of-parts test are performed on weapons selected at random by government inspectors from six-thousand-rifle shipment lots that have completed all other Colt quality control tests. Four weapons are used in the endurance test, ten in the interchangeability test. In the endurance test, each weapon of the four is fired six thousand times in eight hours, with periodic forced-air cooling and regular disassembly and washing of parts. In the interchangeability test, the ten weapons are disassembled, their parts are thoroughly mixed, randomly grouped, and reassembled into ten (hopefully) acceptable performing weapons. In either case if any weapon is rejected because of malfunctions or failure to function, the whole set of four or ten is rejected and a new set randomly chosen from the same shipment. The second set is then tested in the same manner. If the second set must also be rejected, the entire shipment of six thousand rifles is rejected by the government and must be totally reprocessed.

During the endurance test, the Colt workers reported, "It is standard practice that if the gun should fail to feed and fail to fire, we pull back the charging handle, recharge the gun and continue firing without the government men detecting it. The Colt's weapon technician would keep the government agent occupied during the cover up. If a weakened extractor spring is causing trouble, the Colt's men might give you a new spring without the government man knowing it."[3]

A similar pattern was revealed in the interchangeability tests. Out of view of government inspectors, Colt workers were ordered to inspect the test weapons for parts that might need replacement: "We always

changed the parts whether it was before the breakdown or after reassembly. Orders for switches were
given by the quality control man or the range master."[4]
Frequently, workers were required to come to the plant
before or after the regular work day to put in overtime—again, beyond the view of government inspectors
and contrary to government regulation—in order to
"prepare" the weapons for the interchangeability test:
"I have seen the whole upper receiver—the barrel—
changed during overtime, with the new receiver selected from outside the test group. I have seen the
guns test-fired during overtime, and corrected, to insure
that good results would be had during the government-
witnessed regular test-firing."[5]

Who are the workers who signed the affidavits
charging such astonishing, if not criminal, irregularities? And why did they speak out?

"The lead poisoning. That's what did it for me,"
Wayne Handfield told one of the authors. When the
company first installed a "dry tank" for bullet testing,
Handfield and others became concerned about the possibility of inhaling or otherwise absorbing lead. When
rifles are fired in the dry tank, the bullets pass through
a series of baffles. As a result, the bullets are pulverized
to dust and tiny particles. "We told them two years
back we'd have a problem with the dry tanks. We even
filed a grievance. But they didn't listen. Then after we
had the blood tests that showed the lead in our blood,
they were content to let the situation go on. It seemed
so callous to me. They just didn't give a damn."

William Sklar, a law student at the University of
Connecticut Law School and a volunteer at the Connecticut Citizens Action Group, literally stumbled on
the M–16 situation when he spoke to Handfield and
other Colt workers about their complaints of lead pollution in the West Hartford plant. The company's attitude toward the lead hazard jolted Handfield out of
going along with the company on the M–16 test tampering. "I'm sorry I didn't say something about that sooner.
Weapons go back a long way with me. When I got the
job in the plant, I was real excited. I was going to
work on the 'world's most sophisticated shoulder
weapon'—that's what they call it. Then I saw what was

going on and I got disillusioned. But I got in a rut. You lose perspective, you know, about a job and security. I might have let it go if this lead business hadn't come up."

Handfield is a gun purist: "I've loved guns since I was a boy. To me weapons are things of beauty." He has always read avidly "anything about armies and war" and at age sixteen he exaggerated his age in order to join the National Guard unit in his hometown, Florence, Massachusetts. At seventeen he quit school and joined the Army for the first of his two stints in the military. In 1964 he went to work at Colt's main plant in Hartford as a filer on small-arms pistols. When a job came open in the West Hartford plant, where the M–16s are made, he bid for it and got it. For Handfield, the gun enthusiast, this was the ultimate. But he was soon disillusioned, both with the M–16 and with Colt.

He was the first of the weapons testers to get sick from exposure to lead-filled dust. "I was tired at the end of the day, which isn't like me. I wanted to sleep all the time. Colt had promised to give us blood tests every three months, but they gave us only one test when we first started using the dry tank. So I went and got a blood test. The level of lead in my blood was .07 ppm [parts per million]. Then everybody else got tests too."

When the company still failed to put in a ventilation system or institute other precautionary measures, Handfield, incensed, went to the *Hartford Courant* in June, 1971. It was the *Courant* story that led CCAG representatives to contact Handfield and other Colt workers. For two weeks after the newspaper's story on the lead problem "company VIPs were in and out of the plant." Also, after the story, Handfield was given a three-day suspension for "saying something to a foreman," which he says was a bogus charge.

Later that summer, Handfield filed a complaint with the United States Labor Department under the Federal Occupational Safety and Health Act. Government investigators came in, and by early fall Colt had installed a ventilation system that Handfield says has reduced the dust.

Handfield, who is married and the father of three children, was again suspended, this time indefinitely, when it became generally known at the plant that CCAG was looking into possible test tampering. This time he was again told that he had been suspended for "saying something to a supervisor," but three days later he was back at work, having produced a witness who denied the foreman's charge. The "supervisory personnel are nice to me now," he says. "The people I work with consider me something like a hero. I don't know why."

Vic Martinez, a fifty-four-year-old veteran of twenty-two years service in the Marine Corps, joined Colt in October, 1961, as an archery equipment inspector at the Hartford plant. In 1968 he became a process inspector at the West Hartford plant. In May of that year he went onto the range as a targeter and range inspector for the M–16.

"I began to notice these irregularities right away. The minute I saw what was happening, swapping the parts and all the rest, I wanted to get it stopped. But who would believe one man? No one would stick together then. They were afraid they would lose their jobs." Then blood tests revealed that the people who worked in the range had high levels of lead in their blood. Martinez had the highest level on the first tests, with .08 ppm. He asked to be taken out of the range and was, along with three others.

William Sklar of CCAG contacted Martinez, as he would later other Colt workers, about the lead situation. As he talked, Martinez began to describe what else disturbed him, primarily the dishonesty in the testing procedures. This was the first time he had told anyone outside the plant about the problem. Previously, "every time something would happen I informed the government men. But I guess they were in the same boat we were in. Their superiors would tell them to smooth it over and nothing would happen."

When Sklar asked Martinez if he would make the problem public, "I was a little leery. You must understand, I had my wife to consider, it wasn't just me. So I first questioned her, told her I might lose my job and that the company might blackball me." But his wife supported him, and he decided to do it, particularly since he liked and trusted Sklar. "My reasoning was, being a Marine twenty-two years, that the men in the field were put in a position where it could happen that their gun just wouldn't fire. I was in the service and what was happening to them could have happened to me.

"Don't get me wrong. The M–16 is a beautiful little weapon. You can't beat it. But it's only as good as its parts. If you cover up malfunctions, then there's no sense in having tests. You've got to catch these defects and have the guns in A–1 condition before they go out of the plant and before they are in the hands of the boys in the field. There, your life depends on your gun. How many boys have died because their guns didn't fire or because a part didn't fit? We'll never know. It's too late to uncover these things in the field."

At the time of this writing, neither Martinez nor the other Colt whistle blowers have suffered serious repercussions at the plant, despite persistent rumors that they would soon "get the ax." Since November 2, 1971, Martinez has been back on the range, but "they haven't given me the chance to check on many of these things. The barrel-bending is still going on. They do that where everybody can see it." Martinez acknowledges that the majority of his colleagues are "scared stiff" of losing their jobs, but some are "glad these irregularities have come out."

The final chapter of the Colt episode is yet to be written. The results thus far, in terms of getting action from Congress, the Department of Defense, or the Justice Department have been disappointing at best. Congressman Les Aspin (D., Wis.), a first-termer on the House Armed Services Committee, published the CCAG report and later the affidavits of the Colt workers in the *Congressional Record* and sought hearings on the matter before his committee. Committee Chairman F. Edward Hébert (D., La.) referred the matter to the Defense Department. Connecticut Senator Abraham Ribicoff requested that the Senate Armed Services Committee look into the matter. The Defense Department's response was subsequently released as "Fact Sheet— M–16 Rifle," which Senator Barry Goldwater published

in the *Congressional Record*.[6] The Army Material
Command, the fact sheet reported, would begin an
"expedited" investigation, but it went on to state that
the Army had conducted tests on the rifle since November, 1967, that "clearly refute the allegations" in
the CCAG report. One reads the fact sheet's four
paragraphs in vain to find *any* of the allegations of
the Colt workers refuted. Colt Firearms president Paul
Benke later announced an investigation into the irregularities, but specifically declined to "formally rebut"
the report, though he also asserted that no one at
Colt has ever "knowingly" shipped any defective guns
out of the factory to any customer. Thus, both the
government and the company have denied the charges
before the investigations which each have announced.
The FBI has started an investigation, but early press
reports reflect some concern at precisely what the
FBI is investigating. CCAG spokesmen fear the bureau
might be investigating the workers and CCAG rather
than the substance of the report and the affidavits.[7]

15

Whistle Blowers Beyond the Headlines

It would be a mistake to assume that whistle blowers always reach the headlines. The opposite is probably closer to the truth. As Ernest Fitzgerald has said, "The only thing that makes me unique at all is that I have not gone away quietly, whereas most of the others have." Most whistle blowers are relatively unheralded, their reports buried in bureaucratic crypts, their fates unknown to the public even when the public benefits by their courage and honesty. They are whistle blowers who have spoken out far from the centers of power and the national press, and thus have not gained public attention. Or they have quietly given their information to those who they believed could take corrective action and have played only a background role in the ensuing debate. In some cases, they have acted anonymously to bring their information before the public.

This chapter touches briefly on a number of whistle blowers, some practically unknown or little known outside their organizations. In some cases, the reader will recognize the issue but not the name of the individual who first brought that issue to public attention. In other instances, he may recall a news story and wonder what has happened to the person who spoke out. Each case offers an alternative for action when the time comes that a man or woman cannot justify the organization's behavior and must choose between his or her view of the public interest and duty to an employer.

1. Carl W. Houston and Stone and Webster

In February, 1970, Carl Houston went to work as a welding supervisor on the construction of a nuclear power plant in Surry, Virginia. An engineer, he was an employee of the Stone and Webster Engineering Company of Boston, Massachusetts, which was overseeing construction of the plant owned by the Virginia Electric Power Company.

The first day on the job Houston noted defects in the welding of steel pipes, some of which would carry cooling water to and from the nuclear reactor. He informed the company the same day. In succeeding days he found more defects and was soon writing Stone and Webster in Boston in an effort to have corrections made.[1]

The danger of poorly welded pipes was critical, Houston pointed out. If cooling water were lost through a break in the pipes, temperatures within the reactor would rise with extreme rapidity. Though a nuclear explosion would be highly unlikely, in such a "big accident," as nuclear power experts have described the eventuality, the entire reactor would melt within a few hours, perhaps rupturing both the containment vessel surrounding it and the containment slab under it. Large quantities of radioactive material at very high temperatures would be released in the neighborhood of the plant through steam explosions. A molten mass of reactor material would sink into the ground to remain hot and radioactive for years, possibly contaminating underground water reservoirs and creating a long-lasting threat to all life in the vicinity of the plant.

The emergency cooling system that would be activated in such a situation has never been tested in any nuclear power plant, and Houston understandably doubted its effectiveness. The Union of Concerned Scientists, a group of nuclear physicists, engineers, and environmental experts including Dr. Henry W. Kendall of MIT, Dr. Ian A. Forbes of the Lowell Institute of Technology, and Dr. James J. MacKenzie of MIT share Houston's concerns about the adequacy of the emergency system.[2] As Dr. Ralph Lapp, a member of the Manhattan Project team, which developed the first American atomic bomb, has pointed out, the untested system would have to work perfectly within the first five to ten seconds after a break in the cooling system in order to prevent disaster.[3] Faced with this uncertainty and doubts about the resolution of other nuclear power safety issues, Senator Mike Gravel (D., Alaska) has introduced a bill which would impose a national moratorium on reactor construction until the fail-safe system to control the "big accident" has been designed and proven and until other safety issues have been resolved.

But Carl Houston's efforts were in vain. The company replied with increasing irritation to his pleas for better welding.

Two months after he signed on the job, Houston resigned after he was told by a Stone and Webster welding inspector that he was to be fired for "lack of experience in welding," a charge Houston found hard to take seriously, since he had been a journeyman welder for twenty-four years and his engineering experience was mostly in welding.

From April to June he wrote letters trying to get some action on the faulty welding. He wrote Governor Linwood Holton of Virginia and Senator Harry Byrd without replies. He wrote the Atomic Energy Commission with the same result. Finally, he wrote Tennessee Senators Albert Gore and Howard Baker, both of whom contacted the AEC. In mid-July, AEC officials visited Houston, who had moved to Johnson City, Tennessee. They promised to investigate eight of his allegations.

In August the AEC began an investigation of the Surry plant, which lasted for two months. They confirmed Houston's reports of defective welding. Late in October in a letter to Stanley Ragone of the Virginia Electric Power Company, John G. Davis, director of Region III of AEC's division of compliance, confirmed defects in welding, testing of welding rods, and the pouring of concrete, none of which met AEC construction standards. On December 28 the then AEC Chairman Glenn T. Seaborg wrote Senator Gore that "the general validity of Mr. Houston's eight allegations was verified."

The AEC then proposed, according to Houston, to bring all welding and other construction methods up to standards but *not* to correct past defects. AEC representatives told Houston that if there were failures in the operation of the plant, the plant emergency safety system would prevent danger. Houston pointed out that the safety devices to control the heat in the reactor if the normal cooling system failed had never been tested in an actual crisis. He had strong doubts that they would prove adequate.

In April, 1971, the AEC ran six tests on the safety devices in a plant in Idaho Falls, Idaho. All failed. As reported by Thomas O'Toole in the *Washington Post,* "the cooling water that bathed the heated elements was allowed to escape, as it would in a 'loss of coolant' accident that might result from a ruptured pipe. Emergency or backup coolant was then pumped into the reactor vessel to keep the nuclear core cool while procedures were begun to shut the core down.

"Test engineers discovered that high steam pressures kept almost all of the emergency cooling water out of the pressure vessel. One description of the test suggested that the pressurized steam blew the emergency coolant out through an outlet before the water even reached the hot core.

"A second problem occurred when the tests showed that the temperatures of some of the fuel elements in reactor cores might go higher than anticipated during a loss of coolant."[4]

Houston had already predicted these possible failures in the emergency cooling system.

Despite his accuracy, the AEC has not responded to Houston's criticism of the welding in the Surry, Virginia, plant with efforts that he deems adequate. Nor does he have much faith that the agency will insure proper construction in the future. Houston contends that the AEC has insufficient manpower to keep a close eye on the building of nuclear power plants. He is also critical of an AEC policy decision to delegate all quality control at the project level to the owner of each project. The AEC fails to understand, he believes, "that the owner's primary objective is frequently to meet the date scheduled for completion of construction" rather than to take all necessary safety precautions.

In the Surry plant, the need for enforced standards is especially critical, he believes. Virginia is one of the states that have not even adopted the minimum codes and standards of the American Society of Mechanical Engineers; welders at the Surry plant are therefore not bound to comply with ASME standards.

For his pains, Houston has been out of work ever since he left Stone and Webster in April, 1970. He is living in Johnson City, where he has attempted with little success to start a private consulting business. His applications for full-time jobs have been constantly rejected. He believes, though he cannot prove, that he has been blackballed in the construction industry since he criticized his former employer.

In October, 1970, Houston brought suit against Stone and Webster claiming slander and breach of contract. The suit was not heard in federal district court in Richmond until a year later, in October, 1971. At that time, the breach of contract charge was dismissed on grounds that Houston had submitted his resignation. Then Stone and Webster asked that the name of its Virginia agent be joined as defendant along with the company, to which the judge agreed. The case was then remanded to state court. The case thus promises to stretch into a lengthy legal battle far beyond Houston's scant financial means. He has already had to sell his house in Johnson City, Tennessee, to pay his attorney's legal fees. He has also used up six thousand dollars of savings and borrowed five thousand from friends, relatives, and a local bank to support his wife and three children.

He is still trying to force the Atomic Energy Commission to take action on past welding defects at the Surry plant. Virginia Lieutenant Governor Henry Howell has intervened in the matter, and the AEC has scheduled a hearing in February at which Houston will testify.

2. Henry M. Durham and Lockheed

In the midst of the controversy over the proposed bail-out of the Lockheed Aircraft Corporation with a $250 million federal loan guarantee, a former Lockheed employee publicly charged the company with inefficient and wasteful management.

Backed with a sheaf of documentation, Henry M. Durham, a former assistant division manager at Lockheed-Georgia, said bluntly that many of Lockheed's troubles were the company's own fault.

According to documents Durham gave to the *Washington Post,* mostly memoranda he had written to his superiors, inefficient supply practices at Lockheed accounted for a substantial part of the $2 billion overrun on the C-5A transport plane.

In the fall of 1969, Durham found that numerous parts issued and presumably installed on sections of the C-5A were missing. By certifying that these sections were complete, Durham contended, Lockheed received payment from the Air Force for work that still had to be done.

In the spring of 1970, Durham reported to his superiors that the company's methods for ordering "very small parts" (VSPs) and disorderly storage that resulted in parts being thrown away had raised the cost of VSPs from $560,000 per aircraft to over $1 million per aircraft.

Other parts, he reported in another memo to his immediate superior, were purchased and then returned to stock because they weren't needed. Such practices, Durham told the *Post,*[5] wasted "thousands and thousands of dollars. It happened on all ships, constantly."

Durham went on to relate other examples of mismanagement that he had observed and documented in memos to his bosses. Most of the problems, he believes, were kept from the top company management by lower-ranking employees anxious not to rock the boat.

Durham's attempts to improve Lockheed's supply program led, he says, to his demotion in the spring of 1970, with a twenty-dollar-a-week pay cut. He protested, even taking his case to the president of Lockheed-Georgia, R. H. Fuhrman. This interview had no results except, as Durham later wrote Lockheed chairman Daniel Haughton, "I was ostracized, criticized, pushed into a corner, and eventually downgraded."

Rather than take a demotion, Durham said he would leave Lockheed. Haughton replied that he would ask for an investigation but ended his letter, "I hope you find a job that you will be happy with." Durham has not heard of any investigation of his case.

In the next few months, Durham was twice asked to return to Lockheed. The second time he agreed, taking a job at eighty dollars a week below his former salary at the Chattanooga, Tennessee, plant, one hundred miles from his home in Marietta, Georgia.

Once in Chattanooga, however, Durham said he continued to find "shabby performance," and he continued to protest. Finally, in May, 1971, he again left the company. Durham says he asked to be laid off. W. P. Frech, director of manufacturing at Lockheed-Georgia, told the *Post* that Durham left when he was told he would have to take a "downgrade" because of employment cuts.

Durham's public disclosures of mismanagement in July, 1971, brought immediate disclaimers from his former bosses who said, in effect, that Durham didn't know what he was talking about. However, Senator William Proxmire asked Durham to testify before his Subcommittee on Economy in Government. He did on September 29, 1971, reiterating and amplifying the story he gave the *Post*.

At the hearings Durham also reported what had happened to him and his family since he made his accusations public. They were ostracized by friends in Marietta, Georgia, and subjected to "an apparent organized telephone attack threatening in almost every instance my life and frequently the lives of my wife and children. We took these cases rather lightly at first, but the offensive language and brutal tones of the voices we listened to quickly made us realize that some of these people, at least, had murder in their minds."

Now Durham is trying to start a business selling Aerosol products in the Atlanta area. His wife has gone to work to support the family.

Morton Mintz, the reporter who wrote the story for

the *Post,* found Durham an "unlikely" whistle blower. For most of his nineteen years at Lockheed, Mintz reported, Durham worked eleven-hour days and seven-day weeks. His devotion to his company was such that "if Lockheed wanted it, I assumed it was good."

Why, then, did he blow the whistle? In a letter to Fuhrman, he wrote, "I have been very disappointed with my superiors for lacking the fortitude and courage to go to the top if necessary to get serious problems corrected. . . . I realize now that it is because certain members of management feel they must conform and not rock the nice, tight little boat they have constructed. I believe *one cannot afford to jeopardize the company by conforming to such standards.* One must operate with directness and integrity in the best interests of the company, not the individual." (Emphasis added.)

3. George B. Geary and U.S. Steel

George Geary, a sales executive with the United States Steel Corporation's oil and gas industry supply division in Houston, Texas, strongly objected to the sale of a new type of pipe which he believed was inadequately tested and likely to fail under high pressure. He told the company that in his judgment use of the pipe could result in serious physical injury to customers and the public as well as property damage. He urged his immediate superiors to perform more tests before marketing the product.

Geary was not an engineer, but during his fourteen years with U.S. Steel, he had had extensive experience with the technical aspects of tubular steel products manufactured for use by the oil and gas industry.

Despite his reservations, mid-level managers decided to pursue the sales program for the pipe. Geary reluctantly agreed to participate but carried his objections to officials in U.S. Steel's main office, who were ultimately responsible for the product. Because of his good reputation with the company and the potential seriousness of his assertions, these officials ordered an immediate re-evaluation of the new line of pipe. Shortly thereafter, the product was withdrawn from sale pending major retesting.

Geary was discharged on July 13, 1967. The reason given: insubordination. Apparently, even though he may have saved the company substantial costs had the pipe been prematurely marketed and saved users of the pipe from physical and financial injury, he had ignored the rules of the game and breached the etiquette of hierarchical management.

Unlike whistle blowers who lack the means or the persistence to pursue available legal remedies, Geary has sought and continues to seek relief in a number of legal forums. Through a damage suit, his attorney hopes to develop a new principle of law: that any employee, under appropriate circumstances, can sue and obtain compensation for "wrongful discharge." Heretofore, only members of labor unions have had similar protection when their collective bargaining agreements contain provisions limiting discharges to cases in which the employer can show "just cause."

Geary's application for unemployment compensation also raised a question similar to that of dismissal for "just cause" before the Unemployment Compensation Board of Review of the Pennsylvania Department of Labor and Industry. Under the applicable laws, if an employer can show that the employee was discharged for "willful misconduct," the latter can be denied unemployment compensation even though he would otherwise be entitled to benefits. U.S. Steel chose to seek such a finding in Geary's case. After several hearings and appeals, the Pennsylvania Board of Review held on May 3, 1968:

> No company places a man in the position held by the claimant and pays him the salary received by the claimant simply to have him quietly agree to all proposals. The claimant did not refuse to follow orders, but, in fact, agreed to do as instructed despite his opposition to the program proposed. Although he may have been vigorous in his opposition and offended some superiors by going to a vice president, it is clear that *at all times the claimant was working in the best interest of the company* and that the welfare of the

company was primary in his mind. Under these circumstances, giving due regard to the claimant's position with the company, his conduct cannot be deemed willful misconduct. [Emphasis added]

The board was not making a determination on the separate question of whether or not Geary had been wrongfully discharged. Nevertheless, its decision indicates that judicial bodies are capable of reasoned judgments about an employee's conduct with respect to his employer in a whistle blowing situation.

4. Warren Braren and the National Associaion of Broadcasters

As manager of the New York office of the Code Authority of the National Association of Broadcasters, Warren Braren was responsible for seeing that television commercials complied with the code standards for honest and accurate advertising. He particularl? urged the NAB to take steps against cigarette commercials considered in violation of the standards. His superiors were reluctant to take decisive action against tobacco companies, which contributed millions to broadcast treasuries. These differences between Braren and Code Authority leaders became increasingly tense during the late nineteen-sixties as public opposition to the broadcasting of cigarette commercials grew.

In 1969, congressional hearings were held to determine the legislative course to follow expiration of the first federal cigarette-labeling act. Tobacco interests lobbied vigorously against regulation of cigarette advertising, as did broadcast interests. NAB president Vincent Wasilewski testified before the House Commerce Committee in April, 1969, arguing against regulation on the grounds that the NAB code enforcement program provided sufficient "self-regulation" in the public interest. The committee was unaware that Braren, within the NAB, had been arguing that the Code Authority's regulation was far from adequate.

Not long afterwards, on May 1, 1969, as a result of their longstanding differences, the NAB president asked for Braren's resignation.

Shortly after resigning, Braren went to Congressman

Brock Adams (D., Wash.) and disclosed confidential NAB reports which illustrated the failure of "self-regulation" with respect to cigarette advertising. On June 10, Congressman Adams held a news conference and released Braren's information. The House committee had issued its report on the Public Health Cigarette Smoking Act three days earlier, but on hearing of Braren's criticism of NAB regulation, Chairman Harley Staggers hastily called a meeting of the Commerce Committee to hear Braren and NAB representatives discuss his charges.

Braren told committee members that they had been misled into believing that the NAB Code Authority exercised effective regulation over cigarette ads. The Code Authority stuck to its guns and Congressmen from the tobacco states subjected Braren to vicious cross-examination on his motives for speaking out. They attempted to discredit his testimony as the bitterness of a recently fired employee. They also asked why Braren had not come forward while the hearings were still in session and why he had not gone to the chairman when he did speak. Braren admitted that, not versed in the byzantine code of congressional protocol, he had gone to the only committee member with whom he was acquainted. He delayed coming in the first place, he said candidly, while he struggled to decide whether to let the matter go or end the possibility of further employment in his profession by speaking out. "It is not an easy decision, I can assure you, to face the eventual possibility of never being able to work again in your chosen profession," he told the congressmen.

Braren accurately predicted his employment future. The industry has not touched him since. He served for a time as executive director of the National Citizens Committee for Broadcasting, a public interest group, and is now assistant director of Consumers Union.

5. *Kermit Vandivier and B. F. Goodrich*

Kermit Vandivier had worked as a scientific writer for the B. F. Goodrich Company for six years when he was assigned, in early 1968, to write reports on raw data developed from tests of the brakes for the A-7D aircraft. Goodrich was building the A-7D brakes for the Air Force under subcontract from the Ling-Temco-Vought Company. In the course of his work, Vandivier was ordered to falsify figures so that test results which had not met contract specifications would appear to have been successful.

He followed instructions under protest until his conscience would no longer let him remain silent. In addition to the implication of fraud, he feared for the lives of A-7D pilots who would have no knowledge of the actual brake test failures. In June, 1968, he went to the FBI. The local agent promised to begin an investigation but urged him to remain on the job. Five months later, having heard no further word from the FBI, he resigned in protest.

Before he quit, Vandivier had already lined up a job as a reporter with a local newspaper, the *Troy* (Ohio) *Daily News*. Later, the paper ran an exposé on the A-7D scandal.

In August, 1969, Vandivier and another former Goodrich employee, Searle Lawson, an aeronautical engineer, testified before the Joint Economic Committee of Congress. It was revealed at the hearings that the Air Force had been seriously concerned with the performance of the brake before Vandivier's story became public knowledge, but had been refused access to the raw test data (which would have demonstrated the falsifications) on the grounds that such information was "proprietary."

As a result of Vandivier's testimony and a subsequent Air Force investigation, the A-7D brakes were withdrawn and substitutes developed. The Air Force took issue with Vandivier's contention that the brakes constituted a serious threat to the safety of test pilots, but by its action supported his allegations concerning falsification of test data. No action was taken against Goodrich or any of its employees.

6. Carl Thelin and General Motors

When Ralph Nader's *Unsafe at Any Speed* was published in 1965, Carl Thelin was working as an engineer for General Motors. His specialty was design of chassis suspension systems and steering mechanisms. (One of his design innovations culminated in the experimental vehicle which eventually became the Oldsmobile To-ronado.) In addition, he provided engineering liaison for General Motor's legal staff and in that capacity found himself in the middle of the Corvair issue.

Thelin and his associates were charged with devel-oping engineering and technical support for General Motors' defense in damage suits brought by Corvair victims or their families. They conducted accident in-vestigations, produced films to be shown to juries, and held seminars on vehicle dynamics for defense lawyers who would have to question witnesses. Thelin also pre-pared an index and critique of materials considered important in the Corvair litigation.

In the course of piecing together these materials, Thelin discovered inexplicable gaps in company rec-ords. He refused to accept explanations that the missing records never existed. When he persisted, he was finally provided with documents which he later described as "dynamite." He was warned, however, that these pa-pers were never to be shown to anyone who might be called on to testify in behalf of General Motors. Later, Thelin himself was removed from cases when General Motors executives thought he might show the records to potential witnesses.

Several years later, Gary Sellers, a legal consultant to Ralph Nader, discovered in a review of some of the Corvair papers that Carl Thelin's name cropped up re-peatedly. Sellers went to see Thelin, who by then had moved to Buffalo, New York, to head the design and test section of the automotive safety department at the Cornell Aeronautical Laboratory. Thelin revealed to Sellers, and on a separate occasion to *Washington Post* reporter Morton Mintz, that General Motors had con-cealed test reports from its own witnesses to prevent their surfacing in court. According to Thelin, one of the documents proved that with suspension systems like those installed on later models the early Corvairs would have been almost impossible to roll over. It revealed further that top General Motors officials knew this even before the first Corvair was offered for sale.

Thelin said that when Nader's book first came out

he had accepted uncritically the "straight party line" of his company. Later he came to believe that General Motors was obligated at least to produce the suppressed documents. When Sellers, Mintz, and, later, investigators from Senator Ribicoff's Government Operations subcommittee sought his cooperation in finding the truth, he said he had no choice but to help them.[6]

7. George Caramanna and General Motors

George Caramanna was a member of the General Motors team that designed and tested the Corvair. From mid-1957 to 1970 he was senior design and development technician with the research and development section of Chevrolet. In 1970, Caramanna resigned and moved to California for family reasons and began operating his own service station in Spring Valley near San Diego. When new revelations about the Corvair were reported late that year, principally those made by Carl Thelin, Caramanna began to reconsider his earlier decision to remain silent about the defects of the car.

In early May, 1971, he contacted Alexander Auerbach of the *Los Angeles Times* and unfolded a new chapter in the history of the Corvair. Auerbach's story appeared in the *Los Angeles Times* on May 28, 1971.

General Motors had never publicly conceded the unsafe characteristics of the 1960–1963 Corvairs, even though the company instituted several "product improvements" in the 1964 and 1965 models that substantially reduced the car's tendency to roll over unexpectedly. Caramanna's first-hand knowledge conflicted sharply with the official company line.

According to Caramanna, the very first Corvair, a prototype, rolled over in its first trial run. Contrary to claims by General Motors, the rollover was purely accidental and not part of any test program. Production models suffered the same fate, he told Auerbach, adding that "it doesn't have to be at high speed. It can happen at thirty miles per hour or even less in a sharp turn."

More disturbing was his report that the research and development section had been directed to design modifications for racing versions of the Corvair which were not put on the car sold to the public. "You could not turn it over the way we fixed it," he said. He contended that the modifications were simple and inexpensive. They included a stabilizer bar, for which a mounting spot was embossed into the body of the regular Corvair three years before the bar itself became standard equipment. Auerbach noted in his story for the *Los Angeles Times* that General Motors engineer Charles Rubly said in 1960 that the roll stabilizer bar was left off the early Corvair because "we felt the slight amount of gain realized did not warrant the cost." Caramanna maintained that several engineers and technicians on the project, including himself, had told Chevrolet officials point blank that without the stabilizer bar the car was unsafe.

Finally, Caramanna supplied the missing link to the mysterious General Motors test films used by defense counsel in many of the hundreds of suits filed by Corvair crash victims or their families. The film showed a Corvair being put through rigorous test maneuvers without mishap. Caramanna confirmed that the car was a standard Corvair without special adjustments. However, he revealed that he had developed special driving techniques to counter the car's inherent tendency to roll over. The ordinary driver, Caramanna pointed out, would tend to take corrective action that would have precisely the opposite results and substantially accentuate the roll tendency.

8. Ronald Ostrander and Proctor and Gamble

Ronald Ostrander was project engineer on the Procter and Gamble research team which developed Tide laundry detergent in the late nineteen-forties. In December, 1970, he wrote Congressman Henry Reuss (D., Wis.), chairman of the House Conservation and Natural Resources Subcommittee, that "the most important knowledge bearing on. . . . the subject [of phosphate detergents] apparently is known to a limited number of people and I am one of that number."

Ostrander revealed that the optimum amount of detergent for effective washing is substantially less than recommended by most manufacturers. Housewives, he wrote, could achieve better results at substantially less cost while reducing by ninety percent the amount of phosphates entering the water. Most manufacturers call for a minimum of one and one-quarter cups of detergent for top loader washing machines and one-half cup for front loaders, when in fact one-eighth cup would do well for both, he said.

Procter and Gamble, which Ostrander still describes as a "marvelous" company, initially instructed consumers to use much smaller amounts of Tide than other laundry products. But the company discovered, he said, that housewives preferred to see large quantities of suds in the mistaken belief that suds represent cleaning power. Old habits were hard to break and manufacturers apparently decided not to attempt to break a profitable one.

Ostrander left Procter and Gamble in 1949 to take over a family business. Except for a stint with the Army Chemical Corps during World War II, he had been with the company since he graduated from engineering school in 1935. He was not a "disgruntled employee," as Procter and Gamble spokesmen were to charge twenty-one years later in response to his letter to Congressman Reuss. On the contrary, he had planned from the first to leave the company before he became too dependent on its tempting, but late-vesting, pension plan. He remained through the Tide project only because he found it exciting. Both then and later, Ostrander viewed the project as an intriguing industrial version of the supersecret Manhattan Project, which developed the first American atom bomb. When the project was complete, he left satisfied with the company and his own performance.

Now fifty-nine, Ostrander is with the Wisconsin Department of Natural Resources, largely because of a personal commitment to help achieve a better environment. That commitment grew out of his efforts to alert first his friends, then the local media, then the Federal Water Quality Administration, and finally Congress to the truth about optimum use of detergents. His experience suggests that older professionals and technically skilled citizens have much to offer, that one can embark on a second career in the public interest, and that it is never too late to blow the whistle.

As a direct result of Ostrander's letter, Congressman Reuss has called on the Federal Trade Commission to conduct a major investigation based on Ostrander's charges. That investigation is now in progress.

9. Frank Serpico and David Durk and the N.Y.P.D.

One of the major facts that came out during the Knapp Commission investigations of corruption in the New York City Police Department was the effort by two members of the force to get something done about graft within police ranks and the refusal of high-ranking police officials to listen to them.

Patrolman Frank Serpico and Sergeant David Durk were the two policemen responsible for the exposure of misconduct among "New York's Finest" over the past several years and, ultimately, for the convening of the Knapp Commission. The effort took five years of contacting one police official after another, a fruitless appeal to City Hall and, finally, an appeal to the public through the press.

Frank Serpico grew up in the Bedford-Stuyvesant section of Brooklyn and joined the New York City Police Department in 1959 after graduating from City College. As he was to describe it later, he found a well-developed system of shakedowns and payoffs within the department involving not only patrolmen but higher-ups who either actively participated or tolerated the graft.

He also found that the pressure to join the system was intense, and, as he consistently refused to become a part of it, Serpico was increasingly isolated from his fellow policemen.

In 1966, a Bronx gambler offered Serpico and his partner a bribe, which the partner accepted. Serpico turned down his share of the payoff, three hundred dollars, and got in touch with Detective David Durk, a close friend. An Amherst graduate, Durk had been working successfully to recruit college graduates for the New York police. He, too, had become concerned about the demoralizing effects of corruption within police ranks.

Serpico and Durk began contacting officials in the department who had the power and the responsibility to investigate departmental corruption. But nothing happened, and Serpico particularly became mistrustful of his superiors. He feared that they would not back him up in his allegations, and he was under no illusion about the risk he took in making his information known.

As months went by and no action was taken, Durk arranged a meeting with Jay Kriegel, special counsel to Mayor Lindsay on police matters. He and Serpico asked that their identity not be disclosed and that the mayor, whom they offered to meet, not inform their superiors in the police department of the meeting. Reports of that offer vary, but the undisputed fact is that neither he nor Kriegel acted on their information.

The mayor later told the Knapp Commission that "I could not under any circumstances as mayor accept those ground rules. Police Commissioner Leary had been on board for a year and three months at this point. It would have undermined him totally. It would have been a signal to him of no confidence, and if I'd been a police commissioner under those circumstances I expect I'd have handed in my resignation. . . ."

Kriegel told the commission that he did not tell the mayor of Durk and Serpico's belief that the top police command was not acting on their allegations, because of their request for secrecy. Durk, however, said that Kriegel refused to act because it might stir up the police and implied that the city could not afford that with the possibility of summer riots near.

In spite of the official rebuffs, Serpico and Durk kept trying. Durk next went to see the person responsible for policing official misconduct, Commissioner of Investigation Arnold Fraiman. Fraiman barely listened to him and told Durk at one point that Serpico seemed to him a "psycho."

Finally, in October, 1967, a year after Serpico first stated his charges, the police department launched an investigation. Serpico and others believe that it did so only after officials learned that he had talked to Kriegel and Fraiman. That investigation led to indictments against nine patrolmen and one lieutenant. For Serpico it was a bitter victory because not one higher-ranking official was involved, which meant to him that the system of graft could continue relatively uninterrupted.

As a last resort, Serpico and Durk went to the press. The *New York Times* investigated their allegations and in May, 1970, published a long article on police corruption. Here at last they had found a lever that brought some response. Mayor Lindsay heard about the *Times* article one day before it was to be published and appointed a commission to study police misconduct. That body became the Knapp Commission, which during six months of hearings in late 1971 uncovered lengthy evidence of payoffs to police.

New York City Police Commissioner Patrick Murphy has praised Serpico's efforts as "the highest form of loyalty to . . . fellow officers." It is apt praise, particularly in view of Serpico's concern for the kinds of oppression to which patrolmen, in particular, are subject when their superiors encourage a system of corruption or simply close their eyes to it. However, others in the department, those who have most to fear from his allegations, have not been so generous. In February, 1971, Serpico was shot in the head by a narcotics pusher. While he was recovering in a hospital, he received a "get well" card signed "with sincere sympathy . . . that you didn't get your brains blown out, you rat bastard. Happy relapse."

Yet it is not his fellow policemen, it is his superiors against whom Serpico is most bitter. On the witness stand of the Knapp Commission, which called him to testify only after criticism by the newspapers, Serpico urged reform so that "police officers in the future will not experience the same frustration and anxiety that I was subjected to for the past five years at the hands of my superiors because of my attempt to report corruption."

Durk also told the commission why he and Serpico gave five years of their lives to reform their organization:

"We wanted to believe in the rule of law. We wanted

to believe in a system of responsibility. But those in high places everywhere, in the police department, in the D.A.'s office, in city hall, were determined not to enforce the law and they turned their heads when law and justice were being sold on every streetcorner.

"We wanted to serve others, but the department was a home for the drug dealers and thieves. The force that was supposed to be protecting people was selling poison to their children. And there could be no life, no real life for me or anyone else on the force when, every day, we had to face the facts of our own terrible corruption.

"I saw that happening to men all around me, men who could have been good officers, men of decent impulse, men of ideals, but men who were without decent leadership, men who were told in a hundred ways every day go along, forget the law, don't make waves, and shut up.

"So they did shut up. They did go along. They did learn the unwritten code of the department. They went along and they lost something very precious: they weren't cops anymore. They were a long way towards not being men any more."[7]

10. Gordon Rule and the Air Force

A ranking civilian procurement official in the Naval Material Command, Gordon Rule has publicly criticized Navy procurement practices on two separate occasions. Several years ago, he complained to procurement policy makers about the Navy's mishandling of the F–111B fighter contracts, which had resulted in enormous cost overruns. He later revealed the substance of his in-house criticisms in testimony before a subcommittee of the Joint Economic Committee.

For his efforts to protect the public purse, he was passed over for the Legion of Merit, which was awarded to several of his subordinates. The Navy subsequently reversed itself and granted him the Distinguished Service Medal. Rule also got a delayed promotion.

On May 24, 1971, he returned to the same joint committee and revealed that the Navy awarded two contractors $135.5 million in claims without determining whether the government was legally obligated to pay anything. One of the contractors was a subsidiary of the Lockheed Aircraft Corporation, then seeking a $250 million loan guarantee from the federal government. In response to a question from Senator Proxmire, Rule described the proposed guarantee as "most unwise." "If we do this for Lockheed," he said, "we're setting a precedent we'll never live down. . . . If their management is so lousy, let them go broke."

The Navy has taken no action against Rule as yet for his heretical statements.

11. John McGee and the Navy

John McGee, a civilian employee of the Navy, was serving as fuel inspector in Thailand when he became concerned that Navy procedures in handling Armed Forces fuel in Thailand were not providing adequate protection against theft. McGee's attempts to raise these issues with his superiors were frustrated. No one in the Navy, it appeared, was interested. So in March, 1968, he contacted Senator Proxmire's office.

Senator Proxmire instigated an investigation by the General Accounting Office that sustained McGee's allegations of laxity. The GAO found 5.5 million gallons of fuel in Thailand stolen or unaccounted for between January and October, 1967. The report was made public in January, 1969.

The immediate response of the Navy to McGee's allegations was to reprimand him, deny him a pay raise and threaten him with discharge. After Senator Proxmire intervened, however, the reprimand was withdrawn and McGee cleared of any charges.

Having weathered bureaucratic reprisals, McGee has now been promoted from a GS–11 to a GS–12. He is assigned to an interim project office in Pensacola, Florida.[8]

12. Ronald Ridenhour and My Lai

An Army enlisted man left the service to investigate and reveal an incident that led to one of the most sustained examinations of Army procedures in this century, the My Lai massacre. Ronald Ridenhour pieced together the My Lai story with information from fellow soldiers in Vietnam. He disclosed the information through extensive correspondence with Department of Defense officials, members of the House Armed Services Committee and other congressmen seven months before the tragedy became public knowledge.

The results—the inquiries, charges, and trials of Army personnel who were responsible—are well known. One of those involved, General Samuel Koster, who commanded the unit which participated in the massacre and received a demotion for his failure to thoroughly investigate the incident, commented later that the only difference between My Lai and many other similar tragedies in Vietnam was Ronald Ridenhour.

13. Oscar Hoffman and the Navy

Not all whistle blowers in the military fare so well as the preceding ones. Oscar Hoffman, a pipe fitter assigned to inspect pipes on ships under construction for the Navy, did not. While working at Todd Shipyards in Seattle, Hoffman submitted to his Navy supervisor several reports on unsatisfactory work by the contractor. On several occasions these reports were rejected. Then Hoffman was ordered to destroy some fifty of his reports. He refused.

When Navy management learned that Hoffman was planning to file a grievance to correct the conditions, they retaliated with a reprimand. Despite a ruling by a Navy hearing officer that the reprimand was improper, the Navy did not return Hoffman to his former duties but sent him to Tacoma, Washington, to monitor the construction of a ferry boat. Having formally assigned him to Tacoma, the Navy proceeded to abolish his job. Hoffman was fired through a "reduction in force."

The Navy lieutenant who had rejected Hoffman's reports and then improperly issued a reprimand was promoted to lieutenant commander.

Stymied in his attempts to protect the taxpayer and resolve his difficulties with the Navy, Hoffman informed Senator Proxmire and the Joint Economic Committee of the shoddy work he had observed. Then later events proved that had his criticism been heeded earlier, the taxpayer could indeed have been saved huge sums and Navy personnel would have avoided unnecessary risks. One of the ships constructed by Todd Shipyards during the period when Hoffman was attempting to call attention to unsatisfactory welds suffered damage from fire while anchored in Hawaii. Investigation indicated that a number of welds in the piping were faulty.

Despite an (otherwise) unblemished record, Hoffman has been unable to find a position with any other Navy command. He is currently pursuing legal actions seeking reinstatement.[9]

14. Kenneth S. Cook and the Air Force

Kenneth S. Cook was an Air Force weapons analyst assigned to Holloman Air Force Base in New Mexico. A highly educated and competent physicist,[10] Cook complained in 1966 that Lieutenant Colonel Roderick W. Clarke, Acting Commanding Officer, was distorting scientific reports of the defense against intercontinental ballistic missiles and exaggerating claims for the effectiveness of defense systems. Cook was highly disturbed by what he saw as a lack of scientific honesty.

When Cook found that his pleas for incorporating the full pro-and-con analysis arguments in study reports were not heeded, he sent a confidential letter on November 2, 1966, to Brigadier General Ernest Pinson, Commanding General of the Office of Aerospace Research at the Pentagon. In the letter he stated his charges of information manipulation.

On November 22, 1966, Cook was called in by his commanding officer, who informed him that he had a copy of Cook's "confidential" letter to General Pinson. What followed was a Kafkaesque nightmare. Cook's top-secret security clearance was summarily removed without explanation. Then he was ordered to submit to an examination by military medical personnel. According to Cook, the most vehement of the latter was a psychologist who was deputy commander of the NASA "monkey lab." Then, before a military medical panel where he was not permitted legal counsel, he was found mentally and physically incapable of performing further service for the Air Force or elsewhere within the government.

Cook's attempts to alter the verdict or simply to present the testimony of his own doctors were futile. His only recourse from the Air Force's action was the Civil Service Commission, which upheld the decision in a hearing at which neither Cook nor his representatives were permitted to be present. Lieutenant Colonel Paul Grissom, consultant in psychiatry and neurology in the Office of the Surgeon General, stated that the action was an injustice. Two lieutenant colonels and colleagues of Cook at Holloman gave testimony to the Civil Service Commission that it was one of the worst examples of getting rid of an employee. Their efforts were to no avail.

Cook's case is now being pursued by the American Civil Liberties Union and may become a test case in protecting the rights of whistle blowers who simply appeal privately to their superior's superior.

Cook's suit was filed in August, 1969, against the Air Force and Civil Service Commission, challenging the finding of his incompetence and the procedure which allowed him no hearing or means of defending himself. One of the primary facets of the case, which Cook is trying to challenge, is a provision in the Civil Service Code that the authority of the Civil Service Commission is final in such mental disability retirement cases.

Having been declared incompetent, Cook cannot find work. Now residing in Alexandria, Virginia, he spends all of his time researching his case and offering help to Congress in exposing incompetence in military research and development studies.

15. Peter Gall and HEW

The firing of Leon Panetta, director of the Office of Civil Rights in the Department of Health, Education, and Welfare, was met with unprecedented protest within HEW.[11] One of those concerned was Peter Gall, a special assistant to Panetta for press relations. Gall had long been troubled by the administration's vacillation on civil rights policy. He admired Panetta, who he felt was attempting to follow firm guidelines in enforcing Title VI of the Civil Rights Act, and felt that his dismissal compromised the administration.

Shortly after Panetta's dismissal was announced on February 17, 1970, HEW employees began to let the administration know their views. Within a few weeks a petition with close to two thousand signatures was presented to Secretary Finch, protesting the government's position on school desegregation. As a result, Finch promised to meet with employees and discuss the department's position on civil rights.

Other employees felt that stronger measures were called for and were not content to let the matter rest with HEW. Gall joined with a number of HEW employees in drafting a letter to President Nixon expressing their dismay over the action. (The letter was signed by 125 employees.) But he soon concluded that he could not remain a spokesman for a civil rights policy —or nonpolicy—that he opposed. He would have to resign.

Gall and Paul Rilling, an HEW regional director in Atlanta who also felt he could not stay with the department, decided to coordinate their departures and publicize their protest by issuing their letters of resignation to the press. They did so on March 3, the same day that the employees' letter was delivered to the White House. In his letter to Secretary Finch, Gall said, "I cannot any longer try to justify to the public the actions of this Administration regarding either the subject of civil rights generally, or its treatment of your Office for Civil Rights in particular."

Writing later in the *Washington Monthly*, Gall noted that "the protests in HEW raise a crucially important— although perhaps ultimately unanswerable—question: What is the correct balance between a bureaucrat's right under the First Amendment to express his views as a citizen and his obligation to follow the policies of his seniors, especially that senior of seniors, the President?"

His own answer was that a direct protest—in this case an employee's letter addressed to the President— is entirely justifiable. To do it quietly, without press coverage, as some employees suggested, would "have been a waste of everyone's time. . . . There was every reason to believe that the letter would not even have come to the attention of the President if it had been dropped off quietly at the White House mail room."

In similar fashion, he felt that a statement to the press on his own resignation gave force and meaning to his dissent.

Gall is now writing a book with Panetta about civil rights in the Nixon administration.[12]

16. Interior Department Dissenters

The Environmental Quality Act of 1970 requires that every federal agency file a public "environmental impact statement" before taking or approving any action that might substantially affect the environment. The purpose of the statement is to encourage thorough agency consideration of the ecological consequences of a plan and to provide more thorough public scrutiny of agency actions.

When the Trans-Alaska oil pipeline was proposed, the Interior Department was required to prepare and file such a statement. The draft statement finally drawn up painted a glowing picture of the pipeline and downplayed or omitted references to some of the potential environmental risks of the pipeline construction and operation.

Certain employees in the department's Bureau of Land Management were outraged by the proposed statement, which they saw as seriously deficient, particularly in view of information which they knew was available to the department.

Washington columnist Jack Anderson received from environmentalist sources a copy of a Bureau of Land Management memorandum that clearly spelled out the risks to the Alaskan environment which Interior spokesmen had publicly discredited. Anderson published excerpts of the memorandum, but Interior refused to make it available until Congressman Les Aspin (D., Wis.) published a copy in the *Congressional Record*.

The Department of Interior now maintains that it is rethinking its position on the pipeline. The whistle blowers remain unidentified.

The "leaked" memo has become a time-honored tactic for Washington bureaucrats to express their dissatisfaction with the policies of an administration, and for an administration to float trial balloons to test public reaction without risking criticism. Syndicated columnists such as Jack Anderson, and before him Drew Pearson, rely heavily on this form of insider expression to give their readers insights into the functioning of government, though Anderson is rarely the instrument of an "official" leak. The pervasiveness of the phenomenon has led some commentators to suggest that the practice may play an accepted role in molding opinion and in shaping policy.[13]

17. Health Employees for Change and the Public Health Service

In December, 1970, President Nixon signed the Lead-based Poison Prevention Act, a measure his administration had vigorously opposed. He failed, however, to mention the act in his first health message to the Ninety-first Congress and also failed to request appropriations for implementation of the act in his budget message.

By May, 1971, it had become clear to many concerned doctors and medical professionals in the Public Health Service that the administration would seek little if any funding for the lead-poisoning prevention program. Many felt that an unprecedented public break with the administration was the only hope of heading off this move. On May 10, 1971, a group calling itself "Health Employees for Change" (HEC) released to the press a position paper criticizing their agency and the President for continued foot-dragging on the appropriations. Their statement began:

> In spite of the Administration's concern for prevention and health maintenance, there has been little support for action programs to deal with a clearly preventable disease that kills hundreds and leaves thousands of children with some form of measurable brain damage each year: Lead Poisoning.[14]

HEC was not merely an ad hoc attempt to meet the crisis of May, 1971. One hundred or more young physicians and health professionals within the Public Health Service had been holding open, informal meetings for several years to discuss various aspects of administration and PHS health policy. All employees, including superiors at every level, were welcomed. Members of the group prepared discussion papers on various topics for consideration at the open meetings. Though discussions often involved sharp criticism of the status quo within the agency, no attempt was made to seek publicity or involve outsiders.

In the lead poisoning issue, HEC spokesmen tried to elicit a response from the administration and the agency to what they considered reasonable, nonemotional criticism by professionals who had been hired to do more than shuffle papers and follow orders. But their efforts—like those by professionals and citizens outside the agency—proved futile. "Going public" was their last resort.

By coincidence, the HEC statement was released one day before the President announced a massive federal commitment to seek a cure for cancer. The administration proposed $330 million in the first year for a separate cancer research organization. In contrast, the administration announced a month later that it would request $2 million for lead poisoning prevention for fiscal year 1972.[15] (New York City's existing program alone is funded at $2.4 million.)

HEC members are by no means certain that their efforts won even these paltry sums. But they believe they were able to call attention to the situation to powerful voices outside the administration who will not remain silent on the issue in the future.

Asked whether their open criticism of the President's health program has led to reprisals, one active member of Health Employees for Change commented, "None at all. But worse, we had the strange feeling that no one really cared." A number of high-level administrators wrote off the criticism to a few "two-year docs," commissioned Public Health Service officers with only a two-year commitment to the agency, he said. But this is not the case, according to HEC activists. Only about one-quarter to one-third of the professionals involved were "short-timers." Many were older physicians and professionals with a clear career stake in what is happening at PHS.

It is too early to judge the ultimate effect of Health Employees for Change. One outsider—a doctor and former Public Health Service officer—believes that the service is one of the most exciting places in the federal health establishment because of their efforts. As for administration response to date, the only substantiated reaction has been a flurry of "memo-rattling" by mid-level managers who may be threatened by the new voices.

18. Dr. Robert S. McCleery and FDA

In December, 1968, the National Academy of Sciences completed a study of twenty-eight hundred drugs that had entered the market between 1932 and 1962. Its findings were startling. Medical experts agreed that certain drugs were dangerous and should be removed from the market immediately.

The study was commissioned by the Food and Drug Administration, which is responsible for protecting the public from hazardous and ineffective drugs. But instead of moving to follow the report's recommendations, the FDA began a long and tedious series of consultations—many of them with drug companies. It became obvious to some FDA staff members that it would be months or years before action was taken, even on drugs reportedly most hazardous.

Among the concerned staff was Dr. Robert S. McCleery, special assistant for medical communication. As he said later, "FDA's methods for getting drugs off the market were influenced by political and economic factors which, in my judgment, had no place in matters of such serious scientific and public concern."

In February, 1969, convinced that the agency needed prodding from the outside as well as from within, Dr. McCleery resigned.

He did not blow the whistle publicly—for the obvious reason that a one-day announcement by a little known government employee would have minimal effect. Instead, he chose to "try to make the system work."

First, he went to the House Intergovernmental Relations Subcommittee headed by Congressman L. H. Fountain (D., N. C.). The committee had long been aware of FDA's effectiveness, or lack of it. McCleery was able to give Congressman Fountain enough additional information to convince him to hold hearings on the question of removal of dangerous drugs.

McCleery helped organize the hearings as a member of the subcommittee staff from February to October, 1969. As a result, the FDA's methods for dealing with drug hazards, as well as the study by the National Academy of Sciences, became a matter of public record.

Unfortunately, according to McCleery, the FDA did not appreciably change its methods even after extensive congressional scrutiny. So McCleery went a step further. He helped prepare a law suit against the FDA, asking the court to order the agency to take antibiotic combinations, such as Parke-Davis's Panalba, off the market. Medical experts were virtually unanimous in judging these drugs to be hazards.

In June, 1970, a suit was filed in federal district court by the National Council of Senior Citizens and two public health officers. That suit is still pending.

McCleery also wrote a sharply critical report of quality control within the medical profession, *One Life —One Physician*, while working for the Center for Study of Responsive Law. The report was issued in the fall of 1970.

McCleery is a whistle blower through the system. Rather than take his case directly to the public, he went to the institutions that are supposed to check abuses of executive power, the Congress and the courts. As his experience suggests—and as he himself says—this kind of whistle blowing is often not enough by itself. The system in this case has gone nearly three years without responding fully to a disclosure of imminent public hazards.

19. Dr. Harvey Minchew and FDA

Another FDA staff member chose another route on the same issue. Dr. B. Harvey Minchew resigned as acting director of FDA's Bureau of Medicine in May, 1969, when he became convinced that the agency was not responding adequately to the drug hazards detailed in the National Academy of Sciences report. A memo he wrote to his superiors in March urging immediate action had been ignored, as had other informal efforts. Soon after his departure, he helped investigative reporters get the story to the public.

20. Philip I. Ryther and the FAA

Philip I. Ryther was a twenty-six-year veteran of government service when he was forced into early retirement as evaluation chief of the Federal Aviation Administration. The reprisal followed Ryther's efforts to establish stricter regulations of air charter planes.

Ryther had filed a report severely critical of air charter abuses and the applicable FAA regulations six months before the air crash of a chartered plane snuffed out the lives of the Wichita State University football team on October 2, 1970. His immediate superior held up the report for five weeks. Ryther then by-passed channels and contacted the deputy administrator, who indicated that he was unimpressed. The administrator of the agency refused to answer his inquiries and indicated through subordinates that he had no comment on the report.

Seven weeks after filing his report, Ryther was called on the carpet at a special meeting of his superiors for ignoring proper channels. Ryther responded that between the date of his report and the meeting at least 170 persons had been killed in accidents in general aviation, eventualities he had warned against in his report.

On August 19 eleven pages of "charges" were filed against him, including charges that he spent $5.25 for a dinner a year earlier, missed two hours of work (on a day when he was involved in a five-car accident on his way to work), and initialed his own time card rather than leaving it to the authorized clerk. He was subsequently promised that the charges would be dropped if he resigned.

Ryther's "retirement" was approved on October 2, 1970, the day of the Wichita State disaster. He insists that the plane would not have crashed had the recommendations of his report been adopted. Many of them were implemented three-and-a-half weeks after the crash. Ryther did not reveal his story to the press until after he left the FAA.

21. Dr. X

Dr. X is a government inspector, one of those "forgotten men of the consumer movement" who stand at the precise point where industry and bureaucratic pressures are likely to meet. A veterinarian, Dr. X was the inspector in charge of a federally inspected poultry plant. He had a reputation in the inspection service of being "tough on the plants" and of supporting the inspectors under him.

Conditions in the plant to which Dr. X was assigned were far from ideal. At one point he estimated that forty-eight percent of the birds leaving the plant were contaminated. Even his superiors referred to it as a problem plant. But when new plant management was installed, conditions began to deteriorate even further. The new management, inexperienced and openly hostile to the inspection service, began to threaten to oust Dr. X, who doggedly listed all violations and discrepancies and made every effort to have them corrected.

In the fall of 1970, Dr. X's immediate superior in the inspection force removed his right to control the speed of plant production, as unnecessary to insure a wholesome product. The move not only limited Dr. X's ability to improve conditions but also undermined his authority with plant managers. Dr. X felt his authority could not be maintained without the support of his superiors. He also believed that the production issue should be brought to the attention of Ralph Nader. He sent letters to Mr. Nader and Mrs. Virginia Knauer, the President's consumer advisor, describing conditions in the plant.

In December, 1970, grossly substandard conditions forced Dr. X to request that the plant slow the speed of the production line. The plant managers refused and proceeded to run several thousand pounds of birds they knew would be unsalable. Although the regional office of the Consumer and Marketing Service agreed that Dr. X had acted properly, they rewarded him with a notice in January, 1971, that he would be transferred.

The handling of Dr. X's letter to Mrs. Knauer is a classic illustration of bureaucratic response to criticism. After some delay, Mrs. Knauer's office forwarded the substance of Dr. X's charges (but not his name) to the administrator of the Consumer and Marketing Service of the Department of Agriculture. The administrator then referred the charges to the regional office with jurisdiction over Dr. X's plant. Early one morning Dr. X was visited by the USDA officer in charge who asked him to respond to (his own) charges about the plant! Dr. X restated the need for improvement in the plant and suggested that the way to accomplish this was to support inspectors in the field.

The final irony came when the administrator of the Consumer and Marketing Service replied to Mrs. Knauer's letter by informing her that the service had transferred the plant inspector—the very individual who had raised the issues. Later Mrs. Knauer's office sent the Consumer and Marketing Service a perfunctory letter informing them that the complaint had been lodged by the very plant inspector whose removal the service felt "solved" the problem.

The Public Interest Research Group of Washington is assisting Dr. X in challenging his transfer and has provided an attorney to represent the inspector in administrative procedures in the Department of Agriculture. The Group believes that Dr. X's case involves not only important issues of consumer protection and the integrity of USDA's meat and poultry inspection service, but also basic questions about the support to which whistle blowers are entitled when they insist on doing their job properly.

III

Prescriptions for Change

16

The Corporation

There is more law today running in favor of individual rights in the armed services than there is in any of our major corporate communities. I see no reason why the industrial army should not be at least as democratic as the other one. In fact, there is no good reason in the world why The People should not participate generally in the processes of our private governments.
—David Bazelon in *Paper Economy*, 1963

The men and women featured in this book are full-time citizens. When they went to work for large organizations they did not trade one set of responsibilities for another—they merely added their duties as employees to those they felt as citizens. And at critical moments under compelling circumstances, they chose to be citizens first and employees second. This is what whistle blowing is all about.

How should and how can our legal system, our corporations, and our government respond to the citizen-employee? One way, of course, is to ignore him; another, to suppress and punish him. But if the whistle blowers treated here have one thing in common, it is that they cannot—indeed, they will not—be ignored. Suppression must also be self-defeating in the long run for the organizations that practice it. It will make martyrs of its victims, it will enrage their allies within and outside the organization, it will discourage internal self-correction, and it will stifle the very qualities that make for an effective and loyal employee. Under such conditions, self-renewal for the organization itself becomes highly improbable.

The corporation and organizations of employees that represent or purport to represent corporate employees —professional societies and labor unions—are in the best position to respond to the challenge of citizen-employees. Each organization should freely experiment with different approaches consistent with its own needs and the needs of its members. Since professional societies frequently compete among themselves and with labor unions for members, and since corporations frequently compete with each other for the best talent, it is to the interest of each to develop wise and beneficial approaches. Finally, professional societies, unions, and corporations, if we are to believe their leaders and apologists, should be sufficiently flexible to make the kinds of changes necessary to accommodate this new type of citizen-employee.

Professional societies should reformulate their codes of ethics to make them relevant to the employment relationship as well as to the client-professional relationship. The Code of Professional Responsibility of the American Bar Association, for example, does not directly deal with the lawyer who is employed on a full-time basis by a corporation. The explanatory notes to the code do suggest that when he gives business advice, the lawyer who is "house counsel" is subject to different obligations. But it does not explain how business advice differs from legal advice, nor does it suggest what the lawyers' obligations are when business and legal advice are inextricably mixed together. And the two are often indivisible. The distinction is critical to the internal logic of the code, since *all* lawyers, whether serving one employer-client or a number of clients, are required to "exercise independent judgment". One resolution to this dilemma would be to impose duties on *employers* as well as on employed lawyers. The American Association of University Professors (AAUP) does precisely that to preserve academic tenure for its members. Institutions which do not provide procedures to protect or which do not in fact protect the academic independence of faculty members are subject to censure. AAUP can in turn significantly limit the ability of the institution to recruit the teachers it wants.[1] Professional societies could establish similar mechanisms to censure employers that ignore the ethical obligations of society members.

Professional societies should establish independent appeal procedures for corporately employed members who have exhausted whatever procedures are available in the corporation. Similarly, they could offer to arbitrate disputes when the corporation is unable or unwilling to provide any internal mechanism for dealing fairly with dissent. If a firm refuses arbitration, the society should nevertheless proceed to make a determination and to make its decision public. Independent appeals procedures could complement the type of internal due process that enlightened corporate managers should establish. Unfortunately too many of these societies are either so subservient[2] to industry or so involved in defining their own identity that it is unlikely that these changes will occur in the absence of vigorous efforts by individual members.

Societies should also intervene on behalf of members involved in controversies over the application of their professional ethics. Charles Pettis reports that the American Society of Civil Engineers, through its executive director, has attempted to clear his name with potential employers. When a professional's dispute becomes a matter of public concern, the society should intervene, whether or not it is requested to do so, at least to the extent of offering its services as a reasonably disinterested but expert referee. And societies should actively seek employment for members fired for behaving ethically.

Few societies have become involved in legislative controversies unless broad "pocketbook" interests of members are at stake. Of the major engineering societies, only the National Society of Professional Engineers engages in any extensive lobbying effort. The other societies could, if they chose, organize separate lobbying arms and still preserve their own preferred tax status. They could promote legislation to protect members from employer retaliation for obedience to the law. A scientist who refuses to file a false report with a federal regulatory agency should not be forced to pay for his employer's attempted misconduct by involuntarily giving up his livelihood. Likewise, an engineer who reports an employer's illegal conduct to "appropriate authorities," as he must under the NSPE code of ethics when that conduct threatens public health or safety, ought to be protected from retaliatory firing, demotion, or transfer. The government agency authorized to prevent the illegal conduct can also be given the power to penalize a vindictive employer and to order compensation for the employee. But agencies will not be given additional authority unless groups that purport to represent the interests of engineers and other professionals demand that legislatures grant it.

Societies could contribute to other legislative efforts as well. For example, those with members employed by large corporations ought to be leading the fight to require that pensions "vest"[3] early and that pension rights be transferable from one employer to another. The fear of losing a pension is one of the invisible chains that limit an employee's freedom to speak out or refuse to do work that might wantonly imperil others. The American Chemical Society (ACS) has been trying to organize a central pension fund for members much like the one that college teachers enjoy. They have met stiff opposition from large corporations that employ chemists and from the pension fund industry. Since employer participation (voluntary or not) is essential to the success of such a fund, the society could alternatively compel by statute the same result. At this writing the ACS has given no serious consideration to throwing down the gauntlet with such verve. If ACS continues to hesitate, older chemists, except those fortunate enough to be college teachers, will continue to be the indentured servants of their corporate masters, unable to dissent and unable to blow the whistle without fear of losing far more than current income.

Typical of the corporation's power to influence more than the salaries of its employees is its power to sever pension rights even after retirement. DuPont's pension plan, for example, allows the company to cancel a retired employee's rights to receive benefits if he has involved himself in "any activity harmful to the interest of the company." Such vague language cannot help but have a chilling effect on many forms of employee dissent and dissent by retired employees.

Finally, professional societies, especially those that have paid lip service to professional responsibility in the past, ought to investigate the extent of dissent and whistle blowing among their members. The American Society of Planning Officials (ASPO) recently published a study by staff member Earl Finkler entitled *Dissent and Independent Initiative in Planning Offices.*[4] Finkler surveyed planning office directors as well as staff members to come up with the first comprehensive inquiry into dissent in his profession. He explored attitudes, put together five case studies based on real controversies, and developed tentative guidelines for dissent for both employers and employees. ASPO is to be commended for sponsoring such a study. But its executive director, Israel Stollman, apparently tried to dissociate the society from Finkler's effort. In an unprecedented "dissent" to the report, he wrote, "The normal path of internal review for each PAS [Planning Advisory Service] report that we issue produces staff agreement on its content. The report remains an individual statement of the author but falls within a broad range of ASPO policies and views. This report by Earl Finkler does not entirely fall within this broad range." Whether ASPO uses the Finkler study as the basis for further inquiry and action is highly problematical. If it does not, it will have missed an opportunity that few other societies have had for concrete action to protect dissenters.

Labor unions are sometimes cited as the ideal alternative to both new legal protections for whistle blowers and to internal channels for free employee expression. In theory the union may, through the collective bargaining process, demand both substantive rights to protest work that threatens the public and procedural devices for a fair hearing when those rights are asserted. In practice, this potential has been neglected. First, according to union spokesmen, collective bargaining agreements today simply do not prohibit discharge and other forms of retaliation for protests directed against company policies and practices other than those traditionally associated with pay scales, work rules, retirement benefits, and job classification. Article 14, Section 1 of the United Auto Workers contract with

Ford, for example, specifically reserves all "designing" and "engineering" questions to management. Second, grievance procedures have not been considered appropriate forums for challenging the work product as well as working conditions. UAW officials, for example, agreed with Edward Gregory on the carbon monoxide leakage problem, but took action only on the issue of whether or not his transfer was authorized under the collective bargaining agreement. The *real* reason for his transfer, his persistent complaints about safety defects in the automobiles he was assigned to inspect, were considered by the union beyond its authority. Third, unions traditionally have been mesmerized by bread-and-butter issues to the exclusion of others. Some of the professional unions affiliated with the AFL-CIO, however, have recently expressed an interest in pursuing noneconomic concerns of professional employees. They have a significant self-interested motivation, of course, since professionals have resisted collective bargaining as a threat to their status as professionals. If professional societies continue to avoid the issue of professional independence for their employed members, unions will have a growing appeal, especially to younger professional employees. Several professional unions have successfully organized new bargaining units by convincing potential members that collective bargaining is the only effective means to make ethical norms and professional autonomy integral elements of the employment relationship. Representatives of the American Federation of State, County, and Municipal Employees told the authors that younger professionals in government service have been amazingly responsive to this approach.

Until the trade union movement rejects management's tendency to view employees—professional as well as nonprofessional—as obedient cogs and moral neuters rather than as responsible citizens, workers will be unable, for example, to object publicly to unsafe products, environmental hazards, and fraudulent sales practices without fear of retaliation. The experience of steelworker Gilbert Pugliese demonstrates that in the absence of strong pressures from the membership, unions, or at least their local leaders, are not likely to come to the immediate aid of a single embattled member.[5] On June 5, 1969, Pugliese refused to pump any more oil into the Cuyahoga River from the Cleveland plant of the Jones and Laughlin Steel Corporation. The Cuyahoga River, one of the most polluted rivers in America, has been officially described by the city of Cleveland as a "fire hazard." Jones and Laughlin was under pressure from pollution abatement officials at the time and declined to make an issue of Pugliese's refusal. He did not receive a similar order until July 14, 1971. Pugliese, fifty-nine years old with eighteen-year seniority and six years away from pensioned retirement, adamantly refused. The only union official nearby, the assistant chief grievance official, tried to persuade him to follow orders and file a protest later. But Pugliese refused and was suspended for five days for breach of discipline with the strong likelihood that he would be fired at the end of that period.

Pugliese then called everyone he could think of to get action. But he got no response from the pollution agencies nor from the local media. Finally, a former news reporter put in a few calls on his behalf. By the end of the next day he had become a *cause célèbre* in Cleveland and beyond. He was told by a fellow worker, "This puts the union on the spot and they've got to do something now after all the publicity." On the next day other workers were threatening a wildcat strike unless Pugliese received his job back. The union's chief grievance official immediately returned from Washington—he was attending the second week of industry-wide negotiations with the steel companies — and Pugliese's grievance began moving through regular channels. By the afternoon of the second day, Pugliese had been reinstated with pay. When he returned to work on Saturday, July 17, the company was installing drums and pumps to dispose of the oil. Ironically, this was precisely the method he had recommended when he first refused to pour the oil into the river in June, 1969.

Corporations, if they are as flexible, adaptive, and innovative as they purport to be, should be able to accommodate the citizen-employee. Mack Hanan, managing director of Hanan and Son, a New York City management consulting firm specializing in long-term corporate planning, recently recommended that corporations for compelling reasons of self-interest adopt their own "bill of rights for employees" to deal with what he describes as "the new organization man."[6] He writes that the best of the new organization men and women —"the very ones who are most able to help their companies grow—are being lost by businesses which appear reluctant to adjust to the new realities." In the meantime these men and women "see the corporation as having an arbitrary kind of power over individual employees that is unmatched in the rest of the real world because there is no recourse from its exercise and no appeal from its verdicts."

Hanan's proposed bill of rights would emphasize "the free expression of personal beliefs of a social, economic, or political nature within or without the confines of the corporation" rather than rights to object to company policy or action. Its adoption would represent a significant breach in the love-it-or-leave-it philosophy of employment. This would certainly be true if some of Hanan's other recommendations were also adopted. He suggests, for instance, the appointment of an internal ombudsman to whom employees can present complaints. Hanan's ombudsman would be authorized to intervene on behalf of the employee and, most importantly, to dramatize and publicize *outside the corporation* complaints that do not receive proper management attention. Given the present attitudes of top managers, it might also be necessary to adopt a special bill of rights, legally enforceable, for the truly committed ombudsman. No internal mechanism can operate unless last-resort appeals to the outside are explicitly recognized *and* protected.

The corporate ombudsman is not a new proposal. Isidore Silver, writing in the *Harvard Business Review* in 1967, provided a detailed plan for just such a company watchdog based on the experience of various countries with governmental ombudsmen. Silver's corporate ombudsman for employees would be on the staff of the president of the company but would have to be independent and not merely another management functionary. "In corporate terms," writes Silver, "he must have a long-term contract at substantial pay."[7] He points out that other forms of grievance review—for example, "open door" policies providing access to top executives and multi-step personnel office appeals—are totally inadequate to ensure justice or to serve even the corporation's interest.

Many of the proposals of Hanan and Silver are worthy of immediate adoption by giant corporations and by other large organizations, including labor unions, as initial steps in the right direction. They can not be passed off as stopgap public relations gimmicks to pacify restive managers and professionals. The concerns which manifest themselves in whistle blowing will not fade away. Organizations which ignore them or which attempt to suppress them will.

The Xerox Corporation recently announced a program to grant selected employees—28,500 of its 38,000 United States employees are eligible—leaves of absence to work on "social welfare projects."[8] This is a promising new approach which should be watched closely by other large corporations. The crunch will come, however, if one or more employees become involved in projects that Xerox management believes to be in conflict with company policy—or if, for instance, an employee who may have a reputation within the company for complaining about in-plant pollution at one of Xerox's manufacturing facilities seeks a sabbatical to join an occupational safety and health research group. Xerox may certainly assert the right to avoid such situations as a matter of policy. But if it does, it will severely limit one of the most imposing aspects of the program —its explicit recognition that citizenship is not something that can be held in abeyance during the work day or subordinated to the interests of a powerful employer.

17

The Government

Most of what has already been said about the interaction between employee organizations and corporations applies with equal force to the interaction of the
same organizations with government. Since government
employees do not generally have the right to strike,
however, and since the civil service system purports to
take the place of any need for militant unions or com-
bative professional societies, government employees
are in a different situation. Accordingly, their organizations would be expected to adopt slightly different
strategies. What changes are or should be forthcoming
in government employer-employee relationships?

The Pickering case, decided by the Supreme Court
in 1968,[1] validated the proposition that the government-
as-employer does not have the same freedom to control
employee behavior as the corporation-as-employer, even
when its employees act or speak in ways contrary to
certain governmental policies. The Court said that a
school board could not fire a teacher who had written
a letter critical of the board to a local newspaper. Even
Justice William H. Rehnquist, who feels that the "government is entitled to demand at least a large part of
the same personal loyalty owed by any employee to
his employer," has recognized that the Supreme Court's
opinion in the Pickering case requires that public employees be allowed to exercise at least part of their
First Amendment right of free speech against the government.[2] The still unresolved constitutional question
is no longer *whether* the public employee is free to
criticize his or her employer, but *how much* freedom he
has.

Any government agency, of course, can grant more freedom to its employees than the Constitution requires it to give as a minimum, whatever that minimum is finally determined to be. Congress, the state legislatures, the various civil service commissions, and government agencies are therefore free to move well beyond the Pickering case.

Ernest Fitzgerald had framed and hung on the wall of his office in the Department of the Air Force the following Code of Ethics for Government Service:

Any person in Governmental service should:

Put loyalty to the highest moral principles and to country above loyalty to persons, party, or Government department.

Uphold the Constitution, laws, and legal regulations of the United States and of all governments therein and never be a party to their evasion.

Give a full day's labor for a full day's pay, giving to the performance of his duties his earnest effort and best thought.

Seek to find and employ more efficient and economical ways of getting tasks accomplished.

Never discriminate unfairly by the dispensing of special favors or privileges to anyone, whether for remuneration or not; and never accept, for himself or his family, favors or benefits under circumstances which might be construed by reasonable persons as influencing the performance of his governmental duties.

Make no private promises of any kind binding upon the duties of office, since a Governmental employee has no private word which can be binding on public duty.

Engage in no business with the Government, either directly or indirectly, which is inconsistent with the conscientious performance of his governmental duties.

Never use any information coming to him confidentially in the performance of governmental duties as a means for making private profits.

Expose corruption wherever discovered.

Uphold these principles, ever conscious that public office is a public trust.

(This Code of Ethics was agreed to by the House of Representatives and the Senate as House Concurrent Resolution 175 in the Second Session of the 85th Congress. The Code applies to all Government Employees and Office Holders.)

As the notation indicates, this code is not the product of wishful thinking by malcontents in the bureaucracy. It expresses the will of Congress that civil servants be more than mindless and amoral automatons. Unfortunately the Congress did not provide penalties for violations of the code. It is merely a strong admonition to all concerned. But if it were applied vigorously and if it were accompanied by rigorous action on behalf of employees, the code would legitimize ethical whistle blowing as an instrument of policy influenced and directed by employees acting as citizens.

THE NEED FOR OMBUDSMEN

Government agencies should encourage internal dissent and internal whistle blowing up through the hierarchy as an early warning system for abuses and as a means of spotting operational deficiencies otherwise shielded by layers of bureaucracy. And they should go further: They should establish employee ombudsmen empowered to go public with an employee's protest if the agency fails to listen. The Code of Ethics for Government Service requires, in effect, that *each* civil servant serve as an ombudsman for the public interest. If he is blocked within the agency he has no choice—if he is to act consistently with the code—but to go outside the agency.

In April, 1971, Secretary of the Navy John H. Chafee wrote Admiral Bernard A. Clarey, president of the Flag Selection Board, which selects captains for promotion to rear admiral:

> I would hope that you would select a few iconoclasts— original, provocative thinkers who would stimulate the Navy to constantly re-examine its premises and whose selection would encourage those in the lower ranks to do likewise, with the realization that they are not just tolerated but in fact welcomed.[3]

The difficulty, perhaps not fully comprehended by the Secretary, is that candidates for these iconoclast slots are likely to have been weeded out in the lower ranks. Oscar Hoffman, whose tale is recounted in Chapter 15, was a civilian employee of the same Navy out of which Chafee expects his provocative admirals to emerge.

At least one federal agency, the Manpower Administration in the Department of Labor, has developed an internal whistle blowing mechanism for spotting "questionable activities" that may involve fraud, criminal malfeasance, gross mismanagement, and conflicts of interest. The Special Review Staff of the Assistant Secretary for Manpower solicits reports from any person within the agency, from top to bottom, and intervenes selectively to correct serious problems at any level. A spokesman for the staff told one of the authors, "We do our best to convince everyone that brownie points are gained by freely surfacing problems and requesting assistance in their solution, and not by trying to cover up and ending with a larger problem when the initial one erupts, as it almost inevitably does." The mandate of the Special Review Staff, which was created in a reorganization of the Manpower Administration in March, 1969,[4] does not extend to whistle blowing beyond the agency, nor is the staff in any sense independent of the assistant secretary, who also has line responsibility for the very situations the staff might uncover. It is still an important first step in assuring employee access to the highest levels within the agency.

An ideal internal agency ombudsman would include the following elements:

1) Its director and staff would be entirely independent of any other office or division within the agency.

2) Its director would report directly to the agency head and would be empowered to contact persons outside the agency, including those in other departments or branches of government, when the agency head refuses to listen or, without justification, takes no action.

3) The director and his staff should be insulated from the normal budgetary procedures. He should be able to go directly to Congress for his appropriations and he should be accountable solely to the legislature, much as the General Accounting Office today reports to and is accountable only to Congress.

4) The director should be appointed by Congress. Tenure should be protected and should be of suffi-

cient duration to insulate him or her from the partisan pressures of any one term of Congress. The director should be free to appoint his or her own staff.

5) The ombudsman should be empowered to intervene in any agency or civil service proceeding involving an employee of the agency against whom action has been taken in retaliation for communication with or support of the ombudsman's office.

6) The office should have complete access to all agency files and records with limitations on the disclosure of personnel or citizen files unless the individuals concerned consent to disclosure.

7) The ombudsman himself should be held accountable if he fails to perform his duty properly. Aggrieved employees might be given, for example, the right to seek judicial review if the ombudsman fails to act without just cause or if he acts in an arbitrary manner against the interests of the employee.

THE NEED FOR CIVIL SERVICE REFORM

Perhaps only a lawyer—or a civil servant who has been through the wringer—can appreciate the tortured logic of current civil service procedures. Originally designed to provide procedural safeguards for the employee, they make it difficult for the conscientious supervisor to discharge an incompetent and they unfairly burden the "troublemaker" who does his job too well and then tries to defend himself from harassment or worse.

The following is a rough outline of current procedures. Practices do differ from agency to agency, but these seem to be the predominant ones. An important distinction to keep in mind is the difference between "adverse" and "non-adverse" actions. "Non-adverse" actions involve agency actions that on paper at least are not directed against particular employees but rather involve reorganizations, staffing changes, office transfers, and the like that would theoretically apply to any person in the position. "Adverse" actions include the dismissal or demotion of particular individuals.

If the action taken against the employee is "non-adverse" under current regulations, he or she may request and will ordinarily be granted an informal meeting with the supervisor. At such an interview, and at most similar informal proceedings, the civil servant may or may not be accompanied by counsel or a witness, depending on the regulations of the particular agency or, in some cases, on the whim of the responsible official. If this meeting proves unsatisfactory, the employee may either seek a further informal meeting with the supervisor's superior or with some other higher official, or seek a formal consideration of his grievance. Ordinarily, at least one informal meeting is required before the grievance is considered by a grievance officer representing the head of the agency. Normally, an informal meeting is then arranged with the grievance officer, who, on the basis of this meeting, presents a formal recommendation to the agency head. If the grievance is denied in this recommendation, an appeal is usually open to the personnel officer of the full department under which the agency operates unless the agency is independent, in which case the appeal is to the agency's personnel officer.

The personnel officer may, at his discretion, grant a formal hearing, and may, again at his discretion, allow witnesses to testify and allow adverse witnesses to be cross-examined. The personnel officer then issues a final decision on the grievance under the signature of the agency head. The substance of this decision is *not* appealable to any other agency—including the Civil Service Commission—or to any court, though a "procedural" appeal is available to the Civil Service Commission if the employee feels his agency has failed to follow its own procedural rules.

In "adverse" action cases, the employee must be given thirty days notice of the action to be taken. He has the right to respond within five to ten days. His immediate supervisor can either reaffirm the proposed action, deny the merits of the response, or postpone the action for further consideration. The supervisor's original decision, which except in extraordinary cases is rarely modified at this early stage, may then be appealed to a higher level within the agency or to the Civil Service Commission. A specially designated hearing examiner

presides at the agency hearing, and the employee has
the right to counsel but does not have the right to an
open hearing. If he has elected to appeal within the
agency, he forfeits any appeal on the merits of his
case to the Civil Service Commission, but may go
directly to federal court if the agency action is upheld.
Again, however, the Civil Service Commission, as in
the case of "non-adverse" actions, may review procedural matters if the employee feels the agency has
violated its own rules.

If he does decide to go to the Civil Service Commission rather than take his final appeal within the agency,
he first goes to a hearing examiner, then to the Board
of Appeals and Review, and finally, at their discretion,
to the full commission. If the final decision at the
commission is unsatisfactory he may then appeal to a
federal district court.

These appeal processes appear to be unnecessarily
complex and they are. They are time-consuming, expensive, and emotionally exhausting. And what is worse,
in most agencies the original action—adverse or non-
adverse—remains in effect until final disposition. Unless the employee has independent financial resources
or the support of a wealthy private benefactor or organization while he is pursuing his remedies, his final
victory will be a Pyrrhic one. Nevertheless, at any point
in the process he may receive a favorable decision
rendering further action unnecessary. And his opportunity for a fair hearing is immensely greater than that
available to his corporately employed counterpart.

Under the Veterans Preference Act, veterans of the
military services are entitled to special civil service
review of certain "non-adverse" actions. Ernest Fitzgerald's is just such a case. Fitzgerald was not "fired";
rather, his job was abolished under an allegedly de-
partment-wide reorganization. This is not technically
an adverse action, a consideration of little comfort to
the person whose job is suddenly abolished in retaliation for speaking out. But Fitzgerald has already won
an important legal victory which may be valuable in
the more widely available appeal procedures. A federal
district court has ordered that the hearing granted
veterans under the Veterans Preference Act must be

an open hearing to meet the due-process requirements of the Constitution.

In the absence of an unlikely revolution in the attitudes of the Civil Service Commission and the personnel management officials in the agencies of the federal government, the Civil Service Act should be amended and the commission reorganized. The reform should include safeguards for employees who are obliged for reasons of conscience or ethics to blow the whistle on agency action or inaction that threatens the health or safety of citizens or that involves fraud, corruption, gross mismanagement, or conflict of interest. Mechanisms to minimize potential abuses by whistle blowers would also be written into the law. A detailed discussion of the Civil Service System is beyond the scope of this book,[5] but a review of the experiences of employees whose stories are recounted here suggests a few of the needed reforms.

New legal rights. Civil servants should be given more substantive rights, and these rights should be written into law rather than left to the unlimited discretion of the various agencies. Under the present civil service regime, the few rights that employees have are "procedural": They have a right not to be fired without some form of appeal, but once into the appellate process management can defend almost any action on the grounds that it was "in the interest of the service." And management's own view of the interest of the service is not subject to serious challenge. The employee should have the right, for example, to complain about public health and safety hazards and to go outside established channels if those channels are closed or unavailing. Employees should likewise have the right, without fear of retaliation, to communicate with Senators and Representatives and with congressional committees. They should have the right to rely on the Code of Ethics for Government Service to justify their actions.

The widely held belief that government managers face insurmountable obstacles in discharging even incompetent personnel is a gross exaggeration. The procedural steps that must be taken to discharge someone are a deterrent to swift personnel actions in *routine* situations. Thus, if an incompetent or nonproductive employee can be ignored—if he does not pose a threat to the sovereignty of management—his work will often be assigned to someone else, or the manager will find some other way to work around him, and he will continue on the payroll. But the services of trouble-makers, especially those whose eagerness poses a personal threat to a supervisor or manager, can be and are easily terminated.

There is also a procedural gap in existing civil service law that tends to be of little or no concern to the ineffectual employee but that seriously hamstrings the defense of the employee who tries too hard and is discharged for it. Civil servants cannot subpoena witnesses to appear in any hearings that arise out of their discharge. They may thus be unable to get into the hearing record important matters bearing on their case. The lack of any subpoena power may also effectively prevent the appearance of favorable witnesses who would appear and testify if ordered but who might fear for their own jobs if they offered to appear voluntarily.

A special tribunal for employees. The Civil Service Commission and the personnel management offices of the various agencies should be divested of any responsibility for adjudicating disputes between employees and agency management. When these two responsibilities are placed in the same agency or office, conflicts of interest are inevitable. The commission or the personnel office must, in effect, represent the interests of management *and* see that the employee's rights against management are vindicated. All too often when the interests of management are weighed against the interests of a single employee the employee loses. This may be inevitable when the weighing is done by an agency or office that devotes substantial energy to representing the interests of management in personnel matters. One method of separating these two functions would be to establish an entirely separate administrative court for personnel matters. Its sole mission would be to investigate and decide issues arising between employees and agency management. Such a tribunal should be specifically empowered to challenge any assertion by management that a particular personnel action is in the interest of the service by requiring management to prove it.

Job protection during appeals. When an employee objects to a personnel action affecting his status, he should be privileged to continue in his current status pending a final decision on his case. Employees who attempt to overturn agency action against them either through the Civil Service Commission, through an agency's own employee appeals process, or in the courts may suffer the consequences of discharge during the entire appeals process. And all the steps of an appeal may take years. Thus even if an employee is reasonably certain he will someday be vindicated and receive all lost back pay, he may take no action because of the fear that he might not be able to support his family in the interim.

Reimbursement for costs. When an employee is ultimately vindicated, the Civil Service Commission or the court should be authorized to order an agency to reimburse the employee for all costs associated with his challenge of the agency's action, including an allowance for reasonable attorney's fees. Even if an employee is willing and able to survive an extended period of unemployment, he may not be willing to risk going deeply into debt to obtain satisfaction. Similarly, few attorneys are in a position to invest large amounts of time and money with little hope of receiving reasonable compensation. Ernest Fitzgerald has doggedly pursued every appeal open to him, but only because the American Civil Liberties Union was willing to underwrite the costs of the litigation.[6]

Intervention by citizens. Citizens directly interested in the disposition of cases involving civil servants should be permitted to intervene on their behalf both in administrative proceedings and in any judicial proceeding involving the employee. Victims or potential victims of the agency action that was the subject of the employee's disclosure or complaint would, of course, be directly interested.

Some of these proposals, if adopted, may cost us some of the stability we have come to expect from civil administration. But we are now paying a much higher price than this for a kind of well-oiled, imaginary efficiency in the operation of government that is in fact grossly inefficient. Too often, "stability" means ease of access for special interests, gross neglect of the will of Congress, and disregard of the interests of ordinary citizens. Nevertheless, some attention will have to be paid to resolving some very practical problems created by these suggestions.

Agency management will continue to have a strong interest in the loyalty and obedience of employees in circumstances other than those which may justify a protest or a public disclosure. After an employee has confronted his superiors in the procedures outlined in the reform proposal, it may be necessary that he move out of his particular office. In the Pickering case, the Supreme Court emphasized that had the teacher's letter to the editor created such tensions in his work situation that it would have been impossible for him to teach, the school board might have taken some action against him. Presumably he could have been reassigned to another school or given substantially different duties. Federal agencies should likewise be permitted to show the need for such transfers. But any new duties should be consistent with the experience and background of the employee.

The bureaucratic "Siberia treatment" should not be permitted. This is the tactic of moving a civil servant to an office with a telephone and perhaps even a secretary, but without any responsibility or with responsibilities totally inconsistent with his expertise and training. Ernest Fitzgerald spent his last year at the Air Force monitoring the performance of Air Force bowling alleys in Thailand.

Fitzgerald himself has suggested that an employee unwanted because he blew the whistle in the public interest should be granted "livelihood" rather than "job" security until he can find another position commensurate with his talents. In such a case, the employee should also be given the opportunity to present his side of the story in communications between the agency and any potential employer. He should also have the opportunity to examine any and all personnel files or data banks that contain information about him, and he should have the right to enter his comments and his own evidence into these records.

WHEN NOT TO BLOW THE WHISTLE

Any system of law or administration that protects whistle blowers must also deal with potential abuses. There are several obvious types of possible misconduct to control.

The whistle blower does not have the facts straight. If the whistle blower manufactures facts or falsifies evidence, he or she clearly deserves no protection whatsoever. But suppose he has access only to some of the facts but suspects that certain details, if disclosed, would reveal a serious threat to public health or safety? At the time of disclosure, he might reasonably be expected to indicate the limited state of his own knowledge in order to be entitled to protection later. Second, if the whistle blower's suspicions were totally irrational to the extent that no person with his background or training and in his position reasonably could have entertained them, it might also be undesirable to protect him. These kinds of determinations are made by judges and juries every day. There is no reason to believe that they would be any more difficult in whistle-blowing cases, if both sides have access to competent experts and other witnesses and if both are represented by competent counsel.

The whistle blower is a "disgruntled" employee, that is, he might be motivated by a desire to vindicate a personal dispute. The law does not generally take into account motives to determine guilt or innocence or to fix liability. This is because second-guessing someone's mental processes is a difficult if not impossible exercise. Suppose an employee, disgruntled because he has not been promoted, decides to reveal that the head of his agency has deliberately lied to a congressional committee about a serious public health menace? It may be difficult for the agency to prove, or for him to contradict, any allegation that he blew the whistle *because* he was disgruntled. And his true motives, the ones that no one can know with any degree of certainty, might have been mixed. So it might not be

fair to deny this particular employee a protected
status. On the other hand, the fact that he was disgruntled would still be relevant in judging the reliability
of his information.

*The whistle blower has disclosed confidential in-
formation in return for money or the promise of some
other benefit.* Though the law generally does not examine motives, there are important exceptions. A land-
owner, for example, may build a fence on his property
for almost any reason, but if he does it to harass
a neighbor, a court may order him to pull down the
"spite fence." And someone who uses a legal process
such as a subpoena for some ulterior and illegal purpose
may be liable for damages. Suppose the hypothetical
whistle blower just discussed releases the same information in return for a fee from a personal enemy of the
agency head? Protection could and should be denied
on the grounds that public policy should not encourage,
indeed it should condemn, the sale of confidences.

*The whistle blower decides to blow the whistle in
order to save his job.* An employee about to be discharged for a legitimate reason or an employee whose
job is about to be abolished may try to protect himself
by, for example, communicating with a congressional
committee and then plead that he cannot be discharged
for blowing the whistle in the public interest. Conversely, an agency might seek to justify the dismissal
of a whistle blower on legitimate grounds purportedly
unconnected with the fact that he spoke out or made
damaging information public. In either case the problem is how to determine with reasonable certainty the
causal relationship, if any, between these events. One
possible solution is to shift to the employer the burden
of proof to justify the discharge. The employer is, after
all, in the best position to gather all the facts necessary
to explain and to justify its decision.

Whether or not the burden is shifted, the employer is
also in the best position to selectively marshal the facts
to support its point of view. And it will be difficult
for an outsider, no matter how objective or disinterested, to second-guess the agency's judgment that
certain facts are sufficient grounds for dismissal,
independent of the whistle blowing. So the employee

will have to be given the means to place additional facts in the record as well as to challenge the decision-making process that ended with the decision to discharge him. As already suggested, he should be permitted to subpoena and examine under oath his superiors and his co-workers, including those who may have transferred, changed jobs, or left the government entirely. He should also be provided a transcript of their testimony and any cross-examination. He should also be permitted to subpoena relevant documents from agency files, including his own personnel file. (Today in many agencies employees are not even permitted to examine their own personnel file!) Finally, he should also be allowed to introduce in evidence any facts showing that his treatment was different from that of other employees in cases not involving whistle blowing. If he can show that other employees would have been discharged had the criteria applied to him been applied even-handedly, the court or administrative tribunal considering his case might conclude that his discharge was a reprisal.

These are not the only possible limitations on the proposed rights of whistle blowers. Personnel files, for example, should remain sacrosanct. Genuine national security information should also be protected. But a bureaucrat's decision to use a rubber stamp marked "Confidential" or "Secret" should always be subject to challenge.[7] A requirement that intra-agency or intra-governmental channels of communication be explored first might also be desirable, but should not apply when even the use of those channels places the whistle blower in jeopardy.

18

The Law

Professor Arthur S. Miller in his statement before the Conference on Professional Responsibility described the legal picture for potential whistle blowers as "a glum one." The simple fact is that a "love-it-or-leave-it" philosophy permeates the law of private employment relationships. Nevertheless, there have been a number of developments in related areas of the law that can form the basis for a repudiation of the old shibboleths. In addition, there are widely accepted principles which can be reshaped by creative lawyers, judges, and legislators into viable protections for the whistle blower. Many of these guideposts for change are indicated below. It is hoped that legal scholars, sympathetic legislators, and counsel for whistle blowers can build upon this list and expand the analysis of each item.

The First Amendment and the Corporation. In the Pickering case the Supreme Court said:

> teachers may [not] constitutionally be compelled to relinquish the First Amendment rights they would otherwise enjoy as citizens to comment on matters of public interest in connection with the operation of the public schools in which they work.[1]

Pickering had been fired for writing a letter to the editor of a local newspaper critical of school board policies. Had Pickering been a teacher at a private trade school and written to criticize the policies of a conglomerate which owned the school, the Supreme Court undoubtedly would have said that the First Amendment doesn't apply to action against free speech by nongov-

ernmental bodies. Lawyers, of course, would have no
difficulty understanding the logic of this distinction. The
First Amendment, indeed the entire Bill of Rights, was
written to curb the power of the federal government,
and the Fourteenth Amendment to curb the power of
state and local governments. A number of authorities,
Professor Miller and Adolf Berle among them, have
suggested that, short of formal amendment to the Constitution, constitutional protections could be extended
to protect citizens from corporate as well as governmental action.[2]

Their theory is that since many corporations have
the attributes of government—in terms of their size and
wealth, and their ability to control the lives of employees and affect the lives of other citizens—citizens
should reasonably enjoy the same protections against
them that they enjoy against government. Furthermore,
the very existence of a corporation is a manifestation
of governmental power—the legislature's grant of a
charter for corporate organization. The Supreme Court
has not accepted this line of reasoning except, to a limited extent, in one case involving a "company town"
and another involving a large regional shopping center.[3]

Even if the First Amendment were extended to limit
corporate action abridging free speech, the problem of
protecting the disclosure of certain confidential information would remain. Had Pickering supported his
criticism of the school board with a document from
the board's confidential files, the Court might have come
to a very different conclusion on the propriety of his
discharge. It might have said, for instance, that the release of confidential information is not itself "speech"
within the First Amendment. But the line between disclosure and speech cannot be well defined. None of
the whistle blowers discussed in this book appropriated
documents, nor did they publish "trade secrets" which
in themselves had economic value, nor did they publish classified information the release of which might
threaten the national security. In most cases they simply
"spoke the truth," or in Ernest Fitzgerald's phrase,
"committed truth." Nevertheless, when purloined documents, trade secrets, or specifically classified informa-

tion are involved, issues quite different from and more complicated than free speech arise. In these areas, too, old rules and new developments can form the basis for lifting the legal veil of secrecy.

"Just cause" provisions in collective bargaining agreements. Under the National Labor Relations Act, employees may not be discharged for engaging in legitimate unionization efforts, nor may they be dismissed for filing charges of violations of the act or testifying in proceedings of the National Labor Relations Board. The act does not, however, protect whistle blowing involving matters not covered by the act. Thus, the union member who complains about an unfair labor practice cannot be fired, but the member who complains about in-plant pollution (not an unfair labor practice) can be.

But the act does approve of and protect collective bargaining agreements, many of which contain "just cause" provisions stating that members cannot be fired "without just cause" but rarely indicating what is and what is not a proper cause for dismissal. Labor agreements generally establish a grievance mechanism through which members may complain about contract violations and other problems encountered on the job. Though the member files the grievance, the union represents him in the grievance procedures. If the union and the employer are unable to settle a grievance to their mutual satisfaction, the grievance may "go to arbitration." At that point an independent professional arbitrator is called in to make a decision binding on both parties.

There have been a number of arbitration decisions involving whistle-blowing situations. The arbitrators in these cases usually rely heavily on the old rule that disloyalty, in the words of a 1953 Supreme Court opinion, is "an elemental cause for discharge,"[4] but they sometimes find that a superior public interest intervenes to protect the employee.

In a case involving a cab driver who had reported that his employer was rigging meters to overcharge passengers, a California arbitrator eloquently explained:

> There is evidenced in this case a tension between an employee's private loyalty to his employer and his public loyalty to the community. Each citizen has a

duty of citizenship imposed and enforced by law to disclose criminal conduct of which he becomes aware. That duty never ceases as long as he has the knowledge and it remains undisclosed. The fact that his disclosure would be of "incalculable damage" to his employer can hardly be thought to reduce that duty of disclosure. When disclosure to management reasonably appears to the employee to be a futility because of their apparent involvement can it justly be held to constitute the "grossest misconduct" if public disclosure is assured and in fact results from disclosure to a competitor? . . . [The meter irregularities] quite clearly were contrary to the public interest and warranted disclosure.[5]

But there are a number of serious problems with "just cause" provisions. First, they apply to a relatively small percentage of the work force: union membership is down to twenty percent and an even smaller percentage have "just cause" provisions in their contracts. Second, the employee is almost totally at the mercy of the union, which can decide that his grievance has no merit. His only remedy if the union refuses to support his case is to sue the union for failing to fulfill its duty of fair representation. Needless to say, it is usually worth neither the effort nor the expense. Finally, contracts do not generally spell out "unjust" causes, so that arbitrators have very little to rely on except their own sense of what is right in a particular case.

The law of agency. In the law an employee is the "agent" of his or her employer. According to the Restatement of Agency, an agent has three primary obligations to his principal: the duty of obedience, the duty of loyalty, and the duty of confidentiality. But all of these duties are qualified. The "reasonable" directions of the employer must be obeyed, for example, but the employee can rely on business or professional ethics to determine what is reasonable. And the employee is under no duty to obey an order to perform an illegal or an unethical act. Likewise, an employee has a duty not to speak or act disloyally, except, in the words of the Restatement, "in the protection of his own interests and those of others." The Restatement then gives the following example:

> A, employed by P, a life insurance company, in good
> faith advocates legislation which would require a
> change in the policies issued by the company. A has
> violated no duty to P.

Finally, even though an employee must keep his employer's secrets, he may reveal confidential information,
according to the Restatement, "in the protection of a
superior interest of himself or of a third person."

Whistle blowers cannot, however, take unrestrained
comfort in these limitations on an agent's or an employee's duties. An employer's right to terminate the
relationship at will is, unfortunately, not limited by
agency principles. This is so because the employer has
no legal duty to keep an employee on, regardless of
any limitations on the *employee's* duties. Therefore, the
discharged whistle blower cannot seek a court order
to compel his or her reinstatement relying simply on
the law of agency. But he can assert these limitations
on his duties as one of his defenses to a legal action
by his employer. Suppose, for example, a person resigns
and then brings evidence of illegal activity by his employer to law enforcement authorities. Suppose further
that while the authorities are deciding whether to take
any action, the employer sues the former employee
for violating the duty of confidentiality. This is precisely what happened in a recent English case.[6] The
Court of Appeal refused to strike the employee's defense that he had no duty to keep confidential information about a price-fixing agreement and substantial
deception. One of the judges wrote that "any misconduct of such a nature that it ought in the public interest to be disclosed to others" is not protected by the
duty of confidentiality. The court was well aware of
potential abuses. The same judge said that had the disclosures been made out of spite or malice or for a reward he might have decided differently. But the court
clearly was not willing to sacrifice the principle of protecting the employee in this situation for fear of possible abuse in other cases.

Suits for malicious discharge. The legal principle
which allows an employer to discharge his employees
for any reason and without risking legal retaliation by
his employee was succinctly stated by a Tennessee court

in 1884: All employers "may dismiss their employees at will . . . for good cause, for no cause, or even for cause morally wrong, without being thereby guilty of legal wrong."[7] Until the National Labor Relations Law was upheld in 1937, the Supreme Court had said that state laws which limited the employer's freedom to fire for any reason were unconstitutional.[8]

Professor Lawrence E. Blades has written a pioneering assault on the doctrine of employment at will. In a 1967 *Columbia Law Review* article,[9] he forcefully argues that employees ought to be allowed to sue for "malicious discharge" and to receive compensation for lost wages, expenses, and other damages caused by improper action by an employer. Such a suit should be available, he argues, when a person is discharged for refusing to support the employer's political position, for declining to participate in immoral or unlawful activity, or for refusing to compromise professional ethics. This new remedy would grant the employer the right to discharge anyone for any reason (in the absence of a contract limiting that right), but would preserve at least part of the employee's livelihood by allowing him to recover damages.

The law of trade secrecy. Law protecting trade secrets arose in a variety of commercial settings. In the typical case, an employee or ex-employee revealed information to a competitor for a price or for new and perhaps more remunerative employment. Courts deciding these cases recognized that businesses have a legitimate interest in keeping certain information out of the hands of competitors. It is generally assumed by nonlawyers as well as nonexpert lawyers that "trade secrets" consist of certain specific classes of information. *Virtually any information,* however, can be protected as a trade secret if the possessor takes reasonable steps to keep it secret and if he claims it is valuable to him. In law suits against those who have disclosed trade secrets, the central issue is generally *not* whether the particular kind of information involved should be treated as a trade secret, but rather, whether it was taken "wrongfully." Thus, courts decide whether the employee or recipient obtained the information "unfairly," or whether a breach of confidence or breach

of a contract was involved. And to decide these questions they rely on general notions of equity and fairness
and on other areas of the law, such as the law of agency
and the law of contracts.

This is not to say that the whistle blower who reveals
confidential corporate information to the public is immune to law suits or does not run the risk of adverse
court rulings. On the contrary, he is at the mercy of the
court—and of the advocacy skills of his attorney.
Counsel must argue that there can be no breach of
confidence in revealing information the suppression of
which might well be lethal to innocent victims. Or he
must argue that there is a superior public interest in,
for example, protecting the integrity of a regulatory
scheme created to protect the public from the very pred-
atory practices that the whistle blower revealed. Here
is an example of the kind of "trade secret" that should
not, and perhaps cannot, be protected: The Campbell
Soup Company has developed a process to inspect for
botulism in its products. The United States Department
of Agriculture has the details of this process on file
and at Campbell's request has refused to disclose it
to the public and to other companies on the grounds
that it is a trade secret. Mr. Samuel Cochran, Jr., of
Bedford, New York, died fifteen hours after eating
vichyssoise produced by one of Campbell's smaller
competitors, the now bankrupt Bon Vivant Company.
He died of botulism poisoning.

Government employees are prohibited from revealing "trade secrets" and other confidential business information by federal criminal statute.[10] And most of the
regulatory laws contain provisions which prohibit such
disclosures. Government agencies usually recognize
without question an industry's claim that any particular information is a legitimate trade secret or otherwise
deserves confidential treatment. For years, for example,
the Department of the Interior recognized industry's
claim that the amount and identity of pollutants entering our waterways from a particular plant was a trade
secret. When the Corps of Engineers finally decided
to enforce the Refuse Act of 1899 by requiring permits
for discharges, the Environmental Protection Agency,
under mounting congressional and public pressure, de-

manded and received from the Corps agreement that the information on permit applications would be public. Very few of the industries concerned complained. We must conclude that the information did not contain such valuable trade secrets after all. But had the environmental agency accepted the original position of industry—the position that Interior had blithely accepted the year before—federal civil servants might have faced criminal prosecution for any unauthorized disclosure!

Clearly, the concept of trade secrecy must be modified when the public has a superior interest or when the corporation is unable to justify the need for confidentiality. Section 208 (b) of the Clean Air Act as amended in 1970 is an example of one of the changes needed in regulatory laws as they apply to trade secrecy. Under this section, pollution data submitted to the Environmental Protection Agency is public *unless* an industry requests confidential treatment *and* submits its request to public scrutiny and comment. The administrator must then decide whether that class of data ought to be secret. His decision is based not only on bald assertions by industry, but also on comments from citizens, and his decision can be reviewed later by a court.

Recently, the National Commission on Reform of Federal Criminal Laws advanced a potentially far-reaching proposal for changing the criminal statute prohibiting disclosures by civil servants.[11] The commission's recommendation would in effect permit a civil servant to defend himself on the grounds that release of the information was in the public interest. The employee could not assert this defense if his agency had classified that particular class of information secret by formal regulation. This is a significant qualification, but the proposal is a substantial improvement over the uncertain prior law.

Criminal penalties against the corporation. Several states have made it a crime for corporations to coerce their employees in certain ways. In at least seven states, for example, it is illegal for an employer to interfere with an employee's political activity. But criminal statutes, even if they were to include additional prohibitions against coercion of whistle blowers, would have serious drawbacks. The most obvious is that the prosecutor can always choose not to pursue a matter for almost any reason. There have in fact been very few prosecutions under the existing laws, partly because the coerced employee is the only person in a position to file a complaint—and he may not want to risk losing his job. And as Professor Blades has pointed out, these particular laws do not provide for specific redress to employees. Thus, even if an employee files a complaint as a matter of principle and the employer is subsequently fined or jailed for his misdeeds, the employee will still have to suffer the consequences of the coercion without remedy.

Yet the criminal sanction should not be rejected completely. Counsel for the employee can argue that the criminal prohibition *implies* that persons harmed by a violation have the right to sue for damages. Generally, in our legal system, if the client is in the class of persons that the legislature intended to protect and if the harm that resulted is the very type the legislature sought to prevent, courts frequently grant relief. Unfortunately, no courts have apparently taken this position in suits brought under the anticoercion statutes.[12] These statutes could be amended to include a right to a private law suit against violators. Our federal antitrust laws include such multiple sanctions. But even without significant amendment—and even if courts refuse to grant the right to a suit for damages—criminal sanctions should still remain on the books as a fail-safe protection against the most severe instances of coercion or retaliation and for the highly visible cases.

Federal interference-with-witnesses laws. By federal statute it is a crime to coerce a witness giving testimony under subpoena in federal proceedings. A similar provision makes it a crime to coerce witnesses before congressional committees. But those laws have not helped whistle blowers in the past. In 1953 a United States Court of Appeals refused to allow employees to seek damages for discharge in retaliation for their testimony before a federal grand jury against their employer, the Humble Oil and Refining Company.[13] These employees were subpoenaed to testify. They would have risked citation for contempt of court had they refused and prosecutions for perjury had they lied, yet the court said that their employer could be compelled to answer only to a federal prosecutor, not to them, for punishing them for testifying truthfully. And Senator Proxmire has tried in vain to get the Justice Department to prosecute—or even to investigate—those persons responsible for Ernest Fitzgerald's discharge after he testified before the Joint Economic Committee. As Fitzgerald said at the Conference on Professional Responsibility, "Would John Mitchell put Melvin Laird in jail?"

Senator Richard M. Nixon of California introduced an amendment to this statute on April 26, 1951. He told the Senate:

> Mr. President. I have introduced in the Senate today a bill to make it a violation of law for any officer of the Federal Government to dismiss or otherwise discipline a Government employee for testifying before a committee of Congress. . . . There is too much at stake to permit foreign policy and military strategy to be established on the basis of half truths and the suppression of testimony.
>
> Unless protection is given to witnesses who are members of the armed services or employees of the Government, the scheduled hearings will amount to no more than a parade of yes men for administration policies as they exist.[14]

The Federal Fair Labor Standards Act. This statute prohibits the discharge of employees who complain of or testify about violations of federal wage and hour laws. The discretion to enforce the prohibition and to seek damages or reinstatement is left primarily with the Secretary of Labor. Under certain circumstances a complainant can sue the employer on his own behalf, but since there is no adequate provision for recovering attorney's fees, few attorneys are willing or able to commit substantial resources to law suits under the act. So unless the Secretary of Labor takes up his case or unless the employee has independent financial resources to support a law suit, he may be left with a right without a remedy.

But this provision and others like it, even if inadequate as presently drawn, are significant precedents for including employee protection provisions in other federal regulatory laws.

The Muskie amendments to existing federal water quality legislation. Amendments to federal water quality legislation currently under consideration by Congress contain just such a provision. Under the Senate version of the amendments—the so-called Muskie amendments, which have been approved by the Senate Public Works Committee and by the full Senate—an employee cannot be discharged, harassed, or discriminated against for reporting suspected violations of the federal water quality law to federal authorities. This proposal (reproduced in the Appendix), if approved by House and Senate conferees, will be a historic precedent for similar amendments to regulatory legislation in which employee cooperation can be an important element of law enforcement.

There are, however, imperfections in the Muskie version of employee protection. Only the Secretary of Labor, for example, is empowered to go to court on behalf of an aggrieved employee; and the proposed section allows him very wide discretion in making this decision. At the very least, any similar provision should authorize an employee to seek his own remedy in the event that the Secretary of Labor fails to act to protect his rights within a specified period of time. The ideal employee protection provision would also allow a court to award full attorney's fees and other costs incurred by an employee seeking a remedy.

The Universal Military Training and Service Act of 1948. The draft law may be an unlikely place to find an employee protection section, but it does prohibit discrimination in employment against returning veterans. Under its provisions, an ex-serviceman is entitled, with certain limited exceptions, to be reinstated in the job he held before entering the armed forces. To protect this right Congress provided that a reinstated veteran cannot be discharged except for "just cause" for a period of one year after his return. This is, of course, the same language generally used in collective bargaining agreements to protect members from retaliatory or malicious discharge. The provision is enforced by the local United States attorney, who may seek an order of reinstatement with back pay in federal court. If the employee fails to interest the United States attorney in acting on his behalf, he may personally petition a federal court for reinstatement with back pay. This is limited protection for a very limited class of persons, but it is one more breach in the wall of employer freedom to fire for any reason.

The Federal Automobile Dealer Franchise Act of 1956. The so-called Dealer's Day in Court Act in effect prohibits automobile manufacturers from terminating dealerships without just cause.[15] A massive lobbying effort by the National Association of Automobile Dealers was a significant factor in the adoption of the legislation. Two dealer–whistle blowers, however, persuaded many congressmen and senators that noneconomic issues—including the right to free speech—were involved.

Lee Anderson, a former General Motors dealer in Pontiac, Michigan, testified before Senator O'Mahoney's Antitrust and Monopoly Subcommittee that his dealership had been terminated for "disloyalty." Specifically, in a speech he delivered at a local Rotary Club meeting, he charged that the Pontiac Division executives bought cars from the factory at a discount. These "disloyal" utterances were reported in a trade paper, *Automotive News.* He lost his dealership shortly thereafter. Pontiac denied any connection between the two events.

J. E. Travis, a Buick dealer in St. Charles, Missouri, publicly argued for protected territories for established dealers. This point of view was very unpopular in Detroit, where rigorous competition among dealers in the same makes was then company policy. Travis was a former president of the state auto dealers association and had been in the business for thirty-five years. His franchise was canceled—for poor sales, according to General Motors. Travis's sales had in fact declined somewhat in the face of discount dealer competition in nearby St. Louis. But in view of his record his fellow dealers and a number of key senators were convinced that his outspoken position on protected territories was the real reason for his termination. Travis's only satisfaction was the support his testimony gave to the bill under consideration.

The Dealer's Day in Court Act is not a perfect model for employer-employee relations. But it does demonstrate that legislation can effectively redress "natural" imbalances in bargaining power between parties in a continuing economic relationship to one another. A relatively small number of suits have been filed under the act, and few have been entirely successful. But as Professor Stewart Macauley, of the University of Wisconsin Law School, has pointed out, the mere existence of the law—and the potential power of organized dealers reflected in its passage—has probably had more of an impact than the new legal rights it created.

Unconscionable contracts. A contract can be so unfair as a result of disparities in bargaining power between two parties that a court will nullify the whole agreement or parts of it, or even rewrite some of the terms of the agreement, to better protect the disadvantaged party. Whether or not there is a written agreement, the relationship between an employer and his employee is essentially contractual: one party pays salary or wages in return for work performed by the other. Though courts have traditionally been reluctant to interfere in any way with this or any other form of contract, they have increasingly done so when the terms are so favorable to one party as to "shock the conscience" or when one party has to accept excessively burdensome collateral terms to get what he really wants out of the bargain. Some courts, for example, have refused to enforce contracts in which a low-income purchaser must mortgage all of his personal possessions in order to purchase a single appliance on credit.

Often the same *type* of agreement that might be approved by a court if between two merchants or businessmen will not be tolerated between a merchant and a consumer, especially a poor consumer. Though they may not discuss it in their opinions, the judges in these cases are piercing legal formalisms with considerations of fairness and equity to base their decisions on such factors as the awareness of the consumer, the lack of any real bargaining between the parties, and society's interest in discouraging such practices.

A court could consider similar factors in examining employment agreements the terms of which can be dictated by a single employer or by all employers with the same interest in muzzling employees. In a few cases judges have invalidated agreements in which the employee was forced to give up important rights that he or she already had, but none have apparently gone so far as to give the employee new rights. To protect a whistle blower on a contract theory a court would clearly have to read into the contract some very significant new terms. In reaction to such a suggestion a judge might say that it would be more proper for a legislature than for a court to take such a giant step or that the employee should turn to collective bargaining rather than to the courts to exact such terms from an employer. But the issue cannot be so easily avoided. Judges have been and can be persuaded that they ought not "pass the buck" to others whenever tough policy questions underlie the decision in a case before them.

Retaliatory eviction. Recently some courts have said that a landlord cannot evict a tenant for reporting housing code violation to government authorities.[16] They reason that although a landlord generally has the right to evict for any reason, he cannot do so in order to frustrate the public policy of requiring that all housing meet certain minimum standards. Of course there are significant differences between a landlord's relationship to his tenants and an employee's relationship to his employees. But in either case there may be superior, legislatively defined public policies making it reasonable, if not necessary, for a court to interfere in the relationship.

There is also a First Amendment aspect to these cases. If a court or other public agency, the police for example, aids a landlord by ordering the eviction of a tenant for reporting a law violation, it supports the suppression of a form of speech. Thus, even though the First Amendment might not directly limit the landlord, it would still limit any arm of government that inhibited speech by making it possible for the landlord to retaliate. This approach has not yet been accepted by the high courts. Many jurists believe that it would set a precedent for vastly expanding the First Amendment to limit virtually any private action affecting speech or expression. Whether these fears are justified or not, the fact is that the Supreme Court has used precisely this kind of reasoning to extend *other* constitutional guarantees and to limit libel and slander suits by public figures against their critics. For example, in *Shelly v. Kramer* the Supreme Court ruled that state courts could not enforce racially restrictive covenants. The Court's reasoning: Although the subdivider's action in writing the anti-Negro provisions into land conveyances was *not* a violation of the equal protection clause, any court that *applied* the restriction in a private law suit would violate that clause of the Bill of Rights. And in the libel and slander area the Court reasoned that although a public figure, like a corporation, suing for libel would *not* violate the First Amendment, a court which entertained the suit might be doing so under certain circumstances.

Equal Employment Opportunity Laws. Title VII of the Civil Rights Act of 1964 outlaws discrimination in employment for reasons of race, color, religion, sex, or national origin. The Equal Employment Opportunity Commission (EEOC) has certain limited powers to prevent all of these forms of discrimination. But it does not have the power to intervene on behalf of persons discriminated against for speaking out against the practices or policies of their employer or for releasing information critical to the protection of the public health or safety. Giving the EEOC jurisdiction in such cases would be a logical extension of its present authority—or a new agency or commission could be created and given this responsibility.

The task of the new commission, or of the EEOC were its jurisdiction expanded, would be somewhat more complicated than finding discrimination under present law. Under the Civil Rights Act, it is *never* proper to single out employees for special treatment on the basis of race, color, religion, sex, or national origin. But it may or may not be proper for an employer to take some action against the employee who blows the whistle. This is so because whistle blowing may or may not itself be proper, depending on such factors as the magnitude of the alleged evil, the validity of the charge made by the whistle blower, and the motives of the whistle blower. The EEOC or other agency will have to make these and other determinations in every case. It will have to guard against abuses as well as protect justifiable whistle blowing.

Conclusion. Existing laws thus provide a framework for protecting whistle blowers, though they are far from satisfactory at present. Still, the tools are available. It remains for courageous and innovative lawyers, judges, and legislators to reshape old laws, to apply the precedents at hand to new circumstances, and to develop new doctrines and laws to defend the ethical whistle blower.

Whatever legal mechanisms emerge—and there is clearly a wide variety of possibilities—they should, as a minimum

—extend First Amendment guarantees to prohibit interference with expression within private as well as public organizations;

—create guarantees of due process, including open hearings, the right to subpoena and cross-examine witnesses, the right to obtain all relevant documentary evidence, the right to counsel, and the right to appeal to independent authority;

—distinguish sharply between individual privacy and organizational secrecy, but recognize that individual privacy *within* organizations is also entitled to protection; and

—establish legal standards to balance an institution's interest in secrecy against the public's interest in disclosure.

We have included in the Appendix a draft proposal for reform of the federal civil service system incorporating these and other elements. The proposal should be applicable to state civil service systems with minor changes, and any private organization should be able to use it as a guide in establishing its own system for dealing fairly with potential whistle blowers. Congress could, of course, enact an extensive reform of the employee-employer relationship to include unorganized as well as organized workers in private and public institutions. A better approach might be to establish as a matter of law a number of new rights which could then be applied by organizations and ultimately by the courts to individual cases. The series of rights written into our proposal for civil service reform could be adapted to serve this purpose.

No new system of law will develop without the active intervention of citizens concerned with the issues raised by the whistle blowers of the last few years. And no system of law will be meaningful unless the ethic of professional and individual responsibility is embraced by organizations and the persons who serve them. It is a tall order, but it is far closer to being filled than any would have dreamed possible a short time ago.

IV

Strategies for Whistle Blowers

19

To Blow the Whistle

There is no tried and true formula for blowing the whistle effectively and safely. Every person is unique and every situation is different; that which has proved successful in one instance may be totally inappropriate in another. Still, it is imperative that a person considering such a bold action do so with as much forethought as he can muster. We have attempted in the following pages to set down some of the more important questions that a person contemplating blowing the whistle will have to resolve before he puts together his own strategy. Our suggestions are drawn primarily from the experiences of the men and women in this book and from common sense. They are necessarily tentative and form only an outline for action. They are intended merely to help the potential whistle blower organize his thoughts and review all the options.

1) PRECISELY IDENTIFY NOT ONLY THE OBJECTIONABLE ACTIVITY OR PRACTICE, BUT ALSO THE PUBLIC INTEREST OR INTERESTS THAT ARE THREATENED AND THE MAGNITUDE OF THE HARM THAT WILL RESULT FROM NONDISCLOSURE. As a potential whistle blower you must clearly define the issue for yourself before you can hope to enlist the support of others within your organization or on the outside. The nature of the issue in turn will largely determine the succeeding steps to be taken. The practice or activity, for example, might be covered by existing regulatory legislation or it might be the subject of intensive legislative scrutiny by a committee of Congress. If similar practices are the subject of intense pub-

lic debate, citizens' groups may be willing and able to
follow up on your information. And the more widespread the abuse which you can document the better,
for the electorate and the elected consider one complaint a peccadillo, but many of them an issue. You
must identify the threatened interest in order to determine which outside group or authority, if any, should
be contacted. Is it a health or safety interest? And if so,
does it involve an immediate threat of the sort that can
be removed only by quick and effective action? Clearly,
where imminent hazards to health are involved, you
have a strong case for blowing the whistle loud and
clear to outside authorities.

You have to identify the interest to help you decide
whether or not to blow the whistle within the organization. In some cases both the public and corporate
managers share a strong interest in the same corrective
action. George Geary objected to selling what he considered to be inadequately tested oilfield tubing for
United States Steel. He followed his immediate superior's order to sell the pipe despite his reservations, but
appealed to top management to recall the pipe pending
further tests. Management's review substantially confirmed Geary's position. The pipe was then recalled,
perhaps saving the lives and property of purchasers and
other citizens, and incidentally saving U.S. Steel from
the law suits and unfavorable publicity that might have
resulted.

You can never be certain that your disclosure will
have any effect. But you must be convinced that without disclosure there is little hope that significant damage
to health, safety, or some other well-defined public interest can be avoided. The greater the harm that is sure
to result if you remain silent, the more reason you have
to speak out and the likelier you are to find support.
Blowing the whistle on trivia is never justified. It exposes you and your family and your organization to
unnecessary risks, and it may make it more difficult
for others to speak to reveal important matters.

2) VERIFY THE ACCURACY OF YOUR KNOWLEDGE OF THE
SITUATION. In a sense, the burden of proof is on the
whistle blower from the outset. And it is a heavy bur-

den. An error of fact, even if it involves a minor point or a collateral issue, may seriously undermine the integrity of other information you provide authorities and the public. Accurate and complete information is also a precondition to obtaining the assistance of any outside organization. Public interest groups, law enforcement and regulatory agencies, legislators, and even newspaper reporters have limited resources and little spare time. You must provide them with reliable information to expect fast and effective action on your behalf. Ideally, it should be possible for the outside party—or for higher authorities within the organization—to verify your position without merely relying on your word. You should be able, for example, to refer them to other individuals or to available documents which will confirm key facts supporting your position.

Accuracy is also important for anticipating the response of the organization and its allies. Anticipate the worst. If your motives are impugned, for example, your case should be able to stand on its own merit. Ronald Ostrander was described by Procter and Gamble as a "disgruntled employee." In fact, Ostrander left the company not in protest or even out of disenchantment, but rather to take over the operation of a family business which he had inherited. But Procter and Gamble did not effectively contradict the fact that package directions recommended the use of eight to ten times more detergent than necessary for the best cleaning results.

3) IDENTIFY ETHICAL STANDARDS AS WELL AS LAWS, RULES, AND REGULATIONS THAT SUPPORT YOUR DECISION TO BLOW THE WHISTLE. Government employees and members of organized professional groups are subject, at least nominally, to formal, written ethical codes. They are rarely enforced, but they provide important guidelines for a potential whistle blower. These codes, with varying degrees of specificity, dedicate one's primary allegiance to the public interest. The code of ethics for United States government employees is quite clear: "Put loyalty to the highest moral principles and to country above loyalty to persons, party, or government," and "expose corruption wherever discovered." The government code was adopted by the Eighty-fifth Congress as

House Concurrent Resolution 175. It is therefore an expression of the highest legislative authority in the country and not merely a codification of the personal ethical preferences of civil servants.

In the preamble to its code of ethics, the National Society of Professional Engineers recognizes that the individual must serve more than one master: "The Engineer will serve with devotion his employer, his clients, and the public. . . ." Section 2 of the code is quite explicit:

> The Engineer will have proper regard for the safety, health, and welfare of the public in the performance of his professional duties. If his engineering judgment is overruled by nontechnical authority, he will clearly point out the consequences. He will notify the proper authority of any observed conditions which endanger public safety and health.
>
> a. He will regard his duty to the public welfare as paramount.
>
> b. He shall seek opportunities to be of constructive service in civic affairs and work for the advancement of the safety, health and well-being of his community.
>
> c. He will not complete, sign, or seal plans and/or specifications that are not of a design safe to the public health and welfare and in conformity with accepted engineering standards. If the client or employer insists on such unprofessional conduct, he shall notify the proper authorities and withdraw from further service on the project.

Other sections of the NSPE code buttress this commitment. Section 13, for example, warns members not to associate with "enterprises of questionable character" and not to become professionally associated with "engineers who do not conform to ethical practices."

These ethical maxims not only condemn wrongful conduct, they inveigh against the failure to act responsibly. Thus, under the NSPE code, the failure to report "observed conditions which endanger public safety and health" to proper authorities is as unacceptable as creating those conditions through incompetence or the misapplication of professional know-how.

Even lawyers are permitted to report clients' plans for future criminal conduct by Disciplinary Rule 4-

101(c) of the American Bar Association's Code of Professional Responsibility.

Our criminal law has long imposed on all citizens the obligation to report criminal misconduct. The failure to do so, at least where some effort is made to conceal knowledge of the crime,[1] is itself a crime called "misprision." The person guilty of misprision may have had absolutely nothing to do with the commission of the crime or preparations leading up to the crime.

Many federal laws encourage citizens to report misconduct by providing monetary rewards for doing so. For example:

—The Secretary of the Treasury is authorized to pay a reward for information on violation of the internal revenue laws.[2] 26 U.S.C. §7623

—He may also pay informers twenty-five percent of the recovery for information leading to the collection of customs revenue from smugglers.[3] 19 U.S.C. § 1619

—The Secretary of Agriculture may be required by a federal court to pay one-half of any civil penalties collected for falsified reports filed by cotton dealers to persons who reveal the misrepresentations.[4] 26 U.S.C. § 7263

—The Commissioner of Narcotics is authorized to pay rewards for information leading to the seizure of contraband narcotics.[5] 21 U.S.C. § 199

—The Commandant of the Coast Guard is required to divide the fifty-dollar fine that may be collected from seamen found to possess sheath knives between the informer and a "fund for the relief of sick and disabled seamen." 46 U.S.C. § 710

The last example may provide no great incentive to the modern merchant mariner, but it demonstrates that Congress has from early times considered citizen cooperation an important instrument of law enforcement. The recently rediscovered reward provision in the Refuse Act of 1899 is now widely recognized by conservationists and environmental groups, if not by the Justice Department, as a valuable incentive to encourage ordinary citizens to spot water polluters.

None of these provisions draw any distinction be-

tween employees and other persons who might seek
rewards but, as a practical matter, employees or former
employees of an offender are likely to have access to
the kinds of information necessary for conviction.

4) DEVELOP A PLAN OF ACTION: CONSIDER THE PER-
SONAL COSTS AND THE LIKELY RESPONSE OF ALLIES AND
ANTAGONISTS WITHIN AND OUTSIDE THE ORGANIZATION.
There is obviously no single plan of action that will be
effective in all circumstances. Indeed some of the men
and women whose experiences are recounted in this book
have said that they did not really plan to blow the whistle. Ernest Fitzgerald, for example, says that he merely
candidly answered Senator Proxmire's questions at a
public hearing. Dr. Jacqueline Verrett did the same
when interviewed by television newsmen.

Whistle blowers have acted in a number of distinctly
different ways. We have set down some of these in the
hope that others can use them to decide whether, when,
and how to blow the whistle. Our list is not complete,
nor is any one plan necessarily exclusive of the others.
Above all, they must be read with the understanding
that every situation that might require such a heavy
investment of personal courage is unique and not subject to simple analysis.

Blowing the whistle within the organization. Formal
channels for bringing a situation to the attention of top
management should be pursued first, if such channels
exist. In the law there is an analogous principle called
"exhaustion of remedies," by which a person wishing
to file suit must try to obtain satisfaction from the responsible governmental agency before his case will be
heard in court. One reason courts usually apply this
principle is to avoid, if possible, the high costs of litigation to both parties and to the legal system. Would-be
whistle blowers should pursue internal remedies first
for parallel reasons, if they can.

Going to management first minimizes the risk of retaliatory dismissal, as you may not have to go public
with your demands if the corporation or government
agency takes action to correct the situation. It may also
strengthen your case if you ultimately go outside the
organization, since the managers are likely to point out

any weaknesses in your arguments and any factual deficiencies in your evidence in order to persuade you that there is really no problem. Before the public accepts your position they will want to have some assurance that you are responsible and likely to be accurate. One indication that you are a responsible person—and one test of the strength of your convictions—is your willingness to submit your evidence to those who purport to be in the best position to act on it, the organization's top managers. Giving your employer a chance to respond not only enhances your credibility; it tends to minimize the effect of later efforts to impugn your motives or to accuse you of unfairness and disloyalty.

Officers David Durk and Frank Serpico of the New York Police Department discovered first hand the efficacy of pursuing internal avenues first. They went to the *New York Times* with their story of massive corruption in the department *after* trying for several years to get through to Mayor Lindsay. Police corruption might not have been big news, but their repeated failures to get action clearly was. And their credibility with the newspaper was enhanced immeasurably by the fact that they had tried literally every recourse within the department and within the city government before reaching outside.

Blowing the whistle within the organization is not, however, appropriate in every case. As George Geary discovered at United States Steel, it may cost you your job even if your position is completely vindicated by the company. Geary never spoke to an outsider until he sought counsel for his legal challenge to the company's action against him. The pipe he complained about was recalled for testing in line with his recommendation—but he was fired. So there are situations— Geary's may have been one of them—in which seeking relief inside the organization may be too costly to the employee or may be just as costly as going outside. In other circumstances "exhausting one's remedies" may unnecessarily jeopardize the very interests the whistle blower wants to protect. If, for example, a newly discovered defect in a consumer product poses such an imminent hazard to human life that any delay might result in death or serious injury, you should contact au-

thorities who can act immediately to remove the product from the retail market. The legal doctrine of
exhaustion has a related limitation: You are not required to exhaust other remedies before seeking relief
from a court if to do so would result in a denial of
justice.

*Resignation with a strong public statement of the rea-
sons.* Neither John Gardner when he resigned as Secretary of Health, Education, and Welfare under President
Johnson, nor Walter Hickel when he resigned as Secretary of the Interior under President Nixon used the
opportunity to protest policies with which they disagreed and which may have led to their departures.
There was speculation in the press that Gardner was
either unhappy with his department's budget or upset
with the Vietnam war. Hickel's private letter to the
President concerning youthful protests and the war received a lot of attention, but it apparently reached the
press by mistake.[6] He had no intention of resigning at
the time. When he did leave months later he did not
mount a platform to try to vindicate his position.

Gardner and Hickel may in fact have left for totally
personal reasons, or, more likely perhaps, they may
have felt that a public protest would be improper or
inappropriate. Silence seems to have become an unwritten rule for many departing top officials. James Reston,
commenting on this pattern, wrote:

> One thing that is fairly clear from the record is that
> the art of resigning on principle from positions close
> to the top of the American Government has almost
> disappeared. Nobody quits now, as Anthony Eden and
> Duff Cooper left Neville Chamberlain's Cabinet, with
> a clear and detailed explanation of why they couldn't
> be identified with the policy any longer. . . . Most of
> those who stayed on at the critical period of escalation
> gave to the President the loyalty they owed to the
> country. Some . . . are now wondering in private life
> whether this was in the national interest.[7]

But there are signs that the pattern is changing. On
three occasions in the winter of 1969–70, key government employees, including an agency head, resigned or
were asked to resign and then publicly articulated their
disagreements with the Nixon administration.

In August, 1969, Gary Greenberg, a senior trial attorney in the Civil Rights Division of the Justice Department and sixty-four of his colleagues — almost ninety percent of all nonsupervisory lawyers in the division—signed a written protest against the administration decision to delay the enforcement of desegregation orders in Southern schools. They maintained that further delay was clearly contrary to the Constitution they had sworn to uphold and that it could not be supported by any legal argument. Greenberg was asked to resign when, at the request of several judges, he stated his personal views in the course of a proceeding before the United States Court of Appeals in St. Louis. Though Greenberg did not technically resign in protest, he clearly did not leave the department quietly.

Terry Lenzner, former director of the Office of Legal Services in the Office of Economic Opportunity (OEO) publicly rebuked the Nixon Administration for subordinating the legal services program to local political powers. Lenzner and Frank Jones, another top Legal Services official, held a press conference on November 20, 1971, the day after their dismissal. Shortly thereafter all ten regional Legal Services directors signed and submitted a statement protesting the firings and supporting the Lenzner-Jones criticism of political influence in Legal Services. Since then key senators and congressmen, as well as the American Bar Association, have sought to block efforts to fracture the Legal Services program or to subordinate it to local or bureaucratic interests.

In June, 1970, Peter Gall, a special assistant to the director of the Office of Civil Rights at HEW, resigned to protest the forced resignation of the director, Leon Panetta. Gall and the Atlanta regional director, Paul Rilling, who also resigned, circulated statements to the press outlining the real reasons for Panetta's dismissal. Gall's story is presented in some detail in Chapter 15.[8]

Resignation followed by a reasonable period of silence. Dr. A. Dale Console, one-time medical director for E. R. Squibb and Sons, and a participant in the Conference on Professional Responsibility, chose this course of action. He did not express his concern about what he considered unethical and highly deceptive prescription drug marketing practices until a number of years after he left Squibb. This was no strategy decision, but a delayed realization of the implications of silence. In some cases the whistle blower may not realize the significance of his knowledge until later developments reveal it to him. Ronald Ostrander, for example, knew that Procter and Gamble and other detergent manufacturers recommended the use of excessive quantities of their products, but no one knew the significance of phosphate pollution until many years later.

Primarily, of course, delayed whistle blowing gives the individual an opportunity to start a new career or otherwise secure a livelihood for his family before his employer has any opportunity to retaliate. Dr. Console argues that it also tends to reduce the persuasiveness of charges that the individual is acting out of spite or to satisfy some other personal grievance. Procter and Gamble's charge, for example, that Ostrander was a disgruntled employee sounded somewhat foolish, since he had left the company twenty years earlier. But unless the whistle blower can tie his revelations to a *current* issue, he may have no impact whatsoever.

There are two serious problems with this approach. First, many of the situations which demand action by insiders are of such a magnitude or require such immediate attention that comfortable delays are intolerable. Charles Pettis blew the whistle on the trans-Andean highway while he continued to serve as chief consulting engineer because to do otherwise would have cost both the Peruvian and United States governments millions of dollars and perhaps the lives of many more workmen. Second, the drama and poignancy of the disclosure may be lost unless the whistle blower has a well-established reputation or speaks out at a time when other circumstances have made his information vital, as, for example, during an important Congressional hearing or an important public controversy.

Blowing the whistle outside the organization. This is the classic form of whistle blowing. It is often the most effective, but it can also be the most difficult. It certainly involves the greatest risk to the whistle blower, who may lose his job or destroy his career in the process. There are at least three variations of blowing the whistle outside the organization: remaining totally anonymous; revealing your identity only to those who will then, in effect, blow the whistle for you; or identifying yourself openly.

Ernest Fitzgerald has called anonymous whistle blowers "secret patriots." But anonymity, though it may be a means of protection from retaliatory dismissal or harassment, has serious drawbacks. Those who receive information from an anonymous insider have a heavy burden of substantiating and cross-checking the data. And the "secret patriot's" motives are immediately suspect, and there may be no way of allaying these suspicions. If he is later identified, he is far more likely to be vilified as a "rat fink" or a "spy" than his counterpart who openly confesses the reasons for his concern. Finally, anonymity tends to weaken the significance of the disclosure, since the whistle blower is unwilling to put his job on the line, or to subject himself to the public scrutiny he directs on his organization.

There are, however, certain circumstances in which anonymity may be justified: if the whistle blower is able to provide information which is independently verifiable, if he would be unable to support his family except in his present job, *and* if there is no other reasonable means to assure the confidentiality of his communication.

Recently, an anonymous whistle blower (or perhaps one who revealed his or her identity only to an outside contact) provided columnist Jack Anderson with an internal memorandum allegedly written by Dita Beard, Washington lobbyist for the International Telephone and Telegraph Corporation (ITT), to a high company official. The memo suggested that the corporation's pledge to provide substantial financial support for the 1972 Republican National Convention had a significant impact on negotiations between ITT and the Antitrust Division of the Justice Department concerning an out-of-court settlement of a suit to divest ITT of the recently acquired Hartford Fire Insurance Company.

Anderson printed excerpts of the memo in his nationally syndicated column the day after the Senate Judiciary Committee had completed its consideration of the nomination of Richard Kleindienst to be Attorney General. The publication of the memo and the subsequent investigation by Anderson and his associate Brit Hume led Kleindienst to request that the hearing be reconvened to clear up the cloud created by his participation in the alleged "deal." The hearings, which are continuing at this writing, have given the American public a rare insight into the relationship between giant corporations and high government officials. Both Kleindienst and former Antitrust Division chief Richard McLaren, in attempting to disprove the existence of a bargain, have spread across the public record evidence of private informal meetings between various ITT officials and representatives of the Justice Department as well as the White House and of interference by White House political operatives in the antitrust law enforcement process. McLaren, an outspoken critic of conglomerate mergers who had developed a series of challenges against conglomerates under existing laws, though still believing his position would be vindicated by the Supreme Court, was persuaded to settle the case on the basis of flimsy, politically backed evidence.

The "confidential whistle blower"—one who reveals himself to a third party with the understanding that his name will not be used without his consent—may, like the anonymous whistle blower, be protecting himself while sacrificing the chances of generating effective action. Like his anonymous counterpart he acts in the face of a strongly held belief that persons or organizations ought to be able to face their accusers. Underlying this belief is the notion that the veracity and even the integrity of those who claim to speak the truth should be subject to challenge. Those who use information from a confidential whistle blower must challenge him as relentlessly and thoroughly as he would be challenged were his identity revealed. They must play the role of the devil's advocate and play it well. They must insure that the whistle blower's disclosures will stand alone and that they can be thoroughly supported by an independent examination of the underlying facts.

Until our organizations and our laws make significant concessions to the need to recognize and protect individual and professional responsibility of employees, confidential appeals to those independent of the organization will remain absolutely necessary. Ultimately, of course, blowing the whistle is not easy. There is no perfect shield against firing, transfer, demotion, or any other form of retaliation. There is likewise no method that will guarantee curing the situation that threatens the public. Ernest Fitzgerald, for example, feels that he has barely dented the Defense Department's massive giveaways to the defense industry. And despite engineer Carl Thelin's revelations, all Corvairs have not been recalled.

Yet each initiative has made a significant first step by generating broader awareness, facilitating the participation of others in the cause, and building citizen pressure on authorities to act in the public interest. Perhaps it will compel more bystanders to ask themselves the question, if one person accomplished this much, how much more could be done if a few more people bent their arms to the oars?

5) SELECT AN APPROPRIATE OUTSIDE CONTACT. Suppose the decision is made to contact someone outside the organization. Where should you go? You should first consider contacting one or more government agencies that may have jurisdiction in the area of your concern. Even if you are a civil servant, there may be another agency with a direct interest in the matter. Under the National Environmental Policy Act of 1969, for example, all agencies considering major actions that might have a significant effect on the environment must file a draft "environmental impact statement" with the Council on Environmental Quality. The council in turn must circulate draft statements for comment to all other agencies who may have an interest in the proposal. Under the Air Quality Amendments of 1970 the Environmental Protection Agency (EPA) must comment on the draft. When a final statement is issued, any citizen may sue to block a project on the basis that the statement is inadequate. It was during this very process that employees within the Interior Department released a memorandum charging that Interior's draft impact statement on the proposed Alaska pipeline was

incomplete. EPA then severely criticized the draft statement, and citizens groups have blocked the project in
court pending a redraft of the statement.

The procedures established by agencies to receive
reports and complaints from citizens vary greatly. Some
simply refuse to act on anonymous complaints, but
will consider action on the basis of information provided by an identified person who wishes his name with-
held from third parties. The Occupational Safety and
Health Administration, for example, will not act on
anonymous complaints, but does guarantee confidentiality to workers who complain of unsafe or unhealthy
working conditions and identify themselves. Under the
1899 Refuse Act, one-half of the fine collected in the
successful prosecution of a water polluter is to be paid
to persons who give the information leading to conviction. Employees or former employees are, of course,
entitled to collect the reward. And some courts have
said that under the "qui tam" doctrine, a citizen can
sue the polluter on behalf of the government for the
fine and still collect his reward if the United States
attorney fails to act. Clearly, the Refuse Act—which
was largely ignored for the first seventy years it was
on the books—contemplates citizen involvement in the
enforcement process.

In many communities, citizens' groups and police
departments encourage citizens to report drug traffick-
ing, anonymously if they desire, to a special address
or telephone number.[9] Few communities have set up
similar mechanisms for citizens to report polluting industries or corruption. One exception is New York
City, where United States attorney Whitney North Seymour recently announced a post office address to which
citizens can send reports of possible corruption in government. Seymour's office will accept anonymous communications and will guarantee confidentiality if
requested. Whether or not there is a special procedure
like the one in New York City, you should communicate with the state or United States prosecutor's office
or a law enforcement agency if criminal activity might
be involved.

Remember, however, that prosecutors have virtually
unlimited discretion to press a case or to drop it. They

can select what goes before a grand jury and they can settle a case without trial. So when you contact a United States attorney or a district attorney, be prepared to persuade him that he ought to act by showing that there is or will be substantial evidence available and that significant damage will be done to an identifiable group or interest if he fails to prosecute.

You should also consider contacting state or federal legislators. Your United States senator or representative usually has several staff members assigned to "casework." They can act as informal ombudsmen for you in your relations with agencies in the executive branch. More importantly, you may have an issue of political significance to your representative. The best way to find out is to contact his or her office. Finally, your senator or representative may be a member of a committee that deals with issues related to the matter you are bringing to his attention.

Do not limit your contacts to your own legislators. Others may have a strong interest in the matter because of their committee assignments. Henry Durham, the former Lockheed employee who publicly supported Ernest Fitzgerald's charges of mismanagement, did not contact his own congressman or senator. Instead, he brought his evidence to Senator Proxmire, who had already shown a deep interest in military procurement generally and in Lockheed's C–5A air transport contract in particular.

Durham also believed that the senators and representatives from Georgia might have ignored him for political reasons. Lockheed is a major employer in the state and one of the largest employers in the Atlanta area. In fact, you should always consider political implications before contacting persons in political office. Officers Durkin and Serpico attempted to contact Mayor Lindsay just before an election about an issue—police corruption—that might have damaged his chances of reelection. On another occasion they were told by a Lindsay aide that the city administration would delay action to avoid angering policemen on the eve of a "long hot summer."

If government agencies and legislators are unresponsive, you may be forced to contact a citizens' group,

the press, or some other unofficial action group. You
may even have to organize your own group. One
Weyerhauser employee did just that to protest his
company's plan to build a logging road through the
area where he lived. He organized his neighbors and
together they generated enough unfavorable publicity
to convince the company to reverse itself. The Weyerhauser executive who told the story to one of the
authors of this book said that the company seriously
considered firing the employee, but decided he was
too valuable. They also may have admired his courage.

If you cannot organize your own constituency or if
you prefer to try other unofficial means first, you
should proceed with considerable thought and some
caution. Which citizens' group, which newsman, which
interested outsider you contact will depend on a host
of factors, such as the nature of the situation which
must be reported; the geographic scope of the problem
(i.e., whether it is of local, state or national significance); the type of organization you work for; the
accessibility of the citizens' group or of a key newsman who can be trusted to keep your confidence.
Here are a few practical suggestions:

   —Try to be selective. Even if you have no interest
in confidentiality and wish to alert the whole world to
a problem, scatter-shot salvos are usually ineffective.
Mimeographed barrages are easily discounted by
those who receive them as products of crackpots.
And you may unnecessarily affront potential listen-
ers. An investigative reporter, for example, is interested in an exclusive story. If he knows or has
reason to believe that his colleagues in competing
media have the same story at the same time, he may
be less interested in dedicating the necessary time
to pursuing the matter. And it may be tactically dis-
advantageous to bring in the whole world before you
have seen the response of your initial outside contact.
He may point out weak points in your case; he may
demand that you cross-check or find further support
or evidence for a particular contention. He may
prevent integrity and credibility from being destroyed

if you are about to make unsubstantiated or poorly thought out allegations.

—Contact local groups or media first, unless they are likely to be biased against you or unless the situation clearly has national significance. If you decide to contact a national organization, try to select one with the strongest interest in developments in your locale. The National Wildlife Federation, 1412 Sixteenth Street NW, Washington, D.C. 20036, publishes a directory of environmental and conservation groups in the United States. The Clearinghouse for Professional Responsibility, P.O. Box 486, Washington, D.C. 20044, maintains a file on local, state, and national citizens' groups active in many areas of public concern.

—Do your homework on the media, and help them with their homework. Investigative reporters are assigned to stories which require development and analysis. They are not limited to crisis-oriented, single-event reporting that newspapermen call "spot news." Rather, they are expected to develop stories too complex or too important to be treated routinely. Consequently, if you decide to tell your story to the media, try to interest an investigative reporter. Unfortunately, finding such a reporter, especially outside the very large metropolitan areas, may be a serious problem, and once you do find one you may have a difficult time interesting him or her in your situation. They are typically burdened with many assignments, face an endless series of deadlines, and, if they have established reputations, have a number of stories as important as yours from which to choose. You must come to the reporter fully prepared: develop a complete picture of the situation you wish to disclose and write it down beforehand. If you plan to submit a lengthy explanation, summarize or outline it separately so the reporter can get the essence of what you have to say without having to read page after page of supporting material and elaboration. This technique is equally applicable to any communication with an outside group or person you might wish to interest in taking some action. If the daily newspapers or broadcast media are not interested, consider approaching the more specialized journals like the *New Republic,* the *Nation,* the *Progressive, Washington Monthly, Environment,* or the *Texas Observer.* Frequently, once a smaller periodical has developed a story, the mass media will pick it up.

—Contact the Clearinghouse for Professional Responsibility, P.O. Box 486, Washington, D.C. 20044. The Clearinghouse was established to receive and disseminate information from professional and non-professional employees of large public and private organizations whose activity might imperil or endanger the public health, safety, or welfare.

The Clearinghouse strictly protects the mail sent to P.O. Box 486 in order to insure that any correspondent who so desires may have his letter held in confidence. The Clearinghouse does not act directly on the reports it receives. Instead, the writer is advised of the possible courses of action that may be available to him. He is told, for example, how to get in touch with a government agency, private group, or individual who might be interested in taking action on his information or complaint. The Clearinghouse may offer to communicate with an agency or group in his behalf. If he risks placing himself in some form of legal jeopardy, the Clearinghouse will warn him of the possibility. In some cases it may be necessary for the potential whistle blower to seek legal advice before taking any further action. When unsupported or poorly substantiated allegations are made, the correspondent will be asked to develop his position more fully or will be referred to someone who can help him strengthen his case. The Clearinghouse does not provide legal counsel to employees discharged or otherwise harassed for acting as their consciences dictate, but it will attempt to find legal counsel, attempt to enlist the aid of professional societies or other employee organizations, and suggest employment alternatives.

Underlying the struggle of persons within organizations and those without is the Nuremberg principle. Whatever the particular violation and wherever ultimate responsibility rests, this principle and those articulated by all the whistle blowers in this book have one common denominator: no organization, not even an army which demands discipline of the highest order or a nation which makes punishment for treason the price of disloyalty, can be the final arbiter of the rightness or wrongness of its actions. The individuals within the organization are on notice that the defense of "following orders" is fundamentally defective because there exists with respect to every organization a higher law, a higher principle, a higher morality. Organizations and those who direct them are on notice that subordinates—and this generation of whistle blowers should serve as conclusive evidence of the fact—will no longer remain serfs. The challenge for both the individual and the organization is to develop personal and institutional responses to accommodate these principles.

Notes

4. Whistle Blowing and the Law

1. "Power to the Corporation," *Industry Week*, January 4, 1971.

5. A. Ernest Fitzgerald

1. "The Dismissal of A. Ernest Fitzgerald by the Department of Defense," Hearings before the Subcommittee on Economy in Government of the Joint Economic Committee, Congress of the United States, November 17–18, 1969, p. 161.
2. Ibid., p. 12.
3. Ibid., p. 18.
4. Ibid., p. 150.
5. Ibid., p. 159.
6. Ibid., p. 45.
7. Ibid., p. 8.
8. Ibid.
9. Ibid., p. 10.
10. Ibid.
11. Ibid., p. 11.
12. Ibid., pp. 777–78.
13. *Congressional Record*, January 22, 1970.
14. Hearings, p. 11.
15. Ibid., pp. 130–131.
16. "Hearings on Military Posture," Armed Services Committee, May 7, 1969, p. 2693.
17. Hearings, Subcommittee on Economy in Government, p. 113.
18. Whistle Blowers Conference, January 30, 1971.
19. *Washington Post*, November 3, 1971, p. A-3.
20. *Washington Post*, November 23, 1971, p. A-2.
21. Conference.
22. Conference.
23. Conference.

6. Dr. John W. Gofman and Dr. Arthur R. Tamplin

1. Ralph E. Lapp, *New Republic*, January 23, 1971, p. 21. See also *New York Times Magazine*, February 7, 1971, p. 16.

2. The Federal Radiation Council was composed of the Secretaries of Health, Education, and Welfare (chairman), Labor, Defense, Commerce, and Agriculture, the Chairman of the Atomic Energy Commission, and the Special Assistant to the President for Science and Technology. The actual formulation of the standards, however, was accomplished by a special committee of the National Academy of Sciences which "relied heavily on data and information and standards of the National Council on Radiation Protection and the International Commission on Radiological Protection," according to the press office of the Atomic Energy Commission. See also Philip M. Boffey, "Radiation Standards: Are the Right People Making Decisions?" *Science*, vol. 171, February 26, 1971, p. 780.

3. "Epidemiologic Aspects of Cancer," *Ca—A Cancer Journal for Clinicians 19*, 1, pp. 27–35, 1969.

4. "Unanticipated Environmental Hazards Resulting from Technological Intrusions," reprinted in *Environment*, vol. 11, no. 2, March, 1969, pp. 9–28.

5. "Low Dose Radiation, Chromosomes, and Cancer," 1969 IEEE Nuclear Science Symposium, Sheraton-Palace Hotel, San Francisco, October 29, 1969.

6. Hearings, Senate Subcommittee on Air and Water Pollution, November, 1969.

7. Ibid.

8. Speech at Pitzer College, Claremont Colleges, January 14, 1971.

9. Dr. John Totter told William Hines of the *Chicago Sun-Times* in a taped interview on May 4, 1970: "Gofman, for example, has accused me of never reading it [the handbook]. Well, I'd like to know how many handbooks he has read. They're not for that purpose."

10. Letter from Dr. John Totter to Dr. Arthur Tamplin, August 21, 1969.

11. "AEC Staff Comments on Papers and Congressional Testimony by Dr. John W. Gofman and Dr. Arthur R. Tamplin."

12. "Staff Report on Allegations Made by Drs. Tamplin and Gofman of Censorship and Reprisal by the Atomic Energy Commission and the Lawrence Radiation Laboratory at Livermore," July 21, 1970, Atomic Energy Commission.

13. Interview with William Hines.

14. Bob Potter of the AAAS.

15. Philip M. Boffey, "Radiation Standards: Are the Right People Making Decisions?" *Science*, vol. 171, February 26, 1971, p. 780.

16. *Washington Post*, June 8, 1971, p. A-20.

17. Dr. James T. Brennan (NCRP), Department of Radiology, University of Pennsylvania Hospital, October 15, 1970, over TV Channel 16, Scranton, Pa.; also Dr. Richard M. Chamberlain (NRCP), Department of Radiology, University of Pennsylvania Hospital, August 20, 1970, to the Pennsylvania Senate, transcript p. 248.

18. "Government is the Most Dangerous of Genetic Engineers," *Washington Post*, Sunday, July 19, 1970 (based on Professor

Lederberg's testimony before Rep. Flood's House Appropriations Subcommittee).

19. *Bulletin of Atomic Scientists*, September, 1970.
20. Egan O'Connor quotes from "Health Implications of Fallout from Nuclear Weapons Testing through 1961," Report no. 3 of the Federal Radiation Council, May, 1962, Appendix B.
21. *Bulletin of Atomic Scientists*, September, 1970, p. 10.
22. Whistle Blowers Conference, January 30, 1971.
23. Egan O'Connor quotes Gofman in a review of the Gofman-Tamplin book in *Environmental Action*, February 8, 1971.
24. See Lauriston Taylor, AEC Commissioner, and H. J. Dunster, former chairman of the ICRP committee on radiation standards, who reviewed Gofman and Tamplin's book in *Nuclear Engineering*, a United Kingdom publication. Congressman Chet Holifield has publicly called them "irresponsible," as has Dr. John Totter of the AEC. Ralph Lapp refers to them as "overnight converts to a radiation religion," *New Republic*, January 23, 1971.
25. *Nuclear Engineering* (United Kingdom).
26. Dr. John W. Gofman, speech at Pitzer College, Claremont Colleges, January 14, 1971.

7. *Edward Gregory*

1. Statement at Whistle Blowers Conference, January 30, 1971.
2. Ibid.
3. Interview.
4. *Detroit News*, February 27, 1969.
5. *Newsweek*, March 10, 1969.
6. *Detroit News*, March 2, 1969.
7. No. 70 00394 06 23.
8. No. 71 00189 01 25.
9. No. 71 00177 01 25.
10. No. 71 00181 01 25.
11. Interview.
12. Conference.
13. Interview.

8. *Jacqueline Verrett*

1. Whistle Blowers Conference, January 30, 1971.
2. James S. Turner, *The Chemical Feast* (New York: Grossman Publishers, 1970), pp. 12–13.
3. Ibid., p. 13.
4. Ibid.
5. Conference.
6. Conference.
7. Conference.
8. Conference.
9. *The Chemical Feast*, p. 16.
10. Ibid., p. 25.

11. Ibid., p. 26.
12. Conference.
13. Conference.
14. Conference.

9. William I. Stieglitz

1. *Washington Post*, February 3, 1967, p. 11.
2. *New York Times*, February 3, 1967, pp. 1, 15.
3. Whistle Blowers Conference, January 30, 1971.
4. *Technology Review* (MIT alumni journal), February, 1971, pp. 30–31.
5. "Motor Vehicle Safety," Hearings of the House Subcommittee on Health and Safety, Committee on Interstate and Foreign Commerce, July, 1959, p. 234.
6. Ibid., p. 227.
7. Conference.
8. Conference.
9. "HR 13229 and Other Bills Relating to Safety," Hearings of the House Committee on Interstate and Foreign Commerce, April, 1966, p. 898.
10. Conference.
11. *New York Times*, February 3, 1967, pp. 1, 15.
12. Conference.
13. *New York Times*, February 3, 1967, pp. 1, 15.
14. "The Implementation of the National Traffic and Motor Vehicle Safety Act of 1966," Hearings of the Senate Committee on Commerce, March, 1967, p. 158.
15. Conference.
16. Conference.
17. Conference.
18. Conference.
19. Conference.
20. Conference.

10. Fumio Matsuda

1. According to family legend, the people who lived on the slopes of the mountain were irate. They surrounded the family's house with burning torches, but the family did not yield.
2. There was some publicity in the spring of 1971 about an infiltrator who attempted to learn the names of the secret backers and to discredit Matsuda and the Users Union.

11. A. Dale Console

1. "Competitive Problems in the Drug Industry," Hearings of the U.S. Senate Monopoly Subcommittee of the Select Committee on Small Business, March 14, 1969, p. 4501.
2. Ibid., p. 4501.

3. Ibid., p. 4503.
4. Ibid., p. 4501.
5. Ibid., p. 4503.
6. Ibid., pp. 4493–4.
7. Ibid., p. 4496.
8. Ibid., p. 4501.
9. Ibid., p. 4479.
10. Ibid., p. 4480.
11. Whistle Blowers Conference, January 30, 1971.
12. Conference.
13. Conference.
14. Conference.
15. Conference.

12. Christopher Pyle and Ralph Stein

1. Whistle Blowers Conference, January 30, 1971.
2. Conference.
3. *Washington Post*, March 3, 1971.
4. Conference.
5. "CONUS Revisited: The Army Covers Up," *Washington Monthly*, August, 1970, p. 50.
6. Ibid.
7. Ibid.
8. Ibid., p. 51.
9. Ibid.
10. Conference.
11. "CONUS Revisited," p. 51.
12. Conference.
13. *Washington Post*, March 25, 1971.
14. *Washington Post*, February 26, 1971.
15. Ibid.
16. Conference.

13. Charles Pettis

1. "Allegations of Mismanagement of a Peruvian Highway Project Financed with U.S. Assistance Funds," by the Comptroller General of the United States, December 2, 1971.
2. Ibid., p. 47.
3. Ibid., p. 53.
4. *Washington Monthly*, May, 1971, pp. 24–27.

14. The Colt Workers

1. The report is reproduced in 117 *Congressional Record* (daily ed.), November 5, 1971, p. E-11894.
2. Affidavit of Richard J. Welch, 117 *Congressional Record* (daily ed.), November 10, 1971, p. E-12051.
3. Affidavit of Victor L. Martinez, 117 *Congressional Record* (daily ed.), November 10, 1971, p. E-12051.

4. Affidavit of Robert J. Gregoire, 117 *Congressional Record* (daily ed.), November 10, 1971, p. E-12052.
5. Affidavit of Victor L. Martinez, 117 *Congressional Record* (daily ed.), November 10, 1971, p. E-12051.
6. 117 *Congressional Record* (daily ed.), November 22, 1971, p. S-19403.
7. *Hartford Times*, December 4, 1971, p. 1.

15. Whistle Blowers Beyond the Headlines

1. Paul C. Edwards, "A-Power Plant Near Completion," *Washington Post*, August 19, 1971, p. G-1-3.
2. *New York Times*, March 12, 1972, p. 64.
3. Ralph E. Lapp, *A Citizen's Guide to Nuclear Power* (Washington: The New Republic, 1971), a New Republic Pamphlet.
4. Thomas O'Toole, *Washington Post*, May 28, 1971, p. A-4.
5. Morton Mintz, *Washington Post*, July 18, 1971, pp. 1, 8.
6. Based on discussions with Gary Sellers and on Morton Mintz's article in *Washington Post*, September 27, 1970.
7. From Durk's testimony before the Knapp Commission reprinted in the *Washington Post*, December 20, 1971, p. A-18.
8. See *Washington Monthly*, May, 1971, pp. 34–35.
9. "The Acquisition of Weapons Systems," Hearings before the Subcommittee on Economy in Government of the Joint Economic Committee, 91st Congress, 2d Session, 1969, pp. 544–555.
10. See *American Men of Science,* 1954, 1960, and 1964. See also *Congressional Record*, February 28, 1969, p. S-2184.
11. Panetta's "resignation" was announced simultaneously to the public and to him.
12. *Washington Monthly*, June, 1970, pp. 75–83.
13. See, for example, Blumberg, "Corporate Responsibility and the Employee's Duty of Loyalty and Obedience," 24 *Oklahoma Law Review*, August, 1971, p. 306.
14. An estimated 400,000 children are poisoned each year, including 12,000 to 16,000 who require medical treatment and 3,200 who suffer moderate to severe brain damage from ingesting lead-based paints. *Congressional Record* (daily ed.), May 10, 1971, p. E-4177.
15. *Congressional Record* (daily ed.), June 4, 1971, p. E-5453.

16. The Corporation

1. This is not to suggest that the AAUP is a perfect model. It is in fact reluctant to get into what it considers local disputes unless it deems the threat to academic freedom to be of sufficient magnitude. It likewise grants wide discretion to institutions and to local faculty committees in dealing with individual cases.
2. Societies such as the Society of Automotive Engineers (SAE) and the American Society of Mechanical Engineers (ASME) rely so heavily on company-paid membership and facilities

and company-defined roles and meetings that the working committees and procedures are dominated by professional employees who are on company missions. Independence of decision is seriously lacking.

3. When a pension "vests," the employee will receive all or part of it at age sixty-five, for example, even if he retires immediately after vesting.

4. Available from ASPO, 1313 E. 16th St., Chicago, Ill. 60637, $6 prepaid.

5. Barbara and John Ehrenreich recount the Pugliese story in "Conscience of a Steelworker," *The Nation*, September 27, 1971, p. 268.

6. *Harvard Business Review*, July–August, 1971.

7. "The Corporate Ombudsman," *Harvard Business Review*, May–June, 1967.

8. *Wall Street Journal*, September 9, 1971.

17. The Government

1. *Pickering* v. *Board of Education*, 391 U.S. 563 (1968).

2. Remarks of William H. Rehnquist, "Public Dissent and the Public Employee" (speech before the Federal Bar Association, Washington, D.C., September 18, 1970).

3. *Washington Post*, April 17, 1971.

4. Secretary's Order No. 14-69, U.S. Dept. of Labor, March 14, 1969.

5. These reforms and others will be discussed at length in *The New Spoils System*, a study of the civil service and the Civil Service Commission by Robert Vaughn, scheduled for release in the summer of 1972. See also Appendix D of this book.

6. ACLU attorneys are volunteers, but the ACLU underwrites out-of-pocket expenses for cases its members undertake.

7. Daniel Ellsberg's disclosure of the Pentagon Papers sharply focuses the need to reform the current system of classification and to define any exception for national defense information so that the classification of any piece of information can be challenged in the proceeding in which the employee appeals his or her discharge. The former deputy assistant for security in the Air Force, William C. Florence, wrote, "Literally millions of documents are needlessly classified alongside of the relatively few—I would estimate from 1 to 5 percent in the Pentagon—which must legitimately be guarded in the national interest." *Washington Post*, December 12, 1971, p. C-1.

President Eisenhower's former press secretary, James Hagerty, dramatically confirmed Florence's analysis in testimony before Congressman William Moorhead's Government Information subcommittee. Hagerty reported that he would often have the President declassify documents personally to avoid red tape. "And the only thing that was Top Secret about that was what he [the President] would say when he had to go through such nonsense." *Washington Post*, March 7, 1972, p. A-8.

252 WHISTLE BLOWING

18. The Law

1. *Pickering* v. *Board of Education*, 391 U.S. 563 (1968).
2. See, for example, Adolf Berle, *Twentieth Century American Capitalism*, 1954, and his *Three Faces of Power*, 1967; Arthur S. Miller, "The Corporation as a Private Government in the World Community," 46 *Virginia Law Review*, 1960, p. 1539.
3. Respectively, *Marsh* v. *Alabama*, 360 U.S. 501 (1946) and *Amalgamated Food Employees Union* v. *Logan Valley Plaza*, 391 U.S. 308 (1968).
4. *NLRB* v. *Local 1229, IBEW*, 346 U.S. 464 (1953).
5. *Yellow Cab of California*, 65-1 ARB Par. 8256,44 LA 174,-445 (164) (Edgar A. Jones, Arbitrator).
6. *Initial Services, Ltd.* v. *Putterill*, 1967, *Wisconsin Law Review* 1032 (1968). For a discussion of this case and other legal aspects of whistle blowing, see Philip I. Blumberg, "Corporate Responsibility and the Employee's Duty of Loyalty and Obedience: A Preliminary Inquiry," *Oklahoma Law Review*, vol. 24, no. 3, August, 1971, pp. 279–318.
7. *Payne* v. *Western & A.R.R.*, 81 Tenn. 507 (1884).
8. State anti–yellow dog contract laws were overturned in *Adair* v. *United States*, 208 U.S. 161 (1908) and in *Coppage* v. *Kansas*, 236 U.S. 1 (1915). The NLRA was upheld in *NLRB* v. *Jones & Laughlin*, 301 U.S. 1 (1937).
9. Lawrence E. Blades, "Employment at Will vs. Individual Freedom: On Limiting the Abusive Exercise of Employer Power," 67 *Columbia Law Review* 1404 (1967).
10. Section 1905 of Title 18 of the U.S. Code.
11. See Working Papers of the Commission, Vol. I, p. 723, July, 1970.
12. See Professor Blades's article cited in Note 9.
13. *Odell* v. *Humble Oil & Refining Co.*, 201 F2d 123 (10th Cir. 1953).
14. *Congressional Record*, April 26, 1951.
15. The most exhaustive study of this act and the factors involved in its passage is Professor Stewart Macaulay's "Changing a Continuing Relationship Between a Large Corporation and Those Who Deal with It: Automobile Manufacturers, Their Dealers, and the Legal System, Parts I and II," in *Wisconsin Law Review*, Summer and Fall issues, 1965.
16. *Edwards* v. *Habib*, 397 F2d 687 (D.C. Cir. 1968). See also Note, 3 *Harvard Civil Rights—Civil Liberties Law Review* 193 (discussion of the lower court's treatment of the case).

IV. Strategies for Whistle Blowers

1. In the relatively infrequent prosecutions for the crime of misprision, most courts require that there be some evidence that the defendant concealed something from the authorities. See the case of *Lancey* v. *U.S.*, 356 F2d 407 (9th Cir. 1967) interpreting the federal crime, "misprision of a felony," 18 U.S.C. Section 4.

2. 26 U.S.C. Section 7623.
3. 19 U.S.C. Section 1619.
4. 26 U.S.C. Section 7263.
5. 21 U.S.C. Section 199.
6. Or so Hickel explained in his book, *Who Owns America*.
7. *New York Times*, March 9, 1969.
8. The experiences of Greenberg, Lenzner, and Gall are also treated at length in the *Washington Monthly* of December, 1969; June, 1970; and January, 1971, respectively.
9. For example, Blackman's Development Center in Washington, D.C., solicits confidential and anonymous reports on narcotics peddlers, and *Chicago Today*, a newspaper, has established a Secret Witness Bureau to "receive, pass on, and reward information that will help police to solve any of five major crimes." *Chicago Today*, May 26, 1971, p. 26.

Appendix A

Program of the Conference on Professional Responsibility

Mayflower Hotel—Colonial Room
Washington, D.C.
Saturday, January 30, 1971

9:00–9:10 AM	Peter Petkas: Introductions and Welcome
9:10–9:30	Ralph Nader: The Principles of Whistle Blowing
9:30–9:45	Questions and Answers
9:45–10:15	Professor Arthur S. Miller, George Washington Law School: "Whistle Blowing and the Law"
10:15–10:30	Questions and Answers
10:30–11:00	Robert Townsend: Whistle Blowing and the Corporation
11:00–11:15	Questions and Answers
11:15–11:45	Senator Proxmire: his views and experiences
11:45–Noon	Questions and Answers
Noon–12:45 PM	Lunch
12:45–1:30	First Panel Presentations

1. A. Ernest Fitzgerald (formerly with Air Force): C-5A and cost overruns
2. Ralph Stein (former Army enlisted man): Army intelligence operations against civilians
3. Edward Gregory (inspector at Fisher Body Plant, St. Louis): 2.5 million Chevrolets recalled with defective exhaust systems
4. William Stieglitz (former director, Motor Vehicle Performance Services, National Traffic Safety Agency)

1:30–1:45	First Panel Q&A
1:45–2:30	Second Panel Presentations

1. Dr. John Gofman and Dr. Arthur Tamplin (Lawrence Radiation Lab): AEC radiation guidelines
2. Dr. Dale Console (former medical director, E. R. Squibb Co.): AMA and the pharmaceutical industry
3. Dr. Jacqueline Verrett (FDA): cyclamates

2:30–2:45	Second Panel Q&A
2:45–3:00	Coffee Break
3:00–4:00	First Panel Roundtable: Discussion and audience participation
4:00–5:00	Second Panel Roundtable: Discussion and audience participation
5:00–5:45	Peter Petkas: Summation and Prospectus

Appendix B

Codes of Ethics

The following are taken from the codes of ethics or other official statements on professional responsibility of some of the leading professional societies in the United States.

The Engineer's Code*

Preamble

The Engineer, to uphold and advance the honor and dignity of the engineering profession and in keeping with high standards of ethical conduct:

—*Will be honest and impartial, and will serve with devotion his employer, his clients, and the public;*

—*Will strive to increase the competence and prestige of the engineering profession;*

—*Will use his knowledge and skill for the advancement of human welfare.*

Section 2—The Engineer will have proper regard for the safety, health, and welfare of the public in the performance of his professional duties. If his engineering judgment is overruled by non-technical authority, he will clearly point out the consequences. He will notify the proper authority of any observed conditions which endanger public safety and health.

a. He will regard his duty to the public welfare as paramount.

b. He shall seek opportunities to be of constructive service in civic affairs and work for the advancement of the safety, health and well-being of his community.

c. He will not complete, sign, or seal plans and/or specifications that are not of a design safe to the public health and welfare and in conformity with accepted engineering standards. If the client or employer insists on such unprofessional conduct, he shall notify the proper authorities and withdraw from further service on the project.

Section 7—The Engineer will not disclose confidential information concerning the business affairs or technical processes of any present or former client or employer without his consent.

a. While in the employ of others, he will not enter promotional efforts or negotiations for work or make arrangements for other employment as a principal or to practice in connection with a specific project for which he has gained particular and specialized knowledge without the consent of all interested parties.

Section 13—The Engineer will not associate with or allow the use of his name by an enterprise of questionable character, nor will he become professionally associated with engineers who do not conform to ethical practices, or with

* From the Code of Ethics for Engineers of the National Society of Professional Engineers, NSPE Publication No. 1102, as revised, January, 1971

persons not legally qualified to render the professional services for which the association is intended.

a. He will conform with registration laws in his practice of engineering.

b. He will not use association with a nonengineer, a corporation, or partnership, as a "cloak" for unethical acts, but must accept personal responsibility for his professional acts. Note: In regard to the question of application of the Code to corporations vis-a-vis real persons, business form or type should not negate nor influence conformance of individuals to the Code. The Code deals with professional services, which services must be performed by real persons. Real persons in turn establish and implement policies within business structures. The Code is clearly written to apply to the Engineer and it is incumbent on a member of NSPE to endeavor to live up to its provisions. This applies to all pertinent sections of the Code.

The Civil Engineer's Code*

For attainment of the broad goal of quality living, the American Society of Civil Engineers recommends that the individual civil engineer dedicate himself to the following objectives in relation to his work, to his clients and to his professional affiliations, and to his role as citizen in a democratic society.

1) In relation to his work, the civil engineer must recognize the effect his efforts will have on the environment. He is, therefore, obligated to increase his knowledge and competence in incorporating ecological considerations in his design.

2) In relation to his client, the civil engineer must inform the latter of the environmental consequences compared with the benefits of the services requested and the design selected, recommending only responsible courses of action. He must be prepared to relinquish his services in the event the client insists on a course of action which can be demonstrated to have undesirable consequences to the environment. The engineer must also seriously weigh social and national considerations and alternatives when appropriate, in addition to the apparent lowest-cost and technical aspects of a project.

3) In relation to ASCE, the civil engineer must fully utilize mechanisms within the Society which lend support to his own individual efforts to implement environmental considerations. Active support by the Society will enable him to deal more effectively with clients reluctant to accept such factors in their projects.

4) In his role as a citizen, the civil engineer must recognize the urgent need for adequate legislation and enforcement to protect the environment. He must, therefore, take the lead in development, modification and support of government programs, to insure adequate environmental protection.

* From a position paper of the American Society of Civil Engineers' Council on Environmental Systems published in the Society's magazine, *Civil Engineering*, September, 1971

The Chemist's Creed*

to the public
to propagate a true understanding of chemical science, avoiding premature, false, or exaggerated statements, to discourage enterprises or practices inimical to the public interest or welfare, and to share with other citizens a responsibility for the right and beneficent use of scientific discoveries.

to my science
to search for its truths by use of the scientific method, and to enrich it by my own contributions for the good of humanity.

to my profession
to uphold its dignity as a foremost branch of learning and practice, to exchange ideas and information through its societies and publications, to give generous recognition to the work of others, and to refrain from undue advertising.

to my employer
to serve him undividedly and zealously in mutual interest, guarding his concerns and dealing with them as I would my own.

to myself
to maintain my professional integrity as an individual, to strive to keep abreast of my profession, to hold the highest ideals of personal honor, and to live an active, well-rounded, and useful life.

to my employees
to treat them as associates, being ever mindful of their physical and mental well-being, giving them encouragement in their work, as much freedom for personal development as is consistent with the proper conduct of work, and compensating them fairly, both financially and by acknowledgment of their scientific contributions.

to my students and associates
to be a fellow learner with them, to strive for clarity and directness of approach, to exhibit patience and encouragement, and to lose no opportunity for stimulating them to carry on the great tradition.

to my clients
to be a faithful and incorruptible agent, respecting confidence, advising honesty, and charging fairly.

* Approved by the Council of the American Chemical Society, September 14, 1965

Excerpts from the
Code of Professional Responsibility
of the American Bar Association

Disciplinary Rule 1–102   Misconduct
(A) A lawyer shall not:
  (1) Violate a Disciplinary Rule.
  (2) Circumvent a Disciplinary Rule through actions of another.
  (3) Engage in illegal conduct involving moral turpitude.
  (4) Engage in conduct involving dishonesty, fraud, deceit, or misrepresentation.
  (5) Engage in conduct that is prejudicial to the administration of justice.

Disciplinary Rule 2–110   Withdrawal from Employment
(B) Mandatory withdrawal.
  A lawyer representing a client before a tribunal, with its permission if required by its rules, shall withdraw from employment, and a lawyer representing a client in other matters shall withdraw from employment if:
  (1) He knows or it is obvious that his client is bringing the legal action, conducting the defense, or asserting a position in the litigation, or is otherwise having steps taken for him, merely for the purpose of harassing or maliciously injuring any person.
  (2) He knows or it is obvious that his continued employment will result in violation of a Disciplinary Rule.
(C) Permissive withdrawal.
  If DR 2–110 (B) is not applicable, a lawyer may not request permission to withdraw in matters pending before a tribunal, and may not withdraw in other matters, unless such request or such withdrawal is because:
  (1) His client:
    (a) Insists upon presenting a claim or defense that is not warranted under existing law and cannot be supported by good faith argument for an extension, modification, or reversal of existing law.
    (b) Personally seeks to pursue an illegal course of conduct.
    (c) Insists that the lawyer pursue a course of conduct that is illegal or that is prohibited under the Disciplinary Rules.
    (d) By other conduct renders it unreasonably diffi-

cult for the lawyer to carry out his employment effectively.

    (e) Insists, in a matter not pending before a tribunal, that the lawyer engage in conduct that is contrary to the judgment and advice of the lawyer but not prohibited under the Disciplinary Rules.

(2) His continued employment is likely to result in a violation of a Disciplinary Rule.

CANON 4
A Lawyer Should Preserve the Confidences and Secrets of a Client

Disciplinary Rule 4–101   Preservation of Confidences and Secrets of a Client

(A) "Confidence" refers to information protected by the attorney-client privilege under applicable law, and "secret" refers to other information gained in the professional relationship that the client has requested be held inviolate or the disclosure of which would be embarrassing or would be likely to be detrimental to the client.

(B) Except when permitted under DR 4–101 (C), a lawyer shall not knowingly:

    (1) Reveal a confidence or secret of his client.

    (2) Use a confidence or secret of his client to the disadvantage of the client.

    (3) Use a confidence or secret of his client for the advantage of himself or of a third person, unless the client consents after full disclosure.

(C) A lawyer may reveal:

    (1) Confidences or secrets with the consent of the client or clients affected, but only after a full disclosure to them.

    (2) Confidences or secrets when permitted under Disciplinary Rules or required by law or court order.

    (3) The intention of his client to commit a crime and the information necessary to prevent the crime.

    (4) Confidences or secrets necessary to establish or collect his fee or to defend himself or his employees or associates against an accusation of wrongful conduct.

(D) A lawyer shall exercise reasonable care to prevent his employees, associates, and others whose services are utilized by him from disclosing or using confidences or secrets of a client, except that a lawyer may reveal the information allowed by DR 4–101 (C) through an employee.

CANON 5
A Lawyer Shoud Exercise Independent
Professional Judgment on Behalf of a Client

Ethical Consideration 5–24
. . . Although a lawyer may be employed by a business corporation with non-lawyers serving as directors or officers and they necessarily have the right to make decisions of business policy, a lawyer must decline to accept direction of his professional judgment from any layman.

CANON 7
A Lawyer Should Represent a Client
Zealously Within the Bounds of the Law

Ethical Consideration 7–3
Where the bounds of the law are uncertain, the action of a lawyer may depend on whether he is serving as advocate or adviser. A lawyer may serve simultaneously as both advocate and adviser, but the two roles are essentially different. In asserting a position on behalf of his client, an advocate for the most part deals with past conduct and must take the facts as he finds them. By contrast, a lawyer serving as adviser primarily assists his client in determining the course of future conduct and relationships. While serving as advocate, a lawyer should resolve in favor of his client doubts as to the bounds of the law. In serving a client as adviser, a lawyer in appropriate circumstances should give his professional opinion as to what the ultimate decisions of the courts would likely be as to the applicable law.

Ethical Consideration 7–5
A lawyer as adviser furthers the interest of his client by giving his professional opinion as to what he believes would likely be the ultimate decision of the courts on the matter at hand and by informing his client of the practical effect of such decision. He may continue in the representation of his client even though his client has elected to pursue a course of conduct contrary to the advice of the lawyer so long as he does not thereby knowingly assist the client to engage in illegal conduct or to take a frivolous legal position. A lawyer should never encourage or aid his client to commit criminal acts or counsel his client on how to violate the law and avoid punishment therefor.

Ethical Consideration 7–8
A lawyer should exert his best efforts to insure that decisions of his client are made only after the client has been in-

formed of relevant considerations. A lawyer ought to initiate this decision-making process if the client does not do so. Advice of a lawyer to his client need not be confined to purely legal considerations. A lawyer should advise his client of the possible effect of each legal alternative. A lawyer should bring to bear upon this decision-making process the fullness of his experience as well as his objective viewpoint. In assisting his client to reach a proper decision, it is often desirable for a lawyer to point out those factors which may lead to a decision that is morally just as well as legally permissible. He may emphasize the possibility of harsh consequences that might result from assertion of legally permissible positions. In the final analysis, however, the lawyer should always remember that the decision whether to forgo legally available objectives or methods because of non-legal factors is ultimately for the client and not for himself. In the event that the client in a non-adjudicatory matter insists upon a course of conduct that is contrary to the judgment and advice of the lawyer but not prohibited by Disciplinary Rules, the lawyer may withdraw from the employment.

Ethical Consideration 7–10
The duty of a lawyer to represent his client with zeal does not militate against his concurrent obligation to treat with consideration all persons involved in the legal process and to avoid the infliction of needless harm.

Ethical Consideration 7–17
The obligation of loyalty to his client applies only to a lawyer in the discharge of his professional duties and implies no obligation to adopt a personal viewpoint favorable to the interests or desires of his client. While a lawyer must act always with circumspection in order that his conduct will not adversely affect the rights of a client in a matter he is then handling, he may take positions on public issues and espouse legal reforms he favors without regard to the individual views of any client.

Ethical Consideration 7–27
Because it interferes with the proper administration of justice, a lawyer should not suppress evidence that he or his client has a legal obligation to reveal or produce. In like manner, a lawyer should not advise or cause a person to secrete himself or to leave the jurisdiction of a tribunal for the purpose of making him unavailable as a witness therein.

Disciplinary Rule 7–102   Representing a Client Within the Bounds of the Law
(A) In his representation of a client, a lawyer shall not:

(3) Conceal or knowingly fail to disclose that which he is required by law to reveal.

(4) Knowingly use perjured testimony or false evidence.

(5) Knowingly make a false statement of law or fact.

(6) Participate in the creation or preservation of evidence when he knows or it is obvious that the evidence is false.

(7) Counsel or assist his client in conduct that the lawyer knows to be illegal or fraudulent.

(8) Knowingly engage in other illegal conduct or conduct contrary to a Disciplinary Rule.

(B) A lawyer who receives information clearly establishing that:

(1) His client has, in the course of the representation, perpetrated a fraud upon a person or tribunal shall promptly call upon his client to rectify the same, and if his client refuses or is unable to do so, he shall reveal the fraud to the affected person or tribunal.

(2) A person other than his client has perpetrated a fraud upon a tribunal shall promptly reveal the fraud to the tribunal.

Principles of Medical Ethics*

Preamble
These principles are intended to aid physicians individually
and collectively in maintaining a high level of ethical conduct. They are not laws but standards by which a physician
may determine the propriety of his conduct in his relationship with patients, with colleagues, with members of allied
professions, and with the public.

Section 1
The principal objective of the medical profession is to render
service to humanity with full respect for the dignity of man.
Physicians should merit the confidence of patients entrusted
to their care, rendering to each a full measure of service
and devotion.

Section 2
Physicians should strive continually to improve medical
knowledge and skill, and should make available to their
patients and colleagues the benefits of their professional
attainments.

Section 3
A physician should practice a method of healing founded
on a scientific basis; and he should not voluntarily associate
professionally with anyone who violates this principle.

Section 4
The medical profession should safeguard the public and itself
against physicians deficient in moral character or professional competence. Physicians should observe all laws, uphold the dignity and honor of the profession and accept its
self-imposed disciplines. They should expose, without hesi-
tation, illegal or unethical conduct of fellow members of
the profession.

Section 5
A physician may choose whom he will serve. In an emergency, however, he should render service to the best of his
ability. Having undertaken the care of a patient, he may
not neglect him; and unless he has been discharged he may
discontinue his services only after giving adequate notice.
He should not solicit patients.

Section 6
A physician should not dispose of his services under terms
or conditions which tend to interfere with or impair the
free and complete exercise of his medical judgment and skill

* Adopted by the American Medical Association in 1957

or tend to cause a deterioration of the quality of medical care.

Section 7

In the practice of medicine a physician should limit the source of his professional income to medical services actually rendered by him, or under his supervision, to his patients. His fee should be commensurate with the services rendered and the patient's ability to pay. He should neither pay nor receive a commission for referral of patients. Drugs, remedies or appliances may be dispensed or supplied by the physician provided it is in the best interest of the patient.

Section 8

A physician should seek consultation upon request; in doubtful or difficult cases; or whenever it appears that the quality of medical services may be enhanced thereby.

Section 9

A physician may not reveal the confidences entrusted to him in the course of medical attendance, or the deficiencies he may observe in the character of patients, unless he is required to do so by law or unless it becomes necessary in order to protect the welfare of the individual or of the community.

Section 10

The honored ideals of the medical profession imply that the responsibilities of the physician extend not only to the individual, but also to society where these responsibilities deserve his interest and participation in activities which have the purpose of improving both the health and the well-being of the individual and the community.

Appendix C

The Muskie Amendments*

* From S.2770, an act to amend the Federal Water Pollution Control Act (the so-called Muskie amendments), passed unanimously (86–0) by the Senate, November 2, 1971. A similar, somewhat stronger, provision appears in the Coal Mine Safety Act, Public Law 91–173, signed into law, December 30, 1969.

Employee Protection

Sec. 507(a) No person shall discharge, or in any other way discriminate against, or cause to be discharged or discriminated against any employee or any authorized representative of employees by reason of the fact that such employee or representative of any alleged violator has filed, instituted, or caused to be filed or instituted any proceeding under this Act, or has testified or is about to testify in any proceeding resulting from the administration or enforcement of the provisions of this Act.

(b) Any employee or a representative of employees who believes that he has been discharged or otherwise discriminated against by any person in violation of subsection (a) of this section may within thirty days after such violation occurs, apply to the Secretary of Labor for a review of such alleged discharge or discrimination. A copy of the application shall be sent to such person who shall be the respondent. Upon receipt of such application, the Secretary of Labor shall cause such investigation to be made as he deems appropriate. Such investigation shall provide an opportunity for a public hearing at the request of any party to enable the parties to present information relating to such violation. The parties shall be given written notice of the time and place of the hearing at least five days prior to the hearing. Any such hearing shall be of record and shall be subject to section 554 of title 5 of the United States Code. Upon receiving the report of such investigation, the Secretary of Labor shall make findings of fact. If he finds that such violation did occur, he shall issue a decision, incorporating an order therein and his findings, requiring the party committing such violation to take such affirmative action to abate the violation as the Secretary of Labor deems appropriate, including, but not limited to, the rehiring or reinstatement of the employees or representative of employees to his former position with compensation. If he finds that there was no such violation, he shall issue an order denying the application. Such order issued by the Secretary of Labor under this subparagraph shall be subject to judicial review in the same manner as orders and decisions of the Administrator are subject to judicial review under this Act.

(c) Whenever an order is issued under this section to abate such violation, at the request of the applicant, a sum equal to the aggregate amount of all costs and expenses (including the attorney's fees) as determined by the Secretary of Labor to have been reasonably incurred by the applicant for, or in connection with, the institution and prosecution of such proceedings, shall be assessed against the person committing such violation.

Comments on the Muskie Proposal

The Muskie proposal is deficient in a number of ways:

1) Protection should also be extended to employees who report violations directly to the Administrator of the Act and to those who respond by testimony or otherwise to Congressional inquiries.

2) The employee must notify the Secretary within 30 days of the discharge or other act of discrimination. This gives him very little leeway in which to consider alternative courses of action or to negotiate a settlement directly with his employer. Also, since there is no provision for notifying employees of their rights under the Act, 30 days may pass before an employee even knows of his remedy.

3) The Secretary should be required to complete his investigation and make a decision within a limited period of time, perhaps 90 days. And he should be required to explain the reasons for any decisions against the employee, as he is required to do when he finds *for* the employee.

4) Courts reviewing the actions of the Secretary should have the *express* power of reviewing the adequacy of any remedy granted by the Secretary.

5) In another section of the Muskie bill (Section 505) provision is made for citizen suits against the Administrator for failure to carry out his responsibilities under the Act. But this provision does not expressly permit suits against the Secretary of Labor for failure to carry out the employee protection section. The employee should be given this additional assurance of his rights.

—The Authors

Appendix D

Draft of an Employee Rights and Accountability Act*

A BILL TO expand the rights of federal employees and to insure the accountability of such employees to the citizens of the United States.

Be it enacted by the Senate and House of Representatives of the United States of America in Congress assembled, That this Act may be cited as the "Federal Employee Rights and Accountability Act of 19—."

TITLE I.—FINDINGS AND DECLARATION OF PURPOSE

Sec. 101. Findings.

The Congress hereby finds that:

(a) Employees of the Federal government risk substantial damage to their careers, possible loss of their livelihoods, and other forms of harassment if they express their views about

(1) the management of their agencies;

(2) the failure of their agencies to serve their statutory functions;

(3) the direction of agency policy;

(4) conflicts of public and private interest within their agencies; or

(5) illegal conduct by the agency or its employees.

(b) These risks exist to a large extent without regard to whether views are expressed through appropriate channels within the agency, to committees of Congress which have jurisdiction over the subject matter involved, through the fulfillment of lawful obligations of employees, or to the public at large;

(c) Existing laws, rules, and regulations of the separate

---

* This draft of a proposed Employee Rights and Accountability Act is a result of a request made to Ralph Nader by Senator Proxmire at the Conference on Professional Responsibility. It is keyed to present laws relating to federal government employees, but can be easily modified for adoption by state legislatures. It would *not* affect the rights of nongovernment employees, but many of the ideas contained within it—for example, an employee bill of rights, expanded access for citizen complainants, and expanded personal responsibility—could be incorporated into laws intended to increase the protection of unorganized employees. Senator Proxmire plans to introduce a version of this proposal in Congress in 1972. The principal draftsmen were Peter Petkas and Robert Vaughn, attorneys with Ralph Nader's Corporate Accountability Research Group and Public Interest Research Group, respectively.

agencies and of the Civil Service Commission have proven seriously deficient both for employees and for citizens;

(d) Similarly, citizens, under present laws, rules, and regulations do not have adequate access to the courts to seek the removal of employees and officials who fail to discharge their duties either under the laws which prescribe the responsibilities of federal agencies or those which regulate the conduct of federal employees;

(e) The failure of agencies and their employees to fully implement Congressional enactments is frequently due to the inability of knowledgeable employees to communicate to the Congress and to the public information vital to the oversight functions of Congress and to the public's right to know.

Sec. 102. Declaration of Purpose.

The Congress finds the purpose of this Act to be

(a) To enhance the rights of Federal employees to challenge the actions or failures of their agencies and to express their views, without fear of retaliation, through appropriate channels within the agency, through complete and frank responses to Congressional inquiry, through free access to law enforcement officials, through oversight agencies of both the executive and legislative branches of Government, and through appropriate communication with the public.

(b) To broaden remedies available to citizens to hold government employees accountable for the performance of their duties;

(c) To insure that Acts of Congress enacted to protect individual citizens are properly enforced;

(d) To provide new rights and remedies to guarantee that citizens can have confidence in their government and to insure that public offices are truly public trusts.

TITLE II.—PROTECTION OF EMPLOYEES AND OF CONGRESSIONAL ACCESS TO INFORMATION

Sec. 201. Definitions.

(a) For the purposes of the Act, "employee" (except as otherwise provided by this Act or when specifically modified) is defined as in 5 USC §2105 except that

(1) an employee paid from nonappropriated funds of the Army and Air Force Exchange Service, Army and Air Force Motion Picture Service, Navy Ship's Stores Ashore, Navy exchanges, Marine Corps exchanges, Coast Guard exchanges, and other instrumentalities of the armed forces conducted for the comfort, pleasure, contentment and mental and physical improvement of personnel of the armed forces is deemed an employee for the purposes of this Act; and

(2) an employee appointed by the President with the

advice and consent of the Senate or an employee in a
confidential or policy-determining character as enumerated
in 5 CFR §213.3276 is not an employee for purposes of
this title.

(b) For purposes of this Act, "dismissed" (except as
otherwise provided by this Act or when specifically modified)
shall mean any personnel or manpower action which sepa-
rates an employee or abolishes his position.

(c) For purposes of this Act, "agency" shall include every
authority of the United States subject to the Administrative
Procedure Act and shall also include any organization which
has one or more corporate directors, commissioners, chief
executive officers, or members of a governing body appointed
by the President or an appointee of the President.

Sec. 202. Employee Bill of Rights.

Employees shall have the following rights which the Employee Rights and Accountability Board established in Title
IV of this Act and its agents shall have the duty to defend,
protect, and enforce:

1. The right to freely express their opinions on all public
issues, including those related to the duties they are assigned
to perform, *provided, however*, that any agency may promulgate reasonable rules and regulations requiring that any such
opinions be clearly dissociated from agency or administration policy.

2. The right to disclose information unlawfully suppressed;
information concerning illegal or unethical conduct which
threatens or which is likely to threaten public health or
safety or which involves the unlawful appropriation or use
of public funds; information which would tend to impeach
the testimony of officers or employees of the government
before committees of Congress or the responses of such
officers or employees to inquiries from members of the
Senate or House of Representatives concerning the implementation of programs, the expenditure of public funds,
and the protection of the constitutional rights of citizens and
the rights of government employees under this Act and under
any other laws, rules, or regulations for the protection of
the rights of employees; *provided, however*, that nothing in
this section shall be construed to permit the disclosure of the
contents of personnel files, personal medical reports, or the
disclosure of any other information in such a manner as to
invade the individual privacy of an employee or citizen of
the United States.

3. The right to communicate freely and openly with members of Congress and to respond fully and with candor to
inquiries from committees of Congress and from members
of Congress, *provided, however*, that nothing in this section

shall be construed to permit the invasion of the individual privacy of other employees or of citizens of the United States.

4. The right to assemble in public places for the free discussion of matters of interest to themselves and to the public and the right to notify fellow employees and the public of such meetings.

5. The right to due process in the resolution of grievances and appeals including, but not limited to:

—the right to counsel,

—the right to a public hearing and a copy of the transcript of such hearing,

—the right to cross examine witnesses and to compel the attendance and testimony of witnesses and to compel the production of all relevant documents in the course of such a hearing or other similar proceeding,

—the right to testify and submit evidence on behalf of other employees and of other citizens seeking redress in the courts or in the administrative process.

6. The right to humane, dignified, and reasonable conditions of employment which allow for personal growth and self-fulfillment, and for the unhindered discharge of job and civic responsibilities.

7. The right to individual privacy, *provided, however*, that nothing in this section shall limit in any manner an employee's access to his own personnel file, medical report file or any other file or document concerning his status or performance within his agency.

Sec. 203. Complaints of criminal harassment for Congressional testimony.

(a) Any complaint alleging violation of 18 USC §1505 (which prohibits coercion and harassment of Congressional witnesses) shall be promptly investigated by the Justice Department. Within six months after the filing of a complaint, the Justice Department shall render a decision on whether or not prosecution under that section is warranted. If the Department decides prosecution is not warranted, it shall state with specificity the facts and reasons upon which such decision is based.

(b) If the Justice Department renders a decision pursuant to this section that prosecution is not warranted or if it fails to render a decision as required by this section, any citizen may petition the United States district court for the district in which the alleged violation took place or the United States District Court for the District of Columbia for an order to compel prosecution. If the court finds, after an independent review of the evidence, that a prima facie case exists, it shall order prosecution to be commenced.

(c) In its independent review of evidence the court shall have access to the enforcement file of the Justice Department and to all other relevant documents or files within that department or any agency thereof.

TITLE III.—ACCOUNTABILITY OF EMPLOYEES
Sec. 301. Definitions.

(a) For purposes of this Title, "conflicts of interest" shall include behavior proscribed by 18 USC §§201–224. In addition, "conflicts of interest" may include behavior which the court in the exercise of sound discretion proscribes. In the exercise of its discretion, the court may consider Executive Orders addressed to the subject, rules and regulations governing employee conduct and principles of fiduciary law.

(b) For purposes of this Title, "employee" shall be defined as in section 201 of this Act, except that an employee appointed by the President with the advice and consent of the Senate or an employee in a position of a confidential or policy-determining character as enumerated in 5 CFR §213.3276 shall be an employee for purposes of this Title.

(c) For purposes of this Title, an "employee responsible" is one to whom Congress has delegated authority and any employee to whom such authority has been redelegated.

(d) For purposes of this Title, "consumer protection law" shall include any law intended to protect or which does in fact protect individual consumers from unfair, deceptive, or misleading acts or practices; anticompetitive acts or practices; or non-disclosure or inadequate disclosure of product quality, weight, size, or performance.

Sec. 302. Public employees as fiduciaries.

(a) Any employee who administers, enforces, or implements any health, safety, environmental, or consumer protection law or any rules or regulations promulgated for the enforcement of such laws, is a fiduciary to any individual or class of individuals intended to be protected or who are in fact protected from injury or harm or risk of injury or harm by such laws, rules, or regulations, and, as a fiduciary, is obligated to protect such individuals or class of individuals.

(b) Any individual or class of individuals may commence a civil action on his or its own behalf against any employee or employees in any agency for breach of a fiduciary duty upon a showing that said employee or employees by their acts or omissions have exposed said individual or class of individuals to injury or harm, or risk of injury or harm, from which they are to be protected by the employee or employees. Such action may be brought in the United States district court for the district in which the employee or any one of the employees resides or in the United States District

for the District of Columbia. The district court shall have
jurisdiction to entertain such action without regard to the
amount in controversy or the diversity of citizenship of the
parties. The United States through the Attorney General
shall defend any employee or employees against whom such
action is commenced. Such employee or employees may,
however, at his or their option provide for his or their own
defense.

(c) If the court finds that any employee or employees
have breached their fiduciary duty by any act or omission
or by any series of acts or omissions, the court—

> (1) shall order performance or cessation of per-
> formance, as appropriate;

> (2) may temporarily suspend any person or persons
> without pay from the agency for a period not exceeding
> three months;

> (3) may remove an individual or individuals from
> the agency; or

> (4) may take any other appropriate action against
> any employee or employees within the agency who have
> breached the duties of the fiduciary relationship.

Sec. 303. Curbing fraud and conflicts of interest.

(a)(1) Any citizen shall have a right to commence a suit
in the United States district court of the district in which
he resides or in United States District Court for the District
of Columbia on behalf of the United States to recover funds
which have been improperly paid by the United States while
there exists any conflict of interest on the part of the employee responsible for such payment.

(2) It shall be an affirmative defense to any action
under this section that the defendant did not know or have
reason to know of the conflict of interest.

(b) Any citizen who commences a suit under this section
shall be entitled to 30% of the amount recovered for the
government plus attorney's fees and other costs incidental
to the action.

(c) The right of a citizen to commence and maintain a
suit under this section shall continue notwithstanding any
action taken by the Justice Department or any United States
attorney, *provided, however,* that if the United States shall
first commence suit, a citizen may not commence a suit
under this section, *provided further, however,* that if the
United States shall fail to carry on such suit with due diligence within a period of six months or within such additional time as the court may allow, a citizen may commence
a suit under this section and such suit shall continue notwithstanding any action taken by the Justice Department or
any United States attorney.

Sec. 304. Intent of Congress in Section 303.

In Section 303 of this Title, it is the intent of Congress to create a right of citizens to commence and maintain suits under the provisions of this Title.

TITLE IV.—EMPLOYEE RIGHTS AND ACCOUNTABILITY BOARD

Sec. 401. Definition.

For purposes of this Title, "employee" shall be defined as in section 201 of this Act, except that an employee appointed by the President with the advice and consent of the Senate or an employee in a position of a confidential or policy-determining character as enumerated in 5 CFR §213.3276 shall be an employee for purposes of this Title.

Sec. 402. Establishment of the Employee Rights and Accountability Board.

(a) There is hereby established an Employee Rights and Accountability Board (hereinafter referred to as the "Board"). The Board shall be composed of five members, to be appointed as hereinafter directed. No more than three members of the Board may be of the same political party. No more than two members of the Board may have ever served in personnel, management, or administrative positions in any agency. Three members of the Board shall be attorneys admitted to practice before the bar of any jurisdiction in the United States for three years at the time of appointment. No member shall be eligible for reappointment.

(b) The term of office of each member of the Board shall be six years, except that, (1) of those members first appointed, two shall serve for two years and two shall serve for four years, respectively, from the date of appointment, and (2) any member appointed to fill a vacany occurring prior to the expiration of the term for which his or her predecessor was appointed shall be appointed for the remainder of such term.

(c) The Chairman of the Board shall be elected by the Board to serve a two-year term. The Chairman shall be the chief executive and administrative office of the Board.

(d) All members of the Board shall be compensated at the rate provided for in Executive Level 2 as set out in section 5313 of Title 5 of the United States Code.

(e) Three members of the Board shall constitute a quorum for the transaction of business.

(f) The Board may appoint and fix the compensations of such officers, attorneys, and employees, and make such expenditures as may be necessary to carry out its functions.

(g) Notwithstanding section 206 of the Budget and Accounting Act of 1921 (31 USC §15), the Board shall transmit its estimates and requests for appropriations (including any requests for increases therein) directly to the Senate and House of Representatives.

(h) One member of the Board shall be appointed by the President with the advice and consent of the Senate, two members shall be appointed by the president pro tempore of the Senate, and two members shall be appointed by the Speaker of the House of Representatives; *provided that* the first member appointed by the President shall serve six years, the first members appointed by the president pro tempore of the Senate shall serve two and four years respectively, and the first members appointed by the Speaker of the House of Representatives shall serve four and two years respectively.

Sec. 403. Office of Inspection and Complaint.

(a) The Board shall establish an Office of Inspection and Complaint which shall perform the following functions:

(1) Conduct inspections of all agencies to insure compliance with orders of the Board;

(2) Conduct inspections to provide information on the implementation of rules and regulations of the Board;

(3) Conduct inspections to discover violations of rules and regulations of the Board;

(4) Investigate complaints filed with the Board by citizens and employees pursuant to this Title;

(5) Initiate actions against employees for violations of this Title or rules and regulations promulgated hereunder; and

(6) Perform such other investigative functions as the Board may prescribe.

(b) The Office of Inspection and Complaint shall be administered by an Inspector General, who shall be appointed by the Board for a term of seven years and who shall be removable only for good cause.

Sec. 404. Office of Trial Examiners.

(a) The Board shall establish an Office of Trial Examiners which shall hear and adjudicate complaints filed under this Title.

(b) No person may serve as a trial examiner or perform any of the duties of a trial examiner, who is not admitted to practice before the bar of any jurisdiction in the United States.

(c) The Office of Trial Examiners shall be administered by a Chief Examiner appointed by the Board for a six-year term.

(d) The Office of Trial Examiners shall not be subordinate to any other office under the Board, but shall receive its authority and direction directly from the Board.

Sec. 405. Powers of the Board.

The Employee Rights and Accountability Board shall have, in addition to the authority necessary and proper for carrying out its duties and the duties of its subordinate agencies and officers as specified elsewhere in this Title, the authority to—

(1) Inspect and investigate all aspects of the Federal personnel system, including but not limited to the effectiveness of disciplinary procedures and violations of employee rights;

(2) Appoint and remove all subordinate officials and employees, subject to the rules and regulations of the Board applicable to all civil servants; *provided, however,* that the Inspector General and the Chief Examiner shall be removable only for good cause;

(3) Hear and adjudicate complaints received from Federal agencies and departments, from employees, and from citizens, including employee complaints alleging wrongful dismissal;

(4) Reprimand, suspend, fine, or remove any employee, or take other appropriate disciplinary action, *provided, however,* that any such action shall be taken pursuant to duly promulgated regulations of the Board and shall not be inconsistent with the rights of employees granted by the Act, *provided further, however,* that the Board shall have the power to order any fines or portion thereof assessed pursuant to this section paid to the person, persons, or agency damaged by the employee hereunder fined, upon application and proof of loss;

(5) Establish standards of conduct for all employees pertaining to the performance of duties, conflicts of interests, and improper use of personnel management authority;

(6) Conduct and manage its own litigation without review, clearance, or participation by any agency of the Executive branch, including the Department of Justice;

(7) Review employee complaints filed with the office of Inspection and Complaint which allege that a transfer, reassignment, or manpower separation or readjustment was motivated by malice or taken in retaliation for the exercise of any employee's rights as an employee or as a citizen; and

(8) Promulgate any rules or regulations necessary for the fulfillment of its duties under this Act.

Sec. 406. Complaint procedures.

(a) The Board shall establish a citizen complaint procedure and shall receive and consider complaints from any citizen alleging violation by an employee of any Federal law or any rule or regulation promulgated under any Federal law; violation of any employee code of conduct or standard, including but not limited to those promulgated pursuant to this Act, or any rules or regulations promulgated by the Board; failure of any employee to carry out his duty under any Federal law, rule, or regulation; negligent or improper performance of duty by any employee of the United States.

The citizen complaint procedure established under this section shall include the following provisions:

(1) Complaints shall be filed with the Office of Inspection and Complaint, which shall within 60 days of the receipt of the complaint render a written decision setting forth findings of fact and including either an order dismissing the complaint or initiating prosecution before the Office of Trial Examiners; *provided, however*, that an order of dismissal under this section shall not bar or otherwise limit any other rights of the complainant to raise the same or similar issue before the Board or before any other agency; *provided further, however,* that any order of dismissal shall refer the complainant to any other appropriate Federal, state, or local agency.

(2) If the Office of Inspection and Complaint orders the complaint dismissed, the citizen complainant or any other citizen may appeal the order to the Board within 30 days of the entry of such order.

(3) If upon review of any order of dismissal appealed under this subsection, the Board upholds the order of dismissal, the citizen complainant or any citizen may appeal the order of the Board upholding such dismissal to the United States Court of Appeals of the District of Columbia or the United States Court of Appeals for the district in which the complainant resides.

(4) The Office of Inspection and Complaint shall prosecute all complaints which a trial examiner finds meritorious or which the Board has found meritorious, or which an appropriate appellate court has found meritorious. All such complaints shall be adjudicated as set out in sections 407 and 408.

(b) The Board shall establish an employee complaint procedure and shall receive and consider employee complaints alleging any misconduct enumerated in section 406(a) of this Title as well as violations of any rules or regulations of the Board relating to the rights of employees and an action against an employee or against the interests of any employee by his employer agency motivated by malice.

The complaint procedure established under this subsection shall include the same provisions enumerated in subsection (a) of this section for citizen complaints.

(c) The Board shall establish an agency complaint procedure and shall receive and consider complaints from agencies alleging any misconduct enumerated in section 406(a) of this Title or cause for removal or discipline as specified in the rules and regulations of the Board.

The complaint procedures established under this subsection shall include the following provisions:

(1) Agency complaints against an employee shall be presented directly to the Office of Trial Examiners and shall not be subject to review or consideration by the Office of Inspection and Complaint.

(2) Before any complaint is accepted by the Office of Trial Examiners under this subsection the agency shall

[a] Give advance notice 10 days prior to filing the proposed complaint stating specifically and in detail any and all reasons for the proposed action;

[b] At the time of notice thus required, inform the employee of his right to answer personally and in writing and to submit affidavits in support of his answer;

[c] Provide the employee with a decision on whether or not a complaint will be filed, stating the reasons which have been sustained and informing the employee of his rights before the Office of Trial Examiners, which notice and statement of rights shall have been approved by the Board; and

[d] File the complaint within five days of notification of the employee of the decision to file;

Provided, however, that the employee against whom a complaint has been filed may be suspended with pay during the period herein provided for agency action and such additional time as may be necessary for the agency to obtain a ruling from the trial examiner as prescribed in paragraph (3) of this subsection for suspension pending a final decision on the merits, if his continued presence poses a substantial risk of harm to himself, to his fellow employees, or to the public.

(3) If the employee does not object to the Office of Trial Examiners within 15 days of receiving a decision that a complaint will be filed, the trial examiner to whom the complaint has been assigned shall order the action sought by the agency complainant.

(4) If the employee objects to the action requested by the agency, the trial examiner to whom the complaint has been assigned shall order a hearing; *provided, however, that*, if he finds that the facts alleged in the complaint would, if true, support the conclusion that the employee's continued presence poses a substantial risk of harm to himself, to his fellow employees, or to the

public, the trial examiner may also order that the employee be suspended with pay pending final decision on the merits by the trial examiner.

Sec. 407. Hearing Procedures.

(a) Hearings on any complaints prosecuted by the Office of Inspection and Complaint or by any agency shall be conducted by a trial examiner provided by the Office of Trial Examiners.

(b) Complaint hearings shall conform to the requirements of 5 USC §554 as in effect at the time of approval of this Act.

(c) Any hearing conducted by a trial examiner pursuant to this Title shall be open to the public.

(d) For the purpose of any hearing under this Title, any trial examiner is empowered to administer oaths and affirmations, subpoena witnesses, compel their attendance, take evidence, and require the production of any books, papers, correspondence, memoranda, contracts, agreements, or other records which he deems relevant or material to the inquiry. Such attendance of witnesses and the production of any such records may be required from any place in any State or in any Territory or other place subject to the jurisdiction of the United States at any designated place of hearing.

(e) In case of contumacy by, or refusal to obey a subpoena issued to any person, the Board may invoke the aid of any court of the United States within the jurisdiction in which such hearing is held, or where such person resides or carries on business, in requiring the attendance and testimony of witnesses and the production of books, papers, correspondence, memoranda, contracts, agreements, and other records. And such court may issue an order requiring such person to appear before the trial examiner, there to produce records, if so ordered, or to give testimony touching the matter under investigation or in question; and any failure to obey such order of the court may be punished by such court as a contempt thereof. All process in any such case may be served in the judicial district whereof such person is an inhabitant or wherever he may be found. Any person who, without just cause, shall fail or refuse to attend and testify or to answer any lawful inquiry or to produce any records, if in his or its power to do so, in obedience to the subpoena of the trial examiner, shall be guilty of a misdemeanor and, upon conviction, shall be subject to a fine of not more than $10,000, or to imprisonment for a term of not more than one year, or both.

(f) At least three members of the Board must participate in the deliberation preceding a decision and the decision of any appeal brought before the Board pursuant to this Title.

(g) All decisions of the Board, of trial examiners, and of any other official or employee of the Board required to issue findings of fact or written decisions under this Act or under the rules or regulations of the Board shall be published in a convenient form and made available to the public at reasonable cost.

(h) Any person against whom a complaint has been brought under this section may be represented by counsel or by his agency or both.

Sec. 408. Appeal Procedures.

(a) Any employee or agency party to an action before the Office of Trial Examiners, or any complainant, may appeal the decision of a trial examiner to the Board, *provided, however*, that, with respect to citizen complaints, any citizen who is a member of a class of individuals intended to be protected by the law, rule, or regulation on which the complaint is based and who is affected by the alleged violation, omission, or negligent act, or any employee affected by the alleged violation, omission, or negligent act, may appeal a decision to the Board.

(b) In any appeal taken pursuant to this section, the Board shall review the record and uphold, reverse, or modify the decision of the trial examiner. The Board may order oral argument, on its own motion or on motion timely filed by any party, and provide such other procedures or rules as it deems practicable or desirable in any appeal under this section and consistent with the Employee Bill of Rights in Title II of this Act.

(c) Any employee or agency party to an appeal to the Board, any complainant, any citizen or employee affected by an alleged violation who appealed the decision of the trial examiner, and any other citizen or employee affected by an alleged violation, may appeal the decision of the Board to the United States Court of Appeals for the District of Columbia or the United States Court of Appeals for the district in which the appellant resides, *provided, however*, that the venue for such appeals shall not be such as to cause undue hardship to any employee or citizen.

(d) In any appeal in which official dereliction that may threaten public safety has been alleged, the court may remand the appeal to an appropriate district court for a hearing on the facts.

Sec. 409. Congressional Intent.

It is the intent of Congress that the Board effectuate the following policy through its regulations and decisions:

1. That public employees be made personally accountable for failure to enforce the laws and for negligence, incompetence, or improper performance of their public duties;

2. That the rights of employees to expose corruption, dishonesty, incompetence, or administrative failure be protected;

3. That the rights of employees to contact and communicate with Congress be protected;

4. That employees be protected from reprisal or retaliation for the performance of their duties; and

5. That civil servants be motivated to do their duties justly and efficiently.

Index

BUST OF ROTROU BY CAFFIÉRI

JEAN ROTROU'S

SAINT GENEST

AND

VENCESLAS

Edited with Introduction and Notes

BY

THOMAS FREDERICK CRANE

PROFESSOR OF THE ROMANCE LANGUAGES IN CORNELL UNIVERSITY

R. B. Michell.

INTER-
NATIONAL
MODERN
LANGUAGE
SERIES

GINN & COMPANY

BOSTON · NEW YORK · CHICAGO · LONDON

The Athenæum Press
GINN & COMPANY · PRO-
PRIETORS · BOSTON · U.S.A.

TO

TWO GENERATIONS OF
CORNELL STUDENTS, WITH WHOM ASSO-
CIATION FOR NEARLY FORTY YEARS HAS BEEN
A JOY AND AN INSPIRATION, THIS BOOK, LIKE ALL MY
OTHER WORKS, THE OUTCOME OF STUDY WITH
THEM, IS AFFECTIONATELY DEDICATED
BY THEIR TEACHER AND
FRIEND

PREFACE

My object in preparing the present edition of two of
Rotrou's plays has been to widen the range of reading in
French dramatic literature of the seventeenth century, and to
encourage the beginning of original work on the part of more
advanced students. The study of the serious dramatic literature of the above period is, in the schools at least, confined to
one or two plays of Corneille and Racine, and texts of other
authors cannot be readily procured even for college and university work. Next to the great writers just mentioned comes
Rotrou, and yet no edition of his plays has ever been published
outside of France until the present one, and the only accessible French editions, those of Hémon and Ronchaud, are not
adapted to the use of students from their lack of commentary.
It is very desirable that the student of the French classical
drama should know of the romantic tendencies of the age as
expressed in the tragi-comedy of Rotrou, — tendencies that
resulted in the Romantic drama of the last century. Besides
this, Rotrou is an attractive figure, and I venture to think that
the two plays here presented will be found by American students more interesting than the usual classical plays to which
they are accustomed.

I have endeavored to promote independent study by providing the student with materials for such work and by suggesting
topics of study. The two plays are based upon Spanish ones,
and, as Spanish is now studied in many of the schools, I have
given copious extracts from Rotrou's sources in the hope of
awakening an interest in the Spanish drama of the seventeenth
century. I have purposely refrained from treating exhaustively

such points as Rotrou's style, versification, relations to contemporary dramatists, etc. I had hoped that the student would be led to study these and similar points more fully than my space has permitted me to do, and that he would read *Polyeucte*, for example, and draw his own conclusions as to Rotrou's imitation of Corneille. For this reason abundant extracts have been given from Cellot and Desfontaines, whose works are not easily to be found in this country.

The annotations to the text have purposely been made very full. The plays are not easy reading, and the construction and vocabulary often differ from those of modern French. I have endeavored, however, to make these plays intelligible and to put them within the grasp of the ordinary student, who will find a mass of interesting references imbedded in the notes, which, lest they should escape his attention, are placed at the bottom of the page. I have also kept constantly in view literary criticism, and in the introduction and notes will be found judgments of Rotrou by the most eminent of French critics.

In the large number of extracts reproduced in the introduction and notes I have followed closely the original texts, with the result of an occasional typographical variation which should not be laid to the charge of the printer of this work. The same is true also of titles of books.

I should perhaps apologize for my lengthy treatment of *Cosroès*, a play not included in this volume for lack of space. I trust my extensive analysis will lead some students to read this fine tragedy, which is accessible in the selections of Ronchaud and Hémon.

I do not pretend to have contributed anything new to the study of Rotrou, but only to have arranged the materials of others in an orderly and, I hope, attractive form. My indebtedness to Person, Chardon, Steffens, and Stiefel is great, and, I trust, duly acknowledged. A recent visit to London and Paris enabled me to consult the treasures of the British Museum,

and of the National, Arsenal, and Mazarin Libraries, and I
have seen nearly every book cited in my notes and Bibliography. My thanks are due to my former students, Mr. J. B.
Hopkins, now of Lafayette College, and Mr. A. Gordon, for
the collation of texts at Paris and Ithaca, and to the Library
of Harvard College for the loan of the original editions of
Saint Genest and *Venceslas*.

Since the above was written, over a year ago, Mr. Gordon
has become my colleague and has been of the greatest service
to me in seeing this book through the press.

T. F. CRANE

ITHACA, NEW YORK

CONTENTS

ST. GENEST AND VENCESLAS

INTRODUCTION

I

Jean Rotrou was born in August, 1609, at Dreux, the chief
town of its district in the department of Eure-et-Loir and a
quiet little place of about nine thousand inhabitants some
fifty miles southwest of Paris, now famous for the splendid
mausoleum of the Orléans family.[1] His father, Jean Rotrou,
was a citizen of Dreux, and his mother, Isabelle Facheu, was

---

[1] The exact date of Rotrou's birth is not known. He was baptized Fri-
day, August 24, 1609. See Person, *Notes critiques*, p. 107. He was probably born the 19th or 20th. Dom Liron gives the 19th. The materials for
Rotrou's biography are very scanty. A few extracts from official records are given in Jal, *Dictionnaire critique de biographie et d'histoire*,
Paris, 1872; in Person, *Notes critiques et biographiques sur le Poète
Rotrou*, Paris, 1882; and in Chardon, *La vie de Rotrou mieux connue*,
Paris, 1884. The articles in the eighteenth-century and nineteenth-century biographical dictionaries and literary histories have little worth.
The notices of Rotrou in the list of writers prefixed to Richelet's *Dictionnaire de la langue françoise*, Paris, 1728, and in Dom Liron's *Singu-
larités historiques*, Paris, 1738, formerly considered the most trustworthy
biographies of the poet, have been shown to rest on the precious
Notice biographique sur Jean Rotrou, written about 1698 by the abbé

daughter of Étienne Facheu, a well-to-do citizen of Chartres. The Rotrou family was an old and prominent one, the poet's grandfather, uncle, and cousin having been mayors of Dreux between 1581 and 1650. Besides Jean there were three daughters and a well-known brother, Pierre de Rotrou, seigneur de Saudreville, secretary of the army and commissioner of war under Louis XIII and Louis XIV.[1]

Rotrou's early education was received at Dreux, and when he was twelve or thirteen he was sent to Paris to continue his studies, where he won, we are told, the approval of his teachers. The name of only one of them is known, M. de Bréda, professor of philosophy, who afterwards became curate of the church of Saint-André-des-Arts. Nothing is known of the colleges in Dreux and Paris attended by Rotrou, and we are able only to conjecture what his education was. It will be seen later that he used for his plays Latin, Spanish, and Italian sources, and we may suppose that he was familiar with these three languages. Two of Rotrou's dramas, *Antigone* and *Iphigénie*, are on subjects treated by the Greek dramatists, and we might be led to believe that Rotrou was acquainted with the Greek sources. It is probable, however, that in the composition of the above plays he used only French and Latin

---

L.-F. Brillon (1681–1739), and published by L. Merlet at Chartres in 1885. The editor indicates by italics the passages omitted or misunderstood by Dom Liron. This *Notice* is the only one of the early biographies of real value, and I have incorporated most of it into my Introduction. Next to the *Notice* may be mentioned Person's work cited above and Chardon's invaluable biography. A careful analysis of the works relating to Rotrou's biography will be found in Steffens, *Rotrou-Studien*, pp. 3–29. Additions to this are in Stiefel, *Unbekannte italienische Quellen Jean Rotrou's*, pp. vii–ix, and in Buchetmann, *Jean de Rotrou's Antigone*, pp. viii–xiv, 1–13.

[1] Rotrou's brother Pierre is the subject of a work by Person, *Les papiers de Pierre Rotrou de Saudreville*, etc., Paris, 1883. In Person's *Notes critiques*, p. 104, is given a genealogical table of the Rotrou family.

the influence of the Renaissance, which led to the translation and imitation of the comedies of Plautus and Terence and the tragedies attributed to Seneca. It is an interesting fact, however, that these classical comedies and tragedies were not acted on a popular stage, but were performed in royal or private residences and in the colleges. Many of the sixteenth-century plays were not acted at all. This was the case with the most remarkable dramatic writer of this period, Robert Garnier, only one of whose plays, *Bradamante*, seems to have been performed. The influence of such plays affected only the cultivated classes, and did not reach the people who composed the audience at the Hôtel de Bourgogne. This audience still delighted in the great classes of mediæval literature which had never been prohibited, such as the moralities and farces. It is also probable that mysteries or similar plays continued to be performed occasionally in spite of the formal prohibition of the Parlement.

What the repertory of the Hôtel de Bourgogne was at the beginning of the seventeenth century, when Hardy began his career, can be seen from his early plays, which include the *histoire par personnages* and tragedy ; the former being the dramatization of romantic subjects like *Theagenes and Chariclea*, the latter, tragedies influenced by the more regular taste of the Renaissance, but written for performance and not for reading. Besides these, the farce, *pastorale*, and tragi-comedy were the favorite forms of the new drama.

The question of the unities was not settled until after the appearance of Mairet's *Sophonisbe* in 1634 ; and until the Quarrel of the Cid resulted in the general adoption of the new system the mediæval freedom of the stage prevailed. After a long misconception the stage arrangements of the Middle Ages and the period prior to the adoption of the unities are now well understood and explain the structure of the plays of those times, otherwise difficult of comprehension.

On the mediæval stage the different localities involved in the action were represented by characteristic structures, and the actors concerned remained in or near these "mansions," or passed from one to the other. In the modern drama the action is combined with a succession of scenes; in the mediæval drama the different scenes were always before the spectators and it was the action which was transferred from one scene to another.

When the modern theater was founded in France in 1548 it was impossible to transfer to a relatively small stage the elaborate and complicated mediæval system. In order to economize space the actors who were involved did not remain upon the stage as in the earlier arrangement; the number of localities, or "mansions," was reduced as far as possible, and where the play extended over several performances only the localities needed for each performance were erected upon the stage. Finally, the material difficulties often resulted in the condensation of the play and the suppression of superfluous episodes requiring additional localities. It can easily be seen how the *mise en scène* contributed to simplify the action of the drama and gradually to lead to the adoption of the classical system. An additional difficulty arose about the time of the *Cid* (1636), when spectators were admitted to seats upon the stage. This encroachment upon the space almost compelled the reduction of the scenery to the minimum and the consequent contraction of the action of the play.

In order then to understand the character and mode of performance of the early plays of Rotrou we must remember that the unities had not yet been imposed upon the dramatist and that the stage represented permanently, and always in view of the audience, the different localities in which the action was to take place.[1]

---

[1] Illustrations of the scenery of seventeenth-century plays will be found in Rigal, *Alexandre Hardy et le théâtre français à la fin du xvie et*

Rotrou naturally accepted the general form of drama imposed upon him by the above limitations. It remains to consider briefly how far he was influenced by his predecessors in his choice and treatment of subjects. Unfortunately, all of Hardy's plays have disappeared except the small number, thirty-three, published in the five volumes printed in the author's lifetime.[1] Hardy, like Shakespeare, drew freely from the French translations of Plutarch ; Claudian, Virgil, Ovid, Dares and Dictys, and Quintus Curtius furnished other subjects. Sannazaro, Tasso, and Guarini provided the material for his *pastorales*, and novels of Boccaccio and Cinthio are the basis of the plays of *Gésippe* and *Phraate*. The subjects of only five plays, all tragi-comedies, are taken from the Spanish, — three from the novels of Cervantes, one from a collection by Diego Agreda y Vargas, and one from the *Diana* of Montemayor. Rigal has shown that, while Hardy has used Greek, Latin, Italian, and Spanish sources, he was not necessarily acquainted with these languages, but probably in all cases employed French translations. Another interesting point is that Hardy, so far as we can judge from his extant works, did not draw from what was

au commencement du xviie siècle, Paris, 1889, frontispiece ; Petit de Julleville, *Histoire de la langue et de la littérature française*, Paris, vol. iv, pp. 270, 354 ; and in Rigal, *Le théâtre français avant la période classique*, frontispiece. In the last-named work, pp. 310–321, will be found an account of the *Mémoire* of Laurent Mahelot, a manuscript containing sketches for the scenery of a large number of seventeenth-century plays, of which no less than fourteen are Rotrou's. It is from this manuscript that the illustrations mentioned above are taken. See especially the last-named work of Rigal, pp. 247 et seq., and p. 315. A more elaborate account of the *mise en scène* of the seventeenth century and its influence on the development of the French drama will be found in Rigal, *Alexandre Hardy*, etc., pp. 161–217.

[1] To these should be added *Les chastes et loyales amours de Théagène et Chariclée reduites du Grec de l'Histoire d'Héliodore en huit poëmes dramatiques, ou théâtres consecutifs*, Paris, 1623. See Rigal, *Alexandre Hardy*, etc., pp. 66 and 435, where is given an analysis of this singular tragi-comedy in several *journées*, or separate performances.

soon to be the most prolific source of French imitation, the Spanish drama, and, so far as we know, made no use of the Greek and Latin dramatists.[1]

Although tragi-comedy was known in France as early as the *Bradamante* (1582) of Robert Garnier, it owes its settled form and vogue to Hardy.[2] This form maintained itself by the side of tragedy from the beginning of the seventeenth century until 1636, from which time, in consequence of the establishment of the unities, it gradually sank into obscurity, surviving, however, in the eighteenth-century *comédie larmoyante* and *tragédie bourgeoise*, and in the nineteenth-century romantic drama.[3]

As some seventeen of Rotrou's thirty-five plays are tragi-comedies and follow closely the model of Hardy, it is necessary to consider for a moment what constituted a tragi-comedy, and how it differed from a tragedy. The literary tradition of the sixteenth and seventeenth centuries restricted tragedy to an action involving characters of high rank and ending in a tragic dénouement. This idea excluded a tragic plot ending happily (as in the *Cid*), and also any plot ending happily which involved characters of high rank. In order to employ these two classes of subjects tragi-comedy was evolved.[4] The scope

---

[1] See Rigal, *Alexandre Hardy*, etc., pp. 236 et seq., and E. Martinenche, *La comedia espagnole en France de Hardy à Racine*, Paris, 1900, pp. 43–56.

[2] See Rigal, *Alexandre Hardy*, etc., pp. 428–430.

[3] The best account of the French *tragi-comédie* will be found in Rigal, *Alexandre Hardy*, etc., pp. 221–224 and 428–435, and in Horion, *Explication du théâtre classique*, Paris, 1888, pp. 10–21. See also V. Fournel, *La littérature indépendante*, Paris, 1862, pp. 12–15, and Brunetière, *Études critiques*, 7ᵉ série, Paris, 1903, " L'Évolution d'un genre : La Tragédie," pp. 180–183.

[4] Horion, *op. cit.*, p. 10: " On appelait tragi-comédie, au dix-septième siècle, toute pièce de théâtre dont l'intrigue était tragique, comme celle du *Cid*, où il y a effusion de sang, et le dénoûment heureux ; ou encore toute pièce de théâtre qui n'offrait pas d'intrigue tragique, mais dont les personnages appartenaient à un rang distingué, comme rois, princes, comtes, gentilshommes, et dont le dénoûment était heureux.

of tragi-comedy was somewhat broadened later and as Horion says, p. 12 : " Ce mot [tragi-comédie] a quatre sens au dix-septième siècle; il signifie : 1° toute pièce dont l'intrigue est tragique et le dénoûment heureux ; — 2° toute pièce dont les personnages sont d'un rang distingué et le dénoûment heureux ; — 3° toute pièce dont les personnages sont d'une classe commune et le dénoûment funeste ; — 4° toute pièce qui offre le mélange de situations tragiques et de situations comiques. Les deux premiers sens sont admis par Rotrou et Corneille et la plupart des écrivains, ainsi que par l'opinion publique : les deux autres sont exceptionnels et mal vus du public et des écrivains. Pour cette raison on est autorisé à dire que ce qui détermine le titre de tragi-comédie au dix-septième siècle, c'est le caractère du dénoûment heureux uni à une de ces deux conditions : intrigue tragique ou tout simplement personnages nobles."

The source of the tragi-comedy was frequently the novels of the day and the result was a romantic tone which distinguishes the class.[1] Naturally the unities were not observed, and the

---

Quelquefois, au dix-septième siècle, les deux conditions de l'intrigue tragique et de la distinction des personnages étaient réunies, comme dans le *Cid*, à l'heureuse issue du dénoûment ; quelquefois une des deux premières conditions seulement était réalisée ; peu importait ; ce qui était indispensable, c'est qu'une des deux se rencontrât et, de plus, que le dénoûment n'offrît aucune catastrophe sanglante. Dans ces deux cas, la pièce prenait le titre de tragi-comédie."

[1] Hardy's twelve extant tragi-comedies are taken from the romance of Heliodorus (*Theagenes and Chariclea*), from Lucian (*Toxaris*), Plutarch (*Amatoriae Narrationes*), Boccaccio, Giraldi Cinthio, Cervantes (*Novelas ejemplares*, three plays), Montemayor (*Diana*), Rosset (*Histoire des amants volages de ce temps*), Diego Agreda y Vargas (*Novelas*), Camerarius (*Méditations historiques*). The source of the twelfth play, *Lucrèce*, is not known, but Rigal conjectures some Italian novel. See Rigal, *op. cit.*, pp. 241–245 and 428–503. These tragi-comedies are fully analyzed by Rigal in the work just cited. Rotrou's *Cléagénor et Doristée* is from Sorel's romance of the same name; *Agésilan de Colchos* is from the Spanish romance of *Amadis* ; *Les deux Pucelles* is from

most intricate plots, involving disguises of sex, recognitions, etc., are constant. I cannot characterize the tragi-comedies of Hardy better than to give the words of Rigal, p. 502 : " Cherchons une formule qui résume les caractères des tragi-comédies de notre auteur, et nous n'en trouverons pas de meilleure que celle-ci : ce sont des nouvelles dramatisées. C'est parce que ce sont des nouvelles dramatisées, qu'elles empruntent leurs sujets à de vraies nouvelles, françaises ou étrangères ; — c'est parce que ce sont des nouvelles dramatisées que le dénoûment en est généralement heureux, ainsi qu'il arrive dans ces petits romans, faits pour distraire et pour satisfaire le lecteur ; — c'est pour la même raison, enfin, qu'elles ressemblent aux *comedias* espagnoles, dont on a voulu ne faire que des copies."

Of Rotrou's other immediate predecessors it is necessary to mention only Théophile de Viau, Racan, Pichou, and Jean de Schelandre. The first named, Théophile de Viau (1596–1626), is now remembered only by an unfortunate line in his one play which is a commonplace of quotation as an example of bad taste.[1] His life was an agitated one, and he was notorious for his irreligion and immorality. Accused of the authorship

---

Cervantes's *novela*, *Las dos Doncellas*. The *Astrée*, as is well known, was for many years a storehouse of plots for *pastorales* and tragi-comedies. See N. Bonafous, *Étude sur l'Astrée*, Paris, 1846, pp. 260 et seq., and Rigal, *Alexandre Hardy*, etc., p. 504, who cites the well-known passage from Segrais.

[1] The best life of Théophile de Viau is by K. Schirmacher, *Théophile de Viau, sein Leben und seine Werke*, Leipzig, 1897. There is a popular account of the poet and his brother Paul by Charles Garrisson, *Théophile et Paul de Viau: étude historique et litteraire*, Paris, 1899. I have not seen J. Serret, *Études biographiques sur Théophile de Viau*, Agen, 1864. The play in question may be found in *Théophile de Viau. Œuvres complètes. Nouvelle édition par M. Alleaume*, Paris, 1856 (*Bib. Elz.*), vol. ii, pp. 95–142. The diffusion of the Pyramus story is the subject of a dissertation by G. Hart, *Die Pyramus- und Thisbe-Sage in Holland, England, Italien und Spanien*, Passau, 1891. Boileau's criticism of Théophile may be found in his *Satires*, III, 172; IX, 175; and in the preface to the edition of 1701, to be quoted presently.

of a scandalous book, he was condemned to death at the
stake, and was burned in effigy, having fled from Paris. He
was rearrested, spent two years in prison, was tried again, and
his sentence changed to banishment. He remained, however,
in Paris under the protection of his patron, the Duke de Mont-
morency, in whose house he died in 1626. He was the author
of a considerable amount of interesting poetry, which we cannot
consider here, and of one play on Ovid's story of Pyramus and
Thisbe. The date of the performance of the play (it was
printed in 1623) is uncertain and varies in the opinion of the
critics from 1617 to 1626. The form of the play does not
differ from the other tragi-comedies of the time. It approaches
the regular tragedy by the introduction of the conventional
dream, in which (IV. 2) Thisbe's mother beholds the fate of
Pyramus. Thisbe's mother is also supplied with a *confidente*
who speaks only in the scene above cited. The play has the
usual freedom of the tragi-comedies as to the unities, and was
acted, of course, with the "multiple scene." Fortunately, a
contemporary sketch of the scenery has been preserved, and
affords a clear idea of the way in which the various localities
were represented.[1] The play is written throughout in Alexandrine verse. The fifth act consists of two scenes, each of
which is nothing but a long soliloquy by Pyramus and Thisbe.
It is at the end of the play that Thisbe, finding the dagger with
which Pyramus has slain himself, utters the famous lines :

> Ha ! voicy le poignard qui du sang de son maistre
> S'est souillé laschement : il en rougit, le traistre ![2]

---

[1] In Mahelot's *Mémoire*, reproduced in Petit de Julleville, *Hist. de la
langue et de la litt. française*, vol. iv, p. 220 ; see also p. 261.

[2] Boileau says of these lines in the preface to the edition of 1701 :
"Veut-on voir au contraire combien une pensée fausse est froide et
puérile ? Je ne saurais rapporter un exemple qui le fasse mieux sentir
que deux vers du poète Théophile, dans sa tragédie intitulée *Pyrame
et Thisbé*, lorsque cette malheureuse amante ayant ramassé le poignard

It would be easy to cite other passages equally absurd, as, for example, where Pyramus (V. 1) addresses the lion which he supposes has devoured Thisbe as follows :

> En toy, lyon, mon âme a fait ses funérailles,
> Qui digères des jà mon cœur dans tes entrailles
>
> · · · · · · · · · ·
>
> Toy, son vivant cercueil, reviens me dévorer,
> Cruel lyon, reviens, je te veux adorer.[1]

In spite of these blemishes the play contains many poetical beauties, and, as Rigal says, introduced poetry to the stage, restored to the drama the lyrical elements which Hardy had completely banished from it, and spread the plague of conceits and preciosity.[2]

Racan (1589–1670) also produced but one play, a *pastorale*, *Les Bergeries*, the date of which is also uncertain, but which was probably performed in 1619, under the name of *Arthénice*, and in a shorter version.[3] *Les Bergeries* was inspired by

---

encore tout sanglant dont Pyrame s'était tué, elle querelle ainsi ce poignard [he cites the lines in the text and continues]. Toutes les glaces du Nord ensemble ne sont pas, à mon sens, plus froides que cette pensée. Quelle extravagance, bon Dieu ! de vouloir que la rougeur du sang dont est teint le poignard d'un homme qui vient de se tuer lui-même soit un effet de la honte qu'a ce poignard de l'avoir tué."

[1] Did Rotrou have in mind this passage when he wrote these singular lines in *Cosroès*, V. 4 :

> Ma mère, hélas ! quel fruit en as-tu mis au jour !
> Que n'as-tu dans ton sein causé mes funérailles,
> Et fait mon monument de tes propres entrailles ?

[2] Rigal, " Le théâtre au xviie siècle avant Corneille " in Petit de Julleville, *Hist. de la langue et de la litt. française*, vol. iv, p. 222.

[3] The best account of Racan and of the society of his day is by L. Arnould, *Racan, histoire anecdotique et critique de sa vie et de ses œuvres*, Paris, 1896. *Les Bergeries* may be found in *Œuvres complètes de Racan. Nouvelle édition par M. Tenant de Latour*, Paris, 1857 (*Bib. Elz.*), vol. i, pp. 23–137. The date of the play is fully discussed by Arnould, *op. cit.*, pp. 186 et seq.

d'Urfé's *Astrée*, that storehouse of plots for *pastorales* and tragi-comedies, and the Italian *pastorales*, especially the *Pastor fido* of Guarini. The plot is the usual one of jealousy among the shepherds. The rejected lover employs the services of a magician to show in a crystal to a shepherdess the faithlessness of her adorer. A satyr attempts to abduct a shepherdess and there is the discovery of the long-lost child. The first three acts end with a chorus of shepherds, the fourth with a chorus of priests, and the fifth with an *epithalamium*. Besides these lyrical passages, there are in the second act a *chanson* by Tisimandre and in the fifth act one by Alcidor, which may be the connecting link between the use of the chorus and the introduction of *stances*. Racan's *pastorale* is not original in form or treatment, but contains a large amount of beautiful poetry and is especially successful in the description of the various phases of nature and country life.

The typical tragi-comedy as Rotrou received it from his predecessors may be seen in the two plays by Pichou and Jean de Schelandre. Pichou was born about 1596 in Dijon, where he received a careful education from the Jesuits, and afterwards devoted himself to dramatic composition.[1] Besides the *Folies de Cardenio* (performed in 1625 and printed in 1629), he wrote the *Aventures de Rosiléon,* a *pastorale* taken from the *Astrée* ; a tragi-comedy, *L'Infidèle Confidente,* from a Spanish source [2]; and, in 1630, another *pastorale, Filis de Scire,* from the popular Italian poem of the same name by Count Bonarelli. In the following year Pichou was assassinated. The perpetrator and the reason for this crime were never discovered.

The *Folies de Cardenio* was the first of many plays taken from *Don Quixote,* and is based on the story of Cardenio,

---

[1] See Petit de Julleville, *Hist. de la langue et de la litt. française,* vol. iv, p. 225. Pichou's play, with a notice of the author, is in Fournier, *Le théâtre français au xviie siècle,* Paris, 1871, pp. 257–281.

[2] See Martinenche, *La comedia espagnole,* p. 173.

which, with its various ramifications, occupies so large a space (chapters xxiv–xlvi) in the first part of Cervantes's novel. Don Quixote and Sancho do not appear until the fifth scene of the third act, and then play a very subordinate part. The slaughter of the wine-skin giants is introduced at the conclusion of the play, and Don Quixote goes off at the instance of Dorotée, who is disguised as the unfortunate princess. Sancho is left alone, and the piece ends with a brief soliloquy by him, the last lines of which are :

> O Dieux ! que je connay mon espérance vaine,
> Que j'ay mal employé ma jeunesse et ma peine !

The play is otherwise concerned with the adventures of the two pairs of lovers, Cardenio and Luscinde, and Fernant and Dorotée, and does not differ in form from the usual tragi-comedy of the period. In the second act a letter of Luscinde to Cardenio is introduced, written in eight-syllable and twelve-syllable lines. In the second scene of the third act occurs the first example, so far as I know, of the use of *stances*. They are pronounced by Luscinde and consist of six strophes of eight lines, four of eight and four of twelve syllables, with the following rhyme scheme : *abba*, *cddc* (*a* and *b* eight, *c* and *d* twelve syllables). In the sixth scene of the fourth act there is a lament by Dorotée in seven *stances* (and part of an eighth) of ten lines, all of eight syllables, except the last, an Alexandrine. The scheme is *abba*, *ccdede*. As is stated in the note to *Saint Genest*, ll. 1431–1470, Rotrou may have taken from Pichou's play the idea of *stances*, which he and his contemporaries used so freely for many years.

The last of Rotrou's immediate predecessors whom we have to name is Jean de Schelandre, author of the tragi-comedy of *Tyr et Sidon*.[1] The writer was born about 1585 in the territory

---

[1] See Petit de Julleville, *Hist. de la langue et de la litt. française*, vol. iv, p. 226. The play is in Viollet-le-Duc, *Ancien théâtre françois*, Paris, 1854 (*Bib. Elz.*), vol. viii, pp. 31–225.

of Verdun. He entered the army of Turenne and reached the grade of captain, dying in 1635 of wounds received in Germany. The play above mentioned appeared in 1608, and in a revised form in 1628, which is the edition published in the *Ancien théâtre françois*, vol. viii. That the second edition was intended for performance is shown by the *Advertissement de l'Imprimeur*, " Ceste pièce ayant esté composée proprement à l'usage d'un théâtre public," and by a scheme of abridgment enabling the two parts to be acted in one performance.

The plot is twofold and deals with the adventures of Leonte and Belcar, the sons of the kings of Tyre and Sidon, who in a battle have been captured and sent as prisoners, Leonte to Sidon and Belcar to Tyre. Leonte is treated with great freedom and becomes involved in an intrigue with the young and beautiful wife of an old Sidonian, who discovers the wrong done to him and has Leonte assassinated. These tragic events fill up most of the *Première Journée*, " où sont representez les funestes succez des amours de Leonte et Philoline."

Meanwhile Belcar, who was wounded in battle, is nursed by Cassandre and Meliane, daughters of the king of Tyre, both of whom fall desperately in love with the prisoner. He returns the affection of Meliane, who, when the news of Leonte's death reaches Tyre and Belcar's life is in danger, arranges his escape in a vessel. The nurse Almodice, pitying the despair of Cassandre, substitutes her for her sister. Belcar discovers the fraud when he is out at sea and leaves the ship in a small boat. Cassandre stabs herself and leaps into the sea. Her body is found by fishermen and carried to the spot where Meliane is lamenting the disloyal flight of Belcar. Meliane is arrested on the charge of murdering her sister and is condemned to death. Belcar, who is rescued at sea by his father's ambassadors on their way to Tyre to explain Leonte's death, returns in time to save Meliane. The lovers are united and Almodice, the false nurse, and Zorote, the author of Leonte's death, are burned at the same stake.

With the exception of a *chanson* by Leonte's page, the
entire play is in Alexandrine verse. The whole of the second
journée takes place at Tyre or in the vicinity, except one
brief scene at Sidon. In the first *journée* the scene alter-
nates between Sidon and Tyre, but is largely in the former
place. The play is animated and full of romantic episodes. It
is connected with the earlier drama by the figures of the nurse
and the ribald soldiers who assassinate Leonte, as well as by
the frequent change of scene in the first part, and the mixture
of the comic and tragic elements.

We have now briefly surveyed the French drama as Rotrou
received it, and are fitted to judge more correctly his own
contribution to it.

II

Rotrou's first play *L'Hypocondriaque ou le Mort Amoureux.* — *La Bague de
l'Oubli.* — Beginning of Rotrou's Spanish imitation. — Rotrou's life between
1629 and 1631. — Lost plays. — Legal studies. — Rotrou's *servitude honteuse.* — Rotrou's relations with Chapelain. — *Légende des fagots.* —
Legend of arrest for debt. — Rotrou and Madeleine Béjart. — Rotrou's
relations to Cardinal Richelieu. — Rotrou one of the "Cinq Auteurs." —
His share in the *Comédie des Tuileries.* — Rotrou's plays of this period. —
The collaboration of the "Cinq Auteurs" comes to an end. — Rotrou's gratitude to Richelieu. — Dedicates the *Hercule Mourant* to him. — *Agésilan
de Colchos* dedicated to the Cardinal's niece. — Count de Belin a patron of
Rotrou. — Rotrou's relations to Corneille. — The Quarrel of the Cid. —
Rotrou's share in it. — Rotrou's relations with his contemporaries. — Ro-
trou's remuneration for his plays. — Relations with the Hôtel de Rambouillet.
— Rotrou purchases a magistracy at Dreux. — Marriage in 1640. — Children born of this marriage. — Life at Dreux between 1640 and 1650. —
Private character of Rotrou. — Legend and fact concerning Rotrou's death.
— Contemporary notices of his death. — Colletet's epitaph. — Portraits and
engravings. — Bust by Caffiéri. — Statue erected at Dreux. — Rotrou's fame
in the seventeenth century. — Rotrou in the eighteenth century. — Voltaire's
judgment of Rotrou. — Marmontel's version of *Venceslas.* — The judgment
of the nineteenth century in biographical and critical works. — Sources of
Rotrou's plays. — Linguistic studies on Rotrou.

Rotrou's first play, *L'Hypocondriaque ou le Mort Amoureux*,
was not printed until 1631, but was probably composed and

performed in 1628.[1] The author says in the *Argument* : " Si les censeurs y trouvent des défauts ils doivent être satisfaits par ce mot : Il y a d'excellents poètes mais non pas à l'âge de vingt ans." We shall see presently that Rotrou was attached to the theater of the Hôtel de Bourgogne in the quality of playwright, and it was undoubtedly there that his first play was performed.

The hero, Cloridan, is ordered by his father to make a journey to Corinth, and is obliged to leave Perside, the object of his love. On the way he delivers Cléonice, who has been abducted by her suitor Lisidor and his friend Eristhène, both of whom are killed by Cloridan. Cléonice falls in love with her defender, and intercepting a letter from Perside changes a few words and makes it appear that Perside no longer lives. Cloridan goes mad at the news and faints away. When he recovers he imagines that he is dead and takes Cléonice for Perside. At her supposed disfavor he rushes away to drown himself in a neighboring stream. Perside, meanwhile, and her relative Aliaste (who is in love with Cléonice) consult a fortune teller and receive ambiguous answers to their questions. Perside is told, for example, that fate destines a dead man for her husband, and Aliaste learns that Cléonice prefers a dead man to him. Perside and Aliaste then determine to go in search of Cloridan and learn the truth of the fortune teller's predictions.

In the fourth act Cléonice endeavors in vain to persuade Cloridan that he is alive, but the madman hastens away after an imaginary Perside. In the second scene Cloridan is in bed and resists all the arguments of Erimand, Cléonice's father, and even of Cléonice herself, who finally, to pacify Cloridan, promises to bring Perside to him. Perside and Aliaste, meanwhile, have changed dresses and started on their journey. On

---

[1] See Stiefel, *Über die Chronologie von J. Rotrou's dramatischen Werken*, p. 7.

the way they come across the page who carried Perside's letter and who has been robbed and tied to a tree. He informs the travelers of what has taken place. The scene changes to a tomb with Cloridan in a coffin. Cléonice finally recognizes the futility of her attempts to cure Cloridan, and she determines to transfer her affections to Aliaste. As she is leaving the spot where Cloridan is she meets Aliaste and Perside, and confesses her love for Aliaste and acknowledges her wrong to Perside.

It remains only to restore Cloridan to his senses and that is done by the following expedient. Several persons representing the dead are disposed in tombs and awake apparently from death at the sound of music. They express their regret at having their rest disturbed, and one of them fires a pistol loaded only with powder at Cloridan, who immediately recovers his senses, and the two pairs of lovers are united by their parents.[1]

---

[1] The possible source of *L'Hypocondriaque* was first pointed out by E. Fournier in an essay "La Farce et la Chanson au théâtre avant 1660," prefixed to his edition of the *Chansons de Gaultier Garguille*, Paris, 1858 (*Bib. Elz.*), p. xxxix: "Louis Guyon, en ses *Diverses Leçons* (liv. ii, chap. xxv), parle aussi d'une autre farce jouée en son temps. Il s'agissait d'un pauvre avocat hypocondre, dont le mal était de se croire défunt, et qui, à ce titre, refusant toute nourriture, serait enfin réellement mort de faim, si un neveu de sa femme, qui feignit d'être trépassé, ne lui eût prouvé en mangeant auprès de lui qu'on faisait des repas de bon vivant dans le royaume sombre. 'Cette histoire,' dit Louis Guyon, 'fut réduite en farce imprimée, laquelle fut jouée un soir devant le roi Charles neuvième, moi y étant.' Mais où se trouve maintenant cette farce imprimée? Rotrou semble s'en être inspiré pour sa tragicomédie de *l'Hypocondriaque*, et depuis lui, pour de nouvelles, Carmontelle l'imita dans un de ses plus jolis proverbes, *la Diette*; mais il est probable que, comme nous, il ne la connaissait que par l'analyse qu'en a faite Louis Guyon." Person in the Appendix to *Les papiers de Pierre Rotrou de Saudreville*, pp. 127 et seq., gives some extracts from Carmontelle's *proverbe*, *La Diète*. Steffens, *Rotrou-Studien*, p. 28, cites an article by G. Proffen in *Archiv für Litteraturgeschichte*, xiii, pp. 329–335, in which he pointed out a certain similarity between the plot of Goethe's opera of *Lila* and Rotrou's *Hypocondriaque*. See also Bédier, *Les Fabliaux*, Paris, 1893, p. 431.

The scene changes frequently from the home of Perside and Cloridan to a spot near Corinth where Cloridan rescues Cléonice and where the principal action of the play takes place. There are several other localities represented in a manner which can only be understood by the system of " multiple scenes " which has been explained above. While the play is fantastic it is no more so than the early dramas of Corneille, one of which, the *Illusion Comique* (1636), it resembles in many respects. The play is marked by the extravagant gallantry of the day and the passages describing Cloridan's madness are bombastic. Still, in spite of these defects, the piece contains many poetic beauties and the action is rapid and dramatic.

The success of Rotrou's first play was such that he was led the same year (1628) to begin another which he named *La Bague de l'Oubli*. The abbé Brillon says he composed it in a very short time, and adds : " This piece was even more successful than the first, not only on the stage of the Hôtel de Bourgogne, but in the performances which were given of it at the Louvre and at Saint Germain before their Majesties [Louis XIII and Anne of Austria], and at the Palais-Cardinal before his Eminence the Cardinal de Richelieu." [1] In the preface to this play, which was printed in 1634, Rotrou says : " Je n'ai pas si peu de connaissance de mes ouvrages que de te donner celui-ci pour une bonne chose. C'est la seconde pièce qui est sortie de mes mains, et les vers dont je l'ai traitée n'ont pas cette pureté que depuis six ans la lecture, la conversation et l'exercice m'ont acquise." He further states that he has been obliged to print it because copies were in the hands of all the country troupes of actors, and some had boasted that they would find a printer for it. Rotrou concludes with these words : " Comme ce présent est forcé, je ne veux point que tu m'en sois obligé ; et je te veux seulement

---

[1] Abbé Brillon, *Notice biographique*, p. 12.

avertir, que c'est une pure traduction de l'auteur Espagnol
de Vega. Si quelque chose t'y plaît, donnes-en la gloire à ce
grand esprit et les défauts que tu y trouveras que l'âge où
j'étais quand je l'entrepris te les fasse excuser." [1]

The play is a very amusing comedy, the plot of which turns
on a magic ring which has the power of depriving its possessor
of memory. The most interesting thing, however, about the
piece is the fact that it is the first French play taken from the
Spanish drama, anticipating the *Cid* by eight years. Once
started on the path of Spanish imitation Rotrou followed it to
the end of his life, and nine of his thirty-five plays, two of
them his masterpieces, are from the Spanish drama. [2]

---

[1] This preface, "Au Lecteur," is given by Stiefel, *Über die Chronologie*, etc., p. 8, and by Steffens, *Rotrou-Studien*, p. 48, together with the
dedication to the king Louis XIII. Unfortunately, Viollet-le-Duc, in his
edition of Rotrou, has omitted, with one exception (*Clarice*), the preliminary matter, such as prefaces, dedications, etc., saying of the dedications, vol. iv, p. 342, "Ce sont de véritables épîtres à la Montoron."
Montoron, it will be remembered, was the famous financier and patron
of letters to whom Corneille dedicated his *Cinna*. Ronchaud, *Théâtre
choisi de J. de Rotrou*, prints the preliminary matter of the plays in his
selection, and this is done by Steffens, *Rotrou-Studien*, for *La Bague de
l'Oubli*, *Les Occasions perdues*, and *L'Heureuse Constance*. The Parfait
Brothers cite the dedications, etc., from time to time in their *Histoire
du théâtre françois*.
[2] Rotrou's play is compared with the original, Lope de Vega's *La
Sortija del Olvido*, by Steffens in *Rotrou-Studien*, p. 33. See also Martinenche, *op. cit.*, p. 167. Rotrou's indebtedness to the Spanish drama is
discussed in detail by Steffens and, more generally, by Martinenche in
the works cited above. For the question of the imitation of the Spanish drama in the seventeenth century by French writers the student
should read the admirable article by Brunetière, "Corneille et le théâtre
espagnol" in the *Revue des deux mondes*, January 1, 1903, reviewing
Huszär, *P. Corneille et le théâtre espagnol*, Paris, 1903, Martinenche, *La
comedia espagnole*, and Lanson, *Corneille*, Paris, 1898. For the general
subject of the relations of French to Spanish literature see Lanson,
"Études sur les rapports de la littérature française et de la littérature
espagnole au xviie siècle" in *Revue d'Histoire littéraire de la France*,
1896, pp. 45–70, 321–331 ; 1897, pp. 61–73, 180–194. Puibusque, *Histoire*

Little is known of Rotrou's life between 1629 and 1631.
In the *Avertissement au lecteur* of the second edition of
Cléagénor et Doristée (1635) Rotrou speaks of his play as
" Cette cadette de trente sœurs fera envie aux autres de la
suivre, si elle est traitée favorablement." [1] Nothing is known
of these thirty plays, if indeed they really were written and performed. During this period Rotrou probably also carried on
his legal studies, for he is mentioned in 1636 as " avocat en la
cour de Parlement." [2] In 1632 we have an important reference
which throws light on several years of Rotrou's life. On the
30th of October of that year Jean Chapelain wrote to Godeau :
" Le comte de Fiesque m'a amené Rotrou et son Mécène. Je
suis marri qu'un garçon de si beau naturel ait pris une servitude
si honteuse, et il ne tiendra pas à moi que nous ne l'affranchis-
sions bientôt. Il a employé votre nom, outre l'autorité de son
introducteur, pour se rendre considérable, dit-il, auprès de ma
personne. Mandez-moi si vous prenez part dans l'assistance
et les offices qu'il attend de moi et à quoi je me suis résolu." [3]

---

comparée des littératures espagnole et française, Paris, 1843, is now antiquated and of little value.

[1] Stiefel, *Über die Chronologie*, etc., pp. 12, 21–22, and Parfait, *Hist.
du théâtre françois*, iv, p. 487.

[2] Jal, *Dictionnaire critique de biographie et d'histoire*, Paris, 1872.

[3] *Jean Chapelain, Lettres publiées par P. Tamizey de Larroque*, Paris,
1880–1883, 2 vols. (*Collection de documents inédits, 2e série*), vol. i,
p. 6; and Person, *Notes critiques*, p. 133. A brief account of Charles
Léon, Count de Fiesque (whose name is lacking in all French biographical dictionaries), may be found in V. Cousin, *La société française au
xviie siècle*, Paris, 1886, vol. i, pp. 213–225. He was a brilliant figure
in the society of the time, but he injured himself by his connection with
the plots of the Fronde. He is described by Mlle. de Scudéry in *Le
Grand Cyrus*, ix, pp. 923 et seq., under the name of Pisistrate. Among
other things she says of him : "Au reste, Pisistrate n'aime pas seulement
les vers, il en fait aussi de fort jolis et de fort galants. . . . Mais ce qui
rend Pisistrate le plus louable, c'est qu'il est bon autant qu'on le peut
être, qu'il est ardent et fidèle ami, qu'il est magnifique et libéral, qu'il
est brave et généreux, et que, quoiqu'il ait plus d'ambition qu'il n'en

Guizot was the first to suggest that the *servitude honteuse*
referred to an engagement with the theater of the Hôtel de
Bourgogne to furnish it with plays.[1] In other words, it is
probable that Rotrou succeeded Hardy, who died between
1631–1632, as the regular playwright of the Hôtel de Bourgogne.
This supposition is confirmed by another contemporary allusion, somewhat later (1634), in a satirical comedy by Gaillard :

> Corneille est excellent, mais il vend ses ouvrages.
> Rotrou fait bien des vers, mais il est poète à gages.[2]

Who the Maecenas was who is referred to in Chapelain's letter
is not known. Chardon thinks it was Bellerose, the chief actor
of the Hôtel de Bourgogne.[3]

Rotrou's relations with Chapelain grew more intimate as
time passed, and in 1633 the latter wrote to Balzac : "La
comédie dont je vous ai parlé dans mes précédentes n'est
mienne que de l'invention et de la disposition. Le vers en
est de Rotrou, ce qui est cause qu'on n'en peut avoir de copie,
pour ce que le poète en gaigne son pain." [4] It is clear from
this that Rotrou was still bound to the Hôtel de Bourgogne
and was not at liberty to print his plays.

To this period of Rotrou's life may be referred those legen-
dary stories which were later repeated by his biographers.

---

croit avoir, il n'a pourtant pas l'âme intéressée." The Count de Fiesque
is also mentioned in the *Mémoires* of the Cardinal de Retz, Mlle. de
Montpensier, and Mme. de Motteville. See also Chardon, *La vie de
Rotrou mieux connue*, p. 47, and *Segraisiana*, A la Haye, 1722, p. 181.

[1] Guizot, *Corneille et son temps*, Paris, 1880, p. 366. This work first
appeared in 1813. See also Rigal, *Le Théâtre français avant la période
classique*, p. 108; Chardon, *La vie de Rotrou mieux connue*, pp. 39 et
seq.; and Stiefel, *Über die Chronologie*, etc., pp. 13–14.

[2] Cited by Steffens, *Rotrou-Studien*, p. 6; Chardon, *op. cit.*, p. 55;
Rigal, *op. cit.*, p. 109; and Stiefel, *op. cit.*, pp. 13–14.

[3] Chardon, *op. cit.*, p. 43.

[4] *Jean Chapelain, Lettres*, ed. cit., I, p. 27. For the play referred to in
Chapelain's letter see Stiefel, *op. cit.*, p. 17.

The most famous of these is the so-called " légende des fagots,"
first printed in Titon du Tillet's *Description du Parnasse
François*, Paris, 1727. I give it as it appears in the subsequent
edition of the same work, *Bibliothèque Poëtique*, Paris, 1745,
vol. i, p. 208. " Rotrou était joueur dans sa jeunesse et
il avait trouvé un expédient assez singulier pour s'empêcher
de perdre tout son argent à la fois. Quand les comédiens
lui apportaient un présent pour le remercier d'une de ses
piéces, il jettait ordinairement les pistoles ou les louis sur un
tas de fagots qu'il tenait enfermé, et quand il avait besoin
d'argent, il secouait ces fagots pour en faire tomber quelques
pistoles ; ce qui l'obligeait de laisser toujours quelque chose
en réserve." [1]

The second story is related of a later period of the poet's
life, but may be mentioned here. It first appeared in the
Histoire du théâtre françois by the Brothers Parfait, Paris,
1746, vol. vii, p. 189. " Rotrou, après avoir achevé cette
tragédie (*Venceslas*) se préparait à la lire aux comédiens,
lorsqu'il fut arrêté et conduit en prison, pour une dette
qu'il n'avait pu acquitter ; la somme n'était pas considérable,
mais Rotrou était joueur, et par conséquent assez souvent vis-
à-vis de rien. Il envoya chercher les comédiens, et leur offrit
pour vingt pistoles sa tragédie de *Venceslas*, le marché fut
bientôt conclu, Rotrou sortit de prison, sa tragédie fut jouée,
mais avec un tel succès, que les comédiens crurent devoir

---

[1] See also Person, *Notes critiques*, p. 113, and Stiefel's review of Person in *Literaturblatt für germanishe und romanische Philologie*, 1884,
col. 285 : " Er errt sich jedoch wenn er Nicéron für den ersten hält der
diese "légende " verbreitete. Nicéron hat, wie er selbst angibt, aus
dem " Parnasse français" des Titon du Tillet geschöpft. Die Anekdote
ist jedenfalls noch älter. Nach einer Hs. der Münchener Hof- und
Staatsbibliothek, die etwa 1670–1690 geschrieben ist, möchte man ver-
muthen, dass der Schauspieler La Fleur (Robert Guerin), ein Zeitge-
nosse des Dichters, sie in Umlauf gesetzt habe." For this and the
following story see Steffens, *op. cit.*, pp. 8–9.

joindre au prix qu'ils avaient payé cette pièce, un présent
honnête ; on ne sait si Rotrou l'accepta, la personne de qui
on tient ce récit ayant passé sous silence cette dernière par-
ticularité." At the time to which this story is referred (1647)
Rotrou had long been settled as a magistrate at Dreux, and it
is not likely that he was in financial straits.

What Rotrou's relations were with the actors of the troupe
for which he wrote we do not know. It is interesting, however,
to note that when Rotrou printed, in 1636, his *Hercule Mourant*,
Madeleine Béjart, afterwards famous for her relations with
Molière, then a young girl of eighteen and probably a member
of the company of the Théâtre du Marais, wrote the following
lines which appear before the play :

> Ton Hercule mourant va te rendre immortel :
> Au ciel, comme en terre, il publiera ta gloire,
> Et laissant ici-bas un temple à sa mémoire,
> Son bûcher servira pour te faire un autel.[1]

We have seen above that the second play of Rotrou, *La
Bague de l' Oubli*, was performed at the Louvre and Saint
Germain before the king and queen and at the Palais-Cardinal
before Richelieu. The great cardinal's interest in the theater
is well known, and he was quick to recognize the promise of
Rotrou. The abbé Brillon relates in detail the meeting between
the prelate and the poet. He says : "The great ease with
which he wrote and the applause bestowed upon his works,
added to his own inclination and the earnest entreaties of the
actors to continue a labor which brought him so much praise
and was so useful to them, caused him to seek in the ancient
Latin, Spanish, and Italian poets subjects which might preserve
at the court and with the public the reputation he had there acquired. He discovered in a Spanish author a subject which he

---

[1] An interesting account of Madeleine Béjart will be found in Chardon, *M. de Modène, ses deux femmes et Madeleine Béjart*, Paris, 1886.
For her relations with Rotrou see pp. 57–59.

put on the stage under the title of *Les Occasions perdues*, and treated it with such propriety and with such surprising episodes that this play surpassed the others. I believe he dedicated it to the Count de Fiesque, who honored him with his friendship.

"The cardinal, who was very fond of poetry, knowing that this play had been performed before their Majesties to their satisfaction, commanded the actors to play it at his palace, and his Eminence was so pleased with it that he displayed his satisfaction to many who were present and charged Bellerose, the chief actor of the company, to tell the author that he desired to see him. Rotrou, learning the honor that his Eminence showed him, came shortly afterwards to receive his orders. The cardinal having displayed more kindness than Rotrou had dared to hope, the latter expressed his gratitude in the most respectful terms he could use to show his devotion to his orders and his extreme desire to do something for his pleasure. His Eminence received his deference with his usual amiability and asked him several questions in regard to his family, how he lived, how long he had devoted himself to poetry, and whether he composed easily." The cardinal further told Rotrou that he wished to do something for him at once and would be glad to see him sometimes, and that the abbé de Boisrobert would make this easy if Rotrou would apply to him. Shortly afterwards the abbé de Boisrobert informed Rotrou that his Eminence had granted him a pension of six hundred livres a year.[1]

This must have been in 1633, for in the dedication of the tragedy of *Hercule Mourant* to the cardinal, Rotrou says : " Si je n'ai pas assez de mérite, vous avez assez de bonté et vous êtes trop généreux pour m'ôter jamais l'incomparable faveur que vous m'avez continuée depuis trois ans." [2]

---

[1] Abbé Brillon, *Notice biographique*, pp. 12–13.

[2] This dedication and the ode cited later will be found in Ronchaud, *Théâtre choisi*, vol. i, p. 3. The ode alone is given by Viollet-le-Duc in his edition, vol. ii, p. 5.

In consequence of the cardinal's favor, Rotrou was enrolled among the " Cinq Auteurs," destined to elaborate the dramatic designs of Richelieu. These authors, besides Rotrou, were Corneille, Boisrobert, Lestoile, and Colletet, — all except Corneille and Rotrou original members of the French Academy, and all except Corneille and Rotrou long since forgotten. The product of this collaboration, which lasted from 1635 to 1637, was not important for the history of French literature. Three plays were produced : *La Comédie des Tuileries*, performed at the Arsenal before the queen, March 4, 1635, and first printed in 1638 ; *L'Aveugle de Smyrne*, acted at the Palais-Cardinal before the court, February 22, 1637, and not printed until 1638 ; and *La Grande Pastorale*, which was never printed. The share of the individual authors in the above plays is not known. The third act of the *Comédie des Tuileries* is attributed to Corneille and reprinted in his works. Person, on the contrary, sees in this act and in all the rest of the play the touch of Rotrou.[1]

Meanwhile Rotrou had produced, including the play we have already mentioned, no less than twenty-two dramas. After his first experiment with the Spanish drama (*La Bague de l'Oubli*) he had turned to Plautus, and in his *Ménechmes* (1631) had imitated closely the Latin play of the same name. In *Les Occasions perdues* (1633) he returned to Lope de Vega. If Lanson's statement be correct, *Filandre* (1633–1634) is the first imitation of the Italian drama.[2] This was followed in the same year by the *Pélerine Amoureuse*, based on Girolamo Bargagli's *La Pelligrina*. Of the other plays of this period *Hercule Mourant* (1634) was taken from Seneca ; *Cléagénor et Doristée* (1634) from a

---

[1] The subject of the " Cinq Auteurs " is a very obscure and difficult one and has been neglected by scholars. The best treatment of the question of Rotrou's relations to Richelieu and the " Cinq Auteurs " is by Chardon, *La vie de Rotrou mieux connue*, pp. 68–82. Person's opinion is expressed in his *Notes critiques*, p. 128.

[2] *La Grande Encyclopédie*, article "Rotrou."

romance by Charles Sorel; *L'Heureuse Constance* (1635) from
Lope de Vega; *Agésilan de Colchos* (1636) from the Spanish
romance of *Amadis*; *Les deux Pucelles* (1636) from Cervantes's
novela, Las dos Doncellas; and *Les Sosies* (1636) from Plautus.[1]

There are still left eight plays the originals of which have not
yet been discovered : *Céliane* (1632–1633); *Célimène* (1633);
L'Innocente Infidelité (1634); *Florimonde* (1635); *Clorinde*
(1635); *Amélie* (1636); *La Belle Alphrède* (1636); and
Crisante (1636), of which Lanson says : " pièce archaïque qui
pourrait n'être qu'un arrangement d'une œuvre antérieure ; le
sujet me paraît venir de Plutarque, *De mulierum virtutibus*,
histoire de Chiomara." [2] These plays show the predominating
influence of the Spanish drama, and are distinguished by the
intricacy of their plots, in which abductions, disguises, and
recognitions abound. The unities are disregarded and indeli-
cate situations are not infrequent. At the same time it must
also be said that the language of these plays is often poetical,
and the dialogue is rapid and interesting.

---

[1] There is no separate work on Rotrou's imitations of Plautus ; they
are, however, examined, with other Plautus imitations, by Reinhardstöttner. The imitations of Lope de Vega are treated by Steffens, and the
Italian and Spanish sources by Stiefel. The last-named author, in his article *Über die Chronologie*, etc., p. 36, says that the *Filandre* agrees, so far
as the story is concerned, with Chiabrera's *pastorale, La Gelopea*, 1607.
The *Hercule Mourant* has not yet been compared with its sources. See
Buchetmann, *op. cit.*, p. 248, note. The source of *Cléagénor et Doristée*
was first pointed out, I believe, by Chardon in *La vie de Rotrou mieux
connue*, pp. 195–199.

[2] Lanson, *op. cit.* For *Célimène* see Chardon, *La vie de Rotrou mieux
connue*, pp. 199–201. Chardon considers the *Célimène* and the lost *Florante* as the same piece. For the sources of *Amélie* see Stiefel, *Über die
Chronologie*, etc., p. 27. A curious mistake in regard to *La Belle Alphrède*
has been made by Person and Ronchaud. In the contract for the sale
of certain of Rotrou's plays, first printed by Jal, *Dict. crit. de biographie*,
etc., and to be mentioned later, ten plays are enumerated, among them
Calpède (sic). The names of four of these plays are repeated, and instead of *Calpède* occurs the relatively correct *Alfrède*. Both Person and
Ronchaud suppose that a play named *Calpède* has been lost.

The collaboration of the " Cinq Auteurs " came to an end by the withdrawal of Corneille, who, as it is commonly stated, forfeited the cardinal's favor by his lack of " esprit de suite," the cardinal understanding by this expression the submission which blindly follows the orders of one's superiors.[1] Rotrou, on the contrary, always preserved a feeling of gratitude for his great patron. He dedicated to him the tragedy of *Hercule Mourant* (1636) and prefixed to it an ode addressed to Richelieu.[2] In the first stanza he calls on the Muses, " chaste sisters of the Sun," to open the planet's ears to the poet's prayers :

> En cette agréable saison
> Où les fleurs rompent la prison
> De l'élément qui les enserre,
> Il peut faire, par ses chaleurs,
> A mon esprit comme à la terre
> Produire de nouvelles fleurs.

The powers of the planet, with which the poet identifies Richelieu, are not limited by summers or winters, and produce verse as well as seasons and years, while Ronsard and Malherbe are counted among its labors. The following stanzas

---

[1] Voltaire, *Commentaires sur Corneille*, vol. i, p. 205 (*Remarques sur le Cid*), *Œuvres*, ed. Moland, vol. xxxi, p. 205: " Le cardinal à la fin de 1635, un an avant les représentations du Cid, avait donné dans le Palais-Cardinal, aujourd'hui le Palais-Royal, la *Comédie des Tuileries*, dont il avait arrangé lui-même toutes les scènes. Corneille, plus docile à son génie que souple aux volontés d'un premier ministre, crut devoir changer quelque chose dans le troisième acte qui lui fut confié. Cette liberté estimable fut envenimée par deux de ses confrères, et déplut beaucoup au cardinal, qui lui dit *qu'il fallait avoir un esprit de suite*. Il entendait par esprit de suite la soumission qui suit aveuglement les ordres d'un supérieur." It is possible that the illness of the famous actor Mondory was an important factor in the dissolution of the society of the " Cinq Auteurs." See Chardon, *op. cit.*, p. 73, note 2.

[2] See Ronchaud, *Théâtre choisi*, vol. i, p. 5. This is the second ode to Richelieu. The first was printed separately in 1634, and reprinted the next year at the end of the *Diane* in *Autres œuvres du mesme auteur*. A brief extract is given in Chardon, *op. cit.*, p. 60.

are the most personal of the ode and will give some idea of
Rotrou's lyrical style:

> Mais toi, grand démon de la France,
> Autre soleil de notre temps,
> Qui donnes d'un si beau printemps
> Une si parfaite espérance,
> Richelieu, rare effort des Cieux,
> Juste étonnement de ces lieux,
> Si tu daignes prendre la peine
> De jeter un regard sur moi,
> Quel Apollon peut à ma veine
> Être plus Apollon que toi?
>
> Pour toi, grand duc, elle est ouverte,
> C'est pour toi qu'elle veut couler;
> Ma nef, commençons de cingler,
> Puisque notre Ourse est découverte.
> Je sais bien que sur cette mer
> Il est malaisé de ramer:
> Aussi n'est-il point de voyage
> Qui mérite un si grand effort,
> Et nous ferons un beau naufrage,
> Ou nous trouverons un beau port.

In 1637 Rotrou dedicated his tragi-comedy *Agésilan de
Colchos* to the cardinal's niece, Madame de Combalet, and
there are other proofs in his works of his gratitude to Richelieu. What further favors he received from him we do not
know, but in 1639 we find Rotrou using the title "gentilhomme ordinaire de Monseigneur l'éminentissime cardinal de
Richelieu." [1]

Another patron of Rotrou was the Count de Belin, of a noble
family of Maine, where he possessed near Le Mans a splendid
residence and dispensed boundless hospitality.[2] He was fond

---

[1] Chardon, *op. cit.*, p. 77.

[2] The first adequate account of this interesting patron of Rotrou
was given by Chardon in the fifth chapter, pp. 82 et seq., of the work

of poetry and the drama and numbered among his friends
Scudéry, Mairet, Chapelain, and Rotrou. As early as 1634
Rotrou dedicated to the Count de Belin his *Cléagénor et
Doristée*, and later, in 1636, his *Ménechmes*. He visited the
count at Le Mans in 1637, the period of the famous "Quarrel
of the Cid."[1]

It is impossible to enter here into the details of this complicated question, but it may not be out of place to say a few
words on Rotrou's relations to Corneille.[2] Corneille was born
in 1606, and was consequently three years older than Rotrou,
a difference in age that hardly justifies the legend that Corneille was accustomed to call him his "father," even in a metaphorical sense. This statement was first made, I believe, in
the *Histoire du théâtre françois* by the Brothers Parfait, who
say, vol. iv, p. 405, in speaking of Rotrou's first play : "Voici
le coup d'essai du célèbre Rotrou, poète, à qui le Théâtre Français doit quelques fleurs, et que le grand Corneille appelait son
père." Voltaire in his *Siècle de Louis XIV* (*Œuvres*, ed.
Moland, vol. xiv, p. 123) says : "La première scène et une
partie du quatrième acte de *Venceslas* sont des chefs-d'œuvre.
Corneille l'appelait son père. On sait combien le père fut surpassé par le fils." Taschereau in his *Histoire de la vie et des
ouvrages de P. Corneille*, Paris, 1869, vol. i, p. 206, gives a
variant of the story : "Plus jeune que Corneille de trois ans,

just cited. Further details concerning the Count de Belin and society
in the province of Maine will be found in Chardon, *Scarron inconnu et
les types des personnages du Roman comique*, Paris, 1903, vol. i, chap. iv.

[1] The materials for the history of the "Quarrel" may now be found
very conveniently in A. Gasté, *La Querelle du Cid*, Paris, 1899, in which
all the documents in the case are reprinted. Rotrou's relations to the
"Quarrel" are minutely examined by Chardon, *La vie de Rotrou mieux
connue*, pp. 105–131 ; see also *Scarron inconnu*, vol. i, p. 101.

[2] The literary relations of Rotrou and Corneille form the subject of
the seventh chapter, pp. 163–198, of Jarry, *Essai sur les œuvres dramatiques de Jean Rotrou*. See also some interesting remarks by Stiefel
in *Zeitschrift für franz. Spr. und Lit.*, vol. xxiii (1901), p. 97.

il [Rotrou] avait reçu de celui-ci le nom de maître, parce qu'il l'avait précédé à la scène, où il s'était déjà fait applaudir deux fois avant le succès de *Mélite*."

The only reference to Rotrou on the part of Corneille which has been preserved is in the collection of anecdotes attributed to Ménage (*Ménagiana*, Paris, 1715, vol. iii, p. 306) : " M. Corneille disait : ' M. Rotrou et moi ferions subsister des saltimbanques ' ; pour marquer que l'on n'aurait pas manqué de venir à leurs pièces, quand bien même elles auraient été mal représentées."

Corneille, as we have already seen, was associated with Rotrou in the collaboration of the " Cinq Auteurs " in 1635. The previous year Corneille published his comedy *La Veuve*, which is preceded by no less than twenty-six poems in homage of the author. Among the writers are Scudéry, Mairet, du Ryer, Boisrobert, and Rotrou. The production of Rotrou is termed *élégie*, and consists of forty-eight Alexandrine verses. As this poem is valuable for Rotrou's biography, I shall quote a large part of it.[1]

> Pour te rendre justice autant que pour te plaire,
> Je veux parler, Corneille, et ne me puis plus taire.
> Juge de ton mérite, à qui rien n'est égal,
> Par la confession de ton propre rival.
> Pour un même sujet, même désir nous presse ;
> Nous poursuivons tous deux une même maîtresse :

---

[1] The complete *élégie* will be found in *Œuvres de P. Corneille par Marty-Laveaux* (*Les Grands Écrivains de la France*), Paris, 1862, vol. i, pp. 381-383. At the conclusion of the poem Rotrou says :

> Tout ce que j'ai produit cède à ses moindres attraits ;
> Toute veuve qu'elle est, de quoi que tu l'habilles,
> Elle ternit l'éclat de nos plus belles filles.
> J'ai vu trembler Silvie, Amaranthe et Filis,
> Célimène a changé, ses attraits sont pâlis ;
> Et tant d'autres beautés que l'on a tant vantées
> Sitôt qu'elle a paru se sont épouvantées.

Célimène, of course, is the heroine of Rotrou's play of the same name, first printed in 1636.

La gloire, cet objet des belles volontés,
Préside également dessus nos libertés ;
Comme toi je la sers, et personne ne doute
Des veilles et des soins que cette ardeur me coûte.
Mon espoir toutefois est décru chaque jour
Depuis que je t'ai vu prétendre à son amour.
Je n'ai point le trésor de ces douces paroles
Dont tu lui fais la cour et dont tu la cajoles :
Je vois que ton esprit, unique de son art,
A des naïvetés plus belles que le fard,
Que tes inventions ont des charmes étranges,
Que leur moindre incident attire des louanges,
Que par toute la France on parle de ton nom,
Et qu'il n'est plus d'estime égale à ton renom.
Depuis, ma Muse tremble et n'est plus si hardie ;
Une jalouse peur l'a longtemps refroidie,
Et depuis, cher rival, je serais rebuté
De ce bruit spécieux dont Paris m'a flatté,
Si cet ange mortel qui fait tant de miracles,
Et dont tous les discours passent pour des oracles,
Ce fameux cardinal, l'honneur de l'univers,
N'aimait ce que je fais et n'écoutait mes vers.
Sa faveur m'a rendu mon humeur ordinaire ;
La gloire où je prétends est l'honneur de lui plaire,
Et lui seul réveillant mon génie endormi
Est cause qu'il te reste un si faible ennemi.

This generous praise was followed eleven years later by the
splendid eulogy in *Saint Genest* (ll. 277–286). During this
interval Corneille had produced the amazing series of his
masterpieces, from the *Cid* (1636) to *Rodogune* (1645), and
by the phenomenal success of the first had aroused the jealousy of many who had praised *La Veuve*. It has generally
been said that Rotrou was the only one who defended his
friend, but there is no proof of this. We have seen that at the
outbreak of the "Quarrel" Rotrou was the guest of the Count
de Belin at Le Mans, where Mairet, one of Corneille's most
bitter opponents, was a fellow-guest. It is not likely that

Rotrou escaped the influence of this *milieu* or of his friendship with Scudéry and Boisrobert. The most that he could do would be to attempt to reconcile the chief actors in the " Quarrel," Scudéry and Corneille. This is precisely the rôle he played, if he is the author of one of the documents in the " Quarrel," *L'Inconnu et véritable ami de Messieurs de Scudéry et Corneille* (1637), signed "D. R."[1] In this open letter the writer expresses his esteem for Scudéry and Corneille, whose quarrel is known to all Paris. He blames Scudéry for criticising a member of his own profession, and Corneille for claiming preëminence over Scudéry, " qui a fait une infinité des plus beaux poèmes qui se jouent à présent sur le théâtre." His *Amant Libéral* can walk side by side with the *Cid* without shaming it, even if it should take the right. The writer, " who loves the two poets and the two subjects, and does not pride himself on his great intelligence, finds both authors excellent and esteems them highly, as do many learned people who speak impartially." Claveret, too, is blamed for his share in the " Quarrel," although he might have been irritated by Corneille's contempt. In conclusion the writer says : " La voix publique leur [Scudéry and Corneille] doit conseiller, comme je fais de sa part, d'employer ci-après leur temps à des ouvrages dignes de leurs capacités et non pas s'arrêter à se faire la guerre l'un l'autre à la persuasion de ceux qui aime le trouble et qui craignent de les voir écrire mieux qu'eux." Whatever part Rotrou may have taken in the famous " Quarrel," his admiration for Corneille was not diminished, as is shown by the lines in *Saint Genest*, written in 1645, and by the undoubted influence of the *Cid* and *Polyeucte* upon Rotrou's *Saint Genest*.

Rotrou's relations with his contemporaries are pleasantly described by the abbé Brillon in the following words : " Comme

---

[1] This letter is reprinted in Gasté, *op. cit.*, p. 154, and in Chardon, *op. cit.*, p. 127. See also Gasté, *op. cit.*, *Introduction*, p. 33.

Rotrou ne travaillait que pour la troupe de l'Hôtel de Bourgogne et que Corneille l'aîné ne donnait ses ouvrages qu'à
celle du Marais dont Mondory était le chef, il semblait que
ces différents objets devaient causer quelque jalousie entre ces
deux poètes qui se suivaient de fort près : mais, bien loin que
cela fût, ils étaient liés d'une amitié réciproque et parlaient de
leurs ouvrages avec toute l'estime qu'ils devaient ; et cela a
paru plusieurs fois par des élégies qu'ils faisaient à la louange
l'un de l'autre, lesquelles ils mettaient bien souvent à la tête
de leurs ouvrages.

"Les poètes qui travaillaient encore pour le théâtre en ce
temps-là étaient MM. de Scudéry, Mairet, Colletet, du Ryer
et Benserade : ils firent quelques pièces de théâtre, mais en
petite quantité, qui furent bien reçues ; et il y en avait encore
quelques autres dont les ouvrages n'étaient pas suivis. Rotrou
vivait parfaitement bien avec les uns et les autres, et ils étaient
tous de ses amis.

"Les autres auteurs contemporains qui étaient des personnes
distinguées et dont les ouvrages qu'ils ont laissés sont encore
estimés de tout le monde, étaient M. Godeau, évêque de Vence
et de Grasse, M. de Vaugelas, Chapelain, Sillon, Conrart, de
Lestoile, Furet, qui étaient tous amis de Rotrou." [1]

Thirty years of the poet's life had now passed in the precarious profession of playwright. We are fortunate in possessing
two contracts of sale, which give us an idea of the remuneration received by Rotrou from the publishers of his plays. [2] His
salary or pay from the theatre is, of course, another matter.
The first contract is dated March 11, 1636, and is for the sale
of four plays— *Les Ménechmes*, *Céliane*, *Célimène* and *Amélie* —
to Antoine de Sommaville and Toussainct Quinet for the sum

---

1 Abbé Brillon, *Notice biographique*, pp. 16–17.
2 First published by Jal, *Dict. crit. de biographie*, etc., article *Rotrou*,
and reprinted in Ronchaud, *Théâtre choisi*, vol. i, pp. xxii–xxiii. See
also Stiefel, *Über die Chronologie*, etc., p. 21.

of seven hundred and fifty "livres tournois." The author is described as "noble homme Me Jean de Rotrou, advocat en la cour de Parlement, demeurant à Paris, aux Marets du Temple, rue Neuve Sainct-François, paroisse de Sainct-Gervais." The "livre tournois" is the *livre* of twenty *sous* and is equivalent to a little less than the franc. Of course the purchasing power of money in the seventeenth century was greater than at the present day, but still the price of the four plays, a hundred and fifty dollars, was small.

The second contract, dated January 17, 1637, is for the sale to Antoine de Sommaville of ten plays — *La Pélerine Amoureuse, L'Heureux Naufrage, L'Innocente Infidelité, Crisante, Filandre, Florimonde, Alphrède, Agésilan de Colchos, Les Deux Pucelles,* and *Les Sosies.* The price is fifteen hundred "livres tournois," and the printer is at liberty to publish the first six plays whenever he wishes; the last four, however, cannot be issued until six months from the date of the sale. The price of the plays in the second sale was somewhat less than in the first. Besides throwing light upon the pecuniary circumstances of the poet the above contracts enable us to date a number of plays.

During the period preceding 1639 Rotrou had evinced much promise but had produced no plays worthy of preservation. He was now to take a step which changed the whole course of his life and made him a great dramatic author, although apparently it was calculated to have exactly the opposite effect. In the letters of Chapelain already cited is one to the Marquis de Montausier, dated November 20, 1639, at Paris.[1] In it Chapelain says : " Les dames [de Clermont d'Entragues] sont revenues de Mézières. Si M. de Chavroche fait bien, il vous envoyera la lettre en rime que Ration [Rotrou] écrivit, au nom de M. [Mlle.] de Mézières à Mlle. de Rambouillet. Elle est jolie. Le docteur de poète comique se fait lieutenant au bailliage de

---

[1] *Jean Chapelain, Lettres,* ed. cit., I, p. 531.

Dreux." Chardon was happy enough to conjecture that the mysterious "Ration" was an error for Rotrou and to find among the papers of Conrart at the Arsenal the very poem in question addressed under the name of " Sœur Morale " by Mlle. de Mézières to Julie d'Angennes.[1] The letter of Chapelain is precious, not only for giving the approximate date of Rotrou's retirement to Dreux, but also for giving a hint as to Rotrou's relations with the Hôtel de Rambouillet.

We have seen that Rotrou is mentioned in 1636 as "avocat en la cour de Parlement," and the office which he purchased in 1639 at Dreux was one of the minor magistracies of France. The position of " lieutenant-particulier au bailliage de Dreux " was that of a subordinate magistrate who acted during the absence of the " lieutenant-général " as judge in certain royal courts.[2]

The following year (July 9, 1640) Rotrou married at Mantes Marguerite Camus, " fille de noble homme Jehan Camus, conseiller du roi et élu en l'élection de Mantes et d'honorable femme dame Françoise Apoil." [3] Six children were born of this marriage, three of whom died in infancy. Of the other three the son Jean became a priest and died in 1706, the two daughters entered convents. Thus the poet left no posterity, and the family was continued through the collateral line of Rotrou's brother Pierre.[4]

Nothing whatever is known of Rotrou's life at Dreux for the next ten years. He evidently took his magisterial duties seriously, and he continued in his leisure moments to write for the stage, producing ten plays, comprising his masterpieces.[5] In

---

[1] Chardon, *op. cit.*, pp. 150–168.

[2] *Ibid.*, pp. 145–147. For the office in question see A. Chéruel, *Dictionnaire historique des institutions*, etc., vol. ii, p. 663.

[3] Jal, *op. cit.*, and Chardon, *op. cit.*, p. 149.

[4] Chardon, *op. cit.*, p. 11, and Person, *Notes critiques*, p. 103.

[5] See Stiefel, *Über die Chronologie*, etc., pp. 43–44, and *Unbekannte ital. Quellen*, p. 43. Chardon, *op. cit.*, p. 147, says: " Il ne renonça pas

the preface to *Clarice*, published in 1643 (the *privilège* and *achevé d'imprimer* are of 1642), Rotrou says, in speaking of the plays of the Italian Sforza d'Oddi, from whom he had taken the *Clarice*: "Si son langage est beau, son invention ne l'est pas moins: deux ou trois de ses pièces sur qui j'ai jeté les yeux, et qui ne doivent rien à celles que j'ai déjà mises en notre langue, feraient encore admirer cet incomparable comique sur la scène française, si l'inclination qui me reste pour le théâtre, et la passion que j'ai d'avoir l'honneur de divertir encore le premier esprit de la terre, me peuvent faire trouver, parmi mes occupations nécessaires, le temps de leur version." At the end he says: "Je ne te demande point de part en sa gloire; aussi n'en ai-je point en ses fautes s'il s'y trouve d'autres que celles de l'impression, dont encore je ne te puis répondre puisque je demeure à seize lieues de l'imprimerie, et que le soin de te donner mes pièces correctes doit être celui de mes libraires. Adieu." In the dedication of *Bélisaire*, published in 1644, the author says: "Il y a longtemps que je vous cherchais dans mes veilles quelque reconnaissance de l'honneur que vous m'avez fait autrefois, Monseigneur, de souffrir, et les représentations de mes ouvrages, et les protestations de mes très humbles services. Mais comme l'établissement de mes affaires ne m'a pas permis depuis longtemps un grand commerce avec les Muses, je me suis acquitté bien tard de cette dette." Rotrou probably maintained his relations with his former friends, as we shall see was the case with Madame de Clermont d'Entragues. One is tempted to compare the last ten years of Rotrou's life with Shakespeare's

---

cependant à la poésie, puisque c'est de cette dernière période de sa vie, de ce temps de puissante maturité, que datent tous ses chefs-d'œuvre dans les différents genres qu'il ait abordés, dans la tragédie et la comédie, comme dans la tragi-comédie elle-même. C'est en effet à dater de 1645 qu'il produit *La Sœur*, *Le Véritable Saint Genest*, *Don Bernard de Cabrère*, *Venceslas*, *Cosroès*, *Don Lope de Cardone*."

after his retirement to Stratford, but to make the parallel perfect the great English dramatist should have produced none of his masterpieces before that date. Much more picturesque than Stratford, with one great exception, Dreux is also situated on a sluggish stream that slowly winds through the very heart of the little town. On the north a high hill, once crowned by the fortress, now bears the splendid Chapelle Saint-Louis, the mausoleum of the Orléans family. From the park surrounding the chapel one looks down upon the densely built town, dominated by three edifices which Rotrou must have daily seen: the Hôtel de Ville, a charming building of the sixteenth century, of a style marking the transition from Gothic to Renaissance; the gloomy chapel of the city hospital, of the same century, with its enormously high-peaked roof; and the church of Saint Peter, where the remains of the poet would naturally have rested, a structure in every style from that of the twelfth to that of the seventeenth century. Scattered through the town are many wooden houses of the sixteenth century, exactly like those in Stratford about which the memory of Shakespeare clings. In a narrow street leading from the square in which stands the statue of Rotrou is an old house with a court. At the end of the court, in a niche at the height of the second story, is a bust of the poet, of no artistic worth. Legend declares that Rotrou was born in the neighboring house.[1]

There is every reason to suppose that Rotrou's life during the ten years from 1640 to 1650 was a happy and useful one.

---

[1] For the history and antiquities of Dreux the following works may be consulted: Œillet des Murs, *Histoire des comtes du Perche de la famille des Rotrou de 943 à 1231*, Nogent-le-Rotrou, 1856; *Documents historiques sur le comté et la ville de Dreux par E. Lefèvre*, Chartres, 1859 (cited by Chardon); E. de Rotrou, *Dreux, ses antiquités: Chapelle St.-Louis*, Dreux, 1864; and Lemenestrel, *Jean Rotrou dit " Le Grand" : Ses ancêtres et ses descendants*, Dreux, 1869. I bought at Dreux two little guides: *Notice historique et géographique sur la ville de Dreux et ses environs*, and *Notice sur Dreux par A. Lefebvre*, Dreux, 1895. Dreux

He must have felt the constant growth of his genius, and his material circumstances were such that he no longer wrote under the pressure of pecuniary necessity. His death in the very prime of his age and genius (he was not quite forty-one years old) afforded a noble example of civic devotion and Christian fortitude. According to the abbé Brillon Rotrou was inclined to a life of devotion, as the following anecdote shows. "M. Godeau . . . lui disait, un peu avant son décès, qu'il lui donnait encore une année ou deux pour s'exercer avec les muses profanes, après quoi il comptait fortement qu'il s'attacherait aux ouvrages de dévotion, où il était assuré qu'il réussirait merveilleusement bien. Ce conseil, bien loin de n'être pas agréable à Rotrou, entra bien avant dans l'inclination dans laquelle il se trouvait de penser sérieusement et solidement à sa principale affaire, et il s'y attachait si fortement qu'environ deux ans avant sa mort, il ne manquait guère de jour d'aller deux heures devant le Saint-Sacrement prier et méditer avec une profonde dévotion sur nos plus sacrés mystères." [1]

Legend has made free with the circumstances of his death, but we are fortunate in having the account of the abbé Brillon which is undoubtedly correct. I cannot do better than to give it in the writer's exact words. "En l'année 1650, la ville de Dreux, dont il était un des principaux officiers, fut affligée d'une dangereuse maladie. C'était une fièvre pourprée, avec des transports au cerveau, dont on mourait presque aussitôt que l'on en était attaqué, et qui enlevait en un jour jusqu'à

---

has other distinguished sons besides Rotrou. Among them may be mentioned Godeau, bishop of Grasse and Vence, one of the *habitués* of the Hôtel de Rambouillet and a prominent figure in the society of the seventeenth century; the architects Métézeau; Philidor the musician and famous chess player; and General de Billy, from whom the *quai* at Paris is named, killed at the battle of Jena, 1806.

[1] Abbé Brillon, *Notice biographique*, p. 17.

25 ou 30 personnes des plus considérables de la ville. Cela obligea son frère, qui était depuis longtemps à Paris, de lui écrire et de le prier fortement de sortir d'un lieu aussi périlleux que celui où il était et de venir chez lui, ou bien qu'il se retirât dans une terre qui lui appartenait et qui n'était éloignée que de dix lieues de Dreux et de Paris, et où l'air était admirable. Il lui fit réponse qu'étant seul dans la ville qui pût veiller à faire garder la police nécessaire pour essayer de la purger du mauvais air dont elle était infectée, il n'en pouvait sortir, le lieutenant-général en étant absent et le maire venant de mourir ; que c'était la raison pour laquelle il avait remercié Madame de Clermont d'Entragues de la grâce qu'elle lui voulait faire de lui donner un logement dans son château de Mézières, qui n'était éloigné de Dreux que d'une petite lieue, et qui l'empêchait aussi d'accepter l'offre qu'il lui fasait. 'Ce n'est pas,' ajoutait-il, 'que le péril ne soit fort grand, puisqu'au moment que je vous écris, les cloches sonnent pour la vingt-deuxième personne qui est morte aujourd'hui. Elles sonneront pour moi quand il plaira à Dieu. Je suis, etc.'

"Cette lettre fut la dernière qu'il écrivit ; car, peu de temps après, ayant été attaqué d'une fièvre pourprée avec de grands assoupissements, il demanda les Sacrements qui lui furent administrés dans une parfaite connaissance et qu'il reçut avec une parfaite résignation à la volonté de Dieu, qui le retira de ce monde peu de temps après, le . . . jour de . . . l'année 1650, âgé de 40 ans, regretté non seulement de ses proches et de ses amis, mais encore de tous les habitants de la ville de Dreux et des lieux circonvoisins, dont il était estimé et parfaitement aimé."[1]

---

[1] Abbé Brillon, *op. cit.*, pp. 17–18. See Person, *Notes critiques*, p. 109, where will be found the letter supposed to have been written by the poet to his brother a few days before his death. It is this letter which furnishes a part of the inscription on the monument mentioned later. See also abbé Brillon, *op. cit.*, p. 9, where the editor, L. Merlet, characterizes this letter as it deserves.

The abbé left the day of the death blank, but we know otherwise that it was June 27, and that the poet was buried the following day in some spot now unknown.[1]

Rotrou's death apparently passed unnoticed by his contemporaries. A word by Scarron in the *Roman comique*, where one of the characters says, " Il avait perdu un bon ami en feu Rotrou," and an epitaph by Colletet, one of the " Cinq Auteurs," are the only homages paid to the memory of one who was so generous in praise of his fellow-poets.[2] Here is

---

[1] Person, *Notes critiques*, p. 108, and Chardon, *op. cit.*, p. 177.

[2] The reference in the *Roman comique* is in the eighth chapter of the first part, Paris, Garnier Frères, p. 24. The speaker is the poet Roquebrune, for whom see Chardon, *La Troupe du Roman comique dévoilée*, Le Mans, 1876, pp. 123 et seq. Chardon, *La vie de Rotrou mieux connue*, p. 176, note 2, reprints an epitaph attributed to Corneille, first published in *Petite Bibliothèque des Théâtres*, Paris, 1784, p. 8 :

> L'illustre de Rotrou renferme en ce cercueil
> Et l'honneur de Thémis et la gloire des Muses,
> Qui versent, à ses pieds, mille larmes confuses,
> Par le ressentiment de leur extrême deuil.
> Ce fut un grand génie, un juge incorruptible ;
> Mais son corps, comme un autre, et mortel et passible,
> Est sorti de la vie et repose en ce lieu ;
> Aussi, son bel esprit, tout rempli de lumière,
> Aspirant de courir à sa source première,
> S'élève de la terre et s'en retourne à Dieu.

The following reference to Rotrou, a few years after his death, I have not seen quoted before. It occurs in J. Loret, *La Muze historique*, ed. Livet, Paris, 1877, vol. ii, p. 412 (December 8, 1657).

> Ny les vers d'une illustre Muze
> Dont le beau Nom termine en uze,
> Ny les Vers de Monsieur Scarron,
> Ny ceux de l'Abbé de Tiron,
> Ny ceux de l'excellent Malerbe,
> Au stil élégant et superbe,
> Ny ceux du feu sieur de Rotrou,
> Qui bûvoit, dit-on, comme un trou,
> Ny, mesmes, ceux du grand Corneille,
> Ne font pas tous crier merveille.

Perhaps Loret wanted a rhyme for Rotrou and chose the most convenient, like Boileau in the case of Faret, who, thanks to the poet, is inseparably connected in the mind of posterity with *cabaret*.

the epitaph, first published in Titon du Tillet's *Le Parnasse français*, Paris, 1735 :

> Passant vois en Rotrou l'impuissance du sort,
> Il est mort et pourtant son nom se renouvelle ;
> Car si de si beaux vers la grâce est immortelle,
> N'a-t-il pas de quoi vivre en dépit de la mort ?

Corneille's silence is inexplicable. It is true that for ten years Rotrou had lived in a little provincial town and his relations with Paris had probably not been very close. This may explain why he was not made a member of the French Academy, a fact that has sorely puzzled his later biographers.[1]

The frequenters of the *foyer* of the Théâtre-Français often pause before the striking bust of Rotrou by Caffiéri, which may well represent the poet of the period before 1639. The artist (Jean-Jacques Caffiéri, 1725–1792) says that he used for his bust an original painting loaned to him by M. de Rotrou, auditor of accounts and great-grand-nephew of the poet.[2]

---

[1] See Person, *Notes critiques*, p. 146; Chardon, *La vie de Rotrou mieux connue*, p. 173. Steffens, *Rotrou-Studien*, p. 10, cites Delavigne, *La tragédie chrétienne au xviie siècle*, Toulouse, 1847, p. 89. I give the citation from Steffens as I have been unable to procure the work. "Sa résidence à Dreux fut peut-être le seul motif qui l'empêcha d'être admis à l'Académie Française. On sait que pour le même motif de non-résidence [à Paris], Corneille se vit préférer deux fois, M. Salomon d'abord, avocat général du Grand Conseil en 1644; puis en 1646 du Ryer." Rotrou's non-election to the Academy warrants his inclusion in A. Houssaye's superficial *Histoire du 41me fauteuil de l'Académie Française*, Paris, 1894, pp. 37–41.

[2] This bust is reproduced in the frontispiece of this work. For Caffiéri see J. Guiffrey, *Les Caffiéri*, Paris, 1877, where, p. 337, may be found a fine etching by Leloir of the bust of Rotrou. Guiffrey says of this bust, p. 337 : "Suivant son habitude, le sculpteur n'avait rien négligé pour rendre aussi fidèle que possible le portrait du poète tragique. Il explique, dans le livret du Salon, qu'il a travaillé d'après un portrait original appartenant à un arrière-petit-neveu du poète ; il joint même à sa notice un abrégé de la vie de Rotrou communiqué par son descendant. Mais, à côté de ces qualités secondaires, quelle vie, quelle intelligence l'artiste a su imprimer à cette figure distinguée ! De fines

Arsène Houssaye well says of this masterpiece of the sculptor :
"Pour moi le type du poète, c'est le marbre de Rotrou au
foyer de la Comédie-Française. Que dis-je, le marbre? c'est
la vie elle-même, c'est la poésie qui rêve, c'est la passion qui
se souvient, c'est l'homme à l'image de Dieu, c'est le symbole
de toutes les muses, c'est l'Apollon des modernes."

There is also an engraving of no great worth by E. Desrochers, an engraver of the eighteenth century, who produced
a series of some six hundred portraits of distinguished men.

In 1867 was unveiled at Dreux a bronze statue of Rotrou
by the sculptor Allasseur.[1] It represents the magistrate rather
than the poet and is based on the Caffiéri bust. On the front
of the pedestal are the words: "A la mémoire du poète Jean

---

moustaches, les cheveux épars, la chemise entr'ouverte, une collerette
de dentelle carrée sur le cou, un nœud de rubans sur l'épaule droite, un
manteau à larges plis couvrant à demi tous ces détails, vraie tête de
poète et d'inspiré, et en même temps type de cavalier accompli, presque
de raffiné, tels sont les traits caractéristiques de ce chef-d'œuvre. Mais
ce que les mots sont impuissants à rendre, c'est le jeu de la physionomie,
l'intensité de vie et d'expression gravée dans tous les traits, surtout
dans les yeux et la bouche." See also Chardon, *La vie de Rotrou mieux
connue*, p. 181, and especially Chardon, *M. de Modène, ses deux femmes et
Madeleine Béjart*, p. 58, note 1 : "Il faut cependant bien se garder de
lui supposer la tête quasi fascinatrice du buste de Caffiéri, qui nous a
donné un Rotrou complètement apocryphe. Depuis que j'ai écrit mon
livre sur le poète de Dreux, j'ai pu voir chez M. de Rotrou, grâce à sa
parfaite obligeance, les deux seuls portraits authentiques de l'auteur de
Saint Genest. L'un le seul vrai, en réalité, est le Rotrou en magistrat
d'après lequel a été faite la gravure de Desrochers. L'autre est un
Rotrou *appollonisé*, ainsi que me le disait si justement son possesseur. Il
tient une lyre dans la main, sa tête est ceinte d'une couronne de lauriers ;
il est vêtu d'une tunique retenue par une agrafe. Il faut déjà bien de
la complaisance pour retrouver une ressemblance vague avec le premier
portrait. Quant au buste de Caffiéri, fait d'après la communication, par
la famille, du portrait de Rotrou en *Parnassien*, c'est simplement une
œuvre de fantaisie magnifique, mais qui ne ressemble en rien à son
modèle."

[1] For the ceremonies of the unveiling of the statue see Lemenestrel,
Jean Rotrou dit " Le Grand," etc., pp. 99–139.

Rotrou, lieutenant-particulier au bailliage de Dreux, né à Dreux, le 21 août 1609, mort le 28 juin 1650, victime de son dévouement pour ses concitoyens." On the left is mentioned the legacy of M. Lamésange, former mayor of Dreux, who left to the city the necessary funds for the statue; on the right are the names of Rotrou's principal dramas. On the fourth face of the pedestal are engraved the following words, taken from the letter supposed to have been written by the poet to his brother a few days before his death, but which is now known to be a forgery: " Le salut de mes concitoyens m'est confié, j'en réponds à ma patrie; je ne trahirai ni l'honneur ni ma conscience; ce n'est pas que le péril où je me trouve ne soit fort grand puisqu'au moment où je vous écris les cloches sonnent pour la vingt-deuxième personne qui est morte aujourd'hui : Ce sera pour moi quand il plaira à Dieu."

Only two of Rotrou's plays, *St. Genest* and *Venceslas*, have survived, and in the stage history of these plays, given in the next chapter, and in the Bibliography, may be read the story of Rotrou's reputation. I shall here indicate in a rapid way some of the vicissitudes of his posthumous fame. We have seen that there are few contemporary references to the poet and that his death passed almost unnoticed.[1] Fourteen years after Rotrou's death we find a reference to him by one of the greatest of French dramatists, who also paid him the sincerest

---

[1] A few unimportant contemporary references which I have not mentioned may be found in Steffens, *Rotrou-Studien*, p. 7. They are by Scudéry and La Pinelière, a dramatic and satiric poet of the time, now entirely forgotten. Stiefel in his review of Steffens in *Zeitschrift für franz. Spr. und Lit.*, vol. xv, p. 35, gives some unimportant additions to Steffens's references. They are : a reference in Tallemant des Réaux, *Historiettes*, one in Sorel, *Bibliothèque françoise*, p. 183 (not 153 as Stiefel gives it), and a letter from Chapelain to the Count de Belin, which had already been printed by Person (*Venceslas*, p. 145) and Chardon (*Vie de Rotrou*, p. 105). See also the reference in Loret quoted above, p. 43, note 2.

compliment of imitation. In the preface to his first tragedy, *La Thébaïde*, 1664, Racine says : " Ce sujet avait été autrefois traité par Rotrou, sous le nom d'*Antigone*. Mais il faisait mourir les deux frères dès le commencement de son troisième acte . . . et il avait réuni en une seule pièce deux actions différentes, dont l'une sert de matière aux *Phéniciennes* d'Euripide, et l'autre à l'*Antigone* de Sophocle. Je compris que cette duplicité d'actions avait pu nuire à sa pièce, qui d'ailleurs était remplie de quantité de beaux endroits." [1]

The eighteenth century did little for Rotrou. Besides brief, and mostly incorrect, references in biographical dictionaries and histories of the theater, only three critics of eminence mentioned Rotrou. Voltaire, in his *Lettre à M. Scipion Maffei* (1744), says : " Si l'amour n'est pas tragique, il est insipide, et s'il est tragique, il doit régner seul, il n'est pas fait pour la seconde place. C'est Rotrou, c'est le grand Corneille même, il le faut avouer, qui, en créant notre théâtre l'ont presque toujours défiguré par ces amours de commande, par ces intrigues galantes, qui, n'étant point de vraies passions, ne sont point dignes du théâtre." [2] In his *Commentaires sur Corneille* Voltaire has occasion to speak of Rotrou several times. He says, in his remarks on *Médée* : " Rotrou n'avait encore rien fait qui approchât même du médiocre. Il ne donna son *Venceslas* que quatorze ans après la *Médée*, en 1649, lorsque Corneille, qui l'appelait son père, fut devenu son maître et que Rotrou ranimé par le génie de Corneille, devint digne de lui être comparé dans la première scène de *Venceslas*, et dans

---

[1] *Œuvres de J. Racine*, ed. P. Mesnard, Paris, 1885 (*Les Grands Écrivains de la France*), vol. i, p. 403. I believe it was Raynouard, *Journal des Savants*, 1823, pp. 286–287, who first called attention to Racine's imitation of Rotrou. Later (1868) Jarry in his *Essai sur les œuvres dramatiques de Jean Rotrou*, pp. 127–138, added considerably to Raynouard's references, and mentioned besides the imitation of Rotrou by Molière, Regnard, Piron, Legrand, and La Motte.

[2] *Œuvres*, ed. Moland, vol. iv, p. 182.

le quatrième acte. Encore même, cette pièce de Rotrou était-elle une imitation de l'auteur espagnol Francesco Roxas."[1] In criticising the first scene of the first act of *Polyeucte*, Voltaire remarks : "C'est le style de Rotrou, avec plus de force, d'élégance et de richesse."[2] Of Rotrou's relations to Corneille, he says : "Il [Corneille] était un des Cinq Auteurs. . . . Il n'avait trouvé d'amitié et d'estime que dans Rotrou, qui sentait son mérite ; les autres n'en avaient pas assez pour lui rendre justice."[3]

The *Siècle de Louis Quatorze* contains this very inadequate notice of Rotrou : "Rotrou (Jean) né en 1609, le fondateur du théâtre. La première scène et une partie du quatrième acte de *Venceslas* sont des chefs-d'œuvre. Corneille l'appelait son père. On sait combien le père fut surpassé par le fils. *Venceslas* ne fut composé qu'après le *Cid* ; il est tiré entièrement, comme le *Cid*, d'une tragédie espagnole. Mort en 1650."[4] In the *Dissertation sur la tragédie* Voltaire says : "Les modernes ont encore, plus fréquemment que les Grecs, imaginé des sujets de pure invention. Nous eûmes beaucoup de ces ouvrages du temps du cardinal de Richelieu ; c'était son goût, ainsi que celui des Espagnols. . . . Le *Venceslas* de Rotrou est entièrement dans ce goût, et toute cette histoire est fabuleuse. Mais l'auteur voulut peindre un jeune homme fougueux dans ses passions, avec un mélange de bonnes et de mauvaises qualités ; un père tendre et faible ; et il a réussi dans quelques parties de son ouvrage."[5] The *Appel à toutes les Nations de l'Europe* contains the following passage : "Mairet ouvrit donc la véritable carrière où Rotrou entra, et celui-ci alla plus loin que son maître. On joue encore sa

---

[1] *Œuvres*, ed. cit., vol. xxxi, p. 180.

[2] *Ibid.*, p. 372.

[3] *Ibid.*, p. 205.

[4] *Ibid.*, vol. xiv, p. 123.

[5] *Ibid.*, vol. iv, p. 496.

tragédie de *Venceslas*, pièce très défectueuse à la vérité, mais dont la première scène et presque tout le quatrième acte sont des chefs-d'œuvre." [1] Voltaire blames the exaggeration of Rotrou and cites in the *Dictionnaire Philosophique* some lines from the *Hercule Mourant* with the remark : "On voit par ces vers combien l'exagéré, l'ampoulé, le forcé, étaient encore à la mode ; et c'est ce qui doit faire pardonner à Pierre Corneille." [2] In another place (*Remarques sur les Observations de Scudéri*) he says : "Rotrou est l'auteur d'*Hercule*, pièce remplie de vaines déclamations." [3]

Marmontel's relations with Rotrou are more interesting and form a curious chapter in the literary history of the eighteenth century.[4] At the instance of Madame de Pompadour Marmontel undertook in 1759 a revision of Rotrou's *Venceslas*, in which he modernized the language and changed the dénouement, making Cassandre kill herself in the presence of Ladislas after he became king. When the play was performed Lekain, the famous actor of the Théâtre-Français, recited his lines according to the original version, entirely disregarding Marmontel's changes. In order to do this both the Rotrou and Marmontel versions had to be rearranged. Marmontel was exceedingly angry and the result was a bitter quarrel with Lekain and his supporters, which cost Marmontel the loss of his journal *Le Mercure* and a brief detention in the Bastille.

The changes made by Marmontel will be more properly considered in the next chapter in connection with the play

---

[1] *Œuvres*, ed. cit., vol. xxiv, p. 217.

[2] *Ibid.*, vol. xix, p. 45.

[3] *Ibid.*, vol. xxxi, p. 246.

[4] The story will be found in detail in the valuable book recently published by S. Lenel, *Un Homme de Lettres au xviii*e *siècle : Marmontel d'après des documents nouveaux et inédits*, Paris, 1902, chap. v, pp. 168–189. See also Person, *Histoire du Venceslas*, pp. 68–78.

itself. It is sufficient to say here that after printing his version in 1759 Marmontel later published (1773) a splendid edition of *Venceslas*, together with Mairet's *Sophonisbe* and du Ryer's *Scévole*. This edition contains a brief life of Rotrou, an examination of *Venceslas*, and copious remarks upon the text, which is the original one of Rotrou. The life is a fairly correct and sympathetic one, and ends with these words : " Rotrou n'a rien mis d'aussi héroïque dans ses ouvrages que ce trait qui couronne sa vie ; et il est beau de voir dans un poète tragique, un caractère plus grand lui-même et plus intéressant que tous ceux qu'il a peints." As to his literary merit, Marmontel says : " Rotrou fut ce que pouvait être dans ce temps-là un homme de talent, sans beaucoup de génie, qui avait pris Hardi pour modèle, et qui ne croyait pouvoir faire mieux que de copier les Espagnols et de traduire les Latins." Marmontel's judgment on *Venceslas* will be considered later. I have incorporated into my notes his most important ones. They give, like the remarks of Voltaire on Corneille, an interesting idea of the taste of the eighteenth century and the extensive changes which had already taken place in the language.

The name of Rotrou was not forgotten even during the terrors of the Revolution. Between 1786 and 1798 J. F. de La Harpe delivered his famous lectures on ancient and modern literature, and devoted part of one lecture to an examination of *Venceslas*. His judgment, as we shall see later, does not differ from that of Marmontel.

During the Empire the memory of Rotrou was kept alive by Talma's rendition of Ladislas in *Venceslas* (see chap. iv, p. 115), and in 1811 the French Academy offered a prize for the best poem on the death of Rotrou. The prize was awarded the following year to C. H. Millevoye (1782–1816). It cannot be praised very highly ; a brief extract will convey an idea of its character.

D'un frère vainement le fidèle message
A rappelé ses pas sur un autre rivage :
Sa vertu rougirait d'hésiter un instant.
Il voit venir la mort, il la voit, . . . il l'attend.
Immuable, il répond au frère qui l'implore :
" Pour la vingtième fois, j'entends depuis l'aurore
" Sonner l'airain fatal. . . . Je l'entends sans effroi.
" Ce soir, si Dieu l'ordonne, il sonnera pour moi ! "
Il disait ; mais, vaincu par tant de vigilance,
L'homicide fléau se retire en silence.
    .   .   .   .   .   .

Cependant du héros la grande âme exhalée
Aux âmes des martyrs dans les cieux s'est mêlée.
Par d'ineffables chants les séraphins ravis
Fêtent l'hôte nouveau des lumineux parvis :
Mais du haut de ce trône où, près de Borromée,
Il s'assied ombragé des palmes d'Idumée,
O rivages de l'Eure ! ô bords délicieux !
Il vous cherche toujours, et jusque dans les cieux,
Gardant le souvenir de sa ville chérie,
Il forme encor des vœux pour sa douce patrie.[1]

It was not until 1820 that the complete works of Rotrou were made accessible for the first time to the student, in the edition of Viollet-le-Duc, and since then the selections published by Ronchaud and Hémon have still further contributed to a knowledge of the poet's dramas.[2]

---

[1] The poem is reprinted in Lemenestrel, *Jean Rotrou dit " Le Grand,"* Dreux, 1869, pp. 32–36.

[2] The edition of Viollet-le-Duc does not seem to have attracted much attention at the time it was published. It did, however, call forth the valuable review, already cited, by Raynouard in the *Journal des Savants*. The edition of Viollet-le-Duc leaves much to be desired. I have compared only two of the plays in his edition, *Saint Genest* and *Venceslas*, with the original editions. Viollet-le-Duc has modernized the orthography, disregarded the scene divisions of the original, and added to and changed the stage directions. He has also substituted modern words for antiquated ones, as *donner* for *bailler*, etc. Misprints are frequent. Although Hémon says he has consulted the original editions for his text, he has, at least in *Saint Genest* and *Venceslas*, simply

The celebration at Dreux in 1867 called forth nothing of permanent value for Rotrou's biography or the criticism of his works, and it was not until 1882 that the first scientific study of Rotrou began with the *Notes critiques et biographiques sur Rotrou* by L. Person, afterwards reprinted in the appendix to the same author's *Histoire du Venceslas de Rotrou.* To these valuable works Person added, in the same and following years, *Histoire du Véritable Saint-Genest de Rotrou* and *Les papiers de Pierre Rotrou de Saudreville.*[1]

The first attempt at a scientific biography of Rotrou was made by Henri Chardon in an article in the *Revue historique et archéologique du Maine,* 1883, "La vie de Rotrou mieux connue," reprinted separately in 1884. This is by far the most valuable contribution yet made to the study of Rotrou's life. About the same time L. Merlet published a brief biographical sketch in the *Bibliothèque chartraine* (1882) and the precious *Notice biographique* by the abbé Brillon (1885).

The investigation of the sources began in 1891 with three independent investigations : Vianey's *Deux sources inconnues de Rotrou* (Italian sources of *La Sœur* and *La Pèlerine amoureuse*) ; Steffen's *Rotrou-Studien : Jean de Rotrou als Nachahmer Lope de Vega's* ; and A. L. Stiefel's *Unbekannte italienische Quellen Jean de Rotrou's.* Later Stiefel continued his valuable investigation of the sources by two articles in the *Zeitschrift für französische Sprache und Litteratur* (1901, 1906), " Über die Quellen Jean de Rotrou's *Cosroès* " and " Über Jean Rotrou's spanische Quellen." To the above should be added the

---

followed Viollet-le-Duc, correcting the obvious misprints. In a few cases he has restored lines omitted by Viollet-le-Duc, but he may have done this from Ronchaud's edition, published a year before Hémon's. Ronchaud's text is, in the main, an exact reproduction of the original editions, with some modifications in capitalization and punctuation.

[1] A very valuable review of Person's three works will be found in Stiefel's article cited p. 25, note 1.

same author's indispensable article in the same journal (1894), "Über die Chronologie von J. Rotrou's dramatischen Werken." The classical sources of Rotrou's plays have been examined by K. von Reinhardstöttner in his *Plautus : Spätere Bearbeitungen plautinischer Lustspiele*, 1886, and by F. E. Buchetmann in *Jean de Rotrou's Antigone und ihre Quellen*, 1901.

The linguistic interest in Rotrou began in 1882 with a dissertation by a German scholar, K. Sölter, and an article by a French professor, A. Benoist, in the *Annales de la Faculté des lettres de Bordeaux*. To these may be added another German dissertation by M. Franzen, 1892. These contributions are defective in that all make use of the inadequate text of the Viollet-le-Duc edition. Much yet remains to be done in this field.

It is impossible to examine in detail here the large number of biographical and critical works on Rotrou produced in the last fifty years. The most important are mentioned in the Bibliography and cited in this Introduction. The critical estimate of the last century will be considered in the following chapter, which deals in a general way with Rotrou's dramas.

III

Classification of Rotrou's plays. — Distinction between comedy and tragi-comedy. — Rotrou's originality. — His method of imitation. — In the Plautus plays. — In the plays taken from Italian and Spanish sources. — *Laure Persécutée*. — Rotrou's style and language. — Gallantry of the seventeenth century. — Tone of conversation. — Conventional expressions. — Theory of love. — Exaggerated use of antitheses. — *Précieux* expressions. — Sententious expressions. — Play upon words. — Rotrou's language and construction. — Rotrou's versification. — Hiatus. — Rhyme. — Cæsura. — *Enjambement*. — Poetic licenses.

Rotrou's thirty-five extant plays are divided into tragedies, tragi-comedies, and comedies.[1] According to the title-pages

---

[1] There is no doubt as to the genuineness of the thirty-five plays published by Viollet-le-Duc. He has added in the fifth volume a tragedy, *L'Illustre Amazone*, ascribed to Rotrou, but without good reason. Five

seven are tragedies (I give in parentheses the date of composition or performance according to Stiefel) : *Hercule Mourant*
(1634), *Crisante* (1636), *Antigone* (1638), *Iphigénie* (1640),
Bélisaire (1642–1644), *Saint Genest* (1645), and *Cosroès*
(1648). If we bear in mind what has been said earlier, p. 10,
in regard to the signification of the word " tragi-comedy," it
will be seen that *Iphigénie* is, properly speaking, a tragi-comedy,
and it is so given in Viollet-le-Duc's edition. *Venceslas* (1647)
is generally termed a tragedy, but it is a tragi-comedy precisely
in the same sense as is the *Cid*.

At first sight the distinction between the twelve comedies
and the sixteen tragi-comedies is not always clear, but here
too Rotrou follows exactly the definition given on p. 10, note 4.
The comedies contain no tragic plot and involve no characters
of high rank.[1] Otherwise the intrigue is as complicated and
romantic as in the tragi-comedies. *La Belle Alphrède* (1636),
for instance, contains a shipwreck, attack by pirates, disguises
of sex, and recognitions. The comedies are : *La Bague de
l'Oubli* (1628), *Les Ménechmes* (1631), *Diane* (1632–1633),
Célimène (1633), *Filandre* (1633–1634), *Florimonde* (1635),

---

plays are supposed to be lost : *Lisimène*, *Don Alvare de Lune*, *Florante
ou les dédains amoureux*, *La Thébaïde*, and *Amarillis*. Of these it is
likely that *La Thébaïde* is only another name for the *Antigone*. It is
possible that *Lisimène* is an error for *Célimène*, and the same is the
case with *Florante ou les dédains amoureux*, as has been shown by
Chardon, *La vie de Rotrou mieux connue*, pp. 199 et seq. The *Amarillis*
is nothing but the same *Célimène* transformed after Rotrou's death into
a *pastorale* by Tristan l'Hermite, as was pointed out as early as 1745
by the Brothers Parfait in their *Histoire du théâtre françois*, vol. iv,
p. 412 ; see also N. M. Bernardin, *Tristan l'Hermite*, Paris, 1895,
pp. 495–503. This leaves *Alvare de Lune*, about which nothing is
known. See, for the subject of the lost plays, Steffens, *Rotrou-Studien*,
pp. 29–31.

[1] The only exceptions are *Les Sosies*, where Jupiter is a character,
and *La Bague de l'Oubli*, where the characters are noble, but the
intrigue is not tragic.

Clorinde (1635), *La Belle Alphrède* (1636), *Les Sosies* (1636), *Les Captifs* (1638), *Clarice* (1641), and *La Sœur* (1645).

The sixteen tragi-comedies follow very closely the seventeenth-century understanding of the *genre* : noble characters, tragic plot, happy dénouement. These characteristics are not always found together, as, for example, in Rotrou's first play *L'Hypocondriaque* (1628) (the plot of which has already been given on p. 19) the characters are not noble, and the plot is not, strictly speaking, tragic, but the ending is happy. The whole tone of the play entitles it to inclusion in the class of tragi-comedy. The same may be said of *La Pélerine amoureuse* (1633–1634), *Amélie* (1636), and *Les deux Pucelles* (1636). In *Cléagénor et Doristée* (1634) the characters are not noble, but the plot is tragic and the ending happy. The same may be said of *Céliane* (1632–1633).

The ten remaining tragi-comedies all involve persons of high rank, end happily, and have a more or less tragic plot, although this last is not necessary. These tragi-comedies are : *Les Occasions perdues* (1633), *L'Heureux Naufrage* (1633), *L'Innocente Infidelité* (1634), *L'Heureuse Constance* (1635), *Agésilan de Colchos* (1636), *Laure Persécutée* (1638), *Célie* (1644–1645), *Don Bernard de Cabrère* (1646), *Venceslas* (1647), and *Don Lope de Cardone*.[1]

Before examining Rotrou's dramatic genius, it will be necessary to consider briefly the question of his originality. The three influences which are evident in Rotrou's plays—the classical, the Italian, and the Spanish—are characteristic of the time in which he lived. French tragedy is not an evolution of the mediæval mysteries, but the result of the study and imitation of the classical drama in the sixteenth century.[2] The Italian

---

[1] Printed in 1650 after Rotrou's death. The date of composition is uncertain ; Stiefel gives two alternative dates, 1646–1647 and 1649–1650 ; see *Über die Chronologie*, p. 47.

[2] See article by Brunetière already cited, " L'Évolution d'un genre : La Tragédie," p. 176.

and Spanish influences — the result partly of political, partly of geographical, causes — molded most powerfully French society and literature in the seventeenth century.[1] Rotrou naturally and unavoidably took his material from the three categories mentioned above, just as Shakespeare did from the first two. To demand from the sixteenth-century or seventeenth-century dramatist originality, so far as the invention of plot is concerned, is to ask the impossible and to ignore all the literary conditions of the period. The question is admirably put by Brunetière in an article already cited, " Corneille et le théâtre espagnol " : [2] " *Quis primus* — qui des deux est le poète, celui qui " invente," ou celui qui " achève "? celui qui " crée," ou celui qui " fait vivre "? et quel est le créateur, celui qui " trouve la matière," ou celui qui " lui donne une forme "? Ici encore, nous n'avons qu'à consulter l'histoire, ou plutôt l'expérience, et nous verrons qu'en littérature comme en art, l'invention proprement dite, la découverte ou la " trouvaille " du sujet n'est rien, ou assez peu de chose ; et tout dépend de l'usage que l'artiste ou le poète en sait faire. . . . De quelles sources Lope de Vega, Calderon, Alarcon, Tirso de Molina ont-ils tiré les sujets de leurs *Comedias*? C'est une recherche que je ne sache pas qu'on ait encore faite. Mais nous connaissons les sources de Racine, qui semble avoir affecté de ne porter à la scène aucun sujet qu'un Rotrou, qu'un Scudéri, qu'un la Calprenède n'y eussent traité avant lui. Nous connaissons les sources de Shakspeare, et toute la critique est tombée d'accord que, pour être imitée des nouvelles de Bandello et de Luigi da Porta, — qui sont elles-mêmes des chefs-d'œuvre, — l'originalité de son *Roméo et Juliette* n'en était pas diminuée. Et nous connaissons encore les sources d'Euripide, de Sophocle, et d'Eschyle, lesquels n'en

---

[1] See Crane, *La Société française au dix-septième siècle*, New York, 1889, pp. xiv and xv.

[2] *Revue des deux mondes*, January 1, 1903, pp. 191–192.

sont pas moins tout ce qu'ils sont, pour avoir l'un après l'autre traité les mêmes sujets, et les avoir tous ou presque tous reçus d'une tradition légendaire dont il ne semble pas qu'ils aient altéré les grandes lignes. Leurs *Agamemnon*, leurs *Électre*, leurs *Oreste* ne sont, à proprement parler, que des " adaptations." Leur originalité, quelle qu'elle soit, consiste donc en autre chose que dans l' " invention " de leurs sujets, au sens littéral, mais peu littéraire, du mot. S'ils sont poètes, ce n'est pas pour les avoir " trouvés." Ce qui fait l'intérêt ou la valeur de leurs tragédies, comme aussi bien des drames de Shakspeare, et des " comédies " de Calderon ou de Lope de Vega, n'a qu'un lointain rapport avec le sujet de leurs pièces, puisque les mêmes sujets, en d'autres mains, n'ont pas rendu les mêmes effets, ni produit les mêmes chefs-d'œuvre."

The student will have an opportunity in this work to compare two of Rotrou's plays with their sources and to draw his own conclusions as to the poet's originality. Thanks to Steffens, Reinhardstöttner, Stiefel, and Buchetmann the student can examine Rotrou's method of imitation in a large number of other plays, the originals of which are not easily accessible.[1] Of the thirty-five plays of Rotrou the sources of some twenty-six are known more or less exactly, and it is unlikely that the nine remaining plays are original with Rotrou, so far as the plots are concerned.[2]

---

[1] The classical scholar will find an interesting subject of study in the comparison of *Hercule Mourant*, *Iphigénie*, and the three plays from Plautus with their originals. This has not been thoroughly done. Another equally interesting topic would be the comparison of Rotrou's plays with those on similar subjects by Racine, Molière, etc.

[2] The following recapitulation of the sources of Rotrou's plays may be useful to the student. I have arranged them in the order of classical, Italian, Spanish, and miscellaneous, and have indicated the place where the source is discussed; for full titles of works mentioned see Bibliography. *Les Ménechmes*: Plautus, *Menaechmi*, Reinhardstöttner, pp. 549 et seq.; *Les Sosies*: Plautus, *Amphitruo*, Reinhardstöttner, pp. 174 et seq.; *Les Captifs*: Plautus, *Captivi*, Reinhardstöttner, p. 339 et seq.;

It is impossible in the space at my command to examine in detail Rotrou's method of imitation.[1] In a general way it may be said that Rotrou uses his material very freely. There are exceptions, of course, and he follows his original more closely, for example, in the three Plautus plays than elsewhere, yet even here he makes many changes demanded by the taste

---

Hercule Mourant: Seneca, Buchetmann, p. 248, note; *Antigone*: Sophocles, Buchetmann, *op. cit.*; *Iphigénie*: Euripides, Buchetmann, p. 247, note; *Filandre*: Chiabrera, *La Gèlopea*, Stiefel, *Über die Chronologie*, p. 36; *La Pélerine amoureuse*: Girolamo Bargagli, *La Pelligrina*, Stiefel, *Unbekannte ital. Quellen*, p. 4, Vianey, *Deux sources inconnues de Rotrou*; *Clarice*: Sforza d'Oddi, *L'Erofilomachia*, Stiefel, *Unbekannte ital. Quellen*, p. 44; *Célie*: Giovan Batista della Porta, *Gli duoi Fratelli rivali*, Stiefel, *Unbekannte ital. Quellen*, p. 49; *La Sœur*: della Porta, *La Sorella*, Stiefel, *Unbekannte ital. Quellen*, p. 103; *La Bague de l'Oubli*: Lope de Vega, *La Sortija del Olvido*, Steffens, p. 33; *La Diane*: Lope de Vega, *La Villana de Xetafe*, Stiefel, "Über Jean Rotrou's spanische Quellen," *Zeitschrift für franz. Spr. und Lit.*, vol. xxix (1906), pp. 195–234; *Les Occasions perdues* Lope de Vega, *La Occasion Perdida*, Steffens, p. 50; *L'Heureux Naufrage:* Lope de Vega, *El Naufragio Prodigioso* (?), Steffens, p. 89; *L'Heureuse Constance*: Lope de Vega, *El Poder vencido y el Amor premiado* and *Mirad á quien alabais*, Steffens, p. 63; *Laure Persécutée*: Lope de Vega, *Laura Perseguida*, Steffens, p. 91; *Le Véritable Saint Genest*: Lope de Vega, *Lo Fingido Verdadero*, Person, *Hist. du Véritable Saint-Genest*; *Don Bernarde de Cabrère*: Lope de Vega, *La adversa fortuna de Don Bernardo de Cabrera*, Steffens, p. 89; *Venceslas*: Francisco de Rojas, *No hay ser padre siendo rey*, Person, *Hist. du Venceslas*; *Les deux Pucelles*: Cervantes, *Las dos Doncellas*, Ronchaud, *Théâtre choisi de Rotrou*, vol. i, p. xxxi; *Bélisaire*: Mira de Mescua, *El exemplo mayor de la desdicha y gran Capitan Belisario*, Steffens, p. 89; *Cléagénor et Doristée*: Sorel's romance of the same name, Chardon, *La vie de Rotrou mieux connue*, pp. 195 et seq.; *Agésilan de Colchos*: *Amadis*, Jarry, *Essai*, p. 51; *Cosroès*: L. Cellot, *Chosroës*, Stiefel, *Zeitschrift für franz. Spr. und Lit.*, vol. xxiii, pp. 69–188. The possible source of *L'Hypocondriaque* has been mentioned, p. 20, note 1. The plot of *Crisante*, as has already been stated, appears to have been taken from Plutarch, *De Mulierum virtutibus*, story of Chiomara. The sources of the eight remaining plays have not been discovered, but, as I have said, it is not likely that they are original with Rotrou.

[1] This has been done by Jarry, *Essai sur les œuvres dramatiques de Jean Rotrou*, chaps. iv, v, pp. 77–125.

of his audiences. In *Les Ménechmes* he transforms the courtesan Erotium into a coquettish widow, Erotie, who at the end of the play marries Ménechme-Sosicle. In *Les Captifs,* the comedy from which Plautus carefully banished all love intrigue, Rotrou introduces a love story, and the play ends with a double marriage between Philocrate and Olympie, Hegio's daughter, and Tyndare and Philénie, entrusted by her father's will to the guardianship of Hegio and betrothed to the son afterwards stolen. In order to work in his love story Rotrou is obliged to make considerable changes in his original. These are very cleverly done and the result is a most interesting comedy, lacking, it is true, the severe beauty of the original, but more in accord with the taste of the day. A few passages from the play, all belonging to Rotrou, will serve also to illustrate some of the characteristics of the French poet's style.

In the first scene of the first act Philénie reveals to Olympie her love for Tyndare and gives the following much-quoted definition of love : [1]

---

[1] I had finished my introduction when my attention was called to the fact that Rotrou in the passage which follows imitated a similar passage in the tragedy of *La Hadriana* by Luigi Groto, known from his blindness as Il Cieco d'Adria (born at Adria in 1541 and died at Venice in 1585). Unfortunately the Italian play is not within reach and I am obliged to content myself with the analysis and extracts given by P. A. Daniel in *The New Shakspere Society*, series iii. Originals and Analogues. Part I, London, 1875. Mr. Daniel in his introduction, p. xxix, cites a passage from Groto which bears a striking similarity to Romeo's antithetical definition of love in *Romeo and Juliet*, I. 1:

> Why, then, O brawling love! O loving hate!
> O any thing, of nothing first create!
> O heavy lightness! serious vanity!
> Mis-shapen chaos of well-seeming forms!
> Feather of lead, bright smoke, cold fire, sick health!
> Still-waking sleep, that is not what it is!

The passage in Groto is as follows:

> Fu il mio male un piacer senza allegrezza ;
> Un voler, che si stringe, ancor che punga.
> Un pensier, che si nutre, ancor che ancida.

Vous l'entendez, la douleur qui me presse
Se peut dire un plaisir où manque l'allégresse,
Un agréable écueil, un redoutable port ;
Un penser qu'on nourrit et qui donne la mort ;
Un pénible travail qu'au séjour où nous sommes
Les dieux ont envoyé pour le repos des hommes ;
Une captivité qui s'aime en ses liens ;
Un bien source de maux, un mal source de biens :
Un principe de vie, et sa fin tout ensemble ;

Un' affano che 'l ciel dà per riposo.
Un ben supremo, fonte d' ogni male.
Un male estremo, d'ogni ben radice.
Una piaga mortal, che mi fec' io.
Un laccio d' or dov' io stessa m' avvinsi.
Un velen grato, ch' io bevei per gli occhi.
Giunto un finire e un cominciar di vita.
Una febre, che 'l gelo, e 'l caldo mesce.
Un fel, più dolce assai, che mele, ò manna.
Un bel foco, che strugge, e non risolve.
Un giogo insopportabile, e leggiero.
Una pena felice, un dolor caro.
Una morte immortal piena di vita.
Un' inferno, che sembra il Paradiso.

The reader will be pleased to see Mr. Daniel's excellent translation :

My sickness was a pleasure without joy ;
A will embracing yet repelling still,
A care which nourisheth, and yet which slays,
A labour given by heaven as a rest.
A supreme good the source of every ill,
An extreme ill the root of every good,
A mortal wound inflicted by myself,
A golden snare in which myself I 've catched.
A pleasant poison drank in at my eyes;
Together ending and beginning life.
A fever mixed with freezing and with heat,
A gall than honey and manna sweeter far,
A beauteous flame that burns yet not destroys,
An insupportable and lightsome yoke,
A happy suffering and a cherisht grief,
A death immortal brimming o'er with life,
A Hell that seems as 't were a Paradise.

It would be interesting to inquire whether Rotrou has made other use
of Groto.

Une fièvre qui fait et qu'on brûle et qu'on tremble ;
Une manne funeste, un fiel délicieux ;
Un savoureux poison qui se boit par les yeux ;
Une douce amertume, une douceur amère ;
Une charge à la fois et pesante et légère ;
Une mourante vie, un renaissant trépas ;
Une flamme qui brûle et ne consume pas ;
Un ciel où l'on se plaint, un enfer où l'on s'aime.
Une belle prison qu'on se bâtit soi-même.

OLYMPIE

L'esprit est bien confus alors que le discours
Pour montrer un secret cherche tous ces détours :
C'est d'amour, en un mot, que votre cœur soupire.

Pseudole the gaoler (one of Plautus's *lorarii*) has his love
affair, too, with Hegio's maid Célie, and like the *gracioso* in
the Spanish *comedia* presents a burlesque of the more serious
affection of his betters. A good specimen of Rotrou's humor
is afforded by two scenes (III. 3, and IV. 2), in one of which
Pseudole reveals to his prisoner Tyndare his love for Célie, and
in the other presents in person his completed letter to his mistress. Tyndare has just expressed his fear that Philénie does
not love him, and Pseudole replies :

Je suis fort ignorant en matière d'amour ;
Mais quand le soleil luit, je sais bien qu'il est jour.
Après ce que j'ai vu, douter qu'elle vous aime
Serait douter d'un feu plus clair que le jour même :
Mais pour moi je l'en loue, et cette affection
N'est ni sans jugement ni sans proportion :
Je tiens pour les amants et souffre leur folie,
Depuis l'heureux moment que j'en tiens pour Célie.
Comme eux je l'entretiens de soupirs et de vœux ;
Comme eux j'aime à rêver, je soupire comme eux ;
Je me forge comme eux des chimères cornues,
Fais des châteaux en l'air et bâtis dans les nues ;
Comme eux, pour tout dire, j'ai l'esprit de travers,
Et je deviens plaisant jusqu'à faire des vers.

En voulez-vous entendre ? « O Célie ! ô Célie !
« Je mets le monde aux fers, et ta beauté me lie ;
« De geôlier que j'étais je suis ton prisonnier.»

TYNDARE

Après ?

PSEUDOLE

    Je cherche encor la rime du dernier.
J'en suis demeuré là.

TYNDARE

    La pensée est fort belle.

PSEUDOLE

Mais ce méchant métier trouble bien la cervelle :
Je me laisse emporter jusqu'à suer parfois,
M'arracher les cheveux et me ronger les doigts ;
Et quand j'ai tant rêvé que ma veine en est lasse,
Je déteste la muse et maudis le Parnasse.

However, the verses are completed and offered to Célie :

CÉLIE

Comment, tu fais des vers ?

PSEUDOLE

    Ah ! mon ange, est-ce vous ?

CÉLIE, *en riant*

Mon ange !

PSEUDOLE

Eh bien ! mon ciel, mon soleil, mon aurore !

CÉLIE

J'excuse la fureur qui te possède encore :
Car on dit qu'au métier dont tu te veux mêler,
Certain esprit de feu vous meut, vous fait parler,
Et jusques à tel point quelquefois vous transporte,

Que la raison lui cède et n'est pas la plus forte.
Quoique pauvre servante et qu'assez simple à voir,
Je m'enquête de tout et je veux tout savoir.
Crois-moi, pour ton repos, laisse ta poésie,
Elle t'aurait bientôt brouillé la fantaisie.
Quitte-moi de bonne heure Apollon et sa cour :
Pour être bientôt fou, c'est assez de l'amour.
Cet art donne au plus sage une mauvaise estime :
Prends garde à la raison, et laisse-là la rime.
Mais voyons.

PSEUDOLE

Ils sont beaux, car ils t'ont pour objet.
Qui rencontrerait mal sur un si beau sujet ?

(*Il lit*)

« A Célie, *galimatias*
« Geôlière des geôliers, adorable Célie,
« J'en mets d'autres aux fers, et ta beauté me lie ;
« J'emprisonne le monde, et suis ton prisonnier ;
« Possédant les plaisirs où l'Amour nous convie,
« Et sans cueillir les fruits de l'amoureuse vie,
« Ne laisse pas couler ton âge printanier.»

(*A Célie*)

Que t'en semble ?

CÉLIE

Ils sont beaux et passent mon mérite.

PSEUDOLE

Ce mot de *printanier*, ce me semble, est d'élite ;
Mais trouves-tu mal dit, *geôlière des geôliers* ?
Ce n'est point là parler en termes d'écoliers.
Tels qu'ils sont après tout, ils sont vers de caprice :
On sait bien que cet art n'est pas mon exercice ;
Ce sont fruits de l'amour et de l'oisiveté
Que pour te divertir je voue à ta beauté.
Mais du discours enfin venons-en à la chose,
Des souhaits à l'effet, et des vers à la prose :
Tous deux de sort égal et de condition,
Soyons-les de désir et d'inclination.

Is this not a faint echo of Mascarille's impromptu in the *Précieuses Ridicules*?

In *Les Sosies* Rotrou makes no important changes. He substitutes a long and tiresome prologue by Juno for the one by Mercury attributed to Plautus. Although Rotrou's play is almost an exact translation of the *Amphitruo*, still he has impressed his own genius upon his version. Mercury is the true French witty valet, Alcmene is more refined and dignified, and Jupiter is a less sensual and more impassioned lover. When Molière came to treat the same subject he paid Rotrou the great compliment of imitating him as well as Plautus.[1]

In the *Hercule Mourant* Rotrou has introduced a subsidiary love plot (that of Iole and Arcas), and has disfigured his hero by making him talk like an *habitué* of the Hôtel de Rambouillet. The same tone of gallantry, the same romantic air, distinguishes Rotrou's other imitations of the classical drama, on which I cannot dwell here. The changes which he introduced were all in accord with the taste of his time, as is shown by the fact that so great a poet as Racine adopted them in his turn.[2]

Rotrou's relations to his Italian and Spanish sources have been fully discussed by Stiefel and Steffens, and the two plays in the present edition offer sufficient examples of his method in this field. His imitation is never slavish and he expands a hint of his original into a beautiful passage or scene. A good example of this, the only one I have space for, is in the *Laure Persécutée*, the best, perhaps, of Rotrou's tragi-comedies.

Orantée, son of the king of Hungary, is betrothed to the *infanta* of Poland, but is in love with Laure, a lady of unknown birth. The king, in order to separate his son from his unworthy

---

[1] For Molière's imitation of Rotrou see *Molière, Œuvres*, ed. E. Despois et P. Mesnard, vol. vi, "Amphitrion," and Reinhardstöttner, *op. cit.*, p. 183. The classical scholar will find a pleasant piece of work in comparing the three versions.

[2] See Jarry, *op. cit.*, pp. 126 et seq.

love, orders his arrest, and Laure escapes for the time by assuming the attire of a page.   Orantée's attendant, Octave, concocts
a plot with the help of Laure's confidante and convinces Orantée that his mistress is faithless.   In his misery Orantée cannot
give Laure up, and in the fourth act he is represented at the
door of Laure's house accompanied by his treacherous friend
Octave.   After indulging in his grief in the most exaggerated
manner, he directs Octave to knock at Laure's door.   Octave
exclaims in amazement,

Seigneur!

ORANTÉE
Frappe, te dis-je.

OCTAVE
Mais songez-vous à quoi votre transport m'oblige?

ORANTÉE
Ne me conteste point.

OCTAVE
Quel est votre dessein?

ORANTÉE, tirant son poignard
Fais tôt, ou je te mets ce poignard dans le sein.

OCTAVE
Eh bien, je vais heurter.

ORANTÉE
Non, n'en fais rien, arrête:
Mon honneur me retient quand mon amour est prête,
Et l'une m'aveuglant, l'autre m'ouvre les yeux.

OCTAVE
L'honneur assurément vous conseille le mieux.
Retirons-nous.

ORANTÉE

        Attends que ce transport se passe.
Approche cependant ; sieds-toi, prends cette place,
Et, pour me divertir, cherche en ton souvenir
Quelque histoire d'amour de quoi m'entretenir.

OCTAVE, *assis*

Écoutez donc. Un jour . . .

ORANTÉE

                Un jour cette infidèle
M'a vu l'aimer au point d'oublier tout pour elle ;
Un jour j'ai cru son cœur répondre à mon amour ;
J'ai cru qu'un chaste hymen nous unirait un jour ;
Un jour je me suis vu comblé d'aise et de gloire,
Mais ce jour-là n'est plus. Achève ton histoire.

OCTAVE

Un jour donc, en un bal, un seigneur . . .

ORANTÉE

                Fut-ce moi ?
Car ce fut en un bal qu'elle reçut ma foi ;
Que mes yeux, éblouis de sa première vue,
Adorèrent d'abord cette belle inconnue,
Qu'ils livrèrent mon cœur à l'empire des siens,
Et que j'offris mes bras à mes premiers liens.
Mais quelle tyrannie ai-je enfin éprouvée !
Octave, c'est assez, l'histoire est achevée.

This much admired passage is imitated from Lope de Vega, but let the student compare it with the Spanish : [1]

ORANTEO

. . . llama en esa puerta.

---

[1] I have been obliged to use the Spanish text in Steffens, *Rotrou-Studien*, p. 98, which is very corrupt. I have corrected it as well as I could.

OTAVIO

¿Como señor, que llame dices?

ORANTEO

¡ Llama !

OTAVIO

No me mandes que llame.

ORANTEO

Viva el cielo
Que te atraviese con aquesta daga.

OTAVIO

¡ Yo llamaré !

ORANTEO

No llames, tente, espérate.

OTAVIO

¿ Qué, ya no he de llamar ?

ORANTEO

No, que me vence
Un vergonzoso honor, y en este medio
Que tan ciego me viste, abrió mis ojos,
Y me enseñó mi error, escucha, siéntate.

OTAVIO

¿ Adonde ?

ORANTEO

En este suelo.

OTAVIO

Por mí siéntome.

ORANTEO

¿ Entretenerme en algo no pudieras ?

OTAVIO

Si hiciera luna, no faltaran naipes.

ORANTEO

Cuéntame un cuento.

OTAVIO

Un cuento, soy contento.
Ya ya comienzo: Érase que se era . . .

ORANTEO

Dí que era hoy, quando era yo con Laura,
Mas acabaste el cuento.

Rotrou has communicated to his scene a poetical spirit and sentiment which remind us of Shakespeare.

It is now time to turn to other characteristics of Rotrou, such as style, language, versification, and technique. It will, however, be necessary first to say something about the society of the day which is reflected in the plays of Rotrou.

The refinement in French society in the seventeenth century which culminated in the *précieux* movement was largely due, as is well known, to the Hôtel de Rambouillet, which represents the stream of Italian influence. This Italian influence modified profoundly the forms of social life, introducing into France the diversions of Italy and, above all, the conception of Platonic love.[1] This conception of love is embodied in d'Urfé's famous romance of *Astrée*, and the later modifications of it are represented in Mlle. de Scudéry's novels *Le Grand Cyrus* and *Clélie*. These novels reproduce undoubtedly the tone of polite conversation and " their characters speak the language of the Hôtel de Rambouillet and the *Samedis*, and

---

[1] I have treated this subject in the introduction to my *La Société française au dix-septième siècle*, New York, 1889, and in my edition of Boileau's *Les Héros de Roman*, Boston, 1902.

as these romances purposely depict the society of the seventeenth century, Cyrus, Alexander, and Brutus make love in the affected style from which the heroes of Corneille and Racine are not free and into which Molière himself frequently falls." [1]

From the time of *Mélite* (1629) the French drama endeavored to represent the conversation of polite society and to assume the tone of gallantry which characterized it. The consequence was a conventional mode of expression which frequently impairs the enjoyment of even the masterpieces of the French classical drama. The very vocabulary has become formal and conventional, and *feu* (*feux*), *flamme* (*flammes*), are the usual synonyms of *amour*. Corneille makes old Horace, (*Horace*, II. 7), say, "Écoutez-vous vos flammes," i.e. the objects of your love. Both Corneille and Rotrou use *brasier* and *braise* in the same sense. We find also the frequent formulas : *allumer le feu, allumer la flamme,* "to cause love"; *beau feu, belle flamme,* "love"; *les fers, les chaînes,* "the fetters of love" or simply "love," etc. For example, in *Laure Persécutée*, III. 8,

---

[1] See my edition of Boileau's *Les Héros de Roman*, p. 132. Brunetière, "Corneille et le théâtre espagnol," *Revue des deux mondes*, January 1, 1903, p. 201, has the following remark which confirms my earlier statement : "L'amour, dans le théâtre de Corneille, n'est habituellement que de la "galanterie"; et, de cette "galanterie," dans une société qui vivait, comme la société de l'hôtel de Rambouillet, les intrigues amoureuses de l'*Astrée*, de l'*Endymion* ou du *Polexandre*, le poète, pour en trouver autour de lui des modèles, n'avait qu'à ouvrir les yeux. C'est à cet égard encore qu'il est bien de son temps, et du monde où il fréquente. La "galanterie," dans le théâtre de Corneille, ne se sépare point du langage qui lui sert d'expression, et on n'aime point tant chez lui les belles personnes, que la beauté des sentimens qu'elles inspirent, ou l'honneur qu'elles font à leurs galans de s'en laisser aimer." Some excellent remarks on "galanterie" may also be found in Saint-Marc Girardin, *Cours de littérature dramatique*, Paris, 1886, vol. iii, pp. 102 et seq., and Horion, *Explication du théâtre classique*, Paris, 1888, pp. 153, 213, 361, 392, and 627. This valuable work of Horion is indispensable for the teacher of the French classical drama, and I am much indebted to it in this Introduction.

Orantée, supposing Laure to be faithless, tells his father that he is ready to accept the match he has proposed for him :

> Tous mes fers sont brisés, toute ma flamme est morte :
> Choisissez les liens qu'il vous plaît que je porte ;
> Ordonnez-moi le feu qui brûlera mon cœur ;
> Le triomphe tout prêt n'attend que le vainqueur.

So *bel œil, beaux yeux,* for the object of one's affection, a beautiful woman, as in *Horace,* II. 5 :

> Que les pleurs d'une amante ont de puissants discours !
> Et qu'un bel œil est fort avec un tel secours !

And in *Polyeucte,* I. 1 :

> Sur mes pareils, Néarque, un bel œil est bien fort.

And in the same work, II. 1 :

> Pourrai-je voir Pauline et rendre à ses beaux yeux
> L'hommage souverain que l'on va rendre aux Dieux ?

It is unnecessary to cite other formulas relating to different subjects.[1] The use of the figure of oxymoron is frequent, as in *Horace,* III. 2, " ces cruels généreux " ; *Cinna,* III. 3, " cette aimable inhumaine."

The fashionable theory of love could be reconstructed from many passages like those in *Horace,* III. 4 :

> Je le vois bien, ma sœur, vous n'aimâtes jamais ;
> Vous ne connaissez point ni l'amour ni ses traits :
> On peut lui résister quand il commence à naître,
> Mais non pas le bannir quand il s'est rendu maître,
> Et que l'aveu d'un père, engageant notre foi,
> A fait de ce tyran un légitime roi :
> Il entre avec douceur, mais il règne par force ;
> Et, quand l'âme une fois a goûté son amorce,
> Vouloir ne plus aimer, c'est ce qu'elle ne peut,
> Puisqu'elle ne peut plus vouloir que ce qu'il veut :
> Ses chaînes sont pour nous aussi fortes que belles.

---

[1] This has been done by G. H. Kinne, *Formulas in the Language of the French Poet-Dramatists of the Seventeenth Century,* Boston, 1891, a dissertation for the doctor's degree at Strasburg.

And the following from *Cinna*, III. 1 :

> L'amour rend tout permis.
> Un véritable amant ne connaît point d'amis;
> Et même avec justice on peut trahir un traître
> Qui pour une maîtresse ose trahir son maître.[1]

It is unnecessary to cite any more examples. The play of *Venceslas* is full of the various expressions of gallantry, and they have been indicated in the notes.

The exaggerated use of antitheses is also found in Rotrou, who, in this respect, only follows the example of his contemporaries. The student will recall the numerous instances in Corneille's *Horace*, such as in I. 2 :

> Ce jour nous fut propice et funeste à la fois ;
> Unissant nos maisons, il désunit nos rois :
> Un même instant conclut notre hymen et la guerre,
> Fit naître notre espoir et le jeta par terre.

Rotrou in *Venceslas*, l. 769, speaks of

> Efforts d'un cœur mortel pour d'immortels appas,

and in l. 1588 :

> Et vos bras me sont-ils des faveurs ou des chaînes?

The most conspicuous example of the use of antitheses has already been given in the extract from *Les Captifs* on p. 60.

Exaggerated expressions and *précieux* language are frequent, as, for example, *Saint Genest*, ll. 621–622 :

> Et vous voudriez souffrir que dans cet accident
> Ce soleil de beauté trouvât son occident?

and l. 1059 :

> Le fer, solide sang des veines de la terre.

---

[1] Hémon, *Théâtre de Pierre Corneille*, Paris, 1886, vol. ii, " Cinna," ll. 735–736, compares with this passage three from Rotrou:

L'amour excuse tout.	*Clorinde*, IV. 3.
Qui pèche par amour pèche légèrement.	*Crisante*, II. 4.
L'amour fait tout commettre et fait tout excuser.	*Célie*, V. 3.

The use of sententious expressions, which dates back to
Garnier and the imitation of Seneca's tragedies, is also common.[1] Examples are found in *Saint Genest*, ll. 199–201 :

> Ainsi souvent le Ciel conduit tout à tel point
> Que ce qu'on craint arrive, et qu'il n'afflige point,
> Et que ce qu'on redoute est enfin ce qu'on aime ;

and in *Venceslas*, ll. 646–650 :

> Mais les difficultés sont le champ des vertus ;
> Avec un peu de peine on achète la gloire.
> Qui veut vaincre est déjà bien près de la victoire ;
> Se faisant violence, on s'est bientôt dompté,
> Et rien n'est tant à nous que notre volonté.

Rotrou also plays upon words frequently, as in *Venceslas*,
ll. 679–682 :

> Je mettrai de ma main mon rival en ma place,
> Et je verrai leur flamme avec autant de glace
> Qu'en ma plus violente et plus sensible ardeur
> Cet insensible objet eut pour moi de froideur.[2]

The language and construction of Rotrou are those of the
first half of the seventeenth century, while Vaugelas and the
Academy were establishing the rules which have since prevailed.[3] Many words have changed their meaning or disappeared altogether, genders have changed, many verbs are
construed differently from the present usage, the rules for the
inflection of the present participle were not yet fixed, the distinction between the adverbial and prepositional use of certain

---

[1] See notes to the passages cited in text.

[2] For other examples of play upon words see Jarry, *op. cit.*, p. 271.

[3] I have used for grammatical references, as the most accessible to
the student, Haase, *Syntaxe française du xviie siècle, traduite par M.
Obert*, Paris, 1888. The number of the sections corresponds with that
of the original German edition, Oppeln and Leipzig, 1888. A convenient
résumé may be found in Brunot, " La Langue de 1600 à 1660," in Petit
de Julleville, *Hist. de la langue et de la litt. française*, vol. iv. For special
works on Rotrou's grammar and lexicography see Bibliography.

words had not yet been made, and the use of the negative particles differed considerably from the present custom. Examples of the above are indicated in the notes of the present edition and are grouped in the special index.

When Rotrou began his poetical career in 1628 the principal rules which were to govern French versification for two centuries had already been established by Malherbe.[1] These rules regard the avoidance of the hiatus, the *enjambement*, rhyme, inversion, and poetic licenses. It is impossible to examine in detail here the prosody of Rotrou, and I shall confine my remarks almost entirely to the plays in the present edition. It may be said in general that these plays, written at the end of the first half of the century, conform almost exactly to the established rules, and do not differ from the plays of Rotrou's contemporaries, Corneille, etc.

The hiatus is carefully avoided, as by Corneille (Souriau, p. 123). The division of syllables differs occasionally from modern usage and from Corneille's. *Fléau, Saint Genest* 379, 1005, is a monosyllable, the seventeenth-century pronunciation being *flô*. The second person plural ending -*iez* is one syllable : *Saint Genest* 1, *Venceslas* 371, *sauriez* ; but in *Saint Genest* 621 *voudriez* is scanned as three syllables, where the same word in *Venceslas* 471 is two syllables, and so generally, though in *Venceslas* 474, 774, *feriez* and *osiez* are counted as of two syllables (same usage in Corneille, Souriau, p. 120). So with the termination -*ions*, which is considered one syllable, *Saint Genest* 1736, *souffrions* (Souriau, p. 120). Rotrou uses *meurtrier, Venceslas* 1375, 1388, 1508, 1858, as a dissyllable,

---

[1] See M. Souriau, *L'Évolution du vers français au dix-septième siècle*, Paris, 1893. There is no work on Rotrou's verse, and the brief remarks of Jarry, *op. cit.*, p. 298, are all that I have been able to find on the subject. It is taken for granted that the student is acquainted with the ordinary rules of French versification and with the structure of the seventeenth-century Alexandrine verse.

contrary to Corneille's usage (Souriau, p. 120), who gives the word three syllables, which is the present usage.

The most noticeable feature of Rotrou's rhyme is the frequency of "rich rhyme," or rhyme which involves the similarity of the preceding consonant, e.g. *empire–soupire*. Of the 875 couplets in *Saint Genest*, 404, or nearly one half, end in rich rhyme; and of the 933 couplets in *Venceslas*, 440, a somewhat smaller percentage, end in the same kind of rhyme. It is true that in this computation I have included what may be called "obligatory rich rhyme," such as the endings in *é, er, ée, i, ie, u,* and *ment,* which require the similarity of the preceding consonant, the so-called *consonne d'appui*. Examples of the above are so frequent in both plays that instances need not be quoted here. Still, when this large class of obligatory rich rhymes is deducted it leaves so great a proportion of rich rhymes that it is evident that the poet is seeking them. A certain number of "double" or "superfluous" rhymes (called also *rimes opulentes*) are to be found in Rotrou: *Saint Genest* 371–372, *exciter–réciter*; 789–790, *détroner–couronner*; 833–834, *absolu–résolu*; 999–1000, *assurée–azurée*; *Venceslas* 1113–1114, *contenir–obtenir*, etc.

In general, Rotrou allows himself the same liberties taken by Corneille, and rhymes, *Venceslas* 1389–1390, *interdit–dit* (Souriau, p. 130, rhyme of simple and compound), and similarly, *Saint Genest* 817–818, *Dieu–adieu*. So with words derived from the same root, *Saint Genest* 1393–1394, *remis–commis* (Souriau, p. 131). Rotrou, like Corneille, constantly rhymes long and short vowels: *Venceslas* 1175–1176, *Madame–âme*; *Saint Genest* 133–134, *audace–grâce*; 507–508, *âge–hommage*; *Venceslas* 287–288, *satisfasse–grâce* (Souriau, p. 135). The so-called "Normandy rhyme," frequent in Corneille, is seldom found in Rotrou; examples are, however, found in *Saint Genest* 1017–1018, *triompher–fer*; 1473–1474, *cher–toucher*; *Venceslas* 1405–1406, *toucher–cher* (Souriau, p. 137). A few special cases

are the rhyme of *étois* with *voix* in *Saint Genest* 435–436
(Souriau, p. 134) and the frequent rhyme of words now pronounced differently, such as, *Venceslas* 1649–1650, 1737–
1738, 1785–1786, *ennemis–fils* (Souriau, p. 142). Rotrou,
like Corneille, frequently rhymes a diphthong in which synær-
esis has taken place with one divided by diæresis (Souriau,
p. 136) : *Saint Genest* 447–448, 501–502, 593–594, *glorieux–cieux* ; 521–522, 605–606, 1097–1098, *précieux–cieux* ;
649–650, *furieux–dieux* ; 749–750, *dieux–aïeux* ; 1409–
1410, *contageux–dieux* ; *Venceslas* 57–58, *yeux–odieux* ; 521–
522, *vicieux–yeux* ; 617–618, *séditieux–yeux* ; 637–638, *yeux–
furieux* ; 1529–1530, *yeux–glorieux*, etc.

Rotrou also employs the trite and hackneyed rhymes so
frequently used by Corneille : *Saint Genest* 5–6, *songes–mensonges* ; 1635–1636, *hommes–sommes* ; 787–788, *terre–tonnerre*
(Souriau, p. 132) ; likewise, not frequently, the adverbial rhyme,
Venceslas 665–666, *seulement–bassement* ; and the infinitive in
-er : *Saint Genest* 371–372, *exciter–réciter*, *Venceslas* 741–742,
juger–ranger ; 773–774, *éclater–tenter*, etc. Rotrou also follows
Corneille's example in the use of adjectives in rhyme, but not
so frequently : *Venceslas* 1411–1412, *capable–coupable* ; *Saint
Genest* 639–640, *souhaitable–coupable* ; 1207–1208, *sensible–
invincible*, etc.

In general, Rotrou's rhymes are correct and varied, and a
large proportion of them belong to the more difficult class of
rimes riches. I have noted only a few incorrect or unsatisfactory rhymes, such as *Venceslas* 1365–1366, *jamais–succès* ;
1679–1680, *prévue–vaincue* ; 673–674, *confusion–nom*.

In regard to the cæsura Rotrou conforms, like Corneille, to
the rule of Malherbe that the cæsura should never separate
two words connected by meaning and grammatical construction. I have noticed no violation of this rule and no tendency
on the part of Rotrou to shift the cæsura to any other position
than the hemistich, or sixth syllable of the Alexandrine verse.

Rotrou follows also with great care the rule which forbids *enjambement*, or the running over from one line to the next of the sense or meaning, unless it fills the whole of the line into which it overflows. It must be remembered, however, that *enjambement* is permitted where the sense is interrupted or suspended. There are many examples of this in both plays, e.g. *Saint Genest* 950–951; *Venceslas* 353–354; 360–361; 717–718; 908–909; 930–931; 1265–1266; 1467–1468; 1469–1470; 1509–1510; 1532–1533; 1757–1758, etc. There is also a partial *enjambement* which is permitted. This is where the *rejet*, or overflow, consists of proper names, titles, apostrophes, in some cases verbs, which are thrown over into the second line with which they have no definite connection. I have noticed no case of this in *Saint Genest*; in *Venceslas* there is one, 286–287. Of actual *enjambement* there are very few cases. The following are all I have observed: *Saint Genest* 657–658, where, however, the *rejet* fills the hemistich (Souriau, p. 162), as is also the case in 669–670. The cases of formal *enjambement* are more frequent in *Venceslas*, e.g. 1019–1020, where, however, the *rejet* fills the hemistich and is the permissible *rejet* of address, and 1235–1236, where the *enjambement* might be considered the result of suspension or interruption; the same may be said of 1295–1296; in 1312–1313 the *rejet* fills the hemistich, as is also the case with 1527–1528. These are the few exceptions to the strict rule of the seventeenth century on the subject of the *enjambement*, and these few instances belong to what may be called the permissible *enjambement*.

The very few so-called "poetic licenses," affecting orthography, inversion, etc., are treated in the notes and need not be repeated here. In conclusion, it may be said that Rotrou's verse is easy and correct and that he deviates from the strict rules of his day less frequently than Corneille.

IV

Corneille's tragedy of *Polyeucte* was performed towards the end of the year 1640, some five years before Rotrou's *Saint Genest*.[1] It is not likely that Rotrou was directly inspired by Corneille to compose a Christian tragedy. The success of *Polyeucte*, however, encouraged a number of mediocre writers to compose plays of a class that had fallen into disrepute since the decree of Parlement in 1548.[2] The immediate cause of Rotrou's drama was probably a play by Desfontaines entitled *L'Illustre comédien ou le martyre de Saint Genest*.[3] The author,

---

[1] *Œuvres*, ed. Marty-Laveaux (*Les Grands Écrivains de la France*), vol. iii, p. 468. Hémon, *Théâtre de Pierre Corneille*, "Polyeucte," p. 26, maintains that it was at the beginning of 1643.

[2] See p. 6 of present work. An account of this revival will be found in P. V. Delaporte, *Du merveilleux dans la littérature française sous le règne de Louis XIV*, Paris, 1891, pp. 334 et seq.; Hémon, *Théâtre de Pierre Corneille*, "Polyeucte," pp. 12 et seq.; and Horion, *Explication du théâtre classique*, pp. 263 et seq. I have not been able to see Delavigne, *La tragédie chrétienne au xviie siècle*, Toulouse, 1847.

[3] A full analysis of Desfontaines's play is given in the Appendix, and the student can judge for himself whether Rotrou is indebted to it. A comparison of the play of Desfontaines with *Polyeucte* would be very

who flourished in the first half of the seventeenth century, is believed to have been born at Caen, but nothing is known of his birth, profession, or the time of his death.[1] He was the author of some fifteen plays, several of them on religious subjects, of little literary worth. The play in question was printed in 1645, the *privilège* being dated " dernier Avril, 1645," and the *achevé d'imprimer* the 8th of May, 1645. In the *Advis au Lecteur* the author says that he has been obliged to follow his Royal Highness on his journey to Bourbon and consequently was unable to see his play through the press or to furnish the usual preliminary *épître*. Person thinks that the journey to Bourbon probably occupied the early months of 1645, and that therefore the play of Desfontaines was written or performed in 1644.[2] Rotrou's play was printed in 1647, the *privilège* being dated March 2, 1647, and the *achevé d'imprimer* May 26, 1647. Stiefel[3] places the date of composition in 1645, after the play of Desfontaines, and before the *Théodore* (1645) of Corneille. The title of Rotrou's play would seem to indicate that it was subsequent to that of Desfontaines.[4] This was not the first time that Rotrou had been inspired by Desfontaines. In 1644 Rotrou printed his tragi-comedy of *Bélisaire*, which three years

---

instructive. It would be seen that the fourth act of Desfontaines follows closely Corneille's play.

[1] Desfontaines was a member of the company of Molière's Illustre Théâtre in 1644. See E. Soulié, *Recherches sur Molière et sur sa famille*, Paris, 1863, p. 38, and " Document X," p. 175 in same work.

[2] *Histoire du Véritable Saint-Genest*, p. 79.

[3] *Über die Chronologie*, etc., p. 46.

[4] Person, *Histoire du Véritable Saint-Genest*, p. 79. Bernardin, *Devant le rideau*, Paris, 1901, p. 134, says: " Fut-elle représentée? J'en doute; car la pièce de Rotrou est intitulée *Le Véritable Saint Genest*, conformément à l'habitude prise par les libraries d'alors pour distinguer les pièces " vraiment représentées " de celles sur les mêmes sujets qu'ils appelaient "contrefaites." Mais il est probable du moins que ce fut l'œuvre si médiocre de Desfontaines, imprimée en 1645, qui donna à Rotrou l'idée de lire la pièce espagnole et d'en tirer son *Saint Genest*."

before had been preceded by a play on the same subject by Desfontaines.[1]

Although Desfontaines was the immediate source of Rotrou's inspiration, it was Lope de Vega who furnished the general plan of *Le Véritable Saint Genest* by his *comedia de santos*, *Lo Fingido Verdadero*.[2] This play has been printed but twice, — in *Parte xvi* of the *Comedias*, Madrid, 1621 and 1622, and in the fourth volume of the *Obras de Lope de Vega publicadas por la Real Academia Española*, Madrid, 1894. As the play contains no *figura del donayre* or *gracioso*, it may, according to Rennert, be considered as dating from before 1600. It is, however, possible that this figure was deliberately omitted.[3] The play is not mentioned in the original list (1603) of his dramas published by Lope de Vega himself in *El Peregrino en su Patria*, but is contained in the supplementary list in the sixth edition (1618).[4] The latest editor, Menéndez y Pelayo, contents himself with saying, after mentioning the above facts, that the play in question was consequently written before 1618.[5]

The same editor says (p. xl) that Lope de Vega probably took his plot from the *Vida de San Ginés representante, mártir*, contained in the *Flos Sanctorum* of P. Rivadeneira.[6] The source of Rivadeneira's version of the legend is the *Passio Sancti Genesii mimi* in Ruinart's *Acta Martyrum*.[7] As the

---

[1] *Über die Chronologie*, etc.. p. 44.

[2] It is difficult to translate the title of Lope's play. It refers, of course, to Genest's feigning to be converted and afterwards being really converted. A sufficient translation is " Pretense become Truth."

[3] Rennert, *The Life of Lope de Vega*, Philadelphia, 1904, p. 489.

[4] *Ibid.*, pp. 476 et seq.

[5] *Obras de Lope de Vega publicadas por la Real Academia Española*, Madrid, 1894, p. xxxix.

[6] Vol. ii, p. 375. Menéndez y Pelayo reprints this "Vida" in the work cited, pp. xl-xliii.

[7] I have used the edition of Ratisbon, 1859, p. 312. Ruinart's version is reprinted in the *Acta Sanctorum*, August 25, August, vol. v, p. 122, with variants from a manuscript of Utrecht.

legend is a brief one, I give the following translation for the use of those to whom Ruinart and the *Acta Sanctorum* are not accessible.

The Passion of Saint Genest

1. The blessed Genest was the chief in Rome in the art of acting, and used to stand and sing on a platform called *themele*, and imitate the actions of men. One day the emperor Diocletian, as a cruel tyrant who hated the Christians, wished to give an exhibition of the mysteries of the Christian religion. In the presence of the emperor and of all the people who were gathered for that purpose Genest, reclining on the stage as though he were ill, demanded baptism, and acted the play in these words: " Ho! friends, I feel heavy, I wish to be lightened." They answered: " How can we make you light, if you are heavy? Are we carpenters to plane you down?" These words aroused the laughter of the people.

2. Genest replied: " Fools, I wish to die a Christian." " Why?" they asked. To whom Genest replied: " That I may be found in that day as one who has fled to God." A priest and an exorcist were immediately summoned, and, by the inspiration of God, Genest became a believer. When the others sat down about his bed they asked him: " Son, why did you send for us?" Genest, no longer feigning, but with a sincere heart, replied: " Because I desire to receive the grace of Christ, that, regenerated by it, I may be saved from being destroyed by my sins." When they had performed the mysteries of the sacraments and put on him a white robe, he was seized by the soldiers, as a part of the play, and presented to the emperor in order that he might argue about the name of Christ after the fashion of the holy martyrs. Standing on an elevated spot, he thus addressed the assembly:

3. " Give ear, emperor, and all the army, wise men and people of this city! Whenever I heard even the name 'Christian' I shuddered and mocked those who persisted in their belief. Even my parents and relatives I detested for the sake of the name 'Christian,' and held the Christians in such derision that I carefully scrutinized their mysteries that I might perform before you a play made out of their sanctification. But when the water touched my body and in answer to the question I replied that I believed, I saw above

me a hand coming down from heaven, and shining angels standing over me, who read from a book all the sins of my youth and washed them in the same water with which I was sprinkled in your presence, and afterwards showed me the book whiter than snow.[1] Now therefore, glorious emperor, and all ye people, who have beheld these mysteries, believe with me that Christ is the true Lord; He is the light and the truth, He is merciful, and through Him you may obtain forgiveness."

4. At these words the Emperor Diocletian, furiously angry, after Genest had been cruelly beaten, delivered him up to the prefect Plautianus in order that he might be forced to offer sacrifice to the gods.[2] After he had been stretched upon the rack and tortured by prolonged rending by the "claws," he was also burned with flames. He persisted, however, in his belief, declaring: "There is no king but the One I have seen and I adore and worship Him, and if for His worship I should be slain a thousand times I shall be His as I was at first. The tortures cannot tear Christ from my lips and heart. Truly, indeed, I grieve that I sinned in shuddering at His holy name in saintly men, and that like a rude soldier I began very late to adore the true king." He won the crown of martyrdom by decapitation. Then the prefect Plautianus, hearing these words, ordered him to be beheaded instantly. The blessed martyr Genest was beheaded the 25th of August, under the dominion of our Lord Jesus Christ, who lives and reigns for ever and ever. Amen.[3]

---

[1] In the Utrecht MS. the version is: "When therefore I was baptized with water, and likewise the book sprinkled, it was made whiter than snow, so that it showed not even a sign of the former writing."

[2] In the Utrecht MS. is the following version: "Then the emperor's fury was kindled and he ordered all the actors who had performed with Genest to be brought into his presence and severely beaten with rods, supposing that they likewise were believers. But they began to blaspheme the holy name and said with curses: 'We had different intentions; he has become mad, and abandoned his happiness to assume the sorrows of Christianity. For this reason let him alone suffer what he alone has done.' Then the emperor, more fiercely enraged against Genest," etc.

[3] Another version cited by Mostert, *Ausgaben und Abhandlungen*, xciii, p. 51, says: "Complevit autem martirium suum in bona confessione sanctus Genesius sub die viii K. Septembris, sub Diocletiano imperatore, regnante domino nostro Jesu Cristo."

The date of the martyrdom of Saint Genest is assigned to
the year A.D. 303 by Baronius,[1] but Ruinart thinks that it took
place earlier, although it is not certain when it occurred.[2]

The legend of Saint Genest was popular during the Middle
Ages, and a mystery *L'Ystoyre et la vie de Saint Genis* has
been preserved.[3]

Rotrou is not original even in the play intercalated in *Saint
Genest*, but has borrowed it from L. Cellot, from whom he took

---

[1] *Annales ecclesiastici*, Barri-Ducis, 1864, vol. iii, p. 404.

[2] Tillemont, *Mémoires pour servir à l'histoire ecclésiastique*, Paris,
1701, vol. iv, p. 694, contends that Diocletian was not in Rome from
A.D. 286 to A.D. 303, and then not until November. It is better, he
thinks, to place the date in A.D. 285 or 286. The Bollandists, *Acta
Sanct.*, August, vol. v, p. 119, place it indefinitely: "exeunte seculo iii
aut ineunte iv." Allard, *La Persécution de Dioclétien*, Paris, 1890, vol. iv,
p. 11, note 3, inclines to the date A.D. 285.

[3] This mystery of the fifteenth century is described in Petit de
Julleville, *Les Mystères*, Paris, 1880, vol. ii, pp. 520 et seq., and an analysis and extracts are given by Person, *Histoire du Véritable Saint-Genest*,
pp. 7, 86, 97–103. The complete mystery has been edited by W. Mostert and E. Stengel and published in *Ausgaben und Abhandlungen*,
xciii, Marburg, 1895. Some remarks are there given on the popularity
of the legend, and a Latin *Passio Sancti Genesii*, somewhat different
from the one given by Ruinart, is compared with the text of the
mystery. The martydom of Saint Genest has also been the subject of
an oratorio by the German composer Löwe, the text of which is given
in *Damaris, Eine Zeitschrift von Ludwig Giesebrecht*, Stettin, 1860,
"Der heilige Genesius in der Legende, im Drama und im Oratorium,"
pp. 297–322. The article is a popular one and compares the legend,
the play by Rotrou, and the oratorio. I have not been able to see V.
Jacob, "La Légende de St. Genest," in *L'Austrasie*, Metz, 1856, vol. iv,
pp. 277–284. For further references to Saint Genest see U. Chevalier,
*Répertoire des sources historiques du Moyen Age: Bio-Bibliographie.
Nouvelle édition*, Paris, 1905, vol. i, p. 1690. Chevalier gives A.D. 286
as date of martyrdom. Saint Genest was not the only actor who was
converted while ridiculing on the stage the mysteries of the Christian
religion. There were at least three others, — Saint Gelasius or Gelasinus
(*Acta Sanct.*, February 27, February, vol. iii, p. 680), Saint Ardalio (*Acta
Sanct.*, April 14, April, vol. ii, p. 213) and Saint Porphyrius (*Acta Sanct.*,
September 15, September, vol. v, p. 37).

three years later his last great tragedy, *Cosroès*.[1] Cellot's play, *Sanctus Adrianus, Martyr*, from which extracts are given in the Appendix,[2] is based on the legend in the *Acta Sanctorum*, September 8, September, vol. iii, p. 218.[3]

The legend of Saint Adrian is too long to be given here, but the headings of the five chapters may prove of interest.

---

[1] Louis Cellot was born at Paris in 1588 and entered the Jesuit order in 1605. For many years he was a teacher of Hebrew, Greek, and Latin. He was the head of several colleges belonging to the order and was provincial of France. He died at Paris on the 20th of October, 1658. He wrote four plays, an epic, and miscellaneous poetry, all in Latin, besides various theological works. A list of his writings, as well as a more detailed biography, will be found in *Bibliothèque des écrivains de la compagnie de Jésus par A. de Backer et C. Sommervogel*, Liège et Paris, 1869, vol. i, coll. 1159–1160. See also Stiefel's article, "Jean Rotrou's *Cosroès* und seine Quellen" in *Zeitschrift für franz. Spr. und Lit.*, vol. xxiii, pp. 69–188. Stiefel in the *Literaturblatt für germ. und roman. Philologie*, 1884, coll. 284–287, suggests as a possible source Lope de Vega's play *San Adrian y Natalia*, which, however, has not been preserved. He also suggests the possible use of the play. *El mejor representante, San Gines*, by Cancer, Rosete, and Martinez, which was not published, however, until 1668. It might have circulated earlier in manuscript, but I am assured by Mr. Gordon who read the play for me in London that Rotrou made no use of it. I have since read the play in the Ticknor collection in the Boston Public Library and I agree with Mr. Gordon.

[2] Some additional extracts are given by Person in *Les papiers de Pierre Rotrou de Saudreville*, pp. 108–123.

[3] There are other versions in Surius, *Vitae sanct.*, 1618, vol. ix, pp. 88–93, and Voragine, *Legenda aurea*, ed. Graesse, 1846, pp. 597–601. See also the *Breviarium Romanum*, September 8. It is possible that Rotrou may have used two works that I have not been able to see: G. Hardigny, *La vie et miracles de St. Adrien*, Luxemburg, 1636, and B. Ruteau, *Vie et martyre de St. Adrien*, Athies, 1637. There is no question, however, about Rotrou's use of Cellot's tragedy. For further references to Saint Adrian see U. Chevalier, *Répertoire des sources historiques*, vol. i, p. 54. The date of Saint Adrian's martyrdom is given as A.D. 303 at Nicomedia by Chevalier, "circa A.D. 310" by the Bollandists. There is a fifteenth-century mystery on Saint Adrian, for which see Petit de Julleville, *Les Mystères*, vol. ii, pp. 36, 466–467. The *Revue des langues romanes*, 1890, pp. 269–280, contains a thirteenth-century Provençal prose version of a *Passio Sancti Adriani Martyris*.

" I. Maximian fostering idolatry at Nicodemia, twenty-three Christians are arrested and, having boldly proclaimed their faith, are subjected to various torments. II. Adrian joins the martyrs and is thrown into prison with them. Natalia, his wife, visits him, and encourages him to endure martyrdom. She is visited by him. Adrian having bribed the jailers, returns home to Natalia, who, suspecting him of escaping from prison, upbraids him, but when she understands the cause of his coming accompanies him back to prison. III. Natalia serves Adrian and the other martyrs in prison. Adrian, with the others, is led before Maximian and bravely endures various torments. IV. Natalia, with other women, serves the martyrs in prison, assuming for the purpose the dress of a man. Martyrdom of Adrian and the other saints. V. The bodies of the saints are miraculously snatched from the flames and carried to Byzantium by the Christians. Natalia is sought in marriage, but flees to Byzantium and there dies near the bodies of the martyrs."

After this general account of the sources of Rotrou's *Saint Genest*, it will now be proper to consider Rotrou's use of his principal source, Lope de Vega's *Lo Fingido Verdadero*. It may be said at once that there are very important differences between the French and Spanish plays, resulting from the different dramatic theories of the two countries. The entire first act of the Spanish play is taken up with the events which lead to the accession of the emperor Diocletian. The Roman army is in Asia under the command of the emperor Aurelian, who has with him one son, Numerianus ; the other, Carinus, a profligate, is at Rome. The soldiers complain of the fatigues and dangers to which they are exposed by the emperor. Two of the officers, Maximian and Diocletian, also express similar feelings. A peasant girl, Camila, enters, selling bread, and Diocletian, who has no money, offers to pay her when he is emperor of Rome. Camila predicts that he will become emperor when he has killed a wild boar (*jabalí*). A storm bursts and the emperor Aurelian is killed by a thunderbolt. His son Numerianus is proclaimed consul by the soldiers and by his father-in-law Apro.

The scene changes to Rome, where Carinus is shown, roaming about the streets at night with two musicians, a servant Celio, and Rosarda dressed as a man. The band calls on Ginés, who is represented as *un gran letrado*, "a great scholar." He is copying the parts of a comedy by "Aristoceles" on the subject of Pasiphae. Incidentally he informs Carinus that his best actress has become a Christian and gone to do penance in the deserts (*peñas*) of Marseilles. On leaving Ginés Carinus is attacked and killed by the consul Lelius, whose wife he has wronged.

The Roman army returns to Rome on account of the illness of Numerianus, who is carried in a closed litter. His father-in-law Apro confesses to Felisardo that he has killed Numerianus in order to reign in his stead. When the death of Numerianus is discovered Apro asks the army to elect him emperor, but Felisardo reveals Apro's crime, and Diocletian, recalling the prediction of Camila, slays Apro (= Latin *aper* = Spanish *jabalí*, wild boar) and is proclaimed emperor.

Rotrou has not used any part of Lope de Vega's first act, owing to the necessity of limiting the action of his play on account of the unities. As a concession to the gallantry of the day he begins his play with the marriage of the emperor's daughter, and only incidentally refers in ll. 25–30 to Diocletian's humble marriage.

Lope's second act begins with the arrangements for the celebration of the accession of Diocletian, who appoints Maximian as Caesar and associates him with himself in the government of the empire. Camila enters and asks, as a reward for the bread which she gave to Diocletian, the privilege of free access at all times to the emperor. The actor Ginés appears and is asked to furnish a comedy for the celebration. He suggests a number of plays, the *Andria*, the *Miles Gloriosus*, etc., which the emperor declines with a curious statement of his taste in regard to the drama : " Give me a new plot (*fábula*) which contains more invention, although it lacks art. For I have the taste of a Spaniard in this matter, and provided they offer me what is probable I never consider carefully the rules; their strictness rather wearies me, and I have noticed that those who take pains to observe the art never attain to nature."

Diocletian leaves the choice to Ginés, saying, however, that he hears that Ginés's greatest success is in the rôle of lover. Ginés is left with Pinabelo, the member of his troupe who acts the part of servants, and in the interview which follows we learn that Ginés is in love with Marcela, an actress of his company, who, however, has bestowed her affections on Octavio, a fellow-actor. Pinabelo recommends the dismissal of Octavio, and that Ginés should ask Marcela's hand of her father. Ginés replies that the former is impossible, and as to the latter, " Marriage is a union of the wills, and union is impossible where characters are different." He further states that the comedy which he has arranged for performance before the emperor is written to allow him, Ginés, to express his love for Marcela and to illtreat Octavio.

The emperor, Maximian, Camila, and two senators take their seats and the performance begins with a *loa*, or compliment to the emperor. After this the play begins, consisting of several scenes between Ginés (Rufino), Marcela (Fabia), Fabricio (Tebandro), Octavio, and Pinabelo as servant, in which the principal actors at times forget their rôles and express their own feelings of love and jealousy. At the end Celio informs Ginés that Fabia and Octavio have fled and Ginés bursts into a passion of jealousy and rage. The emperor is delighted with this exhibition of Ginés's powers, but is informed by the senator Lelio that this is nothing in comparison with Ginés's ability to represent the part of a Christian. The emperor commands Ginés the next day to represent, by way of mockery, one of those who refuse the incense due to Mars, Venus, Jupiter, and Mercury, in order that he may see a lifelike picture of a Christian firm amid so many tortures. The act concludes with the entrance of Fabricio, the real as well as the feigned father of Marcela (Fabia), who informs Ginés that Octavio and his daughter have fled in earnest and are on their way to embark at Ostia.

It was impossible for Rotrou to use this act of Lope de Vega's and diminish the interest and unity of his subject by two subordinate plays. It is not until the third act of Lope de Vega's drama that the true subject of the play finally appears, and even here Rotrou departs widely from his original, for his subordinate play is a regular drama extending through three acts of the main play, and, what is more important and interesting, dealing with the life of a real martyr, Saint Adrian, whereas in Lope de Vega's play no particular martyr is represented.

Lope de Vega's third act begins with a dialogue between Diocletian and Camila, whom he has made his wife in gratitude for her generosity. Rutilio announces that the wild beasts are in the arena, and proceeds to give a long and detailed description of the curious animals. Camila expresses her unwillingness to accompany Diocletian if prisoners are to be thrown to beasts of such names. The emperor declares that Rome shall see them only as a curiosity and orders the play to be made ready. Ginés enters and the emperor asks news of Marcela. Ginés replies that her father went in search of her and married her to Octavio. The emperor then demands the comedy which is to be

> La imitación
> Del cristiano bautizado
> Porque es un extremo en tí.

The emperor and his wife withdraw in order to allow Ginés to prepare the stage. Marcela enters and asks the subject of the play, and a scene of recrimination between Marcela and Ginés, and between Marcela and her husband, follows, all of which has nothing to do with the real subject of the play.

After Marcela and Octavio depart Ginés declares that it is time to think of the character which will give pleasure to the emperor, who desires to behold a Christian steadfast in his faith. While rehearsing his part he grows more and more earnest, and finally implores the Lord to bestow upon him baptism, since without baptism he cannot approach the Lord.

At this moment music is heard, and doors open at the top of the stage, displaying a picture of the Virgin with Christ in his Father's arms and martyrs on the steps of the throne. Ginés wonders how he can have desired baptism, since it is not in his part. He continues his efforts and asks the saints to intercede for him, concluding with the words, "What fancies I entertain with my desire to imitate perfectly that Christian whom the emperor commands me to imitate!" A voice from within exclaims, "Thou shalt not imitate him in vain, Ginés, thou shalt be saved." While Ginés is plunged in amazement at the vision and voice, Fabio enters and informs Ginés that Marcela has returned home and treats her family harshly, refusing to play the part of the angel in the play to be performed before the emperor. There is a touch of comedy in the confusion of Fabio with the angel who addressed Ginés. Fabio is ordered to take Marcela's place and act the angel.

The emperor, Camila, Maximian, and Léntulo enter and Marcela appears and recites the *loa*. Ginés enters then as a prisoner and guarded by a captain and three soldiers. Almost from the beginning Ginés departs from the words of his rôle to the confusion of his fellow-actors. The spectators also take part in the action by their criticisms. Ginés again demands baptism and an angel appears and invites him to ascend and receive it. The miraculous ceremony takes place in full sight of the audience, who suppose it to be a part of the play.

When Fabio appears as the angel he is told that the scene of the baptism is ended, and when he protests that he has not appeared his declaration is received with incredulity and the emperor takes part in the altercation, affirming that he and the other spectators have seen him. Ginés finally solves the mystery by stating that a *paraninfo* from heaven with a divine voice has acted all of Fabio's rôle. He then declares that he is a Christian and baptized. The emperor's wrath, he continues, will constitute the second act, and he, Ginés, will represent the martyr in the third. The emperor sentences him to death and withdraws with Camila and Maximian, commanding Léntulo and Sulpicio to examine the troupe.

Each actor enters in turn, is questioned as to the rôle he plays, and finally all together are asked if they are Christians. They all deny that they are and are sentenced by Léntulo to immediate banishment from Rome. They depart and Ginés enters in chains. The *alcaide* who has orders to impale him wonders that a person who has so often ridiculed the martyrs should persist in being a Christian. Ginés explains that he ridiculed the Christians while he was a member of the demon's company; now he is a member of Christ's, and proceeds to enumerate the various parts played by the saints.

The last scene is in the Campus Martius, through which are passing the former company of Ginés on their way to exile. They bid farewell to Rome and blame Ginés for their misfortunes. He is revealed impaled and addressing "en el acto postrero" the surrounding people. He declares that he represented the wretched fables of this world. The human comedy, which was all folly, has ceased and the divine comedy, which Ginés is now acting, has begun. He is on his way to heaven to receive his reward, and awaits the second part early on the morrow. Octavio pronounces the final words:

> Aquī acaba la comedía
> Del mejor representante.

The changes which Rotrou has made while imitating Lope de
Vega illustrate in a very interesting manner the differences in
taste and dramatic principles between the French and Spanish
writers, or rather between French and Spanish art.

The laws of the unities, firmly established in France from
the time of the *Sentiments de l'Académie sur le Cid*, in 1638,
rendered it impossible for Rotrou to use the first two acts of
Lope de Vega, which are taken up with the history of the accession of Diocletian. Genest appears only incidentally. Rotrou
alludes to the emperor's previous history only in the scornful
words uttered by Valeria, Diocletian's daughter, in regard to
her father's marriage, in ll. 25–30. Rotrou's play begins with
the insipid obligatory love affair between Valeria and Maximian, introduced by the hackneyed device of the " tragic dream."
Genest enters to pay his respects to the emperor, and the
remainder of the first act is taken up with a literary discussion
between Genest and Diocletian, and the latter's decision that
Genest shall act the part of a Christian martyr. The second
act of Rotrou begins with the preparations for the play and
the rehearsal of their parts by Genest and Marcelle. While
Genest is alone the voice from heaven declares :

> Poursuis, Genest, ton personnage;
> Tu n'imiteras point en vain ;
> Ton salut ne dépend que d'un peu de courage,
> Et Dieu t'y prêtera la main.

From this time on the play within the play proceeds regularly
until Genest's declaration of his conversion in the fourth act.

Rotrou has used little of Lope de Vega's second act. The
literary discussion between Diocletian and Genest is condensed,
and employed by Rotrou in his first act. Lope de Vega has
greatly attenuated the interest of his play by introducing into
it two subordinate plays, one entirely secular and turning on
Genest's love for Marcela. This play simply serves to display
the histrionic ability of Genest, although even this is impaired

by the fact that for part of the time he is not acting at all but simply expressing his real feelings.

It is not until Lope de Vega's third act that the true subject of the play appears, the conversion and martyrdom of Genest. In the Spanish play Genest merely represents the conversion and martyrdom of *a* Christian, whereas in Rotrou the interest is greatly increased and the artistic effect enhanced by the fact that a regular play is introduced on the subject of a particular martyr, and that one who had suffered under Maximin, who is represented both as spectator and actor. It is therefore impossible to compare Rotrou with Lope de Vega for a large part of the French play, and a glance at the Appendix will show how few are the verbal imitations by Rotrou. He has, it is true, imitated the general tendency of the Spanish subordinate play, the rehearsal by Genest, the heavenly voice, the act of baptism (which in the Spanish play is a miracle which takes place in the sight of the audience, but in the French drama is performed behind the scenes), the examination of the company of actors and actresses (not so detailed as in the Spanish play), and there are a certain number of verbal imitations. The conclusion is quite different in the two plays. In the Spanish play the company is banished from Rome and behold their expiring companion as they depart. In Rotrou they are not molested, but are simply urged to use their influence with Genest, and the fifth act of Rotrou is largely devoted to Marcelle's effort to persuade Genest to abandon his new belief. She fails and the whole band afterward beg Diocletian to pardon Genest. The emperor finally consents to forgive him if he will renounce his error and if

> De sa voix sacrilège il purge le blasphème,
> Et reconnaît les dieux auteurs de l'univers.

The French play ends with the usual obligatory recital of the catastrophe by the prefect Plancien.

The play of *Saint Genest*, from its religious character, has not enjoyed the same popularity as *Venceslas*, but a glance at the Bibliography will show that it has been frequently reprinted. I am unable to give any statement of its popularity as shown by the number of representations. I can find no reference to its performance during the eighteenth century, and it would have been improbable that a play of such a nature could please an audience of that time.[1] Four times in the nineteenth century *Saint Genest* was performed, — in 1845 at the Odéon, in 1874 at the Porte-Saint-Martin (in March and November), and in 1900 at the Odéon.[2]

Although *Saint Genest* was seldom performed in the nineteenth century, it did not cease to attract the attention of

---

[1] The only imitation of Rotrou in the eighteenth century with which I am acquainted is Campistron's tragedy of *Adrien* in *Œuvres de M. de Campistron*, Paris, 1750, vol. ii, pp. 187–285. In this insipid work Adrien is substituted for Maximin and married to Valérie, the daughter of Diocletian. She is a Christian. The emperor determines to celebrate the marriage of his daughter by a general persecution of the Christians. Valérie reveals her faith to her husband, who is miraculously converted in the course of the interview. Valérie and Adrien are denounced to the emperor, who orders the latter to be put to death. In the third scene of the fifth act Adrien appears in the presence of Valérie, who, like Natalie, supposes he has purchased his life by recanting. He explains, however, that he has been exposed in the arena to the wild beasts and miraculously delivered; and so has come

> Pour vous chercher, Madame, et mourir à vous yeux ;
> Car je ne doute point que d'un nouveau supplice,
> Plus ardent que jamais César ne me punisse.

Diocletian commands him to be killed at once, but spares the life of Valérie. The death of Adrien has made a profound impression, and multitudes in the army and city are converted by his example. Diocletian in despair resigns his throne and leaves to his successor Maximin the care of punishing Valérie and the other Christians. It will be seen that Campistron's tragedy is a composite of the two plays involved in *Saint Genest*. The imitation of Rotrou is not a verbal one, but consists in the similarity of tone and situations.

[2] See Person, *Histoire du Véritable Saint-Genest*, pp. 91–95, and Bernardin, *Devant le rideau*, p. 144.

critics, and there are frequent references to it in literary histories, essays, etc. I have enumerated these in the Bibliography, and shall mention here only those of exceptional importance as bearing upon the general question of Rotrou's rank in French literature.

The most valuable of these criticisms is that of Sainte-Beuve, contained in his history of Port-Royal.[1] In the fifth chapter Sainte-Beuve has described the famous "Journée du Guichet," when the young abbess of Port-Royal, Angélique Arnauld, refused to allow her father to enter the cloister. This act of austerity and self-renunciation leads the writer to speak of Corneille's *Polyeucte*, of which he considers *Saint Genest* "the true and direct continuation." The seventh chapter is largely devoted to a comparison between the two plays. After saying "Rotrou est de beaucoup inférieur à Corneille; mais quand il monte, c'est dans le même sens et sur les mêmes tons; il aide à mesurer l'échelle," he divides dramatic geniuses into two classes: the sovereign creators, like Shakespeare, Molière, Walter Scott, "si dramatique en ses romans," Goethe in part, who remain calm in the midst of their creations and do not identify themselves with their works; and such writers as Corneille, Schiller, Marlowe, Rotrou, Crébillon, Werner — "tout en bas, mais encore dans son sein, Ducis." The poet of this class "ne dirige pas son talent, il le suit; il marche, pour ainsi dire, dans son talent, au moment de l'effusion, comme un homme ivre; il ne sait pas au juste où il est; il trébuche par places, et il se noie. Il est comme l'acteur qui, dans son rôle pathétique, verserait de vraies larmes, pousserait de vrais soupirs et qui, par cet abandon de lui à son rôle, atteindrait

---

[1] Book I, chap. vii. I have used the fourth edition, Paris, Hachette, 1878, vol. i, pp. 147–174. The work was originally a course of lectures delivered before the Academy of Lausanne in 1837, and first published in 1840.

mainte fois à des accents extraordinaires, mais bientôt retomberait et ne saurait trop où se reprendre dans les intervalles."
He continues : " Donc, en ce second ordre de poëtes dramatiques où le grand Corneille est au premier rang, le bon Rotrou ne vient lui-même qu'au second ; mais il vient tout derrière et par moments presque coude à coude avec Corneille. Il n'en parut jamais plus près que le soir de cette tragédie : *Saint Genest comédien païen représentant le mystère d'Adrien.*" Then follows, pp. 151–169, a careful analysis and criticism of *Saint Genest*. The most important of these critical remarks are cited in the notes to *Saint Genest* and need not be repeated here. In conclusion (after praising *Don Bernard de Cabrère* and *Venceslas*) Sainte-Beuve says, without a very accurate idea of Rotrou's life : " Rotrou passe pour n'avoir pas été heureux. Il pratiquait, à ce qu'il paraît, dans sa vie, le train assez aveugle et hasardé de ses pièces ; on raconte qu'il allait être mis en prison pour dettes, quand *Venceslas* le tira d'affaire. Il réalise l'idée vulgaire qu'on se fait du poëte, ardent, impétueux, endetté, inégal en conduite et en fortune. Les poëtes anglais Dryden, Otway, étaient ainsi. La dignité des Lettres chez nous commença plus tôt, après le moment de Rotrou toutefois. A plusieurs traits énergiques, rudes et négligés, tant du talent que du caractère, il me fait encore l'effet d'un exact contemporain de Mézeray, — d'un Mézeray de la poésie. Cette vie de Rotrou, si en rapport avec son talent, reçut un dernier trait de ressemblance par l'acte héroïque qui la couronna. On sait qu'après s'être rangé probablement et s'être marié, tenant à Dreux, sa ville natale, une charge civile et de judicature, il se voua, durant une peste, au service de ses concitoyens privés de leurs autres magistrats, et qu'il mourut à la peine : trépas de sacrifice, digne des grands traits dont son œuvre dramatique est semée. On peut dire aussi de lui, au sens le plus sérieux, qu' *il voulut*

D'une feinte, en mourant, faire une vérité.

" Il n'avait que quarante et un ans, l'âge même auquel était mort Régnier, son quasi-compatriote et son parent en plus d'un point. Mais pour Rotrou quelle fin plus noble, vraiment faite pour rendre jaloux au cœur les plus généreux dramatiques de cette famille et pour tenter un Schiller !

" *Saint Genest* et *Polyeucte* sont les deux seules tragédies sacrées qui puissent passer, avec toutes les différences, pour des échantillons et des abrégés perfectionnés du genre des mystères."

The most eminent of living critics, F. Brunetière, has judged Rotrou most harshly from the narrow classic point of view. In his *Manuel de l'histoire de la littérature française* (1898), p. 127, he dismisses Rotrou with the contemptuous remark : " Et que Mairet, ou même Rotrou, n'ayant laissé qu'un nom et pas une œuvre, ils ne sont bons à connaître qu'en ' fonction ' de Corneille." In the article already cited, " L'Évolution d'un genre : La Tragédie," p. 183, he says : " Ni Mairet, ni Rotrou, — ni ce Tristan l'Hermite dont on a voulu récemment faire ' un précurseur de Racine,' — n'ont connu, je ne dis pas les ressources, mais l'objet de leur art ; ils en ont rejeté les contraintes, sans se douter que ces contraintes, y compris celle des trois unités, faisaient l'une des conditions de l'impression tragique ; ils ont littéralement ' prostitué ' l'histoire, comme Rotrou, dans son *Wenceslas*, à des inventions de leur cru, dont elle n'est que le passeport ou l'enseigne mensongère."

A little later in the same article, p. 193, speaking of Crébillon's tragedies, he says : " Ou, si l'on veut encore, et, avec une affectation de grandeur qui n'aboutit qu'à l'enflure, comme leur étalage de force n'aboutit qu'à l'horreur inutile, elles nous rappellent la tragi-comédie de Rotrou, le *Wenceslas* ou le *Saint-Genest*. Certes, on sent bien que Corneille et Racine ont passé par là : Crébillon les imite ou les copie sans vergogne. C'est son métier de faire des pièces comme un autre ferait des pendules. Mais relisons là-dessus *Wenceslas*

ou *Saint-Genest* ; c'est ici la même confusion du *dramatique*
et du *romanesque* ; ce sont les mêmes inventions ; c'est la
même incuriosité de tout ce qui s'appelle des noms de style,
de psychologie, et de vérité dans l'art. La tragédie est
ramenée par les œuvres de ce bonhomme, comme qui dirait
à ses premiers débuts; et, non seulement, de ses illustres
prédécesseurs, il n'a pas retenu les leçons, mais s'il les avait
systématiquement dédaignées, on ne voit pas en quoi ses
prétendues tragédies différeraient d'elles-mêmes. Le style en
serait-il plus archaïque peut-être ? "

In regard to Rotrou's style the same critic in the article in the
Revue des deux mondes already cited, " Corneille et le théâtre
espagnol," says, p. 195 : " Parmi les contemporains de Corneille, lisez Rotrou, par exemple, ou Tristan l'Hermite, ou
Quinault, ou Thomas, frère de Pierre, La Calprenède ou du
Ryer : vous les trouverez toujours au-dessous, ou au-dessus,
ou à côté, dans les parages ou dans les environs de ce qu'ils
auraient voulu dire. Leur langue est celle de Corneille, — leur
vocabulaire, et aussi leur syntaxe, — mais un don leur a été
refusé, qui est celui d'égaler leur pensée par l'expression, et,
quoi qu'ils disent, et qui n'est pas toujours plus mal pensé ni
moins vivement senti que du Corneille, ce qui leur fait défaut,
c'est le don de nous procurer, à nous spectateurs ou lecteurs,
la sensation du définitif et de l'achevé."

Another eminent modern critic, E. Deschanel, has judged
Rotrou very differently in his somewhat paradoxical work, *Le
Romantisme des classiques* (*Première série*), Paris, 1883. An
entire chapter, the ninth, pp. 261–287, is devoted to *Saint
Genest*. Deschanel defends the mingling of the tragic and
comic elements in the seventeenth-century tragi-comedy and
says, p. 262 : " Quoique ni Rotrou, ni Corneille, ni Racine
n'aient connu Shakspeare, — qui cependant à cette époque
avait déjà produit tous ses chefs-d'œuvre (mais les communications avec l'Angleterre n'étaient pas alors aussi faciles

qu'aujourd'hui), — on peut dire que le théâtre de Rotrou a quelque chose de Shakspearien, du moins dans la mesure que comportait l'esprit français. C'est ce que je vais tâcher de mettre en lumière le plus simplement possible, en étudiant la pièce de *Saint Genest*." Deschanel then gives a sympathetic account of Rotrou's life, and an analysis of the play in question with its sources, being the first, I believe, to point out Rotrou's use of Cellot's *Sanctus Adrianus*. In conclusion the critic says, pp. 285–287 : " Pour conclure, le *Saint Genest* est une pièce originale et émouvante, dans laquelle on admire la facilité des vers, le large flot des métaphores et des images, leur nouveauté hardie et juste, leur éclat, leur fraîcheur, leur abondante floraison. Il y en a de vraiment belles. En parlant des jeunes martyrs encore enfants, de quels traits, de quelle couleur le poète sait peindre ces douces victimes, fières

> De tendre une gorge assurée
> A la sanglante mort qu'ils voyaient préparée,
> Et tomber sous le coup d'un trépas glorieux,
> Doux fruits à peine éclos, déjà mûrs pour les cieux !

" Ce vers charmant se trouvait en germe dans un mot de la tragédie latine de Louis Cellot : *Jam matura Deo*. Mais quel parti le poète français a su tirer de ce simple trait si court ! — Ailleurs, parlant du martyr qui va répandre son sang pour la croix de Jésus-Christ, il trouve ces deux autres beaux vers :

> Il brûle d'arroser cet arbre précieux
> Où pend pour nous le fruit le plus chéri des cieux.

"Ailleurs, sur la même idée, il ne se gêne pas pour répéter les mêmes rimes, mais avec une image nouvelle et hardie :

> Sur un bois glorieux
> Qui fut moins une croix qu'une échelle des cieux.

" Il y a des vers d'un jet puissant et dru, comme ces deux-ci :

> Après les avoir vus, d'un visage serein,
> Pousser des chants aux cieux dans des taureaux d'airain.

"Ou bien, les quatre autres qui suivent, sur cette idée que les martyrs chrétiens étant habitués à regarder la mort en face, elle s'apprivoise pour eux :

> La mort, pour la trop voir, ne leur est plus sauvage ;
> Pour trop agir contre eux, le feu perd son usage ;
> En ces horreurs enfin le cœur manque aux bourreaux.

Aux bourreaux, et non aux victimes.

"En résumé, dans la partie tragique, l'intérêt de l'action, avec la beauté des sentiments et des vers ; puis, la variété curieuse de la partie familière, qui sert de cadre au tableau ; tout cela ensemble forme une œuvre qui, ce me semble, attache, émeut, captive. Ajoutez-y en pensée, — il le faut, — le jeu des acteurs, les décors, le double théâtre, le mouvement de la scène. Et j'espère que nous dirons ensemble, comme Sainte-Beuve : ' *Saint Genest*, en plein dix-septième siècle, est la pièce la plus romantique qu'on puisse imaginer.' "

Of the more recent critics of Rotrou I shall cite but two. The first is Hippolyte Parigot, who devotes a chapter to *Saint Genest* in his *Génie et métier*, Paris, 1894, pp. 75–85. Parigot's criticisms deal chiefly with the complicated action of the drama and the difficulty of distinguishing between Genest the individual and Genest the actor in the rôle of Adrien. The same is true to a certain extent of the other actors who have a two-fold rôle. He says, p. 83 : "Nous touchons ici au défaut le plus intime du sujet. Écoutez les premiers vers du rôle d'Adrien :

> Ne délibère plus, Adrien, il est temps
> De suivre avec ardeur ces fameux combattants ;
> Si la gloire te plaît, l'occasion est belle ;
> La querelle du ciel à ce combat t'appelle.

Et comparez la dernière stance du rôle de Saint Genest au cinquième acte.

> Puisqu'on ne vainc qu'en combattant,
> D'une vigueur mâle et guerrière
> Courons au but de la carrière,
> Où la couronne nous attend.

" C'est-à-dire que du premier acte au dernier, le personnage n'a point fait un pas : Adrien prépare Genest, et Genest répète Adrien. Notez, je vous prie, que je ne parle pas des fragments du rôle que l'acteur repasse et qui reviendront dans le rôle débité, et que j'en ai au rôle entier, celui d'Adrien joué par Genest, celui de Genest calqué sur Adrien, le double rôle de saint Adrien et de saint Genest. Si, au début, le martyr qu'on représente s'exhorte à la mort en beaux vers, c'est aussi en vers fort beaux que l'acteur s'entraîne à mourir. Même musique, même voix, même sentiment : il y a substitution de personne, et voilà tout le progrès. Quelle péripétie vraiment dramatique prétendait tirer Rotrou d'un caractère qui n'avance pas? La plus soudaine et la plus attendue, la plus piquante et la moins pathétique, est le transport de Genest et l'acte de foi qu'il improvise. La scène est d'un beau mouvement, et l'effet théâtral sans portée. Témoin l'impression produite sur la cour, qui l'écoute.

> Voyez avec quel art Genest sait aujourd'hui
> Passer de la figure aux sentiments d'autrui.

" D'un comédien aussi exercé aucun jeu n'étonne. En vain Genest s'exalte, en vain Lentule reste court, et Marcelle demeure stupide ; cette catastrophe encore ne provoque qu'une incrédule admiration.

> Pour tromper l'auditeur abuser l'acteur même
> De son métier, sans doute, est l'adresse suprême.

" Il faut que Dioclétien intervienne, et crie aux artistes : 'Qui trompe-t-on ici?' pour que du même coup la péripétie soit claire et manifeste ; tant il est vrai que ce rôle compliqué de Genest est, à l'origine, frappé d'impuissance, et que, d'un mot, un personnage secondaire tranche la situation et dénoue la crise. C'est que les actes de foi trop répétés éveillent moins d'émotion que de scepticisme, et qu'au théâtre le scepticisme tue tout ce qu'il effleure d'un sourire.

"Aussi la pièce de *Saint Genest* a-t-elle disparu de la scène, en dépit des beaux vers qui s'y trouvent et des agréments que l'auteur y a semés d'une main prodigue. L'éditeur anonyme d'une édition déjà ancienne, que j'ai sous les yeux, écrit ces lignes un peu naïves : 'Il est peut-être digne de remarque, que cette variété des tons employés par Rotrou, que la vérité des divers sentiments qu'il a décrits et mis en jeu, furent la cause principale de l'oubli dans lequel est tombée cette tragédie.'

"Hélas! non. *Saint Genest* est un sujet imprudemment choisi, malgré une imitation heureuse et des beautés de détail, par un dramaturge qui procédait d'instinct, et savait peu son métier."

The last of the recent critics of *Saint Genest* whom I shall cite is N. M. Bernardin, who devotes to that play a lecture delivered at the Odéon theater and published in *Devant le rideau*, Paris, 1901, pp. 123–144. After a brief sketch of Rotrou's life and an account of the sources of *Saint Genest* Bernardin continues, pp. 140–144 : "Mais si le *Martyre d'Adrien* [the intercalated play] est froid, combien vivant est le *Martyre de Saint Genest*, et combien amusant, au sens où les peintres prennent ce mot ! Comme Corneille avait habilement découpé le chef-d'œuvre du *Cid* dans le drame énorme de Guilhem de Castro, Rotrou, avec ce bon sens tout français, que nous avons bien tort de dédaigner, vu qu'il est beaucoup plus rare que l'esprit, lequel, on le sait, court les rues, Rotrou a fait un choix très judicieux parmi les traits de mœurs et de caractères, parmi les détails pittoresques prodigués dans sa pièce par Lope de Vega ; il en a joint quelques autres fort heureusement trouvés, et il a peint ainsi un tableau très réaliste et très curieux, qui reste unique dans la galerie de nos tragédies classiques.

"Il est assez piquant déjà, avec sa galanterie héroïque, le premier acte, qui nous montre les fiançailles de la princesse Valérie, une précieuse, avec Maximin, ce berger, que son courage et ses exploits ont élevé jusqu'à l'empire ; et la scène n'est certes point banale où l'acteur Genest s'entretient avec les souverains de l'art dramatique et du répertoire, le comédien déclarant hautement sa préference pour les auteurs anciens, les princes penchant plutôt pour les modernes, dont la nouveauté les séduit.

" Mais le second acte est un délicieux, un exquis tableau de genre, dans lequel se trouvent en germe tout l'*Impromptu de Versailles*, de Molière, et le second acte, si pittoresque, d'*Adrienne Lecouvreur*. . . . N'est-il pas vrai que, si le mot *amusant* n'existait pas, il faudrait l'inventer pour l'appliquer à ce deuxième acte de *Saint Genest* ?

> Combien d'actes de tragédies
> Dont on ne peut en dire autant !

Et toujours les applaudissements et les réflexions des princes soulignent et commentent les vers du *Martyre d'Adrien*, dont la représentation est même un instant interrompue par l'entrée brusque de Genest, qui vient se plaindre que les coulisses sont envahies par les courtisans trop galants, et réclamer, au nom de la morale, l'intervention de l'empereur.

"Au quatrième acte, le trouble apporté dans la représentation par la conversion subite de Genest est rendu avec un sentiment de la mesure tout à fait remarquable, et je trouve encore dans l'interrogatoire des comédiens par le préfet un trait bien curieux et bien xviie siècle : ' Que représentiez-vous ? ' demande Plancien à Albin ; et le comédien répond humblement : ' Les assistants.' C'est, Messieurs, que la foule était toujours à cette époque, vu la petitesse de la scène, composée d'un seul personnage. Et voilà comment Léandre pourra répondre encore, dans les *Plaideurs*, à la même question posée par Perrin Dandin : ' Moi, je suis l'assemblée.'

" L'heureuse création de la princesse Valérie a permis à Rotrou de donner un peu plus d'intérêt à son dénouement, en laissant espérer jusqu'à la dernière minute que la catastrophe

pourra être écartée. La princesse amène les comédiens aux
pieds de l'empereur son père ; elle intercède pour eux, et
Dioclétien est près de s'attendrir, quand le préfet vient annoncer que tout est fini. Et, tandis que les comédiens s'éloignent
en larmes, l'épais et vulgaire Maximin emmène en plaisantant
la princesse Valérie, tant il est vrai que jusqu'à la fin la comédie accompagne la tragédie dans cette pièce extraordinaire ;
ainsi dans *Roméo et Juliette* les musiciens plaisantent auprès du
corps inanimé de la jeune fille. Et, de fait, si l'on peut, à
propos d'un de nos vieux poètes tragiques, évoquer le souvenir
de Shakespeare, c'est à propos de Rotrou. Quelle que soit
la distance qui les sépare, ce rapprochement n'en est pas moins
pour Rotrou fort glorieux."

It is now time to turn our attention to *Venceslas*, the history
of which is briefer and less interesting in many respects than
that of *Saint Genest*. The sole source of Rotrou's play is the
drama by the Spanish writer Don Francisco de Rojas y Zorrilla,
entitled *No hay ser padre siendo rey* (" One cannot be father
when one is king ").[1] The author was born in Toledo, October 4, 1607. Almost nothing is known of his life, and the
date of his death is uncertain.[2] He published at Madrid in

---

[1] There is no foundation for the suggestion of Person, *Histoire du
Venceslas*, p. 33, that Rotrou used two plays for his *Venceslas*, one
known to us, another which remains to be discovered.

[2] For the little that is known of Rojas see notice by Don Ramon de
Mesonero Romanos in his edition of *Comedias escogidas de Don Francisco de Rojas Zorilla*, Madrid, 1861, in Rivadeneyra, *Biblioteca de autores
españoles*. Bibliographical details will be found in La Barrera, *Católogo
bibliográfico y biográfico del teatro antiguo español*, Madrid, 1860. See
also A. F. von Schack, *Geschichte der dramatischen Literatur und
Kunst in Spanien*, 2te Ausgabe, Frankfurt-am-Main, 1854, vol. iii, pp.
295–328; Ticknor, *History of Spanish Literature*, fourth American edition, Boston, 1872, vol. ii, pp. 491–495; Fitzmaurice-Kelly, *Littérature
espagnole, traduction de H.-D. Davray*, Paris, 1904, pp. 341–342, where
the indebtedness of French dramatists to Rojas is mentioned. The
form of the name even is doubtful. In his plays the author calls himself

1640 and 1645 two parts or collections of his dramatic works, promising a third which never appeared. These two parts contain twelve plays each, and *No hay ser padre siendo rey* is the second play in the first part. Besides these twenty-four plays, a large number of others (fifty-five) were published under his name, and he was the author of ten plays in collaboration with other writers. The thirty plays published by Don Ramon de Mesonero Romanos in Rivadeneyra's *Biblioteca* probably comprise all the authentic works of Rojas which have come down to us.

Nothing is known of the source of Rojas's play, and any inquiry into this subject is fruitless and unnecessary since Rotrou followed his original closely in all the historical details of his play.[1]

Francisco de Rojas y Zorilla, although the last appellation was not that of his mother, nor the second name of his father.

[1] I cannot do better than to give the conclusions of Person on the subject. He says, *Histoire du Venceslas*, pp. 30 et seq.: "On doit se demander d'abord ce que le sujet de *Venceslas* peut avoir d'historique: Francisco de Rojas s'était bien gardé de désigner par un nom propre le héros de sa pièce: il l'appelle simplement le roi de Pologne: Rey de Polonia. Ses deux fils seulement ont un nom: l'aîné s'appelle Rugero principe (c'est Ladislas); le cadet, Alejandro infante (c'est Alexandre). Mais Rotrou qui jusqu'à *Cosroès* traitera l'histoire avec une si complète désinvolture (voir notamment *Crisante* et cette étrange tragédie de *Bélisaire* dans laquelle l'Imperatrice Théodora laisse tomber une paire de gants à franges que le vainqueur des Vandales ne daigne même pas ramasser), Rotrou, disons-nous, n'était pas embarrassé pour si peu: il a nommé son héros. Où a-t-il pris ce nom de Venceslas? Est-ce dans Dubravius, dans Aeneas Sylvius, dans Nevgebaverus?

"Nous avons consulté toutes ces histoires, *Historiae rerum bohemicarum* ou *rerum Poloniae*. Nous avons rencontré bien des Venceslas et des Vladislas, mais aucun d'eux ne ressemble aux personnages de Rotrou. L'un est successivement roi de Bohême, de Hongrie et de Pologne, de 1283 à 1305. Il avait envoyé son fils en Hongrie: il le rappelle, craignant à cette distance l'effet des mauvais conseils et des mauvais exemples: *vita filii dissolutior quam inerti otio vinoque et prodigis epulis fere quotidie transigebat* (*Dubravii historia bohemica*, 1552, p. cxvi), et il lui offre sa couronne de Pologne. Ailleurs c'est un Vladislas

Rojas does not give a name to his "Rey de Polonia," and it is not certain where Rotrou found the appellation of "Venceslas."[1] Of the other characters in Rojas, Rotrou retains

---

cubitalis (id est pusillae staturae) qui à partir de 1305 fait le malheur de la Pologne, *ob feros intemperantesque mores quibus vitam suam, nunc grassando et spoliando, nunc per stupra et adulteria corpus volutando foede contaminabat* (*Icones et vitae principum regum Poloniae a Salmone Nevgebavero de Cadano*, MDCXX).

"Faut-il reconnaître dans ces portraits l'impétueux et farouche Ladislas? Mais à combien d'autres princes, de ce pays et de ce temps-là surtout, ne pourrait-on pas rapporter un pareil signalement? Et où se trouve la filière historique, le fait précis, la date exacte, la trace enfin de cette Thébaïde polonaise, de la condamnation prononcée par le père devenu le justicier de sa famille, et de l'intervention populaire qui arrache au souverain l'acquittement de l'assassin, comme Horace avait été condamné par les duumvirs et absous par le peuple?

"Voilà un problème intéressant que nous laissons à notre grand regret à résoudre aux historiens, nous contentant, faute de mieux pour l'instant, de dire avec la plupart des dictionnaires que le héros de la tragédie de Rotrou est Venceslas le Vieux, mort en 1306."

This question is discussed also by A. Giesse in an article published in the *Jahresbericht über das Realprogymnasium und Progymnasium zu Homburg v. d. Höhe*, 1892, "Étude sur le Venceslas, tragédie de Rotrou." The author does not throw any new light on the question, but gives some additional details concerning *Venceslas le Vieux*, who died in 1305 and not in 1306, as Person says. Giesse thinks it cannot be proved that Rojas was acquainted with the history of Poland, while it is more than likely that Rotrou was, to some extent, familiar with the period in question. How, he asks, could he have fallen upon such names as Courlande and Cunisberg without having read some pages of the history of the period in question?

[1] Person says further in a note, p. 32, *op. cit.*: "L'auteur anonyme qui en 1722 dénonce au *Mercure de France* l'existence du *No hay ser Padre Siendo Rey* de Francisco de Rojas, regrette que Rotrou n'ait pas pris un sujet vraiment historique. 'Que n'a-t-il choisi,' dit-il 'le personnage d'Eacus, roi d'Égine, qui vit son fils Pélée tuer Phoque, un autre de ses fils, et fut obligé de pardonner à Pélée?' La mort de 'Phoque' est sans doute fort dramatique; mais je ne sais pourquoi nous aimons mieux encore, pour légendaire qu'elle soit, la mort de l'infant Alexandre. Du reste ce nom de *Venceslas* devait hanter depuis longtemps l'imagination de Rotrou, car nous le trouvons déjà en 1635, dans la première édition de *La Bague de l'Oubli* (à Paris, chez François

"Alejandro, infante," "Duque Federico," and "Casandra, duquesa." For "Clavela, criada" of Casandra, Rotrou has substituted "Léonor, suivante" of Théodore; "Coscorron," the servant of Casandra, is omitted as well as "Roberto," the confidant of the prince, who in Rojas is named "Rugero" instead of "Ladislas." The entire rôle of "Théodore" is, as will be seen, the invention of Rotrou, as is also the part of "Octave, gouverneur de Varsovie." The following analysis of the play of Rojas will give the principal points of resemblance and difference between the two plays.

The king of Poland enters with his suite, his two sons, Alexander and Roger, and Duke Frederick. The king calls for a chair and seats himself, complaining that the gout drags him down in spite of himself. He then dismisses his suite and all but Roger (the Ladislas of the French play). We learn from a remark of the duke to the king that the brothers have just been quarreling. The king then pronounces a long address to his son, in which he recalls the death of his wife, the burden of the empire, and the fierce and intractable character of Roger, who hates the duke (the king's favorite), quarrels with his brother, and neglects his studies. He advises him to turn his anger against the Arabs or the Turks, and concludes by declaring that if Roger does not take warning and change his conduct, he will be king as well as father:

Si soy padre, seré rey.

Targa, au premier pilier de la grand'salle du Palais, devant la chapelle, au Soleil d'or); après une épître au Roi et un avertissement au Lecteur, le poète nous donne un long argument de sa pièce, qui commence en ces termes: 'Alfonce, jeune roi de Sicile, nouvel héritier du Royaume, par la mort de Venceslas son père, passionnément amoureux de Liliane, fille d'Alexandre duc de Terre-Neuve, ... etc.' Et plus loin le nom de Venceslas revient une seconde fois dans l'argument. Il fallait que ce nom eût bien de l'attrait aux yeux de Rotrou, pour qu'il en fît sans nécessité, dans un argument, le nom du père d'un roi de Sicile!"

The reader will recall what Brunetière has said about Rotrou's "prostitution" of history in the passage quoted above on p. 95.

Roger then proceeds to answer his father in detail, repeating what he said to his companions on the occasion of a hunting party in the mountains. He complains that his father retains the scepter although he, Roger, is competent to wield it. He hates his brother and the duke because one reigns in the king's eyes and the other in the state. The duke is a flatterer and a talebearer ; he aspires to what Roger seeks, and tries to win what he has won. His brother supports the duke, and even turns his sword against him, Roger. He ends with the most frightful threats against the two. The king, terrified at this outbreak, dissimulates his anger, and seeks to soothe his son by embracing him, declaring that he is in the right, and that he will share his crown with him.

At this moment Alexander enters and the king commands the brothers to be reconciled. After much difficulty on the part of Roger this is done, and the king orders them to remain prisoners in their apartments. The scene ends by the king declaring in an aside that he is going to visit Alexander, and Alexander, in the same manner, states that he is going to see his " esposa."

Then follows a scene between Coscorron and Clavela, servants of the Duchess Casandra, who inform each other that both the brothers, Roger and Alexander, are in love with Casandra, but that she is married to Alexander. The duchess enters and dismisses the servants and then admits Alexander by a secret door. He is very dejected and relates to his wife a dream he had the preceding night, in which he was attacked and wounded by his brother. The lovers are alarmed by a knock on the door and their friend and confidant, Duke Frederick, enters and tells them that the partisans of Roger and Alexander have met in the vestibule of the palace and quarreled. Roger endeavors to separate them and then himself engages in the combat like an infuriated bull. The king enters and puts the partisans of Alexander under arrest. He then proceeds to Alexander's room and, not finding him there, sends in search of him with orders to throw him into prison. The duke advises Alexander to fly to a villa of his in the neighborhood, and states that he has a horse awaiting him. Alexander tears himself from his wife and departs.

The second act (*jornada*) opens, some twenty or thirty days later, with a scene between Roger and his confidant Robert, in which the former recapitulates the grounds of his hatred for the Duke Frederick, whom he is determined to kill. Coscorron enters and is bribed by Roger to watch that night in Casandra's apartment and admit him. In the next scene Casandra informs Clavela that she has written to the king, asking him to protect her against Roger. Clavela retires and leaves her mistress alone. Coscorron and Roger enter secretly and the latter conceals himself. Casandra hears a noise and discovers Coscorron. After questioning him she dismisses him. Roger extinguishes the light and endeavors to seize the duchess, who escapes into an adjoining room, leaving Roger groping around in the dark. At that moment Alexander enters and the brothers clutch each other. Alexander calls for help and Casandra appears with a light, while the brothers separate and draw their swords. Each of the three indulges in lengthy asides, and Roger declares that he has come in search of the duke and is determined to kill him. Alexander explains his presence by saying that the duke is secretly married to Casandra and has given him a key to his apartment, where he, Alexander, may remain until the king's anger against him is appeased. Clavela enters and informs her mistress that the king is in the house, brought there by her letter, and that the duke accompanies him.

The duchess makes the brothers withdraw to separate rooms near by. The king enters and asks whether Roger is concealed in the house. Casandra denies it and says he has not come. The king is about to retire, when the duke advises him to

search the house. The first room he enters is the one where
Alexander is hidden. He comes out and falls at his father's
feet. The king vents his feelings in a lengthy aside and orders
the prince to follow him. Casandra is left alone and summons
Roger, whom she commands to leave by a door opening into
the street. She declares that if he does not obey at once she
will call the king, who has not yet left the house. She repels
his advances and declares that her honor and her husband are
dearer to her than the prince's love. He asks, " Who is your
husband ? " and she replies, " The duke," adding in an aside,
" Aquí importa deslumbrarle." Roger declares that he will kill
him, and finally yielding to Casandra's repeated entreaties
departs with the words, " Tell the duke to beware."

At the opening of the third act of Rojas's play Coscorron
and Robert encounter Roger, agitated and wounded, with
his sword broken. He relates to his confidant that after
Casandra forced him to leave her house and declared herself
the wife of the duke, he, Roger, had sought his rival everywhere, and finally returned late at night to Casandra's abode,
and by means of a pass-key entered her room and found her
sleeping by the side of her husband. He could not see his
face, and as the light expired he killed him and escaped to the
street by climbing down the balcony. There he had encountered a singular vision, a formless skeleton under a black veil,
which, when asked who it was, replied,

Rugero, el Principe, soy.

Roger fell dismayed to the ground and was found by his friend.

At that moment the king enters and demands an explanation from Roger of his presence in that spot at so early an
hour, as well as of his disturbance and bloody hands. Roger
evades his question, as does also Coscorron when the king
addresses him. Roger finally determines to speak and informs
the king that he has killed the one whom the king loves best. As

he utters these words the duke appears and states that Casandra wishes to speak with the king. The amazement of Roger, who supposes that he has killed the duke, is boundless, and he asks himself, "Whom, O heavens, have I slain?" Casandra appears in mourning and relates the events of the past night, revealing her marriage to Alexander and the rivalry for her affections between the brothers. She describes Alexander's return and her awakening to find her husband dead at her side. She pursued the murderer, she says, whose face was hidden by his cloak, and who escaped by way of the balcony. She then denounces Roger as the murderer and calls on the king for justice, exclaiming, "Be king, although you are father." In order to arouse the king's wrath she produces the bloody dagger with which Roger slew his brother. The king addresses her as his daughter, declaring that he will know how to look out for her, since he has to avenge himself as well as her. He commands Roger to surrender his sword and puts him under the guard of the duke. Casandra again calls on the king to avenge her, but this time he replies, "I do not think to take vengeance, but to bestow punishment; this I promise you." The scene ends with these words by the king: "Two sons heaven gave me; one I have lost, and to avenge him I must lose the other."

In the next scene Roger appears in chains imprisoned in a tower. He gives vent to his sorrow for the death of his brother, whom, it seems, he really loved. The king and the duke enter the prison and an affecting interview takes place between the father and son. Roger at first supposes from his father's tokens of affection that he has come to pardon him, and is overwhelmed when he learns he must die. He endeavors to move the king by declaring that he did not intend to kill his brother. The king replies that he punishes him not for the person he murdered but for the murder. Roger asks what father ever punished his son with death as an act of justice or from change of affection. The king answers by citing the case of Trajan, who deprived his guilty son of an eye, and, that his son might not be blinded in accordance with the law which he had broken, sacrificed one of his own. He also mentions Darius, who put to death his son for breaking a certain law, and had made from his skin a seat in which he sat while administering justice. Roger pleads with him in vain and ends by asking him if it is possible for the king, being a father, to punish him thus. The king departs with the words which furnish the title of the play : " It is impossible to be a father while one is a king."

Coscorron enters and in a mock-serious scene confesses his share in the transaction. He betrayed his mistress (who but a servant should do this?) and acted as pander to Roger for his gold. Suppose he should go to the king and acknowledge that he has killed Alexander. He sees in imagination the reward and the punishment of this noble self-sacrifice, and ends by saying that he will try what hanging is, so that no one may say that he has not known all that was to be known in the world. He is interrupted by the entrance of the king accompanied by the duke and Casandra, who both plead for Roger's life. The king is unmoved and says that in punishing Roger now he is only sparing the punishment of some future crime which he surely will commit if he is now pardoned.

Cries of " Long live Prince Roger ! " are heard within, and the duke informs the king that no sooner did Roger appear on his way to execution than the people revolted at the idea of his punishment, delivered him from the hands of justice, and are now bringing him to the palace ; in fact, Roger is at the door awaiting the king's commands. The king sends the duke to another apartment for a large platter covered with a cloth. He is to bring this and at the same time tell Roger to enter. Roger's first words are an appeal for clemency. The king bids him wait a moment until the duke returns, who bears a salver on which is the royal crown covered with a cloth. The king addresses his son saying that the people who demand the life of the prince in opposition to the king's commands evidently wish him to resign his crown, and he, the king, has found a way not to be a king in order to punish, but to be a father in order to pardon. With these words he places his crown on Roger's head. Roger exclaims in amazement, " What are you doing? " The king replies that it is necessary, for being king he cannot pardon him, but being father he cannot condemn him. Roger owes him no thanks, for if he were king he would have to behead him, but as father he forgives him, and adds that he will henceforth care for the duchess. Roger asks the pardon of the duke and Casandra and concludes with the customary appeal to the audience for their favor and approval.

The changes which Rotrou has made in this play are fewer than in *Saint Genest*. The only substantive change has been the introduction of a secondary love plot. He has created a princess, sister to Ladislas (Roger), with whom the duke Frederick is in love, and we have a tiresome subplot like that of the Infante in the *Cid* of Corneille and of Aricie in the *Phèdre* of Racine.

The first act of Rotrou follows Rojas closely, and many passages are almost literally translated. After the king has forced Ladislas to be reconciled with his brother, Rotrou adds a scene (I. 3) in which Ladislas is obliged to become reconciled with the duke also. It is during this scene that the duke is on the point of revealing his love for the princess and asking the king for her hand as a reward for his victories. Ladislas interrupts the duke, supposing that he is about to ask for Cassandre's hand. In the next scene Ladislas reveals the cause of his hatred for the duke, in whom he sees a rival for Cassandre's love.

In Rotrou's second act the princess (Théodore) begs Cassandre to accept Ladislas's love. She, however, fears his fierce and fickle character and refuses to accept his hand. Ladislas enters and urges his suit in person. Cassandre repulses his advances and finally insinuates that her heart has already bestowed itself. Ladislas bursts into fury against his rival and Cassandre withdraws, leaving the brother and sister alone. In the course of this interview Ladislas reveals to the princess that the duke, with whom she is in love, is his rival with Cassandre. The princess is filled with amazement and despair, and refuses to see the duke under the pretext of indisposition. Alexander enters and expresses his surprise, referring to Ladislas's passion for Cassandre in such a way as to make the princess sure that her suspicions that the duke is in love with Cassandre are well founded.

In the third act Alexander, in an interview with Frederick, asks him whether Cassandre can be the object of his love. Frederick indignantly repels the implied charge of betraying Alexander and urges him to put an end to Cassandre's troubles by marrying her. At this moment Cassandre, in great agitation, enters from the apartment of the princess and informs Alexander that she has been urged to accept the hand of Ladislas. Alexander calms her and proposes a marriage that very night. Ladislas enters and declares that Cassandre's scorn for him has awakened his own. He requests his brother to conduct her from the room and bids the duke remain. He then offers to serve the duke if he will declare the object of his love. Frederick gives an evasive answer, although he is given an opportunity of confessing his love for the princess and clearing up the suspicions of Ladislas and of the princess herself. The king enters and declares his intention to reward Frederick for his services to the state by granting him the object of his affections. Frederick is again on the point of revealing his secret, when Ladislas once more closes his lips by an insolent defiance of his father and the declaration that Frederick's death will follow if he obtains his reward. The king is about to order his son's arrest, when Frederick intercedes; but the king bids him not to be disturbed by the threats of Ladislas, for he, the king, will place the duke so high that Ladislas cannot reach him to do him harm.

The fourth act opens with a scene between the princess and her *confidente*, in which the princess describes a dream in which she beheld her brother murdered. The fact reported by the *confidente* that Ladislas has spent the night out of his apartment increases her agitation. At that moment her brother Ladislas enters covered with blood and scarcely able to stand. The prince relates the occurrences of the night. Learning that the duke and Cassandre were to be married that night he had entered the palace and lain in wait for the duke. At last he heard the door opened at his name, and rushing out had stabbed the duke thrice and killed him. The princess is overwhelmed by this unexpected news and retires fainting in her *confidente's* arms.

From the third scene on Rotrou follows his model closely. The king enters with his guards and questions Ladislas, who replies that he has murdered the duke. As he utters these words the duke enters, to the profound amazement of Ladislas, who, in an aside, exclaims:

> Si le duc est vivant, quelle vie ai-je éteinte?
> Et de quel bras le mien a-t-il reçu l'atteinte?

Frederick announces Cassandre, who enters and denounces Ladislas, as in the Spanish play. The imitation, as may be seen from the Appendix, is often a verbal one.

The fifth act of Rotrou opens with an insipid love scene between the princess and the duke. From the third scene on the imitation of Rojas is very close. The pathetic scene between the father and son, the entreaties of the duke and Cassandre for Ladislas's life, the tumult of the populace, the abdication of the king, etc., — all is closely imitated from Rojas. In the French play the princess and the duke are united, and Ladislas offers his crown to Cassandre. There is a striking resemblance between the close of Rotrou's drama and Corneille's *Cid*. In both a woman is asked to accept a lover whose hands are dyed with the blood of a father or a husband. In both an appeal is made to time, to soften her sorrow, and the result can easily be foreseen.

The Spanish original conforms much more closely to the French theory of the unities than does the play of Lope de Vega, on which *Saint Genest* was based, and consequently few changes were necessary on this score. In Rojas's play the scene moves from the palace to Casandra's house and from the prison of Rugero to the royal abode. Rotrou uses only one locality, a room in the royal palace, from which opens the apartment of the Princess Théodore. The time of the Spanish play extends over about a month; in the French drama it is restricted to twenty-four hours. As a matter of fact parts of two days are involved, as in the *Cid*, but this does not constitute a real violation of the rule. The result of the limitation of time in the French play is the usual overcrowding of the incidents.

Rotrou has made no important changes in his characters, except in the case of Ladislas, who is represented in the Spanish play as a man of ungovernable temper, whose pursuit of Casandra is caused by the basest motives. In Rotrou, while Ladislas retains his fiery disposition, his passion for Cassandre has gradually undergone a refining change, and as early as the first interview between Ladislas and Cassandre the former reproaches himself with the nature of his former passion and offers the apology of his youth (see ll. 479–512). It is true that afterwards, under the influence of his ungovernable temper, he insults the duchess and apparently reverts to his earlier baseness; but this must be taken in connection with his jealous rage and the provocation he thinks the duchess has given him. He expresses himself in a way very unusual on the French stage at that time, and incurs the severe censure of Marmontel. Rotrou has also omitted the two servants obligatory in the Spanish drama and substituted the *confidente* of Théodore.

The general result of Rotrou's changes is a play more compact and dramatic than the original, while the repulsive character of the hero has been softened and rendered more attractive.

A glance at the Bibliography will show that *Venceslas* has been reprinted uninterruptedly since the first edition of 1648, and it has never entirely lost its place in the répertoire of the French theater. The stage history of *Venceslas* has been given very completely by Person, *Histoire du Venceslas*, pp. 66–95, and need not be repeated here. Suffice it to say that *Venceslas* was frequently acted in the seventeenth century. In the eighteenth century the style of the play seemed antiquated and it was seldom performed. About the middle of the century, 1759, Marmontel made his famous revision, already alluded to on p. 49 of the present work. The character of this revision will be considered in a moment. Marmontel's changes were not favorably received, and the play continued to be acted in a somewhat modified form of the original, but infrequently. Early in the last century it was often acted with Talma in the rôle of Ladislas. It does not appear to have been performed after 1816 until 1842, and not again until 1867, at Dreux, during the ceremonies of the inauguration of the statue of Rotrou already mentioned. Since then it has been acted only twice, in 1873 and 1875, at the *matinées littéraires* given by Ballande at the Théâtre de la Gaîté and the Théâtre de la Porte-Saint-Martin.

Voltaire's estimate of Rotrou has already been given in chapter II, pp. 47–49. *Venceslas* is mentioned only briefly and incidentally. The revision by Marmontel has been alluded to before, p. 49, as well as the subsequent edition, in 1773, of the play in its original form.

In the *Examen du Venceslas* in that edition Marmontel
pronounces judgment on the play as a whole.[1] The following
extracts will suffice to give Marmontel's point of view. "Le
sujet de cette pièce est vraiment tragique : il est terrible,
touchant et moral. Les trois caractères sur lesquels l'action
roule, sont grands et fortement conçus. Les caractères subor-
donnés sont en action et à leur place. Le nœud de l'intrigue
est une erreur très vraisemblable, et prolongée avec assez
d'art. Il n'y a guère d'action mieux combinée, ni de groupe
mieux composé. L'intérêt croît d'acte en acte, et tout est
bien conduit jusqu'à la conclusion, qui blesse également la
bienséance et la vérité, mais qui peut être aisément changée.
. . . Rotrou était sans doute un de ceux qui dégradaient le
moins un sujet héroïque ; mais s'il rencontrait quelquefois
l'expression noble et vraie, il donnait beaucoup plus souvent
dans la bassesse ou dans l'enflure. Sa versification était lâche
et traînante, son style inculte, négligé à l'excès, souvent embarrassé dans des constructions obscures et pénibles, et qui
pis est, d'une indécence et d'une grossièreté choquante : je
dis choquante, pour le goût d'à présent ; car celui de son
siècle n'était pas encore assez délicat pour en être blessé.

"Il serait donc injuste de reprocher à Rotrou, d'avoir
manqué à des convenances qui n'en étaient pas encore ; mais
en quoi il n'est pas excusable, c'est d'avoir noirci sans raison
le personnage intéressant de sa pièce.

"Que Ladislas soit fougueux, violent, emporté dans les
accès de sa passion, c'est en cela qu'il est tragique ; mais c'est
pour lui qu'on doit trembler et s'attendrir ; c'est lui qui doit
arracher des larmes ; c'est à lui qu'on doit s'attacher ; c'est
lui qu'on doit voir avec frémissement monter sur l'échafaud ;

---

[1] I have used the reprint of the edition of 1773 found in *Œuvres de
Marmontel*, Paris, 1820, vol. vii, pp. 354–458. The reprint does not
give the text of the plays annotated by Marmontel. The extracts given
above will be found on pp. 436–439.

c'est lui qu'on doit voir avec joie de l'échafaud passer au
trône; et dans le moment que son père, pour le sauver, lui
met la couronne sur la tête, tous les cœurs doivent applaudir.
Il faut donc que son caractère soit celui d'un prince naturellement bon, mais égaré, rendu furieux et coupable par des passions qu'il n'a pu dompter. Tout ce qui annonce la dureté, la
méchanceté d'un cœur naturellement féroce, est donc une tache
dans ce caractère, et tout le rôle est plein de ces traits odieux.

"... J'ai dit quel était le mérite de cette pièce. Quant à
l'exécution, elle était au-dessus des forces de Rotrou. A l'exception des scènes du père et du fils, où la grandeur et
l'intérêt des choses ont élevé l'âme du poète et soutenu son
style, tout le reste est faible, négligé, mal écrit; et l'on ne
peut trop regretter qu'un sujet si beau ne soit pas tombé dans
les mains ou d'un Racine ou d'un Voltaire."

Marmontel then alludes to his version of the play and the
reception it met with at the hands of the critics [1] and the
public, and continues: "Je laisse à des lecteurs tranquilles le
soin de voir et de juger; et de toutes les corrections que j'ai
faites au *Venceslas*, il n'y en a qu'une sur laquelle je me per-
mettrai d'insister: c'est le dénoûment de l'intrigue.

"On me fit dans le temps une sorte de violence pour
renoncer à ce changement. Je me défiais de moi-même; et
quoiqu'au spectacle de la cour on m'eût félicité d'avoir fini
par un coup de théâtre qui remplissait l'idée du caractère de
Cassandre, et qui, en punissant Ladislas, donnait à l'action
plus de moralité, et au dénoûment plus de vraisemblance;
cependant, comme au spectacle de Paris le public, par un
froid silence, avait paru ou surpris ou fâché de ne pas retrouver l'ancien dénoûment, je cédai aux instances qu'on me fit

---

[1] Marmontel cites a passage from a letter by Voltaire, which may be
found in the edition of Voltaire's works already cited, vol. xlv, p. 491:
"J'ai lu hier le *Venceslas* que vous avez rajeuni. Il me semble que vous
avez rendu un très-grand service au théâtre."

pour le rétablir. J'y ai réfléchi depuis, et au bout de quinze ans, j'y ai réfléchi de sang froid. Or il répugne encore à présent et à mon âme et à mes principes, que Ladislas sorte du théâtre, impuni, couronné, heureux dans son amour, par l'espérance révoltante qu'on lui donne d'épouser Cassandre ; au lieu qu'il est également et dans le caractère de Cassandre, et dans la vérité de sa situation, et dans la bonté théâtrale des mœurs, qu'elle se tue, et mette au désespoir le coupable impuni qu'on vient de couronner. Voilà sur quoi j'insiste. Par le crime arriver au bonheur, est une chose monstrueuse à présenter sur le théâtre.

" Je reviens donc à ma première idée, et je supplie le lecteur de comparer avec réflexion ce dénoûment à celui de Rotrou.

SCÈNE DERNIÈRE

VENCESLAS, LADISLAS, LE DUC, THÉODORE, CASSANDRE, OCTAVE, ET LE PEUPLE

VENCESLAS

Peuple, dans Venceslas ne voyez plus qu'un père.
Vous avez désarmé ma justice sévère ;
Vous avez mis le prince au-dessus de la loi ;
C'est me chasser du trône, et l'élire pour roi.

CASSANDRE

Lui mon roi ! des forfaits le trône est le refuge !
Le crime est couronné par les mains de son juge !

VENCESLAS

Cassandre, la justice a ses droits limités :
La clémence a les siens ; je les ai consultés.

LADISLAS

J'ai, pour vous, accepté la vie et la couronne,
Madame ; ordonnez-en : je vous les abandonne.
Mon amour malheureux n'a que trop éclaté.

CASSANDRE

Que dis-tu, Ladislas ? te serais-tu flatté
Que du sang de ton frère encor toute fumante,
Ta main pourrait charmer les yeux de son amante ?
Penses-tu que le crime heureux et couronné,
Dans le fond de mon cœur en soit moins condamné ?
Règne, jouis du trône, et du jour que te laisse
Une pitié barbare, une indigne faiblesse ;
Règne, fais s'il se peut oublier le passé
A ce père trop tendre, à ce peuple insensé :
De leur lâche bonté je ne suis point complice.

LADISLAS

Ma grâce est en vos mains.

CASSANDRE, en se frappant

Voilà donc ton supplice.

LADISLAS, au désespoir, et voulant se tuer

Dieux !

VENCESLAS, en l'embrassant

Mon fils !

LADISLAS

Je vivrai ; je vous dois cet effort.
Coupable et malheureux je subirai mon sort.
O Cassandre ! ô mon frère ! en supportant la vie,
Je serai trop puni de vous l'avoir ravie."

It would take too much space to enumerate the other changes made by Marmontel in his revision published in 1759. This edition is scarce and the student will have to content himself with the version published by Viollet-le-Duc in his edition of Rotrou's works, vol. v, pp. 265–324, which, as Lenel has pointed out, contains changes by Colardeau and others, although Viollet-le-Duc expressly says " avec les corrections faites en 1759 par Marmontel." This version of the play is the one used when the tragedy is acted. I have given in my notes copious extracts from Marmontel's "Remarques," which are interesting as showing the changes that have taken place in taste and language between the seventeenth and eighteenth centuries.

Marmontel was followed by La Harpe (see chapter II, p. 50), who devoted to an analysis of *Venceslas* part of the fifth chapter of his *Cours de littérature ancienne et moderne*, Paris, 1825, vol. viii, pp. 125–141. He says: "De tous ceux qui ont écrit avant Corneille, c'est celui qui avait le plus de talent; mais comme son *Venceslas*, la seule pièce de lui qui soit restée, est postérieure aux plus belles du père du théâtre, on peut le compter parmi les écrivains qui ont pu se former à l'école de ce grand homme. Il fit plus de trente pièces, tant tragédies que comédies et tragi-comédies: plusieurs sont empruntées du théâtre espagnol ou de celui des Grecs; mais il a plus imité les défauts du premier que les beautés du second: il n'a pas même évité la licence grossière et les pointes ridicules qui déshonoraient la scène, et dont Corneille l'a purgée le premier." He then analyzes the play and his judgment does not differ from that of Marmontel. He blames Rotrou for making Ladislas so repulsive by his vices, and criticises the ending of the play: "Ce dénouement est défectueux dans la partie morale, puisque le prince est récompensé. Cependant il ne révolte point, et il faut en savoir gré à l'auteur: c'est une preuve qu'il a su intéresser en faveur de Ladislas, et qu'il a connu ce secret de l'art qui consiste à faire excuser et plaindre les attentats qu'un moment de fureur a fait commettre, et qui ne sont pas réfléchis." La Harpe then examines each character and criticises Rotrou's "oubli des convenances." He concludes with the words: "Heureusement ces détails si vicieux, et les longueurs et les vers ridicules, sont faciles à supprimer; et, à l'aide de ces retranchements et de quelques corrections, l'ouvrage s'est soutenu au théâtre avec un succès mérité. Son ancienneté le rend précieux, et, au défaut d'élégance, le style un peu suranné a un air de vétusté et de naturel qui ne lui messied pas, et qui donne même un nouveau prix aux beautés en rappelant leur époque."

The critical estimates of *Venceslas* in the nineteenth century will be found in the general works relating to Rotrou and in the literary histories, which it has not been my purpose to cite. Some criticism of *Venceslas* has already been mentioned in the second chapter in dealing with the general subject of Rotrou's literary reputation. It is, however, surprising that *Venceslas* did not attract the attention of the nineteenth-century critics as did *Saint Genest*, — a fact probably accounted for by the more novel form and character of the latter play.

I greatly regret that the limits of the present work have not permitted the inclusion of *Cosroès*, a noble play, which deserves more than a mere mention. It was the last play by Rotrou and was composed in 1648 and first printed in 1649. For a long time *Cosroès* was considered the only original play of Rotrou, but it has been shown that it was taken from Cellot, who furnished, as has been seen, the plot for the play intercalated in *Saint Genest*.[1] An analysis of *Cosroès* will show its interesting character and ethical connection with *Venceslas*.[2]

Cosroès, king of Persia, has married as his second wife Sira, by whom he has a son Mardesane. The heir to the throne is Siroès, the son by the first marriage, whose wife is Narsée,

---

[1] The credit of this discovery belongs to E. Deschanel, who made it known in his *Le Romantisme des Classiques*, Paris, 1883, pp. 268–287, a work already cited for its criticism of *Saint Genest*, on p. 96 of this Introduction. Since then the subject of Rotrou's indebtedness to Cellot for *Cosroès* has been treated in a masterly manner by A. L. Stiefel in the *Zeitschrift für franz. Spr. und Lit.*, vol. xxiii, pp. 69–188, in the article already mentioned.

[2] An analysis of *Cosroès* and a critical estimate of the play will be found in Saint-Marc Girardin, *Cours de littérature dramatique*, vol. ii, pp. 30–39.

supposed to be the daughter of Sira, but in reality the daughter of the powerful minister Palmiras. The play opens with an angry scene between the queen and her stepson, whom she accuses of want of respect for her son Mardesane, declaring that she will perish or her son will reign. At these words Siroès lays his hand upon his sword, saying that before this happens his sword must become useless, his heart insensible, and his arm paralyzed. Mardesane enters at this moment and the infuriated queen accuses Siroès of an attempt upon her life. Mardesane deprecates his mother's zeal and expresses his own preference for a life of quiet. Siroès does not believe he can withstand the temptations of power and deny his mother's wishes, and concludes by solemnly warning him that if he aspires to the throne he must first kill him (Siroès); otherwise he cannot long hope to be his master. Mardesane withdraws at the approach of Palmiras, who, we learn, has incurred the disfavor of the queen. Siroès cannot banish from his mind the fatal words of the queen, and Palmiras urges him to defend his claims to the throne, by violence if necessary. Cosroès himself obtained the throne by slaying his own father, Hormisdas, and many of his subjects would gladly " see the first act of parricide punished by a second one." Siroès exclaims :

> Laisser ravir un trône est une lâcheté,
> Mais en chasser un père est une impiété.

While Siroès is torn by the conflict of ambition and filial respect, Pharnace enters with the astonishing news that the king intends to crown Mardesane in the presence of the army. Siroès recalls the queen's words :

> Mais, je périrai, traître, ou mon fils régnera ;

and cries :

> Oui, oui, qu'elle périsse, et nous, régnons, Pharnace.

The act closes with the urgent advice of Palmiras:

> Le besoin presse ; allons, ne perdons plus de temps ;
> Pratiquons-nous les grands, gagnons les habitants ;
> Employons nos amis, et, la brigue formée,
> Observons Mardesane, ouvrons-nous à l'armée,
> Et, promettant d'entendre au traité des Romains,
> Intéressons Émile à nous prêter les mains.

The second act opens with a scene between Cosroès, Sira, and the king's officer, Sardarigue. The king is recovering from one of his attacks of madness produced by remorse for his father's murder. Sira urges him to abdicate and thus forget his crime. Cosroès yields to the advice and wiles of his wife and declares that he will elect Mardesane, and see without regret, in his old age, his scepter in a more capable hand and his innocent son succeed a guilty father. Sardarigue asks if this can be done without a crime against the right of primogeniture and the laws of the state. Sira craftily exposes the dangers which the king will run if he chooses Siroès, who would remove all obstacles to his independent reign, and declares that Siroès, that very morning, had drawn his sword on her. The king is horrified and promises to protect Sira, who points out that if Mardesane is elected he will reign only in his father's name. Sardarigue, when called on to summon the council and arrange the coronation ceremony, ventures to express his fears of the result, but the king orders him to arrest Siroès and guard him carefully. Mardesane then enters and learns from the king of his choice of a successor. The gentle and noble character of Mardesane is revealed in his reply. He seeks to avoid the honor which belongs rightly to his brother, and conjures the king for once not to listen to the prayers of his wife, but " to save his (Mardesane's) virtue from a mother's love." The king informs him of the arrest of Siroès, which will prevent all opposition, and commands

Mardesane to accept the crown. The prince yields with regret, assured of his own ruin, and cries out to his mother :

> Ah, Madame, quel fruit me produit votre amour.

At that point Siroès enters and demands an explanation of the rumor he has heard. He declares his respect for the queen, and, if it were permissible to extol his own services, recalls that he has lately saved the life of Mardesane in battle. The queen refers to the pretended attack upon her by Siroès, and the king commands him to receive as from him the order which will shortly be brought. All withdraw with the exception of Siroès, and Sardarigue and guards enter. Sardarigue delivers the order of arrest, but at the same time expresses his own devotion to Siroès, and declares that it is time for him to show himself to the camp and overthrow the queen's intrigues. Siroès breaks into grateful thanks for Sardarigue's support and the act closes with the words of Siroès :

> Allons, lançons plutôt que d'attendre la foudre ;
> Avisons aux moyens dont nous devons résoudre :
> Mais faites-moi régner pour régner avec moi,
> Et vous donner plutôt un compagnon qu'un roi.

At the beginning of the third act Sira expresses to her *confidente*, Hormisdate, her joy at the success of her plots ; Mardesane is seated on the throne, Palmiras disgraced, and Siroès arrested. Hormisdate ventures to suggest that this great success involves great dangers, that fortune is fickle and the people deceitful. Sira replies that the arrest of Siroès relieves her of fear, but that she desires to prevent his release, and begs Hormisdate to accomplish her design, asking whether she (the queen) can rely implicitly upon the zeal of Artanasde, the brother of Hormisdate. When Hormisdate replies in the affirmative the queen gives her a dagger and a bowl of poison, and asks her to transmit these by her brother to Siroès in prison, leaving to the prince the choice of the mode of death. If he refuses to choose, Artanasde is to murder him.

Hormisdate is overwhelmed with horror, but yields and departs
with the foreboding :

> Mais je crains de vous rendre un service fatal,
> Et, j'ose dire plus, que j'en augure mal.

Then Sardarigue and guards enter and when the queen asks if
he has executed his order, he replies that he has not, but has
another which he must carry out to his regret, — the arrest of
the queen.

SIRA

Quelle audace est la vôtre !

Moi, téméraire ?

SARDARIGUE

Vous.

SIRA

De quelle part ?

SARDARIGUE

Du roi.

SIRA

Imposteur ! Cosroès t'impose cette loi ?

SARDARIGUE

Cosroès n'a-t-il pas déposé la couronne ?

SIRA

Qui donc ? est-ce mon fils, traître, qui te l'ordonne ?

SARDARIGUE

Votre fils m'ordonner ! en quelle qualité ?

SIRA

De ton roi, de ton maître, insolent, effronté !

SARDARIGUE

Siroès est mon roi, Siroès est mon maître :
La Perse sous ces noms vient de le reconnaître.

Sira calls in vain on her suite and the guards for protection and threatens Sardarigue with condign punishment. As she is led away she encounters Siroès and Palmiras. A rapid dialogue of single lines then ensues, but Palmiras interposes to cut the interview short and the infuriated queen is led to prison by Sardarigue and guards.

Siroès exclaims that his reign begins under sad auspices if he owes to it blood and punishments. Palmiras explains the critical state of the kingdom and endeavors to soothe the regrets of Siroès for his treatment of his father; but remorse has begun its work and Siroès compares the diamond points in the crown to the cares which fate bestows.

> Et ce vain ornement marque bien la rigueur
> Des poignantes douleurs qui nous percent le cœur.

While Siroès is in this frame of mind his wife, Narsée, enters and upbraids him for the arrest of her mother, the queen. Siroès excuses himself by the necessity of the case and declares :

> Et ce sont nos bourreaux que je fais arrêter.

NARSÉE

> Nos bourreaux, les auteurs du jour qui nous éclaire !

SIROÈS

> Les auteurs de l'affront qu'ils nous ont voulu faire.

NARSÉE

> Un empire vaut-il cette inhumanité ?

In an impassioned address Narsée calls on Siroès to destroy all that can arouse his fears and suspicions, and to sacrifice the daughter with the mother. Siroès is overcome by his wife's appeal and orders the guards to obey her directions and especially to place Sira in her daughter's hands. The conclusion of this fine scene is marred by the tone of gallantry in the answer of

Siroès to Narsée's question : " Cette faveur vous coûte trop de peine?"

> Je n'ai qu'un seul regret, que mon amour extrême,
> En hasardant mes jours, se hasarde lui-même,
> Et qu'au point du succès dont je flattais mes vœux,
> L'heur de vous posséder me devienne douteux.

Narsée declares that her fate is inseparable from his and that she can promise him

> un bouclier invincible
> En la garde d'un cœur surveillant et sensible,
> Qui de vos ennemis vous parera les coups,
> Ou qu'il faudra percer pour aller jusqu'à vous.

It will be remembered that at the beginning of the last act Sira intrusted to Hormisdate a dagger and bowl of poison to be transmitted by her brother, Artanasde, to Siroès in prison. Artanasde at once communicates to his king the design of his stepmother and shows him her fatal gift. When Siroès breaks forth into reproaches and cries :

> O redoutable esprit, ô marâtre cruelle !
> Trop pieuse Narsée, et mère indigne d'elle !

Artanasde reveals to him the fact that Narsée is not the daughter of Sira, but of Palmiras, formerly in the service of the queen, who substituted his own child for the queen's daughter, who died while an infant under the charge of Hormisdate. Siroès, doubtful at first, is finally convinced by Artanasde, whom he charges to keep the dagger and poison and dismisses with expressions of gratitude.

Sardarigue enters and informs Siroès that the soldiers espousing his cause are bringing to him as prisoners Cosroès and Mardesane. Siroès asks who gave the order for their arrest, and when he learns that it was the spontaneous act of the army, bursts into tears at this conspicuous example of the fickleness of fortune. He asks for time to prepare himself for

the interview with his father. After his departure Narsée
enters and commands Sardarigue to liberate the queen; while
Sardarigue hesitates to obey Palmiras appears and forbids him
to act. In the scene which follows between Narsée and Palmiras, largely a rapid dialogue of single lines, the latter pro-
fesses the most profound respect for Narsée and, without
revealing the secret of her birth, assures her that she has no
interest in the captivity or death of the queen. Narsée is
shocked at the apparent cruelty of these words, and Palmiras
is on the point of confessing himself her father when Artanasde
enters in great agitation and begs Palmiras to come at once to
Siroès, who, having seen his father in a fit of madness, is so
disturbed that he wavers in his designs. Unless this irresolu-
tion can be overcome, all that has been accomplished by Palmiras will be in vain. Palmiras, like a true courtier, exclaims:

> De nos têtes, ô ciel, détourne ton courroux!
> Sauve un roi trop pieux de sa propre faiblesse,
> Et ceux qu'en son parti sa fortune intéresse.

He leaves Artanasde and his sister Hormisdate to explain to
Narsée what he had left unsaid, and the act closes with an
aside from the perplexed Narsée:

> Dieux! quelle est cette énigme, et qu'y puis-je comprendre?
> Quel jour puis-je tirer de tant d'obscurité,
> Et quelle foi devrai-je à cette vérité?

The fifth act opens with a scene between Sira and Sardarigue, in which the queen expresses her deadly hatred of Siroès
and desires liberty only that she may die his murderer.
Siroès then enters with his retinue and seats himself upon the
throne. Sira confesses all her crimes and declares that she
has sworn to die or see her son reign, and that if liberty were
offered her she would employ it for the destruction of Siroès.
The king upbraids her for the fatal results of her ambition
which have ruined her husband and son. Sira begs for sentence

and dismissal from the presence of Siroès, whose sight is unendurable to her :

> Tyran, délivre-moi de l'horreur de tes yeux ;
> Chaque trait m'en punit, chaque regard m'en tue,
> Et mon plus grand supplice est celui de ta vue.

Siroès calls upon his satraps to pronounce judgment and, showing to Sira the dagger and poison which she sent to him, asks whether she considers them sufficient witnesses against her. She replies :

> Quand j'ai tout avoué, je n'ai rien à répondre ;
> Je prends droit par moi-même, et mon plus grand forfait
> Est, non d'avoir osé, mais osé sans effet.

And Siroès answers :

> Les instruments du mal le seront du supplice :
> Choisissez l'un des deux, et faites-vous justice.

Sira declares that this is a favor she did not dare to hope for, and chooses the poison, saying that its taste will be sweet in default of Siroès's blood, which she would have drawn with joy from his breast. She asks as another favor :

> Tyran, fais que mon fils y précède mes pas,
> Pour le voir, par sa mort, exempt de l'infamie
> De recevoir des lois d'une main ennemie ;
> Vivant, de son crédit tu craindrais les effets.

Siroès replies :

> Vos vœux sont généreux, ils seront satisfaits.
> Qu'il entre, Sardarigue, et remenez la reine.

> SIRA, *avec emportement*
> Reine est ma qualité, quand tu sais qu'elle est vaine !
> Hier, j'étais ta marâtre, et je tiens à grand bien
> De mourir aujourd'hui pour ne t'être plus rien.
> (*Elle sort avec Sardarigue et les gardes*)

Palmiras asks the king to ascribe the queen's vain words to her despair, and Siroès expresses his desire to spare her life if

the interests of his authority would permit. Palmiras answers
in the sentementious manner of the political tragedy of the
seventeenth century :

> Remettant l'intérêt qui touche sa personne,
> Un roi ne peut donner celui de la couronne,
> Et, s'il voit que l'État coure quelque danger,
> Est contraint de punir, s'il ne se veut venger.
> Sa justice est le bien de toute la province ;
> Ce qu'il pourrait sujet, il ne le peut pas prince ;
> Et l'indulgence enfin qui hasarde un État
> Est le plus grand défaut qu'ait un grand potentat.

Mardesane is then led before Siroès, who recalls his former
warning that Mardesane, if he aspired to the throne, should
not spare his brother, and asks if the scepter of Persia is an
easy burden. Mardesane answers that to be able to taste its
sweetness a longer trial would be needed. The rapid dialogue
that follows, in speeches of one or two lines, grows more and
more bitter. Siroès demands by what right Mardesane had
seized the throne. He replies :

> Par droit d'obéissance, et par l'ordre d'un père.

SIROÈS

> Contre un droit naturel quel père m'est contraire ?

MARDESANE

> Quel ? le vôtre et le mien qui, juge de son sang,
> A selon son désir disposé de son rang.

SIROÈS

> Il a fondé ce choix dessus votre mérite.

MARDESANE

> Je n'ai point expliqué la loi qu'il m'a prescrite.

SIROÈS

> Vous exécutez mal la foi que vous donnez ;
> Je vous la tiendrai mieux que vous ne la tenez.

MARDESANE

Généreux, j'aime mieux avouer une offense
Que, timide et tremblant, parler en ma défense.

SIROÈS

Juste, j'ai plus de lieu de vous faire punir
Que, lâche, d'un affront perdre le souvenir.

MARDESANE

Vous en vengeant, au moins, vous n'aurez pas la gloire
D'avoir été prié d'en perdre la mémoire.

SIROÈS

Vous avez trop de cœur.

MARDESANE

     Assez pour faire voir
Une grande vertu dans un grand désespoir.

SIROÈS

Mais il se produit tard.

Mardesane in two speeches of great dignity and beauty declares
that the scepter has inspired him with the feelings of a king,
and that in spite of the untoward accident which has befallen
him he still preserves an independent heart, and to save his
life would not offer a prayer to Siroès's vanity. He contrasts
his own conduct with that of Siroès, when the latter was arrested. He, Mardesane, respected him deprived of his rights,
scarcely consented to dictate the law to him, and might perhaps
have laid the crown at his feet. But, after the bloody plot of
Siroès and his contempt for the laws of nature, he declares:

Je ne vous cèle point que, si quelque aventure
Remettait aujourd'hui le sceptre entre mes mains,
Pour vous le rendre plus tous respects seraient vains,
Et, dépouillant pour vous tous sentiments de frère,
Je me ferais justice et vengerai mon père.
Voilà tout le dessein que j'ai de vous toucher,
Et tout ce qu'à ma peur vous pouvez reprocher;
J'en laisse à décider à votre tyrannie.

Siroès, enraged at Mardesane's inflexible spirit, orders him to
be led to execution and put to death in his mother's sight.
Mardesane is defiant to the last and departs with the words:

> Allons, règne, tyran, règne enfin sans obstacle;
> J'ai reçu de mon père, avecque son pouvoir,
> Celui d'aller trouver la mort sans désespoir.

The following scene (Siroès, Palmiras, Pharnace) prepares
us for the interview between father and son. Siroès declares
that he cannot purchase the sweetness of empire at the cost
of a father's life, and to Pharnace's admonition that this ten-
der feeling is untimely and the quiet of the state must be
assured, he cries:

> Je m'en démets, cruels; régnez, je l'abandonne,
> Et ma tête à ce prix ne veut point de couronne;
> Mon cœur contre mon sang s'ose en vain révolter;
> Par force ou par amour il s'en fait respecter.
> A mon père, inhumains, donnez un autre juge,
> Ou dans les bras d'un fils qu'on lui souffre un refuge.

He continues in the same strain until his father enters. Scarcely
has Cosroès expressed his horror at the unnatural conduct of
his son when the contrite Siroès falls at his father's feet and
renounces his rights to become again his son:

> Est-il un bras de fils qu'un soupir, une larme,
> Un seul regard d'un père aisément ne désarme?
> Si contre vous, hélas! j'écoute mon courroux,
> Je porte dans le sein ce qui parle pour vous;
> Dedans moi, contre moi, vous trouvez du refuge,
> Et, criminel ou non, vous n'avez point de juge.
> Paisible, possédez l'État que je vous rends;
> Vous pouvez seul, Seigneur, régler mes différends;
> Arbitre entre vos fils, terminez leur dispute
> En retenant pour vous le rang qu'ils ont en butte;
> Ne le déposez pas aux dépens de mes droits,
> Entretenez en paix votre sang sous vos lois.

Cosroès cannot believe the words of Siroès while Mardesane and the queen are captives, and Siroès at once orders their release. After Cosroès, Sardarigue, and the guards have departed, Palmiras, as usual, indulges in gloomy reflections on the probable results of Siroès's action. Siroès declares that he would prefer death to the inhumanity of disregarding the voice of nature.

At this moment Narsée enters and informs Siroès that Mardesane has killed himself rather than die an infamous death. Although Narsée has learned the secret of her birth she could not withhold her attentions from Sira, but, seeing her weeping over her son's body and calling on the fates and hostile gods, she withdrew unable to utter a word, and as she departed she saw borne in the bowl of poison which Siroès had ordered for Sira's punishment.

The play ends with the entrance of Sardarigue, who relates in the conventional manner the final catastrophe:

> Ah! Sire, malgré vous le destin de la Perse
> Vous protège et détruit tout ce qui vous traverse.

SIROÈS

> Qu'est-ce encor?

SARDARIGUE

> Cosroès, rentré dans la prison,
> Ayant vu que la reine y prenait le poison,
> Prompt, et trompant les soins et les yeux de la troupe,
> Avant qu'elle eût tout pris, s'est saisi de la coupe,
> Et, buvant ce qui reste: « Il faut, » nous a-t-il dit,
> Voyant d'un œil troublé Sira rendre l'esprit
> Et nager dans son sang Mardesane sans vie,
> « Il faut du sort de Perse assouvir la furie,
> « Accorder à mon père un tribut qu'il attend,
> « Laisser à Siroès le trône qu'il prétend,
> « Et de tant de tyrans terminer la dispute. »
> Là, tombant, quelque garde a soutenu sa chute;
> Et nous . . .

SIROÈS, *furieux*

Et bien, cruels, êtes-vous satisfaits?
Mon règne produit-il d'assez tristes effets?
La couronne, inhumains, à ce prix m'est trop chère.
Allons, Madame, allons suivre ou sauver un père.

PALMIRAS

Ne l'abandonnons point.

SARDARIGUE, *à part*

Ses soins sont superflus;
Le poison est trop prompt, le tyran ne vit plus.

In conclusion it may be said that it is not difficult to assign Rotrou to his proper place in the dramatic literature of the first half of the seventeenth century. He easily stands first among the contemporaries of Corneille. This alone would not be high praise, for Mairet, Scudéry, du Ryer, La Calprenède, Tristan, and Benserade were not formidable rivals in the serious drama, and Rotrou's comedies do not suffer from a comparison with those of Boisrobert, Desmarests, Cyrano, Scarron, and Thomas Corneille. There is, of course, no question here of Racine, whose *Andromaque* did not appear until 1667, that is, seventeen years after Rotrou's death. The only one with whom Rotrou can be justly compared is the great Corneille, and the comparison offers many interesting points of study. They began their literary careers about the same time and under the same conditions; they were even fellow-workers under Richelieu. Both accepted the prevailing form of the drama, tragi-comedy, and one, Rotrou, never excelled in any other. Corneille, on the other hand, became the founder of the classical tragedy and imparted to it the form with which it was invested during its long lease of life from 1639 to 1830, the dates of *Horace* and of *Hernani*.

It is futile to inquire what the result would have been if the Quarrel of the Cid had not shaped Corneille's literary future;

the drama of Rotrou shows the inevitable trend of tragi-comedy. Although Rotrou made great advances in his art in the last ten years of his life, it is not reasonable to claim that, had it been prolonged, he would have attained a higher place in French dramatic literature. *Laure Persécutée* (1638) is the best of his tragi-comedies; *La Sœur* (1645) the best of his comedies; and the plays in this volume (1645 and 1647) — *Cosroès* is probably of 1648 — the best of his tragedies. But all these plays show an advance only in the art and not in the underlying principles of this art. Rotrou was essentially a romantic poet and the form of tragi-comedy was the one best adapted to his genius. This form appeals to the countrymen of Shakespeare, and Rotrou will probably be more favorably judged by them than by his own compatriots.

After all, the main question is one of accomplishment, and the masterpieces of Corneille and Racine will always be the best defenders of a literary form with which the Romantic world is not in sympathy. *Saint Genest*, *Venceslas*, *Cosroès*, great plays though they be, can hardly make us wish that the form to which they belong had prevailed over the form of classical tragedy.

LE VÉRITABLE SAINT GENEST

TRAGÉDIE DE MR. DE ROTROU

1645

The text of *Saint Genest* and *Venceslas* is, with modernized orthography, that of the original editions of 1648, which I have used in the copies at Paris and in the Harvard College Library (see Bibliography for full description). I have corrected only such errors as are manifestly typographical; all other changes are mentioned in the notes. I have not thought it worth while to give the variants of Viollet-le-Duc and Hémon, as they have no independent value; the stage directions added by the former editor have occasionally been given in brackets, where they were necessary for the understanding of the text. The edition of Ronchaud, as has already been said, follows the original editions very closely, except in some minor points of capitalization, punctuation, etc. See p. 51, note 2.

ACTEURS

DIOCLÉTIEN, empereur
MAXIMIN, empereur
VALÉRIE, fille de Dioclétien
CAMILLE, suivante
PLANCIEN, préfet
GENEST, comédien
MARCELLE, comédienne
OCTAVE, comédien
SERGESTE, comédien
LENTULE, comédien
ALBIN, comédien
DÉCORATEUR
GEÔLIER

ADRIEN, représenté par Genest
NATALIE, par Marcelle
FLAVIE, par Sergeste
MAXIMIN, par Octave
ANTHISME, par Lentule
GARDE, par Albin
GEÔLIER

SUITE DE SOLDATS ET GARDES

1648 omits "Un Page" who appears in Act I, scenes 2 and 4. *Dioclétien* is given by 1648 always in the form *Diocletian*. I have followed the usual form. This is also the case with *Adrien*, always *Adrian* in 1648. *Anthisme* appears in the form *Anthyme* in 1648, Act IV, scene 5.

Diocletian was born in A.D. 245 of most obscure family, his parents being slaves. He entered the army, and, rapidly rising, was proclaimed emperor by the soldiers in A.D. 284. He slew with his own hand Arrius Aper, who was accused of the murder of the emperor Numerianus, in order to fulfill a prophecy made to him while a youth by a Gaulish Druidess, that he should ascend a throne as soon as he had slain the wild boar (*aper*). In A.D. 286 he associated with himself in the government M. Aurelius Valerius Maximianus, like himself born of humble parents, conferring on him first the title of Caesar and afterwards that of Augustus. In A.D. 292 he still further divided his power by appointing two Caesars, Galerius and Constantius. The former, surnamed Armentarius from his profession of herdsman, is known as Galerius Valerius Maximianus, and was married by Diocletian to his daughter Valeria. He is the *Maximin* of Rotrou's play, and became emperor on Diocletian's abdication in A.D. 305.

Valeria, the daughter of Diocletian and Prisca, was married to Galerius, as stated above, in A.D. 292. After her husband's death, in A.D. 311, she and her mother were treated with great cruelty by his successor Maximinus, and were finally put to death by the emperor Licinius in A.D. 315.

For the legend of *Adrien*, whose martyrdom took place in Nicomedia under Galerius about A.D. 310, see Introduction, p. 83, note 3.

The scene is at Rome, and the time, strictly speaking, should be A.D. 292, the date of the marriage of Valeria to Galerius. It is, however, impossible to reconcile the various dates of the martyrdom of Saint Genest, placed by Baronius in A.D. 303, and of Adrian, referred by Tillemont to A.D. 309 and by the editors of the *Acta Sanctorum* to A.D. 310. Rotrou, for the purpose of his play, makes the martyrdom of Adrian precede that of Saint Genest. See Introduction, p. 82.

The usual designation for the dramatis personae in the seventeenth century is *acteurs*, with or without the article. The word *personnages* was sometimes employed, and later became the usual term.

ACTE PREMIER

Scène I

Valérie, Camille

CAMILLE

Quoi ! vous ne sauriez vaincre une frayeur si vaine?
Un songe, une vapeur vous causent de la peine,
A vous sur qui le Ciel déployant ses trésors,
Mit un si digne esprit dans un si digne corps !

VALÉRIE

Le premier des Césars apprit bien que les songes   5
Ne sont pas toujours faux et toujours des mensonges ;
Et la force d'esprit dont il fut tant vanté,

The references to Haase, *Syntaxe française du xvii⁰ siècle, traduite par M. Obert*, Paris, 1898, are by sections and remarks, and will apply to the original German edition, Oppeln and Leipzig, 1888. The *Lexiques de Corneille, Racine, Molière*, etc., are the *lexiques* accompanying the editions of those authors in *Les Grands Écrivains de la France*, Paris, Hachette et Cie.

---

2. une vapeur: Littré, *Dict.*, "Nom employé dans le xvii⁰ siècle pour désigner des accidents subits qui portaient au cerveau." In modern French usually in the plural and meaning "the blues."

3. déployant sur: "in whom Heaven revealing its treasures," etc. *A vous* repeats emphatically the *vous* before *causent* of the preceding line.

5. For Calpurnia's dream see Shakespeare's *Julius Caesar*, II. 2. For the "Dream" in French tragedy see P. V. Delaporte, *Du merveilleux dans la littérature française sous le règne de Louis XIV*, Paris, 1891, pp. 144 et seq. The dream was a usual part of the machinery of the tragedy. The most famous is the one in *Athalie*, II. 5. There is also a dream in *Venceslas*, ll. 1157–1170.

Pour l'avoir conseillé, lui coûta la clarté.

Le Ciel, comme il lui plaît, nous parle sans obstacle ;

S'il veut, la voix d'un songe est celle d'un oracle, 10

Et les songes, surtout tant de fois répétés,

Ou toujours, ou souvent, disent des vérités.

Déjà cinq ou six nuits à ma triste pensée

Ont de ce vil hymen la vision tracée,

M'ont fait voir un berger avoir assez d'orgueil 15

Pour prétendre à mon lit, qui serait mon cercueil,

Et l'empereur, mon père, avecque violence,

De ce présomptueux appuyer l'insolence.

Je puis, s'il m'est permis, et si la vérité

Dispense les enfants à quelque liberté, 20

De sa mauvaise humeur craindre un mauvais office ;

Je connais son amour, mais je crains son caprice,

8. Pour l'avoir conseillé : i.e. for having persuaded him that dreams were false. — **clarté :** = *vie*.

14. vil : "base, unworthy."— **tracée :** for agreement see note to l. 542.

15. orgueil : "presumption."

16. prétendre à mon lit : "aspire to my hand." *Lit* (*couche*, l. 27) constantly in French tragedy for "marriage." Here translate : "aspire to share my couch, which would be my coffin."

17. avecque : instead of *avec*, for metrical reasons, to obtain an additional syllable. See l. 87 and frequently. In the seventeenth century both forms were used in prose, *avec* before a vowel and *avecque* before a consonant. See *Lexique de Corneille*, I, p. 101, and Vaugelas, *Remarques sur la langue françoise, Nouvelle édition par A. Chassang*, Paris, 1880, I, pp. 424–429.

19. puis : see *Lexique de Corneille*, II, p. 210. In his early plays Corneille used *je peux*, but changed it to *je puis* after 1644. Vaugelas, *Remarques*, I, p. 143, says : "Je ne pense pas qu'il le faille tout à fait condamner ; mais je sais bien que *je puis* est beaucoup mieux dit, et plus en usage." At present *peux* is used unless the subject follows, as *puis-je*.

20. Dispense à : antiquated, "to authorize to do." Translate : "if truth permits children some liberty." See *Lexique de Corneille*, I, p. 310. *Polyeucte*, III. 2 : "serais-je dispensée A suivre, à son exemple, une ardeur insensée ? "

21. office : "service."

Et vois qu'en tout rencontre il suit aveuglément
La bouillante chaleur d'un premier mouvement.
Sut-il considérer, pour son propre hyménée,   25
Sous quel joug il baissait sa tête couronnée,
Quand, empereur, il fit sa couche et son État
Le prix de quelques pains qu'il emprunta soldat,
Et, par une faiblesse à nulle autre seconde,
S'associa ma mère à l'empire du monde?   30
Depuis, Rome souffrit et ne réprouva pas
Qu'il commît un Alcide au fardeau d'un Atlas,
Qu'on vît sur l'univers deux têtes souveraines,
Et que Maximien en partageât les rênes.
Mais pourquoi pour un seul tant de maîtres divers   35
Et pourquoi quatre chefs au corps de l'univers?
Le choix de Maximin et celui de Constance
Étaient-ils à l'État de si grande importance
Qu'il en dût recevoir beaucoup de fermeté,
Et ne pût subsister sans leur autorité?   40
Tous deux différemment altèrent sa mémoire,

---

23. For omission of subject of *vois*, see *Lexiques de Racine*, I, p. cxviii,
and *de Molière*, I, p. clxxx; Vaugelas, *Remarques*, II, pp. 143 et seq.,
382; and Haase, 8, A. In this particular case *je* has already been used
twice in the preceding line. — **rencontre**: "occasion, juncture," now
feminine, but originally masculine and as late as the eighteenth century.
Dict. de l'Académie, 1694: "On dit rencontre d'affaires, pour dire con-
joncture. Quelques-uns le fasoient masculin, et il l'est en cette phrase:
En ce rencontre." See *Lexique de Corneille*, II, p. 288.

24. **mouvement**: "impulse."

27. **sa couche**: = "his hand." See l. 16.

28. **soldat**: "as a soldier." Appositional use without article.

32. **Qu'il commît un Alcide au fardeau d'un Atlas**: i.e. did not blame
him for associating a Hercules (called Alcides from his grandfather
Alceus) with an Atlas in bearing the burden of the world, the Roman
empire. The reference is to Diocletian's choice of Maximian as a colleague, or joint emperor, in A.D. 286, and the proclamation in A.D. 292
of Constantius and Galerius as Caesars. See note, pp. 139, 140. *Commettre*, "intrust, confide," sometimes used with *en*; see l. 795.

L'un par sa nonchalance, et l'autre par sa gloire.

Maximin, achevant tant de gestes guerriers,

Semble au front de mon père en voler les lauriers;

Et Constance, souffrant qu'un ennemi l'affronte,   45

Dessus son même front en imprime la honte.

Ainsi, ni dans son bon, ni dans son mauvais choix

D'un conseil raisonnable il n'a suivi les lois,

Et, déterminant tout au gré de son caprice,

N'en prévoit le succès ni craint le préjudice.   50

CAMILLE

Vous prenez trop l'alarme, et ce raisonnement

N'est point à votre crainte un juste fondement.

Quand Dioclétien éleva votre mère

Au degré le plus haut que l'univers révère,

Son rang, qu'il partageait, n'en devint point plus bas,   55

Et, l'y faisant monter, il n'en descendit pas ;

Il put concilier son honneur et sa flamme,

Et, choisi par les siens, se choisir une femme.

Quelques associés qui règnent avec lui,

Il est de ses États le plus solide appui :   60

S'ils sont les matelots de cette grande flotte,

Il en tient le timon, il en est le pilote,

Et ne les associe à des emplois si hauts

Que pour voir des Césars au rang de ses vassaux.

43. **achevant** : gerundive use of present participle ; see ll. 45, 429, and Haase, 91.

46. **Dessus** : = *sur*, see l. 686, and *Venceslas*, ll. 1334, 1359.

50. **succès** : " result."

57. **flamme** : = *amour*. See Introduction, p. 69, for the gallantry of the seventeenth century. In the conventional poetic language of the time *flamme* or *flammes* and *feu* or *feux* are common substitutes for *amour*.

59. **Quelques associés qui règnent** : this form was more frequent in the seventeenth century than at the present day. See Haase, 45, R. iv.

Voyez comme un fantôme, un songe, une chimère,   65
Vous fait mal expliquer les mouvements d'un père,
Et qu'un trouble importun vous naît mal à propos
D'où doit si justement naître votre repos.

VALÉRIE

Je ne m'obstine point d'un effort volontaire
Contre tes sentiments en faveur de mon père,   70
Et contre un père, enfin, l'enfant a toujours tort.
Mais me répondras-tu des caprices du sort?
Ce monarque insolent, à qui toute la terre
Et tous ses souverains sont des jouets de verre,
Prescrit-il son pouvoir? et, quand il en est las,   75
Comme il les a formés, ne les brise-t-il pas?
Peut-il pas, s'il me veut dans un état vulgaire,
Mettre la fille au point dont il tira la mère,
Détruire ses faveurs par sa légèreté,
Et de mon songe, enfin, faire une vérité?   80
Il est vrai que la mort, contre son inconstance,
Aux grands cœurs, au besoin, offre son assistance,
Et peut toujours braver son pouvoir insolent;
Mais, si c'est un remède, il est bien violent.

----

68. **D'où**: "whence"; i.e. you are disturbed for a reason from which your peace of mind should spring. See ll. 199–201.

74. **jouets de verre**: = "fragile playthings."

75. **Prescrit-il son pouvoir**: "does he relinquish his power?" i.e. does he lose his power by prescription (lapse of time)?

77. **Peut-il pas**: for omission of *ne* see Haase, 101, and important note in *Lexique de Corneille*, II, p. 110. See also *Lexique de Mme. de Sévigné*, I, pp. xxxvii and lviii; *Lexique de Molière*, I, p. cxlviii; Vaugelas, I, p. 342; and Chassang, *French Grammar*, p. 412, R. III: Vaugelas, II, p. 294, limits the omission of *ne* to interrogative sentences.

81–84. The threat of suicide by Valérie is one of the commonplaces of French classical tragedy. See frequent declarations of Sabine in *Horace*, II. 6, 7; IV. 7; V. 3; and *Venceslas*, ll. 1701–1702.

CAMILLE

La mort a trop d'horreur pour espérer en elle ;　　85
Mais espérez au Ciel, qui vous a fait si belle,
Et qui semble influer avecque la beauté
Des marques de puissance et de prospérité.

Scène II

Un Page, Valérie, Camille

LE PAGE

Madame . . .

VALÉRIE

　　Que veux-tu ?

LE PAGE

　　　　　L'empereur, qui m'envoie,
Sur mes pas avec vous vient partager sa joie.　　90

VALÉRIE

Quelle ?

LE PAGE

　　L'ignorez-vous ?　Maximin, de retour
Des pays reculés où se lève le jour,
De leurs rébellions, par son bras étouffées,
Aux pieds de l'empereur apporte les trophées,
Et de là se dispose à l'honneur de vous voir.　　95

(*Il s'en va*)

CAMILLE

Sa valeur vous oblige à le bien recevoir.
Ne lui retenez pas le fruit de sa victoire :
Le plus grand des larcins est celui de la gloire.

---

87. **Et qui semble influer** : *influer* is here used in its original sense
(Lat. *influere*), but with a causative meaning : "to cause to flow into,
to shed, to give." See A. Benoist, *Notes sur la langue de Rotrou*, in
Annales de la Faculté des Lettres de Bordeaux, vol. iv (1882), p. 385,
and l. 1449.

VALÉRIE

Mon esprit, agité d'un secret mouvement,
De cette émotion chérit le sentiment;   100
Et cet heur inconnu, qui flatte ma pensée,
Dissipe ma frayeur et l'a presque effacée.
Laissons notre conduite à la bonté des dieux.

(*Voyant Maximin*)

O ciel! qu'un doux travail m'entre au cœur par les yeux!

SCÈNE III

DIOCLÉTIEN, MAXIMIN, VALÉRIE, CAMILLE, PLANCIEN, GARDES,
SOLDATS

(*Il se fait un bruit de tambours et de trompettes*)
(*Maximin baise les mains de Valérie*)

DIOCLÉTIEN

Déployez, Valérie, et vos traits et vos charmes;   105
Au vainqueur d'Orient faites tomber les armes;
Par lui l'empire est calme et n'a plus d'ennemis.
Soumettez ce grand cœur qui nous a tout soumis;
Chargez de fers un bras fatal à tant de têtes,
Et faites sa prison le prix de ses conquêtes.   110
Déjà par ses exploits il avait mérité
La part que je lui fis de mon autorité;
Et sa haute vertu, réparant sa naissance,
Lui fit sur mes sujets partager ma puissance.

101. **heur**: for *bonheur*. *Heur* fell into disuse towards the end of the
seventeenth century. See *Lexique de Corneille*, I, p. 480; Corneille
used the word frequently as late as 1682.

104. **doux travail**: "pleasant agitation," example of the rhetorical
figure known as oxymoron. — **entre au cœur**: for use of *à* for *dans*, see
Haase, 121, B.

105–110. Notice the affected gallantry of the time. See Introduction,
p. 69.

Aujourd'hui que, pour prix des pertes de son sang,　　115
Je ne puis l'honorer d'un plus illustre rang,
Je lui dois mon sang même, et, lui donnant ma fille,
Lui fais part de mes droits sur ma propre famille.
Ce présent, Maximin, est encore au-dessous
Du service important que j'ai reçu de vous;　　120
Mais, pour faire vos prix égaux à vos mérites,
La terre trouverait ses bornes trop petites;
Et vous avez rendu mon pouvoir impuissant,
Et restreint envers vous ma force en l'accroissant.

MAXIMIN

La part que vos bontés m'ont fait prendre en l'empire　　125
N'égale point, Seigneur, ces beaux fers où j'aspire.
Tous les arcs triomphants que Rome m'a dressés
Cèdent à la prison que vous me bâtissez;
Et, de victorieux des bords que l'Inde lave,
J'accepte, plus content, la qualité d'esclave,　　130
Que, dépouillant ce corps, vous ne prendrez aux cieux

121–124. That is, Maximin's services have been so great that Diocletian cannot find a suitable reward within the narrow confines of the earth, and by increasing Diocletian's authority Maximin has diminished his power to recompense him adequately. Compare *Venceslas*, ll. 339–340.

128. la prison: i.e. union with Valérie. See l. 110.

129. de victorieux: *de* here indicates change in state or condition. See Littré, s.v. *de*, p. 953, col. 3. "From being victorious over the shores bathed by the Indus, I accept the rank of slave." See l. 382, and *Venceslas*, l. 1399.

131. Que: is to be construed with *plus content* of the preceding line. "The more gladly since Diocletian remains upon this earth, and does not, laying off his mortal body, assume the rank in heaven earned by his virtues." For omission of *pas* with negative see Haase, 100; Chassang, *French Grammar*, p. 413; *Lexiques de Corneille*, II, p. 107; *de Racine*, p. 336; and *de Molière*, I, p. cxlvi. See ll. 155, 184, and *Venceslas*, ll. 623, 774, 911, and 968.

Le rang par vos vertus acquis entre les dieux :
Mais oser concevoir cette insolente audace
Est plutôt mériter son mépris que sa grâce,
Et, quoi qu'ait fait ce bras, il ne m'a point acquis   135
Ni ces titres fameux, ni ce renom exquis
Qui des extractions effacent la mémoire
Quand à sa vertu seule il faut devoir sa gloire.
Quelque insigne avantage et quelque illustre rang
Dont vous ayez couvert le défaut de mon sang,   140
Quoi que l'on dissimule, on pourra toujours dire
Qu'un berger est assis au trône de l'empire,
Qu'autrefois mes palais ont été des hameaux,
Que qui gouverne Rome a conduit des troupeaux,
Que pour prendre le fer j'ai quitté la houlette,   145
Et qu'enfin votre ouvrage est une œuvre imparfaite.
Puis-je, avec ce défaut non encor réparé,
M'approcher d'un objet digne d'être adoré,
Espérer de ses vœux les glorieuses marques,
Prétendre d'étouffer l'espoir de cent monarques,   150
Passer ma propre attente, et me faire des dieux,
Sinon des ennemis, au moins des envieux ?

---

137. extractions : = "lowly birth." Benoist, p. 368 : "L'emploi des substantifs abstraits au pluriel était beaucoup plus fréquent au xviie siècle
que de nos jours. Rotrou en est plein."

147. non encor : according to Littré more correct than the usual *pas
encore*. *Encor* for *encore* for the sake of the meter.

148. d'un objet digne d'être adoré : i.e. Valérie. *Objet* in seventeenth-
century drama is equivalent to *femme aimée*. See l. 836; *Venceslas*,
l. 1520; and *Lexiques de Corneille*, II, p. 120, and *de Molière*, II,
p. 200.

149. vœux : the original meaning is "vow," then "promise," then
prayer offered to the gods for some desire or wish. In the gallantry
of the seventeenth century it indicates the desire expressed to the
object of one's affection to be loved by her. It may generally be
translated by "love, affections." See *Venceslas*, l. 298.

150. étouffer : here, "frustrate, disappoint."

DIOCLÉTIEN

Suffit que c'est mon choix, et que j'ai connaissance
Et de votre personne et de votre naissance,
Et que, si l'une enfin n'admet un rang si haut,   155
L'autre par sa vertu répare son défaut,
Supplée à la nature, élève sa bassesse,
Se reproduit soi-même et forme sa noblesse.
A combien de bergers les Grecs et les Romains
Ont-ils pour leur vertu vu des sceptres aux mains?   160
L'histoire, des grands cœurs la plus chère espérance,
Que le temps traite seule avecque révérence,
Qui, ne redoutant rien, ne peut rien respecter,
Qui se produit sans fard et parle sans flatter,
N'a-t-elle pas cent fois publié la louange   165
De gens que leur mérite a tirés de la fange,
Qui par leur industrie ont leurs noms éclaircis,
Et sont montés au rang où nous sommes assis?
Cyrus, Sémiramis, sa fameuse adversaire,
Noms qu'encore aujourd'hui la mémoire révère,   170
Lycaste, Parrasie, et mille autres divers,
Qui dans les premiers temps ont régi l'univers;

169. 1648 has *Cyrès*; Ronchaud, *Cyre*.

---

153. **Suffit que** : = *Il suffit que*. See *Lexiques de Corneille, de Racine*,
and *de Molière* ; and Benoist, p. 408.

155-156. **l'une** : i.e. *votre naissance*. — **L'autre** : i.e. *votre personne*.

159. Some of these shepherds are mentioned presently.

169. **Cyrus** : Cyrus, the founder of the Persian empire, was reared as
the son of the herdsman who saved his life when he was to be killed
by exposure. Semiramis also, according to legend, was exposed by her
mother Derceto and was brought up by the chief shepherd of the royal
herds.

171. **Lycaste, Parrasie** : the former was son of Minos and Itone, and
was king of Crete; the latter was a son of Lycaon, from whom Par-
rhasia in Acadia was believed to have derived its name. I find no
reference to their humble birth or that they were shepherds.

Et récemment encor, dans Rome, Vitellie,
Gordien, Pertinax, Macrin, Probe, Aurélie,
N'y sont-ils pas montés, et fait de mêmes mains   175
Des règles aux troupeaux et des lois aux humains?
Et moi-même, enfin, moi, qui, de naissance obscure,
Dois mon sceptre à moi-même et rien à la nature,
N'ai-je pas lieu de croire, en cet illustre rang,
Le mérite dans l'homme et non pas dans le sang,   180
D'avoir à qui l'accroît fait part de ma puissance,
Et choisi la personne, et non pas la naissance?

> (*A Valérie*)

Vous, cher fruit de mon lit, beau prix de ses exploits,
Si ce front n'est menteur, vous approuvez mon choix,
Et tout ce que l'amour pour marque d'allégresse   185

185. **pour marque.** So in 1648. Viollet-le-Duc and, following his
example, Hémon have *imprime*. It is possible that the text of 1648 is
a misprint for *peut marquer*, which would give a good reading, or it
may be an instance of Rotrou's careless writing.

---

173. **Vitellie** : Vitellius, emperor from January to December 22, A.D. 69.

174. **Gordien**, etc.: there were three emperors of this name in the
third century, no one of whom seems to fit the description of Rotrou;
Pertinax, emperor A.D. 193, was of humble origin, as were also Macrinus,
A.D. 217-218, and Probus, A.D. 276-282, but not Aurelius (M. Aurelius
Antoninus), A.D. 161-180. Finally, Diocletian, as he states himself in
l. 177, was of most obscure parentage.

175. **N'y sont-ils pas montés, et fait de mêmes mains** : where several
compound tenses occur in the same sentence the auxiliary verb is often
omitted after the first. See Haase, 149, R. 1, and *Lexiques de Corneille*,
I, p. lxxvi, and *de Racine*, p. 121. Here, however, the construction is
incorrect, for the omitted auxiliary is *avoir*, not *être*. See ll. 181-182,
ll. 904-906, and *Venceslas*, l. 824.

181. **D'avoir à qui**, etc.: the translation going back to l. 179, seems
to be: "Have I not cause to believe (that) in this noble rank (of mine)
merit is in the man and not in the blood, (as a reason) for having shared
my power with the one (Maximin) who increases it, and for having
chosen the person and not the birth."

183. **cher fruit de mon lit** : usual conventional circumlocution for *fille*
or *fils*.

184. **n'est menteur** : for omission of *pas* see note on l. 131.

Sur le front d'une fille amante, mais princesse,
Y fait voir sagement que mon élection
Se trouve un digne objet de votre passion.

VALÉRIE

Ce choix étant si rare, et venant de mon père,
Mon goût serait mauvais s'il s'y trouvait contraire.   190
Oui, Seigneur, je l'approuve, et bénis le destin
D'un heureux accident que j'ai craint ce matin.

(*Se tournant vers Camille*)

Mon songe est expliqué : j'épouse en ce grand homme
Un berger, il est vrai, mais qui commande à Rome.
Le songe m'effrayait, et j'en chéris l'effet,   195
Et ce qui fut ma peur est enfin mon souhait.

193–194. **Mon songe est expliqué**, etc.: Sainte-Beuve, *Port-Royal*, I,
pp. 152–153, says : "Tout cela, convenons-en, est fort mauvais ; nulle
part mieux qu'en ce commencement on ne touche du doigt les défauts
du temps et du talent de Rotrou, l'emphase, la vaine pompe. Toutes
ces premières conversations ne sont que des tirades ampoulées, où la
seule idée qui se développe incessamment, dans une indigeste recrudescence d'images, est le contraste de l'ancienne condition de berger
avec la pourpre et la gloire actuelle de Maximin. Ce souvenir pas-
toral revient dans toutes les bouches, dans celle de Valérie, de Maximin
lui-même, de Dioclétien qui cherche des autorités et des précédents :

> A combien de bergers les Grecs et les Romains
> Ont-ils, pour leur vertu, vu des sceptres aux mains ?

et il énumère. — Rotrou ne savait pas assez le monde pour comprendre
que plus ces défauts de naissance sont réels et sensibles, moins on les
étale. Ses deux empereurs, Dioclétien et Maximin, se posent tout
d'abord dans le mauvais moule des bronzes solennels, dans toute la
roideur d'un empereur équestre. On retrouve ici chez Rotrou, mais
grossis, tous les défauts de Corneille : c'est comme un frère cadet
qui ressemble à son aîné, mais en laid. Les Romains de Corneille en
sont et en restent à Lucain ; ceux de Rotrou vont au Stace et au
Claudien."

195. l'effet: "the fulfillment."

MAXIMIN, *lui baisant la main*

O favorable arrêt, qui me comble de gloire,
Et fait de ma prison ma plus digne victoire !

CAMILLE

Ainsi souvent le Ciel conduit tout à tel point
Que ce qu'on craint arrive, et qu'il n'afflige point,   200
Et que ce qu'on redoute est enfin ce qu'on aime.

Scène IV

Un Page, Dioclétien, Maximin, Valérie, Camille, Plancien,
GARDES, SOLDATS

LE PAGE

Genest attend, Seigneur, dans un désir extrême,
De s'acquitter des vœux dus à Vos Majestés.
    (*Il sort*)*

DIOCLÉTIEN

Qu'il entre.

CAMILLE, *à Valérie*

Il manquait seul à vos prospérités ;
Et, quel que soit votre heur, son art, pour le parfaire,   205

---

* So in 1648. This stage direction should of course come after Diocletian's words. Viollet-le-Duc and Hémon have. (*Le page sort*) after
Qu'il entre. In the original edition the minor stage directions are
printed in the margin and not always placed correctly.

199-201. This sententious speech of Camille is characteristic of early
French tragedy, and the plays of Garnier are filled with maxims and
sententious speeches. See P. Kahnt, *Gedankenkreis der Sentenzen in
Jodelle's und Garnier's Tragödien und Seneca's Einfluß auf derselben*,
Marburg, 1887. See *Venceslas*, ll. 646-650.

203. De s'acquitter des vœux, etc. : = " to pay the homage due your
Majesties."

Semble en quelque façon vous être nécessaire.
Madame, obtenez-nous ce divertissement
Que vous même estimez et trouvez si charmant.

Scène V

Genest, Dioclétien, Maximin, Valérie, Camille, Plancien,
gardes, soldats

genest

Si parmi vos sujets une abjecte fortune
Permet de partager l'allégresse commune,   210
Et de contribuer, en ces communs désirs,
Sinon à votre gloire, au moins à vos plaisirs,
Ne désapprouvez pas, ô généreux monarques,
Que notre affection vous produise ses marques,
Et que mes compagnons vous offrent par ma voix,   215
Non des tableaux parlants de vos rares exploits,
Non cette si célèbre et si fameuse histoire
Que vos heureux succès laissent à la mémoire
(Puisque le peuple grec, non plus que le romain,
N'a point pour les tromper une assez docte main),   220

220. 1648 has *tromper*, probably a misprint for *tracer* which Viollet-le-Duc and Hémon have.

209. abjecte : "humble." See *Lexique de Corneille*, I, p. 17 : "En 1664, Raillet écrit ce mot de la même manière (*abjet*) dans son *Triomphe de la Langue françoise* (p. 16), et c'est encore cette forme que Furetière préfère en 1690, dans son Dictionnaire. Nicot (1606) et l'Académie (1694) donnent *abject*."

214. produise ses marques : = *donner des marques, donner des témoignages de, des preuves de.* "That our affection should give you proofs of itself."

216. tableaux parlants, etc.: "speaking pictures (scenes) of your unusual deeds."

Mais quelque effort au moins par qui nous puissions dire
Vous avoir délassés du grand faix de l'empire,
Et, par ce que notre art aura de plus charmant,
Avoir à vos grands soins ravi quelque moment.

DIOCLÉTIEN

Genest, ton soin m'oblige, et la cérémonie   225
Du beau jour où ma fille à ce prince est unie,
Et qui met notre joie en un degré si haut,
Sans un trait de ton art aurait quelque défaut.
Le théâtre aujourd'hui, fameux par ton mérite,
A ce noble plaisir puissamment sollicite,   230
Et dans l'état qu'il est ne peut, sans être ingrat,
Nier de te devoir son plus brillant éclat :
Avec confusion j'ai vu cent fois tes feintes
Me livrer malgré moi de sensibles atteintes ;
En cent sujets divers, suivant tes mouvements,   235
J'ai reçu de tes feux de vrais ressentiments ;

232. 1648 omits a word before *devoir*. Viollet-le-Duc has *lui devoir ;*
Hémon, *te devoir*. I have followed the latter.

---

221. **par qui :** for *qui* referring to things, with preposition, see Haase,
32 ; *Venceslas*, ll. 1764, 1767.

228. **trait :** = "display."

233. **feintes :** the characters assumed by the actor, "impersonations."

234. **sensibles atteintes :** translate : "have deeply impressed me."
Sensible is a favorite word with Rotrou, and became fashionable in the
eighteenth century with Rousseau and his followers. It means that
which produces an effect upon the senses, and the translation will vary
according to the context. See ll. 1276, 1432, and *Venceslas*, ll. 681 and
1857.

236. **J'ai reçu, etc. :** translate : "your ardor has aroused true feeling
in me." That is, the assumed feelings of the actor have awakened the
corresponding real feelings in Diocletian. In modern French the word
ressentiment is used only in the sense of "resentment," but in the
seventeenth century it was employed in a wider sense of any deep feeling produced by anything. See *Lexique de Corneille*, II, p. 299.

Et l'empire absolu que tu prends sur une âme
M'a fait cent fois de glace et cent autres de flamme.
Par ton art les héros, plutôt ressuscités
Qu'imités en effet et que représentés,   240
Des cent et des mille ans après leurs funérailles,
Font encor des progrès, et gagnent des batailles,
Et sous leurs noms fameux établissent des lois :
Tu me fais en toi seul maître de mille rois.
Le comique, où ton art également succède,   245
Est contre la tristesse un si présent remède
Qu'un seul mot, quand tu veux, un pas, une action
Ne laisse plus de prise à cette passion,
Et, par une soudaine et sensible merveille,
Jette la joie au cœur par l'œil ou par l'oreille.   250

GENEST

Cette gloire, Seigneur, me confond à tel point . . .

DIOCLÉTIEN

Crois qu'elle est légitime, et ne t'en défends point.
Mais passons aux auteurs, et dis-nous quel ouvrage
Aujourd'hui dans la scène a le plus haut suffrage,
Quelle plume est en règne, et quel fameux esprit   255
S'est acquis dans le cirque un plus juste crédit.

246. For *présent* Viollet-le-Duc and Hémon have *pressant*.

---

238. **de glace . . . de flamme:** "chilled . . . and inflamed me."
242. **Font encor des progrès,** etc.: "still advance and win battles."
Littré, "progrès, suite de succès militaires et autres."
244. **en toi :** = "by your acting."
248. **Ne laisse plus de prise à cette passion :** "leaves that passion
(*tristesse*) no more power."
252. **ne t'en défends point :** "do not deny it."
254. **dans la scène a le plus haut suffrage :** = "is the most popular on
the stage."
255. **en règne :** antiquated for *en faveur*.
256. **cirque :** = "theater."

GENEST

Les goûts sont différents, et souvent le caprice
Établit ce crédit bien plus que la justice.

DIOCLÉTIEN

Mais, entre autres encor, qui l'emporte, en ton sens?

GENEST

Mon goût, à dire vrai, n'est point pour les récents :   260
De trois ou quatre au plus peut-être la mémoire
Jusqu'aux siècles futurs conservera la gloire ;
Mais de les égaler à ces fameux auteurs
Dont les derniers des temps seront adorateurs,
Et de voir leurs travaux avec la révérence   265
Dont je vois les écrits d'un Plaute et d'un Térence,
Et de ces doctes Grecs, dont les rares brillants
Font qu'ils vivent encor si beaux après mille ans,
Et dont l'estime enfin ne peut être effacée,
Ce serait vous mentir et trahir ma pensée.   270

DIOCLÉTIEN

Je sais qu'en leurs écrits l'art et l'invention
Sans doute ont mis la scène en sa perfection ;
Mais ce que l'on a vu n'a plus la douce amorce
Ni le vif aiguillon dont la nouveauté force ;

259. **qui l'emporte, en ton sens** : " who in your judgment excels ? "
270. **trahir ma pensée** : " belie my thought."
272. **scène** : = "drama."
273. **ce que l'on a vu** : i.e. the works of the older dramatists mentioned in ll. 266-267. — **la douce amorce** : = " charm, attraction."
274. **Ni le vif aiguillon**, etc. : translate : " nor the powerful stimulus of novelty "; lit. " the stimulus with which novelty forces (or goads us)." *Forcer* is here used absolutely, without an object. This absolute use of many verbs generally employed with an object or in the reflexive form is very common in Corneille. See *Lexique de Corneille*, I, p. lxiv.

Et ce qui surprendra nos esprits et nos yeux,   275
Quoique moins achevé, nous divertira mieux.

GENEST

Nos plus nouveaux sujets, les plus dignes de Rome,
Et les plus grands efforts des veilles d'un grand homme,
A qui les rares fruits que la muse produit
Ont acquis dans la scène un légitime bruit,   280
Et de qui certes l'art comme l'estime est juste,
Portent les noms fameux de Pompée et d'Auguste ;
Ces poèmes sans prix, où son illustre main
D'un pinceau sans pareil a peint l'esprit romain,
Rendront de leurs beautés votre oreille idolâtre,   285
Et sont aujourd'hui l'âme et l'amour du théâtre.

VALÉRIE

J'ai su la haute estime où l'on les a tenus ;
Mais leurs sujets enfin sont des sujets connus ;
Et quoi qu'ils aient de beau, la plus rare merveille,

277-286. These lines contain a panegyric of Corneille, who at this date, 1645, had produced the following tragedies : *Le Cid* (1636); *Horace*, *Cinna* (1640) ; *Polyeucte* (1643) ; *Pompée* (1643–1644); *Rodogune* (1644–1645); *Théodore* (1645). The plays alluded to in the text are *Cinna ou la clémence d'Auguste* and *Pompée*. For relations between Rotrou and Corneille see Introduction, p. 32.

277. **Nos plus nouveaux sujets** : i.e. the latest subjects of tragedy.

279. **les rares fruits** : seven tragedies in nine years (besides *Le Menteur* and *La suite du Menteur*), four at least masterpieces of the art !

285. **Rendront de leurs beautés**, etc.: "will make your ears worship their beauties." See what has been said in Introduction, p. 71, on Rotrou's language.

286. **l'âme et l'amour du théâtre** : for *âme* as term of affection see Molière, *Amphytrion*, I. 4 :

> Adieu, Cléanthis, ma chère âme,

Voltaire, *Alzire*, II. 3 :

> Toi, l'âme de ma vie,

and *Lexique de Corneille*.

Quand l'esprit la connaît, ne surprend plus l'oreille. 290
Ton art est toujours même, et tes charmes égaux,
Aux sujets anciens aussi bien qu'aux nouveaux ;
Mais on vante surtout l'inimitable adresse
Dont tu feins d'un chrétien le zèle et l'allégresse,
Quand, le voyant marcher du baptême au trépas, 295
Il semble que les feux soient des fleurs sous tes pas.

MAXIMIN

L'épreuve en est aisée.

GENEST *

　　　Elle sera sans peine,
Si votre nom, Seigneur, nous est libre en la scène ;
Et la mort d'Adrien, l'un de ces obstinés,
Par vos derniers arrêts naguère condamnés, 300
Vous sera figurée avec un art extrême,
Et si peu différent de la vérité même,
Que vous nous avoûrez de cette liberté
Où César à César sera représenté,
Et que vous douterez si, dans Nicomédie, 305
Vous verrez l'effet même ou bien la comédie.

* 1648 by a misprint has *Dioclétien* instead of *Genest*.

---

291. **même** : for omission of the article see Haase, 28, D, and *Lexiques de Corneille*, II, p. 80, and *de Molière*, I, p. xcvi.

298. **Si votre nom**, etc. : i.e. if we are allowed to use your name, to impersonate you on the stage.

299. **Adrien** : for the martyrdom of Adrian see Introduction, p. 83.

301. **figurée** : "represented."

303. **avoûrez** : for *avouerez*. Quicherat, *Petit traité de versification française*, p. 9 : "L'*e* muet placé dans le corps de certains mots après une voyelle, allonge cette voyelle, mais ne compte pas lui-même pour une syllabe : Je paie-rai, je loue-rai, nous avoue-rons, je me fie-rai, je remue-rai, dénue-ment. Aujourd'hui cet *e* se remplace souvent par un accent circonflexe." See also L. E. Kastner, *A History of French Versification*, Oxford, 1903, p. 18. See *Venceslas*, ll. 704, 816, 973, 1447.

306. **l'effet même** : "the very fact."

MAXIMIN

Oui, crois qu'avec plaisir je serai spectateur
En la même action dont je serai l'acteur.
Va, prépare un effort digne de la journée
Où le Ciel, m'honorant d'un si juste hyménée,   310
Met, par une aventure incroyable aux neveux,
Mon bonheur et ma gloire au-dessus de mes vœux.

310. **juste hyménée** : i.e. a marriage so well proportioned to his merit.
311. **neveux** : "posterity." See *Venceslas*, l. 947.

ACTE DEUXIÈME

Scène I (*Le théâtre s'ouvre*)

Genest, *s'habillant, et tenant son rôle, considère le théâtre, et dit au décorateur* ; Le Décorateur*

GENEST

Il est beau ; mais encore, avec peu de dépense,
Vous pouviez ajouter à sa magnificence,
N'y laisser rien d'aveugle, y mettre plus de jour,   315
Donner plus de hauteur aux travaux d'alentour,
En marbrer les dehors, en jasper les colonnes,
Enrichir leurs tympans, leurs cimes, leurs couronnes,
Mettre en vos coloris plus de diversité,
En vos carnations plus de vivacité,   320
Draper mieux ces habits, reculer ces paysages,
Y lancer des jets d'eau, renfondrer leurs ombrages,

* 1648 omits *Le Décorateur* from the characters of the scene.

---

315. aveugle : "dark, obscure." See Racine, *Œuvres*, IV, p. 116 :

Sombre nuit, aveugles ténèbres.

316. travaux d'alentour : = "the surroundings."

317. En marbrer les dehors : i.e. paint the exterior to resemble marble and give the columns the appearance of jasper.

318. tympans, . . . cimes, . . . couronnes : the space inclosed within a pediment or arch ; the summits of the pediments ; *couronnes* probably for *couronnes de corniche*, the coping of the cornice.

321. reculer ces paysages : i.e. give greater distance to, throw more into the background, these landscapes.

322. renfondrer : antiquated for *renfoncer*, "make the shadows stand out, deepen the shadows." See Godefroy, *Dictionnaire de l'ancienne langue française*.

Et surtout en la toile où vous peignez vos cieux
Faire un jour naturel au jugement des yeux,
Au lieu que la couleur m'en semble un peu meurtrie.   325

LE DÉCORATEUR

Le temps nous a manqué plutôt que l'industrie ;
Joint qu'on voit mieux de loin ces raccourcissements,
Ces corps sortant du plan de ces refondrements ;
L'approche à ces dessins ôte leurs perspectives,
En confond les faux jours, rend leurs couleurs moins vives,   330
Et, comme à la nature, est nuisible à notre art
A qui l'éloignement semble apporter du fard :
La grâce une autre fois y sera plus entière.

GENEST

Le temps nous presse ; allez, préparez la lumière.

[Le Décorateur sort]

SCÈNE II

GENEST seul, se promenant, et lisant son rôle, dit comme en
repassant, et achevant de s'habiller

« Ne délibère plus, Adrien, il est temps   335
« De suivre avec ardeur ces fameux combattants :

325. **meurtrie** : "dull."

327. **Joint que** : a conjunction now antiquated but in constant use in the seventeenth century. See Haase, 137, 5, R. 2. The usual translation is "in addition to," or here simply "besides." — **raccourcissements** : "foreshortenings."

328. **Ces corps sortant**, etc. : = "these masses standing out from the background."

330. **faux jours** : "the artificial light," i.e. the lights and shadows of the painted scene.

331–332. **est nuisible . . . apporter du fard** : translate : "is detrimental to our art, which distance seems to embellish." For figurative use of *fard* see *Lexiques de Corneille*, I, p. 424, and *de Molière*, I, p. 475.

336. **combattants** : i.e. the Christian martyrs.

« Si la gloire te plaît, l'occasion est belle ;
« La querelle du ciel à ce combat t'appelle ;
« La torture, le fer et la flamme t'attend ;
« Offre à leurs cruautés un cœur ferme et constant ; 340
« Laisse à de lâches cœurs verser d'indignes larmes,
« Tendre aux tyrans les mains et mettre bas les armes ;
« Toi, rends la gorge au fer, vois-en couler ton sang,
« Et meurs sans t'ébranler, debout et dans ton rang.

  (*Il répète encore ces quatre derniers vers*)

« Laisse à de lâches cœurs verser d'indignes larmes, 345
« Tendre aux tyrans les mains et mettre bas les armes ;
« Toi, rends la gorge au fer, vois-en couler ton sang,
« Et meurs sans t'ébranler, debout et dans ton rang.»

Scène III

Marcelle, *achevant de s'habiller, et tenant son rôle* ; Genest *

MARCELLE

Dieux ! comment en ce lieu faire la comédie?
De combien d'importuns j'ai la tête étourdie ! 350
Combien, à les ouïr, je fais de languissants !
Par combien d'attentats j'entreprends sur les sens !
Ma voix rendrait les bois et les rochers sensibles ;

---

 345. 1648 omits the repeated lines and has only: *Laisse à de lâches cœurs*, etc. I follow Viollet-le-Duc for convenience of reader.
 * 1648 omits *Genest*.

---

 338. querelle : "cause."
 339. For the use of a singular verb with several coördinate subjects see Haase, 146 ; *Lexiques de Corneille*, I, p. lxx ; *de Racine*, p. cx ; *de Molière*, I, p. clxiii ; *de Mme. de Sévigné*, I, p. xxxix.
 349. faire la comédie : = "act."
 350. De combien d'importuns, etc. : translate : "How many troublesome persons have annoyed me."
 351-352. Combien, à les ouïr, etc. : translate : "According to them how many lovers I make, with how many wiles I attack their senses !"

Mes plus simples regards sont des meurtres visibles ;
Je foule autant de cœurs que je marche de pas ;　　　355
La troupe, en me perdant, perdrait tous ses appas.
Enfin, s'ils disent vrai, j'ai lieu d'être bien vaine.
De ces faux courtisans toute ma loge est pleine ;
Et, lasse au dernier point d'entendre leurs douceurs,
Je les en ai laissés absolus possesseurs.　　　360
Je crains plus que la mort cette engeance idolâtre
De lutins importuns qu'engendre le théâtre,
Et que la qualité de la profession
Nous oblige à souffrir avec discrétion.

GENEST

Outre le vieil usage où nous trouvons le monde,　　　365
Les vanités encor dont votre sexe abonde
Vous font avec plaisir supporter cet ennui,
Par qui tout votre temps devient le temps d'autrui.
Avez-vous repassé cet endroit pathétique
Où Flavie en sortant vous donne la réplique,　　　370
Et vous souvenez-vous qu'il s'y faut exciter ?

MARCELLE, *lui baillant son rôle*

J'en prendrais votre avis, oyez-moi réciter :
(*Elle répète*)

355. **Je foule autant de cœurs**, etc.: translate: "at every step I
tread a heart under foot."

356. **perdrait**: the conditionals here and in l. 353 depend on *à les
ouïr*, l. 351 ; i.e. from what they say one would suppose that, etc.

358. **loge**: "dressing room."

361. **idolâtre**: translate: "who idolize me."

362. **lutins**: the primary meaning is "hobgoblin, sprite, imp"; then
applied to persons, generally children, "mischievous rogues." Translate here as adj. with *importuns*: "mischievous bores whom the theater
breeds."

369. **repassé**: "rehearsed."

370. **réplique**: "cue."

372. **J'en prendrais votre avis**: "I would like to have your opinion."
—**oyez-moi**: *ouïr* is now used only in the infinitive and compound

« J'ose à présent, ô Ciel, d'une vue assurée,
« Contempler les brillants de ta voûte azurée,
« Et nier ces faux dieux, qui n'ont jamais foulé   375
« De ce palais roulant le lambris étoilé.
« A ton pouvoir, Seigneur, mon époux rend hommage ;
« Il professe ta foi, ses fers t'en sont un gage ;
« Ce redoutable fléau des dieux sur les chrétiens,
« Ce lion altéré du sacré sang des tiens,   380
« Qui de tant d'innocents crut la mort légitime,
« De ministre qu'il fut, s'offre enfin pour victime,
« Et, patient agneau, tend à tes ennemis
« Un col à ton saint joug heureusement soumis.»

GENEST

Outre que dans la cour que vous avez charmée   385
On sait que votre estime est assez confirmée,
Ce récit me surprend, et vous peut acquérir
Un renom au théâtre à ne jamais mourir.

MARCELLE

Vous m'en croyez bien plus que je ne m'en présume.

389. 1648 has *Vous en croyez.* I follow Viollet-le-Duc, Ronchaud, and Hémon.

---

tenses. Corneille still employs the present ind. *oy*, the imp. *oyez*, and the fut. *orrai.* See *Lexique de Corneille*, II, p. 141. The obsolete tenses are now replaced by *entendre.* — **réciter :** used absolutely. See ll. 274, 451.

376. **De ce palais roulant le lambris étoilé :** lit. "the starry ceiling of this revolving palace." To tread the ceiling seems to us absurd and we should prefer the Shakespearean conception in the *Merchant of Venice*, V. 1 :
Look how the floor of heaven
Is thick inlaid with patines of bright gold.

382. **De ministre qu'il fut :** before he became a Christian Adrian was himself a zealous persecutor of the Christians ; see Introduction, p. 83.

388. **Un renom . . . à ne jamais mourir :** "imperishable, undying fame." *A* is here the preposition of definition. See *Venceslas*, l. 1365.

GENEST

La cour **viendra** bientôt ; commandez qu'on allume.   390

(*Elle rentre*)

Scène IV

Genest *seul, repassant son rôle, et se promenant*

GENEST

« Il serait, Adrien, honteux d'être vaincu ;
« Si ton Dieu veut ta mort, c'est déjà trop vécu.
« J'ai vu, Ciel, tu le sais par le nombre des âmes
« Que j'osai t'envoyer par des chemins de flammes,
« Dessus les grils ardents, et dedans les taureaux,   395
« Chanter les condamnés et trembler les bourreaux.

(*Il répète ces quatre vers*)

« J'ai vu, Ciel, tu le sais par le nombre des âmes
« Que j'osai t'envoyer par des chemins de flammes,
« Dessus les grils ardents, et dedans les taureaux,
« Chanter les condamnés et trembler les bourreaux.»   400

(*Et puis, ayant un peu rêvé, et ne regardant plus son
rôle, il dit*)

Dieux, prenez contre moi ma défense et la vôtre ;
D'effet comme de nom je me trouve être un autre ;
Je feins moins Adrien que je ne le deviens,
Et prends avec son nom des sentiments chrétiens.

---

397. 1648 omits the repeated lines as above, l. 345, and has *J'ai vu, Ciel, tu le sais*, etc.

---

392. Si ton Dieu, etc.: "if your God requires your death, you have already lived too long," i.e. it is time for you to die.

395. Dessus les grils ardents, et dedans les taureaux : the adverbs *dessus* and *dedans* were used in the seventeenth century frequently as prepositions; see Haase, 126, 128. See ll. 46, 686, 1033, *Venceslas*, ll. 569, 644, 1246, 1334, 1359, etc. ; and *Lexiques de Malherbe*, pp. 158, 172, and *de Corneille*, I, p. 290, etc.

Je sais, pour l'éprouver, que par un long étude   405
L'art de nous transformer nous passe en habitude ;
Mais il semble qu'ici des vérités sans fard
Passent et l'habitude et la force de l'art,
Et que Christ me propose une gloire éternelle
Contre qui ma défense est vaine et criminelle ;   410
J'ai pour suspects vos noms de dieux et d'immortels,
Je répugne aux respects qu'on rend à vos autels ;
Mon esprit, à vos lois secrètement rebelle,
En conçoit un mépris qui fait mourir son zèle,
Et, comme de profane enfin sanctifié,   415
Semble se déclarer pour un crucifié.
Mais où va ma pensée, et par quel privilège
Presque insensiblement passé-je au sacrilège,
Et du pouvoir des dieux perds-je le souvenir ?
Il s'agit d'imiter et non de devenir.   420

(*Le ciel s'ouvre avec des flammes, et une voix s'entend,*
qui dit)

UNE VOIX

Poursuis, Genest, ton personnage ;
Tu n'imiteras point en vain ;
Ton salut ne dépend que d'un peu de courage,
Et Dieu t'y prêtera la main.

405. **pour l'éprouver** : "by my experience." — **étude** (Lat., *studium*) :
was masculine until the seventeenth century, but finally the feminine
termination led to the present gender. See Benoist, p. 371.

406. **L'art de nous transformer**, etc. : "the art of assuming other
characters becomes in us a habit."

411. **J'ai pour suspects** : "I regard as suspicious."

414. **fait mourir** : "destroys." An important function of *faire* is to
transform intransitive verbs into transitive as here.

415-416. **Et, comme de profane**, etc. : "and (my spirit), as if at last sancti-
fied from being profane, seems to declare itself for one who was cruci-
fied," or, "after having been profane." See note on l. 129 for this use of *de*.

421-424. It is not usual in the French classical drama to depart from
the use of the Alexandrine verse. It is done, however, in the case of

GENEST, *étonné, continue*

Qu'entends-je, juste Ciel, et par quelle merveille,   425
Pour me toucher le cœur, me frappes-tu l'oreille?
Souffle doux et sacré qui me viens enflammer,
Esprit saint et divin qui me viens animer,
Et qui, me souhaitant, m'inspires le courage,
Travaille à mon salut, achève ton ouvrage,   430
Guide mes pas douteux dans le chemin des cieux,
Et pour me les ouvrir dessille-moi les yeux.
Mais, ô vaine créance et frivole pensée,
Que du ciel cette voix me doive être adressée!
Quelqu'un, s'apercevant du caprice où j'étois,   435
S'est voulu divertir par cette feinte voix,

stances to be noted later, and sometimes letters are given in prose.
Here Rotrou wished to emphasize the speech of the heavenly character
and so puts it in the form of a stanza of four lines, three of eight and
one of twelve syllables, with alternate rhyme.

429. me souhaitant: "with my consent, voluntarily." This construction corresponds to the Latin abl. abs., *me volente*, or to the predicative
acc., *me volentem*.

432. Et pour me les ouvrir dessille-moi les yeux: "and unclose my
eyes in order to open them." *Dessiller*, more properly *déciller* (Lat., *de*
and *cilium*, "eyelid"), was originally a technical term in fowling. In
order to train the falcon his eyelids were sewed together and unsewed
when his training was accomplished. See *Venceslas*, l. 495.

434. doive: the subjunctive depends on *créance* and *pensée*, which are
equivalent to the verbs from which they are derived.

435. caprice où j'étois: "the capricious mood (*or* humor) in which I
was." — **étois**: I have, with this one exception, modernized the seventeenth-century form of the imperfect and conditional tenses of verbs,
printing *ai* for *oi*. In this one case it was necessary to retain the earlier
form in order to make a permissible rhyme with *voix* in the following
line. See Introduction, p. 75.

436. S'est voulu divertir: for *a voulu se divertir*. At the present day,
when a verb in the infinitive follows another in the indicative, the
objective personal pronoun is placed before the infinitive. In the
seventeenth century, on the contrary, the pronoun almost always preceded the indicative. In this case such verbs as *pouvoir, vouloir, penser,
oser*, etc., followed by the infinitive of a reflexive verb, were treated

Qui d'un si prompt effet m'excite tant de flamme,
Et qui m'a pénétré jusqu'au profond de l'âme.
Prenez, dieux, contre Christ, prenez votre parti,
Dont ce rebelle cœur s'est presque départi ; 440
Et toi contre les dieux, ô Christ, prends ta défense,
Puisqu'à tes lois ce cœur fait encor résistance,
Et dans l'onde agitée où flottent mes esprits
Terminez votre guerre, et m'en faites le prix.
Rendez-moi le repos dont ce trouble me prive. 445

Scène V

LE Décorateur, *venant allumer les chandelles*, Genest

LE DÉCORATEUR

Hâtez-vous, il est temps ; toute la cour arrive.

GENEST

Allons, tu m'as distrait d'un rôle glorieux
Que je représentais devant la cour des cieux,
Et de qui l'action m'est d'importance extrême,
Et n'a pas un objet moindre que le ciel même. 450
Préparons la musique, et laissons-les placer.

LE DÉCORATEUR, *s'en allant, ayant allumé*

Il repassait son rôle et s'y veut surpasser.

[*Ils sortent*]

---

themselves as reflexive verbs in the compound tenses, but always without agreement of the participle. See Haase, 68, R. ii.

437. flamme : "zeal."

451. placer : used absolutely "indiquer les places dans une cérémonie, dans une assemblée," Littré. Here, "let the audience be
seated."

Scène VI

DIOCLÉTIEN, MAXIMIN, VALÉRIE, CAMILLE, PLANCIEN,
SUITE DE SOLDATS, GARDES

VALÉRIE

Mon goût, quoi qu'il en soit, est pour la tragédie :
L'objet en est plus haut, l'action plus hardie,
Et les pensers pompeux et pleins de majesté   455
Lui donnent plus de poids et plus d'autorité.

MAXIMIN

Elle l'emporte enfin par les illustres marques
D'exemple des héros, d'ornement des monarques,
De règle et de mesure à leurs affections,
Par ses événements et par ses actions.   460

PLANCIEN

Le théâtre aujourd'hui, superbe en sa structure,
Admirable en son art, et riche en sa peinture,
Promet pour le sujet de mêmes qualités.

MAXIMIN

Les effets en sont beaux, s'ils sont bien imités.
Vous verrez un des miens, d'une insolente audace,   465

---

455. pensers : poet. for *pensées*. Corneille used this word frequently,
Racine and Molière occasionally; see note in *Lexique de Corneille*, II,
p. 173.

457-459. Elle l'emporte enfin, etc. : translate : " It (tragedy) excels
by the famous proofs it gives of the example of heroes, of the honor of
sovereigns, of the government and moderation of their passions."

458. exemple : for omission of the definite article see *Lexique de
Corneille*, I, p. xxxiii et seq.

465. un des miens : sc. *sujets*, not to be confused with the *sujet* of
l. 463, which means the subjects of the tragedies or plays performed in
the " théâtre aujourd'hui."

Au mépris de la part qu'il s'acquit en ma grâce,
Au mépris de ses jours, au mépris de nos dieux,
Affronter le pouvoir de la terre et des cieux,
Et faire à mon amour succéder tant de haine
Que, bien loin d'en souffrir le spectacle avec peine,   470
Je verrai d'un esprit tranquille et satisfait
De son zèle obstiné le déplorable effet,
Et remourir ce traître après sa sépulture,
Sinon en sa personne, au moins en sa figure.

DIOCLÉTIEN

Pour le bien figurer, Genest n'oubliera rien :   475
Écoutons seulement et trêve à l'entretien.

(*Une voix chante avec un luth*)
(*La pièce commence*)

SCÈNE VII

GENEST *seul sur le théâtre élevé*
DIOCLÉTIEN, MAXIMIN, VALÉRIE, CAMILLE, PLANCIEN,
GARDES, *assis*, SUITE DE SOLDATS

GENEST, *sous le nom d'*ADRIEN

Ne délibère plus, Adrien, il est temps
De suivre avec ardeur ces fameux combattants :
Si la gloire te plaît, l'occasion est belle ;
La querelle du ciel à ce combat t'appelle ;   480
La torture, le fer et la flamme t'attend ;
Offre à leurs cruautés un cœur ferme et constant ;
Laisse à de lâches cœurs verser d'indignes larmes,
Tendre aux tyrans les mains et mettre bas les armes ;

---

473. **remourir** : not in the Dictionary of the Academy, nor in Hatzfeld and Darmesteter. It is in Littré : "mourir une seconde fois." See ll. 297-300. Adrien was to die a second time on the stage.

Toi, rends la gorge au fer, vois-en couler ton sang,   485
Et meurs sans t'ébranler, debout et dans ton rang.
La faveur de César, qu'un peuple entier t'envie,
Ne peut durer au plus que le cours de sa vie ;
De celle de ton Dieu, non plus que de ses jours,
Jamais nul accident ne bornera le cours :   490
Déjà de ce tyran la puissance irritée,
Si ton zèle te dure, a ta perte arrêtée.
Il serait, Adrien, honteux d'être vaincu ;
Si ton Dieu veut ta mort, c'est déjà trop vécu.
J'ai vu, Ciel, tu le sais par le nombre des âmes   495
Que j'osai t'envoyer par des chemins de flammes,
Dessus les grils ardents, et dedans les taureaux,
Chanter les condamnés et trembler les bourreaux ;
J'ai vu tendre aux enfants une gorge assurée
A la sanglante mort qu'ils voyaient préparée,   500
Et tomber sous le coup d'un trépas glorieux
Ces fruits à peine éclos, déjà mûrs pour les cieux.

489. **De celle de ton Dieu**, etc. : an example of the frequent inversions
in Rotrou ; see Introduction, p. 75. *De celle* (*faveur*) is limited by *le*
cours at the end of the following line.

499. **J'ai vu tendre aux enfants**, etc. : " I have seen children presenting," etc. The construction is the common one of the indirect object
for direct after verbs of seeing, etc., followed by the infinitive of an
active verb with a direct object. See Haase, 90, and Mätzner, *Syn-*
tax der neufranzösischen Sprache, Berlin, 1843, I, p. 195. See *Venceslas*,
ll. 232, 1478, 1537, and 1644.

502. **Ces fruits à peine éclos** : " these fruits (*les enfants* of l. 499)
scarcely out of the blossom." This is one of Rotrou's finest lines. Curnier, *Étude sur Rotrou*, p. 72, note, cites, as parallel passages, Malherbe :

> Avant que d'un hiver la tempête et l'orage
> A leur teint délicat pussent faire dommage,
> S'en allèrent fleurir au printemps éternel,

and Prudentius, *Hymnus Epiphaniae* :

> Salvete, flores martyrum,
> Quos lucis ipso in limine
> Christi insecutor sustulit,
> Ceu turbo nascentes rosas.

J'en ai vu que le temps prescrit par la nature
Était près de pousser dedans la sépulture,
Dessus les échafauds presser ce dernier pas,   505
Et d'un jeune courage affronter le trépas.
J'ai vu mille beautés en la fleur de leur âge,
A qui, jusqu'aux tyrans, chacun rendait hommage,
Voir avecque plaisir meurtris et déchirés
Leurs membres précieux de tant d'yeux adorés.   510
Vous l'avez vu, mes yeux, et vous craindriez sans honte
Ce que tout sexe brave et que tout âge affronte !
Cette vigueur peut-être est un effort humain?
Non, non, cette vertu, Seigneur, vient de ta main ;
L'âme la puise au lieu de sa propre origine,   515
Et, comme les effets, la source en est divine.
C'est du ciel que me vient cette noble vigueur
Qui me fait des tourments mépriser la rigueur,
Qui me fait défier les puissances humaines,
Et qui fait que mon sang se déplaît dans mes veines,   520
Qu'il brûle d'arroser cet arbre précieux
Où pend pour nous le fruit le plus chéri des cieux.
J'ai peine à concevoir ce changement extrême,
Et sens que, différent et plus fort que moi-même,
J'ignore toute crainte, et puis voir sans terreur   525
La face de la mort en sa plus noire horreur.
Un seul bien que je perds, la seule Natalie,

F. Clément, *Carmina e poetis Christianis excerpta*, Paris, 1880, p. 98,
note 7, cites Statius, *Silvae*, Bk. III, 3, 12 :

> Mediâ cecidere abrupta juventâ
> Gaudia, florentesque manu scidit Atropos annos,
> Qualia pallentes declinant lilia culmos,
> Pubentesque rosae primos moriuntur ad Austros.

503. **J'en ai vu que:** "I have seen those whom."

520–521. **que mon sang se déplaît**, etc.: i.e. my blood is restless in
my veins, longs to leave them and water the cross (*arbre précieux*).

525–530. The situation is the same as in Corneille's *Polyeucte*, IV.
2 and 3.

Qu'à mon sort un saint joug heureusement allie,
Et qui de ce saint zèle ignore le secret,
Parmi tant de ferveur mêle quelque regret.   530
Mais que j'ai peu de cœur, si ce penser me touche !
Si proche de la mort, j'ai l'amour en la bouche !

Scène VIII

FLAVIE, *tribun, représenté par* SERGESTE, *comédien* ; ADRIEN ;
DEUX GARDES

FLAVIE

Je crois, cher Adrien, que vous n'ignorez pas
Quel important sujet adresse ici mes pas ;
Toute la cour en trouble attend d'être éclaircie   535
D'un bruit dont au palais votre estime est noircie,
Et que vous confirmez par votre éloignement.
Chacun selon son sens en croit diversement :
Les uns, que pour railler cette erreur s'est semée,
D'autres, que quelque sort a votre âme charmée,   540

534. adresse ici mes pas : conventional expression for "brings me here."

535. attend de : antiquated for *attend que*, but in that case, of course, the construction of the rest of the line would have to be entirely changed. Corneille uses this form in *Horace*, I. 2 :

Cher amant, n'attends plus d'être un jour mon époux.

536. votre estime : i.e. the esteem in which you are held. This is the objective use of the possessive. See *Venceslas*, ll. 51, 57.

540. sort : "magic spell." — **a votre âme charmée** : for *a charmé votre âme*. In Old French the order of words was freer and the object of a compound tense could be placed between the auxiliary and the participle, the latter then agreeing in gender and number with its object. This construction is in modern French admissible only in poetry and for the sake of rhyme. It was frequent before Corneille and began to be antiquated in his day. The following examples are from *Horace* :

Aucun étonnement n'a leur gloire flétrie.

D'autres, que le venin de ces lieux infectés
Contre votre raison a vos sens révoltés ;
Mais surtout de César la croyance incertaine
Ne peut où s'arrêter, ni s'asseoir qu'avec peine.

ADRIEN

A qui dois-je le bien de m'avoir dénoncé ?   545

FLAVIE

Nous étions au palais, où César empressé
De grand nombre des siens, qui lui vantaient leur zèle
A mourir pour les dieux ou venger leur querelle ;
« Adrien, a-t-il dit, d'un visage remis,
« Adrien leur suffit contre tant d'ennemis :   550
« Seul contre ces mutins il soutiendra leur cause ;
« Sur son unique soin mon esprit se repose :
« Voyant le peu d'effet que la rigueur produit,
« Laissons éprouver l'art où la force est sans fruit ;
« Leur obstination s'irrite par les peines ;   555
« Il est plus de captifs que de fers et de chaînes ;
« Les cachots trop étroits ne les contiennent pas ;
« Les haches et les croix sont lasses de trépas ;

> Quelle horreur d'embrasser un homme dont l'épée
> De toute ma famille a la trame coupée.
> Le seul amour de Rome a sa main animée.

See *Lexique de Corneille*, I, p. lvii, and Mätzner, *Franz. Gram.*, p. 491, and *Syntax*, I, p. 362. See *Saint Genest*, ll. 11, 14, 167, 492.

541. le venin de ces lieux infectés : i.e. the poison of those infected places where the Christian doctrine was preached.

544. Ne peut où s'arrêter, etc. : "cannot come to a decision or rest at ease." A clumsy construction ; we should expect *ne ... ni ... ni*, but *s'arrêter* needed a qualification, hence *où* instead of *ni*.

545. le bien : = *le bonheur*.

546–547. César empressé, etc. : "Caesar, thronged about by a crowd of courtiers."

549. un visage remis : "a tranquil countenance." *Remis* in the sense of "calm, tranquil," is antiquated ; see *Lexique de Corneille*, II, p. 285.

« La mort, pour la trop voir, ne leur est plus sauvage ;

« Pour trop agir contre eux, le feu perd son usage ;   560

« En ces horreurs enfin le cœur manque aux bourreaux,

« Aux juges la constance, aux mourants les travaux.

« La douceur est souvent une invincible amorce

« A ces cœurs obstinés, qu'on aigrit par la force.»

Titien, à ces mots, dans la salle rendu,   565

« Ha ! s'est-il écrié, César, tout est perdu.»

La frayeur à ce cri par nos veines s'étale ;

Un murmure confus se répand dans la salle :

« Qu'est-ce ? a dit l'empereur, interdit et troublé.

« Le ciel s'est-il ouvert ? le monde a-t-il tremblé ?   570

« Quelque foudre lancé menace-t-il ma tête ?

« Rome d'un étranger est-elle la conquête ?

« Ou quelque embrasement consume-t-il ces lieux ? »

« — Adrien, a-t-il dit, pour Christ renonce aux dieux.»

ADRIEN

Oui, sans doute, et de plus à César, à moi-même,   575

Et soumets tout, Seigneur, à ton pouvoir suprême.

559–562. La mort, pour la trop voir, etc.: Sainte-Beuve, *op. cit.*, pp. 157–158, says: "Une autre qualité poétique dans le style de Rotrou, et qui lui est commune avec Corneille, qu'il a peut-être même à un degré plus évident encore, c'est le vers plein, tout d'une venue, de ces vers qui emportent la pièce. Fréquents chez Regnier, fréquents chez Molière, assez fréquents chez Corneille, plus rares chez Racine, Boileau, et dans cette école de poëtes à tant d'égards excellents, ces grands vers qui se font dire *ore rotundo*, à pleine lèvre, ces vers tout eschyliens qui auraient mérité de résonner sous le masque antique, ne font faute dans Rotrou." As examples Sainte-Beuve cites the above lines and ll. 821–822.

559. pour la trop voir : "on account of seeing it too frequently."

560. Pour trop agir, etc.: translate: "because employed too much against them fire loses its properties, its effect, is powerless."

562. travaux : "torments, tortures."

567. s'étale : "spreads." We should employ some other figure, such as "fear chills our blood," or "heart."

576. soumets : first person singular ; for omission of subject see note on l. 23.

FLAVIE

Maximin, à ce mot, furieux, l'œil ardent,
Signes avant-coureurs d'un funeste accident,
Pâlit, frappe du pied, frémit, déteste, tonne,
Comme désespéré, ne connaît plus personne,   580
Et nous fait voir au vif le geste et la couleur
D'un homme transporté d'amour et de douleur.
Et j'entends Adrien vanter encor son crime !
De César, de son maître, il paie ainsi l'estime,
Et reconnaît si mal qui lui veut tant de bien !   585

ADRIEN

Qu'il cesse de m'aimer, ou qu'il m'aime chrétien.

FLAVIE

Les dieux, dont comme nous les monarques dépendent,
Ne le permettent pas, et les lois le défendent.

ADRIEN

C'est le Dieu que je sers qui fait régner les rois,
Et qui fait que la terre en révère les lois.   590

FLAVIE

Sa mort sur un gibet marque son impuissance.

ADRIEN

Dites mieux, son amour et son obéissance.

FLAVIE

Sur une croix enfin . . .

578. accident : here simply "event, occurrence," not "accident."
581. au vif : "vividly." Ordinarily the expression is used only with
verbs like *trancher*, *piquer*, *toucher*, and *couper*.
591–599. This rapid dialogue of repartee is characteristic of Corneille ;
see *Polyeucte*, IV. 3 ; V. 3, etc. ; also ll. 1603–1604 of *Saint Genest*.

ADRIEN

Sur un bois glorieux,
Qui fut moins une croix qu'une échelle des cieux.

FLAVIE

Mais ce genre de mort ne pouvait être pire.   595

ADRIEN

Mais, mourant, de la mort il détruisit l'empire.

FLAVIE

L'auteur de l'univers entrer dans un cercueil !

ADRIEN

Tout l'univers aussi s'en vit tendu de deuil,
Et le ciel effrayé cacha ses luminaires.

FLAVIE

Si vous vous repaissez de ces vaines chimères,   600
Ce mépris de nos dieux et de votre devoir
En l'esprit de César détruira votre espoir.

ADRIEN

César m'abandonnant, Christ est mon assurance ;
C'est l'espoir des mortels dépouillés d'espérance.

---

597. **L'auteur de l'univers entrer dans un cercueil**: for the use of the pure infinitive in exclamatory sentences see Mätzner, *Franz. Gram.*, p. 474. — **cercueil**: lit. "coffin," but used in French figuratively for "tomb" or "grave." See *Venceslas*, l. 259.

600. **Si vous vous repaissez**, etc. : "If you glory in these idle fancies."

602. **En l'esprit de César**, etc. : a clumsy mode of expression. The meaning is "will ruin your expectations which depend on Caesar's favor."

604. **espoir — espérance** : Littré says : "espoir a un sens plus général, plus indéterminé qu'espérance. A part cette nuance, espoir et espérance se confondent."

FLAVIE

Il vous peut même ôter vos biens si précieux.   605

ADRIEN

J'en serai plus léger pour monter dans les cieux.

FLAVIE

L'indigence est à l'homme un monstre redoutable.

ADRIEN

Christ, qui fut homme et Dieu, naquit dans une étable.
Je méprise vos biens et leur fausse douceur,·
Dont on est possédé plutôt que possesseur.   610

FLAVIE

Sa piété l'oblige, autant que sa justice,
A faire des chrétiens un égal sacrifice.

ADRIEN

Qu'il fasse, il tarde trop.

FLAVIE

                    Que votre repentir . . .

ADRIEN

Non, non, mon sang, Flavie, est tout prêt à sortir.

FLAVIE

Si vous vous obstinez, votre perte est certaine.   615

ADRIEN

L'attente m'en est douce, et la menace vaine.

FLAVIE

Quoi ! vous n'ouvrirez point l'oreille à mes avis,
Aux soupirs de la cour, aux vœux de vos amis,

---

606. **monter dans les cieux** : usually *monter aux cieux*.
612. **égal** : "impartial." See *Lexique de Corneille*, I, p. 342.

A l'amour de César, aux cris de Natalie,
A qui si récemment un si beau nœud vos lie?   620
Et vous voudriez souffrir que dans cet accident
Ce soleil de beauté trouvât son occident?
A peine, depuis l'heure à ce nœud destinée,
A-t-elle vu flamber les torches d'hyménée :
Encor si quelque fruit de vos chastes amours   625
Devait après la mort perpétuer vos jours !
Mais vous voulez mourir avecque la disgrâce
D'éteindre votre nom avecque votre race,
Et, suivant la fureur d'un aveugle transport,
Nous être tout ravi par une seule mort !   630
Si votre bon génie attend l'heure opportune,
Savez-vous les emplois dont vous courez fortune?
L'espoir vous manque-t-il? et n'osez-vous songer
Qu'avant qu'être empereur Maximin fut berger?
Pour peu que sa faveur vous puisse être constante,   635
Quel défaut vous défend une pareille attente?
Quel mépris obstiné des hommes et des dieux
Vous rend indifférents et la terre et les cieux,
Et, comme si la mort vous était souhaitable,
Fait que pour l'obtenir vous vous rendez coupable,   640
Et vous faites César et les dieux ennemis?
Pesez-en le succès d'un esprit plus remis ;

622. **Ce soleil de beauté**, etc.: an example of Rotrou's affected style ;
see Introduction, p. 71.

625. **Encor si**: "if at least." For the form *encor* see note on l. 147.

628. **avecque**: see note on l. 17.

630. **tout ravi**: i.e. without leaving any posterity. See ll. 625–626.

632. **courez fortune**: "run the risk of," i.e. have the chance of obtaining.

634. **avant qu'**: antiquated for *avant de*, with infinitive; see Haase,
88, and *Lexique de Corneille*, I, pp. 98–99.

641. **Et vous faites César**, etc.: "you render Caesar and the gods hostile to yourself."

642. **Pesez-en le succès**, etc.: "Weigh the result of this with a calmer
mind."

Celui n'a point péché, de qui la repentance
Témoigne la surprise et suit de près l'offense.

ADRIEN

La grâce dont le ciel a touché mes esprits 645
M'a bien persuadé, mais ne m'a point surpris ;
Et, me laissant toucher à cette repentance,
Bien loin de réparer, je commettrais l'offense.
Allez, ni Maximin, courtois ou furieux,
Ni ce foudre qu'on peint en la main de vos dieux, 650
Ni la cour, ni le trône, avecque tous leurs charmes,
Ni Natalie enfin avec toutes ses larmes,
Ni l'univers rentrant dans son premier chaos,
Ne divertiraient pas un si ferme propos.

FLAVIE

Pesez bien les effets qui suivront mes paroles. 655

ADRIEN

Ils seront sans vertu, comme elles sont frivoles.

FLAVIE

Si raison ni douceur ne vous peut émouvoir,
Mon ordre va plus loin.

ADRIEN

Faites votre devoir.

643–644. **de qui ... l'offense** : i.e. whose immediate repentance shows that the sin was committed inadvertently.

647. **Et, me laissant toucher à cette repentance** : "and, allowing my-self to be moved by this repentance." After *se laisser* (and sometimes *faire*) the active infinitive is often employed for the passive, in which case the preposition of agency (*par* usually) is expressed by *à*. See Haase, 125, R. 2, and *Lexiques de Corneille*, I, p. 11 ; *de Racine*, p. 5 ; and *de Molière*, I, p. 7. See *Venceslas*, l. 293.

656. **vertu** : "power," or "strength" ; like Lat., *virtus*.

FLAVIE

C'est de vous arrêter et vous charger de chaînes,
Si, comme je vous dis, l'une et l'autre sont vaines. 660

[*On enchaîne Adrien*]

ADRIEN, *présentant ses bras aux fers, que les gardes lui attachent*

Faites ; je recevrai ces fardeaux précieux
Pour les premiers présents qui me viennent des cieux,
Pour de riches faveurs et de superbes marques
Du César des Césars et du roi des monarques ;
Et j'irai sans contrainte où, d'un illustre effort, 665
Les soldats de Jésus triomphent de la mort. [*Ils sortent tous*]

Scène IX

DIOCLÉTIEN, MAXIMIN, ETC.

DIOCLÉTIEN

En cet acte, Genest à mon gré se surpasse.

MAXIMIN

Il ne se peut rien feindre avecque plus de grâce.

659. **C'est de vous arrêter et vous charger de chaînes** : in prose the
preposition *de* before *arrêter* would regularly be repeated before *charger* ;
see Haase, 145, and *Lexiques de Corneille*, I, pp. 12, 255 ; *de Racine*, I,
p. cxxii ; *de Molière*, I, p. clxxxvii.

660. **l'une et l'autre** : i.e. *raison ni douceur* in l. 657.

661. **Faites** : this is the representative (*verbum vicarium*) use of *faire*
expressed in English by "do," the understood verbs being those in l. 659.
In this sense *faire* is generally followed by an accusative, e.g. *Horace*,
II. 5 : "Et je te traiterais comme j'ai fait (i.e. ai traité) mon frère."
See Haase, 71 ; and *Lexiques de Corneille*, I, p. 419 ; *de Racine*, I, p. 217 ;
de Molière, I, p. 468 ; and *de Mme. de Sévigné* I, p. 410.

663. **marques** : "signs, tokens," i.e. of regard. See *Lexique de Corneille*, II, p. 73.

668. **Il ne se peut rien feindre** : reflexive for passive ; see Haase, 72 ;
Lexiques de Racine, I, p. xcii ; *de Molière*, I, p. civ.

VALÉRIE, *se levant*

L'intermède permet de l'en féliciter,
Et de voir les acteurs.

DIOCLÉTIEN

Il se faut donc hâter.   670

ACTE TROISIÈME

Scène I

DIOCLÉTIEN, MAXIMIN, VALÉRIE, CAMILLE, PLANCIEN, SUITE DE GARDES, ET DE SOLDATS

VALÉRIE, *descendant du théâtre*

Quel trouble ! quel désordre ! et comment sans miracle
Nous peuvent-ils produire aucun plaisant spectacle ?

CAMILLE

Certes, à voir entre eux cette confusion,
L'ordre de leur récit semble une illusion.

MAXIMIN

L'art en est merveilleux, il faut que je l'avoue ;　　　　675
Mais l'acteur qui paraît est celui qui me joue,
Et qu'avecque Genest j'ai vu se concerter.
Voyons de quelle grâce il saura m'imiter.

Scène II

MAXIMIN, *représenté par* OCTAVE, *comédien* ; ADRIEN, *chargé de fers* ; FLAVIE ; SUITE DE GARDES ET DE SOLDATS

MAXIMIN, *acteur*

Sont-ce là les faveurs, traître, sont-ce les gages
De ce maître nouveau qui reçoit tes hommages,　　　　680
Et qu'au mépris des droits et du culte des dieux
L'impiété chrétienne ose placer aux cieux ?

ADRIEN

La nouveauté, Seigneur, de ce maître des maîtres
Est devant tous les temps et devant tous les êtres :
C'est lui qui du néant a tiré l'univers,   685
Lui qui dessus la terre a répandu les mers,
Qui de l'air étendit les humides contrées,
Qui sema de brillants les voûtes azurées,
Qui fit naître la guerre entre les éléments,
Et qui régla des cieux les divers mouvements ;   690
La terre à son pouvoir rend un muet hommage,
Les rois sont ses sujets, le monde est son partage ;
Si l'onde est agitée, il la peut affermir ;
S'il querelle les vents, ils n'osent plus frémir ;
S'il commande au soleil, il arrête sa course :   695
Il est maître de tout, comme il en est la source ;
Tout subsiste par lui, sans lui rien n'eût été ;
De ce maître, Seigneur, voilà la nouveauté.
Voyez si sans raison il reçoit mes hommages,
Et si sans vanité j'en puis porter les gages.   700

683–698. This passage should be compared with the similar one in
Polyeucte, III. 2 :

> Le Dieu de Polyeucte et celui de Néarque
> De la terre et du ciel est l'absolu monarque,
> Seul être indépendant, seul maître du destin,
> Seul principe éternel, et souveraine fin.
> C'est ce Dieu des chrétiens qu'il faut qu'on remercie
> Des victoires qu'il donne à l'empereur Décie ;
> Lui seul tient en sa main le succès des combats ;
> Il le veut élever, il le peut mettre à bas ;
> Sa bonté, son pouvoir, sa justice est immense ;
> C'est lui seul qui punit, lui seul qui récompense.
> Vous adorez en vain des monstres impuissants.

684. devant : antiquated for *avant*; see Haase, 130, and *Lexiques de
Corneille*, I, p. 298; *de Racine*, p. 150; *de Molière*, I, p. 324; and *de Mme.
de Sévigné*, I, p. 277.

694. querelle : "rebukes."

700. porter les gages : i.e. his chains were a token of his homage.

Oui, ces chaînes, César, ces fardeaux glorieux,
Sont aux bras d'un chrétien des présents précieux ;
Devant nous, ce cher maître en eut les mains chargées,
Au feu de son amour il nous les a forgées ;
Loin de nous accabler, leur faix est notre appui, 705
Et c'est par ces chaînons qu'il nous attire à lui.

MAXIMIN, *acteur*

Dieux ! à qui pourrons-nous nous confier sans crainte,
Et de qui nous promettre une amitié sans feinte,
De ceux que la fortune attache à nos côtés,
De ceux que nous avons moins acquis qu'achetés, 710
Qui sous des fronts soumis cachent des cœurs rebelles,
Que par trop de crédit nous rendons infidèles?
O dure cruauté du destin de la cour,
De ne pouvoir souffrir d'inviolable amour,
De franchise sans fard, de vertu qu'offusquée, 715
De devoir que contraint, ni de foi que manquée !
Qu'entreprends-je, chétif, en ces lieux écartés,
Où, lieutenant des dieux justement irrités,
Je fais d'un bras vengeur éclater les tempêtes,
Et poursuis des chrétiens les sacrilèges têtes, 720
Si, tandis que j'en prends un inutile soin,
Je vois naître chez moi ce que je fuis si loin?
Ce que j'extirpe ici dans ma cour prend racine ;
J'élève auprès de moi ce qu'ailleurs j'extermine.
Ainsi notre fortune, avec tout son éclat, 725
Ne peut, quoi qu'elle fasse, acheter un ingrat.

715. **de vertu qu'offusquée** : "any virtue but (that which is) dimmed,
obscure." For this use of *que* see Haase, 138, R. 2. The same meaning
is found twice in the next line. See also Mätzner, *Syntax*, II, p. 218,
and *Lexiques de Corneille*, II, p. 248 ; *de Racine*, p. 245 ; *de Molière*, II,
p. 356 ; and *de Mme. de Sévigné*, II, p. 274.

ADRIEN

Pour croire un Dieu, Seigneur, la liberté de croire
Est-elle en votre estime une action si noire,
Si digne de l'excès où vous vous emportez,
Et se peut-il souffrir de moindres libertés ?   730
Si jusques à ce jour vous avez cru ma vie
Inaccessible même aux assauts de l'envie,
Et si les plus censeurs ne me reprochent rien,
Qui m'a fait si coupable, en me faisant chrétien ?
Christ réprouve la fraude, ordonne la franchise,   735
Condamne la richesse injustement acquise,
D'une illicite amour défend l'acte indécent,
Et de tremper ses mains dans le sang innocent :
Trouvez-vous en ces lois aucune ombre de crime,
Rien de honteux aux siens, et rien d'illégitime ?   740
J'ai contre eux éprouvé tout ce qu'eût pu l'enfer :
J'ai vu couler leur sang sous des ongles de fer,

---

737. 1648 has *innocent* for *indécent*, a misprint caused by the ending
of the following line. Viollet-le-Duc and Hémon have *indécent*.

---

730. **Et se peut-il souffrir** : see note on l. 668.
731. **Si jusques à ce jour** : in poetry *jusque* may take an *s* in order to
make an additional syllable in the line. See *Venceslas*, ll. 950, 1482.
733. **censeurs** : "censorious." The word is usually a substantive.
Benoist, p. 376 : "D'autres mots, quoique substantifs ou employés sub-
stantivement, sont traités comme des adjectifs, et reçoivent des degrés
de comparaison."
737–738. **défend l'acte indécent, Et de tremper**, etc. : *défend* is here construed with two complements of a different nature. See Benoist, p. 401,
and *Lexiques de Corneille*, I, p. lxxii ; *de Racine*, p. cxv ; and *de Molière*, I,
p. clxxiv.
738. **ses mains** : " one's hands."
741–744. See ll. 786–789, *Venceslas*, ll. 36–40. For the use of several
lines beginning with the same word or words see Darmesteter and Hatzfeld, *Le seizième siècle en France*, p. 160, note 2. This is very common
in Théophile de Viau, on which see Schirmacher, p. 303.
742. **ongles de fer** : instrument of torture in the shape of a claw.

J'ai vu bouillir leur corps dans la poix et les flammes,
J'ai vu leur chair tomber sous de flambantes lames,
Et n'ai rien obtenu de ces cœurs glorieux   745
Que de les avoir vus pousser des chants aux cieux,
Prier pour leurs bourreaux au fort de leur martyre,
Pour vos prospérités, et pour l'heur de l'empire.

MAXIMIN, *acteur*

Insolent! est-ce à toi de te choisir des dieux?
Les miens, ceux de l'empire et ceux de tes aïeux   750
Ont-ils trop faiblement établi leur puissance
Pour t'arrêter au joug de leur obéissance?

ADRIEN

Je cherche le salut, qu'on ne peut espérer
De ces dieux de métal qu'on vous voit adorer.

MAXIMIN, *acteur*

Le tien, si cette humeur s'obstine à me déplaire,   755
Te garantira mal des traits de ma colère,
Que tes impiétés attireront sur toi.

ADRIEN

J'en parerai les coups du bouclier de la foi.

MAXIMIN, *acteur*

Crains de voir, et bientôt, ma faveur négligée
Et l'injure des dieux cruellement vengée.   760
De ceux que par ton ordre on a vus déchirés,

744. **flambantes lames**: lit. "flaming blades," i.e. red-hot knives.
756. **traits de ma colère**: "strokes, blows of my anger."
759. **ma faveur négligée**: "my slighted favor."
761. **De ceux que**, etc.: governed by *Les plus cruels tourments* in l. 764. An example of the inversion so common and necessary in verse.

Que le fer a meurtris et le feu dévorés,
Si tu ne divertis la peine où tu t'exposes,
Les plus cruels tourments n'auront été que roses.

ADRIEN

Nos corps étant péris, nous espérons qu'ailleurs   765
Le Dieu que nous servons nous les rendra meilleurs.

MAXIMIN, *acteur*

Traître ! jamais sommeil n'enchantera mes peines
Que ton perfide sang, épuisé de tes veines,
Et ton cœur sacrilège, aux corbeaux exposé,
N'ait rendu de nos dieux le courroux apaisé.   770

ADRIEN

La mort dont je mourrai sera digne d'envie,
Quand je perdrai le jour pour l'auteur de la vie.

765. étant péris : "after our bodies have perished." *Périr* is usually conjugated with *avoir*. Littré says that when conjugated with *être* it expresses more especially condition, but adds that this shade of difference is not always observed. Jarry cites Corneille's *Andromède*, III. 4 :

> Ce cheval ailé fût péri mille fois,
> Avant que de voler sous un indigne poids.

This use of *être* with *périr* is frequent in Madame de Sévigné ; see *Lexique*, IV, p. 200.

766. rendra : "will restore."

768. Que : "until." This locution is formed with the *ne* in l. 770, and followed by the subjunctive in the same line ; l. 769 should begin with the repeated *que*, which is omitted for metrical reasons. *Que*, in such cases, may generally be translated by "without," and so above : "without (*or* until) your treacherous blood . . . having appeased (*or* has appeased) the wrath of our gods." See Mätzner, *Franz. Gram.*, pp. 396, 509 ; *Syntax*, II, 193 ; and *Lexiques de Corneille*, II, p. 248 ; *de Racine*, p. 426 ; and *de Molière*, II, p. 358. See *Venceslas*, l. 484.

MAXIMIN, *acteur* [*à Flavie*]

Allez ; dans un cachot accablez-le de fers ;
Rassemblez tous les maux que sa secte a soufferts,
Et faites à l'envi contre cet infidèle . . .   775

ADRIEN

Dites ce converti.

MAXIMIN, *acteur*

Paraître votre zèle ;
Imaginez, forgez ; le plus industrieux
A le faire souffrir sera le plus pieux :
J'emploîrai ma justice où ma faveur est vaine,
Et qui fuit ma faveur éprouvera ma haine.   780

ADRIEN [*à part*] *s'en allant*

Comme je te soutiens, Seigneur, sois mon soutien :
Qui commence à souffrir commence d'être tien.

Scène III

MAXIMIN, *acteur*, GARDES

(*Flavie emmène* ADRIEN *avec des gardes*)

MAXIMIN, *acteur* [*à part*]

Dieux, vous avez un foudre, et cette félonie
Ne le peut allumer et demeure impunie !
Vous conservez la vie et laissez la clarté   785
A qui vous veut ravir votre immortalité,
A qui contre le Ciel soulève un peu de terre,

775. **Et faites à l'envi,** etc. : "and vie with each other in showing your
zeal against this disloyal . . ." *Faites* belongs with *paraître* in next line.

777. **forgez** : "invent."

782. **être tien** : for *être le tien*, see ll. 862, 1537. For omission of the
article see Haase, 17, R, and Mätzner, *Syntax*, I, p. 434.

787. **A qui contre le Ciel soulève un peu de terre** : does this mean that
Genest incites against Heaven a little dust, i.e. himself ? This would

A qui veut de vos mains arracher le tonnerre,
A qui vous entreprend et vous veut détrôner
Pour un Dieu qu'il se forge et qu'il veut couronner !   790
Inspirez-moi, grands dieux, inspirez-moi des peines
Dignes de mon courroux et dignes de vos haines,
Puisqu'à des attentats de cette qualité
Un supplice commun est une impunité.

                    (*Il sort*)

SCÈNE IV

FLAVIE, *ramenant* ADRIEN *à la prison* ; ADRIEN, LE
                GEÔLIER, GARDES

FLAVIE, *au geôlier*

L'ordre exprès de César le commet en ta garde.   795

LE GEÔLIER

Le vôtre me suffit, et ce soin me regarde.

SCÈNE V

NATALIE, FLAVIE, ADRIEN, LE GEÔLIER

NATALIE

O nouvelle trop vraie ! est-ce là mon époux ?

FLAVIE

Notre dernier espoir ne consiste qu'en vous :
Rendez-le-nous à vous, à César, à lui-même.

seem to be the case, as in the other lines *qui* is the subject of the following verb.

789. **entreprend :** "attacks."

795. **commet en ta garde :** see l. 32, where the more common *à* is employed.

799. **Rendez-le-nous à vous,** etc : is *nous* here merely the ethical dative, or is it used for disjunctive form, *à nous*, on account of meter ?

NATALIE

Si l'effet n'en dépend que d'un désir extrême . . .   800

FLAVIE

Je vais faire espérer cet heureux changement.
Voyez-le.

> (*Flavie s'en va avec les gardes et le geôlier se retire*)

ADRIEN

Tais-toi, femme, et m'écoute un moment.
Par l'usage des gens et par les lois romaines,
La demeure, les biens, les délices, les peines,
Tout espoir, tout profit, tout humain intérêt,   805
Doivent être communs à qui la couche l'est.
Mais que, comme la vie et comme la fortune,
Leur créance toujours leur doive être commune,
D'étendre jusqu'aux dieux cette communauté,
Aucun droit n'établit cette nécessité.   810
Supposons toutefois que la loi le désire,
Il semble que l'époux, comme ayant plus d'empire,
Ait le droit le plus juste ou le plus spécieux
De prescrire chez soi le culte de ses dieux.
Ce que tu vois enfin, ce corps chargé de chaînes,   815
N'est l'effet ni des lois ni des raisons humaines,
Mais de quoi des chrétiens j'ai reconnu le Dieu,
Et dit à vos autels un éternel adieu.
Je l'ai dit, je le dis, et trop tard pour ma gloire,

---

801. **Je vais faire espérer,** etc.: does this mean "I am going to cause (others) to hope for this happy change?"

807. **Mais que:** "provided." For this use, now obsolete, see Haase, 137, 4, and Mätzner, *Syntax,* II, p. 175.

817. **Mais de quoi:** = *mais de ce que,* "but because I have recognized, but for having recognized, etc." For this obsolete use see Haase, 42, R. 4, and Benoist, p. 396.

Puisqu'enfin je n'ai cru qu'étant forcé de croire,   820
Qu'après les avoir vus, d'un visage serein,
Pousser des chants aux cieux dans des taureaux d'airain,
D'un souffle, d'un regard jeter vos dieux par terre,
Et l'argile et le bois s'en briser comme verre.
Je les ai combattus : ces effets m'ont vaincu ;   825
J'ai reconnu par eux l'erreur où j'ai vécu ;
J'ai vu la vérité, je la suis, je l'embrasse ;
Et si César prétend par force, par menace,
Par offres, par conseil, ou par allèchements,
Et toi ni par soupirs ni par embrassements,   830
Ébranler une foi si ferme et si constante,
Tous deux vous vous flattez d'une inutile attente.
Reprends sur ta franchise un empire absolu ;
Que le nœud qui nous joint demeure résolu ;
Veuve dès à présent, par ma mort prononcée,   835

820. **je n'ai cru qu'étant forcé de croire** : " I believed only when I was compelled to believe."

821. **les** : refers to *chrétiens* in l. 817.

825. **ces effets** : " these results," i.e. those enumerated in ll. 822–824.

830. **ni par soupirs ni par embrassements** : the negation is implied ; in English "either . . . or" is employed ; see Haase, 140, R. 2, and Benoist, p. 397.

833–838. The idea seems an echo of *Polyeucte*, IV. 4, where Polyeucte resigns Pauline to Sévère.

835–838. **Veuve dès à présent**, etc. : Sainte-Beuve, *op. cit.*, pp. 160–161, says : "On ramène Adrien dans sa prison. Sa femme Natalie (représentée par Marcelle, cette comédienne un peu coquette de tout à l'heure) le vient trouver ; mais, au premier mot qu'elle essaie, Adrien, moins galant que Polyeucte, et qui n'a pas les délicatesses et politesses de ce *cavalier* d'Arménie, lequel, même à travers son enthousiasme, accueillait Pauline en disant :

> Madame, quel dessein vous fait me demander ?

Adrien coupe court au dessein qu'il suppose à Natalie :

> . . . Tais-toi femme, et m'écoute un moment !

A part cette incivilité du début, la tirade est belle, grande et finalement touchante. Les délicatesses pourtant de la scène entre Polyeucte

Sur un plus digne objet adresse ta pensée ;
Ta jeunesse, tes biens, ta vertu, ta beauté,
Te feront mieux trouver que ce qui t'est ôté.
Adieu : pourquoi, cruelle à de si belles choses,
Noyes-tu de tes pleurs ces œillets et ces roses ?   840
Bientôt, bientôt le sort, qui t'ôte ton époux,
Te fera respirer sous un hymen plus doux.
Que fais-tu ? tu me suis ! Quoi ! tu m'aimes encore ?
Oh ! si de mon désir l'effet pouvait éclore !
Ma sœur, c'est le seul nom dont je te puis nommer,   845
Que sous de douces lois nous nous pourrions aimer !

(L'embrassant)

Tu saurais que la mort, par qui l'âme est ravie,
Est la fin de la mort plutôt que de la vie,

et Pauline s'y font à un autre endroit regretter. Au lieu de ce noble et
généreux don que Polyeucte veut faire de Pauline à Sévère, Adrien, qui
voit déjà Natalie veuve, se montre trop empressé de la donner à n'importe qui." Sainte-Beuve then cites the lines 835–838, and continues :
" Loin d'être héroïque et magnanime comme chez Polyeucte, le don ainsi
exprimé, jeté comme au hasard, n'est plus même élevé ni décent. Cette
noble nature de Rotrou avait du vulgaire, du bas. Corneille d'ordinaire
est noble, ou enflé, ou subtil, ou au pis un peu comique de naïveté : il
n'est pas vulgaire. Rotrou l'est ; il avait de mauvaises habitudes dans
sa vie, du désordre, le jeu ; il n'avait pas toujours gardé les mœurs de
famille, il fréquentait la taverne et certainement très-peu l'hôtel de
Rambouillet."

836. objet : see note on l. 148. — adresse : for <i>adresse à</i>, on account of
meter.

838. mieux trouver que ce qui, etc. : <i>mieux</i> is here substantive : " find
a better one than he who is taken from you."

840. ces œillets et ces roses : lit. " these pinks and these roses." Can
Rotrou be punning on <i>œillets</i> (" little eyes, eyelets ") and refer it to
Natalie's eyes and the roses to her cheeks ?

842. respirer : = <i>vivre</i>, as in English : " breathe," meaning " live."

844. si de . . . éclore : translate : " if my desire could be fulfilled."

845. Ma sœur : see l. 1138. Since Adrien's conversion Natalie had
regarded him in the light of a brother. This changed relation of husband and wife after conversion is common in the history of early Christianity. In the legend of Adrian in the <i>Legenda Aurea</i>, p. 598, after

Qu'il n'est amour ni vie en ce terrestre lieu,
Et qu'on ne peut s'aimer ni vivre qu'avec Dieu.   850

NATALIE, *l'embrassant*

Oh ! d'un Dieu tout-puissant merveilles souveraines !
Laisse-moi, cher époux, prendre part en tes chaînes !
Et, si ni notre hymen ni ma chaste amitié
Ne m'ont assez acquis le nom de ta moitié,
Permets que l'alliance enfin s'en accomplisse,   855
Et que Christ de ces fers aujourd'hui nous unisse ;
Crois qu'ils seront pour moi d'indissolubles nœuds
Dont l'étreinte en toi seul saura borner mes vœux.

ADRIEN

O ciel ! ô Natalie, ah ! douce et sainte flamme,
Je rallume mes feux et reconnais ma femme.   860
Puisqu'au chemin du ciel tu veux suivre mes pas,
Sois mienne, chère épouse, au delà du trépas ;
Que mes vœux, que ta foi . . . Mais, tire-moi de peine :
Ne me flatté-je point d'une créance vaine ?
D'où te vient le beau feu qui t'échauffe le sein ?   865
Et quand as-tu conçu ce généreux dessein ?
Par quel heureux motif . . .

859. 1648 has *O ciel ! ô Natalie ! ah ! sainte flamme*, a word or words
having been omitted. Viollet-le-Duc has *douce et sainte flamme*, and I
have followed his text. Hémon has same text.

Natalia has visited her husband for the first time in prison and encouraged him to persevere, he addresses her with these words : "Vade, soror
mea, tempore passionis nostrae accersam te, ut videas finem nostrum."
854. moitié : constantly in verse for "wife" ; cf. English "better half."
Corneille uses the word frequently ; see *Lexique*, II, p. 96. See *Venceslas*, l. 473.
858. étreinte : "clasp, bond."—borner : would regularly be followed
by *à* ; here *en* is a peculiarity of Rotrou's language. See l. 795, where
en is also used for *à*.
862. Sois mienne : see note on l. 782.

NATALIE

Je te vais satisfaire ;
Il me fut inspiré presque aux flancs de ma mère,
Et presque en même instant le ciel versa sur moi
La lumière du jour et celle de la foi.   870
Il fit qu'avec le lait, pendante à la mamelle,
Je suçai des chrétiens la créance et le zèle ;
Et ce zèle avec moi crut jusqu'à l'heureux jour
Que mes yeux, sans dessein, m'acquirent ton amour.
Tu sais, s'il t'en souvient, de quelle résistance   875
Ma mère en cet amour combattit ta constance ;
Non qu'un si cher parti ne nous fût glorieux,
Mais pour sa répugnance au culte de tes dieux.
De César toutefois la suprême puissance
Obtint ce triste aveu de son obéissance ;   880
Ses larmes seulement marquèrent ses douleurs ;
Car qu'est-ce qu'une esclave a de plus que des pleurs ?
Enfin, le jour venu que je te fus donnée :
« Va, me dit-elle à part, va, fille infortunée,
« Puisqu'il plaît à César ; mais surtout souviens-toi   885
« D'être fidèle au Dieu dont nous suivons la loi,
« De n'adresser qu'à lui tes vœux et tes prières,
« De renoncer au jour plutôt qu'à ses lumières
« Et détester autant les dieux de ton époux
« Que ses chastes baisers te doivent être doux. »   890
Au défaut de ma voix, mes pleurs lui répondirent.
Tes gens dedans ton char aussitôt me rendirent,

887. 1648 has *tes vœux ni tes prières*, an evident misprint corrected
by Viollet-le-Duc.

---

868. **flancs** : poetical for " bosom, womb."
877. **Non qu'un si cher parti**, etc. : " not but that we were proud of so
precious a match."
882. **Car qu'est-ce qu'une esclave**, etc. : " for what more does a slave
possess but tears ? "

Mais l'esprit si rempli de cette impression
Qu'à peine eus-je des yeux pour voir ta passion,
Et qu'il fallut du temps pour ranger ma franchise   895
Au point où ton mérite à la fin l'a soumise.
L'œil qui voit dans les cœurs clair comme dans les cieux
Sait quelle aversion j'ai depuis pour tes dieux ;
Et, depuis notre hymen, jamais leur culte impie,
Si tu l'as observé, ne m'a coûté d'hostie ;   900
Jamais sur leurs autels mes encens n'ont fumé ;
Et, lorsque je t'ai vu, de fureur enflammé,
Y faire tant offrir d'innocentes victimes,
J'ai souhaité cent fois de mourir pour tes crimes,
Et cent fois vers le ciel, témoin de mes douleurs,   905
Poussé pour toi des vœux accompagnés de pleurs.

ADRIEN

Enfin je reconnais, ma chère Natalie,
Que je dois mon salut au saint nœud qui nous lie.
Permets-moi toutefois de me plaindre à mon tour :
Me voyant te chérir d'une si tendre amour,   910
Y pouvais-tu répondre et me tenir cachée
Cette céleste ardeur dont Dieu t'avait touchée ?
Peux-tu, sans t'émouvoir, avoir vu ton époux
Contre tant d'innocents exercer son courroux ?

NATALIE

Sans m'émouvoir ! Hélas ! le Ciel sait si tes armes   915
Versaient jamais de sang sans me tirer des larmes.
Je m'en émus assez ; mais eussé-je espéré

---

899. 1648 has *le* for *leur*. I have followed Viollet-le-Duc's correction.

895. **ranger** : this word means practically the same as *soumise* in next line, "subject, subdue."
902. **fureur** : "zeal."
906. **Poussé** : for omission of auxiliary see note on l. 175.

De réprimer la soif d'un lion altéré,
De contenir un fleuve inondant une terre,
Et d'arrêter dans l'air la chute d'un tonnerre?   920
J'ai failli toutefois, j'ai dû parer tes coups;
Ma crainte fut coupable autant que ton courroux.
Partageons donc la peine aussi bien que les crimes:
Si ces fers te sont dus, ils me sont légitimes;
Tous deux dignes de mort, et tous deux résolus,   925
Puisque nous voici joints, ne nous séparons plus;
Qu'aucun temps, qu'aucun lieu, jamais ne nous divisent:
Un supplice, un cachot, un juge nous suffisent.

ADRIEN

Par un ordre céleste, aux mortels inconnu,
Chacun part de ce lieu quand son temps est venu: 930
Suis cet ordre sacré, que rien ne doit confondre;
Lorsque Dieu nous appelle, il est temps de répondre;
Ne pouvant avoir part en ce combat fameux,
Si mon cœur au besoin ne répond à mes vœux,
Mérite, en m'animant, ta part de la couronne   935
Qu'en l'empire éternel le martyre nous donne:
Au défaut du premier, obtiens le second rang;
Acquiers par tes souhaits ce qu'on nie à ton sang,
Et dedans le péril m'assiste en cette guerre.

NATALIE

Bien donc, choisis le ciel et me laisse la terre.   940
Pour aider ta constance en ce pas périlleux,
Je te suivrai partout et jusque dans les feux;
Heureuse si la loi qui m'ordonne de vivre
Jusques au ciel enfin me permet de te suivre,

933. **Ne pouvant avoir part,** etc.: Natalie had not been summoned by Heaven to meet a martyr's death; all she could do was to encourage her husband.

Et si de ton tyran le funeste courroux   945
Passe jusqu'à l'épouse, ayant meurtri l'époux.
Tes gens me rendront bien ce favorable office
De garder qu'à mes soins César ne te ravisse
Sans en apprendre l'heure et m'en donner avis,
Et bientôt de mes pas les tiens seront suivis;   950
Bientôt . . .

ADRIEN

   Épargne-leur cette inutile peine;
Laisse m'en le souci, leur veille serait vaine.
Je ne partirai point de ce funeste lieu
Sans ton dernier baiser et ton dernier adieu :
Laisses-en sur mon soin reposer ton attente.   955

SCÈNE VI

FLAVIE, GARDES, ADRIEN, NATALIE

FLAVIE

Aux desseins importants, qui craint, impatiente.
Eh bien, qu'obtiendrons-nous ? vos soins officieux
A votre époux aveugle ont-ils ouvert les yeux ?

NATALIE

Nul intérêt humain, nul respect ne le touche ;
Quand j'ai voulu parler, il m'a fermé la bouche,   960
Et, détestant les dieux, par un long entretien,
A voulu m'engager dans le culte du sien.
Enfin, ne tentez plus un dessein impossible,
Et gardez que, heurtant ce cœur inaccessible,

---

956. **impatiente** : for *s'impatiente*, "is impatient." For omission of the reflexive pronoun see Haase, 61, and Benoist, p. 387.

957. **officieux** : here, as generally, in a good sense, "obliging, kind."

959. **respect** : "employé avec le sens de considération, raison d'agir," Benoist, p. 368.

Vous ne vous y blessiez, pensant le secourir, 965
Et ne gagniez le mal que vous voulez guérir ;
Ne veuillez point son bien à votre préjudice ;
Souffrez, souffrez plutôt que l'obstiné périsse ;
Rapportez à César notre inutile effort,
Et, si la loi des dieux fait conclure à sa mort, 970
Que l'effet prompt et court en suive la menace :
J'implore seulement cette dernière grâce.
Si de plus doux succès n'ont suivi mon espoir,
J'ai l'avantage au moins d'avoir fait mon devoir.

FLAVIE

O vertu sans égale, et sur toutes insigne ! 975
O d'une digne épouse époux sans doute indigne !
Avec quelle pitié le peut-on secourir,
Si, sans pitié de soi, lui-même il veut périr ?

NATALIE

Allez ; n'espérez pas que ni force ni crainte
Puissent rien où mes pleurs n'ont fait aucune atteinte ; 980
Je connais trop son cœur, j'en sais la fermeté,
Incapable de crainte et de legèreté.
A regret contre lui je rends ce témoignage ;
Mais l'intérêt du Ciel à ce devoir m'engage.
Encore un coup, cruel, au nom de notre amour, 985

970. **conclure** : a legal term, "to vote for, decide," speaking of judges.

978. **soi** : for *lui*. The restriction of *soi* to an indefinite subject (*on, chacun, quiconque, nul, personne*, or an infinitive used indefinitely) was not common until after the middle of the seventeenth century. See Haase, 13 ; Mätzner, *Syntax*, I, p. 255 ; *Lexique de Corneille*, II, p. 336 ; Vaugelas, *Remarques*, I, p. 275 and Chassang, *French Grammar*, p. 277. See *Venceslas*, l. 1386 ; the modern usage is found in l. 1354.

985–992. Notice the ambiguity of Natalie's address to her husband in Flavie's presence.

985. **Encore un coup** : = *encore une fois*, frequent in Corneille ; see *Lexique*, I, p. 226, and *Lexique de Molière*, I, p. 245.

Au nom saint et sacré de la céleste cour,
Reçois de ton épouse un conseil salutaire :
Déteste ton erreur, rends-toi le Ciel prospère ;
Songe et propose-toi que tes travaux présents,
Comparés aux futurs, sont doux ou peu cuisants.   990
Vois combien cette mort importe à ton estime,
D'où tu sors, où tu vas, et quel objet t'anime.

ADRIEN

Mais toi, contiens ton zèle, il m'est assez connu,
Et songe que ton temps n'est pas encor venu ;
Que je te vais attendre à ce port désirable.   995
Allons, exécutez le décret favorable
Dont j'attends mon salut plutôt que le trépas.

FLAVIE, *le livrant au geôlier et s'en allant*

Vous en êtes coupable, en ne l'évitant pas.
      [*Il sort. Le geôlier et les gardes emmènent Adrien*]

Scène VII

NATALIE, *seule*

J'ose à présent, ô Ciel, d'une vue assurée,
Contempler les brillants de ta voûte azurée,   1000
Et nier ces faux dieux, qui n'ont jamais foulé
De ce palais roulant le lambris étoilé.
A ton pouvoir, Seigneur, mon époux rend hommage ;
Il professe ta foi, ses fers t'en sont un gage ;
Ce redoutable fléau des dieux sur les chrétiens,   1005
Ce lion altéré du sacré sang des tiens,
Qui de tant d'innocents crut la mort légitime,
De ministre qu'il fut, s'offre enfin pour victime,

1008. **De ministre**, etc. : see note on l. 129.

Et, patient agneau, tend à tes ennemis
Un col à ton saint joug heureusement soumis.   1010

Rompons, après sa mort, notre honteux silence ;
De ce lâche respect forçons la violence,
Et disons aux tyrans, d'une constante voix,
Ce qu'à Dieu du penser nous avons dit cent fois.

Donnons air au beau feu dont notre âme est pressée ;   1015
En cette illustre ardeur mille m'ont devancée ;
D'obstacles infinis mille ont su triompher,
Cécile des tranchants, Prisque des dents de fer,
Fauste des plombs bouillants, Dipne de sa noblesse,
Agathe de son sexe, Agnès de sa jeunesse,   1020
Tècle de son amant, et toutes du trépas ;
Et je répugnerais à marcher sur leur pas !

                                        (*Elle rentre*)

1014. **du penser**: "in thought." See note on l. 455.

1015. **Donnons air au beau feu**, etc. : translate : "Let us fan the noble flame which consumes our heart."

1018–1021. *Saint Cecilia*, the patroness of music, is said to have suffered martyrdom in A.D. 230. After she had survived the flames she was put to death with the sword (*tranchants* of l. 1018). The church celebrates her festival on November 22. *Saint Prisca*, martyred about A.D. 275, has her festival on January 18. The *Martyrologium Romanum* says : "Sub Claudio Imperatore post multa tormenta martyrio coronata est." *Saint Fausta* was martyred under Maximian, and her death is commemorated on September 20. *Martyrologium Romanum*, May 15, says of Saint Dympna : "In Brabantia sanctae Dympnae virginis et martyris, filiae Regis Hiberniae, quae pro fide Christi et virginitate servanda, a patre jussa est decollari." This took place at Gheel in Brabant in the seventh century. *Saint Agatha* was martyred under Decius in A.D. 251 and her festival occurs February 5. She suffered incredible tortures among which was "mamillarum abcissionem," to which the text perhaps refers. *Saint Agnes* was martyred about A.D. 304, it is said at the age of thirteen. She has two festivals, January 21 and 28. The *Martyrologium* quotes the words of Saint Jerome, "quae et aetatem vicit et tyrannum." There are six *Theclas* in the *Martyrologium Romanum*, the one referred to in the text being probably the Thecla martyred at Iconium under Nero. Her festival is celebrated September 23. She forsook, as was so often the case, her betrothed Thamaris.

Scène VIII

GENEST, DIOCLÉTIEN, MAXIMIN, VALÉRIE, CAMILLE, PLANCIEN,
GARDES *

GENEST

Seigneur, le bruit confus d'une foule importune
De gens qu'à votre suite attache la fortune,
Par le trouble où nous met cette incommodité,   1025
Altère les plaisirs de Votre Majesté,
Et nos acteurs, confus de ce désordre extrême . . .

DIOCLÉTIEN, *se levant, avec toute la cour*

Il y faut donner ordre, et l'y porter nous-même.
De vos dames la jeune et courtoise beauté
Vous attire toujours cette importunité.   1030

* 1648 has *Genest, Dioclétien, Maximin, etc.*

1023-1030. There seems to be no reason for this scene except to
bring about the end of Act III by affording the emperor a pretext for
leaving the stage.

ACTE QUATRIÈME

Scène I

DIOCLÉTIEN, MAXIMIN, VALÉRIE, CAMILLE, PLANCIEN, GARDES,
descendant du théâtre

VALÉRIE, *à Dioclétien*

Votre ordre a mis le calme, et dedans le silence
De ces irrévérents contiendra l'insolence.

DIOCLÉTIEN

Écoutons : car Genest, dedans cette action,
Passe aux derniers efforts de sa profession.

Scène II

ADRIEN, FLAVIE, GARDES, DIOCLÉTIEN, MAXIMIN, VALÉRIE,
CAMILLE, PLANCIEN, SUITE DE GARDES

FLAVIE

Si le Ciel, Adrien, ne t'est bientôt propice,   1035
D'un infaillible pas tu cours au précipice.
J'avais vu, par l'espoir d'un proche repentir,
De César irrité le courroux s'alentir ;
Mais, quand il a connu nos prières, nos peines,
Les larmes de ta femme et son attente vaines,   1040
L'œil ardent de colère et le teint pâlissant :
« Amenez, a-t-il dit d'un redoutable accent,

1036. tu cours : in modern French the future would be employed.

204

« Amenez ce perfide, en qui mes bons offices
« Rencontrent aujourd'hui le plus lâche des vices ;
« Et que l'ingrat apprenne à quelle extrémité   1045
« Peut aller la fureur d'un monarque irrité. »
Passant de ce discours, s'il faut dire, à la rage,
Il invente, il ordonne, il met tout en usage,
Et, si le repentir de ton aveugle erreur
N'en détourne l'effet et n'éteint sa fureur . . .   1050

ADRIEN

Que tout l'effort, tout l'art, toute l'adresse humaine
S'unisse pour ma perte et conspire à ma peine :
Celui qui d'un seul mot créa chaque élément,
Leur donnant l'action, le poids, le mouvement,
Et prêtant son concours à ce fameux ouvrage,   1055
Se retint le pouvoir d'en suspendre l'usage ;
Le feu ne peut brûler, l'air ne saurait mouvoir,
Ni l'eau ne peut couler qu'au gré de son pouvoir ;
Le fer, solide sang des veines de la terre
Et fatal instrument des fureurs de la guerre,   1060
S'émousse, s'il l'ordonne, et ne peut pénétrer
Où son pouvoir s'oppose et lui défend d'entrer.
Si César m'est cruel, il me sera prospère ;
C'est lui que je soutiens, c'est en lui que j'espère ;
Par son soin, tous les jours, la rage des tyrans   1065
Croit faire des vaincus et fait des conquérants.

1043. mes bons offices : " my kind services," or simply " my kindness."

1047. s'il faut dire : in prose *s'il faut le dire.* For omission of object of transitive verb see *Lexiques de Racine*, p. 297 ; and *de Molière*, I, p. clxxxi. It is possible that *dire* is here used absolutely ; see *Lexique de Molière*, I, p. 336.

1059. Le fer, solide sang, etc. : notice the use of *fer* in a double sense, " iron " and " sword." A good example of Rotrou's inflated style ; see Introduction, p. 71.

1063. il me sera prospère : *il* refers to *Celui qui* of l. 1053.

FLAVIE

Souvent en ces ardeurs la mort qu'on se propose
Ne semble qu'un ébat, qu'un souffle, qu'une rose ;
Mais, quand ce spectre affreux sous un front inhumain,
Les tenailles, les feux, les haches à la main,   1070
Commence à nous paraître et faire ses approches,
Pour ne s'effrayer pas il faut être des roches,
Et notre repentir, en cette occasion,
S'il n'est vain, pour le moins tourne à confusion.

ADRIEN

J'ai contre les chrétiens servi longtemps vos haines,   1075
Et j'appris leur constance en ordonnant leurs peines.
Mais, avant que César ait prononcé l'arrêt
Dont l'exécution me trouvera tout prêt,
Souffrez que d'un adieu j'acquitte ma promesse
A la chère moitié que Dieu veut que je laisse,   1080
Et que, pour dernier fruit de notre chaste amour,
Je prenne congé d'elle en le prenant du jour.

FLAVIE

Allons, la piété m'oblige à te complaire ;
Mais ce retardement aigrira sa colère.

ADRIEN

Le temps en sera court ; devancez-moi d'un pas.   1085

1068. **ébat** : " frolic, sport, pastime." Littré : " Aujourd'hui *ébat* ne se dit guère qu'au pluriel. Il serait bon de faire comme Rotrou et de maintenir l'usage du singulier."

1073-1074. **Et notre repentir,** etc. : that is, if our repentance is delayed until the hour of punishment approaches it is either useless, does not save us, or results in our confusion, or shame.

1084. **sa colère** : i.e. Caesar's, l. 1077.

FLAVIE

Marchons : le zèle ardent qu'il porte à son trépas
Nous est de sa personne une assez sûre garde.

UN GARDE

Qui croit un prisonnier toutefois le hasarde.

ADRIEN

Mon ardeur et ma foi me gardent sûrement ;
N'avancez rien qu'un pas, je ne veux qu'un moment.   1090
(*Ils s'en vont*)

Scène III

ADRIEN, *seul, continue*

Ma chère Natalie, avec quelle allégresse
Verras-tu ma visite acquitter ma promesse !
Combien de saints baisers, combien d'embrassements
Produiront de ton cœur les secrets mouvements !
Prends ma sensible ardeur, prends conseil de ma flamme ; 1095
Marchons assurément sur les pas d'une femme :
Ce sexe qui ferma, rouvrit depuis les cieux ;
Les fruits de la vertu sont partout précieux ;
Je ne puis souhaiter de guide plus fidèle.
J'approche de la porte, et l'on ouvre. C'est elle.   1100

1086. 1648 has, by a misprint, *le zèle ardent que je porte au trépas.*
Viollet-le-Duc, followed by Hémon, corrects, *qu'il porte à son trépas* ;
Ronchaud, *qui le porte au trépas.*

1088. le hasarde : i.e. runs the risk of losing him ; lit. "exposes him to risk."

1096. assurément : " signifie, comme dans Corneille : avec assurance,"
Benoist, p. 390. See *Lexique de Corneille*, I, p. 81.

Scène IV

NATALIE, ADRIEN

ADRIEN, *la voulant embrasser*

Enfin, chère moitié . . .

NATALIE, *se retirant, et lui fermant la porte*

Comment ! seul et sans fers ?
Est-ce là ce martyr, ce vainqueur des enfers,
Dont l'illustre courage et la force infinie
De ses persécuteurs bravaient la tyrannie ?

ADRIEN

Ce soupçon, ma chère âme . . .

NATALIE

Après ta lâcheté,　　　1105
Va, ne me tiens plus, traître, en cette qualité :
Du Dieu que tu trahis je partage l'injure ;
Moi, l'âme d'un païen ! moi, l'âme d'un parjure !
Moi, l'âme d'un chrétien qui renonce à sa loi !
D'un homme enfin sans cœur et sans âme et sans foi !　　　1110

ADRIEN

Daigne m'entendre un mot.

NATALIE

Je n'entends plus un lâche
Qui dès le premier pas chancelle et se relâche,
Dont la seule menace ébranle la vertu,
Qui met les armes bas sans avoir combattu,

1105. **ma chère âme** : see note on l. 286.
1112. **chancelle et se relâche** : "wavers and grows slack."

Et qui, s'étant fait croire une invincible roche, 1115
Au seul bruit de l'assaut se rend avant l'approche.
Va, perfide, aux tyrans à qui tu t'es rendu
Demander lâchement le prix qui t'en est dû ;
Que l'épargne romaine en tes mains se desserre ;
Exclu des biens du ciel, songe à ceux de la terre ; 1120
Mais, parmi ses honneurs et ses rangs superflus,
Compte-moi pour un bien qui ne t'appartient plus.

ADRIEN

Je ne te veux qu'un mot : accorde ma prière.

NATALIE

Ah ! que de ta prison n'ai-je été la geôlière !
J'aurais souffert la mort avant ta liberté. 1125
Traître, qu'espères-tu de cette lâcheté ?
La cour s'en raillera ; ton tyran, quoi qu'il die,
Ne saurait en ton cœur priser ta perfidie.
Les martyrs, animés d'une sainte fureur,
En rougiront de honte et frémiront d'horreur ; 1130
Contre toi, dans le ciel, Christ arme sa justice ;
Les ministres d'enfer préparent ton supplice,
Et tu viens, rejeté de la terre et des cieux,
Pour me perdre avec toi, chercher grâce en ces lieux ?
 (*Elle sort furieuse, et dit en s'en allant*)
Que ferai-je, ô Seigneur ! puis-je souffrir sans peine 1135
L'ennemi de ta gloire et l'objet de ta haine ?

1115. **s'étant fait croire**, etc.: i.e. having made others believe him a
firm rock. See note on l. 436.

1116. **l'approche** : i.e. of the enemy.

1119. **l'épargne romaine** : "the Roman treasury."

1127. **die** : for *dise*, an archaic form of the present subjunctive still
permissible for the sake of rhyme. See *Lexiques de Corneille*, I, p. 306,
de Racine, p. 155, and *de Molière*, I, p. xcix.

1134. **chercher grâce en ces lieux** : i.e. to seek my pardon.

Puis-je vivre et me voir en ce confus état
De la sœur d'un martyr, femme d'un apostat,
D'un ennemi de Dieu, d'un lâche, d'un infâme?

ADRIEN

Je te vais détromper. Où cours-tu, ma chère âme?   1140

NATALIE

Ravir dans ta prison, d'une mâle vigueur,
La palme qu'aujourd'hui tu perds faute de cœur,
Y joindre les martyrs, et d'une sainte audace
Remplir chez eux ton rang et combattre en ta place ;
Y cueillir les lauriers dont Dieu t'eût couronné,   1145
Et prendre au ciel le lieu qui t'était destiné.

ADRIEN

Pour quelle défiance altères-tu ma gloire ?
Dieu toujours en mon cœur conserve sa victoire ;
Il a reçu ma foi, rien ne peut l'ébranler,
Et je cours au trépas, bien loin d'en reculer.   1150
Seul, sans fers, mais armé d'un invincible zèle,
Je me rends au combat où l'empereur m'appelle ;
Mes gardes vont devant, et je passe en ce lieu
Pour te tenir parole et pour te dire adieu.
M'avoir ôté mes fers n'est qu'une vaine adresse   1155
Pour me les faire craindre et tenter ma faiblesse ;
Et moi, pour tout effet de ce soulagement,
J'attends le seul bonheur de ton embrassement.
Adieu, ma chère sœur, illustre et digne femme ;

1138. **De la sœur**, etc.: i.e. become the wife of an apostate after having been the sister of a martyr. See notes on ll. 129 and 845.

1147. **altères-tu** : "do you impair ?"

1155. **adresse** : "device, trick."

1157. **soulagement** : "relief" (from his fetters).

Je vais par un chemin d'épines et de flamme, 1160
Mais qu'auparavant moi Dieu lui-même a battu,
Te retenir un lieu digne de ta vertu.

Adieu : quand mes bourreaux exerceront leur rage,
Implore-moi du ciel la grâce et le courage
De vaincre la nature en cet heureux malheur, 1165
Avec une constance égale à ma douleur.

NATALIE, *l'embrassant*

Pardonne à mon ardeur, cher et généreux frère,
L'injuste impression d'un soupçon téméraire,
Qu'en l'apparent état de cette liberté,
Sans gardes et sans fers, tu m'avais suscité : 1170
Va, ne relâche rien de cette sainte audace
Qui te fait des tyrans mépriser la menace.
Quoiqu'un grand t'entreprenne, un plus grand est pour toi.
Un Dieu te soutiendra, si tu soutiens sa foi.
Cours, généreux athlète, en l'illustre carrière 1175
Où de la nuit du monde on passe à la lumière ;
Cours, puisqu'un Dieu t'appelle aux pieds de son autel,
Dépouiller sans regret l'homme infirme et mortel ;
N'épargne point ton sang en cette sainte guerre ;
Prodigues-y ton corps, rends la terre à la terre ; 1180
Et redonne à ton Dieu, qui sera ton appui,
La part qu'il te demande et que tu tiens de lui ;
Fuis sans regret le monde et ses fausses délices,
Où les plus innocents ne sont point sans supplices,
Dont le plus ferme état est toujours inconstant, 1185
Dont l'être et le non-être ont presque un même instant,

1161. **auparavant**: = *avant*. The use of *auparavant* as a preposition is obsolete ; see Haase, 130, and note in *Lexique de Corneille*, I, pp. 91–92.

1173. **entreprenne** : see note on l. 789.

1186. **Dont l'être et le non-être**, etc.: translate : "in which (*le monde*) existence and nonentity are almost equal in duration."

Et pour qui toutefois la nature aveuglée
Inspire à ses enfants une ardeur déréglée,
Qui les fait si souvent, au péril du trépas,
Suivre la vanité de ses trompeurs appas.   1190
Ce qu'un siècle y produit, un moment le consomme.
Porte les yeux plus haut, Adrien ; parais homme :
Combats, souffre et t'acquiers, en mourant en chrétien,
Par un moment de mal, l'éternité d'un bien.

ADRIEN

Adieu, je cours, je vole au bonheur qui m'arrive ;   1195
L'effet en est trop lent, l'heure en est trop tardive !
L'ennui seul que j'emporte, ô généreuse sœur,
Et qui de mon attente altère la douceur,
Est que la loi, contraire au Dieu que je professe,
Te prive par ma mort du bien que je te laisse,   1200
Et, l'acquérant au fisc, ôte à ton noble sang
Le soutien de sa gloire et l'appui de son rang.

NATALIE

Quoi ! le vol que tu prends vers les célestes plaines
Souffre encor tes regards sur les choses humaines ?
Si dépouillé du monde et si près d'en partir,   1205
Tu peux parler en homme et non pas en martyr ?
Qu'un si faible intérêt ne te soit point sensible ;
Tiens au Ciel, tiens à Dieu d'une force invincible ;
Conserve-moi ta gloire, et je me puis vanter
D'un trésor précieux que rien ne peut m'ôter.   1210
Une femme possède une richesse extrême,
Qui possède un époux possesseur de Dieu même.

1196. **L'effet** : "the fulfillment."
1200. **du bien** : "wealth, property."
1202. **Le soutien de sa gloire**, etc. : translate : "the means of supporting its splendor and rank."

Toi, qui de ta doctrine assistes les chrétiens,
Approche, cher Anthisme, et joins tes vœux aux miens.

Scène V

Anthisme, Adrien, Natalie

anthisme

Un bruit, qui par la ville a frappé mon oreille,   1215
De ta conversion m'apprenant la merveille
Et le noble mépris que tu fais de tes jours,
M'amène à ton combat, plutôt qu'à ton secours.
Je sais combien César t'est un faible adversaire ;
Je sais ce qu'un chrétien sait et souffrir et faire,   1220
Et je sais que jamais, pour la peur du trépas,
Un cœur touché de Christ n'a rebroussé ses pas.
Va donc, heureux ami, va présenter ta tête
Moins au coup qui t'attend qu'au laurier qu'on t'apprête ;
Va de tes saints propos éclore les effets ;   .   1225
De tous les chœurs des cieux va remplir les souhaits.
Et vous, hôtes du ciel, saintes légions d'anges,
Qui du nom trois fois saint célébrez les louanges,
Sans interruption de vos sacrés concerts,
A son aveuglement tenez les cieux ouverts.   1230

adrien

Mes vœux arriveront à leur comble suprême,
Si, lavant mes péchés de l'eau du saint baptême,
Tu m'enrôles au rang de tant d'heureux soldats

1218. **M'amène à ton combat**, etc. : i.e. brings me to encourage you to combat, rather than to succor you.

1225. **Va de tes saints propos éclore les effets** : translate : "go realize the results of your holy resolutions." *Éclore* is active ; see Benoist, p. 384.

Qui sous même étendard ont rendu des combats.
Confirme, cher Anthisme, avec cette eau sacrée   1235
Par qui presque en tous lieux la croix est arborée,
En ce fragile sein le projet glorieux
De combattre la terre et conquérir les cieux.

ANTHISME

Sans besoin, Adrien, de cette eau salutaire,
Ton sang t'imprimera ce sacré caractère :   1240
Conserve seulement une invincible foi,
Et, combattant pour Dieu, Dieu combattra pour toi.

ADRIEN, *regardant le ciel, et rêvant un peu longtemps, dit enfin*

Ha ! Lentule ! en l'ardeur dont mon âme est pressée,
Il faut lever le masque et t'ouvrir ma pensée :
Le Dieu que j'ai haï m'inspire son amour ;   1245
Adrien a parlé, Genest parle à son tour.
Ce n'est plus Adrien, c'est Genest qui respire
La grâce du baptême et l'honneur du martyre ;
Mais Christ n'a point commis à vos profanes mains

1234. **sous même étendard** : see note on l. 291.

1236. **est arborée** : "is erected." The figure seems to us rather mixed ; the meaning, however, is clear : baptism everywhere plants the cross, being the outward token of admission to the Christian church.

1239–1240. **Sans besoin . . . de cette êau salutaire**, etc. : the frequent difficulty in early times of administering the rite of baptism led the church to accept as a substitute for the material ceremony what was known as *baptismus desiderii* and *baptismus sanguinis* (based on Matt. x. 39, "He that findeth his life shall lose it : and he that loseth his life for my sake shall find it," and similar passages in Mark and John). These were recognized by the Council of Trent, Sessio VI, cap. iv, "sine lavacro regenerationis, aut ejus voto, etc." See Hinschius, *Das Kirchenrecht*, Berlin, 1888, IV, p. 54. See also notes to the story of "Der ungetaufte Priester" in Gering's *Islendzk Aeventyri*, Halle, 1884, p. 63.

1247. **respire** : "longs for." See *Lexiques de Corneille* and *de Racine*.

1249. **à vos profanes mains** : it must not be forgotten that it is the converted Genest who is speaking and that the rôle of Anthisme was acted by a pagan.

Ce sceau mystérieux dont il marque ses saints. 1250
 (*Regardant au ciel, dont l'on jette quelques flammes*) *
Un ministre céleste, avec une eau sacrée,
Pour laver mes forfaits fend la voûte azurée ;
Sa clarté m'environne, et l'air de toutes parts
Résonne de concerts, et brille à mes regards.
Descends, céleste acteur ; tu m'attends, tu m'appelles. 1255
Attends, mon zèle ardent me fournira des ailes ;
Du Dieu qui t'a commis dépars-moi les bontés.
(*Il monte deux ou trois marches et passe derrière la tapisserie*)

MARCELLE, *qui représentait Natalie*

Ma réplique a manqué ; ces vers sont ajoutés.

LENTULE, *qui faisait Anthisme*

Il les fait sur-le-champ, et sans suivre l'histoire,
Croit couvrir en rentrant son défaut de mémoire. 1260

DIOCLÉTIEN

Voyez avec quel art Genest sait aujourd'hui
Passer de la figure aux sentiments d'autrui.

VALÉRIE

Pour tromper l'auditeur, abuser l'acteur même,
De son métier, sans doute, est l'adresse suprême.

---

* Viollet-le-Duc omits this stage direction and Hémon substitutes *d'où* for antiquated *dont*. See Haase, 37, A, and *Lexiques de Corneille*, I, p. 321, *de Racine*, p. 160, and *de Molière*, I, p. lvi. The *l* before *on* is the euphonic *l*.

1251–1257. **Un ministre céleste**, etc.: the celestial minister is seen by Genest alone, who receives the rite, but not in the presence of the audience. In the Spanish original heaven opens and reveals the celestial inhabitants. For the use of the supernatural in the drama of the seventeenth century see Delaporte, and Introduction to this play, p. 77.

1257. **qui t'a commis**: "who has appointed you," i.e. entrusted you with this mission. *Commetre* is used absolutely. See *Venceslas*, l. 669.

Scène VI

FLAVIE, GARDES, MARCELLE, LENTULE, DIOCLÉTIEN, ETC.

FLAVIE

Ce moment dure trop, trouvons-le promptement ; 1265
César nous voudra mal de ce retardement ;
Je sais sa violence et redoute sa haine.

UN SOLDAT

Ceux qu'on mande à la mort ne marchent pas sans peine.

MARCELLE

Cet homme si célèbre en sa profession,
Genest, que vous cherchez, a troublé l'action, 1270
Et, confus qu'il s'est vu, nous a quitté la place.

FLAVIE, *qui est Sergeste*

Le plus heureux parfois tombe en cette disgrâce ;
L'ardeur de réussir le doit faire excuser.

CAMILLE, *riant à Valérie*

Comme son art, madame, a su les abuser !

Scène VII

GENEST, SERGESTE, LENTULE, MARCELLE, GARDES, DIOCLÉTIEN,
VALÉRIE, ETC.

GENEST, *regardant le ciel, le chapeau à la main*

Suprême Majesté, qui jettes dans les âmes, 1275
Avec deux gouttes d'eau, de si sensibles flammes,

1271. **confus qu'il s'est vu** : "confused as he has been seen (to be)."
In such expressions *que* is equivalent to *comme*; see *Lexique de Corneille*, II, pp. 242–243. — **nous** : ethical dative.

1276. **deux gouttes** : "a few drops," determinate for indeterminate
number. — **sensibles** : "ardent." See note on l. 234.

Achève tes bontés, représente avec moi
Les saints progrès des cœurs convertis à ta foi !
Faisons voir dans l'amour dont le feu nous consomme,
Toi le pouvoir d'un Dieu, moi le devoir d'un homme ;   1280
Toi l'accueil d'un vainqueur sensible au repentir,
Et moi, Seigneur, la force et l'ardeur d'un martyr.

MAXIMIN

Il feint comme animé des grâces du baptême.

VALÉRIE

Sa feinte passerait pour la vérité même.

PLANCIEN

Certes, ou ce spectacle est une vérité,   1285
Ou jamais rien de faux ne fut mieux imité.

GENEST

Et vous, chers compagnons de la basse fortune
Qui m'a rendu la vie avecque vous commune,
Marcelle, et vous, Sergeste, avec qui tant de fois
J'ai du Dieu des chrétiens scandalisé les lois,   1290

1277. avec moi : i.e. in my person.

1281. l'accueil d'un vainqueur sensible au repentir : i.e. the welcome extended by a conqueror, God, touched by the repentance of a sinner.

1287. la basse fortune, etc. : the actor's profession, which was held in slight esteem in ancient Rome. Saint Augustine cites in his *De Civitate Dei*, II, 13, a passage from Cicero's *De Republica* (IV, 10), in which Scipio declares: "Romani . . . cum artem ludricam scaenamque totam in probro ducerent, genus id hominum [actors] non modo honore civium reliquorum carere, sed etiam tribu moveri notatione censoria voluerunt." See notes by F. Creuzer in Moser's edition of Cicero's *De Republica*, Frankfurt, 1826, pp. 434 et seq.; Alt, *Theater und Kirche*, Berlin, 1846, pp. 277–297, chap. xxi, "Das Schauspielerwesen bei den Römern"; Merrill, *Selected Letters of Pliny*, p. 355, notes; and Martha, *Les moralistes sous l'empire romain*, Paris, 1886, p. 287. See also G. Maugras, *Les Comédiens hors la loi*, Paris, 1887.

Si je puis vous prescrire un avis salutaire,
Cruels, adorez-en jusqu'au moindre mystère,
Et cessez d'attacher avec de nouveaux clous
Un Dieu qui sur la croix daigne mourir pour vous ;
Mon cœur, illuminé d'une grâce céleste . . .   1295

MARCELLE

Il ne dit pas un mot du couplet qui lui reste.

SERGESTE

Comment, se préparant avecque tant de soin . . .

LENTULE, *regardant derrière la tapisserie*

Holà, qui tient la pièce ?

GENEST

Il n'en est plus besoin.
Dedans cette action, où le Ciel s'intéresse,
Un ange tient la pièce, un ange me redresse :   1300
Un ange, par son ordre, a comblé mes souhaits,
Et de l'eau du baptême effacé mes forfaits.
Ce monde périssable et sa gloire frivole
Est une comédie où j'ignorais mon rôle.
J'ignorais de quel feu mon cœur devait brûler ;   1305
Le démon me dictait quand Dieu voulait parler ;
Mais, depuis que le soin d'un esprit angélique
Me conduit, me redresse et m'apprend ma réplique,
J'ai corrigé mon rôle, et le démon confus,
M'en voyant mieux instruit, ne me suggère plus.   1310

1300. 1648 has *me r'adresse*, and the same form in ll. 1308 and 1646. I have retained the modern form with Viollet-le-Duc and Hémon.

1298. **qui tient la pièce :** "who has the play ? " This is said in order to prompt Genest, who has apparently forgotten his part.

1300. **un ange me redresse :** "an angel prompts me," lit. "corrects me."

J'ai pleuré mes péchés, le Ciel a vu mes larmes ;
Dedans cette action il a trouvé des charmes,
M'a départi sa grâce, est mon approbateur,
Me propose des prix, et m'a fait son acteur.

LENTULE

Quoiqu'il manque au sujet, jamais il ne hésite.   1315

GENEST

Dieu m'apprend sur-le-champ ce que je vous récite,
Et vous m'entendez mal, si dans cette action
Mon rôle passe encor pour une fiction.

DIOCLÉTIEN

Votre désordre enfin force ma patience :
Songez-vous que ce jeu se passe en ma présence ?   1320
Et puis-je rien comprendre au trouble où je vous voi?

GENEST

Excusez-les, Seigneur, la faute en est à moi ;
Mais mon salut dépend de cet illustre crime :
Ce n'est plus Adrien, c'est Genest qui s'exprime ;
Ce jeu n'est plus un jeu, mais une vérité   1325
Où par mon action je suis représenté,
Où moi-même, l'objet et l'acteur de moi-même,

1320. ce jeu : "this play, performance."

1321. voi: for *vois*. For the *s* now found in the first persons of the present and preterite (and also in the second person of the imperative), except in the first conjugation and *ai* from *avoir*, see Darmesteter's *Historical French Grammar*, London, 1899, p. 324 : "At the end of the seventeenth century the use of the *s* became general ; the earlier forms are only to be found in the works of a few poets in which they were employed occasionally for the sake of the rhyme." See l. 1589, and *Lexiques de Corneille*, I, p. lxiii, and *de Racine*, p. cvii. The use of the form without *s* is still permitted in poetry ; see Quicherat, *Traité de versification française*, Paris, 1850, pp. 84, 477.

Purgé de mes forfaits par l'eau du saint baptême,
Qu'une céleste main m'a daigné conférer,
Je professe une loi que je dois déclarer.   1330
Écoutez donc, Césars, et vous, troupes romaines,
La gloire et la terreur des puissances humaines,
Mais faibles ennemis d'un pouvoir souverain
Qui foule aux pieds l'orgueil et le sceptre romain :
Aveuglé de l'erreur dont l'enfer vous infecte,   1335
Comme vous des chrétiens j'ai détesté la secte,
Et si peu que mon art pouvait exécuter,
Tout mon heur consistait à les persécuter :
Pour les fuir et chez vous suivre l'idolâtrie,
J'ai laissé mes parents, j'ai quitté ma patrie,   1340
Et fait choix à dessein d'un art peu glorieux
Pour mieux les diffamer et les rendre odieux :
Mais, par une bonté qui n'a point de pareille,
Et par une incroyable et soudaine merveille
Dont le pouvoir d'un Dieu peut seul être l'auteur,   1345
Je deviens leur rival de leur persécuteur,
Et soumets à la loi que j'ai tant réprouvée
Une âme heureusement de tant d'écueils sauvée :
Au milieu de l'orage où m'exposait le sort,
Un ange par la main m'a conduit dans le port,   1350
M'a fait sur un papier voir mes fautes passées
Par l'eau qu'il me versait à l'instant effacées ;

1330. une loi : "a religion." Littré : "Il se dit quelquefois de toute religion fondée sur un livre."

1338. heur : see note on l. 101.

1341. un art peu glorieux : see note on l. 1287.

1346. de leur persécuteur : see note on l. 129.

1350-1352. Un ange par la main, etc. : this is taken from the legend. See Ruinart, p. 312 : "Vidi super me manum caelitus venientem, et angelos radiantes super me stetisse, qui omnia peccata quae ab infantia feci recitaverunt de libro, quae mox in ipsa acqua laverunt, in qua in conspectu vestro perfusus sum, et mihi candidiorem nive postmodum ostenderunt."

Et cette salutaire et céleste liqueur,
Loin de me refroidir, m'a consumé le cœur.
Je renonce à la haine et déteste l'envie   1355
Qui m'a fait des chrétiens persécuter la vie;
Leur créance est ma foi, leur espoir est le mien;
C'est leur Dieu que j'adore; enfin je suis chrétien.
Quelque effort qui s'oppose en l'ardeur qui m'enflamme,
Les intérêts du corps cèdent à ceux de l'âme.   1360
Déployez vos rigueurs, brûlez, coupez, tranchez:
Mes maux seront encor moindres que mes péchés.
Je sais de quel repos cette peine est suivie,
Et ne crains point la mort qui conduit à la vie.
J'ai souhaité longtemps d'agréer à vos yeux;   1365
Aujourd'hui je veux plaire à l'empereur des cieux;
Je vous ai diverti, j'ai chanté vos louanges;
Il est temps maintenant de réjouir les anges,
Il est temps de prétendre à des prix immortels,
Il est temps de passer du théâtre aux autels.   1370
Si je l'ai mérité, qu'on me mène au martyre:
Mon rôle est achevé, je n'ai plus rien à dire.

DIOCLÉTIEN

Ta feinte passe enfin pour importunité.

GENEST

Elle vous doit passer pour une vérité.

VALÉRIE

Parle-t-il de bon sens?

MAXIMIN

Croirai-je mes oreilles?   1375

1368-1370. See note on ll. 741-744.

1373. **Ta feinte**, etc.: i.e. your assumption of the rôle of Adrien has
been carried too far. The emperor supposes he is still acting.

GENEST

Le bras qui m'a touché fait bien d'autres merveilles.

DIOCLÉTIEN

Quoi ! tu renonces, traître, au culte de nos dieux ?

GENEST

Et les tiens aussi faux qu'ils me sont odieux,
Sept d'entre eux ne sont plus que des lumières sombres
Dont la faible clarté perce à peine les ombres,   1380
Quoiqu'ils trompent encor votre crédulité ;
Et des autres le nom à peine en est resté.

DIOCLÉTIEN, *se levant*

O blasphème exécrable ! ô sacrilège impie,
Et dont nous répondrons, si son sang ne l'expie !
Préfet, prenez ce soin, et de cet insolent   1385
          (*A Plancien*)
Fermez les actions par un acte sanglant
Qui des dieux irrités satisfasse la haine :
          (*Tous se lèvent*)
Qui vécut au théâtre expire dans la scène ;
Et si quelqu'autre, atteint du même aveuglement,
A part en son forfait, qu'il l'ait en son tourment.   1390

MARCELLE, *à genoux*

Si la pitié, Seigneur . . .

DIOCLÉTIEN

                    La piété plus forte
Réprimera l'audace où son erreur l'emporte.

1378. **tiens :** for omission of subject see note on l. 23.
1379. **Sept d'entre eux :** the sun, moon, Mercury, Venus, Mars, Jupiter, and Saturn.

PLANCIEN

Repassant cette erreur d'un esprit plus remis . . .

DIOCLÉTIEN

Acquittez-vous du soin que je vous ai commis.

CAMILLE, *à Genest*

Simple, ainsi de César tu méprises la grâce !   1395

GENEST

J'acquiers celle de Dieu.
                    (*Dioclétien sort avec toute la cour*)

Scène VIII

OCTAVE, LE DÉCORATEUR, MARCELLE, PLANCIEN

OCTAVE

Quel mystère se passe ?

MARCELLE

L'empereur abandonne aux rigueurs de la loi
Genest, qui des chrétiens a professé la foi.

OCTAVE

Nos prières peut-être . . .

MARCELLE

Elles ont été vaines.

1395. **Simple** : "simpleton." Littré defines *simple* : " Qui se laisse facilement tromper, niais"; and cites Corneille, *Suite du Menteur*, II. 7 :

> Simple, n'as-tu point vu que c'était une feinte,
> Un effet de l'amour, dont mon âme est atteinte ?

See Benoist, p. 373, who says that *simple* can now be employed only as adjective.

PLANCIEN

Gardes !

UN GARDE

Seigneur ?

PLANCIEN

Menez Genest, chargé de chaines,   1400
Dans le fond d'un cachot attendre son arrêt.

GENEST

(*On le descend du théâtre*)

Je t'en rends grâce, ô Ciel ! allons, me voilà prêt :
Les anges, quelque jour, des fers que tu m'ordonnes
Dans ce palais d'azur me feront des couronnes.

Scène IX

PLANCIEN, MARCELLE, OCTAVE, SERGESTE, LENTULE, ALBIN,
GARDES, LE DÉCORATEUR, ET AUTRES ASSISTANTS

PLANCIEN, *assis*

Son audace est coupable, autant que son erreur,   1405
D'en oser faire gloire aux yeux de l'empereur.
Et vous, qui sous même art courez même fortune,
Sa foi, comme son art, vous est-elle commune ?
Et comme un mal souvent devient contagieux . . .

MARCELLE

Le Ciel m'en garde, hélas !

OCTAVE

M'en préservent les dieux !   1410

SERGESTE

Que plutôt mille morts . . .

1407. **courez même fortune** : see notes on ll. 291, 632.

LENTULE

Que plutôt mille flammes . . .

PLANCIEN, *à Marcelle*

Que représentiez-vous ?

MARCELLE

Vous l'avez vu, les femmes,
Si, selon le sujet, quelque déguisement
Ne m'obligeait parfois au travestissement.

PLANCIEN, *à Octave*

Et vous ?

OCTAVE

Parfois les rois, et parfois les esclaves.   1415

PLANCIEN, *à Sergeste*

Vous ?

SERGESTE

Les extravagants, les furieux, les braves.

PLANCIEN, *à Lentule*

Ce vieillard ?

LENTULE

Les docteurs sans lettres ni sans lois,
Parfois les confidents, et les traîtres parfois.

PLANCIEN, *à Albin*

Et toi ?

ALBIN *

Les assistants.

* After *Albin* 1648 adds incorrectly *garde*.

1412. **Que représentiez-vous** : " What rôle did you play ? "
1414. **travestissement** : i.e. to take men's parts.

PLANCIEN, *se levant*

Leur franchise ingénue
Et leur naïveté se produit assez nue.   1420
Je plains votre malheur ; mais l'intérêt des dieux
A tout respect humain nous doit fermer les yeux.
A des crimes parfois la grâce est légitime ;
Mais à ceux de ce genre elle serait un crime,
Et, si Genest persiste en son aveuglement,   1425
C'est lui qui veut sa mort et rend son jugement.
Voyez-le toutefois, et, si ce bon office
Le peut rendre lui-même à lui-même propice,
Croyez qu'avec plaisir je verrai refleurir
Les membres ralliés d'un corps prêt à périr.   1430

1420. se produit assez nue : "reveals itself very plainly."
1429–1430. avec plaisir je verrai refleurir, etc. : " I shall see with pleasure flourishing again the reunited members of a body about to perish."

ACTE CINQUIÈME

SCÈNE I

GENEST, *seul dans la prison, avec des fers*

Par quelle divine aventure,
Sensible et sainte volupté,

1431–1470. This scene consists of what are technically known as *stances*, in this case being of ten lines of eight syllables, with the following rhyme : *ababcddccd* (masculine *b*, *d* ; feminine *a*, *c*). Voltaire in his *Commentaires sur Corneille*, ed. Moland, xxxi, p. 199, says (*Remarques sur Médée, acte* iv, *scène* v) : "Rotrou avait mis les stances à la mode. Corneille, qui les employa les condamne lui-même dans ses réflexions sur la tragédie. Elles ont quelque rapport à ces odes que chantaient les chœurs entre les scènes sur le théâtre grec. Les Romains les imitèrent : il me semble que c'était l'enfance de l'art. Il était bien plus aisé d'insérer ces inutiles déclamations entre neuf ou dix scènes qui composaient une tragédie que de trouver dans son sujet même de quoi animer toujours le théâtre, et de soutenir une longue intrigue toujours intéressante. Lorsque notre théâtre commença à sortir de la barbarie, et de l'asservissement aux usages anciens pire encore que la barbarie, on substitua à ces odes des chœurs qu'on voit dans Garnier, dans Jodelle et dans Baïf, des stances que les personnages récitaient. Cette mode a duré cent années ; le dernier exemple que nous ayons des stances est dans *la Thébaïde*. Racine se corrigea bientôt de ce défaut ; il sentit que cette mesure, différente de la mesure employée dans la pièce, n'était pas naturelle ; que les personnages ne devaient pas changer le langage convenu ; qu'ils devenaient poëtes mal à propos." Voltaire repeats the substance of these remarks when he examines the *Cid*, I. 7. Stiefel, *Über die Chronologie*, etc., p. 25, note 1, says : "Bei Corneille erscheinen die Stances zum ersten Mal in der *Veuve* (1633). Voltaire in den *Commentaires sur Corneille*, bemerkt zu *Médée*, IV. 5 : ' Rotrou avait mis les stances à la mode.' Ich weiss nicht ob Rotrou dieses Verdienst, das nach Voltaire überhaupt keines ist, gebührt, aber sicher ist, dass Pichou schon vor ihm Stances in *Les Folies de Cardenio* (achevé d'imprimer 12 sept. 1629, priv. 20 août 1625 (?) nach Beauchamp) anwendete." Stiefel, *Über die Chronologie*, etc., p. 25, says that

Essai de la gloire future,
Incroyable félicité ;
Par quelles bontés souveraines,   1435
Pour confirmer nos saints propos
Et nous conserver le repos
Sous le lourd fardeau de nos chaînes,
Descends-tu des célestes plaines
Dedans l'horreur de nos cachots?   1440

O fausse volupté du monde,
Vaine promesse d'un trompeur !
Ta bonace la plus profonde

Rotrou used *stances* from 1632 on in almost all his plays. The use of *stances* begins in fact in *Céliane* (1632–1633) and continues until *Saint Genest* (1645). In the earlier plays they are employed two or three times in each play, but usually they are introduced only once. Corneille defends the use of stances in his *Examen* of *Andromède* (1650), and employs them in all his earlier plays and in *Polyeucte* (1640), *Suite du Menteur* (1643), *Héraclius* (1647), *Andromède* (1650), *Œdipe* (1659), and the *Toison d'Or* (1660). Racine, as has been said, used them only once, in *La Thébaïde* (1664). *Stances* are found in Desmaret's *Les Visionnaires* (1640), and are very amusingly burlesqued by Scarron in his *Jodelet*, V. 1. Furetière in the *Roman Bourgeois* (ed. Tulou, Paris, 1883, p. 107) puts into the mouth of one of his ridiculous characters, Vollichon, the following praise of *stances* : "Tout ce que j'y trouve à redire [in Corneille's *Cinna*] c'est qu'il y devrait avoir cinq ou six couplets de vers, comme j'en ai vu dans le *Cid*, car c'est le plus beau des pièces." Petit de Julleville, IV, p. 223, says: "L'influence des Bergeries se marqua seulement dans quelques détails des œuvres postérieures: dans l'emploi des chœurs, . . . dans l'usage des stances, si du moins *La Chanson* de Tisimandre a inspiré à Pichou l'idée d'orner de stances *Les Folies de Cardenio*, et à Rotrou, à Corneille, à Mairet, à bien des autres l'idée d'en faire autant pour un grand nombre de leurs œuvres." See also Corneille, ed. Marty-Laveaux, III, p. 121, note 1; also Corneille, *Examen d'Horace*, and D'Aubignac, *Pratique du Théâtre*, pp. 241–244. Verse other than Alexandrine is found in many of Rotrou's plays and is generally used for letters and, of course, for songs, etc.

1433. Essai: "foretaste, anticipation."
1436. propos: "purposes, resolutions."

N'est jamais sans quelque vapeur ;
Et mon Dieu, dans la peine même   1445
Qu'il veut que l'on souffre pour lui,
Quand il daigne être notre appui
Et qu'il reconnaît que l'on l'aime,
Influe une douceur suprême
Sans mélange d'aucun ennui.   1450

Pour lui la mort est salutaire,
Et par cet acte de valeur
On fait un bonheur volontaire
D'un inévitable malheur.
Nos jours n'ont pas une heure sûre ;   1455
Chaque instant use leur flambeau ;
Chaque pas nous mène au tombeau,
Et l'art, imitant la nature,

1444. vapeur : = *vent*.

1449. Influe : see note on l. 87.

1458–1460. Et l'art, imitant la nature, etc.: where did Rotrou find this comparison of the cradle with the coffin? The only parallel I know is in Calderon's *El Principe Constante*, III. 7 (ll. 488–573 of Krenkel's edition). Don Fernando (" el Principe Constante ") says :

> Bien sé al fin que soy mortal,
> Y que no hay hora segura ;
> Y por eso dió una forma
> Con una materia en una
> Semejanza la razon
> Al ataud y á la cuna.

He then declares that when we accept anything we join our hands palms upward, and when we throw anything away we turn our palms downward. He continues :

> El mundo, cuando nacemos,
> En señal de que nos busca,
> En la cuna nos recibe,
> Y en ella nos asegura
> Boca arriba ; pero cuando,
> Ó con desdén ó con furia,
> Quiere arrojarnos de sí,
> Vuelve las manos que junta,
> Y aquel instrumento mismo

Bâtit d'une même figure
Notre bière et notre berceau. 　　　　　　　　1460

Mourons donc, la cause y convie :
Il doit être doux de mourir
Quand se dépouiller de la vie
Est travailler pour l'acquérir.
Puisque la céleste lumière 　　　　　　　　1465
Ne se trouve qu'en la quittant
Et qu'on ne vainc qu'en combattant,
D'une vigueur mâle et guerrière
Courons au bout de la carrière
Où la couronne nous attend. 　　　　　　　　1470

Scène II

MARCELLE, LE GEÔLIER, GENEST

LE GEÔLIER, *à Marcelle*

Entrez.

(*Il s'en va*)

MARCELLE

Eh bien, Genest, cette ardeur insensée
Te dure-t-elle encore, ou t'est-elle passée ?
Si tu ne fais pour toi, si le jour ne t'est cher,
Si ton propre intérêt ne te saurait toucher,

Forma esta materia muda ;
Pues fué cuna boca arriba
Lo que boca abajo es tumba.

I.e. the cradle turned upside down represents the mound over a grave. Where else is this comparison used ? Is it original with Calderon, and did Rotrou take it from him ?

1465–1470. Puisque la céleste lumière, etc : for this figure see ll. 1175, 1233.

1473. Si tu ne fais pour toi : "if you do not help yourself." *Faire* is intransitive. See Benoist, p. 387.

Nous osons espérer que le nôtre, possible,   1475
En cette extrémité te sera plus sensible,
Que, t'étant si cruel, tu nous seras plus doux,
Et qu'obstiné pour toi, tu fléchiras pour nous :
Si tu nous dois chérir, c'est en cette occurrence ;
Car, séparés de toi, quelle est notre espérance?   1480
Par quel sort pouvons-nous survivre ton trépas?
Et que peut plus un corps dont le chef est à bas?
Ce n'est que de tes jours que dépend notre vie ;
Nous mourrons tous du coup qui te l'aura ravie ;
Tu seras seul coupable, et nous tous, en effet,   1485
Serons punis d'un mal que nous n'aurons point fait.

GENEST

Si d'un heureux avis vos esprits sont capables,
Partagez ce forfait, rendez-vous-en coupables,
Et vous reconnaîtrez s'il est un heur plus doux
Que la mort, qu'en effet je vous souhaite à tous.   1490
Vous mourriez pour un Dieu dont la bonté suprême,
Vous faisant en mourant détruire la mort même,
Ferait l'éternité le prix de ce moment,
Que j'appelle une grâce, et vous un châtiment.

MARCELLE

O ridicule erreur de vanter la puissance   1495
D'un Dieu qui donne aux siens la mort pour récompense !

1475. **possible** : = *peut-être*.   See note in *Lexique de Corneille*, II,
pp. 202–203.

1481. **survivre** : active.   See Benoist, p. 386.

1482. **Et que peut plus un corps**, etc.: see l. 1430.

1484. **qui te l'aura ravie** : the use of the future perfect is much more
common in French than in English, where we often substitute the perfect (*passé indéfini*) for it.   This is the case in modern French, where
the past indefinite is frequently used instead of the future perfect, as in
the seventeenth century.   See Chassang, *French Grammar*, p. 330.   See
also l. 1486 : "We shall be punished for a wrong which we have not
committed."

D'un imposteur, d'un fourbe et d'un crucifié !
Qui l'a mis dans le ciel ? qui l'a déifié ?
Un nombre d'ignorants et de gens inutiles,
De malheureux, la lie et l'opprobre des villes,   1500
De femmes et d'enfants dont la crédulité
S'est forgée à plaisir une divinité,
De gens qui, dépourvus des biens de la fortune,
Trouvant dans leur malheur la lumière importune,
Sous le nom de chrétiens font gloire du trépas   1505
Et du mépris des biens qu'ils ne possèdent pas,
Perdent l'ambition en perdant l'espérance,
Et souffrent tout du sort avec indifférence !
De là naît le désordre épars en tant de lieux ;
De là naît le mépris et des rois et des dieux,   1510
Que César irrité réprime avec justice
Et qu'il ne peut punir d'un trop rude supplice.
Si je t'ose parler d'un esprit ingénu,
Et si le tien, Genest, ne m'est point inconnu,
D'un abus si grossier tes sens sont incapables ;   1515
Tu te ris du vulgaire et lui laisses ses fables,
Et pour quelque sujet, mais qui nous est caché,
A ce culte nouveau tu te feins attaché.
Peut-être que tu plains ta jeunesse passée,
Par une ingrate cour si mal récompensée :   1520
Si César, en effet, était plus généreux,
Tu l'as assez suivi pour être plus heureux :
Mais dans toutes les cours cette plainte est commune ;
Le mérite bien tard y trouve la fortune ;

1504. **la lumière importune** : i.e. weary of life.

1515. **D'un abus si grossier** : Benoist, p. 365 : "*Abus* est employé pour signifier *illusion*, état de quelqu'un qui est abusé."

1519–1528. **Peut-être que tu plains ta jeunesse passée**, etc. : complaints against the court are frequently found in the seventeenth-century drama. Those in Molière's *Femmes Savantes*, IV. 3, will occur to the reader's mind.

Les rois ont ce penser inique et rigoureux   1525
Que, sans nous rien devoir, nous devons tout pour eux,
Et que nos vœux, nos soins, nos loisirs, nos personnes,
Sont de légers tributs qui suivent leurs couronnes.
Notre métier surtout, quoique tant admiré,
Est l'art où le mérite est moins considéré.   1530
Mais peut-on qu'en souffrant vaincre un mal sans remède?
Qui se sait modérer, s'il veut, tout lui succède.
Pour obtenir nos fins, n'aspirons point si haut ;
A qui le désir manque aucun bien ne défaut.
Si de quelque besoin ta vie est traversée,   1535
Ne nous épargne point, ouvre-nous ta pensée ;
Parle, demande, ordonne, et tous nos biens sont tiens.
Mais quel secours, hélas ! attends-tu des chrétiens ?
Le rigoureux trépas dont César te menace,
Et notre inévitable et commune disgrâce?   1540

GENEST

Marcelle, avec regret j'espère vainement
De répandre le jour sur votre aveuglement,
Puisque vous me croyez l'âme assez ravalée,
Dans les biens infinis dont le Ciel l'a comblée,
Pour tendre à d'autres biens, et pour s'embarrasser   1545
D'un si peu raisonnable et si lâche penser.

1529–1530. **Notre métier surtout**, etc.: see note on l. 1287.

1531. **Mais peut-on qu'en souffrant**: "Can one overcome an irremediable wrong except by suffering?" *Que* here is equivalent to *si ce n'est, sinon, excepté,* as in l. 715. See Benoist, p. 395, and *Lexique de Corneille,* II, p. 246.

1535. **Si de quelque besoin,** etc.: "If your life is hampered by some want," lit. "thwarted, crossed."

1537. **nos biens sont tiens**: see note on l. 782.

1542. **De répandre le jour,** etc.: "to enlighten your blindness."

1545. **Pour tendre à d'autres biens**: "to incline toward other possessions." Cf. English, "tend towards." See *Lexiques de Racine,* p. 517, and *de Molière,* II, p. 530.

Non, Marcelle, notre art n'est pas d'une importance
A m'en être promis beaucoup de récompense ;
La faveur d'avoir eu des Césars pour témoins
M'a trop acquis de gloire et trop payé mes soins.　　　1550
Nos vœux, nos passions, nos veilles et nos peines,
Et tout le sang enfin qui coule de nos veines,
Sont pour eux des tributs de devoir et d'amour
Où le Ciel nous oblige, en nous donnant le jour ;
Comme aussi j'ai toujours, depuis que je respire,　　　1555
Fait des vœux pour leur gloire et pour l'heur de l'empire :
Mais où je vois s'agir de l'intérêt d'un Dieu,
Bien plus grand dans le ciel qu'ils ne sont en ce lieu,
De tous les empereurs l'empereur et le maître,
Qui seul me peut sauver, comme il m'a donné l'être,　　　1560
Je soumets justement leur trône à ses autels,
Et contre son honneur ne dois rien aux mortels.
Si mépriser leurs dieux est leur être rebelle,
Croyez qu'avec raison je leur suis infidèle,
Et que, loin d'excuser cette infidélité,　　　1565
C'est un crime innocent dont je fais vanité.
Vous verrez si ces dieux de métal et de pierre

1552. Viollet-le-Duc and Hémon have *dans nos veines*.

1554. 1648 omits incorrectly *nous* before *oblige*. Ronchaud, Viollet-le-Duc, and Hémon have restored it.

1548. **A m'en être promis** : *à* here introduces clause of result in infinitive form after *n'est pas d'une importance* in l. 1547. Translate (beginning in l. 1547) : "Our art is not so important that I have promised myself any great reward," or, more closely, "not important enough to have promised," etc.

1554. **Où** : = *auxquels*. See Haase, 38 ; Chassang, *French Grammar*, § 260 ; and Vaugelas, I, p. 173.

1558. **qu'ils ne sont en ce lieu** : for *qu'ils ne le sont*. The use of the predicative *le* in subordinate comparative clauses is optional at the present time ; for seventeenth-century usage see Haase, 7, R. 2, and Vaugelas, II, p. 425.

1562. **dois** : for omission of subject see note on l. 23.

Seront puissants au ciel comme on les croit en terre,
Et s'ils vous sauveront de la juste fureur
D'un Dieu dont la créance y passe pour erreur :   1570
Et lors ces malheureux, ces opprobres des villes,
Ces femmes, ces enfants et ces gens inutiles,
Les sectateurs enfin de ce crucifié,
Vous diront si sans cause ils l'ont déifié.
Ta grâce peut, Seigneur, détourner ce présage.   1575
Mais, hélas ! tous l'ayant, tous n'en ont pas l'usage ;
De tant de conviés bien peu suivent tes pas,
Et, pour être appelés, tous ne répondent pas.

MARCELLE

Cruel, puisqu'à ce point cette erreur te possède,
Que ton aveuglement est un mal sans remède,   1580
Trompant au moins César, apaise son courroux,
Et, si ce n'est pour toi, conserve-toi pour nous.
Sur la foi de ton Dieu fondant ton espérance,
A celle de nos dieux donne au moins l'apparence,
Et, sinon sous un cœur, sous un front plus soumis,   1585
Obtiens pour nous ta grâce, et vis pour tes amis.

1583. 1648 has incorrectly *Sur la foi d'un Dieu*. Ronchaud, Viollet-
le-Duc, and Hémon have corrected to *de ton*.

1570. **y** : refers to *terre* in l. 1568.

1573. **sectateurs** : generally applied to the "followers" of a heresi-
arch. Rotrou uses the word here either in its good sense, or as the
followers of Christ seemed to the enemies of Christianity.

1576. **tous l'ayant** etc.: i.e. all may enjoy the grace of God, but all do
not avail themselves of it.

1577–1578. **De tant de conviés**, etc.: the reference is of course to the
Parable of the marriage of the king's son in Matt. xxii. 2–14, and
especially verse 14 : "For many are called, but few are chosen."

1584. **l'apparence**: i.e. an apparent belief.

GENEST

Notre foi n'admet point cet acte de faiblesse ;
Je la dois publier, puisque je la professe.
Puis-je désavouer le maître que je sui ?
Aussi bien que nos cœurs, nos bouches sont à lui.   1590
Les plus cruels tourments n'ont point de violence
Qui puisse m'obliger à ce honteux silence.
Pourrais-je encore, hélas ! après la liberté
Dont cette ingrate voix l'a tant persécuté,
Et dont j'ai fait un Dieu le jouet d'un théâtre,   1595
Aux oreilles d'un prince et d'un peuple idolâtre,
D'un silence coupable, aussi bien que la voix,
Devant ses ennemis méconnaître ses lois ?

MARCELLE

César n'obtenant rien, ta mort sera cruelle.

GENEST

Mes tourments seront courts, et ma gloire éternelle.   1600

MARCELLE

Quand la flamme et le fer paraîtront à tes yeux . . .

GENEST

M'ouvrant la sépulture, ils m'ouvriront les cieux.

MARCELLE

O dur courage d'homme !

GENEST

                    O faible cœur de femme !

1589. sui : for *suis*. See note on l. 1321.
1597. aussi bien que la voix : i.e. to disregard in the sight of his enemies his voice as well as his laws; the voice was the divine call in
ll. 421–424.
1603–1604. Cf. ll. 591–599.

MARCELLE

Cruel ! sauve tes jours.

GENEST

Lâche ! sauve ton âme.

MARCELLE

Une erreur, un caprice, une légèreté,   1605
Au plus beau de tes ans, te coûter la clarté!

GENEST

J'aurai bien peu vécu, si l'âge se mesure
Au seul nombre des ans prescrit par la nature ;
Mais l'âme qu'au martyre un tyran nous ravit
Au séjour de la gloire à jamais se survit.   1610
Se plaindre de mourir, c'est se plaindre d'être homme ;
Chaque jour le détruit, chaque instant le consomme ;
Au moment qu'il arrive, il part pour le retour,
Et commence de perdre en recevant le jour.

1606. te coûter le clarté : the use of the pure infinitive (without prepositions) is common in French in exclamatory sentences.   Generally the subject is not expressed; when it is it is usually a personal pronoun.   In the text the three substantives in l. 1605 are the subjects.   See Chassang, *French Grammar*, p. 367; Mätzner, *Syntax*, I, p. 322; and *Lexique de Molière*, I, p. clxxxix.

1607. J'aurai bien peu vécu : see note on l. 1484.

1610. se survit: "lives again."

1614. Et commence de perdre : *commencer* may be followed by an infinitive with either *à* or *de*.   Littré says that the grammarians have endeavored to distinguish between the two, but the distinction is not justified by the usage of writers.   See Vaugelas, II, p. 149 (who maintains that *de* must never be used); Haase, 112, 4, R. 2.   Molière uses *de*; Racine both *de* and *à*; Mme. de Sévigné *de*; Corneille *de*.   See note in *Lexique de Corneille*, I, p. 191.   For the sentiment in this speech of Genest a great number of parallels can be found from Manilius to Young.   The former in his *Astronomica*, IV. 16, says :

Nascentes morimur, finisque ab origine pendet.

MARCELLE

Ainsi rien ne te touche, et tu nous abandonnes ? 1615

GENEST

Ainsi je quitterais un trône et des couronnes :
Toute perte est légère à qui s'acquiert un Dieu.

Scène III

LE GEÔLIER, MARCELLE, GENEST

LE GEÔLIER

Le préfet vous demande.

MARCELLE

Adieu, cruel !

GENEST

Adieu.

[*Marcelle sort*]

Scène IV

LE GEÔLIER, GENEST

LE GEÔLIER

Si bientôt à nos dieux vous ne rendez hommage,
Vous vous acquittez mal de votre personnage, 1620
Et je crains en cet acte un tragique succès.

The latter in *Night Thoughts*, V. l. 717 :

> While man is growing, life is in decrease,
> And cradles rock us nearer to the tomb ;
> Our birth is nothing but our death begun.

Corneille has a similar thought in *Tite et Bérénice*, V. 1 :

> Chaque instant de la vie est un pas vers la mort.

1620. **Vous vous acquittez mal de votre personnage** : "you are per-forming your part badly."

1621. **succès** : see note on l. 50.

GENEST

Un favorable juge assiste à mon procès ;
Sur ses soins éternels mon esprit se repose ;
Je m'assure sur lui du succès de ma cause ;
De mes chaînes par lui je serai déchargé,   1625
Et par lui-même un jour César sera jugé.

(*Il s'en va avec le geôlier*)

SCÈNE V

DIOCLÉTIEN, MAXIMIN, SUITE DE GARDES

DIOCLÉTIEN

Puisse par cet hymen votre couche féconde
Jusques aux derniers temps donner des rois au monde,
Et par leurs actions ces surgeons glorieux
Mériter comme vous un rang entre les dieux !   1630
En ce commun bonheur l'allégresse commune
Marque votre vertu plus que votre fortune,
Et fait voir qu'en l'honneur que je vous ai rendu
Je vous ai moins payé qu'il ne vous était dû.
Les dieux, premiers auteurs des fortunes des hommes,   1635
Qui dedans nos États nous font ce que nous sommes,
Et dont le plus grand roi n'est qu'un simple sujet,
Y doivent être aussi notre premier objet ;
Et, sachant qu'en effet ils nous ont mis sur terre
Pour conserver leurs droits, pour régir leur tonnerre,   1640

1640. 1648 has *leurs tonnerres* incorrectly, as rhyme requires singular.

1624. Je m'assure sur lui, etc. : "I trust to him for the success of my cause." *S'assurer* in this sense may be followed by *dans, en, sur*, and *à*. See *Lexiques de Corneille*, I, pp. 82–83 (*de, sur, à*) ; *de Racine*, pp. 44–45 (same) ; and *de Molière*, I, p. 91 (*sur, à, en*).

1629. ces surgeons glorieux : "may these glorious descendants," etc. *Surgeons* (Lat., *surgere*, "shoot," in botanical sense) is here used figuratively, and in that sense is now obsolete.

1640. pour régir leur tonnerre : i.e. to direct their judgments.

Et pour laisser enfin leur vengeance en nos mains,
Nous devons sous leurs lois contenir les humains,
Et notre autorité, qu'ils veulent qu'on révère,
A maintenir la leur n'est jamais trop sévère.
J'espérais cet effet, et que tant de trépas   1645
Du reste des chrétiens redresseraient les pas :
Mais j'ai beau leur offrir de sanglantes hosties,
Et laver leurs autels du sang de ces impies,
En vain j'en ai voulu purger ces régions,
J'en vois du sang d'un seul naître des légions.   1650
Mon soin nuit plus aux dieux qu'il ne leur est utile ;
Un ennemi défait leur en reproduit mille,
Et le caprice est tel de ces extravagants,
Que la mort les anime et les rend arrogants.
Genest, dont cette secte aussi folle que vaine   1655
A si longtemps été la risée et la haine,
Embrasse enfin leur loi contre celle des dieux,
Et l'ose insolemment professer à nos yeux ;
Outre l'impiété, ce mépris manifeste
Mêle notre intérêt à l'intérêt céleste :   1660
En ce double attentat, que sa mort doit purger,
Nous avons et les dieux et nous-même à venger.

MAXIMIN

Je crois que le préfet, commis à cet office,
S'attend aussi d'en faire un public sacrifice,
D'exécuter votre ordre, et de cet insolent   1665

1650. Viollet-le-Duc and Hémon have *Je vois*.

1641. **Et pour laisser enfin**, etc. : There is a change of subject here,
" And in order that they (the gods, l. 1635), may leave their vengeance
in our hands, etc."

1646. **redresseraient les pas** : i.e. would set their feet again in the
right path.

Donner ce soir au peuple un spectacle sanglant,
Si déjà sur le bois d'un théâtre funeste
Il n'a représenté l'action qui lui reste.

Scène VI

Valérie, Camille, Marcelle, *comédienne*, Octave, *comédien*, Sergeste, *comédien*, Lentule, *comédien*, Albin,
Dioclétien, Maximin, suite de gardes

(*Tous les comédiens se mettent à genoux*)

valérie, *à Dioclétien*

Si, quand pour moi le Ciel épuise ses bienfaits,
Quand son œil provident rit à tous nos souhaits,   1670
J'ose encor espérer que, dans cette allégresse,
Vous souffriez à mon sexe un acte de faiblesse,
Permettez-moi, Seigneur, de rendre à vos genoux
Ces gens qu'en Genest seul vous sacrifiez tous :
(*L'empereur les fait lever*)
Tous ont aversion pour la loi qu'il embrasse,   1675
Tous savent que son crime est indigne de grâce ;
Mais il est à leur vie un si puissant secours
Qu'ils la perdront du coup qui tranchera ses jours.
M'exauçant, de leur chef vous détournez vos armes ;
Je n'ai pu dénier cet office à leurs larmes,   1680

1667–1668. **Si déjà sur le bois**, etc : "if he has not already performed
the remainder of his play upon the stage of a theater fatal to him."
I do not find *bois* elsewhere used for stage; *planches* (cf. English
"boards") is often employed in this sense, as *monter sur les planches*,
"to go on the stage." Can this be an allusion to the "bois glorieux"
of l. 593?

1673. **de rendre à vos genoux**: "to bring back as suppliants to your
feet."

Où je n'ose insister, si ma témérité
Demande une injustice à Votre Majesté.

DIOCLÉTIEN

Je sais que la pitié plutôt que l'injustice
Vous a fait embrasser ce pitoyable office,
Et dans tout cœur bien né tiens la compassion   1685
Pour les ennemis même une juste action ;
Mais où l'irrévérence et l'orgueil manifeste
Joint l'intérêt d'État à l'intérêt céleste,
Le plaindre est, au mépris de notre autorité,
Exercer la pitié contre la piété ;   1690
C'est d'un bras qui l'irrite arrêter la tempête
Que son propre dessein attire sur sa tête,
Et d'un soin importun arracher de sa main
Le couteau dont lui-même il se perce le sein.

MARCELLE

Ha ! Seigneur, il est vrai ; mais de cette tempête   1695
Le coup frappe sur nous, s'il tombe sur sa tête,
Et le couteau fatal, que l'on laisse en sa main,
Nous assassine tous en lui perçant le sein.

1681. **Où je n'ose insister**: *où* refers to *office* in preceding line. See note on l. 1554.

1685. **tiens**: first person. For omission of subject see note on l. 23.

1686. **Pour les ennemis même**: in poetry *même* is sometimes used adverbially, i.e. in the singular form even with plural pronouns and substantives. Sometimes, as in the text, the meaning is ambiguous and the sense would permit equally well either *même pour les ennemis* or *pour les ennemis même*. See Haase, 53, R. 1 ; Vaugelas, I, p. 318 (Vaugelas makes agreement in number obligatory) ; Chassang, *French Grammar*, p. 240; and notes in *Lexiques de Corneille*, II, p. 81, and *de Racine*, p. 318.

1688. **Joint**: for singular verb with several coördinate subjects see note on l. 339.

1691–1692. **C'est d'un bras qui l'irrite**, etc. : i.e. it would be to quell the storm which an arm defying our authority has by its own willfulness drawn down upon his head.

OCTAVE

Si la grâce, Seigneur, n'est due à son offense,
Quelque compassion l'est à notre innocence. 1700

DIOCLÉTIEN *

Le fer qui de ses ans doit terminer le cours
Retranche vos plaisirs en retranchant ses jours :
Je connais son mérite, et plains votre infortune ;
Mais, outre que l'injure, avec les dieux commune,
Intéresse l'État à punir son erreur, 1705
J'ai pour toute sa secte une si forte horreur,
Que je tiens tous les maux qu'ont souffert ses complices,
Ou qu'ils doivent souffrir, pour de trop doux supplices.
En faveur toutefois de l'hymen fortuné
Par qui tant de bonheur à Rome est destiné, 1710
Si par son repentir, favorable à soi-même,
De sa voix sacrilège il purge le blasphème,
Et reconnaît les dieux auteurs de l'univers,
Les bras de ma pitié vous sont encore ouverts.
Mais voici le préfet : je crains que son supplice 1715
N'ait prévenu l'effet de votre bon office.

SCÈNE VII

PLANCIEN, DIOCLÉTIEN, MAXIMIN, VALÉRIE, CAMILLE, MARCELLE, OCTAVE, ETC.

PLANCIEN

Par votre ordre, Seigneur, ce glorieux acteur,
Des plus fameux héros fameux imitateur,
Du théâtre romain la splendeur et la gloire,

---

* 1648 has incorrectly *Flavie* for *Dioclétien*.

1703. **plains** : for omission of subject see note on l. 23.

Mais si mauvais acteur dedans sa propre histoire,　　　　1720
Plus entier que jamais en son impiété,
Et par tous mes efforts en vain sollicité,
A du courroux des dieux, contre sa perfidie,
Par un acte sanglant fermé la tragédie . . .

MARCELLE, *pleurant*

Que nous achèverons par la fin de nos jours.　　　　1725

OCTAVE

O fatale nouvelle !

SERGESTE

O funeste discours !

PLANCIEN

J'ai joint à la douceur, aux offres, aux prières,
A si peu que les dieux m'ont donné de lumières,
(Voyant que je tentais d'inutiles efforts)
Tout l'art dont la rigueur peut tourmenter les corps :　　　　1730
Mais ni les chevalets, ni les lames flambantes,
Ni les ongles de fer, ni les torches ardentes,
N'ont contre ce rocher été qu'un doux zéphyr
Et n'ont pu de son sein arracher un soupir.
Sa force en ce tourment a paru plus qu'humaine ;　　　　1735
Nous souffrions plus que lui par l'horreur de sa peine ;
Et, nos cœurs détestant ses sentiments chrétiens,
Nos yeux ont malgré nous fait l'office des siens ;
Voyant la force enfin, comme l'adresse, vaine,
J'ai mis la tragédie à sa dernière scène,　　　　1740

1728. **A si peu que les dieux m'ont donné de lumières** : "to the little understanding which the gods have bestowed upon me."

1731. **chevalets** : "racks," dim. of *cheval* ; compare our "horse" in carpentry. It is the frame on which the prisoner was stretched.

1738. **Nos yeux ont malgré nous fait l'office des siens** : i. e. we have shed the tears which he did not.

Et fait, avec sa tête, ensemble séparer
Le cher nom de son Dieu qu'il voulait proférer.

DIOCLÉTIEN, *s'en allant*

Ainsi reçoive un prompt et sévère supplice
Quiconque ose des dieux irriter la justice !

[*Il sort*]

VALÉRIE, *à Marcelle*

Vous voyez de quel soin je vous prêtais les mains ;   1745
Mais sa grâce n'est plus au pouvoir des humains.

(*Ils s'en vont tous pleurant*)

MAXIMIN, *emmenant Valérie*

Ne plaignez point, Madame, un malheur volontaire,
Puisqu'il l'a pu franchir et s'être salutaire,
Et qu'il a bien voulu, par son impiété,
D'une feinte en mourant faire une vérité.   1750

1741–1742. **Et fait, avec sa tête,** etc.: the idea that the executioner's
sword cut in two the name of God which Genest was pronouncing, as
well as cut off the martyr's head, seems to us most affected and like a
reminiscence of Ovid.

1750. **D'une feinte en mourant faire une vérité** : Sainte-Beuve, *op. cit.*,
p. 169, says of the last two scenes : "On entrevoit ici un beau dénoûment qui est manqué : on conçoit possible, vraisemblable, selon les
lois de la Grâce et l'intérêt de la tragédie, la conversion de toute la
troupe ; on se la figure aisément assistant au supplice de Genest, et, à
un certain moment, se précipitant tout entière, se baptisant soudainement de son sang, et s'écriant qu'elle veut mourir avec lui. Mais rien
de tel : la piteuse troupe muette est encore à genoux quand le préfet
vient annoncer qu'il est trop tard pour supplier César, et que ce grand
acteur

> Des plus fameux héros fameux imitateur,
> Du théâtre romain la splendeur et la gloire,
> Mais si mauvais acteur dedans sa propre histoire,
> . . . .
> A du courroux des Dieux, contre sa perfidie,
> Par un acte sanglant fermé la tragédie. . . .

Et le tout finit par une pointe de ce grossier, féroce et en ce moment
subtil Maximin, qui remarque que Genest a voulu, *par son impiété*,

D'une feinte en mourant faire une vérité.

C'est pousser trop loin, pour le coup, le mélange du comique avec le tragique : ce dernier acte, du moins, devait finir tout glorieusement et pathétiquement. Mais si Corneille allait quelquefois au hasard, Rotrou s'y lançait encore plus, Rotrou espèce de Ducis plus franc, plus primitif, marchant et trébuchant à côté de Corneille : Ducis pourtant, en sa place, n'aurait point manqué cette fin-là."

The *pointe* ("witticism," "pun") to which Sainte-Beuve alludes is practically a translation of the title of the Spanish original, *Lo Fingido Verdadero*; see what I have said, p. 79, note 2.

I cannot refrain from quoting a final word from Sainte-Beuve's remarks in the work already cited, p. 142 : "La véritable et directe continuation de *Polyeucte* au théâtre se fit par le *Saint Genest* de Rotrou. Le succès de *Polyeucte*, on le voit dans les annales du théâtre français d'alors, excita une sorte de recrudescence de sujets religieux ; les La Serre, les Des Fontaines se mirent en frais de martyres ; les *Sainte Catherine*, les *Saint Alexis* moururent coup sur coup : on ne se souvient que de *Saint Genest*. Rotrou, fortement ému de la pièce sublime de Corneille, et qui ne rougissait pas de paraître suivre en disciple celui qui, par un naïf renversement de rôle, le nommait *son père*, produisit, peu d'années après (1646), cette autre tragédie de la même famille exactement et qui, je l'ai déjà indiqué, ressuscite et clôt sur notre théâtre l'ancien genre des martyres. *Saint Genest* fait le second de *Polyeucte* ; et tous deux sont des rejetons imprévus, au seuil du théâtre classique, d'une culture longtemps florissante au Moyen-Age, mais depuis lors tout à fait tombée. Il arrive souvent ainsi, en littérature, que des séries entières d'œuvres antérieures, appartenant à une période finissante de la civilisation avec laquelle elles s'en vont disparaître elles-mêmes, se retrouvent soudainement dans une dernière œuvre modifiée et supérieure, qui les abrège, les résume et en dispense."

FIN

VENCESLAS

TRAGI–COMÉDIE DE MR. DE ROTROU

1647

ACTEURS

VENCESLAS, roi de Pologne
LADISLAS, son fils, prince
ALEXANDRE, infant
FÉDERIC,[1] duc de Curlande et favori
OCTAVE, gouverneur de Varsovie
GARDES
CASSANDRE, duchesse de Cunisberg
THÉODORE, infante
LÉONOR, suivante

Throughout notes to *Venceslas* the initial M. refers to Marmontel's *Remarques sur le Venceslas de Rotrou*, first published in 1773. I have used the version contained in *Œuvres complètes de Marmontel*, Paris, 1820, VII, pp. 441–458. See above, p. 50.

---

[1] *Féderic* is an adaptation of the Spanish *Federico*. The modern form is *Frédéric*.

ACTE PREMIER

Scène I

Venceslas, Ladislas, Alexandre, gardes

VENCESLAS

Prenez un siège, prince ; et vous, infant, sortez.

ALEXANDRE

J'aurai le tort, Seigneur, si vous ne m'écoutez.

VENCESLAS

Sortez, vous dis-je ; et vous, gardes, qu'on se retire.

> [*Alexandre et les gardes sortent*]

LADISLAS

Que me désirez-vous ?

VENCESLAS

              J'ai beaucoup à vous dire.

   [*A part*]

Ciel, prépare son sein et le touche aujourd'hui.   5

---

2. J'aurai le tort, etc.: i.e. unless you hear my side you will think I am in the wrong. See Benoist, p. 411. M.: "Avoir le tort n'est pas français. On dit avoir tort."

4. Que me désirez-vous : M.: "On dit dans ce sens-là, que désirez-vous de moi ?"

5. le touche : when two imperatives are connected by *et, ou,* or *mais* (sometimes *puis*) the pronoun object of the second imperative stands before it in the seventeenth century. See Haase, 154, and Benoist, p. 399.

LADISLAS, *bas*

Que la vieillesse souffre et fait souffrir autrui !
Oyons les beaux avis qu'un flatteur lui conseille.

VENCESLAS

Prêtez-moi, Ladislas, le cœur avec l'oreille.
J'attends toujours du temps qu'il mûrisse le fruit
Que pour me succéder ma couche m'a produit ;   10
Et je croyais, mon fils, votre mère immortelle
Par le reste qu'en vous elle me laissa d'elle.
Mais, hélas ! ce portrait qu'elle s'était tracé
Perd beaucoup de son lustre et s'est bien effacé
Et, vous considérant, moins je la vois paraître,   15
Plus l'ennui de sa mort commence à me renaître.
Toutes vos actions démentent votre rang :
Je n'y vois rien d'auguste et digne de mon sang ;
J'y cherche Ladislas, et ne le puis connaître.
Vous n'avez rien de roi que le désir de l'être ;   20
Et ce désir, dit-on, peu discret et trop prompt,
En souffre avec ennui le bandeau sur mon front.
Vous plaignez le travail où ce fardeau m'engage,
Et, n'osant m'attaquer, vous attaquez mon âge ;
Je suis vieil, mais un fruit de ma vieille saison   25
Est d'en posséder mieux la parfaite raison :
Régner est un secret dont la haute science
Ne s'acquiert que par l'âge et par l'expérience.

7. **Oyons** : see *Saint Genest*, note on l. 372.

15. **considérant** : construed absolutely ; see Benoist, p. 402.

18. **d'auguste et digne** : M. : "La règle veut que l'article [preposition] *de* soit répété."

19. **et ne le puis connaître** : for omission of subject of *puis* see *Saint Genest*, note on l. 23.

22. **bandeau** : = *diadème*.

25. **Je suis vieil** : *vieil* for *vieux* is not infrequent in the seventeenth century. M. : "On dit je suis vieux, vieil ne s'est conservé que devant les noms qui commencent par une voyelle."

Un roi vous semble heureux, et sa condition
Est douce au sentiment de votre ambition ; 30
Il dispose à son gré des fortunes humaines ;
Mais, comme les douceurs, en savez-vous les peines?
A quelque heureuse fin que tendent ses projets,
Jamais il ne fait bien au gré de ses sujets :
Il passe pour cruel, s'il garde la justice ; 35
S'il est doux, pour timide et partisan du vice.
S'il se porte à la guerre, il fait des malheureux ;
S'il entretient la paix, il n'est pas généreux ;
S'il pardonne, il est mol ; s'il se venge, barbare ;
S'il donne, il est prodigue, et s'il épargne, avare. 40
Ses desseins les plus purs et les plus innocents
Toujours en quelque esprit jettent un mauvais sens,
Et jamais sa vertu, tant soit-elle connue,
En l'estime des siens ne passe toute nue.
Si donc, pour mériter de régir des États, 45
La plus pure vertu même ne suffit pas,
Par quel heur voulez-vous que le règne succède

36-40. For several lines beginning with the same word see *Saint Genest*, note on ll. 741-744.

39. mol : for *mou* ; cf. l. 25. M. : " Le style noble a conservé molle au féminin, en parlant des choses : la molle arène, la molle oisiveté ; il a rejeté mol et mou."

42. jettent un mauvais sens : " arouse an unfavorable feeling." M. : " On dit jeter dans les esprits des soupçons, de l'inquiétude ; mais on dit, présenter un sens. Sens est pris là pour l'aspect et pour l'apparence des choses."

43. tant soit-elle connue : in modern French, *tant qu'elle soit connue*. For omission of *que* and inversion of subject see Haase, 45, G., and *Lexiques de Malherbe*, p. 623, and *de La Fontaine*, II, p. 374.

44. ne passe toute nue : " is considered unalloyed." See *Saint Genest*, l. 1420.

47. heur : see *Saint Genest*, note on l. 101. — que le règne succède, etc. : translate : "should reign successfully," and make *des esprits oisifs* subject. M. : " On ne dit point indéfiniment le règne, pour l'action de régner."

A des esprits oisifs que le vice possède,
　　　(*Le prince tourne la tête et témoigne s'emporter*)
Hors de leurs voluptés incapables d'agir,
Et qui, serfs de leurs sens, ne se sauraient régir?　　　　　50
Ici, mon seul respect contient votre caprice.
Mais examinez-vous et rendez-vous justice ;
Pouvez-vous attenter sur ceux dont j'ai fait choix
Pour soutenir mon trône et dispenser mes lois,
Sans blesser les respects dus à mon diadème,　　　　　55
Et sans en même temps attenter sur moi-même?
Le duc, par sa faveur, vous a blessé les yeux,
Et, parce qu'il m'est cher, il vous est odieux ;
Mais, voyant d'un côté sa splendeur non commune,
Voyez par quels degrés il monte à sa fortune ;　　　　　60
Songez combien son bras a mon trône affermi.
Et mon affection vous fait son ennemi !
Encore est-ce trop peu : votre aveugle colère
Le hait en autrui même et passe à votre frère ;
Votre jalouse humeur ne lui saurait souffrir　　　　　65
La liberté d'aimer ce qu'il me voit chérir ;

51. **mon seul respect** : "only respect for me." See ll. 293, 395. This
is the frequent objective use of the possessive pronoun ; see l. 57.

52. **rendez-vous justice** : "judge yourself."

53. **attenter sur** : (or *à*), "to make a criminal attack upon one" is now
obsolete. See *Lexiques de Corneille, de Racine, de La Fontaine,* and *de
Malherbe.*

57. **Le duc, par sa faveur** : M. : "La faveur dont jouit le duc est la
faveur du roi, non pas la sienne propre. Il fallait dire par son crédit." —
vous a blessé les yeux : "has offended you," lit. "has wounded your eyes."
In this sense *blesser* is used also with *vue* ; see *Lexiques de Corneille,* I,
p. 125, and *de Racine,* p. 65.

59. **voyant d'un côté** : i.e. considering under one aspect only, taking
a partial view of, etc.

63. **Encore est-ce trop peu** : "Yet that is not enough." For this use
of *encore* followed by inversion of subject and verb, see Mätzner,
Syntax, II, pp. 61, 271.

64. **en autrui même** : for *même en autrui* ; see *Saint Genest,* note on
l. 1686.

Son amour pour le duc lui produit votre haine.

Cherchez un digne objet à cette humeur hautaine ;

Employez, employez ces bouillants mouvements

A combattre l'orgueil des peuples ottomans ;   70

Renouvelez contre eux nos haines immortelles,

Et soyez généreux en de justes querelles :

Mais contre votre frère et contre un favori

Nécessaire à son roi plus qu'il n'en est chéri,

Et qui de tant de bras qu'armait la Moscovie   75

Vient de sauver mon sceptre, et peut-être ma vie,

C'est un emploi célèbre et digne d'un grand cœur !

Votre caprice, enfin, veut régler ma faveur :

Je sais mal appliquer mon amour et ma haine,

Et c'est de vos leçons qu'il faut que je l'apprenne !   80

J'aurais mal profité de l'usage et du temps !

LADISLAS *

Souffrez . . .

VENCESLAS †

Encore un mot, et puis je vous entends :

S'il faut qu'à cent rapports ma créance réponde,

* 1648 has *Le Prince*.

† 1648 has everywhere after this *Le Roi* for *Venceslas*, both in headings of scenes and in dialogue. I have followed Viollet-le-Duc in printing uniformly *Venceslas* and *Ladislas* ; see subsequent note at beginning
of Scène II, p. 262.

---

69. bouillants mouvements : "fiery, passionate, impulses."

70. des peuples ottomans : it is probable that Rotrou had in mind the
successes of the Turks in the seventeenth century, and not in the uncertain period of his play. See Introduction, p. 103, note 1.

71. nos haines immortelles : see last note. A king of Poland was
slain by the Turks at the battle of Varna, 1444.

79. Je sais, etc. : i.e. in your opinion I do not know how to bestow
my favor, etc.

81. J'aurais mal profité, etc. : when the past of the conditional is used
in principal propositions some verb like "say," "think," "believe,"
"suppose" is understood. "You think I have not profited by the habit
of reigning and the lessons of age."

Rarement le soleil rend la lumière au monde
Que le premier rayon qu'il répand ici-bas   85
N'y découvre quelqu'un de vos assassinats ;
Ou, du moins, on vous tient en si mauvaise estime
Qu'innocent ou coupable on vous charge du crime,
Et que, vous offensant d'un soupçon éternel,
Aux bras du sommeil même on vous fait criminel.   90
Sous ce fatal soupçon qui défend qu'on me craigne,
On se venge, on s'égorge, et l'impunité règne,
Et ce juste mépris de mon autorité
Est la punition de cette impunité ;
Votre valeur, enfin, naguère si vantée,   95
Dans vos folles amours languit comme enchantée,
Et, par cette langueur dedans tous les esprits
Efface son estime et s'acquiert des mépris :
Et je vois toutefois qu'un heur inconcevable,
Malgré tous ces défauts, vous rend encore aimable, 100
Et que votre bon astre en ces mêmes esprits
Souffre ensemble pour vous l'amour et le mépris.
Par le secret pouvoir d'un charme que j'ignore,
Quoiqu'on vous mésestime, on vous chérit encore.
Vicieux on vous craint, mais vous plaisez heureux, 105
Et pour vous l'on confond le murmure et les vœux.
Ha ! méritez, mon fils, que cette amour vous dure,
Pour conserver les vœux étouffez le murmure,

---

88. **on vous charge du crime** : M. : " Il fallait dire de crimes."

89. **Et que, vous offensant d'un soupçon éternel** : M. : " Offenser quelqu'un d'un soupçon, n'est pas français. On s'offense de, mais on offense par."

91. **Sous ce fatal soupçon**, etc. : i.e. Ladislas is suspected of every crime and it is supposed that he will enjoy immunity on account of his father's love.

98. **son estime** : see note on l. 51 ; "the esteem formerly felt for your bravery."

101. **bon astre** : *astre* is here employed in the astrological sense of a planet influencing one's destiny. See following note.

Et régnez dans les cœurs par un sort dépendant
Plus de votre vertu que de votre ascendant ;   110
Par elle rendez-vous digne d'un diadème :
Né pour donner des lois, commencez par vous-même,
Et que vos passions, ces rebelles sujets,
De cette noble ardeur soient les premiers objets ;
Par ce genre de règne il faut mériter l'autre,   115
Par ce degré, mon fils, mon trône sera vôtre :
Mes États, mes sujets, tout fléchira sous vous,
Et, sujet de vous seul, vous régnerez sur tous.
Mais si, toujours vous-même et toujours serf du vice,
Vous ne prenez des lois que de votre caprice,   120
Et si, pour encourir votre indignation,
Il ne faut qu'avoir part en mon affection ;
Si votre humeur hautaine, enfin, ne considère
Ni les profonds respects dont le duc vous révère,
Ni l'étroite amitié dont l'infant vous chérit,   125
Ni la soumission d'un peuple qui vous rit,
Ni d'un père et d'un roi le conseil salutaire,
Lors, pour être tout roi, je ne serai plus père,
Et, vous abandonnant à la rigueur des lois,
Au mépris de mon sang je maintiendrai mes droits.   130

LADISLAS

Encor que de ma part tout vous choque et vous blesse,
En quelque étonnement que ce discours me laisse,
Je tire au moins ce fruit de mon attention

110. **ascendant** : originally an adjective referring to the rising of a planet at the moment of a person's birth. This planet is supposed to influence one's fate. Then the adjective became, as here, a substantive indicating the influence of the planet, and finally merely a predominating influence ; see l. 857.

116. **vôtre** : for *le vôtre* ; see *Saint Genest*, note on l. 782. M.: "Sera vôtre, n'est point du langage noble ; il fallait dire, sera le vôtre."

130. **Au mépris de mon sang** : "in spite of my family ties."

131. **Encor** : for *encore* ; see *Saint Genest*, note on l. 147.

D'avoir su vous complaire en cette occasion,
Et, sur chacun des points qui semblent me confondre,   135
J'ai de quoi me défendre et de quoi vous répondre,
Si j'obtiens à mon tour et l'oreille et le cœur.

VENCESLAS

Parlez, je gagnerai vaincu plus que vainqueur.
Je garde encor pour vous les sentiments d'un père :
Convainquez-moi d'erreur, elle me sera chère.   140

LADISLAS

Au retour de la chasse, hier, assisté des miens,
Le carnage du cerf se préparant aux chiens,
Tombés sur le discours des intérêts des princes,
Nous en vînmes sur l'art de régir les provinces,
Où, chacun à son gré forgeant des potentats,   145

137. **l'oreille et le cœur** : "your attention and your favor." Ladislas repeats the words used by his father in l. 8.

142. **Le carnage du cerf**, etc : i.e. while they were preparing the quarry (part of the entrails given to the dogs after the chase, so called because wrapped in the skin, *curée* from *cuir*, Lat. *corium*) for the hounds. M. : "Détail inutile, mal exprimé, et peu digne de la tragédie."

143. **Tombés sur le discours**, etc. : translate : "the conversation having fallen upon," etc. Lit. "We having fallen upon the conversation, etc." This is the absolute use of the past participle ; see note on l. 15.

144. **Nous en vînmes** : the *en* refers either to *discours* or *intérêts*, i.e. that part of the conversation relating to the art of governing provinces, or that part of the interests of princes involved in the government of provinces. Marmontel remarks on ll. 143–145 : " Tombés sur les discours, est familier et prosaïque ; les discours des intérêts, n'est pas français ; en venir sur l'art, ne l'est pas davantage ; où, n'a aucun rapport, tout cela est très négligé."

145. **Où, chacun à son gré forgeant des potentats** : i.e. each one of the prince's companions imagining, inventing, ideal rulers, etc. Castiglione's famous work, *Il Cortegiano*, is supposed to have grown out of a society game at the Court of Urbino, in which the company undertake to form in words a perfect courtier (*formar con parole un perfetto cortegiano*).

Chacun selon son sens gouvernant vos États,
Et presque aucun avis ne se trouvant conforme,
L'un prise votre règne, un autre le réforme ;
Il trouve ses censeurs comme ses partisans ;
Mais, généralement, chacun plaint vos vieux ans.   150
Moi, sans m'imaginer vous faire aucune injure,
Je coulai mes avis dans ce libre murmure,
Et, mon sein à ma voix s'osant trop confier,
Ce discours m'échappa, je ne le puis nier :
« Comment, dis-je, mon père, accablé de tant d'âge   155
« Et, sa force à présent servant mal son courage,
« Ne se décharge-t-il, avant qu'y succomber,
« D'un pénible fardeau qui le fera tomber?
« Devrait-il, me pouvant assurer sa couronne,
« Hasarder que l'État me l'ôte ou me la donne?   160
« Et s'il veut conserver la qualité de roi,
« La retiendrait-il pas s'en dépouillant pour moi?
« Comme il fait murmurer de l'âge qui l'accable !
« Croit-il de ce fardeau ma jeunesse incapable?
« Et n'ai-je pas appris, sous son gouvernement,   165
« Assez de politique et de raisonnement
« Pour savoir à quels soins oblige un diadème,
« Ce qu'un roi doit aux siens, à l'État, à soi-même,
« A ses confédérés, à la foi des traités ;
« Dedans quels intérêts ses droits sont limités,   170

---

152. **Je coulai mes avis :** *couler* is transitive. "I let my opinions escape in this free criticism." See *Lexique de Corneille*, I, p. 220. M.: "Couler, dans ce sens-là, n'est que du style très-familier."

157. **avant qu'y succomber :** for *avant d'y succomber* ; see l. 518, and *Saint Genest*, note on l. 634.

160. **Hasarder que l'État**, etc.: in allusion, apparently, to the elective nature of the Polish crown. See l. 539.

166. **et de raisonnement :** M.: "On apprend à raisonner ; mais apprendre du raisonnement, n'est pas français, et ne doit pas l'être."

168. **soi-même :** for *lui-même* ; see *Saint Genest*, note on l. 978.

« Quelle guerre est nuisible et quelle d'importance,
« A qui, quand et comment il doit son assistance ;
« Et pour garder, enfin, ses États d'accidents,
« Quel ordre il doit tenir et dehors et dedans ?
« Ne sais-je pas qu'un roi qui veut qu'on le révère   175
« Doit mêler à propos l'affable et le sévère,
« Et, selon l'exigence et des temps et des lieux,
« Savoir faire parler et son front et ses yeux,
« Mettre bien la franchise et la feinte en usage,
« Porter tantôt un masque et tantôt un visage ;   180
« Quelque avis qu'on lui donne, être toujours pareil,
« Et se croire souvent plus que tout son conseil ?
« Mais surtout, et de là dépend l'heur des couronnes,
« Savoir bien appliquer les emplois aux personnes,
« Et faire, par des choix judicieux et sains,   185
« Tomber le ministère en de fidèles mains ;
« Élever peu de gens si haut qu'ils puissent nuire,
« Être lent à former aussi bien qu'à détruire,
« Des bonnes actions garder le souvenir,
« Être prompt à payer et tardif à punir ?   190
« N'est-ce pas sur cet art, leur dis-je, et ces maximes
« Que se maintient le cours des règnes légitimes ? »
Voilà la vérité touchant le premier point :
J'apprends qu'on vous l'a dite et ne m'en défends point.

VENCESLAS

Poursuivez.

178. **Savoir faire parler et son front et ses yeux** : i.e. to express his feelings by his looks. For three infinitives in succession see *Lexique de Molière*, I, p. cxxvii.

180. **un visage** : i.e. a natural countenance.

181. **être toujours pareil** : M. : "On dit être égal à soi-même. On ne dit point être pareil à soi-même."

182. **Et se croire** : M. : " Dans ce sens-là on dit, s'en croire."

184. **Savoir bien appliquer**, etc. : we should say, "to select carefully persons for offices."

LADISLAS

A l'égard de l'ardente colère   195
Où vous meut le parti du duc et de mon frère,
Dont l'un est votre cœur, si l'autre est votre bras,
Dont l'un règne en votre âme, et l'autre en vos États,
J'en hais l'un, il est vrai, cet insolent ministre
Qui vous est précieux autant qu'il m'est sinistre,   200
Vaillant, j'en suis d'accord, mais vain, fourbe, flatteur,
Et de votre pouvoir secret usurpateur,
Ce duc, à qui votre âme, à tous autres obscure,
Sans crainte s'abandonne et produit toute pure,
Et qui, sous votre nom beaucoup plus roi que vous,   205
Met à me desservir ses plaisirs les plus doux,
Vous fait mes actions pleines de tant de vices,
Et me rend près de vous tant de mauvais offices
Que vos yeux prévenus ne trouvent plus en moi
Rien qui vous représente et qui promette un roi.   210
Je feindrais d'être aveugle et d'ignorer l'envie
Dont, en toute rencontre, il vous noircit ma vie,
S'il ne s'en usurpait, et m'ôtait les emplois

204. **produit** : for *se produit*. The omission of the reflexive pronoun is common in the seventeenth century. See Haase, 61, where a list is given which does not include this verb; it is in Sölter, p. 60. It is omitted also in list in Godefroy, *Lexique comparé de la langue de Corneille*, I, p. 283. See ll. 771, 918, 1033, 1431 ; and *Lexiques de Racine*, p. 497 (and grammatical introduction, p. lxxxviii) ; *de Corneille*, I, p. lxxv ; and *de Molière*, I, p. clxxxii.

206. **Met à me desservir**, etc.: translate : "takes the sweetest pleasure in doing me an ill service." M.: "A me desservir. Ce mot n'est pas du haut style."

207. **Vous fait mes actions**, etc.: "represents to you my actions as so full of," etc.

212. **rencontre** : see *Saint Genest*, note on l. 23. — **il vous noircit ma vie** : M.: "On noircit aux yeux de quelqu'un ; mais on ne noircit pas à quelqu'un quelque chose."

213. **S'il ne s'en usurpait, et m'ôtait les emplois** : M.: "S'en usurpait, n'est pas français ; et, avant le seconde verbe, il fallait répéter la négative."

Qui, si jeune, m'ont fait l'effroi de tant de rois,
Et dont, ces derniers jours, il a des Moscovites   215
Arrêté les progrès et restreint les limites.
Partant pour cette grande et fameuse action,
Vous en mîtes le prix à sa discrétion.
Mais, s'il n'est trop puissant pour craindre ma colère,
Qu'il pense mûrement au choix de son salaire,   220
Et que le grand crédit qu'il possède à la cour,
S'il méconnaît mon rang, respecte mon amour,
Ou, tout brillant qu'il est, il lui sera frivole.
Je n'ai point sans sujet lâché cette parole ;
Quelques bruits m'ont appris jusqu'où vont vos desseins, 225
Et c'est un des sujets, Seigneur, dont je me plains.

VENCESLAS

Achevez.

LADISLAS *

Pour mon frère, après son insolence,
Je ne puis m'emporter à trop de violence,
Et de tous vos tourments la plus affreuse horreur
Ne le saurait soustraire à ma juste fureur.   230
Quoi ! quand, le cœur outré de sensibles atteintes,
Je fais entendre au duc le sujet de mes plaintes,

---

* 1648, *Le Prince.*

---

215. dont: this word refers to *emplois* of l. 213; translate : "and by means of which," i.e. the military offices or duties of which he has deprived Ladislas. M.: "Construction très-vicieuse."

217. Partant, etc. : *partant* refers to the duke and is used absolutely. M.: "Partant devrait se rapporter à vous ; et au contraire il n'est relatif à aucun des termes de la phrase."

223. frivole: "useless." M.: "Il fallait dire, inutile, frivole n'a point ce régime."

224. sujet: "cause." In l. 226 *sujets* may be translated "matters."

228. Je ne puis m'emporter à trop de violence: M.: "Il fallait dire me porter."

232. Je fais entendre au duc, etc.: see *Saint Genest*, note on l. 499.

Et, de ses procédés justement irrité,
Veux mettre quelque frein à sa témérité,
Étourdi, furieux et poussé d'un faux zèle, 235
Mon frère contre moi vient prendre sa querelle,
Et, bien plus, sur l'épée ose porter la main !
Ha ! j'atteste du Ciel le pouvoir souverain
Qu'avant que le soleil, sorti du sein de l'onde,
Ote et rende le jour aux deux moitiés du monde, 240
Il m'ôtera le sang qu'il n'a pas respecté,
Ou me fera raison de cette indignité.
Puisque je suis au peuple en si mauvaise estime
Il la faut mériter du moins par un grand crime,
Et, de vos châtiments menacé tant de fois, 245
Me rendre un digne objet de la rigueur des lois.

VENCESLAS, bas

Que puis-je plus tenter sur cette âme hautaine?
Essayons l'artifice où la rigueur est vaine,
Puisque plainte, froideur, menace ni prison
Ne l'ont pu, jusqu'ici, réduire à la raison. 250
    (*Il dit au prince*)
Ma créance, mon fils, sans doute un peu légère,
N'est pas sans quelque erreur, et cette erreur m'est chère.
Étouffons nos discords dans nos embrassements ;
    (*Il l'embrasse*)
Je ne puis de mon sang forcer les mouvements.
Je lui veux bien céder, et, malgré ma colère, 255

234. **Veux** : for omission of subject see *Saint Genest*, note on l. 23. The subject is also omitted with *fera* in l. 242.

247. **Que puis-je plus tenter** : M. : "Il serait à souhaiter que cette façon de parler fût reçue ; mais on est obligé de dire, que puis-je tenter de plus."

251. **légère** : "rash, hasty."

252. **et cette erreur m'est chère** : because it has brought about an explanation and made possible a reconciliation.

253. **Étouffons nos discords** : M. : "Discords est vieux ; il était énergique, et plus sonore que différents : les poëtes devraient le rajeunir."

Me confesser vaincu, parce que je suis père.
Prince, il est temps qu'enfin sur un trône commun
Nous ne fassions qu'un règne et ne soyons plus qu'un :
Si proche du cercueil où je me vois descendre,
Je me veux voir en vous renaître de ma cendre,   260
Et par vous, à couvert des outrages du temps,
Commencer à mon âge un règne de cent ans.

LADISLAS

De votre seul repos dépend toute ma joie,
Et, si votre faveur jusque-là se déploie,
Je ne l'accepterai que comme un noble emploi   265
Qui, parmi vos sujets, fera compter un roi.

Scène II

ALEXANDRE, VENCESLAS, LADISLAS *

ALEXANDRE

Seigneur?

VENCESLAS

Que voulez-vous? sortez.

ALEXANDRE

Je me retire.
Mais si vous . . .

VENCESLAS

Qu'est-ce encor? que me vouliez-vous dire?
(*A part*)
A quel étrange office, Amour, me réduis-tu,

* 1648 has from here on uniformly *Le Prince* instead of *Ladislas*.
The heading of this scene in 1648 is: *Alexandre, Le Roi, Le Prince.*
See note, p. 253.

---

259. cercueil : see *Saint Genest*, note on l. 597.
260. renaître de ma cendre : the common poetical figure based on the legend of the phenix, which was believed to burn itself and to live again in a new and young phenix which sprang from the ashes.

De faire accueil au vice et chasser la vertu !   270

ALEXANDRE

Que si vous ne daignez m'admettre en ma défense,
Vous donnerez le tort à qui reçoit l'offense ;
Le prince est mon aîné, je respecte son rang ;
Mais nous ne différons ni de cœur ni de sang,
Et, pour un démentir, j'ai trop . . .

VENCESLAS

                     Vous, téméraire,   275
Vous la main sur l'épée, et contre votre frère !
Contre mon successeur en mon autorité !
Implorez, insolent, implorez sa bonté,
Et, par un repentir digne de votre grâce,
Méritez le pardon que je veux qu'il vous fasse.   280
Allez, demandez-lui. Vous, tendez-lui les bras.

ALEXANDRE

Considérez, Seigneur . . .

VENCESLAS

           Ne me répliquez pas.

ALEXANDRE, *bas*

Fléchirons-nous, mon cœur, sous cette humeur hautaine?
Oui, du degré de l'âge il faut porter la peine.

    271. **Que si vous me daignez,** etc. : understand *Je veux vous dire* from
l. 268.

    275. **démentir** : for *démenti*, the now usual participial substantive. In
the sixteenth and at the beginning of the seventeenth centuries *démentie*
or *démentir* were used with same meaning as *démenti*.

    283. **Fléchirons-nous, mon cœur, sous cette humeur hautaine** : M. :
" L'usage d'adresser ainsi la parole à son cœur, à son âme, à ses pensées
(figure dont Rotrou a si fort abusé dans cette pièce) est hereusement
aboli. On regardait cela comme de la poésie, et rien n'est moins poétique que ce qui n'est point naturel."

    284. **Oui, du degré de l'âge il faut porter la peine** : i.e. one must bear
the penalty of his age. Alexandre is the younger son. Littré cites

Que j'ai de répugnance à cette lâcheté !   285
    (*Parlant au prince* [*Ladislas*])
O Ciel ! pardonnez donc à ma témérité,
Mon frère : un père enjoint que je vous satisfasse ;
J'obéis à son ordre, et vous demande grâce ;
Mais, par cet ordre, il faut me tendre aussi les bras.

VENCESLAS

Dieu ! le cruel encor ne le regarde pas !   290

LADISLAS

Sans eux, suffit-il pas que le roi vous pardonne ?

VENCESLAS

Prince, encore une fois, donnez-les, je l'ordonne.
Laissez à mon respect vaincre votre courroux.

LADISLAS, embrassant son frère

A quelle lâcheté, Seigneur, m'obligez-vous !
Allez, et n'imputez cet excès d'indulgence   295
Qu'au pouvoir absolu qui retient ma vengeance.

ALEXANDRE, bas

O nature ! ô respect ! que vous m'êtes cruels !

VENCESLAS

Changez ces différends en des vœux mutuels ;
Et, quand je suis en paix avec toute la terre,

this line under *degré*, and defines this particular use : " Figurément, et
par analogie, le plus ou le moins que présentent les choses intellec-
tuelles ou morales."

   293. Laissez à mon respect : see *Saint Genest*, note on l. 647, and
Venceslas, note on l. 51. M. : " A mon respect, ne dit point au respect
que vous me devez."

   298. différends : here used in the sense of " quarrel, difference." The
Academy since 1798 has used only the spelling in the text. The word is,
of course, the same as the adjective *différent*, and there is no good reason to indicate the substantive by another form. See *Lexique de Corneille*, I, p. 303. — **vœux** : here "affection." Same meaning in l. 310,
" affections." See *Saint Genest*, note on l. 149.

Dans ma maison, mes fils, ne mettez point la guerre.   300
  [*A Ladislas*]
Faites venir le duc, infant. Prince, arrêtez.
                                    (*L'infant sort*)

SCÈNE III

VENCESLAS, LADISLAS

LADISLAS

Vous voulez m'ordonner encor des lâchetés,
Et pour ce traître encor solliciter ma grâce !
Mais pour des ennemis ce cœur n'a plus de place :
Votre sang, qui l'anime, y répugne à vos lois.   305
Aimez cet insolent, conservez votre choix,
Et du bandeau royal qui vous couvre la tête
Payez, si vous voulez, sa dernière conquête ;
Mais souffrez-m'en, Seigneur, un mépris généreux ;
Laissez ma haine libre, aussi bien que vos vœux ;   310
Souffrez ma dureté, gardant votre tendresse,
Et ne m'ordonnez point un acte de faiblesse.

VENCESLAS

Mon fils, si près du trône où vous allez monter,
Près d'y remplir ma place et m'y représenter,
Aussi bien souverain sur vous que sur les autres,   315
Prenez mes sentiments et dépouillez les vôtres.
Donnez à mes souhaits, de vous-même vainqueur,
Cette noble faiblesse, et digne d'un grand cœur,
Qui vous fera priser de toute la province,
Et, monarque, oubliez les différends du prince.   320

---

315. souverain sur vous : M. : "On dit souverain de, et non pas souverain sur." It is true that *de* is more common with *souverain*, but *sur* is found in Corneille and Racine ; see *Lexiques* of these writers.

LADISLAS

Je préfère ma haine à cette qualité.
Dispensez-moi, Seigneur, de cette indignité.

Scène IV

Féderic,* Venceslas, Alexandre, Ladislas, Octave

VENCESLAS

Étouffez cette haine, ou je prends sa querelle.
Duc, saluez le prince.

LADISLAS, *l'embrassant avec peine.* [*A part*]

O contrainte cruelle !

(*Ils s'embrassent*)

VENCESLAS

Et, d'une étroite ardeur unis à l'avenir,   325
De vos discords passés perdez le souvenir.

FÉDERIC

Pour lui prouver à quoi mon zèle me convie,
Je voudrais perdre encore et le sang et la vie.

VENCESLAS

Assez d'occasions, de sang et de combats
Ont signalé pour nous et ce cœur et ce bras,   330
Et vous ont trop acquis, par cet illustre zèle,

---

* 1648 has always *Le Duc* or *Le Duc de Curlande* for *Féderic*. For convenience of reader I have followed Viollet-le-Duc, as in the case of *Venceslas* and *Ladislas*.

---

328. **perdre encore et le sang et la vie**: M.: " On dit bien, perdre la vie ; mais on ne dit pas, perdre le sang. On ne dit pas même dans ce sens-là perdre son sang, mais verser ou donner son sang."

330. **Ont signalé**: " have distinguished, made famous."

Tout ce qui d'un mortel rend la gloire immortelle ;
Mais vos derniers progrès, qui certes m'ont surpris,
Passent toute créance et demandent leur prix.
Avec si peu de gens avoir fait nos frontières   335
D'un si puissant parti les sanglants cimetières,
Et dans si peu de jours, par d'incroyables faits,
Réduit le Moscovite à demander la paix,
Ce sont des actions dont la reconnaissance
Du plus riche monarque excède la puissance :   340
N'exceptez rien aussi de ce que je vous dois ;
Demandez ; j'en ai mis le prix à votre choix :
Envers votre valeur acquittez ma parole.

FÉDERIC

Je vous dois tout, grand roi.

VENCESLAS

                Ce respect est frivole :
La parole des rois est un gage important,   345
Qu'ils doivent, le pouvant, retirer à l'instant.
Il est d'un prix trop cher pour en laisser la garde ;
Par le dépôt, la perte ou l'oubli s'en hasarde.

FÉDERIC

Puisque votre bonté me force à recevoir
Le loyer d'un tribut et le prix d'un devoir,   350

339–340. **Ce sont des actions**, etc. : cf. the *Cid*, IV. 3 :

> Ne sont pas des exploits qui laissent à ton roi
> Le moyen ni l'espoir de s'acquitter vers toi.

For the sentiment compare *Saint Genest*, ll. 121–124. In *Don Lope de Cardone* (1649), II. 4, there is a similar situation, — a grateful king offers his victorious generals whatever they desire.

343. **Envers votre valeur** : construe with *parole*, "claim the performance of my promise to your bravery."

346. **le pouvant** : "when they are able to do so." *Pouvoir* is here transitive.

350. **Le loyer** : M. : " Loyer a vieilli ; c'est une perte pour la poésie."

Un servage, Seigneur, plus doux que votre empire,
Des flammes et des fers, sont le prix où j'aspire ;
Si d'un cœur consumé d'un amour violent
La bouche ose exprimer . . .

LADISLAS

        Arrêtez, insolent ;
Au vol de vos désirs imposez des limites,   355
Et proportionnez vos vœux à vos mérites :
Autrement, au mépris et du trône et du jour,
Dans votre infâme sang j'éteindrai votre amour :
Où mon respect s'oppose, apprenez, téméraire,
A servir sans espoir, et souffrir et vous taire ;   360
Ou . . .

FÉDERIC, *sortant*

        Je me tais, Seigneur, et, puisque mon espoir
Blesse votre respect, il blesse mon devoir.

        (*Il s'en va avec l'infant*)

SCÈNE V

VENCESLAS, LADISLAS, OCTAVE

VENCESLAS

Prince, vous emportant à ce caprice extrême,
Vous ménagez fort mal l'espoir d'un diadème,
Et votre tête encor qui le prétend porter.   365

351–354. **Un servage**, etc. : "servitude" (subjection to the one I love).
These lines express the conventional gallantry of the seventeenth century. For *flammes* and *fers* see *Saint Genest*, note on ll. 105–110. M. :
"Servage a vieilli."

364. **Vous ménagez fort mal**, etc. : i.e. you are acting very rashly if
you hope to attain the crown.

LADISLAS

Vous êtes roi, Seigneur, vous pouvez me l'ôter ;
Mais j'ai lieu de me plaindre, et ma juste colère
Ne peut prendre des lois ni d'un roi ni d'un père.

VENCESLAS

Je dois bien moins en prendre et d'un fol et d'un fils.
Pensez à votre tête, et prenez-en avis.   370

(*Il s'en va en colère*)

Scène VI

LADISLAS, OCTAVE

OCTAVE

O dieux ! ne sauriez-vous cacher mieux votre haine ?

LADISLAS

Veux-tu que, la cachant, mon attente soit vaine,
Qu'il vole à mon espoir ce trésor amoureux,
Et qu'il fasse son prix de l'objet de mes vœux ?
Quoi ! Cassandre sera le prix d'une victoire   375
Qu'usurpant mes emplois il dérobe à ma gloire ?
Et l'État, qu'il gouverne à ma confusion,
L'épargne, qu'il manie avec profusion,
Les siens qu'il agrandit, les charges qu'il dispense,
Ne lui tiennent pas lieu d'assez de récompense,   380

---

370. **et prenez-en avis** : "and be warned" (by the thought of the danger you are incurring : "Pensez à votre tête"). M.: "Tête a deux sens différents, et la relation est fausse. La tête dont le prince doit prendre avis, est l'entendement, la prudence ; la tête qui est en péril et à laquelle il doit penser, est figurément la vie."

376. **Qu'ursurpant mes emplois** : see note on l. 213.

380. **Ne lui tiennent pas lieu**, etc.: translate : "are not a sufficient reward for him, unless," etc.; lit. "do not stand in the place of a sufficient reward, unless," etc.

S'il ne me prive encor du fruit de mon amour,
Et si, m'ôtant Cassandre, il ne m'ôte le jour?
N'est-ce pas de tes soins et de ta diligence
Que je tiens le secret de leur intelligence?

OCTAVE

Oui, Seigneur ; mais l'hymen qu'on lui va proposer　　　385
Au succès de vos vœux la pourra disposer :
L'infante l'a mandée, et, par son entremise
J'espère à vos souhaits la voir bientôt soumise :
Cependant, feignez mieux, et d'un père irrité
Et d'un roi méprisé craignez l'autorité ;　　　　　　390
Reposez sur nos soins l'ardeur qui vous transporte.

LADISLAS

C'est mon roi, c'est mon père, il est vrai, je m'emporte ;
Mais je trouve en deux yeux deux rois plus absolus,
Et, n'étant plus à moi, ne me possède plus.

---

385. **mais l'hymen qu'on lui va proposer** : i.e. with Ladislas.

391. **Reposez sur nos soins**, etc. : " Trust to our care the passion which transports you." M. : " On dit bien se reposer sur ; mais on ne dit guère reposer quelque chose, et encore moins son ardeur."

393. **deux yeux** : i.e. Cassandre. M. : " Style des anciens romans, qu'a rejeté la tragédie."

394. **ne me possède plus** : for omission of subject of verb see *Saint Genest*, note on l. 23. See *Venceslas*, notes on ll. 401, 405.

ACTE DEUXIÈME

Scene I

Théodore,* Cassandre

THÉODORE

Enfin, si son respect ni le mien ne vous touche,   395
Cassandre, tout l'État vous parle par ma bouche :
Le refus de l'hymen qui vous soumet sa foi
Lui refuse une reine et veut ôter un roi ;
L'objet de vos mépris attend une couronne
Que déjà d'une voix tout le peuple lui donne,   400
Et, de plus, ne l'attend qu'afin de vous l'offrir :
Et votre cruauté ne le saurait souffrir ?

CASSANDRE

Non, je ne puis souffrir, en quelque rang qu'il monte,
L'ennemi de ma gloire et l'amant de ma honte,

---

* 1648 adds, after *Théodore*, *Infante*.

395. **si son respect ni le mien**, etc. : strictly speaking *ni* should always be repeated before each of the coördinate objects. This rule was often violated in the seventeenth century, as at the present day. See Haase, 140, R. 3. See *Lexiques de La Fontaine*, II, p. 104, and *de Racine*, p. 339.

397–398. Le refus de l'hymen, etc. : i.e. Ladislas will, in his sister's opinion, refuse the crown unless he can offer it to Cassandre. — **et veut ôter un roi** : "and desires to suppress a king." M.: "Le refus, qui refuse, est une négligence outrée, ou une affectation puérile. Oter exige un régime indirect : ôtez-moi la vie, ôtez-vous de mes yeux."

401. ne l'attend : the subject *il*, referring to Ladislas, is omitted ; see above, note on l. 394.

404. gloire : " good name, fame, reputation."

Et ne puis pour époux vouloir d'un suborneur   405
Qui voit qu'il a sans fruit poursuivi mon honneur ;
Qui, tant que sa poursuite a cru m'avoir infâme,
Ne m'a point souhaitée en qualité de femme,
Et qui, n'ayant pour but que ses sales plaisirs,
En mon seul déshonneur bornait tous ses désirs.   410
En quelque objet qu'il soit à toute la province,
Je ne regarde en lui ni monarque ni prince,
Et ne vois, sous l'éclat dont il est revêtu,
Que de traîtres appâts qu'il tend à ma vertu.
Après ses sentiments, à mon honneur sinistres,   415
L'essai de ses présents, l'effort de ses ministres,
Ses plaintes, ses écrits, et la corruption
De ceux qu'il crut pouvoir servir sa passion,
Ces moyens vicieux aidant mal sa poursuite,
Aux vertueux enfin son amour est réduite ;   420
Et, pour venir à bout de mon honnêteté,

405. ne puis : the omitted subject is *je*; see above, note on l. 394. —
vouloir d'un suborneur : " wish to have a seducer." Littré : " vouloir de,
avec un substantif pour complément, rechercher, accepter."

409. Et qui, n'ayant pour but que ses sales plaisirs : M. : " Ce vers, et
presque tout ce discours de Cassandre, est contraire à la bienséance.
L'art d'exprimer avec délicatesse ce qui blesse la modestie, et de le
voiler aux yeux de l'imagination par une expression vague et légère ;
cet art dont Racine a été le plus parfait modèle, n'était pas connu
avant Corneille, et n'était pas même assez connu de lui."

410. bornait : *borner* is followed by *en*, *dans*, or *à*. See *Lexiques*. M. :
" On dit borner à et non pas borner en."

411. En quelque objet, etc. : " However the whole realm may regard
him." I do not find any other example of *objet* for " regard, consideration." M. : " On dirait aujourd'hui, en quelque estime."

413. Et ne vois : for omission of *je* see notes on ll. 401, 405.

414. appâts : "allurements."

415. à mon honneur sinistres : M. : " Sinistres n'a point ce régime, et
ne se prend qu'à l'absolu."

416. L'essai : i.e. the attempt his presents make to corrupt Cassandre.

417. et la corruption : the bribery of Cassandre's servants, etc.

421. pour venir à bout de mon honnetêté : " to overcome my virtue."
Venir à bout de means " to accomplish, to succeed," and then by an

Il met tout en usage, et crime et piété.
Mais en vain il consent que l'amour nous unisse :
C'est appeler l'honneur au secours de son vice ;
Puis, s'étant satisfait, on sait qu'un souverain   425
D'un hymen qui déplaît a le remède en main :
Pour en rompre les nœuds et colorer ses crimes,
L'État ne manque pas de plausibles maximes.
Son infidélité suivrait de près sa foi :
Seul il se considère ; il s'aime, et non pas moi.   430

THÉODORE

Ses vœux, un peu bouillants, vous font beaucoup d'ombrage.

CASSANDRE

Il vaut mieux faillir moins et craindre davantage.

THÉODORE

La fortune vous rit, et ne rit pas toujours.

CASSANDRE

Je crains son inconstance et ses courtes amours ;
Et puis, qu'est un palais, qu'une maison pompeuse   435
Qu'à notre ambition bâtit cette trompeuse,
Où l'âme dans les fers gémit à tout propos,
Et ne rencontre pas le solide repos ?

THÉODORE

Je ne vous puis qu'offrir, après un diadème.

extension of the meaning it denotes the design also. M. : "Expression
triviale et peu décente."

433. **La fortune vous rit** : see l. 126.

435. **qu'est un palais, qu'une maison**, etc. : "what is a palace but a
splendid house." In modern prose the interrogative would be *qu'est-ce*,
or *qu'est-ce que*. The second *que* is the conjunction equivalent to "but"
or "except." See Haase, 138, R. 2, and *Saint Genest*, note on l. 715. M. :
"On dirait à présent qu'est-ce qu'un palais ? "

439. **Je ne vous puis qu'offrir**, etc. : "I can offer you nothing." *Que* is
here used for *ce que*, representing the Lat. neuter *quod*. See Chassang,

CASSANDRE

Vous me donnerez plus, me laissant à moi-même.   440

THÉODORE

Seriez-vous moins à vous, ayant moins de rigueur?

CASSANDRE

N'appelleriez-vous rien la perte de mon cœur?

THÉODORE

Vous feriez un échange, et non pas une perte.

CASSANDRE

Et j'aurais cette injure impunément soufferte !
Et ce que vous nommez des vœux un peu bouillants,   445
Ces desseins criminels, ces efforts insolents,
Ces libres entretiens, ces messages infâmes,
L'espérance du rapt dont il flattait ses flammes,
Et tant d'offres enfin, dont il crut me toucher,
Au sang de Cunisberg se pourraient reprocher?   450

THÉODORE

Ils ont votre vertu vainement combattue.

French Grammar, p. 286, R. viii; Haase, 42. This usage is generally found in connection with the verbs *avoir*, *savoir*, and *pouvoir* in the negative. Very common expressions are " Je ne sais que faire " and " je n'ai que faire," for " je n'ai rien à faire " and " je n'ai que faire de ": " I have nothing to do with," and hence " I do not need." Molière, *L'Avare*, IV. 5 : " Je n'ai que faire de vos dons." M. : " Cela n'est plus français ; on dit, que puis-je vous offrir, ou, je ne sais que vous offrir."

450. **Au sang de Cunisberg se pourraient reprocher**: translate: "could it be possible for the race of Cunisberg (the family of Cassandre) to be reproached with," etc. The construction of *reprocher* is with indirect object of person reproached and direct object of thing with which one is reproached. In the text *se* belongs to *pourraient* as part of reflexive *se pouvoir*, "to be possible."

CASSANDRE

On en pourrait douter si je m'en étais tue,
Et si, sous cet hymen me laissant asservir,
Je lui donnais un bien qu'il m'a voulu ravir.
Excusez ma douleur ; je sais, sage princesse,   455
Quelles soumissions je dois à Votre Altesse ;
Mais au choix que mon cœur doit faire d'un époux,
Si j'en crois mon honneur, je lui dois plus qu'à vous.

SCÈNE II

LADISLAS, THÉODORE, CASSANDRE

LADISLAS, *entrant à grands pas.* [*A part*]

Cède, cruel tyran d'une amitié si forte,
Respect qui me retiens, à l'ardeur qui m'emporte :   460
Sachons si mon hymen ou mon cercueil est prêt ;
Impatient d'attendre, entendons mon arrêt !
(*A Cassandre*)
Parlez, belle ennemie : il est temps de résoudre
Si vous devez lancer ou retenir la foudre ;
Il s'agit de me perdre ou de me secourir.   465
Qu'en avez-vous conclu ? faut-il vivre ou mourir ?
Quel des deux voulez-vous, ou mon cœur ou ma cendre ?

457. au choix : the use of *à* for *dans* in many cases was frequent in the seventeenth century ; see Haase, 121, and *Lexique de Corneille*, I, p. 6.

459. amitié : for *amour*. See *Lexiques de Corneille*, I, p. 54, and *de Racine*, note, p. 28.

467. Quel des deux voulez-vous, ou mon cœur ou ma cendre : when *ou* is preceded by *lequel* (*quel*) or *qui*, interrogatives, it is usual to govern the substantives by the preposition *de*, which is not translated, and to omit the first *ou* ; in other words, the substantives are attracted into the genitive case, usually following *lequel*, etc., or understood in the interrogative : e.g. " Lequel doit plaire plus, d'un jaloux ou d'un autre." Molière, *Les Fâcheux*, II. 4. See ll. 1393–1394. This construction is not

Quelle des deux aurai-je, ou la mort ou Cassandre?
L'hymen à vos beaux jours joindra-t-il mon destin,
Ou si votre refus sera mon assassin? 470

CASSANDRE

Me parlez-vous d'hymen? et voudriez-vous pour femme
L'indigne et vil objet d'une impudique flamme?
Moi, dieux! moi, la moitié d'un roi, d'un potentat!
Ha! prince, quel présent feriez-vous à l'État,
De lui donner pour reine une femme suspecte! 475
Et quelle qualité voulez-vous qu'il respecte
En un objet infâme et si peu respecté,
Que vos sales désirs ont tant sollicité?

LADISLAS

Il y respectera la vertu la plus digne
Dont l'épreuve ait jamais fait une femme insigne, 480
Et le plus adorable et plus divin objet
Qui de son souverain fit jamais son sujet.
Je sais trop (et jamais ce cœur ne vous approche
Que confus de ce crime il ne se le reproche)
A quel point d'insolence et d'indiscrétion 485

obligatory and the form in the text is common. See l. 1454, where *qui*
takes the place of *lequel*, and l. 1584, where interrogative is understood.
Quel in l. 467, and *quelle* in l. 468, are equivalent to *lequel* and *laquelle*.
See Littré under *ou* (III, p. 875, col. 1) and *de* (II, p. 959, col. 1, D. 11);
Mätzner, *Franz. Gram.*, p. 430; *Syntax*, I, p. 224. M.: "Il fallait dire
lequel des deux."

470. Ou si: interrogative formula; *ou bien si* is also used. It avoids
the necessity of placing the subject after the verb. Corneille, *Le Cid*,
III. 5:

> Justes cieux, me trompé-je encore à l'apparence,
> Ou si je vois enfin mon unique espérance?

473. la moitié: = *femme*; see *Saint Genest*, note on l. 854.

484. Que confus de ce crime il ne se le reproche: lit. "without, being
confused at this crime, reproaching itself for it." See *Saint Genest*,
note on l. 768.

Ma jeunesse d'abord porta ma passion ;
Il est vrai qu'ébloui de ces yeux adorables
Qui font tant de captifs et tant de misérables,
Forcé par leurs attraits si dignes de mes vœux,
Je les contemplais seuls et ne recherchai qu'eux.   490
Mon respect s'oublia dedans cette poursuite.
Mais un amour enfant put manquer de conduite :
Il portait son excuse en son aveuglement,
Et c'est trop le punir que du bannissement.
Sitôt que le respect m'a dessillé la vue,   495
Et qu'outre les attraits dont vous êtes pourvue,
Votre soin, votre rang, vos illustres aïeux
Et vos rares vertus m'ont arrêté les yeux,
De mes vœux aussitôt réprimant l'insolence,
J'ai réduit sous vos lois toute leur violence,   500
Et, restreinte à l'espoir de notre hymen futur,
Ma flamme a consumé ce qu'elle avait d'impur :
Le flambeau qui me guide et l'ardeur qui me presse
Cherche en vous une épouse et non une maîtresse :
Accordez-la, Madame, au repentir profond   505
Qui, détestant mon crime, à vos pieds me confond ;
Sous cette qualité souffrez que je vous aime,

---

488. **Qui font tant de captifs**, etc. : M. : " Des yeux adorables qui font
des captifs et des misérables, sont du style des vieux romans."

492. **un amour enfant**: i.e. a love in its infancy, at the beginning.
There may be a reference to the god of love depicted as a child and
blind ; see next line. M. : " Ce vers, et les deux suivants, sont dignes
d'un madrigal de Trissotin." — **manquer de conduite** : " to behave badly."
A certain number of words like *conduite*, *humeur*, *heur*, etc., are used
absolutely in the sense of "good conduct," "bad humor," "good fortune," etc. See l. 1154, where *déportements* means "bad conduct."

495. **m'a dessillé la vue** : see *Saint Genest*, note on l. 432.

497. **Votre soin** : does this mean "care, solicitude, for her honor"?

503. **Le flambeau**: i.e. the wedding torch. M. : " Un flambeau et une
ardeur qui cherchent une épouse : mauvaise poésie."

507. **Sous cette qualité** : i.e. in the character of a repentant man.

Et privez-moi du jour plutôt que de vous-même :
Car, enfin, si l'on pèche adorant vos appas,
Et si l'on ne vous plaît qu'en ne vous aimant pas,   510
Cette offense est un mal que je veux toujours faire,
Et je consens plutôt à mourir qu'à vous plaire.

CASSANDRE

Et mon mérite, prince, et ma condition
Sont d'indignes objets de votre passion :
Mais, quand j'estimerais vos ardeurs véritables,   515
Et quand on nous verrait des qualités sortables,
On ne verra jamais l'hymen nous assortir,
Et je perdrai le jour avant qu'y consentir.
D'abord que votre amour fit voir dans sa poursuite
Et si peu de respect et si peu de conduite,   520
Et que le seul objet d'un dessein vicieux
Sur ma possession vous fit jeter les yeux,
Je ne vous regardai que par l'ardeur infâme
Qui ne m'appelait point au rang de votre femme,
Et que par cet effort brutal et suborneur   525
Dont votre passion attaquait mon honneur ;
Et, ne considérant en vous que votre vice,
Je pris en telle horreur vous et votre service,
Que, si je vous offense en ne vous aimant pas,
Et si dans mes vœux seuls vous trouvez des appas,   530

---

512. **Et je consens plutôt à mourir**, etc. : this whole speech of Ladislas
is characteristic of the gallantry of the seventeenth century; see Introduction, p. 69.   M. : "C'est complaire qu'il fallait dire."

515. **quand j'estimerais** : with the conditional *quand* is used with the
meaning "granting that, even if."

518. **avant qu'** : see note on l. 157.

519. **D'abord que** : antiquated for *dès que*, "as soon as, when." See
Lexiques de Corneille, I, p. 19, and *de Racine*, p. 8.

521. **Et que** : *que* repeats *D'abord que* of l. 519.

525. **Et que** : *Je ne vous regardai* of l. 523 is understood.

Cette offense est un mal que je veux toujours faire,
Et je consens plutôt à mourir qu'à vous plaire.

LADISLAS

Eh bien ! contre un objet qui vous fait tant d'horreur,
Inhumaine, exercez toute votre fureur ;
Armez-vous contre moi de glaçons et de flammes ;   535
Inventez des secrets de tourmenter les âmes ;
Suscitez terre et ciel contre ma passion ;
Intéressez l'État dans votre aversion ;
Du trône où je prétends détournez son suffrage,
Et pour me perdre, enfin, mettez tout en usage :   540
Avec tous vos efforts et tout votre courroux,
Vous ne m'ôterez pas l'amour que j'ai pour vous :
Dans vos plus grands mépris, je vous serai fidèle ;
Je vous adorerai furieuse et cruelle,
Et, pour vous conserver ma flamme et mon amour,   545
Malgré mon désespoir, conserverai le jour.

THÉODORE

Quoi ! nous n'obtiendrons rien de cette humeur altière !

CASSANDRE

Il m'a dû, m'attaquant, connaître toute entière,

531–532. Cette offense, etc. : this repetition by one character of the
words of another is frequent in French seventeenth-century tragedy.
Corneille's plays are full of examples : see *Horace*, III. 4, ll. 893–894 :
913–914. M.: " Cette affectation de répliquer dans les mêmes termes
ne convient qu'à la comédie."

535. glaçons : met. for "coldness, aversion." M.: "S'armer de glaçons
et de flammes : fausse image, antithèse puérile."

539. détournez son suffrage : see note on l. 160.

546. conserverai : for omission of subject *je*, see note on l. 394.

548. Il m'a dû, m'attaquant, connaître toute entière : M.: " Construction pénible et dure. Quand l'infinitif qui suit le verbe devoir ou
pouvoir a pour régime le pronom personnel, ce pronom peut être placé
indifféremment avant ou après le premier verbe : on observe même que
Racine et les bons écrivains du siècle passé trouvaient plus élégant de

Et savoir que l'honneur m'était sensible au point
D'en conserver l'injure et ne pardonner point.   550

THÉODORE

Mais vous venger ainsi, c'est vous punir vous-même ;
Vous perdez avec lui l'espoir d'un diadème.

CASSANDRE

Pour moi le diadème aurait de vains appas
Sur un front que j'ai craint et que je n'aime pas.

THÉODORE

Régner ne peut déplaire aux âmes généreuses.   555

CASSANDRE

Les trônes bien souvent portent des malheureuses
Qui, sous le joug brillant de leur autorité,
Ont beaucoup de sujets et peu de liberté.

THÉODORE

Redoutez-vous un joug qui vous fait souveraine ?

CASSANDRE

Je ne veux point dépendre, et veux être ma reine ;   560
Ou ma franchise, enfin, si jamais je la perds,
Veut choisir son vainqueur et connaître ses fers.

dire, il m'a dû connaître, il m'a pu tromper : mais lorsqu'on place le
pronom personnel avant le verbe devoir ou pouvoir, il faut que l'infinitif
suive immédiatement, par la raison que si des termes incidents séparent
les deux verbes, la relation n'est plus assez sensible. On dira donc, dès
longtemps il m'a dû connaître, et non pas, il m'a dû dès longtemps connaître ; par ses artifices il m'a pu tromper, et non pas, il m'a pu, par ses
artifices, tromper, ainsi du reste."

550. **D'en conserver l'injure** : i.e. to remember the wrong done to her
honor. M. : "Conserver l'injure, ne dit point, conserver le ressentiment
de l'injure."

560. **Je ne veux point dépendre**, etc. : "I do not wish to be dependent,
and I wish to be queen of myself." M. : "On ne dit point en parlant de
soi-même, être sa reine, être son roi."

THÉODORE

Servir un sceptre en main vaut bien votre franchise.

CASSANDRE

Savez-vous si déjà je ne l'ai point soumise?

LADISLAS

Oui, je le sais, cruelle, et connais mon rival ;   565
Mais j'ai cru que son sort m'était trop inégal
Pour me persuader qu'on dût mettre en balance
Le choix de mon amour ou de son insolence.

CASSANDRE

Votre rang n'entre pas dedans ses qualités,
Mais son sang ne doit rien au sang dont vous sortez,   570
Ni lui n'a pas grand lieu de vous porter envie.

LADISLAS

Insolente, ce mot lui coûtera la vie,
Et ce fer, en son sang si noble et si vanté,
Me va faire raison de votre vanité.

566. **Mais j'ai cru que son sort m'était trop inégal**: M.: "On ne dit point être inégal à quelqu'un ou à quelque chose. On dit inégal en soi-même ; et ce n'est qu'au pluriel que ce mot s'emploie pour exprimer le rapport réciproque d'inégalité: des temps inégaux, des grandeurs inégales ; mais quand même on dirait qu'un homme est inégal à un autre, on ne dirait point, son sort m'est inégal."

569. **Votre rang n'entre pas dedans ses qualités**: i.e. the question of your rank does not enter into his character. For *dedans = dans* see *Saint Genest*, note on l. 395. See also same play, ll. 504, 939, and *Venceslas*, ll. 644, 1246, and 1333.

570. **ne doit rien**: "is not inferior."

571. **Ni lui n'a pas grand lieu de vous porter envie**: M.: " On dit bien avoir lieu ; mais avoir grand lieu n'est pas français. Ni lui n'a pas, ne peut être reçu que dans le langage familier, le style soutenu exige, il n'a pas, et lui, nominatif, est une licence populaire." For the pleonastic negative see Benoist, p. 410.

574. **Me va faire raison de votre vanité**: "will give me satisfaction for your vainglory."

Violons, violons des lois trop respectées.　　　　　575
O sagesse, ô raison, que j'ai tant consultées !
Ne nous obstinons point à des vœux superflus ;
Laissons mourir l'amour où l'espoir ne vit plus.
Allez, indigne objet de mon inquiétude,
J'ai trop longtemps souffert de votre ingratitude ;　　575
Je vous devais connaître, et ne m'engager pas
Aux trompeuses douceurs de vos cruels appas,
Ou, m'étant engagé, n'implorer point votre aide,
Et, sans vous demander, vous ravir mon remède.
Mais contre son pouvoir mon cœur a combattu ;　　585
Je ne me repens pas d'un acte de vertu.
De vos superbes lois ma raison dégagée
A guéri mon amour et croit l'avoir songée ;
De l'indigne brasier qui consumait mon cœur
Il ne me reste plus que la seule rougeur,　　　　　590
Que la honte et l'horreur de vous avoir aimée
Laisseront à jamais sur ce front imprimée.
Oui, j'en rougis, ingrate, et mon propre courroux
Ne me peut pardonner ce que j'ai fait pour vous.
Je veux que la mémoire efface de ma vie　　　　　595
Le souvenir du temps que je vous ai servie :
J'étais mort pour ma gloire, et je n'ai pas vécu
Tant que ce lâche cœur s'est dit votre vaincu ;
Ce n'est que d'aujourd'hui qu'il vit et qu'il respire,
D'aujourd'hui qu'il renonce au joug de votre empire,　　600

585. **son pouvoir** : does this refer to *amour* in l. 578 ?

589. **brasier** : here met. for " flame " (of love) ; see l. 752, and *Lexique de Corneille*, I, p. 136 ; *braise* in same sense is frequent in Corneille. In the next line *rougeur* refers to the color of the metaphorical flame and also to the hue of shame. M. : " La rougeur de brasier qui consume son cœur : métaphore qu'on peut mettre à côté de celle du poignard du Pirame de Théophile :

> Le voilà ce poignard, qui du sang de son maître
> S'est souillé lâchement. Il en rougit, le traître."

600. **D'aujourd'hui** : *ce n'est que* of preceding line is understood.

Et qu'avec ma raison mes yeux et lui d'accord
Détestent votre vue à l'égard de la mort.

CASSANDRE

Pour vous en guérir, prince, et ne leur plus déplaire,
Je m'impose moi-même un exil volontaire,
Et je mettrai grand soin, sachant ces vérités,   605
A ne vous plus montrer ce que vous détestez.
Adieu.   (*Elle s'en va*)

SCÈNE III

LADISLAS, THÉODORE

LADISLAS, *interdit, la regardant sortir*

Que faites-vous, ô mes lâches pensées ?
Suivez-vous cette ingrate ? êtes-vous insensées ?
Mais plutôt qu'as-tu fait, mon aveugle courroux ?
Adorable inhumaine, hélas ! où fuyez-vous ?   610
Ma sœur, au nom d'Amour, et par pitié des larmes
Que ce cœur enchanté donne encore à ses charmes,
Si vous voulez d'un frère empêcher le trépas,
Suivez cette insensible et retenez ses pas.

THÉODORE

La retenir, mon frère, après l'avoir bannie !   615

LADISLAS

Ah ! contre ma raison servez sa tyrannie ;
Je veux désavouer ce cœur séditieux,

611. 1648 by a singular misprint has *Ma haine* instead of *Ma sœur*.
I have followed correction of Viollet-le-Duc, Ronchaud, and Hémon.

---

601. **lui** : refers to *cœur* of l. 598.
602. **à l'égard** : this is the text of the original edition, and apparently
was so written by Rotrou by a slip of the pen for *à l'égal*, "like, as"; it
is used again in l. 978.

La servir, l'adorer, et mourir à ses yeux.
Privé de son amour, je chérirai sa haine,
J'aimerai ses mépris, je bénirai ma peine :   620
Se plaindre des ennuis que causent ses appas,
C'est se plaindre d'un mal qu'on ne mérite pas.
Que je la voie au moins si je ne la possède ;
Mon mal chérit sa cause, et croît par son remède.
Quand mon cœur à ma voix a feint de consentir,   625
Il en était charmé, je l'en veux démentir ;
Je mourais, je brûlais, je l'adorais dans l'âme,
Et le Ciel a pour moi fait un sort tout de flamme.
      (*A part*)
Allez . . . Mais que fais-tu, stupide et lâche amant ?
                                        (*Elle va*)
Quel caprice t'aveugle ? as-tu du sentiment ?   630
Rentre, prince sans cœur, un moment en toi-même.
      (*A Théodore*)
Me laissez-vous, ma sœur, en ce désordre extrême ?

THÉODORE

J'allais la retenir.

LADISLAS

                    Hé ! ne voyez-vous pas
Quel arrogant mépris précipite ses pas ?
Avec combien d'orgueil elle s'est retirée,   635
Quelle implacable haine elle m'a déclarée, ·
Et que m'exposer plus aux foudres de ses yeux,
C'est dans sa frénésie armer un furieux ?

---

623. **si je ne la possède** : for omission of *pas* see *Saint Genest*, note
on l. 131. See also *Venceslas*, ll. 774, 911, and 968.

625–626. **Quand mon cœur à ma voix**, etc. : translate : "When my
heart pretended to be in harmony with my words (those uttered in
ll. 579–602), it was still under Cassandre's spell. I wish now to accuse
it of falsehood in acting as it did." I am not sure that I have translated
je l'en veux démentir correctly.

De mon esprit plutôt chassez cette cruelle ;
Condamnez les pensers qui me parleront d'elle ;   640
Peignez-moi sa conquête indigne de mon rang,
Et soutenez en moi l'honneur de votre sang.

THÉODORE

Je ne vous puis celer que le trait qui vous blesse
Dedans un sang royal trouve trop de faiblesse.
Je vois de quels efforts vos sens sont combattus,   645
Mais les difficultés sont le champ des vertus ;
Avec un peu de peine on achète la gloire.
Qui veut vaincre est déjà bien près de la victoire ;
Se faisant violence, on s'est bientôt dompté,
Et rien n'est tant à nous que notre volonté.   650

LADISLAS

Hélas ! il est aisé de juger de ma peine
Par l'effort qui d'un temps m'emporte et me ramène,
Et par ces mouvements si prompts et si puissants
Tantôt sur ma raison, et tantôt sur mes sens.
Mais quelque trouble enfin qu'ils vous fassent paraître, 655
Je vous croirai, ma sœur, et je serai mon maître :
Je lui laisserai libre et l'espoir et la foi
Que son sang lui défend d'élever jusqu'à moi ;
Lui souffrant le mépris du rang qu'elle rejette,
Je la perds pour maîtresse, et l'acquiers pour sujette :   660
Sur qui régnait sur moi j'ai des droits absolus,

641. **Peignez-moi sa conquête,** etc.: "pretend that it is beneath my rank to win her hand."

644. **Dedans** : see note on l. 569.

646–650. **Mais les difficultés,** etc.: for this sententious manner see *Saint Genest*, note on ll. 199–201.

652. **d'un temps** : usually *tout d'un temps*, "in a moment." The *Lexiques de Corneille*, etc., give only *tout d'un temps*.

660. **l'acquiers** : for omission of subject here and in ll. 662 and 929 see *Saint Genest*, note on l. 23.

Et la punis assez par son propre refus.
Ne renaissez donc plus, mes flammes étouffées,
Et du duc de Curlande augmentez les trophées.
Sa victoire m'honore, et m'ôte seulement   665
Un caprice obstiné d'aimer trop bassement.

THÉODORE

Quoi ! mon frère, le duc aurait dessein pour elle ?

LADISLAS

Ce mystère, ma sœur, n'est plus une nouvelle,
Et mille observateurs que j'ai commis exprès
Ont si bien vu leurs feux qu'ils ne sont plus secrets.   670

THÉODORE

Ha !

LADISLAS

          C'est de cet amour que procède ma haine,
Et non de sa faveur, quoique si souveraine
Que j'ai sujet de dire avec confusion
Que presque auprès de lui le roi n'a plus de nom.
Mais, puisque j'ai dessein d'oublier cette ingrate,   675
Il faut en le servant que mon mépris éclate,
Et, pour avec éclat en retirer ma foi,
Je vais de leur hymen solliciter le roi :

---

667. **le duc aurait dessein** : conditional of possibility, "can the duke
have designs on her ?" See Mätzner, *Syntax*, I, p. 113. M. : "On dit
avoir desseins sur quelqu'un, mais avoir dessein pour quelqu'un n'est
pas français."

669. **que j'ai commis exprès** : "whom I have expressly charged."
Commettre is used absolutely in legal parlance of charging an official
with a certain duty. See *Saint Genest*, note on l. 1257.

677. **Et, pour avec éclat en retirer ma foi** : M. : "Pour ne doit jamais
se séparer ainsi de son verbe."

678. **Je vais de leur hymen solliciter le roi** : M. : "On ne dit pas solliciter quelqu'un de quelque chose."

Je mettrai de ma main mon rival en ma place,
Et je verrai leur flamme avec autant de glace   680
Qu'en ma plus violente et plus sensible ardeur
Cet insensible objet eut pour moi de froideur.

(*Il s'en va*)

Scène IV

Théodore, *seule*

O raison égarée ! ô raison suspendue !
Jamais trouble pareil t'avait-il confondue ?
Sottes présomptions, grandeurs qui nous flattez,   685
Est-il rien de menteur comme vos vanités ?
Le duc aime Cassandre ! et j'étais assez vaine
Pour réputer mes yeux les auteurs de sa peine !
Et, bien plus, pour m'en plaindre et les en accuser,
Estimant sa conquête un heur à mépriser !   690
Le duc aime Cassandre ! Eh quoi ! tant d'apparences,
Tant de subjections, d'honneurs, de déférences,
D'ardeurs, d'attachements, de craintes, de tributs,
N'offraient-ils à mes lois qu'un cœur qu'il n'avait plus ?
Ces soupirs, dont cent fois la douce violence,   695
Sortant désavouée, a trahi son silence,
Ces regards par les miens tant de fois rencontrés,
Les devoirs, les respects, les soins qu'il m'a montrés,
Provenaient-ils d'un cœur qu'un autre objet engage ?
Sais-je si mal d'amour expliquer le langage ?   700

679. **Je mettrai de ma main**, etc. : a somewhat similar situation is in the *Cid*, where the Infante, from a different motive, it is true, encourages the marriage of Chimène and Rodrigue. Compare *Cid*, I. 2:

> Elle aime don Rodrigue et le tient de ma main,

and V. 4:

> Allons encore un coup le donner à Chimène.

681–682. **sensible** : the frequent use of this word by Rotrou has been mentioned in note to l. 234 of *Saint Genest*. See *Venceslas*, ll. 681, 757, 860, 1461, and 1857. For play upon words see Introduction, p. 72.

Fais-je d'un simple hommage une inclination?
Et formé-je un fantôme à ma présomption?
Mais, insensiblement renonçant à moi-même,
J'avoûrai ma défaite, et je croirai que j'aime.
Quand j'en serais capable, aimerais-je où je veux?   705
Aux raisons de l'État ne dois-je pas mes vœux?
Et ne sommes-nous pas d'innocentes victimes
Que le gouvernement immole à ses maximes?
Mes vœux, en un vassal honteusement bornés,
Laisseraient-ils pour lui des rivaux couronnés?   710
Mais ne me flatte point, orgueilleuse naissance:
L'Amour sait bien sans sceptre établir sa puissance,
Et, soumettant nos cœurs par de secrets appas,
Fait les égalités et ne les cherche pas.
Si le duc n'a le front chargé d'une couronne,   715
C'est lui qui les protège, et c'est lui qui les donne.
Par quelles actions se peut-on signaler
Que . . .

Scène V

Léonor,* Théodore

léonor

Madame, le duc demande à vous parler.

théodore

Qu'il entre. Mais, après ce que je viens d'apprendre,
Souffrir un libre accès à l'amant de Cassandre,   720

* 1648 adds, after *Léonor*, *suivante*.

---

704. avoûrai: see *Saint Genest*, note on l. 303.
706–716. **Aux raisons de l'État**, etc.: the same ideas are expressed in
the *stances* of the Infante, *Cid*, V. 2, beginning:

   T'écouterai-je encor, respect de ma naissance.

Agréer ses devoirs et le revoir encor,
Lâche, le dois-je faire? Attendez, Léonor.
Une douleur légère à l'instant survenue
Ne me peut aujourd'hui souffrir l'heur de sa vue :
Faites-lui mon excuse. O Ciel ! de quel poison   725
(Elle sort)

Sens-je inopinément attaquer ma raison?
Je voudrais à l'amour paraître inaccessible,
Et d'un indifférent la perte m'est sensible !
Je ne puis être sienne, et, sans dessein pour lui,
Je ne puis consentir ses desseins pour autrui.   730

Scène VI

Alexandre, Théodore, Léonor

alexandre

Comment ! du duc, ma sœur, refuser la visite !
D'où vous vient ce chagrin, et quel mal vous l'excite?

théodore

Un léger mal de cœur qui ne durera pas . . .

alexandre

Un avis de ma part portait ici ses pas.

théodore

Quel?

alexandre

Croyant que Cassandre était de la partie . . .   735

---

733. **mal de cœur**: translate : " indisposition " ; lit. " qualm." *Cœur*
means not merely " heart," but " breast " and region of the heart.

735. **était de la partie** : translate : " was here " ; lit. " was (one) of
the company."

THÉODORE

A peine deux moments ont suivi sa sortie.

ALEXANDRE

Et sachant à quel point ses charmes lui sont doux,
Je l'avais averti de se rendre chez vous,
Pour vous solliciter vers l'objet qu'il adore
D'un secours que je sais que Ladislas implore.   740
Vous connaissez le prince, et vous pouvez juger
Si sous d'honnêtes lois Amour le peut ranger :
Ses mauvais procédés ont trop dit ses pensées ;
On peut voir l'avenir dans les choses passées,
Et juger aisément qu'il tend à son honneur,   745
Sous ces offres d'hymen, un appât suborneur.
Mais, parlant pour le duc, si je vous sollicite
De la protection d'une ardeur illicite,
N'en accusez que moi ; demandez-moi raison
Ou de son insolence ou de sa trahison.   750
C'est moi, ma chère sœur, qui réponds à Cassandre

---

740. 1648 has *D'un secours que je sais Ladislas l'implore.* The misprint is corrected as in text by Viollet-le-Duc, Ronchaud, and Hémon.

746. 1648 has *Sous ces appas d'hymen*, corrected by Viollet-le-Duc,
du Ronchaud, and Hémon as in text.

---

742. **Si sous d'honnêtes lois Amour le peut ranger :** "whether love can
subject him to the laws of virtue."

746. **un appât suborneur :** "a seductive allurement." See notes on
ll. 405, 414.

748. **De la protection d'une ardeur illicite :** "protection against an unlawful love," i.e. Ladislas's for Cassandre. M.: "Illicite n'est plus que
du style didactique en morale."

751-752. **C'est moi, ma chère sœur,** etc.: translate: "It is I, my dear
sister, who am responsible to Cassandre for an affection which will never
die." It is strange that Rotrou has employed the same figure, "brasier,"
twice in the same act ; see l. 589. Alexandre's reference to the duke's
love is of course ambiguous and he really means his own. For the
affected style of this passage see Introduction, p. 69. M.: "Mauvaise
métaphore en usage autrefois, dont on a senti le ridicule."

D'un brasier dont jamais on ne verra la cendre,
Et du plus pur amour de qui jamais mortel
Dans le temple d'hymen ait encensé l'autel.
Servez contre une impure une ardeur si parfaite.   755

> THÉODORE, *se retirant, appuyée sur Léonor*

Mon mal s'accroît, mon frère ; agréez ma retraite.

> ALEXANDRE, *seul*

O sensible contrainte ! ô rigoureux ennui
D'être obligé d'aimer dessous le nom d'autrui !
Outre que je pratique une âme prévenue,
Quel fruit peut tirer d'elle une flamme inconnue?   760
Et que puis-je espérer sous ce respect fatal
Qui cache le malade en découvrant le mal?
Mais, quoi que sur mes vœux mon frère ose entreprendre,
J'ai tort de craindre rien sous la foi de Cassandre,
Et certain du secours et d'un cœur et d'un bras   765
Qui pour la conserver ne s'épargneraient pas.

---

766. 1648 has *en ne l'épargneraient pas*, and is followed by Ronchaud; Viollet-le-Duc and Hémon have corrected to *s'épargneraient*,
which is undoubtedly the true reading.

---

756. agréez ma retraite : " permit me to withdraw."

757. sensible : " painful "; see note on l. 681. — **ennui :** this word, in
the seventeenth century, had the meaning of "grief, sorrow," which
later became weakened into that of "annoyance," etc. See ll. 1596,
1706; and *Lexiques de Malherbe*, p. 221 ; *de Corneille*, I, p. 368 ; and
de Racine, p. 186.

759. Outre que je pratique, etc.: " Besides employing a prejudiced
mind " (his sister's), i.e. endeavoring to win his sister's influence ostensibly for the duke. M.: " Pratiquer une âme, n'est pas français."

761. ce respect fatal : i.e. the respect he had shown Cassandre in
concealing his love.

764-765. J'ai tort de craindre rien sous la foi, etc. : " I am wrong to
fear anything on the faith of Cassandre, and while I am certain of the
help of a heart and arm " (his own, or the duke's as his friend), etc.
M. : " On dit bien, sous la garde, mais on ne dit pas, sous la foi."

ACTE TROISIÈME

Scène I

Féderic *

Que m'avez-vous produit, indiscrètes pensées,
Téméraires désirs, passions insensées,
Efforts d'un cœur mortel pour d'immortels appas,
Qu'on a d'un vol si haut précipités si bas? 770
Espoirs qui jusqu'au ciel souleviez de la terre,
Deviez-vous pas savoir que jamais le tonnerre,
Qui dessus votre orgueil enfin vient d'éclater,
Ne pardonne aux desseins que vous osiez tenter?
Quelque profond respect qu'ait eu votre poursuite, 775
Vous voyez qu'un refus vous ordonne la fuite.
Évitez les combats que vous vous préparez ;
Jugez-en le péril, et vous en retirez.
Qu'ai-je droit d'espérer, si l'ardeur qui me presse
Irrite également le prince et la princesse ; 780
Si, voulant hasarder ou ma bouche ou mes yeux,

* 1648 has *Le Duc de Cueilland* [sic], *favori.*

---

769. **mortel pour d'immortels,** etc. : see notes on ll. 681, 786. M. :
" Vieille antithèse, que le goût a proscrite." For play upon words see
note on ll. 681–682.

771. **souleviez** : for *vous souleviez.* See note to l. 204.

772. **Deviez-vous pas** : for omission of *ne* see *Saint Genest*, note on
l. 77.

774. **Ne pardonne** : for omission of *pas* see note on l. 623.

779. **l'ardeur qui me presse** : "the love which constrains me." One
of the many conventional expressions in French seventeenth-century
tragedy. It is not registered in Kinne's *Formulas*; see ll. 831, 1099.

Je fais l'une malade et l'autre furieux?
Apprenons l'art, mon cœur, d'aimer sans espérance,
Et souffrir des mépris avecque révérence ;
Résolvons-nous sans honte aux belles lâchetés   785
Que ne rebutent pas des devoirs rebutés ;
Portons sans intérêt un joug si légitime ;
N'en osant être amant, soyons-en la victime.
Exposons un esclave à toutes les rigueurs
Que peuvent exercer de superbes vainqueurs.   790

SCÈNE II

ALEXANDRE, FÉDERIC

ALEXANDRE

Duc, un trop long respect me tait votre pensée ;
Notre amitié s'en plaint et s'en trouve offensée ;
Elle vous est suspecte, ou vous la violez,
Et vous me dérobez ce que vous me celez.
Qui donne toute une âme en veut aussi d'entières,   795
Et, quand vos intérêts m'ont fourni des matières,
Pour les bien embrasser, ce cœur vraiment ami
Ne s'est point contenté de s'ouvrir à demi,

785–786. **belles lâchetés,** etc.: translate : " noble faint-heartedness that
is not offended by attentions that have been spurned."

786. **Que ne rebutent pas des devoirs rebutés** : M.: " Cette façon de
faire jouer un mot avec lui-même, passait autrefois pour une élégance
de style ; un goût plus sévère l'a bannie du langage sérieux." See note
on ll. 681–682.

787. **sans intérêt** : " unselfishly," i.e. without hope of reward.

789. **un esclave** : himself.

794. **Et vous me dérobez,** etc. : " and you keep back from me what
you are hiding from me." *Dérober* is a synonym of *celer*.

795. **d'entières** : repeats the idea of *toute*, *âmes* being understood.

796. **fourni des matières** : " provided occasions." See *Lexique de
Corneille*, II, p. 74.

Et j'ai, d'une chaleur généreuse et sincère,
Fait pour vous tout l'effort que l'amitié peut faire.   800
Cependant vous semblez, encor mal assuré,
Mettre en doute un serment si saintement juré;
Je lis sur votre front des passions secrètes,
Des sentiments cachés, des atteintes muettes,
Et, d'un œil qui vous plaint, et toutefois jaloux,   805
Vois que vous réservez un secret tout à vous.

FÉDERIC

Quand j'ai cru mes ennuis capables de remède,
Je vous en ai fait part, j'ai réclamé votre aide,
Et j'en ai vu l'effet si bouillant et si prompt
Que le seul souvenir m'en charme et me confond.   810
Mais, quand je crois mon mal de secours incapable,
Sans vous le partager il suffit qu'il m'accable,
Et c'est assez et trop qu'il fasse un malheureux,
Sans passer jusqu'à vous, et sans en faire deux.

ALEXANDRE

L'ami qui souffre seul fait une injure à l'autre;   815
Ma part de votre ennui diminûra la vôtre.
Parlez, duc, et sans peine ouvrez-moi vos secrets:
Hors de votre parti je n'ai plus d'intérêts;
J'ai su que votre grande et dernière journée
Par la main de l'amour veut être couronnée,   820

804. des atteintes muettes : this is simply a repetition of *Des senti-ments cachés*, "feelings not spoken of." For another meaning of *atteinte* see note on l. 860.

806. Vois : for omission of subject of verb see *Saint Genest*, note on l. 23.

816. diminûra : for *diminuera*; see *Saint Genest*, note on l. 303, and *Venceslas*, notes on ll. 704, 973, 1447.

819. journée : "battle." Hatzfeld et Darmesteter, *Dict. gén.* : "Ce qui s'est passé de remarquable dans une journée, spécialement un fait d'armes." *Lexique de Malherbe*, p. 346, " D'Ivri la fatale journée," and *Lexique de Corneille*, II, p. 37.

Et que, voulant au roi, qui vous en doit le prix,
Déclarer la beauté qui charme vos esprits,
D'un frère impétueux l'ordinaire insolence
Vous a fermé la bouche et contraint au silence.
Souffrez, sans expliquer l'intérêt qu'il y prend,   825.
Que j'en aille pour vous vider le différend,
Et ne m'en faites point craindre les conséquences :
Il faut qu'enfin quelqu'un réprime ses licences,
Et, le roi ne pouvant nous en faire raison,
Je me trouve et le cœur et le bras assez bon.   830
Mais, m'offrant à servir les ardeurs qui vous pressent,
Que j'apprenne du moins à qui vos vœux s'adressent.

FÉDERIC

J'ai vu de vos bontés des effets assez grands
Sans vous faire avec lui de nouveaux différends ;
Sans irriter sa haine, elle est assez aigrie ;   835
Il est prince, Seigneur, respectons sa furie :
A ma mauvaise étoile imputons mon ennui,
Et croyons-en le sort plus coupable que lui.
Laissez à mon amour taire un nom qui l'offense,
J'ai des respects, encor plus forts que sa défense   840
Et qui plus qu'aucun autre ont droit de me lier,
Tout précieux qu'il m'est, m'ordonnent d'oublier :
Laissez-moi retirer d'un champ d'où ma retraite
Peut seule à l'ennemi dérober ma défaite.

ALEXANDRE

Ce silence obstiné m'apprend votre secret,   845
Mais il tombe en un sein généreux et discret.

824. **contraint**: for omission of auxiliary see *Saint Genest*, note on
l. 175.
826. **différend**: see note on l. 298. See also note on l. 834.
831. **les ardeurs qui vous pressent**: see note on l. 779.
832. **à qui vos vœux s'adressent**: "to whom your love is directed";
for *vœux* see *Saint Genest*, note on l. 149.

Ne me le celez plus, duc, vous aimez Cassandre :
C'est le plus digne objet où vous puissiez prétendre,
Et celui dont le prince, adorant son pouvoir,
A le plus d'intérêt d'éloigner votre espoir.   850
Traitant l'amour pour moi, votre propre franchise
A donné dans ses rets et s'y trouve surprise ;
Et mes desseins pour elle, aux vôtres préférés,
Sont ces puissants respects à qui vous déférez.
Mais vous craignez à tort qu'un ami vous accuse   855
D'un crime dont Cassandre est la cause et l'excuse :
Quelque auguste ascendant qu'aient sur moi ses appas . . .

FÉDERIC

Ne vous étonnez point si je ne réponds pas.
Ce discours me surprend, et cette indigne plainte
Me livre une si rude et si sensible atteinte   860
Qu'égaré je me cherche et demeure en suspens
Si c'est vous qui parlez, ou moi qui vous entends.
Moi, vous trahir, Seigneur ! moi, sur cette Cassandre
Près de qui je vous sers, pour moi-même entreprendre,
Sur un amour si stable et si bien affermi !   865
Vous me croyez bien lâche, ou bien peu votre ami.

---

862. 1648 has *moi qui vous attends*, a misprint corrected by Viollet-le-Duc, Ronchaud, and Hémon.

---

851. **Traitant l'amour pour moi** : "managing my love affair." The duke acted as intermediary between Cassandre and Alexandre, and to screen the latter pretended to be Cassandre's lover. See ll. 864, 886–891.

857. **Quelque auguste ascendant** : see note on l. 110. M. : "Un ascendant est fort, il est fier, il est redoutable ; mais un ascendant n'est pas auguste."

860. **sensible atteinte** : "painful shock"; see notes on ll. 681, 804.

861. **égaré je me cherche** : translate : "I strive to find my way."

863–864. **sur cette Cassandre**, etc. : "I have designs for myself on this Cassandre," etc.

ALEXANDRE

Croiriez-vous, l'adorant, m'altérer votre estime?

FÉDERIC

Me pourriez-vous aimer coupable de ce crime?

ALEXANDRE

Confident ou rival, je ne vous puis haïr.

FÉDERIC

Sincère et généreux, je ne vous puis trahir. 870

ALEXANDRE

L'amour surprend les cœurs, et s'en rend bientôt maître.

FÉDERIC

La surprise ne peut justifier un traître ;
Et tout homme de cœur, pouvant perdre le jour,
A le remède en main des surprises d'amour.

ALEXANDRE

Pardonnez un soupçon, non pas une créance, 875
Qui naissait du défaut de votre confiance.

FÉDERIC

Je veux bien l'oublier, mais à condition
Que ce même défaut soit sa punition,

---

867. **Croiriez-vous, l'adorant, m'altérer votre estime**: "would you think, if you loved her, to change my opinion of you?" For this use of the present participle (gerund) instead of a conditional or relative clause see Haase, 95 ; *Lexique de Molière*, I, p. cxxxviii ; and l. 1816. M. : "M'altérer pour altérer en moi, n'est pas français. Votre estime, ne dit plus l'estime que j'ai pour vous."

874. **A le remède en main**, etc.: i.e. can commit suicide; see *Saint Genest*, note on ll. 81–84.

Et qu'il me soit permis une fois de me taire
Sans que votre amitié s'en plaigne ou s'en altère.   880
Au reste, et cet avis, s'ils vous étaient suspects,
Vous peut justifier mes soins et mes respects,
Cassandre par le prince est si persécutée,
Et d'agents si puissants pour lui sollicitée,
Que, si vous lui voulez sauver sa liberté,   885
Il n'est plus temps d'aimer sous un nom emprunté :
Assez et trop longtemps, sous ma feinte poursuite,
J'ai de votre dessein ménagé la conduite ;
Et vos vœux, sous couleur de servir mon amour,
Ont assez ébloui tous les yeux de la cour.   890
De l'artifice enfin il faut bannir l'usage ;
Il faut lever le masque et montrer le visage :
Vous devez de Cassandre établir le repos,
Qu'un rival persécute et trouble à tout propos.
Son amour en sa foi vous a donné des gages ;   895
Il est temps que l'hymen règle vos avantages,
Et, faisant l'un heureux, en laisse un mécontent.
L'avis vient de sa part, il vous est important.
Je vous tais cent raisons qu'elle m'a fait entendre,
Arrivant chez l'infante, où je viens de la rendre,   900

881. Viollet-le-Duc has *s'il vous était suspect*, and in next line has *mon respect*. This is probably the correct reading, but I have followed in the text the form of 1648.

---

879. Et qu'il me soit permis une fois de me taire : this reticence of the duke and the way in which he is several times prevented by Ladislas from revealing to the king the object of his love seem unnatural and forced. See l. 1108.

886. Il n'est plus temps d'aimer sous un nom emprunté : i.e. the duke's.

889. sous couleur : M. : "Façon de parler qui n'est plus en usage, et qui nous manque."

892. Il faut lever le masque : see l. 180.

896. vos avantages : i.e. over his brother.

898. de sa part : "from her," i.e. Cassandre.

900. où je viens de la rendre : " whither I have just conducted her."

Qui, hautement du prince embrassant le parti,
La mande, s'il est vrai ce qu'elle a pressenti,
Pour d'un nouvel effort en faveur de sa peine
Mettre encore une fois son esprit à la gêne.
Gardez-vous de l'humeur d'un sexe ambitieux :   905
L'espérance d'un sceptre est brillante à ses yeux,
Et de ce soin enfin un hymen vous libère.

ALEXANDRE

Mais me libère-t-il du pouvoir de mon père,
Qui peut . . .

FÉDERIC

Si votre amour défère à son pouvoir,
Et si vous vous réglez par la loi du devoir,   910
Ne précipitez rien, qu'il ne vous soit funeste.
Mais vous souffrez bien peu d'un transport si modeste,
Et l'ardent procédé d'un frère impétueux
Marque bien plus d'amour qu'un si respectueux.

901. **Qui, hautement du prince embrassant le parti**: "who, openly espousing the cause of the prince." M. : "Rien de plus pénible et de plus forcé que la construction de toute cette phrase."

902. **La mande, s'il est vrai,** etc. : "summons her, if her presentiment (Cassandre's) be true," etc.

903. **en faveur de sa peine** : "in favor of his love." *Peine*, conventional gallant expression for "love"; lit. "the trouble caused by his unrequited love."

904. **Mettre encore une fois son esprit à la gêne** : "to constrain her mind once more." Originally *gêne* was used of torture (lit. "to suffer the pains of hell"; Heb., *Gehenna*). *Mettre à la gêne*, "to torment, to rack"; then "to make uncomfortable, to rack one's brains" (in the reflexive). Compare l. 936. See *Lexique de Corneille*, I, p. 460. Molière employs later signification.

911. **Ne précipitez rien, qu'il ne vous soit funeste**: "do not be rash, so that it (your father's power ?) may not be fatal to you." For omission of *pas* in second clause see *Saint Genest*, note on l. 131, and *Venceslas*, ll. 623, 774, 911, and 968.

914. **qu'un si respectueux**: *procédé* is understood. M. : "Un n'est plus reçu comme pronom, s'il n'est précédé de l'article."

ALEXANDRE

Non, non, je laisse à part les droits de la nature,   915
Et commets à l'Amour toute mon aventure :
Puisqu'il fait mon destin, qu'il règle mon devoir ;
Je prends loi de Cassandre ; épousons dès ce soir.
Mais, duc, gardons encor d'éventer nos pratiques ;
Trompons pour quelques jours jusqu'à ses domestiques,   920
Et, hors de ses plus chers, dont le zèle est pour nous,
Aveuglons leur créance et passez pour l'époux ;
Puis, l'hymen accompli sous un heureux auspice,
Que le temps parle après et fasse son office,
Il n'excitera plus qu'un impuissant courroux   925
Ou d'un père surpris, ou d'un frère jaloux.

FÉDERIC

Quoique visiblement mon crédit se hasarde,
Je veux bien l'exposer pour ce qui vous regarde,
Et, plus vôtre que mien, ne puis avec raison
Avoir donné mon cœur et refuser mon nom ;   930
Le vôtre . . .

SCÈNE III

CASSANDRE, ALEXANDRE, FÉDERIC

CASSANDRE, *en colère de chez l'infante*

Eh bien, Madame, il faudra se résoudre
A voir sur notre sort tomber ce coup de foudre.

918. **épousons** : used either absolutely for reflexive or with omission of
reflexive pronoun ; see note on l. 204 ; see also ll. 771 and 1033.

919. **gardons encore d'éventer nos pratiques** : "let us take care to conceal yet our proceedings." M. : "Eventer n'est plus que du style
familier."

922. **Aveuglons leur créance et passez pour l'époux** : notice the change
of person ; "let us deceive their belief and do you pass for the husband."

927. **crédit** : "reputation."

929. **puis** : for omission of subject see note on l. 660.

931. **Eh bien, Madame**, etc. : these words are spoken to the princess,
who is not visible.

Un fruit de votre avis, s'il nous jette si bas,
Est que la chute au moins ne nous surprendra pas.
    (*Avisant l'infant*)
Ha ! Seigneur, mettez fin à ma triste aventure.   935
Mettra-t-on tous les jours mon âme à la torture?
Souffrirai-je longtemps un si cruel tourment?
Et ne vous puis-je, enfin, aimer impunément?

ALEXANDRE

Quel outrage, Madame, émeut votre colère?

CASSANDRE

La faveur d'une sœur pour l'intérêt d'un frère :   940
Son tyrannique effort veut éblouir mes vœux
Par le lustre d'un joug éclatant et pompeux.
On prétend m'aveugler avec un diadème,
Et l'on veut malgré moi que je règne et que j'aime :
C'est l'ordre qu'on m'impose, ou le prince irrité,   945
Abandonnant sa haine à son autorité,
Doit laisser aux neveux le plus tragique exemple
Et d'un mépris vengé la marque la plus ample
Dont le sort ait jamais son pouvoir signalé,
Et dont jusques ici les siècles aient parlé.   950
Voilà les compliments que l'amour leur suscite,
Et les tendres motifs dont on me sollicite.

ALEXANDRE

Rendez, rendez le calme à ces charmants appas ;
Laissez gronder le foudre : il ne tombera pas,

936. **Mettra-t-on tous les jours**, etc. : cf. l. 904.

947. **neveux** : "posterity" ; see *Saint Genest*, note on l. 311. M. :
"On dit à nos neveux."

950. **jusques** : for *jusque* ; see *Saint Genest*, note on l. 731.

951. **leur** : refers to *sœur* and *frère* in l. 940.

954. **Laissez gronder le foudre** : M. : "Foudre n'a conservé les deux
genres que dans la main de Jupiter ; on dit que ce dieu est armé du
foudre ou de la foudre ; mais dans tout autre cas le féminin a prévalu."

Ou l'artisan des maux que le sort vous destine　　　　955
Tombera le premier dessous votre ruine.
Fondez votre repos en me faisant heureux ;
Coupons dès cette nuit tout accès à ses vœux,
Et voyez sans frayeur quoi qu'il ose entreprendre,
Quand vous m'aurez commis une femme à défendre,　　960
Et quand ouvertement, en qualité d'époux,
Mon devoir m'enjoindra de répondre de vous.

FÉDERIC

Prévenez dès ce soir l'ardeur qui le transporte :
Aux desseins importants la diligence importe.
L'ordre seul de l'affaire est à considérer ;　　　　965
Mais tirons-nous d'ici pour en délibérer.

CASSANDRE

Quel trouble, quelle alarme, et quels soins me possèdent !

SCÈNE IV

LADISLAS, ALEXANDRE, CASSANDRE, FÉDERIC

LADISLAS

Madame, il ne se peut que mes vœux ne succèdent ;
J'aurais tort d'en douter, et de redouter rien
Avec deux confidents qui me servent si bien,　　　　970
Et dont l'affection part du profond de l'âme :
Ils vous parlaient sans doute en faveur de ma flamme ?

---

958. **ses vœux** : i.e. Ladislas's.

966. **Mais tirons-nous d'ici** : M. : "Dans ce sens-là on dit, retirons-nous d'ici."

968. **il ne se peut que mes vœux ne succèdent** : for omission of *pas* in the second negation see note on l. 623.

CASSANDRE

Vous les désavoûriez de m'en entretenir,
Puisque je suis si mal en votre souvenir
Qu'il veut même effacer du cours de votre vie   975
La mémoire du temps que vous m'avez servie,
Et qu'avec lui vos yeux et votre cœur d'accord
Détestent ma présence à l'égard de la mort.

LADISLAS

Vous en faites la vaine, et tenez ces paroles
Pour des propos en l'air et des contes frivoles :   980
L'amour me les dictait, et j'étais transporté,
S'il s'en faut rapporter à votre vanité :
Mais, si j'en suis bon juge, et si je m'en dois croire,
Je vois peu de matière à tant de vaine gloire ;
Je ne vois point en vous d'appas si surprenants   985
Qu'ils vous doivent donner des titres éminents ;
Rien ne relève tant l'éclat de ce visage,
Ou vous n'en mettez pas tous les traits en usage.

973. **Vous les désavoûriez de m'en entretenir:** "You would disown them if they did speak to me of it." For *désavoûriez* see note on l. 816.

975. **Qu'il veut même effacer du cours de votre vie:** M.: "Il n'y a pas d'exemple d'une inadvertance pareille : c'est le souvenir qui veut effacer du cours de la vie du prince la mémoire du temps qu'il a servi Cassandre."

978. **à l'égard de la mort:** see note on l. 602.

979. **Vous en faites la vaine,** etc.: "You are proud of it (l. 976), but consider those words (which I addressed to you when I played the lover) as idle words and trifling tales." *Tenez* may be present indicative with subject pronoun omitted, but in that case the meaning is not clear. Cassandre did not think Ladislas's words idle and trifling, as ll. 981–982 show: "if your vanity can be trusted, love dictated them to me and I was carried away by passion." *Faire la vaine* is to play the part of a vainglorious person. See *Lexique de Molière*, II, p. 589.

987. **Rien ne relève tant,** etc.: "nothing enhances so greatly the brilliancy of this countenance, or else you do not employ (call into service) all its features."

Vos yeux, ces beaux charmeurs, avec tous leurs appas,
Ne sont point accusés de tant d'assassinats ;   990
Le joug que vous croyez tomber sur tant de têtes
Ne porte point si loin le bruit de vos conquêtes :
Hors un seul, dont le cœur se donne à trop bon prix,
Votre empire s'étend sur peu d'autres esprits.
Pour moi, qui suis facile et qui bientôt me blesse,   995
Votre beauté m'a plu, j'avoûrai ma faiblesse,
Et m'a coûté des soins, des devoirs et des pas ;
Mais du dessein, je crois que vous n'en doutez pas.
Vous avez eu raison de ne vous pas promettre
Un hymen que mon rang ne me pouvait permettre.   1000
L'intérêt de l'État, qui doit régler mon sort,
Avecque mon amour n'en était pas d'accord :
Avec tous mes efforts j'ai manqué de fortune ;
Vous m'avez résisté, la gloire en est commune :

990. **Ne sont point accusés de tant d'assassinats** : this conventional gallantry is later ridiculed by Molière in the *Précieuses Ridicules*, scene 9 :

MASCARILLE. Mais au moins y a-t-il sûreté ici pour moi ?
CATHOS. Que craignez-vous ?
MASCARILLE. Quelque vol de mon cœur, quelque assassinat de ma franchise.

M. : " Hyperbole ironique, plus ridicule encore."

993. **Hors un seul** : Féderic, whom Ladislas supposes to be Cassandre's suitor.

995. **facile** : " susceptible."

997. **des soins, des devoirs et des pas** : various grades of a lover's attentions. *Pas* in this sense is defined by Littré : " allées et venues, peines qu'on prend pour quelque affaire"; and he cites a line from Lachaussée's *Mélanide*, II. 3, where two of the above words are used :

Je vous promets du moins,
Que je n'épargnerai ni mes pas ni mes soins.

See *Lexiques de Racine*, p. 372, and *de Molière*, II, p. 250.

998. **Mais du dessein** : i.e. his real object in wooing her. M. : " Une si grossière insolence, dite en face à une femme, ne serait pas même soufferte dans la comédie la plus licencieuse."

1003. **j'ai manqué de fortune** : " I have been unfortunate."

1004. **la gloire en est commune** : " the glory of having resisted me is an ordinary glory."

Si contre vos refus j'eusse cru mon pouvoir,   1005
Un facile succès eût suivi mon espoir :
Dérobant ma conquête, elle m'était certaine ;
Mais je n'ai pas trouvé qu'elle en valût la peine,
Et bien moins de vous mettre au rang où je prétends,
Et de vous partager le sceptre que j'attends.   1010
Voilà toute l'amour que vous m'avez causée :
Si vous en croyez plus, soyez désabusée.
Votre mépris, enfin, m'en produit un commun ;
Je n'ai plus résolu de vous être importun ;
J'ai perdu le désir avecque l'espérance,   1015
Et, pour vous témoigner de quelle indifférence
J'abandonne un plaisir que j'ai tant poursuivi,
Je veux rendre un service à qui m'a desservi.
Je ne vous retiens plus ; conduisez-la, mon frère ;
Et vous, duc, demeurez.

CASSANDRE, donnant la main à Alexandre

         Oh ! la noble colère !   1020
Conservez-moi longtemps ce généreux mépris,
Et que bientôt, Seigneur, un trône en soit le prix !

[Elle sort avec Alexandre]

1005. **Si contre vos refus j'eusse cru mon pouvoir** : "if in spite of
your refusals I had trusted my power." M. : "Ce vers et les suivants
présentent une idée infâme et révoltante."

1007. **Dérobant ma conquête** : "if I had carried off (abducted) the
object of my love." For *conquête* in sense of object of love see *Lexique
de Racine*, p. 105.

1009. **rang où je prétends** : "rank to which I aspire," i.e. the throne.

1010. **Et de vous partager le sceptre** : M. : "Vous partager, pour dire
partager avec vous, n'est pas français."

1013. **Votre mépris, enfin, m'en produit un commun** : " Your scorn, at
last, has inspired me with a scorn common (to us both)," i.e. a like
scorn. M. : "Un commun ne dit point un pareil ; m'en produit ne
dit pas m'en inspire ; tout cela est très-mal écrit."

Scène V

Ladislas, Féderic

ladislas, *bas*

Dieux ! avec quel effort et quelle peine extrême
Je consens ce départ qui m'arrache à moi-même,
Et qu'un rude combat m'affranchit de sa loi !   1025
Duc, j'allais pour vous voir, et de la part du roi.

féderic

Quelque loi qu'il m'impose, elle me sera chère.

ladislas

Vous savez s'il vous aime et s'il vous considère :
Il vous fait droit aussi quand il vous agrandit,
Et sur votre vertu fonde votre crédit.   1030
Cette même vertu, condamnant mon caprice,
Veut qu'en votre faveur je souffre sa justice,
Et le laisse acquitter à vos derniers exploits
Du prix que sa parole a mis à votre choix.
Usez donc pour ce choix du pouvoir qu'il vous donne ;   1035
Venez choisir vos fers, qui sont votre couronne ;

1024. **Je consens ce départ:** *consentir* as a transitive verb is antiquated; see *Lexiques de Corneille*, I, p. 208, and *de Molière*, I, p. 226.
Same use in l. 1793.

1025. **Et qu'un rude combat :** "and how hard a struggle."

1029. **Il vous fait droit:** "he does you justice."

1033–1034. **Et le laisse acquitter à vos derniers exploits**, etc.: "and allow
him for your last deeds to pay the reward which his promise has left
in your choice." For omission of the reflexive pronoun see note on
l. 771. M.: "On ne dit pas s'acquitter à."

1036. **Venez choisir vos fers**, etc.: "come choose the object of your
inthrallment which is your recompense." *Vos fers* in the conventional
gallantry of the seventeenth century is the one whose fetters the lover
wears. M.: "Des fers qui sont une couronne. Expression romanesque,
image ridicule."

Déclarez-lui l'objet que vous considérez,
Je ne vous défends plus l'heur où vous aspirez,
Et de votre valeur verrai la récompense,
Comme sans intérêt, aussi sans répugnance.   1040

FÉDERIC

Mon espoir, avoué par ma témérité,
Du succès de mes vœux autrefois m'a flatté ;
Mais, depuis mon malheur d'être en votre disgrâce,
Un visible mépris a détruit cette audace ;
Et qui se voit des yeux le commerce interdit   1045
Est bien vain s'il espère et vante son crédit.

LADISLAS

Loin de vous desservir et vous être contraire,
Je vais de votre hymen solliciter mon père.
J'ai déjà sa parole, et, s'il en est besoin,
Près de cette beauté vous offre encor mon soin.   1050

FÉDERIC

En vain je l'obtiendrai de son pouvoir suprême,
Si je ne puis encor l'obtenir d'elle-même.

1037. l'objet que vous considérez : " the object (of your love) which you have in view."

1039. verrai : omission of subject as frequently ; see *Saint Genest*, note on l. 23.

1043. Mais, depuis mon malheur d'être en votre disgrâce : " but since I have had the misfortune to incur your disfavor."

1045–1046. Et qui se voit des yeux le commerce interdit, etc.: translate : " and he who sees the interchange of glances forbidden in vain hopes and boasts his influence." *Commerce des yeux* is conventional gallantry of the seventeenth century, similar to the *précieux* language ridiculed by Molière.

1050. vous offre : for omission of subject see above, l. 1039.

1051. de son pouvoir suprême : M. : " Son est relatif au terme le plus éloigné ; mauvaise construction de phrase."

LADISLAS

Je crois que les moyens vous en seront aisés.

FÉDERIC

Vos soins en ma faveur les ont mal disposés.

LADISLAS

Avec votre vertu ma faveur était vaine.   1055

FÉDERIC

Mes efforts étaient vains avecque votre haine.

LADISLAS

Mes intérêts cessés relèvent votre espoir.

FÉDERIC

Mes vœux humiliés révèrent mon devoir ;
Et l'âme qu'une fois on a persuadée
A trop d'attachement à sa première idée   1060
Pour reprendre sitôt l'estime ou le mépris,
Et guérir aisément d'un dégoût qu'elle a pris.

Scène VI

VENCESLAS, LADISLAS, FÉDERIC, GARDES

VENCESLAS, à *Féderic*

Venez, heureux appui que le Ciel me suscite,
Dégager ma promesse envers votre mérite.
D'un cœur si généreux ayant servi l'État,   1065

1053. **Je crois que les moyens vous en seront aisés**: "I believe that the means of obtaining her will be easy for you"; *en* = *l'obtenir*.

1057. **Mes intérêts cessés relèvent votre espoir**: "The cessation of my interest improves your hopes," or "The abandonment of my interests." The fact that he has ostensibly given up Cassandre improves Féderic's chance of obtaining her hand.

Vous desservez son prince en le laissant ingrat :
J'engageai mon honneur engageant ma parole ;
Le prix qu'on vous retient est un bien qu'on vous vole :
Ne me le laissez plus, puisque je vous le dois,
Et déclarez l'objet dont vous avez fait choix ;   1070
En votre récompense éprouvez ma justice ;
Du prince la raison a guéri le caprice ;
Il prend vos intérêts, votre heur lui sera doux,
Et qui vous desservait parle à présent pour vous.

LADISLAS, *bas*

Contre moi mon rival obtient mon assistance !   1075
A quelle épreuve, ô Ciel, réduis-tu ma constance !

FÉDERIC

Le prix est si conjoint à l'heur de vous servir
Que c'est une faveur qu'on ne me peut ravir.
Ne faites point, Seigneur, par l'offre du salaire,
D'une action de gloire une œuvre mercenaire.   1080
Pouvoir dire : « Ce bras a servi Venceslas »,
N'est-ce pas un loyer digne de cent combats ?

VENCESLAS

Non, non, quoi que je doive à ce bras indomptable,
C'est trop que votre roi soit votre redevable.
Ce grand cœur, refusant, intéresse le mien,   1085
Et me demande trop en ne demandant rien.

1072. **Du prince** : limited by *le caprice*.

1077. **Le prix est si conjoint,** etc. : M. : "Conjoint pour attaché n'est plus en usage, même dans le style familier. On ne l'emploie qu'en terme de pratique, et au pluriel, pour dire, les époux conjoints, homme et femme : les futurs conjoints."

1084. **soit votre redevable** : "should be your debtor." For *redevable* as substantive see *Lexiques de Malherbe*, p. 544, and *de Corneille*, II, p. 276. For sentiment cf. l. 339 and *Saint Genest*, ll. 119–124.

Faisons par vos travaux et ma reconnaissance
Du maître et du sujet discerner la puissance :
Mon renom ne vous peut souffrir, sans se souiller,
La générosité qui m'en veut dépouiller.   1090

FÉDERIC

N'attisez point un feu que vous voudrez éteindre.
J'aime en un lieu, Seigneur, où je ne puis atteindre :
Je m'en connais indigne, et l'objet que je sers,
Dédaignant son tribut, désavoûrait mes fers.

VENCESLAS

Les plus puissants États n'ont point de souveraines   1095
Dont ce bras ne mérite et n'honorât les chaînes ;
Et mon pouvoir, enfin, ou sera sans effet,
Ou vous répond du don que je vous aurai fait.

LADISLAS, *bas*

Quoi ! l'hymen qu'on dénie à l'ardeur qui me presse
Au lit de mon rival va mettre ma maîtresse !   1100

FÉDERIC

Ma défense à vos lois n'ose plus repartir.

1089. **Mon renom** : M. : " Renom a vieilli ; on dit renommée."

1094. **Dédaignant son tribut** : M. : " Son tribut est pris là pour le tribut que l'on reçoit ; et il doit signifier le tribut que l'on paie."

1096. **chaînes** : like *fers* in l. 1036.

1099. **l'ardeur qui me presse** : see note on l. 779.

1100. **Au lit de mon rival**, etc : "is going to unite my rival and the object of my love."

1101. **Ma défense** : i.e. his refusal to name the object of his love. — **repartir** : "oppose." For this unusual meaning of *repartir* see *Lexique de Molière*, II, p. 402, where the following examples are given : *Tartuffe*, 136, wrong citation ; *Femmes Savantes*, 306, where *repartir* is the equivalent of *répondre*.

LADISLAS, [*à part*]

Non, non, lâche rival, je n'y puis consentir.

FÉDERIC

Et, forcé par votre ordre à rompre mon silence,
Je vous obéirai, mais avec violence.
Certain de vous déplaire en vous obéissant, 1105
Plus que n'observant point un ordre si pressant,
J'avoûrai donc, grand roi, que l'objet qui me touche . . .

LADISLAS

Duc, encore une fois, je vous ferme la bouche,
Et ne vous puis souffrir votre présomption.

VENCESLAS

Insolent !

LADISLAS

J'ai sans fruit vaincu ma passion : 1110
Pour souffrir son orgueil, Seigneur, et vous complaire,
J'ai fait tous les efforts que la raison peut faire ;
Mais en vain mon respect tâche à me contenir,
Ma raison de mes sens ne peut rien obtenir.
Je suis ma passion, suivez votre colère : 1115
Pour un fils sans respect perdez l'amour d'un père ;
Tranchez le cours du temps à mes jours destiné,
Et reprenez le sang que vous m'avez donné ;
Ou, si votre justice épargne encor ma tête,
De ce présomptueux rejetez la requête, 1120
Et de son insolence humiliez l'excès,
Ou sa mort à l'instant en suivra le succès.

(*Il s'en va furieux*)

1103. **rompre mon silence**: M.: "On dit rompre le silence, avec l'article indéfini, au lieu du pronom possessif."

1108. **Duc, encore une fois, je vous ferme la bouche**: see note on l. 879.

Scène VII

VENCESLAS, FÉDERIC, GARDES

VENCESLAS

Gardes, qu'on le saisisse.

FÉDERIC, *les arrêtant*

     Ha ! Seigneur, quel asile
A conserver mes jours ne serait inutile,
Et me garantirait contre un soulèvement?   1125
Accordez-moi sa grâce ou mon éloignement.

VENCESLAS

Qu'aucun soin ne vous trouble et ne vous importune.
Duc, je ferai si haut monter votre fortune,
D'un crédit si puissant j'armerai votre bras,
Et ce séditieux vous verra de si bas,   1130
Que jamais d'aucun trait de haine ni d'envie
Il ne pourra livrer d'atteinte à votre vie,
Que l'instinct enragé qui meut ses passions
Ne mettra plus de borne à vos prétentions,
Qu'il ne pourra heurter votre pouvoir suprême,   1135
Et que tous vos souhaits dépendront de vous-même.

ACTE QUATRIÈME

Scène I

Théodore, Léonor

THÉODORE

Ha, Dieu ! que cet effroi me trouble et me confond !
Tu vois que ton rapport à mon songe répond,
Et sur cette frayeur tu condamnes mes larmes?
Je me mets trop en peine, et je prends trop d'alarmes?   1140

LÉONOR

Vous en prenez sans doute un peu légèrement.
Pour n'avoir pas couché dans son appartement,
Est-ce un si grand sujet d'en prendre l'épouvante,
Et de souffrir qu'un songe à ce point vous tourmente?
Croyez-vous que le prince, en cet âge de feu   1145
Où le corps à l'esprit s'assujettit si peu,
Où l'âme sur les sens n'a point encor d'empire,
Où toujours le plus froid pour quelque objet soupire,
Vive avecque tout l'ordre et toute la pudeur
D'où dépend notre gloire et notre bonne odeur?   1150
Cherchez-vous des clartés dans les nuits d'un jeune homme
Que le repos tourmente et que l'amour consomme?

1139. **Et sur cette frayeur,** etc.: translate: "and do you blame my tears in this state of fear?"

1150. **notre bonne odeur**: "our good reputation." M.: "Bonne odeur, pour bonne renommée n'est plus que du langage familier ou mystique."

1151. **Cherchez-vous des clartés,** etc.: "Do you seek to be enlightened concerning the way a young man spends his nights?" M.: "Tout ce détail dans lequel entre Léonor pour expliquer à Théodore comment il est possible qu'un jeune prince ne couche pas chez lui, blesserait aujourd'hui les bienséances théâtrales."

C'est les examiner d'un soin trop curieux :
Sur leurs déportements il faut fermer les yeux ;
Pour n'en point être en peine, il n'en faut rien apprendre, 1155
Et ne connaître point ce qu'il faudrait reprendre.

THÉODORE

Un songe interrompu, sans suite, obscur, confus,
Qui passe en un instant, et puis ne revient plus,
Fait dessus notre esprit une légère atteinte,
Et nous laisse imprimée ou point ou peu de crainte ;　　1160
Mais les songes suivis, ou dont à tout propos
L'horreur se remontrant interrompt le repos,
Et qui distinctement marquent les aventures,
Sont des avis du Ciel pour les choses futures.
Hélas ! j'ai vu la main qui lui perçait le flanc ;　　1165
J'ai vu porter le coup, j'ai vu couler son sang ;
Du coup d'une autre main j'ai vu voler sa tête ;
Pour recevoir son corps j'ai vu sa tombe prête ;
Et, m'écriant d'un ton qui t'aurait fait horreur,
J'ai dissipé mon songe, et non pas ma terreur.　　1170
Cet effroi de mon lit aussitôt m'a tirée,
Et, comme tu m'as vue, interdite, égarée,

1154. **déportements :** "scandalous conduct," originally "conduct," either good or bad, as in English. This meaning is antiquated and has given way to the special signification of "bad conduct." Compare *humeur*, "bad humor," and *conduite*, l. 492. See *Lexiques de Malherbe*, p. 167, and *de Molière*, I, p. 311. See also the word *heur* in *Saint Genest*, note on l. 101. — **leurs**, refers to *jeune homme*, l. 1151, used in general sense.

1157–1160. **Un songe interrompu**, etc.: for the dream in French tragedy see *Saint Genest*, note on l. 5.

1157. **sans suite :** "incoherent."

1159. **dessus :** = *sur*; see *Saint Genest*, note on l. 46.

1160. **Et nous laisse imprimée ou point ou peu de crainte :** M. : "Imprimée est un solecisme. Ce participe se rapporte, non pas à crainte, mais à peu ou à point, et alors il est indéclinable."

Sans toi je me rendais en son appartement,
D'où j'apprends que ma peur n'est pas sans fondement,
Puisque ses gens t'ont dit ... Mais que vois-je?

SCÈNE II

OCTAVE, LADISLAS, THÉODORE, LÉONOR

OCTAVE

Ha! Madame! 1175

THÉODORE, *à Léonor*

Eh bien?

OCTAVE

Sans mon secours le prince rendait l'âme.

THÉODORE

Prenais-je, Léonor, l'alarme sans propos?

LADISLAS

Souffrez-moi sur ce siège un moment de repos ;
Débile, et mal remis encor de la faiblesse
Où ma perte de sang et ma chute me laisse,   1180
Je me traîne avec peine, et j'ignore où je suis.

THÉODORE

Ha! mon frère!

LADISLAS

Ha! ma sœur! savez-vous mes ennuis?

THÉODORE

O songe, avant-coureur d'aventure tragique,
Combien sensiblement cet accident s'explique !

1179. **mal remis**, etc.: "scarcely yet recovered from the weakness."
1180. **laisse**: for singular verb with two subjects see *Saint Genest*,
note on l. 339, and l. 1187 below.
1183. **avant-coureur d'aventure tragique**: "forerunner of tragic events."
1184. **sensiblement**: "obviously," i.e. in the light of the dream.

Par quel malheur, mon frère, ou par quel attentat   1185
Vous vois-je en ce sanglant et déplorable état?

LADISLAS

Vous voyez ce qu'Amour et Cassandre me coûte.
Mais faites observer qu'aucun ne nous écoute.

THÉODORE, *faisant signe à Léonor, qui va voir si
personne n'écoute*

Soignez-y, Léonor.

LADISLAS

Vous avez vu, ma sœur,
Mes plus secrets pensers jusqu'au fond de mon cœur;   1190
Vous savez les efforts que j'ai faits sur moi-même
Pour secouer le joug de cette amour extrême,
Et retirer d'un cœur indignement blessé
Le trait empoisonné que ses yeux m'ont lancé.
Mais, quoi que j'entreprenne, à moi-même infidèle,   1195
Contre mon jugement mon esprit se rebelle;
Mon cœur de son service à peine est diverti
Qu'au premier souvenir il reprend son parti,
Tant a de droit sur nous, malheureux que nous sommes,
Cet amour, non amour, mais ennemi des hommes!   1200
J'ai, pour aucunement couvrir ma lâcheté,
Quand je souffrais le plus, feint le plus de santé;
Rebuté des mépris qu'elle a faits d'un esclave,
J'ai fait du souverain et j'ai tranché du brave;

1187. **Vous voyez ce qu'Amour,** etc.: M.: "Amour, sans article, signifie le dieu d'amour; et il n'est pas du style grave."

1190. **pensers**: see *Saint Genest*, note on l. 455.

1198. **il reprend son parti**: "it takes her part again."

1201. **aucunement**: = *en quelque façon*. This meaning is now antiquated; see *Lexiques de Malherbe*, p. 46, and *de Corneille*, I, p. 89.

1203-1204. **Rebuté des mépris,** etc.: "disheartened by the contempt
she displayed for a slave, I have played the sovereign and acted the

Bien plus, j'ai, furieux, inégal, interdit, 1205
Voulu pour mon rival employer mon crédit :
Mais, au moindre penser, mon âme transportée
Contre mon propre effort s'est toujours révoltée,
Et l'ingrate beauté dont le charme m'a pris
Peut plus que ma colère et plus que les mépris : 1210
Sur ce qu'Octave, enfin, hier me fit entendre
L'hymen qui se traitait du duc et de Cassandre,
Et que ce couple heureux consommait cette nuit . . .

OCTAVE

Pernicieux avis, hélas ! qu'as-tu produit ?

LADISLAS

Succombant tout entier à ce coup qui m'accable, 1215
De tout raisonnement je deviens incapable,
Fais retirer mes gens, m'enferme tout le soir,
Et ne prends plus avis que de mon désespoir.
Par une fausse porte, enfin, la nuit venue,
Je me dérobe aux miens et je gagne la rue, 1220
D'où, tout soin, tout respect, tout jugement perdu,
Au palais de Cassandre en même temps rendu,

bravo." *Faire*, in the sense "to play a part, pretend to be," is usually
followed by the direct object : *faire le mort*, *faire le magnanime* ; but
it is also construed with the preposition as in the text, and is a synonym
of *trancher de* ; see *Lexique de Corneille*, I, p. 418. M.: "On dit avoir
du mépris, des mépris, pour quelqu'un, on ne dit pas en faire des
mépris, ni du mépris."

1211–1212. Sur ce qu'Octave, etc.: "by reason of Octave's informing
me yesterday of the marriage." For this use of *sur ce que* see *Lexique
de Molière*, II, p. 511.

1217. Fais: for omission of subject, as so often, see *Saint Genest*,
note on l. 23, and below, ll. 1223 et seq. See also Benoist, p. 407.

1219. Par une fausse porte: "By a secret door." *Fausse porte* means
also a sham door made for architectural symmetry (in this sense *porte
feinte* is also employed); or a small door, not ordinarily used ; or, finally,
in a fortress, a postern.

J'escalade les murs, gagne une galerie,
Et cherchant un endroit commode à ma furie,
Descends sous l'escalier, et dans l'obscurité   1225
Prépare à tout succès mon courage irrité.
Au nom du duc enfin j'entends ouvrir la' porte,
Et, suivant à ce nom la fureur qui m'emporte,
Cours, éteins la lumière, et d'un aveugle effort
De trois coups de poignard blesse le duc à mort.   1230

THÉODORE, *effrayée, s'appuyant sur Léonor*

Le duc ! qu'entends-je? hélas !

LADISLAS

               A cette rude atteinte,
Pendant qu'en l'escalier tout le monde est en plainte,
Lui, m'entendant tomber le poignard sous ses pas,
S'en saisit, me poursuit et m'en atteint au bras.
Son âme à cet effort de son corps se sépare ;   1235
Il tombe mort.

THÉODORE

         O rage inhumaine et barbare !

LADISLAS

Et moi, par cent détours que je ne connais pas,
Dans l'horreur de la nuit ayant traîné mes pas,
Par le sang que je perds mon cœur enfin se glace ;
Je tombe, et, hors de moi, demeure sur la place,   1240

1226. **à tout succès** : "for every event."

1233. **m'entendant tomber le poignard sous ses pas** : "hearing my dagger fall at his feet." *Me* is the dative of possession. Marmontel understands the translation to be "hearing me drop my dagger at his feet," and says : "Tomber est neutre, et non pas actif : on ne dit pas, je tombe quelque chose, mais je laisse tomber."

Tant qu'Octave, passant, s'est donné le souci
De bander ma blessure et de me rendre ici,
Où, non sans peine encor, je reviens en moi-même.

THÉODORE, *appuyée sur Léonor*

Je succombe, mon frère, à ma douleur extrême.
Ma faiblesse me chasse et peut rendre évident   1245
L'intérêt que je prends dedans votre accident.
   (*Bas*)
Soutiens-moi, Léonor.   Mon cœur, es-tu si tendre
Que de donner des pleurs à l'époux de Cassandre,
Et vouloir mal au bras qui t'en a dégagé?
Cet hymen t'offensait, et sa mort t'a vengé.   1250
            (*S'en allant*)

SCÈNE III

LADISLAS, OCTAVE

OCTAVE

Déjà du jour, Seigneur, la lumière naissante
Fait voir par son retour la lune pâlissante.

LADISLAS

Et va produire aux yeux les crimes de la nuit.

1241. **Tant qu'Octave:** "until Octave." *Tant que* in the sense of *jusqu'à ce que* is now antiquated, but was common in the seventeenth century, and was followed by the subjunctive. The indicative is here used probably because the statement is one of accomplished action. See Haase, 137, and *Lexique de Corneille*, II, p. 369.

1243. **je reviens en moi-même:** M.:. "Dans un autre sens, on dit bien rentrer en soi-même. Mais pour exprimer, reprendre ses sens, ses esprits, on dit, revenir à soi-même."

1246. **dedans:** for *dans*; see ll. 569, 1333. M.: "On dit prendre intérêt à quelque chose, et non dans quelque chose. Ce vers est d'ailleurs prosaïque, et choquant pour l'oreille."

1249. **Et vouloir mal au bras,** etc.: M.: "Vouloir mal à quelqu'un est du style familier.   Vouloir mal au bras est ridicule."

OCTAVE

Même au quartier du roi j'entends déjà du bruit.
Allons vous rendre au lit, que quelqu'un ne survienne.   1255

LADISLAS

Qui souhaite la mort, craint peu, quoi qu'il advienne.
Mais allons, conduis-moi.

SCÈNE IV

VENCESLAS, GARDES, LADISLAS, OCTAVE

VENCESLAS

Mon fils !

LADISLAS

Seigneur ?

VENCESLAS

Hélas !

OCTAVE

O fatale rencontre !

VENCESLAS

Est-ce vous, Ladislas,
Dont la couleur éteinte et la vue égarée
Ne marquent plus qu'un corps dont l'âme est séparée ?   1260
En quel lieu, si saisi, si froid et si sanglant,
Adressez-vous ce pas incertain et tremblant ?
Qui vous a si matin tiré de votre couche ?
Quel trouble vous possède et vous ferme la bouche ?

1255. **que quelqu'un ne survienne** : "lest some one enter." M. : " Que,
pour de peur que ; cette ellipse est poétique, et devrait être permise
en vers."

LADISLAS, *se remettant sur sa chaise*

Que lui dirai-je, hélas?

VENCESLAS

                    Répondez-moi, mon fils;   1265
Quel fatal accident . . .

LADISLAS

                    Seigneur, je vous le dis :
J'allais . . . j'étais . . . l'Amour a sur moi tant d'empire . . .
Je me confonds, Seigneur, et ne vous puis rien dire.

VENCESLAS

D'un trouble si confus un esprit assailli
Se confesse coupable, et qui craint a failli.   1270
N'avez-vous point eu prise avecque votre frère?
Votre mauvaise humeur lui fut toujours contraire,
Et si pour l'en garder mes soins n'avaient pourvu . . .

LADISLAS

M'a-t-il pas satisfait? Non, je ne l'ai point vu.

VENCESLAS

Qui vous réveille donc avant que la lumière   1275
Ait du soleil naissant commencé la carrière?

LADISLAS

N'avez-vous pas aussi précédé son réveil?

VENCESLAS

Oui, mais j'ai mes raisons qui bornent mon sommeil.
Je me vois, Ladislas, au déclin de ma vie,

1271. **N'avez-vous point eu prise avecque votre frère**: "Have you not quarreled with your brother?" M.: "Avoir prise avec quelqu'un n'est que du style familier."

1274. **M'a-t-il pas satisfait**: for omission of *ne* in interrogative sentences see note on l. 772.

Et, sachant que la mort l'aura bientôt ravie,   1280
Je dérobe au sommeil, image de la mort,
Ce que je puis du temps qu'elle laisse à mon sort :
Près du terme fatal prescrit par la nature,
Et qui me fait du pied toucher ma sépulture,
De ces derniers instants dont il presse le cours,   1285
Ce que j'ôte à mes nuits, je l'ajoute à mes jours.
Sur mon couchant, enfin, ma débile paupière
Me ménage avec soin ce reste de lumière ;
Mais quel soin peut du lit vous chasser si matin,
Vous à qui l'âge encor garde un si long destin?   1290

LADISLAS

Si vous en ordonnez avec votre justice,
Mon destin de bien près touche son précipice :
Ce bras, puisqu'il est vain de vous déguiser rien,
A de votre couronne abattu le soutien :
Le duc est mort, Seigneur, et j'en suis l'homicide ;   1295
Mais j'ai dû l'être.

1281. **Je dérobe au sommeil, image de la mort** : this has been a favorite
image with the poets since the days of Ovid (*Amorum*, II. 9, 41) :

> Stulte, quid est somnus, gelidae nisi mortis imago?

Compare Shakespeare, *Macbeth*, II. 3 :

> Shake off this downy sleep, death's counterfeit,
> And look on death itself !

A large number of quotations from ancient and modern poets will
be found in *Notes and Queries*, first series, IV, 435; IX, 346; X, 229,
356, 412.

1285. **dont il presse** : *il* refers to *le terme fatal* of l. 1283. M.: "Il se
rapporte à terme ; et le terme qui presse le cours des instants, fait une
fausse image."

1287. **Sur mon couchant** : "In my declining years." The figure is taken
from the setting of the sun.

1292. **Mon destin de bien près touche son précipice** : translate : "my fate
will very soon reach a disastrous end." M.: "Il fallait dire, il touche à
son précipice."

VENCESLAS

O dieu ! le duc est mort, perfide !
Le duc est mort, barbare ! et pour excuse, enfin,
Vous avez eu raison d'être son assassin !
A cette épreuve, ô Ciel, mets-tu ma patience ?

Scène V

Féderic, Venceslas, Ladislas, Octave, gardes

FÉDERIC

La duchesse, Seigneur, vous demande audience.   1300

LADISLAS

Que vois-je ? quel fantôme et quelle illusion
De mes sens égarés croît la confusion ?

VENCESLAS

Que m'avez-vous dit, prince, et par quelle merveille
Mon œil peut-il sitôt démentir mon oreille ?

LADISLAS

Ne vous ai-je pas dit qu'interdit et confus,   1305
Je ne pouvais rien dire et ne raisonnais plus ?

VENCESLAS

Ah ! duc, il était temps de tirer ma pensée
D'une erreur qui l'avait mortellement blessée :
Différant d'un instant le soin de l'en guérir,

1297–1298. **et pour excuse, enfin,** etc. : "and you offer as an excuse that
you were right in assassinating him."

1302. **croît ma confusion** : M. : "Croître n'est plus actif, il est neutre."
For singular verb with two subjects see note on l. 1180.

1309–1310. **Différant d'un instant le soin de l'en guérir,** etc. : translate :
"had the care of undeceiving my mind in regard to it (*erreur*) been

Le bruit de votre mort m'allait faire mourir.   1310
Jamais cœur ne conçut une douleur si forte.
Mais que me dites-vous?

FÉDERIC

Que Cassandre à la porte

Demandait à vous voir.

VENCESLAS

Qu'elle entre.

(Il [Féderic] sort)

LADISLAS, bas

O justes cieux!

M'as-tu trompé, ma main? me trompez-vous, mes yeux?
Si le duc est vivant, quelle vie ai-je éteinte?   .   1315
Et de quel bras le mien a-t-il reçu l'atteinte?

SCÈNE VI

CASSANDRE, VENCESLAS, LADISLAS, FÉDERIC, OCTAVE, GARDES

CASSANDRE, aux pieds du roi, pleurant

Grand roi, de l'innocence auguste protecteur,
Des peines et des prix juste dispensateur,

delayed a moment, the report of your death would have killed me."
For the use of the imperfect indicative in the apodosis of a conditional sentence see Mätzner, *Franz. Gram.*, p. 365. Marmontel says the
participle has no relation to anything.

1317–1478. SCENE VI. It is impossible not to see in the whole of this
scene the influence of Corneille's *Cid*, II. 8. There is more pathos in
the scene where Chimène implores the king for vengeance on the death
of a father slain by a lover; but there is more dramatic interest in this
scene in Rotrou where Cassandre asks justice for the death of her
husband, and where both the murdered man and the murderer are the
children of the judge; there are also in parts of this scene echoes of
Horace, V. 2, where Valère accuses Horace before the king. The verbal
imitation of Corneille by Rotrou is rare; one may, however, compare
l. 680 of the *Cid*,

Par cette triste bouche elle empruntait ma voix,

with l. 1420 of *Venceslas*,

Demandent par ma bouche un arrêt légitime.

Exemple de justice inviolable et pure,
Admirable à la race et présente et future,   1320
Prince et père à la fois, vengez-moi, vengez-vous,
Avec votre pitié mêlez votre courroux,
Et rendez aujourd'hui d'un juge inexorable
Une marque aux neveux à jamais mémorable.

VENCESLAS, la faisant lever

Faites trêve, Madame, avecque les douleurs   1325
Qui vous coupent la voix et font parler vos pleurs.

CASSANDRE

Votre Majesté, Sire, a connu ma famille.

VENCESLAS

Ursin de Cunisberg, de qui vous êtes fille,
Est descendu d'aïeux issus de sang royal,
Et me fut un voisin généreux et loyal.   1330

CASSANDRE

Vous savez si prétendre un de vos fils pour gendre
Eût au rang qu'il tenait été trop entreprendre !

VENCESLAS

L'amour n'offense point dedans l'égalité.

1324. **neveux**: see note on l. 947. M. : "On dit, à nos neveux."
1330. **loyal**: M. : "Ce mot a vieilli, et le style héroïque, qui l'a perdu, ne l'a point remplacé."
1331–1332. **Vous savez si prétendre un de vos fils**, etc. : translate : "You know whether in his rank aspiring to one of your sons for his daughter's husband would have been too presumptuous." To aspire to a person's hand is *prétendre la main*, to aspire to marry a person is *prétendre une personne*; but otherwise the sense of "aspiring to" is expressed by the neuter *prétendre* with the preposition *à* ; see l. 1735. M. : "On dit, prétendre à quelqu'un, et non pas, prétendre quelqu'un. On ne dit point, entreprendre à, mais, entreprendre sur. Ces vers sont d'une dureté horrible."
1333. **dedans**: see notes on ll. 569, 1246.

CASSANDRE

Tous deux ont eu dessein dessus ma liberté,
Mais avec différence et d'objet et d'estime ;   1335
L'un, qui me crut honnête, eut un but légitime,
Et l'autre, dont l'amour fol et capricieux
Douta de ma sagesse, en eut un vicieux.
J'eus bientôt d'eux aussi des sentiments contraires,
Et, quoiqu'ils soient vos fils, ne les trouvai point frères :   1340
Je ne les puis aimer ni haïr à demi ;
Je tins l'un pour amant, l'autre pour ennemi ;
L'infant par sa vertu s'est soumis ma franchise,
Le prince par son vice en a manqué la prise ;.
Et, par deux différents, mais louables effets,   1345
J'aime en l'un votre sang, en l'autre je le hais.
Alexandre, qui vit son rival en son frère,
Et qui craignit, d'ailleurs, l'autorité d'un père,
Fit, quoiqu'autant ardent que prudent et discret,
De notre passion un commerce secret,   1350
Et, sous le nom du duc déguisant sa poursuite,
Ménagea notre vue avec tant de conduite

1341. 1648 has *puis*, which Viollet-le-Duc and Hémon have corrected to *pus* in order to agree with the other past tenses in the passage.

1334. dessus : = *sur* ; see *Saint Genest*, notes on ll. 46, 39⅓, 686 ; *Venceslas*, note on l. 1359.

1336. honnête : " virtuous." See *honnêteté*, note on l. 1714.

1338. sagesse : Littré : " En parlant des femmes, modestie, chasteté " ; translate : " virtue."

1344. en a manqué la prise : " has lost his hold on it," i.e. has failed to win my love. M. : " Façon de parler trop peu noble."

1349–1350. Fit . . . De notre passion un commerce secret : translate : " kept our love a secret." — **quoiqu'autant ardent que prudent :** M. : " L'oreille répugne à cette cacophonie."

1352. Ménagea notre vue, etc. : translate : " so conducted himself in our sight."

Que toute Varsovie a cru jusqu'aujourd'hui
Qu'il parlait pour le duc, quand il parlait pour lui.
Cette adresse a trompé jusqu'à nos domestiques ;   1355
Mais, craignant que le prince, à bout de ses pratiques,
Comme il croit tout pouvoir avec impunité,
Ne suivît la fureur d'un amour irrité
Et dessus mon honneur osât trop entreprendre,
Nous crûmes que l'hymen pouvait seul m'en défendre,   1360
Et l'heure prise, enfin, pour nous donner les mains,
Et, bornant son espoir, détruire ses desseins,
Hier, déjà le sommeil semant partout ses charmes . . .
(En cet endroit, Seigneur, laissez couler mes larmes :
Leur cours vient d'une source à ne tarir jamais)   1365
        (*Pleurant*)
L'infant, de cet hymen espérant le succès
Et de peur de soupçon arrivant sans escorte,
A peine eut mis le pied sur le seuil de la porte

1357. 1648 has *tant pouvoir*, corrected by Viollet-le-Duc, Ronchaud, and Hemon to *tout pouvoir*. I have retained correction, as original reading is probably a misprint.

1353. **Que toute Varsovie** : M. : "L'usage veut qu'on dise, tout Varsovie, tout Rome, tout Londres, etc., quoique ces noms de villes soient féminins. Cette bizarrerie apparente de l'usage est fondée sur ce qu'alors tout se rapporte, dans la pensée, au collectif de ville, qui est peuple."

1356. **à bout de ses pratiques** : translate : "having exhausted his plots." M. : "Cette expression n'est plus que du langage familier."

1359. **dessus** : see note on l. 1334.

1361. **l'heure prise** : "the hour having been set." This construction corresponds to the Latin ablative absolute, and is generally considered by Romance grammarians as the absolute accusative ; see Mätzner, *Syntax*, I, pp. 197, 356 ; *Lexique de Corneille*, I, p. lxii ; *de Molière*, I, p. cxliv. See also note on l. 143.

1365. **une source à ne tarir jamais** : "an inexhaustible spring." For infinitive with *à* used attributively see Mätzner, *Franz. Gram.*, p. 479. See below, l. 1492, and *Saint Genest*, l. 388. In this construction the infinitive is sometimes active and sometimes passive, as in ll. 1485, 1574. See *Lexique de Corneille*, I, p. 11.

Qu'il sent, pour tout accueil, une barbare main
De trois coups de poignard lui traverser le sein.   1370

VENCESLAS

O dieu ! l'infant est mort !

LADISLAS, *bas*

          O mon aveugle rage,
Tu t'es bien satisfaite, et voilà ton ouvrage !
    (*Le roi s'assied et met son mouchoir sur son visage*)

CASSANDRE

Oui, Seigneur, il est mort, et je suivrai ses pas
A l'instant que j'aurai vu venger son trépas.
J'en connais le meurtrier, et j'attends son supplice   1375
De vos ressentiments et de votre justice :
C'est votre propre sang, Seigneur, qu'on a versé,
Votre vivant portrait qui se trouve effacé.
J'ai besoin d'un vengeur, je n'en puis choisir d'autre :
Le mort est votre fils, et ma cause est la vôtre ;   1380
Vengez-moi, vengez-vous, et vengez un époux
Que, veuve avant l'hymen, je pleure à vos genoux.
Mais, apprenant, grand roi, cet accident sinistre,
Hélas ! en pourriez-vous soupçonner le ministre ?
Oui, votre sang suffit pour vous en faire foi :   1385
    (*Montrant Ladislas*)
Il s'émeut, il vous parle et pour et contre soi,
Et, par un sentiment ensemble horrible et tendre,
Vous dit que Ladislas est meurtrier d'Alexandre.

    1375. **J'en connais le meurtrier** : until the middle of the seventeenth
century *meurtrier* was a dissyllable. M.: "Meurtrier est de trois
syllables."

    1384. **le ministre** : "the author." See l. 1413. M.: "Le ministre
d'un accident n'est pas français ; il fallait dire, la cause. Ministre suppose une puissance qui domine et commande, et à laquelle on obéit :
ministre de la volonté, de la haine, de la vengeance, etc."

    1386. **contre soi** : for *contre lui* ; see *Saint Genest*, note on l. 978.

Ce geste encor, Seigneur, ce maintien interdit,
Ce visage effrayé, ce silence le dit,   1390
Et, plus que tout, enfin, cette main encor teinte
De ce sang précieux qui fait naître ma plainte.
Quel des deux sur vos sens fera le plus d'effort,
De votre fils meurtrier ou de votre fils mort?
Si vous étiez si faible, et votre sang si tendre   1395
Qu'on l'eût impunément commencé de répandre,
Peut-être verriez-vous la main qui l'a versé
Attenter sur celui qu'elle vous a laissé :
D'assassin de son frère, il peut être le vôtre ;
Un crime pourrait bien être un essai de l'autre :   1400
Ainsi que les vertus, les crimes enchaînés
Sont toujours ou souvent l'un par l'autre traînés.
Craignez de hasarder, pour être trop auguste,
Et le trône et la vie, et le titre de juste.
Si mes vives douleurs ne vous peuvent toucher,   1405
Ni la perte d'un fils qui vous était si cher,
Ni l'horrible penser du coup qui vous la coûte,
Voyez, voyez le sang dont ce poignard dégoutte ;
        (*Elle tire un poignard de sa manche*)
Et, s'il ne vous émeut, sachez où l'on l'a pris ;
Votre fils l'a tiré du sein de votre fils ;   1410

1393-1394. **Quel des deux . . . De votre fils**, etc.: for the construction of *de* after *quel*, etc., see note on l. 467. M. : " Il fallait dire,
lequel des deux." Benoist, p. 380 : " Rotrou emploie quel, quelle, dans
une interrogation directe ou indirecte, au lieu de lequel, laquelle."

1398. **Attenter sur celui qu'elle vous a laissé** : "attack that which
(*celui* = *sang*, " blood, life ") it has (thus far) spared to you."

1399. **D'assassin de son frère** : "from being the assassin of his
brother." See *Saint Genest*, notes on ll. 129, 382.

1402. **l'un par l'autre traînés** : M. : " Il fallait dire, entraînés."

1403. **pour être trop auguste** : translate : "because you are too merciful to punish your son." The word *auguste* is employed for the sake of
rhyme and does not convey the proper meaning. M. : " Terme impropre ;
c'était clément ou débonnaire qu'il fallait dire."

Oui, de ce coup, Seigneur, un frère fut capable ;
Ce fer porte le chiffre et le nom du coupable,
Vous apprend de quel bras il fut l'exécuteur,
Et, complice du meurtre, en déclare l'auteur :
Ce fer qui, chaud encor, par un énorme crime   1415
A traversé d'amour la plus noble victime,
L'ouvrage le plus pur que vous ayez formé,
Et le plus digne cœur dont vous fussiez aimé ;
Ce cœur enfin, ce sang, ce fils, cette victime,
Demandent par ma bouche un arrêt légitime.   1420
Roi, vous vous feriez tort par cette impunité,
Et, père, à votre fils vous devez l'équité.
J'attends de voir pousser votre main vengeresse
Ou par votre justice ou par votre tendresse ;
Ou, si je n'obtiens rien de la part des humains,   1425
La justice du Ciel me prêtera les mains :
Ce forfait contre lui cherche en vain du refuge ;
Il en fut le témoin, il en sera le juge ;
Et, pour punir un bras d'un tel crime noirci,
Le sien saura s'étendre et n'est pas raccourci,   1430
Si vous lui remettez à venger nos offenses.

1413. **de quel bras il fut l'exécuteur** : M. : " Un fer exécuteur d'un bras, n'est pas français."

1415. **Ce fer qui, chaud encor** : M. : " Chaud est banni du style noble ; en pareil cas on dirait, tout fumant."

1427. **cherche en vain du refuge** : M. : " Du refuge n'est pas français : il fallait dire un refuge : du est partitif, et ne s'emploie que pour les choses susceptibles de plus et de moins : c'est ainsi qu'on dirait chercher du secours ou de l'assistance, parce qu'on dit plus d'assistance, et moins de secours ; mais on ne dit point de l'asile, ni du refuge, par la raison qu'asile et refuge sont indivisibles, et qu'on ne dit pas plus de refuge, ni moins d'asile."

1430. **et n'est pas raccourci** : compare Numbers xi. 23, "And the Lord said unto Moses, Is the Lord's hand waxed short ?" Isaiah l. 2, "Is my hand shortened at all, that it cannot redeem ?" Isaiah lix. 1, "Behold, the Lord's hand is not shortened, that it cannot save."

1431. **Si vous lui remettez à venger nos offenses** : translate : "if you leave him to avenge our wrongs." See *Lexique de Corneille*, II, p. 285,

VENCESLAS

Contre ces charges, prince, avez-vous des défenses?

LADISLAS

Non, je suis criminel : abandonnez, grand roi,
Cette mourante vie aux rigueurs de la loi ;
Que rien ne vous oblige à m'être moins sévère ;   1435
Supprimons les doux noms et de fils et de père,
Et tout ce qui pour moi vous peut solliciter.
Cassandre veut ma mort, il la faut contenter ;
Sa haine me l'ordonne, il faut que je me taise,
Et j'estimerai plus une mort qui lui plaise   1440
Qu'un destin qui pourrait m'affranchir du trépas,
Et qu'une éternité qui ne lui plairait pas.
J'ai beau dissimuler ma passion extrême,
Jusqu'après le trépas mon sort veut que je l'aime,
Et, pour dire à quel point ce cœur est embrasé,   1445
Jusqu'après le trépas qu'elle m'aura causé.
Le coup qui me tûra pour venger son injure
Ne sera qu'une heureuse et légère blessure,
Au prix du coup fatal qui me perça le cœur,
Quand de ma liberté son bel œil fut vainqueur :   1450
J'en fus désespéré jusqu'à tout entreprendre ;
Il m'ôta le repos, que l'autre me doit rendre :
Puisqu'être sa victime est un décret des Cieux,

1445. 1648 has at end of line *ombragé*, an evident misprint for *ombrazé*, *embrazé*, *embrasé*.

where three examples are given of *remettre à quelqu'un à faire quelque chose*.

1433–1460. This speech of Ladislas contains echoes of the *Cid*, V. 1, and of *Horace*, V. 2.

1447. tûra : for *tuera* ; see notes on ll. 816, 1602.

1452. Il m'ôta le repos : i.e. *le coup fatal qui me perça le cœur*. — que l'autre : i.e. *le coup qui me tûra*.

Qu'importe qui me tue, ou sa bouche ou ses yeux?
Souscrivez à l'arrêt dont elle me menace ;   1455
Privé de sa faveur, je ne veux point de grâce :
Mettez à bout l'effet qu'amour a commencé,
Achevez un trépas déjà bien avancé ;
Et, si d'autre intérêt n'émeut votre colère,
Craignez tout d'une main qui peut tuer un frère.   1460

VENCESLAS

Madame, modérez vos sensibles regrets,
Et laissez à mes soins nos communs intérêts ;
Mes ordres aujourd'hui feront voir une marque
Et d'un juge équitable et d'un digne monarque ;
Je me dépouillerai de toute passion,   1465
Et je lui ferai droit par sa confession !

CASSANDRE

Mon attente, grand roi, n'a point été trompée,
Et . . .

VENCESLAS

Prince, levez-vous, donnez-moi votre épée.

LADISLAS, *se levant*

Mon épée ! Ha ! mon crime est-il énorme au point
De me . . .

VENCESLAS

Donnez, vous dis-je, et ne répliquez point.   1470

1454. **Qu'importe qui me tue, ou sa bouche ou ses yeux**: see note on l. 467.
1457. **Mettez à bout l'effet** : M. : " Mettre à bout, pour achever, n'est plus du style noble : mettre à bout un effet, n'est pas français."
1460. **Craignez tout d'une main qui peut tuer un frère** : M. : " Ladislas se calomnie lui-même d'une manière atroce et sans raison. Il n'a pas tué son frère à dessein ; pourquoi fait-il entendre à son père qu'il serait capable de le tuer lui-même ? "
1461. **sensibles** : see *Saint Genest*, note on l. 234.
1466. **Et je lui ferai droit par sa confession** : " and I shall judge him from his confession." M. : " Faire droit, n'est plus que du style de Palais."

LADISLAS

La voilà !

VENCESLAS, *la baillant à Féderic*

Tenez, duc.

OCTAVE

O disgrâce inhumaine !

VENCESLAS

Et faites-le garder en la chambre prochaine.
Allez.

LADISLAS, *ayant fait la révérence au roi, et à Cassandre*

Presse la fin où tu m'as destiné,
Sort ! voilà de tes jeux, et ta roue a tourné.

[*Il sort*]

VENCESLAS

Duc?

FÉDERIC

Seigneur?

VENCESLAS

De ma part donnez avis au prince   1475
Que sa tête, autrefois si chère à la province,

1474. Sort ! voilà de tes jeux, et ta roue a tourné : " Fate ! these are
thy freaks, and thy wheel has revolved." Fortune, not Fate, is associated with the emblem of the wheel. See Tibullus, I. 5, 70 : " Ver-
satur celeri Fors levis orbe rotae" ; Ovid, *Trist.*, V. 8, 7 : " Nec metuis
dubio Fortunae stantis in orbe Numen . . . ?" and *Epist. ex Ponto*, II.
3, 56 : " Te fieri comitem stantis in orbe deae." See also Ausonius,
Epig., 12, and Propertius, II. 8, 8, who attributes the wheel to Love.
Fortune's wheel was a favorite figure with Shakespeare ; see *Henry V*,
III. 6 : " And giddy Fortune's furious fickle wheel" ; *As You Like It*,
I. 2 : " Let us sit and mock the good housewife Fortune from her wheel,
that her gifts may henceforth be bestowed equally " ; *Antony and Cleo-
patra*, IV. 15 : " That the false housewife Fortune break her wheel" ;
King Lear, II. 2 : " Fortune, good-night : smile once more ; turn thy
wheel" ; *Hamlet*, II. 2 : " Break all the spokes and fellies from her
wheel" ; *3 Henry VI*, IV. 3 : " Though Fortune's malice overthrow
my state, My mind exceeds the compass of her wheel." See Rotrou's
Bélisaire, IV. 7.

Doit servir aujourd'hui d'un exemple fameux
Qui fera détester son crime à nos neveux.

Scène VII

VENCESLAS, CASSANDRE, OCTAVE, GARDES

VENCESLAS, *à Octave*

Vous, conduisez Madame, et la rendez chez elle.

CASSANDRE, *à genoux*

Grand roi, des plus grands rois le plus parfait modèle,   1480
Conservez invaincu cet invincible sein,
Poussez jusques au bout ce généreux dessein,
Et, constant, écoutez contre votre indulgence
Le sang d'un fils qui crie et demande vengeance.

VENCESLAS

Ce coup n'est pas, Madame, un crime à protéger :   1485
J'aurai soin de punir, et non pas de venger.
      (*Elle s'en va avec Octave, le roi restant*)
O Ciel ! ta providence, apparemment prospère,

1477. **Doit servir aujourd'hui d'un exemple fameux :** M. : "Quoique dans *Cinna*, Corneille ait dit,

> Pour servir dignement
> D'une marque éternelle à ce grand changement,

je ne crois pas que servir d'une marque, servir d'un exemple, soit français ; et je pense qu'on doit dire, à l'indéfini, servir de marque, servir d'exemple."

1478. **Qui fera détester**, etc. : see *Saint Genest*, note on l. 499.

1481. **sein** : = *cœur*. M. : "Impropriété dans l'acception du mot sein, affectation dans l'antithèse, invaincu n'est pas reçu."

1485. **un crime à protéger** : "a crime to be protected." See notes on ll. 1365, 1515.

Au gré de mes souhaits de deux fils m'a fait père,
Et l'un d'eux, qui par l'autre aujourd'hui m'est ôté,
M'oblige à perdre encor celui qui m'est resté !   1490

1488. 1648 has *Au gré de mes forfaits*, an evident misprint, corrected by Viollet-le-Duc and Hémon to *soupirs*, and by Ronchaud to *souhaits*. I have followed the last as probably nearer the true original.

1489–1490. Et l'un d'eux, qui par l'autre, etc.: this is certainly an echo of the famous passage in the *Cid*, III. 3:

> La moitié de ma vie a mis l'autre au tombeau,
> Et m'oblige à venger, après ce coup funeste,
> Celle que je n'ai plus sur celle qui me reste.

ACTE CINQUIÈME

Scène I

Théodore, Léonor

THÉODORE

De quel air, Léonor, a-t-il reçu ma lettre?

LÉONOR

D'un air et d'un visage à vous en tout promettre :
En vain sa modestie a voulu déguiser,
Venant à votre nom, il l'a fallu baiser,
Comme à force imprimant sur ce cher caractère   1495
Une marque d'un feu qu'il sent, mais qu'il veut taire.

THÉODORE

Que tu prends mal ton temps pour éprouver un cœur
Que la douleur éprouve avec tant de rigueur !
J'ai plaint la mort du duc comme d'une personne
Nécessaire à mon père et qui sert sa couronne ;   1500

1492. **à vous en tout promettre** : see note on l. 1365.

1495. **à force** : "perforce." Usually *à force = beaucoup, extrêmement.*
For the use in the text, "compelled, obliged," see *Lexiques de Malherbe,* p. 276, and *de Molière,* I, p. 496. M. : "Construction pénible ;
un baiser qui imprime à force une marque d'un fer, etc., est d'un détail
peu digne de la tragédie."

1497–1498. **pour éprouver un cœur**, etc.: "to put to the test a heart
which sorrow has so sorely tried." Apparently Théodore intends to
rebuke Léonor for repeating details which may cause her to reveal her
own feelings for the duke.

Et, quand on me guérit de ce fâcheux rapport,
Et que j'apprends qu'il vit, j'apprends qu'un frère est mort,
Encor, quoi que nos cœurs eussent d'intelligence,
Je ne puis de sa mort souhaiter la vengeance.
J'aimais également le mort et l'assassin,   1505
Je plains également l'un et l'autre destin ;
Pour un frère meurtri ma douleur a des larmes,
Pour un frère meurtrier ma fureur n'a point d'armes ;
Et, si le sang de l'un excite mon courroux,
Celui . . . Mais le duc vient : Léonor, laissez-nous.   1510

(Léonor s'en va)

Scène II

Féderic, Théodore

féderic

Brûlant de vous servir, adorable princesse,
Je me rends par votre ordre aux pieds de Votre Altesse.

théodore

Ne me flattez-vous point, et m'en puis-je vanter ?

1501. Et, quand on me guérit de ce fâcheux rapport: M.: "On ne guérit pas d'un rapport. Manque d'analogie dans les termes."

1503. quoi que nos cœurs eussent d'intelligence: translate: "whatever agreement there may have been between our hearts," i.e. no matter how much we may have loved each other. For *être d'intelligence*, = *être d'accord*, see *Lexiques de Racine*, p. 279, and *de Corneille*, II, p. 25.

1507. Pour un frère meurtri: M.: "Meurtri n'a plus la signification relative à celle de meurtre et de meurtrier ; il ne se dit plus que de chairs altérées par une contusion violente, et il répond à meurtrissure." Benoist, p. 382 : "meurtrir est employé dans le sens de tuer."

1513. et m'en puis-je vanter: "and can I pride myself on it ? " i.e. on your eagerness to serve me. *Vanter* is used for rhyme and probably all that Rotrou intended to make Théodore say was, " Are you not flattering me ? can I trust your offer of service ? "

FÉDERIC

Cette épreuve, Madame, est facile à tenter :
J'ai du sang à répandre, et je porte une épée,   1515
Et ma main pour vos lois brûle d'être occupée.

THÉODORE

Je n'exige pas tant de votre affection,
Et je ne veux de vous qu'une confession.

FÉDERIC

Quelle? ordonnez-la-moi.

THÉODORE

                              Savoir de votre bouche
De quel heureux objet le mérite vous touche,   1520
Et doit être le prix de ces fameux exploits
Qui jusqu'en Moscovie ont étendu nos lois.
J'imputais votre prise aux charmes de Cassandre,
Mais, l'infant l'adorant, vous n'y pouviez prétendre.

FÉDERIC

Mes vœux ont pris, Madame, un vol plus élevé,   1525
Aussi par ma raison n'est-il pas approuvé.

1520. 1648 has *De quel généreux objet*, which of course is a misprint, as it destroys the metrical correctness of the line. Viollet-le-Duc and Hémon have substituted *heureux*, and I have followed their example.

1515. sang à répandre : see notes on ll. 1365, 1632.
1520. objet : see *Saint Genest*, notes on ll. 148, 836.
1523. prise : "conquest," i.e. the capture of your heart.
1524. l'infant l'adorant : see *Saint Genest*, notes on ll. 43, 45, 429; *Venceslas*, ll. 867, 1846; and *Lexique de Racine*, p. ci.

THÉODORE

Ne cherchez point d'excuse en votre modestie :
Nommez-la, je le veux.

FÉDERIC

Je suis sans repartie,
Mais ma voix cédera cet office à vos yeux :
Vous-même nommez-vous cet objet glorieux :   1530
Vos doigts ont mis son nom au bas de cette lettre.

(*Lui baillant la lettre ouverte*)

THÉODORE, *ayant lu son nom*

Votre mérite, duc, vous peut beaucoup permettre,
Mais . . .

FÉDERIC

Osant vous aimer, j'ai condamné mes vœux,
Je me suis voulu mal du bien que je vous veux ;
Mais, Madame, accusez une étoile fatale   1535
D'élever un espoir que la raison ravale,
De faire à vos sujets encenser vos autels,
Et de vous procurer des hommages mortels.   ·

THÉODORE

Si j'ai pouvoir sur vous, puis-je de votre zèle
Me promettre à l'instant une preuve fidèle?   1540

1528. **Je suis sans repartie** : "I have nothing to answer." A frequent
phrase in the seventeenth century, equivalent to *sans qu'il y ait rien
à dire contre, sans qu'il soit possible de répondre, sans conteste.* See
Lexiques de Corneille, II, p. 293, and *de Molière*, II, p. 401.

1534. **Je me suis voulu mal du bien que je vous veux** : for play on
words see ll. 681–682, 1481. M. : "Jeu d'expression absolument contraire au naturel."

1537. **De faire à vos sujets**, etc. : see ll. 232, 1478, and 1644.

FÉDERIC

Le beau feu dont pour vous ce cœur est embrasé
Trouvera tout possible, et l'impossible aisé.

THÉODORE

L'effort vous en sera pénible, mais illustre.

FÉDERIC

D'une si noble ardeur il accroîtra le lustre.

THÉODORE

Tant s'en faut : cette épreuve est de tenir caché   1545
Un espoir dont l'orgueil vous serait reproché,
De vous taire et n'admettre en votre confidence
Que votre seul respect avec votre prudence,
Et, pour le prix, enfin, du service important
Qui rend sur tant de noms votre nom éclatant,   1550
Aller en ma faveur demander à mon père,
Au lieu de notre hymen, la grâce de mon frère,
Prévenir son arrêt, et, par votre secours,
Faire tomber l'acier prêt à trancher ses jours.
De cette épreuve, duc, vos vœux sont-ils capables ?   1555

FÉDERIC

Oui, Madame, et de plus, puisqu'ils sont si coupables,
Ils vous sauront encor venger de leur orgueil
Et tomber, avec moi, dans la nuit du cercueil.

1542. et l'impossible aisé : with this exaggeration compare the *Cid*,
II. 3, 465 :

L'INFANTE

Et tu sais que mon âme à tes ennuis sensible,
Pour en tarir la source y fera l'impossible.

See *Lexique de Corneille*, II, p. 10.

1545. Tant s'en faut : " Far from it."

1554. Faire tomber l'acier : i.e. from the hand of the executioner.
L'acier, poetic for a weapon made of steel, " ax, sword." See *Lexique
de Corneille*, I, p. 29.

1558. cercueil : see l. 259, and *Saint Genest*, note on l. 597.

THÉODORE

Non, je vous le défends, laissez-moi mes vengeances,
Et, si j'ai droit sur vous, observez mes défenses.   1560
Adieu, duc.   (*Elle s'en va*)

FÉDERIC, *seul*

Quel orage agite mon espoir !
Et quelle loi, mon cœur, viens-tu de recevoir !
Si j'ose l'adorer, je prends trop de licence ;
Si je m'en veux punir, j'en reçois la défense.
Me défendre la mort sans me vouloir guérir,   1565
N'est-ce pas m'ordonner de vivre et de mourir ?
Mais . . .

Scène III

VENCESLAS, FÉDERIC, GARDES

VENCESLAS

O jour à jamais funèbre à la province !
Féderic ?

FÉDERIC

Quoi, Seigneur ?

VENCESLAS

Faites venir le prince.

FÉDERIC, *sortant avec les gardes*

Il sera superflu de tenter mon crédit :
Le sang fait son office, et le roi s'attendrit.   1570

VENCESLAS, *seul, rêvant et se promenant*

Trêve, trêve, nature, aux sanglantes batailles
Qui si cruellement déchirant mes entrailles,

1572. **entrailles**: poetic for "heart, tenderness, affection, pity, feeling";
compare Colossians iii. 12, " bowels of mercies " ; 1 John iii. 17, " bowels
of compassion." See *Lexique de Corneille*, I, p. 372, and *de Racine*, p. 190.

Et, me perçant le cœur, le veulent partager
Entre mon fils à perdre et mon fils à venger !
A ma justice en vain ta tendresse est contraire,   1575
Et dans le cœur d'un roi cherche celui d'un père :
Je me suis dépouillé de cette qualité,
Et n'entends plus d'avis que ceux de l'équité.
Mais, ô vaine constance ! ô force imaginaire !
A cette vue encor je sens que je suis père   1580
Et n'ai pas dépouillé tout humain sentiment.
Sortez, gardes. Vous, duc, laissez-nous un moment.

                                            (*Ils sortent*)

SCÈNE IV

VENCESLAS, LADISLAS

LADISLAS

Venez-vous conserver ou venger votre race?
M'annoncez-vous, mon père, ou ma mort ou ma grâce?

VENCESLAS, *pleurant*

Embrassez-moi, mon fils.

LADISLAS

                        Seigneur, quelle bonté,   1585
Quel effet de tendresse, et quelle nouveauté !
Voulez-vous ou marquer ou remettre mes peines?
Et vos bras me sont-ils des faveurs ou des chaînes?

1574. **à perdre . . . à venger**: see note on l. 1365.

1580. **A cette vue**: the sight of Ladislas who must enter at the words.

1584. **ou ma mort ou ma grâce**: see notes on ll. 467, 1587.

1587. **Voulez-vous ou marquer ou remettre mes peines**: " Do you wish
to indicate (emphasize) my punishment or to pardon me ? " i.e. Is your
embrace a sign of my pardon or the farewell which precedes my death ?

1588. **Et vos bras me sont-ils des faveurs ou des chaînes**: M.: " C'est
dans les situations les plus touchantes que Rotrou semble affecter
l'antithèse ; et c'est là surtout qu'elle est déplacée. Des bras peuvent
être des chaînes ; mais des bras sont-ils des faveurs ? "

VENCESLAS, *pleurant*

Avecque le dernier de leurs embrassements,
Recevez de mon cœur les derniers sentiments.   1590
Savez-vous de quel sang vous avez pris naissance?

LADISLAS

Je l'ai mal témoigné, mais j'en ai connaissance.

VENCESLAS

Sentez-vous de ce sang les nobles mouvements?

LADISLAS

Si je ne les produis, j'en ai les sentiments.

VENCESLAS

Enfin, d'un grand effort vous trouvez-vous capable?   1595

LADISLAS

Oui, puisque je résiste à l'ennui qui m'accable,
Et qu'un effort mortel ne peut aller plus loin.

VENCESLAS

Armez-vous de vertu, vous en avez besoin.

LADISLAS

S'il est temps de partir, mon âme est toute prête.

VENCESLAS

L'échafaud l'est aussi, portez-y votre tête.   1600
Plus condamné que vous, mon cœur vous y suivra ;
Je mourrai plus que vous du coup qui vous tûra.
Mes larmes vous en sont une preuve assez ample ;

1596. **ennui** : see note on l. 757.
1602. **tûra** : see note on l. 1447.

Mais à l'État, enfin, je dois ce grand exemple,
A ma propre vertu ce généreux effort,   1605
Cette grande victime à votre frère mort :
J'ai craint de prononcer, autant que vous d'entendre,
L'arrêt qu'ils demandaient, et que j'ai dû leur rendre.
Pour ne vous perdre pas, j'ai longtemps combattu,
Mais, ou l'art de régner n'est plus une vertu,   1610
Et c'est une chimère aux rois que la justice,
Ou, régnant, à l'État je dois ce sacrifice.

LADISLAS

Eh bien, achevez-le, voilà ce col tout prêt.
Le coupable, grand roi, souscrit à votre arrêt ;
Je ne m'en défends point, et je sais que mes crimes   1615
Vous ont causé souvent des courroux légitimes.
Je pourrais du dernier m'excuser sur l'erreur
D'un bras qui s'est mépris et crut trop ma fureur :
Ma haine et mon amour, qu'il voulait satisfaire,
Portaient le coup au duc, et non pas à mon frère :   1620
J'alléguerais encor que le coup part d'un bras
Dont les premiers efforts ont servi vos États,
Et m'ont, dans votre histoire, acquis assez de place
Pour vous devoir parler en faveur de ma grâce ;
Mais je n'ai point dessein de prolonger mon sort ;   1625

1611. **Et c'est une chimère aux rois que la justice** : "and justice is for kings an idle fancy." For connective *que* when *c'est* is followed by two appositional subjects see *Lexique de Corneille*, II, p. 245 ; and Mätzner, *Franz. Gram.*, p. 344, and *Syntax*, I, p. 12. There are other examples in ll. 1630, 1631–1632.

1613. **Eh bien, achevez-le, voilà ce col tout prêt** : M. : "L'hémistiche tombe sur un *e* muet. Col ni cou n'est plus du style noble : en pareil cas on dit, ma tête."

1616. **des courroux légitimes** : M. : "Courroux n'a point de pluriel."

1618. **D'un bras qui s'est mépris et crut trop ma fureur** : M. : "Il y a un contretemps dans le second hémistiche ; il fallait dire, et a cru."

J'ai mon objet à part, à qui je dois ma mort :
Vous la devez au peuple, à mon frère, à vous-même ;
Moi je la dois, Seigneur, à l'ingrate que j'aime,
Je la dois à sa haine, et m'en veux acquitter :
C'est un léger tribut qu'une vie à quitter ;   1630
C'est peu, pour satisfaire et pour plaire à Cassandre,
Qu'une tête à donner et du sang à répandre,
Et, forcé de l'aimer jusqu'au dernier soupir,
Sans avoir pu, vivant, répondre à son désir,
Suis ravi de savoir que ma mort y réponde,   1635
Et que, mourant, je plaise aux plus beaux yeux du monde.

VENCESLAS

A quoi que votre cœur destine votre mort,
Allez vous préparer à cet illustre effort,
Et, pour les intérêts d'une mortelle flamme,
Abandonnant le corps, n'abandonnez pas l'âme.   1640
Tout obscure qu'elle est, la nuit a beaucoup d'yeux,
Et n'a pas pu cacher votre forfait aux cieux.

(*L'embrassant*)

Adieu, sur l'échafaud portez le cœur d'un prince,

1626. **J'ai mon objet à part** : "I have my particular object." Used
in this adjective sense *à part* means "peculiar, particular, exceptional."
See *Lexique de Corneille*, II, p. 159.

1629. **et m'en veux acquitter** : "and wish to pay my debt."

1630. **C'est un léger tribut**, etc. : see note on l. 1611. Same construction in ll. 1631–1632.

1632. **une tête à donner** : see notes on ll. 1365, 1515.

1635. **Suis ravi** : for omission of pronoun see *Saint Genest*, note on
l. 23, and many other places. M. : "On trouvera cent fois la même faute
dans cette pièce."

1641–1642. **Tout obscure qu'elle est, la nuit a beaucoup d'yeux,** etc. : this
is not in the Spanish original. Where is there a similar thought ? M. :
" La nuit a des yeux, est une métaphore simple, mais penser et dire
que la nuit a beaucoup d'yeux, quoiqu'elle soit obscure, et par là faire
allusion aux étoiles, rien de moins naturel, dans la situation d'un père
qui envoie son fils à la mort."

Et faites-y douter à toute la province
Si, né pour commander et destiné si haut,   1645
Vous mourez sur un trône ou sur un échafaud.
Duc, remmenez le prince.

    (*Le roi frappe du pied pour retenir* le duc*)

      (*Féderic entre avec des gardes*)

     LADISLAS, *s'en allant*

      O vertu trop sévère !
Venceslas vit encor, et je n'ai plus de père !

       [*Il sort*]

SCÈNE V

VENCESLAS, GARDES

VENCESLAS

O justice inhumaine et devoirs ennemis !
Pour conserver mon sceptre, il faut perdre mon fils !   1650
Mais laisse-les agir, importune tendresse,
Et vous, cachez, mes yeux, vos pleurs et ma faiblesse.
Je ne puis rien pour lui, le sang cède à la loi,
Et je ne lui puis être et bon père et bon roi.
Vois, Pologne, en l'horreur que le vice m'imprime,   1655
Si mon élection fut un choix légitime ;
Et si je puis donner aux devoirs de mon rang
Plus que mon propre fils et que mon propre sang.

SCÈNE VI

THÉODORE, CASSANDRE, LÉONOR, VENCESLAS, GARDES

THÉODORE

Par quelle loi, Seigneur, si barbare et si dure,
Pouvez-vous renverser celle de la nature ?   1660

---

* *Retenir* in stage direction of 1648 is evidently an error, corrected by
Viollet-le-Duc and Hémon into *faire venir*.

J'apprends qu'au prince, hélas ! l'arrêt est prononcé,
Que de son châtiment l'appareil est dressé.
Quoi ! nous demeurerons, par des lois si sévères,
L'État sans héritiers, vous sans fils, moi sans frères !
Consultez-vous un peu contre votre fureur :   1665
C'est trop qu'en votre fils condamner une erreur ;
Du carnage d'un frère un frère est incapable ;
De cet assassinat la nuit seule est coupable ;
Il plaint autant que nous le sort qu'il a fini
Et par son propre crime il est assez puni.   1670
La pitié, qui fera révoquer son supplice,
N'est pas moins la vertu d'un roi que la justice.
Avec moins de fureur vous lui serez plus doux :
La justice est souvent le masque du courroux ;
Et l'on imputera cet arrêt si sévère   1675
Moins au devoir d'un roi qu'à la fureur d'un père.
Un murmure public condamne cet arrêt :
La nature vous parle, et Cassandre se tait ;
La rencontre du prince en ce lieu non prévue,
L'intérêt de l'État, et mes pleurs l'ont vaincue ;   1680
Son ennui si profond n'a su nous résister :
Un fils, enfin, n'a plus qu'un père à surmonter.

CASSANDRE

Je revenais, Seigneur, demander son supplice,
Et de ce noble effort presser votre justice ;
Mon cœur, impatient d'attendre son trépas,   1685
Accusait chaque instant qui ne me vengeait pas ;
Mais je ne puis juger par quel effet contraire

    1667. **carnage** : = *meurtre* : M. : " J'ai déjà observé qu'on dit meurtre
pour un seul homme."

    1669. **le sort qu'il a fini** : " the destiny which he has accomplished."

    1679. **La rencontre du prince en ce lieu non prévue** : did Théodore and
Cassandre meet the prince as he was being led away to prison ? See
l. 1688.

Sa rencontre en ce cœur a fait taire son frère !
Ses fers ont combattu le vif ressentiment
Que je dois, malheureuse, au sang de mon amant ;   1690
Et, quoique, tout meurtri, mon âme encor l'adore,
Les plaintes, les raisons, les pleurs de Théodore,
Le murmure du peuple et de l'État entier,
Qui contre mon parti soutient son héritier
Et condamne l'arrêt dont ma douleur vous presse,   1695
Suspendent en mon sein cette ardeur vengeresse,
Et me la font enfin passer pour attentat
Contre le bien public et le chef de l'État.
Je me tais donc, Seigneur ; disposez de la vie
Que vous m'avez promise et que j'ai poursuivie.   1700

     [*A part*]
Au défaut de celui qu'on te refusera,
J'ai du sang, cher amant, qui te satisfera.

VENCESLAS

Vous ne pouvez douter, duchesse, et vous, infante,
Que, père, je voudrais répondre à votre attente :
Je suis par son arrêt plus condamné que lui,   1705
Et je préférerais la mort à mon ennui :

   1706. 1648 has *sa mort*, a misprint corrected by Viollet-le-Duc, Ronchaud, and Hémon to *la mort*.

   1688. Sa rencontre en ce cœur, etc. : i.e. meeting Ladislas (see l. 1679) has silenced in Cassandre's heart his brother's cry for vengeance.

   1691. Et, quoique, tout meurtri, etc. : M. : " Tout meurtri pour dire, tout mort qu'il est, n'est plus français."

   1699. disposez de la vie, etc. : M. : " La vie que vous m'avez promise, signifie, dans son sens naturel, la vie que vous m'avez promis de conserver ; et c'est tout le contraire dans le sens du poète."

   1701–1702. Au défaut de celui qu'on te refusera, etc. : for threat of suicide see *Saint Genest*, ll. 81–84.

   1706. à mon ennui : M. : " Ennui est ridiculement faible, pour exprimer la situation d'un prince, qui porte sa tête sur l'échafaud." See note on l. 757.

Mais d'autre part je règne, et, si je lui pardonne,
D'un opprobre eternel je souille ma couronne ;
Au lieu que, résistant, à cette dureté
Ma vie et votre honneur devront leur sûreté.   1710
Ce lion est dompté : mais peut-être, Madame,
Celui qui, si soumis, vous déguise sa flamme,
Plus fier et violent qu'il n'a jamais été,
Demain attenterait sur votre honnêteté ;
Peut-être qu'à mon sang sa main accoutumée   1715
Contre mon propre sein demain serait armée.
La pitié qu'il vous cause est digne d'un grand cœur ;
Mais, si je veux régner, il l'est de ma rigueur :
Je vous dois malgré vous raison de votre offense,
Et, quand vous vous rendez, prendre votre défense.   1720
Mon courroux résistant, et le vôtre abattu,
Sont d'illustres effets d'une même vertu.

Scène VII

Féderic, Venceslas, Théodore, Cassandre, Léonor, gardes

VENCESLAS

Que fait le prince, duc ?

FÉDERIC

C'est en ce moment, Sire,
Qu'il est prince en effet et qu'il peut se le dire :

1709. **Au lieu que, résistant**, etc. : M. : " Résistant n'a aucun rapport,
et la construction est forcée."

1711. **Ce lion est dompté** : i.e. for a short time.

1712. **vous déguise sa flamme** : "conceals his love from you."

1713. **Plus fier et violent** : M. : "Il eût été mieux de dire, plus fier,
plus violent. Je ne crois pourtant qu'il soit indispensable de répéter
plus, quand les deux mots ont tant d'analogie."

1714. **honnêteté** : " virtue, honor." See *honnête*, note on l. 1336.

1718. **il l'est de ma rigueur** : " he (Ladislas) is worthy of my severity."

1724. **et qu'il peut se le dire** : M. : " Se le dire, ne signifie pas ici, dire
cela à soi-même ; mais se dire soi-même tel ; et dans ce sens-là, se le
dire n'est pas français."

Il semble, aux yeux de tous, d'un héroïque effort,   1725
Se préparer plutôt à l'hymen qu'à la mort.
Et puisque, si remis de tant de violence,
Il n'est plus en état de m'imposer silence,
Et m'envier un bien que ce bras m'a produit,
De mes travaux, grand roi, je demande le fruit.   1730

VENCESLAS

Il est juste, et fût-il de toute ma province . . .

FÉDERIC

Je le restreins, Seigneur, à la grâce du prince.

VENCESLAS

Quoi !

FÉDERIC

        J'ai votre parole, et ce dépôt sacré
Contre votre refus m'est un gage assuré.
J'ai payé de mon sang l'heur que j'ose prétendre.   1735

VENCESLAS

Quoi ! Féderic aussi conspire à me surprendre !
Quel charme contre un père, en faveur de son fils,
Suscite et fait parler ses propres ennemis ?

1727. **si remis de tant de violence**: "so calm after such great violence." Compare l. 1179, and *Saint Genest*, note on l. 549.

1729. **Et m'envier**: M.: "Il fallait dire, et de m'envier." See ll. 1752,
1780. Modern usage requires the repetition of the preposition, but
in the seventeenth century *de* and *à* were constantly not repeated.
See Haase, 145; Vaugelas, II, p. 393; *Lexiques de Corneille*, I,
pp. lxxvii, 12, 255; and *de Molière*, I, p. clxxxvii; Benoist, p. 407.

1733. **et ce dépôt sacré**: "and this sacred pledge (your promise)."
In the next line translate *gage assuré* "a certain guarantee."

1735. **prétendre**: for *prétendre à*; see note on l. 1331.

FÉDERIC

C'est peu que pour un prince une faute s'efface,
L'État qu'il doit régir lui doit bien une grâce : 1740
Le seul sang de l'infant par son crime est versé,
Mais par son châtiment tout l'État est blessé :
Sa cause, quoique injuste, est la cause publique :
Il n'est pas toujours bon d'être trop politique.
Ce que veut tout l'État se peut-il denier ? 1745
Et, père, devez-vous vous rendre le dernier ?

SCÈNE VIII

OCTAVE, VENCESLAS, FÉDERIC, THÉODORE, CASSANDRE,
LÉONOR, GARDES

OCTAVE, *hors d'haleine*

Seigneur, d'un cri commun toute la populace
Parle en faveur du prince et demande sa grâce,
Et surtout un grand nombre, en la place amassé,
A d'un zèle indiscret l'échafaud renversé, 1750
Et, les larmes aux yeux, d'une commune envie
Proteste de périr ou lui sauver la vie ;
D'un même mouvement et d'une même voix
Tous le disent exempt de la rigueur des lois,
Et, si cette chaleur n'est bientôt apaisée, 1755
Jamais sédition ne fut plus disposée.

1739. **C'est peu que pour un prince une faute s'efface** : M.: "Ce vers ne présente pas un sens net ; le poète veut dire que c'est faire peu de chose pour un prince, que de lui pardonner une faute."

1744. **politique** : "prudent, cautious."

1756. **disposée** : "ready, prepared." M.: "Plus disposée pour dire, plus près d'éclater, n'est pas français ; disposée avec mieux, peut être pris à l'absolu ; mais avec plus, il veut un régime."

En vain pour y mettre ordre et pour les contenir,
J'ai voulu . . .

VENCESLAS, à Octave

C'est assez, faites-le-moi venir.

LÉONOR

Ciel, seconde nos vœux.

(Octave va quérir le prince)

THÉODORE

Voyons cette aventure.

VENCESLAS, rêvant et se promenant à grands pas

Oui, ma fille ; oui, Cassandre ; oui, parole ; oui, nature ; 1760
Oui, peuple, il faut vouloir ce que vous souhaitez,
Et par vos sentiments régler mes volontés.

(Le prince et Octave entrent)

SCÈNE IX

LADISLAS, VENCESLAS, FÉDERIC, THÉODORE, CASSANDRE,
LÉONOR, GARDES

LADISLAS, aux pieds du roi

Par quel heur . . .

VENCESLAS, le relevant

Levez-vous : une couronne, prince,
Sous qui j'ai quarante ans régi cette province,
Qui passera sans tache en un règne futur,   1765

1760. **Oui, ma fille ; oui, Cassandre ; oui, parole ; oui, nature** : M. :
"On trouverait ridicule aujourd'hui, avec raison, que le roi mît la
parole qu'il a donné, au nombre des êtres réels ou allégoriques auxquels
il s'adresse."

1764. **Sous qui** : for *qui* used with prepositions and referring to things
see *Lexique de Corneille*, I, p. xlvii ; II, p. 254. Another example in
l. 1764. See *Saint Genest*, note on l. 221.

Et dont tous les brillants ont un éclat si pur,
En qui la voix des grands et le commun suffrage
M'ont d'un nombre d'aïeux conservé l'héritage,
Est l'unique moyen que j'ai pu concevoir
Pour, en votre faveur, désarmer mon pouvoir.   1770
Je ne vous puis sauver tant qu'elle sera mienne :
Il faut que votre tête ou tombe, ou la soutienne ;
Il vous en faut pourvoir, s'il vous faut pardonner,
Et punir votre crime, ou bien le couronner.
L'État vous la souhaite, et le peuple m'enseigne,   1775
Voulant que vous viviez, qu'il est las que je règne.
La justice est aux rois la reine des vertus,
Et me vouloir injuste est ne me vouloir plus.
        (*Lui baillant la couronne*)
Régnez, après l'État j'ai droit de vous élire,
Et donner en mon fils un père à mon empire.   1780

LADISLAS

Que faites-vous, grand roi?

VENCESLAS

                    M'appeler de ce nom,
C'est hors de mon pouvoir mettre votre pardon.
Je ne veux plus d'un rang où je vous suis contraire.
Soyez roi, Ladislas, et moi je serai père.
Roi, je n'ai pu des lois souffrir les ennemis ;   1785
Père, je ne pourrai faire périr mon fils.
Une perte est aisée où l'amour nous convie :

1773. **Il vous en faut pourvoir**: " it (the crown) must be conferred
on you."

1779. **après l'État j'ai droit de vous élire**: "according to the laws of
the state I have the right to choose you." *Après = d'après*; see Haase,
132, C, and *Lexique de Corneille*, I, p. 70. In Poland the throne was elective until 1788, when it was declared hereditary. The king was usually
succeeded by his son, who, however, had to be elected by the senate.

Je ne perdrai qu'un nom pour sauver une vie,
Pour contenter Cassandre, et le duc, et l'État,
Qui les premiers font grâce à votre assassinat :   1790
Le duc pour récompense a requis cette grâce,
Ce peuple mutiné veut que je vous la fasse,
Cassandre le consent, je ne m'en défends plus ;
Ma seule dignité m'enjoignait ce refus.
Sans peine je descends de ce degré suprême :   1795
J'aime mieux conserver un fils qu'un diadème.

LADISLAS

Si vous ne pouvez être et mon père et mon roi,
Puis-je être votre fils et vous donner la loi ?
Sans peine je renonce à ce degré suprême ;
Abandonnez plutôt un fils qu'un diadème.   1800

VENCESLAS

Je n'y prétends plus rien, ne me le rendez pas :
Qui pardonne à son roi punirait Ladislas,
Et sans cet ornement ferait tomber sa tête.

LADISLAS

A vos ordres, Seigneur, la voilà toute prête ;
Je la conserverai, puisque je vous la dois ;   1805
Mais elle régnera pour dispenser vos lois,
Et toujours, quoi qu'elle ose ou quoi qu'elle projette,
Le diadème au front, sera votre sujette.
    (*Il dit au duc l'embrassant*)
Par quel heureux destin, duc, ai-je mérité

1793. **Cassandre le consent** : M. : "Consentir n'a plus le régime direct : on dirait, Cassandre y consent." See note on l. 1024.

1794. **Ma seule dignité**, etc. : " my rank alone forced me to refuse it " (i.e. Ladislas's pardon).

1802. **Qui pardonne à son roi**, etc. : " he who forgives his king would punish Ladislas " (i.e. if he were not king).

Et de votre courage et de votre bonté   1810
Le soin si généreux qu'ils ont eu pour ma vie?

FÉDERIC

Ils ont servi l'État alors qu'ils l'ont servie.
Mais, et vers la couronne et vers vous acquitté,
J'implore une faveur de Votre Majesté.

LADISLAS

Quelle?

FÉDERIC

Votre congé, Seigneur, et ma retraite,   1815
Pour ne vous plus nourrir cette haine secrète
Qui, m'expliquant si mal, vous rend toujours suspects
Mes plus ardents devoirs et mes plus grands respects.

LADISLAS

Non, non, vous devez, duc, vos soins à ma province :
Roi, je n'hérite point des différends du prince,   1820
Et j'augurerais mal de mon gouvernement
S'il m'en fallait d'abord ôter le fondement :
Qui trouve où dignement reposer sa couronne,

1812. **alors qu'** : for *lorsque* ; see Haase, 137, R. ii. The old form is still used in poetry and even in modern prose ; see Mätzner, *Syntax*, II, p. 130.

1815. **Votre congé** : M. : "Cela signifie à présent, le congé que vous avez reçu, et non pas le congé que vous avez donné."

1816. **Pour ne vous plus nourrir cette haine secrète** : M. : "Vous nourrir, pour nourrir en vous, n'est pas français."

1817. **m'expliquant si mal** : "as I have explained myself so badly." See note on l. 867.

1819–1836. In these lines Raynouard, *Journal des Savants*, 1823, p. 286, sees a reference to Cardinal Mazarin, at this time, 1647, at the height of his power.

1820. **différends** : see notes on ll. 298, 826.

1823. **Qui trouve où dignement reposer sa couronne** : "he who finds a worthy resting place for his crown."

Qui rencontre à son trône une ferme colonne,
Qui possède un sujet digne de cet emploi,   1825
Peut vanter son bonheur, et peut dire être roi.
Le Ciel nous l'a donné, cet État le possède ;
Par ses soins tout nous rit, tout fleurit, tout succède ;
Par son art nos voisins, nos propres ennemis,
N'aspirent qu'à nous être alliés ou soumis ;   1830
Il fait briller partout notre pouvoir suprême ;
Par lui toute l'Europe ou nous craint ou nous aime,
Il est de tout l'État la force et l'ornement,
Et vous me l'ôteriez par votre éloignement.
L'heur le plus précieux que, régnant, je respire   1835
Est que vous demeuriez l'âme de cet empire.
   (*Montrant Théodore*)
Et, si vous répondez à mon élection,
Ma sœur sera le nœud de votre affection.

FÉDERIC

J'y prétendrais en vain, après que sa défense
M'a de sa servitude interdit la licence.   1840

THÉODORE

Je vous avais prescrit de cacher vos liens ;
Mais les ordres du roi sont au-dessus des miens,
Et, me donnant à vous, font cesser ma défense.

1837. élection : " choice." See note on l. 1779.

1838. nœud : " bond."

1839–1840. J'y prétendrais en vain, etc. : " I should aspire to her in vain, after she has refused me permission to serve her." M. : " Dans ce sens-là, ma servitude est du style romanesque. La licence de la servitude fait une antithèse puérile."

1841. vos liens : " your bondage to me." *Liens* for " chains, fetters," etc., is one of the commonplaces of the gallantry of the times ; see *Lexiques de Racine*, p. 301, and *de Molière*, II, p. 114. See *Saint Genest*, note on ll. 105–110 ; *Venceslas*, notes on ll. 351, 1036, 1096, etc.

FÉDERIC

Oh ! de tous mes travaux trop digne récompense !
    (*A Ladislas*)
C'est à ce prix, Seigneur, qu'aspirait mon crédit,   1845
Et vous me le rendez, me l'ayant interdit.

LADISLAS

J'ai pour vous accepté la vie et la couronne,
Madame ; ordonnez-en, je vous les abandonne.
Pour moi, sans vos faveurs, elles n'ont rien de doux ;
Je les rends, j'y renonce, et n'en veux point sans vous :   1850
De vous seule dépend et mon sort et ma vie.

CASSANDRE

Après qu'à mon amant votre main l'a ravie !

VENCESLAS

Le sceptre que j'y mets a son crime effacé.
Dessous un nouveau règne oublions le passé ;
Qu'avec le nom de prince il perde votre haine :   1855
Quand je vous donne un roi, donnez-nous une reine.

    1846. me l'ayant interdit : "after you had forbidden me it." See notes on ll. 867, 1817.

    1849. sans vos faveurs : M. : "Cette expression n'est plus décente, lorsqu'on s'adresse à une femme ; on l'emploierait en parlant aux dieux. Rien n'appauvrit tant le langage noble que l'abus que l'on fait des mots les plus honnêtes, pour voiler à demi les choses qui ne le sont pas."

    1850. et n'en veut point : for omission of subject see note on l. 1635.

    1851. dépend et mon sort et ma vie : for singular verb with two subjects see note on l. 1180.

    1854. Dessous : = *sous*. See Haase, 128, A ; Vaugelas, I, p. 217 ; and *Lexiques de Corneille*, I, p. 288, and *de Racine*, p. 146.

CASSANDRE

Puis-je, sans un trop lâche et trop sensible effort,
Épouser le meurtrier, étant veuve du mort?
Puis-je . . .

VENCESLAS

Le temps, ma fille . . .

CASSANDRE

Ha! quel temps le peut faire?

LADISLAS

Si je n'obtiens, au moins permettez que j'espère :   1860
Tant de soumissions lasseront vos mépris
Qu'enfin de mon amour vos vœux seront le prix.

VENCESLAS, *à Ladislas*

Allons rendre à l'infant nos dernières tendresses,
Et dans sa sépulture enfermer nos tristesses.
Vous, faites-moi, vivant, louer mon successeur,   1865
Et voir de ma couronne un digne possesseur.

1857. **sensible effort** : "painful effort." See *Saint Genest*, note on l. 234.

1860. **Si je n'obtiens** : i.e. If I obtain nothing now. *Obtenir* is here used absolutely.

1863–1866. With the conclusion of this scene compare the ending of the *Cid* and Corneille's care in omitting all reference to the Count's funeral. Corneille says in *Examen du Cid* : " Les funérailles du Comte étaient encore une chose fort embarrassante, soit qu'elles soient faites avant la fin de la pièce, soit que le corps ait demeuré en présence dans son hôtel, attendant qu'on y donnât ordre. Le moindre mot que j'en eusse laissé dire, pour en prendre soin, eût rompu toute la chaleur de l'attention, et rempli l'auditeur d'une fâcheuse idée. J'ai cru plus à propos de les dérober à son imagination par mon silence," etc.

FIN

APPENDIX I

PARALLEL PASSAGES IN ROTROU'S *SAINT GENEST* AND IN THE SPANISH ORIGINAL

Saint Genest, ll. 216–220. LOPE DE VEGA, *Lo Fingido Verdadero*, acto segundo (p. 57, Tomo IV. *Obras de Lope de Vega publicadas por la Real Academia Española*).

> Si tus glorias,
> Si tus grandes hazañas, si tu raro
> Divino entendimiento, César ínclito,
> Fuera capaz de versos y de historias,
> Ginés representara tu alabanza,
> Y todos los ingenios que celebra,
> No sólo Roma, pero España y Grecia,
> Se ocuparan, señor, en escribillas.

Saint Genest, ll. 271–276. *Lo Fingido Verdadero*, acto segundo, p. 57.

> Dame una nueva fábula que tenga
> Más invención, aunque carezca de arte;
> Que tengo gusto de español en esto,
> Y como me le dé lo verosímil,
> Nunca reparo tanto en los preceptos,
> Antes me cansa su rigor, y he visto
> Que los que miran en guardar el arte,
> Nunca del natural alcanzan parte.

Saint Genest, ll. 421–424. *Lo Fingido Verdadero*, acto tercero, p. 71.

> (*Con música se abran en alto unas puertas en que se vean pintados una imagen de Nuestra Señora y un Cristo en brazos del Padre, y por las gradas de este trono algunos mártires*)

UNA VOZ DENTRO

> No le imitarás en vano,
> Ginés: que te has de salvar.

359

Saint Genest, ll. 425–436.　*Lo Fingido Verdadero*, acto tercero, p. 72.

> ¡ Válgame el cielo ! ¿ Qué es esto ?
> ¿ Quién me habló ? Pero sería,
> Aunque lejos de este puesto,
> Alguien de mi compañía
> Que me vió tratando desto.
>
> .　　.　　.　　.　　.　　.
>
> La voz que todo mi oído
> Me ha penetrado el sentido,
> Sospecho que fuera bien
> Pensar que es Cristo, si es quien
> Me ha tocado y me ha movido.

Saint Genest, ll. 446–449.　*Lo Fingido Verdadero*, acto tercero, p. 72.

> ¡ Ah, señor !
> No te diviertas en vano ;
> Que sale el Emperador,
> Y que has de hacer falta es llano.
>
> .　　.　　.　　.　　.　　.
>
> Perdona, que divertido
> En imitar al cristiano,
> Fuera me vi de sentido,
> Pensando que el soberano
> Ángel me hablaba al oído.

Saint Genest, ll. 1239–1242.　*Lo Fingido Verdadero*, acto tercero, p. 74.

GINÉS

> ¡ Ay, Señor ! ¡ Quién estuviera,
> Ya que es vuestro, bautizado,
> Por si acaso perdonado
> De aqueste martirio fuera !
> Que si no, bien sé que basta
> Mi sangre.

Saint Genest, l. 1258.　*Lo Fingido Verdadero*, acto segundo, p. 62.

MARCELA

> Esto no está en la comedia ;
> Mira que el César nos mira.

Saint Genest, ll. 1259–1260. *Lo Fingido Verdadero*, acto tercero, p. 74.

> Hace y dice de improviso
> Cosas de que no da aviso.

Saint Genest, ll. 1263–1264. *Lo Fingido Verdadero*, acto segundo, p. 62.

DIOCLECIANO

> Mas pienso que es artificio
> Þeste gran representante,
> Porque turbarse un amante
> Fué siempre el mayor indicio.

Saint Genest, l. 1283. *Lo Fingido Verdadero*, acto tercero, p. 75.

> ¡ Cuál estaba en el bautismo
> Imitando á los cristianos,
> Humilde y puestas las manos !

Saint Genest, l. 1284. *Lo Fingido Verdadero*, acto tercero, pp. 74–75.

> Represéntale Ginés
> Que parece que lo es,
> Y verdadero el suceso
> .   .   .   .   .
> No hay diferencia
> Desto al verdadero caso.

Saint Genest, ll. 1298–1300. *Lo Fingido Verdadero*, acto tercero, p. 75.

> ¡ Hola ! ¡ Apunten !

GINÉS

> ¿ Pues no ves
> Que el cielo me apunta ya,
> Desde que á un ángel oí
> Detrás de su azul cortina :

Saint Genest, ll. 1303–1314; 1365–1370. *Lo Fingido Verdadero*, acto tercero, p. 75.

> Estaba el papel errado :
> Donde Dios decir tenía,

Demonio, amigos, decía
Y donde gracia, pecado,
  Donde cielo hermoso, infierno,
Donde si errara me fuera,
Donde vida, muerte fiera,
Donde gloria, llanto eterno;
  Pero despúes que apuntó
El ángel del vestuario
Del cielo, y lo necesario
Para acertar me enseñó.
  Yo dije á Dios mi papel
Desde el punto de aquel día,
Y aun como el Avemaría
Que también estaba en él.
  Oyeron de mi buen celo
La comedia, y era justo,
Y en verdad que dí gran gusto,
Pues que me llevan al cielo.
  De Dios soy de aquí adelante,
Que siéndolo de su fe,
Dice el cielo que seré
El mejor representante.

Saint Genest, l. 1322. *Lo Fingido Verdadero*, acto tercero, p. 76.

La culpa habrá estado en mí,
Y así no es bien que te espantes.

Saint Genest, ll. 1319–1321. *Lo Fingido Verdadero*, acto tercero, p. 76.

Si la comedia ignoráis,
¿Para qué á hacerla salís?
¿Y por qué también reñís
Cuando en mi presencia estáis?

Saint Genest, ll. 1386–1388. *Lo Fingido Verdadero*, acto tercero, p. 76.

Pues ya quiero hacer mi dicho,
Y morirás en comedia,
Pues en comedia has vivido.

Saint Genest, ll. 1395–1396. *Lo Fingido Verdadero*, acto tercero, p. 76.

> Villano, ¿ por qué has perdido
> La gracia del César?

GINÉS

>   Tengo
> La de Dios.

Saint Genest, ll. 1405–1430. *Lo Fingido Verdadero*, acto tercero, pp. 77–78.

LÉNTULO

> Llamad los representantes,
> Y salgan uno por uno
> Sin que se esconda ninguno.

> (*Sale Marcela*)

MARCELA

> ¿ Qué me mandas ?

LÉNTULO

>   Dí, ¿ quién eres ?

MARCELA

> Marcela.

LÉNTULO

>   ¿ De qué servías
> Á Ginés ?

MARCELA

>   ¿ Ya no lo vías ?
> De representar mujeres.

> (*Sale Octavio*)

LÉNTULO

> Tu, ¿ quién eres ?

OCTAVIO

>   Su marido.

LÉNTULO

> ¿ Qué representáis ?

OCTAVIO

Galanes.

(*Sale Sergesto*)

LÉNTULO

Vos, ¿qué hacéis?

SERGESTO

Yo, los rufianes,
El soldadillo perdido,
    El capitán fanfarrón,
Y otras cosas deste modo,
Y lo represento todo
Cuando se ofrece ocasión.

LÉNTULO

¿Qué haces tú?

(*Sale Albino*)

ALBINO

Yo, los graciosos,
Desdichados, no dichosos,
Si aquí muestras tu furor.
    Hago también los pastores
Si se pierde alguna dama
Y por los montes me llama.

APPENDIX II

PARALLEL PASSAGES IN ROTROU'S *SAINT GENEST*
AND LOUIS CELLOT'S *SANCTUS ADRIANUS*

Saint Genest, ll. 335–348. LUDOVICI CELLOTII *Opera Poetica*,
Paris, 1630, p. 1.

ADRIANUS

> Adriane, jacta est alea : athletam Dei
> Profiteris auctoratus et forti voves
> Servire domino : macte, vinciri imminet,
> Uri, necari : gravius et si quid jubet
> Orci lanista, pectus addictum offeres.
> Aliis locatas tendere ad populum manus,
> Submittere arma, pollicis mitem licet
> Statum rogare ; te decet jugulum dare
> Totumque ferrum recipere, et stantem mori.

Saint Genest, ll. 487–490. LUDOVICI CELLOTII *op. cit.*, p. 1.

> Sed vita prorogetur ; hic certe brevis
> Dabatur honorum meta, Caesareus favor
> Residet omnis. Nempe mortalem aestimas
> Christo probandus ?

Saint Genest, ll. 499–502. LUDOVICI CELLOTII *op. cit.*, p. 1.

> Vidi haud suo pallere tortorem metu,
> Vidi caduca pendulum in vulnus manu
> Fugere sub ictu, colla cum immotus gradu
> Praeberet infans, atque vix lethi capax
> Victrice tenerum laurea impleret caput.
> Haec virgo potuit, potuit in vitae puer
> Limine, Deo maturus.

Saint Genest, ll. 527–532. LUDOVICI CELLOTII *op. cit.*, p. 2.

> Unum est quo latus
> Nudare vereor : socia genialis tori,

365

Natalia ardet veneris innocua face,
Adriane, amat te : genua prensabit manu,
Rigabit ora lacrymis, praesens bonum,
Tot spes futuri, voce quam blanda occinet !

Saint Genest, ll. 554–574. LUDOVICI CELLOTII *op. cit.*, p. 2.

Labor Adriani vincet, et caelo auspice
Quiescet aut elusus aut fessus furor.
Strident catenis oppida, angusti gemunt
Vomuntque turbam carceres, crebra nece
Fessae secures, arma carnificis, reis
Tormenta desunt : dixerat, magno ambitu
Titianus intrat grande dicturus nefas :
Res periit omnis, Caesar ! — Horrendum sonat
Murmur per aulam : Jovius an letho occidit ?
Romam tyrannus occupat ? Largo perit
Urbs Nicomedis igne ? Quid dubios tenes ?
Eloquere, — Christum noster Adrianus colit !

Saint Genest, ll. 679–682. LUDOVICI CELLOTII *op. cit.*, p. 11.

Haec illa meriti gratia ? haec nostris fides
Jurata sceptris ? transfuga et nostri et tui
Oblitus hostem colere ut affectes Deum ?

Saint Genest, ll. 717–724. LUDOVICI CELLOTII *op. cit.*, p. 12.

Num quid aggredior miser,
Elusus, exspes ? Ecce per nemorum avia,
Per clausa Phoebo lustra, et aestiferi canis
Perusta flammis arva, Christicolum insequor
Sacrilega vindex capita, et introrsus mea
Surgunt in aula : quos procul venor, meo
Sub latere crescunt.

Saint Genest, ll. 731–737. LUDOVICI CELLOTII *op. cit.*, p. 13.

Olim Adriano si stetit vita innocens,
Quae Christianum culpa constituit reum ?
Christus fidelem ludere incautos vetat,
Verbo aucupari perfido, fraude illice
Captare gazas ; sanguine innocuo manus
Foedare, veneris scandere illicitae toros . . .

Saint Genest, ll. 749–754. LUDOVICI CELLOTII *op. cit.*, p. 13.

GALERIUS

Tuum est Deos eligere ? judicio placet
Meo petatur, quae mihi petitur salus.

ADRIANUS

A quo impetranda est poscitur : cassa prece
Metalli inane pondus impelli jubes ?

Saint Genest, ll. 802–810. LUDOVICI CELLOTII *op. cit.*, p. 22.

ADRIANUS

Mulier huc aurem et sile. . . .
Communia inter esse consortes tori
Voluêre jura Romuli . . .
Sed aut eosdem jure connubii Deos,
Aut ritu eosdem colere, si varii placent,
Lex nulla jussit, . . .

Saint Genest, ll. 851–856. LUDOVICI CELLOTII *op. cit.*, p. 23.

Christe, tam potens habes,
Tam dulce numen ? Teneo te, pars o mei,
Adriane, mea lux ? Effer evinctas manus :
Nunc Adriani rite convenio in manum
Non falsa conjux : Christus hoc vinclo invicem
Sibique amantes sociat. O thalamum ! o faces
Diu cupitas !

Saint Genest, ll. 865–874. LUDOVICI CELLOTII *op. cit.*, p. 24.

ADRIANUS

Dic autem, soror,
Unde iste subitus pectus invasit calor ?

NATALIA

Fatebor equidem, frater, et totam dabo.
Nataliam, Adriane, unus et mundo intulit
Christoque peperit uterus, in cunis erat
Audire Christum ludus, haerentem uberi,
Christum docebat mater ; acclivi in sinum,

Christum canebat. Crevit interea simul
Aetas, amorque minimis, donec viro
Maturam amasti, frater.

Saint Genest, ll. 884–901. LUDOVICI CELLOTII *op. cit.*, p. 25.

Ultimum est quod te alloquor:
I nata felix, si qua religio movet
Dissidia, tu homini victa succumbas cave,
Quin oro vincas. In novos Christus Lares
Domiducus esto, si datur Christum sequi:
Sin, viva nunquam triste transilias domûs
Limen nefande . . .

> . . . scit verax Deus

Quae vota fudi tacita, quam stabili in minas,
In ferrum, in ignes, robore armavi fidem.
Tibi juncta nunquam thura delubro intuli.

Saint Genest, ll. 1192–1202. LUDOVICI CELLOTII *op. cit.*, p. 54.

NATALIA

Te praesta virum,
Adriane ; tenui poena momento parit
Aeternitatem.

ADRIANUS

Totus in caelum feror.
Hîc condita aevi meta. Sed timeo tibi,
Amata conjux: lege damnatum bona
Sequentur: unde nobilem serves statum
Eripiet hastae Caesare offenso rigor.

Saint Genest, ll. 1211–1212. LUDOVICI CELLOTII *op. cit.*, p. 54.

NATALIA

Nimis est avara cui satis non est, Deo
Dives maritus.

From this point, Cellot, III. 8, Rotrou abandons his original.
In Cellot the sixth scene (Galerius, Adrianus, Anthimus, Metellus)
consists of a long harangue by Anthimus in the presence of the
emperor, who, at the end, orders Adrianus to be led to execution.

The rest of the play of Cellot is filled by various episodes. The Christians are separated; Natalia assumes masculine dress in order to elude Flavius, who seeks her hand, and to penetrate to the dungeon of Adrianus. She meets Flavius, and deceiving him is admitted by him into the prison. Flavius in a long monologue laments that he has incurred Natalia's disfavor. The emperor, hearing that a man has penetrated to the prison of Adrianus, orders the unknown to be brought to his presence. Natalia reveals herself and begs that Adrianus may die last. However, in the fifth act, when the consul orders Adrianus to be executed, "agitque apud eum Natalia ut primus omnium crucietur." In the second scene Natalia encourages Adrianus and supports him in the tortures. In the third scene she contemplates the happiness of Adrianus received up into heaven. Flavius, in the fourth scene, in spite of Natalia's entreaties, orders the body of Adrianus to be cast into the furnace. One hand alone of all the body of Adrianus is preserved and carefully retained by Natalia.

APPENDIX III

ANALYSIS OF DESFONTAINES'S *L'ILLUSTRE COMÉ-DIEN, OU LE MARTYRE DE SAINCT GENEST*

There are, I believe, only two editions of the play by Desfontaines, one printed in 1645 and the other in the following year. Both are in the Bibliothèque Nationale at Paris. The title of the first edition (Yf. Réserve 539) is: L'Illustre / Comedien, / Ov / Le Martyre / De / Sainct Genest. / Tragedie. / A Paris, / Chez Cardin Besongne, au Palais, / au haut de la Montée de la saincte Chappelle, / aux Roses Vermeilles. / M.DC.XLV. / Avec Privilege dv Roy. / 4º. The *privilège* is dated "dernier Avril 1645." "Achevé d'imprimer le 8 may 1645." The author, whose name is nowhere mentioned, in an "Advis au Lecteur" says he has been commanded to follow his Royal Highness on his journey to Bourbon, and has not been present at the printing of his book nor able to furnish the "Epistre liminaire," but the proofs have been submitted to a gentleman of rank, who has corrected them. The second edition is the same as the first, except the date, which is 1646. The copy in the Bibliothèque Nationale (Yf. 4833) has no *privilège*, but has the same "Advis au Lecteur" as in the first edition, and is in octavo.

The list of *acteurs* is as follows: "Diocletian, Empereur Romain; Aquillin, Favory de l'Empereur; Rutile, Conseiller d'Estat de l'Empereur; Genest, Comedien; Aristide, Confident de Genest; Anthenor, Pere de Genest; Pamphilie, Maitresse de Genest; Luciane, Sœur d'Anthenor; Deux Gardes." "La scène est à Rome dans une Salle du Palais de l'Empereur."

In the first scene (Diocletian, Aquillin, Rutile, and two guards) Rutile persuades the emperor to cease his severity towards the Christians and try to win them by kindness. Diocletian declares that severity is necessary. Rutile has a plan to convert the Christians, which is no less than to turn the scaffolds into superb theaters and in them deride the errors and abuses of Christianity:

> Tu sçais combien Genest, cet illustre Comique
> A de grace et d'addresse en tout ce qu'il pratique,
> Et qu'au gré de sa voix, et de ses actions,
> Il peut comme il luy plaist changer nos passions,
> Esgayer nos esprits, les rendre solitaires,
> Amoureux, mesprisans, pitoyables, colères,
> Et par un souverain et merveilleux pouvoir
> Imprimer en nos cœurs tout ce qu'il nous fait voir.
> Commande luy, Seigneur, d'exposer sur la scène
> Les superstitions d'une trouppe peu saine.
>   .   .   .   .
> Si tu doutes encor des traits de sa science
> Tu peux dans ton Palais en faire experience,
> Et par un coup d'essay de cet art merveilleux
> En toy-mesme esprouver ce qu'il pourra sur eux.[1]

The emperor consents and orders Genest to be brought to him at once. Rutile says he is waiting with his company in the next room.

In the second scene (Genest, Pamphilie, Luciane, Anthenor, Aristide, Diocletian, Aquillin, Rutile, a guard) Genest proposes to celebrate the emperor's famous deeds, but Diocletian declares that he wishes another effort of Genest's art, and withdraws, leaving Rutile to explain his will. Rutile then explains his plan:

> Faites voir leurs abus, descouvrez leur erreur,
> Rendez-les des humains et la honte et l'horreur,
> Mocquez-vous de leur foy, riez de leurs mystères,
>   .   .   .   .
> Rendez-les en un mot de tout point ridicules:
> Mais d'ailleurs exaltez Jupiter, nos Hercules,
> Nos Mars, nos Apollons et tous les autres Dieux
> Qu'ont icy de tout temps adoré nos ayeux.

---

[1] In the extracts from Desfontaines's play I have followed the orthography of the original.

Genest replies that nothing could be easier, because these rebels, hated by the gods and men, made him forsake his father and his country; unable to endure their guilty precepts, he freed himself from their crimes by his flight. So that justly animated against them, he will show the errors by which the Christians are charmed, and that their hope is only a fancy, a dream, a folly. Is there anything so absurd as the new mystery that they call "baptism," where, washed by a few drops of water, they think to be raised to heaven? It is by this action, so worthy of derision, that he will begin the *divertissement* which the emperor expects:

> Nous ne sçaurions choisir de plus belle matière,
> C'est là que me donnant une libre carrière,
> Je mettray les Chrestiens en un si mauvais point
> Qu'ils seront insensez, s'ils ne se changent point.

Genest further declares that, without leaving the spot and without any theatrical apparatus, they can arrange their performance. Rutile withdraws and Genest encourages his troupe to win the favor of Caesar. Anthenor asks what history can serve as subject for their plan. Aristide suggests that of Dardaleon[1] or Porphire, who, both favorites of the emperor, were so deceived by the Christians that they became the scorn of the world. Luciane replies that both practiced their profession, and Pamphilie says that baptism was the first action which, soothing the ridiculous grief of these fools, made them lose their wealth and their lives. Genest declares that it is not necessary to seek so far the aid of an historical event:

> Nous pouvons rencontrer dans nostre propre sort,
> De quoy plaire à César qui nous prisera fort
> Si par un trait adroit et de haute industrie
> Il sçait que nous aurons quitté nostre patrie,
> Nos parens et nos biens pour venir en ces lieux,
> Loing de ses ennemis rendre hommage à ses dieux.
> Voicy donc quel sera l'ordre de ce mystère:
> Il faudra qu'Anthenor représente mon père,

[1] Dardaleon is evidently meant for Ardalio, who, as well as Porphyrius, was an actor-martyr. See Introduction, p. 82, note 3.

Et que par un flatteur, quoyque faux entretien,
Il feigne qu'il me veut aussi rendre Chrestien.
Ma sœur qui me portait à cette loi prophane
Avoit, vous le sçavez, de l'air de Luciane,
Qui sçaura, je m'asseure en cette occasion,
Imiter son humeur et son affection.
Aristide d'ailleurs pour vaincre sa folie,
Se dira parmi nous frère de Pamphilie,
Et me conjurera par l'esclat de ses yeux
De ne la point trahir, aussi bien que nos dieux.
Voilà sur ce sujet tout ce qui vous regarde.

At this moment Aquillin enters with presents from the emperor, and the actors burst forth into the most extravagant thanks, with which the first act closes.

The emperor in the second act prepares to witness the play, which begins with the second scene (Genest, Luciane). Luciane endeavors to convert Genest, who cannot follow an unknown one who was

         . . . mis aux liens
Et dans son triste sort abandonné des siens.

Luciane extols this unknown one:

Mais dans l'obscurité son berceau fut illustre.
.   .   .   .
Des Princes d'Orient il receut les hommages,
Et l'astre qui guida ces Mages en ce lieu
Fit bien voir que c'estoit la demeure d'un Dieu.

Genest withstands these arguments and asks to have the subject changed as Anthenor is approaching, who will probably take the side of Luciane. Anthenor asks whether Genest's rebellious heart has yielded. Luciane replies, "As little as a rock which, beaten by the storm, defies the wind and the waves." Genest declares:

Cette comparoison n'est pas mal assortie.
Mon cœur et le rocher ont de la sympathie,
Car si l'un par les vents ne se peut esmouvoir,
Les soupirs ont sur l'autre aussi peu de pouvoir.

A long discussion follows, but Genest remains obdurate, and finally his father casts him off, saying:

> Cessant de m'escouter, cesse aussi de me voir:
> Va, monstre, je suivray la loi que tu me donnes,
> Et t'abandonneray comme tu m'abandonnes.

In the fourth scene (Genest, Pamphilie, Aristide) Genest complains that he is forsaken by all, and he seeks relief in "les divines clartez des yeux de Pamphilie." He explains his situation and bewails his lot. Aristide encourages him, and says that the gods will interest themselves for him, and Pamphilie declares:

> Mais de quelques rigueurs dont le sort vous accable,
> Fussiez-vous en un point encore plus deplorable,
> Je vous puis asseurer que ma fidelité
> Sera jusqu'au tombeau sans inégalité.

Genest does not wish to involve Pamphilie in his misfortunes:

> Ha! Madame! souffrez qu'en ce désordre extrême,
> Ma raison une fois parle contre moy-mesme,
> Et qu'agissant pour vous, elle monstre en ce jour
> Par un estrange effect un véritable amour.

Aristide finally advises Genest, in order to save his inheritance, to feign to follow his father's wishes and to receive, like him, baptism. Genest thinks the effect of this advice would be to offend the gods, and asks Pamphilie,

> A quoy me resoudray-je, aymable Pamphilie?

PAMPHILIE

> Je crains.

ARISTIDE

> Que craignez-vous?

PAMPHILIE

> Tout.

ARISTIDE

> Dieux! quelle folie!
> Vous craignez, dites-vous, Quoy? que deux gouttes d'eau
> De son ardente amour esteignent le flambeau?

PAMPHILIE

Non, mais que cette erreur à la fin ne luy plaise
Et qu'elle n'ayt pour nous une suitte mauvaise.

GENEST

Ha ! ne me croyez pas d'un esprit si peu sain.

PAMPHILIE

Vous pouvez donc agir et suivre ce dessein.

GENEST

Il faut adroitement conduire cette affaire.

The scene and act conclude with Aristide undertaking to see
Genest's father and arrange the stratagem. Genest and Pamphilie are requested by Aristide to meet him at the temple of
the Christians.

At the opening of the third act the emperor praises the skill
of the actors to Rutile, and the play continues in the second
scene :

GENEST

Où suis-je ? Qu'ay-je veu ? Quelle divine flamme
Vient d'esblouir mes yeux, et d'esclaircir mon âme ?
Quelle rayon de lumière espurant mes esprits,
A dissippé l'erreur qui les avoit surpris ?
Je croy, je suis Chrestien ; et cette grace extrême,
Dont je sens les effects est celle du Baptême.

PAMPHILIE

Chrestien ? Qui vous l'a faict ?

GENEST

Je le suis.

ARISTIDE

Resvez-vous ?

GENEST

Un ange m'a faict tel.

ANTHENOR

Devant qui ?

GENEST

Devant tous.

LUCIANE

Personne toutesfois n'a veu cette adventure.

RUTILE, *à l'Empereur*

Il leur va débiter quelque estrange imposture

GENEST

. . . .

Non, Amys, je vous dis des choses véritables,
N'a guères quand icy j'ay paru devant vous,
Les yeux levez au ciel, teste nue, à genoux,
Je voyois, ô merveille à peine concevable !
A travers ce lambris un prodige admirable,
Un ange mille fois plus beau que le soleil,
Et qui me promettant un bonheur sans pareil
M'a dit qu'il ne venoit si je le voulois croire
Que pour me revestir des rayons de sa gloire.

. . . .

L'ange, dont la presence estonnoit mon esprit,
En l'une de ses mains tenoit un livre escrit,
Où la bonté du Ciel secondant mon envie,
Je lisois aisément les crimes de ma vie,
Mais avec un peu d'eau que l'autre main versoit,
Je voyois aussitost que l'escrit s'effaçoit,
Et que par un effect qui passe la nature,
Mon cœur étoit plus calme, et mon âme plus pure.

. . . .

DIOCLETIAN

Cette feinte, Aquillin, commence à me desplaire,
Qu'on cesse.

Genest continues to extol the God of the Christians, and concludes by declaring

Qu'il est seul souverain, seul maistre du tonnerre,
Des cieux, des élémens, des anges, des mortels,
Et digne seul enfin, et d'encens, et d'autels.

The emperor threatens him with punishment if he does not change his language, but he continues :

He bien ! me voilà prest, tyran, allons mourir,
Apportez, apportez ces bienheureuses chaînes,

Instrumens de ma gloire ainsi que de mes peines,
. . . .
Irrite tes bourreaux, invente des tortures,
Et par un sentiment qui ne t'est pas nouveau
Qu'un deluge de sang te venge d'un peu d'eau,
Dont le divin effect m'a donné tant de grâces,
Qu'à tes yeux aujourd'hui je brave tes menaces.

Diocletian orders Rutile to follow the actors and endeavor to
subdue the pride of Genest's invincible heart, to offer him offices,
honors, all that is in Rome, but if he persists the emperor orders
that he be exposed to the

. . . ardeurs d'une flamme cruelle,
Qui sur son corps perfide agissant peu à peu,
Avec mille douleurs le brûle à petit feu.

The emperor then bursts out in a fury against the troupe and
accuses them of having seduced Genest. Pamphilie defends the
company, who, she declares, are innocent, and Anthenor explains
that the supposed relationship in the play does not exist and that
they acted as Christians only by Genest's orders. The others
defend themselves also, and Diocletian finally orders Luciane to
follow Genest and persuade him to renounce his errors. Luciane
suggests that Pamphilie do the same, but she refuses, as it is evident from Genest's action that he never really loved her and his
treason renders him hateful in her eyes. She concludes:

César, si cet ingrat ne change de courage,
Espargne tes bourreaux, il suffit de ma rage,
Tu ne le peux frapper d'un coup plus inhumain,
Laisse désormais cet office à ma main,
Et tu reconnoistras que le fer, et la flamme,
N'ont rien comparable au courroux d'une femme,
A qui par imprudence, ou par légèreté,
On a manqué d'amour ou de fidélité.

Diocletian approves her anger and declares that if Genest does
not change his mind he will abandon him to her rage:

Que tout chargé de fer à tes pieds on l'amène,
Et puis s'il ne se rend, qu'on l'immole à ta hayne.

At the beginning of the fourth act Aristide informs Pamphilie
that nothing has moved Genest and that Rutile has ordered him
to be brought into the presence of Pamphilie. She asks what she
shall do. "Aristide: You know better than I the humor of this
traitor. — Pamphilie: He has deceived me as much and more
than he has you. — Aristide: You are the only one whose anger
he fears." Pamphilie expresses her doubts, but Aristide says it is
Rutile's order and she must make an effort.

In the second scene Pamphilie recites three *stances*, one of
which will suffice here:

> Aveugles tyrans de mon âme,
> Qui régnez sur moi tour à tour,
> Hayne, mespris, vengeance, amour,
> Où se termineront mes fureurs ou ma flamme?
> Hayne, dois-je suivre tes loix?
> Amour, dois-je escouter ta voix?
> Dois-je courir à la vengeance?
> Ou par un plus noble mespris,
> Chercheray-je mon allégeance
> Dans l'oubly des ardeurs dont mon cœur est épris?

At the conclusion of the *stances* Genest and two guards enter
and Pamphilie upbraids him for his wrong to her and ends with
the words:

> Je veux qu'un châtiment aussi rude que prompt
> Dans ton perfide sang en efface l'affront,
> Et montre que par moy ton destin sera pire,
> Que pour avoir choqué ni les dieux ni l'empire.

Genest replies in typical seventeenth-century gallantry:

> Me voilà prest, Madame, et victime enchaisnée,
> Sans regret, à vos pieds j'attends ma destinée.
> . . . .
> Mais si je puis encore espérer quelque grâce,
> Souffrez qu'auparavant le coup qui me menace
> J'ose vous demander quel estrange forfaict
> Vous anime, Madame, à ce cruel effect?

PAMPHILIE

> Quel forfaict, desloyal? ô Dieux, quelle impudence!
> Il est la vertu mesme; et la mesme innocence,

Il n'a jamais manqué ni d'amour ni de foy,
Il n'a jamais trahy ni l'empereur ni moy,
Il ne parla jamais en faveur du baptesme,
Sa bouche n'a jamais proféré de blasphème !
.   .   .   .

Genest explains that formerly he did love her with a sensual
love, but now

Qu'un véritable amour me porte à vous chérir,
Jusqu'à vouloir pour vous tout quitter et mourir.
Me pouvez-vous sans tort appeler infidèle,
Traistre, parjure, ingrat, inconstant, et rebelle ?

Pamphilie asks what name should be applied to him for abandoning her and betraying the gods and his prince. Genest replies
that treachery is innocent and fair and fidelity blamable and
criminal, when a tyrant and gods horrible and pernicious are concerned. How sweet it is to throw off so hateful a yoke and submit
to the laws of an adorable monarch who holds his palace and court
in heaven ! If Pamphilie could receive a ray of grace, she would
esteem little the favor of earthly monarchs. He concludes with a
prayer :

Seigneur, si ta bonté daigne escouter mes vœux,
Accorde à Pamphilie . . .

PAMPHILIE

Arreste, malheureux,
Que veux-tu demander ?

GENEST

Que sa bonté suprême,
Sauve l'autre moitié qui reste de moy-mesme,
Et souffre pour le moins qu'auparavant ma mort,
Je luy tende la main pour la mener au port.
Si j'obtiens dessus vous cette illustre victoire,
Que son heureux effect augmentera ma gloire !
Que mon sort sera doux, que je mourray content,
Si je puis achever ce dessein important !
Ne le différons point, escoutez-moy, Madame.

A long argument follows to prove the powerlessness of the heathen gods:

> Pensez-vous que des dieux de bois, d'or ou de pierre,
> Et dont l'estre est borné dans l'ombre qui l'enserre,
> Des dieux qui ne sont rien que corps inanimez,
> Que la main d'un mortel et le fer ont formez,
> Ayent pu d'une parolle en miracles féconde,
> Créer l'homme, le ciel, l'air, et la terre et l'onde,
> Régler les élémens, semer d'astres les cieux,
> Faire tant de beautez qui brillent à nos yeux,
> Et partout establir cet ordre incomparable,
> Qui maintient l'univers et le rend admirable ?

Genest concludes by begging Pamphilie to accept the favor of the true God, whom he adores:

> Cette mesme faveur est en vostre pouvoir,
> Ne la refusez point, ma chère Pamphilie,
> Que par elle vostre âme à la mienne s'allie,
> Et souffrez qu'aujourd'huy par un si beau bien
> J'unisse pour jamais vostre cœur et le mien.
> Voyez combien pour vous mon amour est extrême.

Pamphilie asks whether he loves her. He answers that he loves her more than himself and declares that he will suffer tortures provided he can purchase for her at the cost of his blood a happiness which she should long for with him.

PAMPHILIE

Hélas !

GENEST

> Vous soupirez, ha ! sans doute la crainte
> Combat vostre désir, et la tient en contrainte,
> Vous redoutez la mort, un tyran vous faict peur.

PAMPHILIE

> Non, non, ne pense pas que je manque de cœur,
> Ces soupirs qu'a produits une sainte tendresse
> Montrent mon repentir, et non pas ma foiblesse,
> Je te suy, cher amant, je te cède, et je croy :
> Ton Dieu règne en mon cœur, et triomphe de moy.

Déjà de ce bonheur je suis toute ravie,
Et regardant tes fers avec un œil d'envie,
Je brûle qu'un tyran n'ordonne à ses bourreaux
De passer en mes mains ces illustres fardeaux.
Ne pouvant les ravir qu'au moins je les soutienne,
Ouy, ces fers sont mes fers, cette chaîne est la mienne,
Puisque par les effects d'une douce rigueur
Elle passe à present de tes mains à mon cœur.

GENEST

Pamphilie, ô transports que me comblez de gloire !

In the fourth scene (Diocletian, Aquillin, Rutile, Genest, Anthenor, Aristide, Luciane, and guards) Pamphilie enters and Rutile tells the emperor that from her looks she has undoubtedly been victorious. Pamphilie exclaims that she has done more than she should have done. Aristide praises the generosity of the emperor, who has overwhelmed them with gifts. Pamphilie upbraids his servility and confesses herself a Christian. Diocletian is enraged and orders Rutile to lead away the insolent ones and reduce them to dust. Rutile and Genest withdraw, and Pamphilie asks whether she is to be separated from Genest. The emperor cries : " No, no, you shall follow him. The same punishment is reserved for you, too."

PAMPHILIE

Comme mesmes tourmens, nous aurons mesme gloire.

ARISTIDE

Mais avant le combat tu chantes la victoire,
La mort aux plus hardis donne de la terreur.

PAMPHILIE

Les lasches comme toy l'ont tousjours en horreur,
Son seul nom te fait peur, mais un noble courage
En affronte les traicts sans changer de visage.

Diocletian says she does wrong to trust to a God who could not save himself from death. Pamphilie then recites five *stances*, of which the first will give a sufficient idea.

> Collosse de boue et d'argile,
>   Qu'idolâtre un peuple fragile,
> Ozes-tu bien tenir ce propos criminel?
> Ozes-tu mesurer ta grandeur à la sienne,
> Et ne connois-tu pas, misérable mortel,
>   Qu'il faut que sa bonté soustienne,
> Que ce Dieu te peut mettre en poudre demain
>   En retirant sa main?

The act ends with Diocletian's words:

> Et mon juste courroux te fera reconnoistre
> Que je suis malgré luy ton seigneur et ton maistre:
> Despeschez, Aquillin, qu'on l'oste, promptement,
> Et qu'on l'aille esgorger aux yeux de son amant.

At the opening of the fifth act Anthenor upbraids Aristide for his sadness and inquires the cause. Aristide replies that it is on account of the approaching punishment of Genest and Pamphilie. Luciane is inflamed with jealousy and, declaring that he loves Pamphilie, withdraws in a rage. Aristide wishes to follow and undeceive her, but Anthenor advises him to let the storm blow over. Diocletian, Rutile, and their suite then enter, and the emperor asks:

> Les tourmens n'ont produit qu'un effet inutile,
> Et ce désespéré souffre sans murmurer
> Tout ce que sans mourir on sçavoit endurer?

RUTILE

> Ouy, César, il endure et brave les supplices,
> On diroit que son cœur y trouve délices
> Et qu'alors que son sang coule de tous costez
> Il nage dans un bain parmy des voluptez.

. . . .

DIOCLETIAN

> Sans doute il s'est muny de la force des charmes,
> Mais qu'a fait Pamphilie en ses tristes alarmes?

Then follows by Rutile a detailed description (fifty-one lines) of the torture of Genest. A few lines will suffice to show its character:

> «Voids, a dit Pamphilie, ô merveilleux vainqueur,
> «Voids, ô mon cher amant, si je manque de cœur,

«Si proche du trépas regarde si je tremble.
«Non, non, je ne crains rien, mourons, mourons ensemble,
«Et puisqu'un sainct hymen nous doit joindre là-haut,
«Que nostre sang versé sur ce cher eschaffaut
«En signe les accords, et soit le premier gage
«Que nous aurons donné de nostre mariage.
«Ces fers nous tiendront lieu de joyaux précieux,
«Ce funèbre appareil de lit délicieux,
«Les bourreaux d'officiers, et toute l'assistance
«De pompe, d'ornement, et de magnificence.»

DIOCLETIAN

Et je crève en mon cœur de despit et de rage
Que de mes propres mains ne le puis-je estouffer.

Rutile continues his account of the torture of Genest, who, apparently, cannot be killed. At length the executioner manages to dispatch Pamphilie.

Genest s'impatiente, et brûle de la suivre.
Il dit que de ses maux le plus grand est de vivre,
Et je crois, ô César, qu'il non faut pas douter :
Mais d'ailleurs s'il ne meurt il est à redouter,
Et je crains que le peuple esmeu de sa constance
Ne se porte à la fin à quelque violence.
Voilà l'occasion qui me ramène icy.

The emperor orders him to return and have Genest executed immediately :

Délivre promptement Rome de cette peste
Avant qu'à nos estats elle soit plus funeste.
Va.

Diocletian laments the constancy of the Christians, whom no torture can free from their blindness :

Mais que veut Aquillin ? il paroit tout esmeu.

The emperor asks whether there has been a revolt. Aquillin answers in the negative, that the people love or fear the emperor's power ; consequently it is not that which disturbs him, but a sad accident. He relates that after having conducted Pamphilie to the place of execution, he was returning to the palace when he saw Luciane, "de quelque desplaisir blessée," throw herself from the bridge into the Tiber. Aristide, seeing the one he loved perish, wished to follow her, but Anthenor endeavored to restrain him. In the mad struggle both fell into the river:

> Attachez l'un à l'autre ils tombent sous les ondes,
> Leur chute fait ouvrir leurs entrailles profondes,
> Qui les ayant trois fois et rendus et repris,
> Pour jamais à la fin estouffent leurs esprits.

Diocletian expresses his pity, but begs Aquillin to reserve his sympathy for him, the emperor, and exclaims:

> Oui, malgré mes grandeurs et les pompes de Rome,
> Je connois, Aquillin, enfin que je suis homme,
> Mais homme abandonné, mais un homme odieux,
> Mais un homme l'horreur des hommes et des dieux.

Aquillin endeavors to comfort him, and concludes with the words:

> Le trône est un azile où ne va pas la crainte,
> Tout le monde sur vous ayant les yeux ouvers,
> Vous ne sçauriez périr qu'avec tout l'univers.

The emperor bursts forth into a long *tirade* (forty-six lines) of remorse and despair. In imagination he sees Genest with Pamphilie:

> Tous deux la palme en main, et tous deux couronnez.
> Chères ombres, pardon, et du ciel où vous estes
> Calmez de mon esprit les horribles tempestes:
> Je fus en vostre endroit cruel et furieux;
> Mais je vous vay ranger au nombre de nos dieux,
> Je vay vous eslever d'illustres mausolées
> Qui toucheront du faistre aux voutes estoilées,
> Et serviront de marque aux siècles à venir
> Et de vostre innocence et de mon repentir.
> Mais, helas! tout à coup ces clartez disparoissent,
> Mon désespoir revient et mes craintes renaissent.
> O dieux, injustes dieux, qui voyez mes ennuis,
> Qui voyez mes tourmens, et l'horreur où je suis,
> Moderez, inhumains, les douleurs que j'endure,
> J'ay vengé vos autels, j'ay vengé vostre injure,

> Et si vous ne voulez qu'on vous croye impuissans
> Vous devez apaiser les tourmens que je sens.
> Mais s'il faut, dieux ingrats, enfin que je périsse,
> Achevez vos rigueurs, et hastez mon supplice.

With these words of Diocletian the play ends. Only the rarity of the work would justify the above lengthy analysis, which shows very clearly that Rotrou owed to Desfontaines nothing but possibly an additional incentive to the composition of a more worthy play on an interesting subject. This we have already seen was the case in another play, *Bélisaire*.

APPENDIX IV

PARALLEL PASSAGES IN ROTROU'S *VENCESLAS* AND IN THE SPANISH ORIGINAL

Venceslas, ll. 8–137. FRANCISCO DE ROJAS, *No hay ser padre siendo rey*, ed. Rivadeneyra, pp. 389–390.

Estadme, Rugero, atento.
. . . .

Decís que estoy ya muy viejo,
(Decís muy bien) y que fuera
Razón, que aquesta corona
Pusiera en vuestra cabeza.
Esto ha de salir de mí,
Que el gobierno y la grandeza
No consiste en procurarla,
Sino sólo en merecerla,
¿ Sabéis á lo que se expone
El que un imperio gobierna ?
No hay cosa bien hecha en él
Que á los suyos lo parezca :
Si es justo, cruel le llaman ;
Si es piadoso, le desprecian ;
Pródigo, si es liberal ;
Avaro, si se refrena ;
Si es pacífico, es cobarde ;
Disoluto, si se alegra ;
Hipócrita, si es modesto ;
Es fácil, si se aconseja.
Pues si la virtud no basta
Al que la virtud conserva,
Vos, todo entregado al ocio,
Al apetito y torpeza,
Mal podréis vivir buen rey

386

Si aun ser bueno no aprovecha.
¿ Y cómo es posible, cómo
(Si ya el cielo no lo trueca),
Que gobierne tanto imperio
Quien á sí no se gobierna?

.   .   .   .

Al duque, que me sustenta
La carga de mis cuidados,
Con rigor y con soberbia
Le queréis quitar la vida

.   .   .   .

Porque le quiero.
Y ahora con vuestro hermano
Habéis tenido allá fuera
Un enojo.

.   .   .   .

En las alarbes fronteras
Gastad esas altiveces,
Y de la gola á las grevas
Sobre el andaluz armado
El rey otomano os vea.
¡ Con tu hermano ! ¡ Bien por Dios !
Y con el Duque, . . .

.   .   .   .

En estas calles y plazas,
Siempre que la aurora argenta
Cuanto ha de dorar con rayos
El padre de las estrellas,
Se hallan muertas mil personas,
Y la desdicha es aquesta ;
Que es tal vuestra mala fama,
Que aunque el vulgo las cometa,
Dice, hecho una lengua todo,
Que tenéis la culpa dellas.

.   .   .   .

Gobernad vuestras acciones

.   .   .   .

Y sois, con acciones nuevas
Comedido en las palabras,
Justiciero en las sentencias,
Piadoso en la ejecución,

Disimulado en la ofensa,
Advertido en los peligros
Y firme en los resistencias.
Si esto hiciéredes, Rugero,
Mi corona, mi grandeza,
Cuanto aquesta espada rige,
Cuanto estas canas gobiernan,
Será vuestro desde luego ;
Pero si no se reserva,
Ni un hermano que os obliga,
Ni un valido que os respeta,
Ni un pueblo que os obedece,
Ni un padre que os amonesta ;
Si soy padre, seré rey.
Porque en tan graves materias,
Quien no premia, no es prudente,
Ni el que no castiga, reina.

RUGERO

Ya que en cualquiera ocasión
Cuanto imagino os molesta,
Hoy me habéis debido en ésta
El cuidado y la atención.
Y aunque llegue á merecer
Con vos nombre de importuno,
Á esos cargos uno á uno
Os tengo de responder.

Venceslas, ll. 141–266. FRANCISCO DE ROJAS, *No hay ser padre siendo rey*, ed. Rivadeneyra, pp. 390–391.

Al descanso ya entregados,
Viéndonos tristes y solos,
Tratamos de murmurar,
Que es éste el manjar del ocio.
Gobernamos tus Estados,
Dispusimos sentenciosos,
Culpamos unos ministros,
Diferenciamos á otros :
Materia que tantos tocan,
Y que la entienden tan pocos.

Ya á murmurar destinados,
Yo, más entonces que todos,
Á tu fama me adelanto
Y á tu impiedad me provoco.
¿ Como (les dije) mi padre
No sacude de los hombros
El peso de esta corona,
Flaco Atlante á tanto globo ?
¿ Piensa, por ventura, piensa
Mi padre que por ser mozo
No sabré regir el cetro
  .   .   .   .   .   .

Ya la política he visto,
Ya tengo previsto el modo
De saber regirse un rey ;
No es difícil, pues con sólo
Ser afable de ordinario,
Ser á veces rigoroso,
Con no ser todo de nadie
Y ser á un tiempo de todos,
Ser remiso en los castigos,
No ser tardo en los negocios,
Con pedir consejo á muchos
Y determinar con pocos,
  .   .   .   .   .   .

Con tener buenos ministros,
(Que en esta parte es el todo),
Ni subir á unos de presto
Ni bajar de presto á otros,
Será un Príncipe perfecto,
Liberal, sabio y dichoso :
  .   .   .   .   .   .

Ya he satisfecho esta parte :
Mas volviendo á los enojos
De tu privado y mi hermano,
Ambos tan tuyos en todo
Que el Duque en tu Estado reina
Cuanto mi hermano en tus ojos,
Digo : que al Duque aborrezco,
Porque lisonjero y loco,
Atrevido, descompuesto

En mi agravio y en su abono
Contigo me ha descompuesto;
Él te enoja si me enojo,
Cuando soy cruel, te avisa;
Calla, cuando soy piadoso;
Si galanteo, lo sabes;
No disimula, si rondo;
Dícete si vengo tarde.
Cállate si me recojo,
Conquista lo que conquisto,
Pretende lo que enamoro.
Y en cuanto á mi hermano, digo,
.   .   .   .

Que he de tomar la venganza
Del fuego á que me provoco,
Si ya en mí, como en su sangre,
La satisfacción no cobro.
¿Bueno es que yo con el Duque,
Ó me incite escandoloso,
Ó imprudente me atropelle
Á decirle mis ahogos,
Y vuelva por él mi hermano
En esa cuadra, y no sólo
Á la defensa se inicte,
Sino que ardiente y furioso
Contra mí el acero empuñe?
.   .   .   .

Si antes que la aurora brode
De luz y esplendor dos polos
.   .   .   .

No he de tomar la venganza
Que debe á mi honor heroico!
.   .   .   .

Que si en todo estoy culpado
Más dicha es, será más logro,
Que si he de llevar la pena
De los delitos de todos,
Sólo ejercite la culpa
Quien ha de pagarlo solo.

REY

(*Ap.* En tanta resolución,
Hoy, que su error no mitigo,
Qué haré? si aquí le castigo
Irrito su indignación.

.   .   .   .)

Puesto que me halle corrido,
Siendo el que me habéis vencido
Vengo á ser el vencedor.
Hoy en vos mi edad reposa;

.   .   .   .   .   .

Los dos uno hemos de ser
Pues tanto amor os abona,
Vuestra será esta corona
Como vuestro mi poder.

RUGERO

Guárdete el cielo, que así
Seré hechura de tu mano.

Venceslas, ll. 267–322. FRANCISCO DE ROJAS, *No hay ser padre siendo rey*, ed. Rivadeneyra, p. 391.

ALEJANDRO

Yo soy.

REY

¿Qué queréis aquí?

Idos.

ALEJANDRO

Quiero hablar con vos.

.   .   .   .   .   .

REY

Llegad, pedidle perdón.

ALEJANDRO

.   .   .   .   .   .

Tus brazos, hermano, pido,
No por haberte ofendido,
Sí por haberte enojado:

.   .   .   .   .   .

RUGERO

.   .   .   .   .   .

Vete, Alejandro, con Dios;
Digo que estás perdonado.

REY

Rugero, lo que he mandado
Es que os abracéis los dos:
Ea, acaba.

RUGERO

Harélo ansí. (*Abrázale*)

Venceslas, ll. 1257–1316. FRANCISCO DE ROJAS, *No hay ser padre siendo rey*, ed. Rivadeneyra, pp. 401–402.

REY

¿ Hijo, Rugero?

RUGERO

Señor . . .

REY

¿ Dónde ahora te adelantas,
La turbación en las plantas
Y el defeto en la color?
¿ Tú levantado, Rugero?
¿ Huir de mi amor intentas?
¿ Todas las manos sangrientas,
Y el semblante todo fiero?
¿ Dónde vas?

RUGERO, *ap.*

¿ Qué le diré?

REY

Dime todo tu dolor.

RUGERO, *turbado*

Digo que sí . . . yo . . . señor,
Iba . . . estaba . . . no lo sé.

.   .   .   .   .   .

REY

¿Y tu hermano?

RUGERO

· No sé dél.

REY

¿No le has visto?

RUGERO

No le he visto.

REY

¿Y de qué es la novedad
De hallarte ya levantado?

RUGERO

¿Pues tambien no ha madrugado
Ahora tu majestad?

REY

Hijo, como el sueño es muerte
Y ya se acaba mi vida,
No quiero que el sueño impida
Lo que me queda de suerte;
Y así si el sueño dejé
En mi cuidado otro empeño,
Pues lo que faltaré al sueño,
Á la vida añadaré.
Y ya como el tiempo quiere
Apresurar mi partida,
Se ha de añadir á la vida
Todo lo que se pudiere.
Pero dime, por tus ojos,
Tu cuidado ó tu dolor,
Pon mi pena y pon mi amor
De parte de tus enojos;
Dime, ¿con quién has reñido?
¿Mas que ha sido con tu hermano?

RUGERO

No, señor.

· · · · · · · ·

(*Sale el Duque*)

DUQUE

La Duquesa quiere hablarte.

RUGERO, *ap.*

¿ Qué es esto ? ¡ válgame Dios !

. . . .

REY

¿ Hijo, qué ibas á decirme ?

RUGERO

Yo no iba á decirte nada.

REY

¿ Y tú, qué quieres contar ?
¿ Cómo así tu labio cesa ?

DUQUE

Que Casandra, la duquesa,
Te quiere, señor, hablar.

REY

Entre..

. . . . . .

RUGERO, *ap.*

. . . . .

¿ Á quién, cielos, dí la muerte ?

Venceslas, ll. 1317–1490. FRANCISCO DE ROJAS, *No hay ser
padre siendo rey*, ed. Rivadeneyra, pp. 402–403.

(*Sale Casandra de luto, y el Duque con ella*)

CASANDRA

Invicto Rey, justiciero,
Rey á quien el cielo ha dado
Mucha templanza en lo airado,
Mucha causa en lo severo :
Oigame tu majestad,
Ó airado ó enternecido,
Que bien merece el oido
Quien ofrece la piedad.

. . . .

¿ Sabéis que soy bien nacida ?

REY

. Vuestro padre, el duque Ursino
Fué tan bueno como yo.

CASANDRA

¿ Fuera de tu honor delito
Que un hijo tuyo, señor,
Se desposara conmigo ?

REY

No hay culpa si hay igualdad.
. . . .

CASANDRA
. . . . . .
¿ Quién pensarás ? El que miras.
    (*Señala á Rugero*)
No lo cuento con indicios,
Él, retórico el semblante,
Presumo que te lo ha dicho,
Atiéndele á los temores,
Y le verás los avisos.
. . . .
Y si mis ruegos no valen,
Si su crueldad no ha podido
Ni ellos reducirte cera
Ni ella administrarte risco,
Abre los ojos y mira
    (*Saca una daga sangrienta*)
El instrumento atrevido
Con que el príncipe Rugero
Violó el corazón más limpio
Que en el templo del amor
Ofrenda fué ó sacrificio.
. . . .
Si cerrares los oídos,
Culparéte la piedad;
. . . .
Y cuando todos me falten
El cielo, que fué el testigo,
Para castigar la culpa
Será juez deste delito.
. . . .

REY

Dadme la espada, Rugero.

RUGERO

Señor, . . . si . . . yo . . . si he querido . . .

REY

No os turbéis, dadme la espada.

RUGERO

Tomad.

REY

Duque Federico,
Á aquesta primera puerta
Llevad á Rugero.

RUGERO, *ap.*

Hoy quiso
La fortuna atar la rueda
Al curso de mis delitos.

. . . .

REY

. . . .

Guardad al Príncipe, Duque,
Y que le aviséis os digo
Que hoy ha de ser un ejemplo
De mi justicia y castigo.

(*Vase el Duque*)

Roberto, id á acompañar
Á Casandra.

CASANDRA

Rey invicto,
No sea, no, tu justicia
Sólo para los principios,
Para el castigo la aguardo,
Venganza pide el delito.

REY

No pienso tomar venganza,
Pero daréle castigo :
Esta palabra os prometo.

. . . .

Dos hijos me ha dado el cielo,
Ya el uno tengo perdido :
¡ Y para vengar aquél
He de perder otro hijo !
(*Vase*)

Venceslas, ll. 1567–1648. FRANCISCO DE ROJAS, *No hay ser padre siendo rey*, ed. Rivadeneyra, pp. 404–405.

REY

Quedaos, no entréis conmigo, porque quiero
Enternecer mis penas con Rugero,
Y no éntre nadie.

.   .   .   .

RUGERO

Señor, ¿ vos en mi prisión ?
¿ Vos á verme tan piadoso,
Negado á lo rigoroso ?
¿ Vos ya sin indignación ?
¿ Vos para darme el perdón
Dejáis la severidad,
Exponéis la majestad
Y olvidáis lo justiciero ?

REY

Dadme los brazos, Rugero.
(*Abrázale*)

RUGERO

Señor, ¿ pues qué novedad
Ha movido vuestro pecho,
Y aún vuestros rigores ? digo
Que hacéis ahora conmigo
Lo que jamás habéis hecho.
¿ Si ya no estáis satisfecho
De mi pena en mis cuidados,
Vos lazos tan ajustados
En vez de rigores fieros ?

REY

Porque han de ser los postreros,
Os los doy tan apretados.

.   .   .   .

¿ Sois mi hijo ?

RUGERO

Soy Rugero.

REY

¿ Sois firme?

RUGERO

Soy animoso.

REY

¿ Valiente?

RUGERO

Soy valeroso.

REY

¿ Osado también?

RUGERO

Soy fiero.

REY

Pues sólo deciros quiero . . .

. . . . . .

Que os prevengáis de valor,
Que bien lo habréis menester.

RUGERO

Pues ¿ qué me queréis decir,
Cuando esperando os estoy?

REY

Quiero deciros que hoy,
Príncipe, habéis de morir.

. . . .

RUGERO

Pues yo á Casandra adoré :
Pensé que al Duque ofendía,
Mintióme la intención mia,
Y al Duque airado busqué.
Y si á mi hermano maté
Un yerro ha sido violento
Que hoy se trueca en escarmiento.

. . . . . .

REY

.   .   .   .

Pero mirad por el alma,
Y quedaos, Príncipe, adios,

.   .   .   .

RUGERO

Pues vamos, pena, á morir :
Pues de su boca escuché
Que él me perdonara padre,
Mas no puede siendo rey.

Venceslas, ll. 1683–1702. FRANCISCO DE ROJAS, *No hay ser padre siendo rey*, ed. Rivadeneyra, pp. 405–406.

CASANDRA

Señor, yo entraba
Por esa cuadra primera,
Á pedir segunda vez
El suplicio á la sentencia
Y ví al príncipe Rugero
Desde esa torre soberbia
Formar los últimos pasos
Y las últimas querellas ;

.   .   .   .

Mi esposo es muerto, señor,
Y cuando el Príncipe muera,
Yo no recojo esta sangre
Porque se derrame aquella,
Si por mí le dabas muerte,
Yo te pido que suspendas
La indignación de tu espada :
Una piedad te lo ruega.

.   .   .   .

Venceslas, ll. 1704–1722. FRANCISCO DE ROJAS, *No hay ser padre siendo rey*, ed. Rivadeneyra, p. 406.

REY

Duquesa, Infante, Señora,
En esta ocasión quisiera
No ser rey por perdonarle ;

Mas será razón que adviertas
Que queda á su indignación
Tu honra y mi vida sujetas.
El que ahora humilde miras,
Mañana con más violencia
Del sagrado de tu casa
Violará las nobles puertas.
Y, como tú me dijiste,
Es evidente sentencia
Que dará muerte á su padre
Quien de su hermano se venga.

. . . .

Venceslas, ll. 1747–1761. FRANCISCO DE ROJAS, *No hay ser padre siendo rey*, ed. Rivadeneyra, p. 406.

DUQUE

        Apenas
El Príncipe en un caballo
Midió la calle primera
Al suplicio, que en la plaza
Determinaba su alteza,
Cuando la plebe conjura
Piadosamente indiscreta
Por el príncipe Rugero
La natural obediencia.
Todos dicen que no puedes,
Aunque justiciero seas,
Dejarles sin heredero;
Y como has oido, alteran,
Trayéndole hasta tu cuarto,
Las pasiones y las lenguas,
Y yo, . . .

REY

Tente, no prosigas

. . . .

Venceslas, ll. 1763–1780. FRANCISCO DE ROJAS, *No hay ser padre siendo rey*, ed. Rivadeneyra, p. 406.

REY

Príncipe, escúchame ahora:
Aquesta corona regia,

Herencia de mis abuelos
Y de su justicia herencia,
Es la que sustituida
Siempre ha estado en mi cabeza;
El pueblo que vivas dice,
Y también su voz me enseña
Que no quiere que yo reine,
Pues deroga mi sentencia.
Atiéndeme ahora á un medio,
Escucha una conveniencia
Para no ser rey en cargos,
Para ser padre en clemencias.

(*Pónele la corona*)

Venceslas, ll. 1781–1800. FRANCISCO DE ROJAS, *No hay ser padre siendo rey*, ed. Rivadeneyra, p. 406.

RUGERO

Gran Señor, ¿qué es lo que haces?

REY

Ponerte esta insignia regia,
Hacer á mi amor un gusto,
Un agasajo á mi pena;
Tú seas rey, yo seré padre;
Siendo sólo padre, es fuerza
Como padre perdonarte,
Y siendo rey, no pudiera;
Pues siendo tú rey ahora,
Es preciso que no puedas
Castigarte tú á ti mismo;
Y ansí, de aquesta manera,
Siendo yo padre, tú rey,
Partimos la diferencia;
Yo no te castigaré;
La plebe queda contenta,
Yo quedaré siendo padre,
Y tú siendo rey te quedas.

RUGERO

Pues tú me dijiste un tiempo,
Bien pienso yo que te acuerdas,

No hay ser padre siendo rey ;
Diga ahora mi obediencia,
No hay ser rey siendo tu hijo,
Pues más quiero en esta empresa
Perder el cetro y la vida,
Que no que tu reino pierdas.

Venceslas, ll. 1801–1803. FRANCISCO DE ROJAS, *No hay ser padre siendo rey*, ed. Rivadeneyra, p. 406.

REY

Hijo, ya estás perdonado ;
Pero no me lo agradezcas,
Que á ser yo rey, te quitara
De los hombros la cabeza ;
. . . . . .

RUGERO

Pues Duque, á mis brazos llega ;
Y á la duquesa Casandra
En esta ocasión me deja
Que los perdones le pida,
Piadosos los cielos quieran
Que te merezca el perdón ;
Y del Senado merezca
Piedad para la censura,
Y aplausos á la comedia.

FIN

BIBLIOGRAPHY

A. BIBLIOGRAPHICAL

BUCHETMANN, F. E., *Jean de Rotrou's Antigone und ihre Quellen: Ein Beitrag zur Geschichte des antiken Einflusses auf die französische Tragödie des siebzehnten Jahrhunderts*, Erlangen und Leipzig, 1901. This work is vol. xxii of *Münchener Beiträge zur romanischen und englischen Philologie herausgegeben von H. Breymann und J. Schick*. It contains a bibliography of the material employed in the work (pages viii–xvi), and an introduction to the study of Rotrou's imitation of classical writers with references to sources bearing on this question (pages 1–32). Buchetmann supplements Steffens and continues the bibliography of Rotrou from 1891 to 1901. Other additions may be found in Stiefel, *Unbekannte italienischen Quellen Jean Rotrou's*, pp. vii–ix.

STEFFENS, G., *Rotrou-Studien. I. Jean de Rotrou als Nachahmer Lope de Vega's: Dissertation zur Erlangung der Doktorwürde*, etc., Oppeln, 1891. The introduction (pages 3–32), "Zur Biographie Rotrou's und zur Geschichte der Rotrou-Forschung," contains an extensive *bibliographie raisonnée* of works on Rotrou down to 1891, with a critical examination of the biographical material relating to Rotrou. There is an important review by Stiefel, with many additions and corrections, of Steffens's dissertation, in *Zeitschrift für französische Sprache und Litteratur*, 1893, vol. xv, pp. 35–40, of *Referate und Rezensionen*.

I have purposely refrained from citing here articles in biographical dictionaries and notices in histories of French literature. Some of the most valuable have been quoted in the introduction. I have mentioned in general only works of importance on which the present account of Rotrou is based, and I have not included the large number of minor works cited in the introduction, which can easily be found by glancing through the index.

B.　BIOGRAPHICAL

I.　Critical

CHARDON, H., *La vie de Rotrou mieux connue*, Paris, 1884.

DIDOT, A. F., *Chefs-d'œuvre tragiques de Rotrou, Crébillon, Lafosse, Scarron et Laharpe*, Paris, 1843. Contains a very good notice of Rotrou with extracts from his miscellaneous poetry.

JAL, A., *Dictionnaire critique de biographie et d'histoire*, Paris, 1872. Contains the two contracts with publishers mentioned in text.

LEMENESTREL, CH., *Jean Rotrou dit " Le Grand" : Ses ancêtres et ses descendants ; Sa vie*, Dreux, 1869.

MERLET, L., *Notice biographique sur Jean Rotrou*, Chartres, 1885. This is the invaluable notice by the abbé Brillon on which the early biographies of Rotrou are based.

PERSON, L., *Notes critiques et biographiques sur le Poète Rotrou*, Paris, 1882. These important notes were reprinted in *Histoire du Venceslas de Rotrou*, pp. 103–148. Reviewed by T de L. (Tamizey de Laroque) in *Revue des Questions historiques*, vol. xxxii, 1882, pp. 342–344 ; and by Marty-Laveaux in *Revue critique d'histoire et de littérature*, vol. xiv, no. 27, pp. 9–10.

　　Les papiers de Pierre Rotrou de Saudreville, secrétaire du Maréchal de Guébriant (Introduction), Paris, 1883. Reviewed by Stiefel in *Litteraturblatt für germanische und romanische Philologie*, 1884, cols. 284–287.

II.　General

CURNIER, LÉONCE, *Étude sur Jean Rotrou*, Paris, 1885. Contributes nothing of value. The second part, " Documents à l'appui," consists merely of analyses of Rotrou's plays with an occasional extract.

GUIZOT, M., *Corneille et son temps*, Paris, 1880. Contains an excellent essay on Rotrou (pages 363–405).

HÉMON, F., *Rotrou : Théâtre choisi*, Paris, 1883. This work is preceded by an essay on " Rotrou et son œuvre," which occupies pages 1–78. This essay is both biographical and critical, but cannot be said to add much to the subject.

HOUSSAYE, A., *Histoire du 41ᵐᵉ fauteuil de l'Académie Française*, Paris, 1894. This work is devoted to the famous Frenchmen who have failed to be elected into the *Académie Française*. It contains a very superficial essay on Rotrou.

JARRY, JULES, *Essai sur les œuvres dramatiques de Jean Rotrou*, Lille, 1868. This work possesses considerable critical value, but is of no importance for Rotrou's biography.

SPORON, WILLIAM, *Jean Rotrou : En litterærhistorisk Studie*, Copenhagen, 1894. A general biographical and critical work of no great originality.

TAILLANDIER, SAINT-RENÉ, *Rotrou : Sa vie et ses œuvres*, Paris, 1865. I have not seen this, but I understand that it is an academic address of no importance.

C. CRITICAL

I. CHRONOLOGY OF PLAYS

STIEFEL, A. L., " Über die Chronologie von J. Rotrou's dramatischen Werken," in *Zeitschrift für französische Sprache und Litteratur*, vol. xvi, 1894, pp. 1–49.

II. SOURCES OF PLAYS

BUCHETMANN, F. E., *Jean de Rotrou's Antigone und ihre Quellen*, Erlangen und Leipzig, 1901. Full title is given above, p. 403.

STEFFENS, G. See p. 403. Steffens discusses Spanish (Lope de Vega) sources of following plays of Rotrou : *La Bague de l'Oubli, Les Occasions perdues, L'Heureuse Constance, Laure Persécutée*. The sources of the following plays are more briefly considered : *La Belle Alphrède, L'Heureux Naufrage, Bélisaire, Don Bernard de Cabrère*, and *Don Lope de Cardone*.

STIEFEL, A. F., *Unbekannte italienischen Quellen Jean de Rotrou's*, in *Zeitschrift für französiche Sprache und Litteratur, V. Supplement*, 1891, pp. 1–159. See Introduction, p. 57, note 2, for contents.

   " Über die Quellen Jean de Rotrou's *Cosroès*," in *Zeitschrift für französische Sprache und Litteratur*, vol. xxiii, pp. 69–188.

   " Über Jean Rotrous spanische Quellen," in *Zeitschrift für französische Sprache und Litteratur*, vol. xxix, pp. 195–234. The first of a series of articles. After alluding incidentally to *L'Hypocondriaque, Les Ménechmes*, and *La Bague de l'Oubli*, the author discusses at length the source of Rotrou's *Diane*, which is Lope de Vega's *La Villana de Xetafe*.

VIANEY, J., *Deux sources inconnues de Rotrou*, Dôle, 1891. Points out the Italian sources of *La Sœur* and *La Pèlerine amoureuse*.

III. Saint Genest

Bernardin, N. M., *Devant le rideau*, Paris, 1901, pp. 123–144, "Le théâtre de Rotrou. Saint Genest."

Parigot, H., *Génie et métier*, Paris, 1894, pp. 75–85, "Saint Genest."

Person, L., *Histoire du véritable Saint-Genest de Rotrou*, Paris, 1882. Reviewed by Stiefel in *Litteraturblatt für germanische und romanische Philologie*, 1884, cols. 284–287; and by A. Morel-Fatio in *Revue critique d'histoire et de littérature*, vol. xiv, no. 37, pp. 201–204.

IV. Venceslas

Giesse, A., "Étude sur le Venceslas," in *Jahresbericht über das Realprogymnasium und Progymnasium zu Homburg v. d. Höhe*, Homburg v. d. Höhe, 1892, pp. 3–12.

Person, L., *Histoire du Venceslas de Rotrou suivie des notes critiques et biographiques*, Paris, 1882. Reviewed by Stiefel in article cited above in *Litteraturblatt*, etc.

Zirwer, Dr. Otto, *Étude sur Venceslas: Tragédie de Rotrou. Programm*, Berlin, 1903.

D. GRAMMATICAL AND LEXICOGRAPHICAL

Benoist, Antoine, "Notes sur la langue de Rotrou," in *Annales de la Faculté des Lettres de Bordeaux*, 1882, vol. iv, pp. 365–412.

Franzen, Mathias, *Über den Sprachgebrauch Jean Rotrou's: Inaugural-Dissertation*, Rheinbach, 1892. 4to, 41 pages.

Sölter, Karl, *Grammatische und lexikologische Studien über Jean Rotrou: Inaugural-Dissertation*, Altona, 1882. 16mo, 68 pages.

The value of the works above mentioned is greatly impaired by the fact that the text used in all cases is the entirely untrustworthy one in Viollet-le-Duc's edition, Paris, 1820.

In this connection may be mentioned a brief *lexique* of Rotrou contained in the Appendix to Jarry, *Essai sur les œuvres dramatiques de Rotrou* (pages 300–324), and a study of the metaphors in the play of *La Sœur* by E. Degenhardt, "Die Metapher bei den Vorläufern Molière's, 1612–1654," in *Ausgaben und Abhandlungen*, lxxii, Marburg, 1888, pp. 49–54.

E. EDITIONS OF *SAINT GENEST* AND *VENCESLAS*

I. Saint Genest

1647. Le / Veritable / St Genest, / Tragedie, / De Mr / De Rotrou. / A Paris, / Chez Tovssainct Qvinet, au Palais, dans / la petite Salle, sous la montee de la Cour des Aydes, / M. DC. XXXXVII. / Auec Priuilege du Roy. / 4to, ii + 104 pages. P. (1) *Extraict du Priuilege du Roy.* March 2, 1647. Antoine de Sommauille is permitted to print, etc.: "Le dit Sommauille a associé au dit Priuilege Toussainct Quinet aussi Marchand Libraire à Paris suiuant l'accord fait entr'eux. Acheué d'imprimer pour la première fois le 26, May, 1647. Les exemplaires ont esté fournis." Paris, Bib. Nat., Yf, 277. *Réserve.* This copy is in a "recueil factice," lettered *Recveil de Comedie* [sic]. *To. 10.* This is the only copy I have found with date of 1647 on title-page. Although the *privilège* was granted to Antoine de Sommaville, I have found no copy bearing his name as printer. He must have transferred his rights to Quinet, who alone printed the work. This edition is, except date, the same as that of 1648. Saint Genest has no dedication.

1648. Le / Veritable / St Genest, / Tragedie, / De Mr / De Rotrou. / A Paris, / Chez Toussainct Quinet, au Palais, dans / la petite Salle, sous la montée de la Cour des Aydes. / MDCXXXXVIII. / Auec Privilege du Roy. / 4to, ii + 104 pages. Exactly the same, except date, as the edition of 1647. Paris, Bib. Nat., Yf, 431 ; Bib. Ars., 10847, B.L.; Bib. Maz., 10918, 12 ; Brit. Mus., 85, i, 11 ; Harvard College Lib., 8585, 85. There is a copy in the Bib. Nat., p. Yf, 38, in a "recueil factice," which differs from the edition of 1647 only in the typographical ornament on page 1.

1666. Saint / Genest, / Tragedie. / No title-page, place, date, or printer. P. (1) *Saint / Genest, / Tragedie.* / P. (2) *Acteurs,* etc. P. (3) *St. Genest, / Tragedie. / Acte Premier,* / etc. On pages 4–76 follows the tragedy. This edition is entered in the catalogue of the Bib. Nat., Paris : "Saint Genest, Paris, G. de Luyne, 1666, 12mo." Yth, 16017–16018. There is a copy in the Brit. Mus., 163, e, 22.

1666. Saint Genest. In *Recueil de tragédies saintes.* Paris, Estienne Loyson, 1666. 12mo. A "recueil factice." See *Catalogue of the Soleinne Collection.*

1705. Saint Genest. In *Théâtre François ou recueil des meilleures pièces de théâtre des anciens auteurs.* Paris, Pierre Ribou, 1705. (3 vols., 12mo.) Vol. ii. Brit. Mus., 242, f. 16–18.

1737. *Saint Genest.* In *Théâtre François ou recueil des meilleures pièces de théâtre.* Paris, 1737. (12 vols., 12mo.) Vol. i, pp. 227–433.

1820. *Saint Genest.* In *Jean Rotrou: Œuvres.* Paris, 1820. (5 vols., 8vo.) Vol. v, pp. 1–84. This is the only edition of Rotrou's complete works and was edited by Viollet-le-Duc.

1862. *Saint Genest.* In *Chefs-d'Œuvre tragiques.* Paris, Librairie de Firmin Didot, etc., 1862. (2 vols., 12mo.) Vol. i, pp. 1–58.

1882. *Saint Genest.* In *Théâtre choisi de J. De Rotrou: Avec une étude par Louis de Ronchaud.* Paris, Librairie des Bibliophiles, 1882. (2 vols., 16mo.) Vol. i, pp. 165–248.

1883. *Saint Genest.* In *Rotrou: Théâtre choisi. Nouvelle édition avec une introduction et des notices par M. Félix Hémon.* Paris, Laplace, Sanchez et Cie., 1883. 12mo. Pp. 280–335.

II. VENCESLAS

1648. *Venceslas, / Tragi-Comedie. / De Mr De Rotrov. / A Paris. / Chez Antoine De Somma- / Ville, au Palais dans la petite Salle / des Mer-ciers, à l'Escu de France. / M. DC. XLVIII. / Avec Privilege du Roy. /* 4to, v + 110 pages. *Privilège 28 Mars, 1648. Achevé d'Imprimer le douzième May, 1648.* Paris, Bib. Nat., p. Yf, 38. *Réserve*; Bib. Ars., 10847, B.L. There is another copy, Bib. Nat., Yf, 377, *Réserve*, exactly like above except that dedication is lacking and title-page is followed directly by *Extraict du Privilege du Roy.* A copy is in Bib. Ars., Theat. N. 17586; Brit. Mus., 85, i, 11; and Harvard College Library, 8585, 84. Venceslas is dedicated to the Prince de Poix. This dedication is printed in Ronchaud, ii, pp. 95–97. Although of no historical value I give it from the original, for the sake of completeness, in a note.[1]

[1] A Monseigneur Monseigneur De Créquy, Prince De Poix, Seigneur De Canaples, de Pont-Dormy, etc. Et premier Gentilhomme de la chambre du Roi. Monseigneur, — Venceslas, encore tout glorieux des applaudissemens qu'il a reçus de la plus grande reine du monde, et de la plus belle cour de l'Europe ne pouvant restreindre son ambition aux caresses et à l'estime du beau monde, ose aujourd'hui se montrer à toute la France, sous l'honneur de la protection que vous lui avez promise; et ne craint point de s'exposer aux ennemis que sa gloire lui peut susciter, ayant pour asile l'une des plus anciennes et plus illustres maisons du royaume, et pour défenseur l'héritier des vertus, comme du sang, des plus fameux appuis de nos rois, et des plus redoutables bras de l'État. Personne n'ignore, Monseigneur, que les grandes actions de ces grands hommes à qui vous avez succedé font presque toute la beauté de notre histoire, et que l'antiquité grecque et romaine n'a rien vu de plus mémorable que ce que les

1648. *Venceslas : Tragédie de Mr. de Rotrou. Suivant la copie imprimée à Paris.* "Hollande. Elzev. 1648. Petit in 12mo." *Catalogue of the Soleinne Collection.* There is also mentioned in the same catalogue : *Recueil de pièces imprimées en Hollande par les Elzeviers, suivant la copie imprimée à Paris, 1648–49. A la Sphère.* Contains *Venceslas,* etc.

1655. *Venceslas, / Tragicomedie / De Mr De Rotrou. / Sur L'Imprimé. / A Paris. / Chez Anthoine De Sommaville. / Au Palais, dans la*

derniers siècles ont vu faire au grand Daguerre, père de l'une de vos aïeules, et au glorieux Connêtable de l'Esdiguierre, votre bisaïeul, dont le premier sortit victorieux de ce fameux duel qu'un de nos rois lui permit à Sedan, où son ennemi combattait avec tant d'avantage, et le second fit sa renommée si célèbre par les batailles de Pontcharra et de Salbertran, et servit la couronne par de si prodigieux succès qu'il en mérita les premières charges. Il fut suivi de l'indomptable maréchal de Créquy, votre aïeul, qui signala par une infinité de preuves la passion qu'il avait pour son prince, et par un illustre et double combat, que la postérité n'oubliera jamais, celle qu'il avait pour sa gloire. La volée de canon qui l'emporta dans le glorieux emploi qui l'occupait en Italie, fait encore aujourd'-hui voler son nom aussi loin que le bruit des actions héroïques peut aller ; et sa vertu se continua en celle de Monsieur de Canaples, votre père, dont la vie et la mort representèrent dignement celles de ses devanciers. Il est impossible de comprendre dans la juste étendue d'une lettre la mémoire de tant de héros, et je laisse à l'histoire les panégyriques des fameux Pont-Dormys, dont l'un fut frère d'armes de l'incomparable Bayard, et mérita de passer en sa créance pour la valeur même ; je dirai seulement, Monseigneur, qu'il ne vous suffit pas d'être riche de la gloire d'autrui, vous ne vous contentez pas des acquisitions qu'on vous a faites, et vous ne vous croiriez pas digne successeur de ces illustres personnes si vous ne leur ressembliez et si vous ne vous deviez la plus belle partie de votre estime ; l'Italie a retrouvé dans le fils la valeur des pères, et le sang que vous coûta l'effort qu'elle fit contre votre vie fut autant une marque de la frayeur que vous lui fîtes que du péril où votre grand cœur vous précipita ; vous avez poussé jusqu'aux bords de la Sègre cette ardeur sans mesure qui vous attache si fortement aux intérêts de votre maître, et, partout où votre courage vous a porté, l'on a si clairement reconnu le sang dont vous sortez que nos ennemis peuvent avec raison douter de la perte de ces grands personnages que vous réparez si dignement. Ces vérités étant très constantes, Venceslas, (Monseigneur), a-t-il lieu de rien redouter sous l'autorité d'un si digne protecteur ? Faites-lui la grâce de le souffrir, puisque vous l'avez daigné flatter de cette espérance, et qu'il se donne à vous sans autre considération que l'honneur d'être vôtre et de m'obtenir de vous la permission de me dire avec toutes les soumissions que je vous dois, Monseigneur, Votre très humble et très obéissant serviteur. ROTROU.

The nobleman to whom the play was dedicated was Charles III, sire de Blanchefort and prince de Poix, duc de Créquy, born about 1623 and dying at Paris, February 13, 1687. He was a distinguished soldier and ambassador to Rome, where in 1662 he was the object of an insult by the papal guard, for which the pope was compelled to offer an apology, disband the Corsican guard who had been guilty of the offense, and erect an obelisk with an inscription commemorating the offense and its punishment.

petite salle des Merciers, / *à l'Escu de France.* / *M. DC. LV.* / 12mo, x + 83 pages.　Paris, Bib. Nat., Yth, 18808.

1705. *Venceslas.* In *Théâtre François ou recueil des meilleures pièces de théâtre des anciens auteurs,* etc.　Vol. i.　Brit Mus., 242, f. 16.

1708. *Venceslas,* / *Tragi-Comedie.* / *De Mr De Rotrou.* / *A Paris,* / *Chez Pierre Ribou, sur le Quay des Augustins, à la descente du Pont-* / *neuf, à l'Image S. Louï.* / *M. DC. XCXVIII.* / *Avec Privilege du Roy.* / 12 mo, i + 92 pages.　Paris, Bib. Nat., Yf, 4871.

1716. *Venceslas, Tragi-Comedie de Mr. de Rotrou.*　Paris, Chez Christophe David, 1716.　In Archives de la Comédie-Francaise.

1718. *Venceslas,* / *Tragi-Comedie.* / *De Mr De Rotrou.* / *A Paris,* / *Chez Pierre Ribou, seul Libraire* / *de l'Académie Royale de Musique,* / *sur* / *le Quay des Augustins,* / *à la descente* / *du Pont Neuf, à l'Image* / *S. Louïs. M. DCC. XVIII.* / *Avec Approbation et Privilege du Roy.* 12mo, 91 pages.　Paris, Bib. Nat., Yth, 18812; Bib. Ars., Theat. N. 10768.

1737. *Venceslas.* In *Théâtre François ou recueil des meilleures pièces de théâtre,* etc.　Vol. i, pp. 463–577.

1759. *Venceslas,* / *Tragedie* / *De Rotrou.* / *Retouchée par M. Marmontel.* / *Prix 30 sols.　A Paris.* / *Chez Sébastien Jorry.　Imprimeur-Libraire,* / *rue et vis-à-vis la Comédie Françoise, au* / *Grand Monarque & aux Cigognes.* / *M. DCC. LIX.* / 8vo, viii + 93 pages.　Paris, Bib. Nat., Yth, 18815; Bib. Ars., Theat. N. 10558.　This is the first edition of Marmontel's version.

1773. *Venceslas.* In *Chefs-d'œuvre dramatiques, ou recueil des meilleures pièces du Théâtre François, tragique, comique et lyrique.　Avec trois discours préliminaires sur les trois genres, et des remarques sur la langue et le goût.　Par M. Marmontel, Historiographe de France, l'un des Quarante de l'Académie Française.　Dédié à Madame la Dauphine.　Paris, MDCCLXXIII.* 4to.　This beautifully printed volume contains Mairet's *Sophonisbe,* du Ryer's *Scévole,* and Rotrou's *Venceslas,* with lives of the authors, examination of plays, and remarks.　All except text of plays may be more conveniently found in Marmontel, *Œuvres complètes,* Paris, 1820, vol. vii. I have used the copy in the library of the Arsenal, Paris, 10173, B.L. There is a copy in the Bib. Nat., Yf, 601.　*Réserve.*

1774. *Venceslas,* / *Tragédie* / *En Cinq Actes,* / *Par M. Rotrou ;* / *Représentée pour la première fois en* / *1647, et réimprimée sur le manuscrit des Comédiens du Roy en 1774.* / *Prix 30 sols.* / *A Paris,* / *Chez la Veuve Duchesne, Libraire, rue Sainte-* / *Jacques, au Temple du Goût.* / *Avec Approbation et Privilège du Roy.* / 12mo, 96 pages.

Paris, Bib. Nat., Yth, 18815. Is this the same edition mentioned in the *Catalogue of the Soleinne Collection*: *Venceslas. Retouché par Colardeau*, Paris, Ve Duchesne, 1774?

1780. *Venceslas.* In *Recueil des meilleures pièces dramatiques faites en France depuis Rotrou jusqu'à nos jours, ou le Théâtre François.* Lyon, Joseph Sulpice Grabit. 8vo. "(Publié par Delisle de Salles.)" *Catalogue of the Soleinne Collection.*

1784. *Venceslas.* In *Petite Bibliothèque des Théâtres, contenant un recueil des meilleures pièces du Théâtre François, tragique, comique, lirrique* [sic] *et bouffon, depuis l'origine des spectacles en France jusqu'à nos jours. Paris, MDCC. LXXIV.* Petit in 12mo. Contains portrait of Rotrou after the bust by Caffiéri, life of Rotrou, catalogue of his plays, and *Venceslas.* Paris, Bib. Ars., 10175, B.L. In the list of Rotrou's plays is this note: "*Venceslas* . . . représentée en 1647, et imprimée à Paris l'année suivante in 4to chez Antoine de Sommaville." The above volume is one of the collection which contains eighty volumes, published between 1784 and 1789. See *Catalogue of the Soleinne Collection.*

1785. *Venceslas.* In *Bibliothèque universelle des Dames.* Paris, 1785–1797. (156 vols., 12mo.) *Théâtre*, vol. i. Brit. Mus., 12206, d, 29.

1803. *Venceslas.* In C. B. Petitot. *Répertoire du Théâtre François.* Paris, 1803–1804. (23 vols., 8vo.) Vol. i. Brit. Mus., 86, e, 1.

1808. *Venceslas.* In *Théâtre des auteurs du second ordre. Tragédie.* Paris, 1808–1810. (40 vols., 12mo.) Vol. i. Brit. Mus., 242, d, 8.

1813. *Venceslas.* In *Répertoire général du Théâtre François.* Paris, 1813. (57 vols., 12mo.) Vol. xxiv. Brit. Mus., 11735, e. Paris, Bib. Nat., Yf, 5242.

1818. *Venceslas:* In *Répertoire général du Théâtre François, Théâtre du second ordre.* Paris, H. Nicolle, 1818. Paris, Bib. Nat., Yf, 5297.

1819. *Venceslas. Tragédie de Rotrou ; Représentée, pour la première fois, sur le Théâtre de l'Hôtel de Bourgogne, par la Troupe royale en 1647 ; et remise au Théâtre avec des changements faits par Marmontel, le Lundi 30 avril 1759. Nouvelle édition, conforme à la représentation. A Paris, Chez Barba, Libraire, au Palais Royal, derrière le Théâtre François, 1819.* 8vo, 99 pages. At bottom of page are Marmontel's changes. Bib. Nat., Yth, 1882.

1820. *Venceslas.* In *Œuvres*, ed. Viollet-le-Duc. Vol. v., pp. 173–262.

1821. *Venceslas.* In *Répertoire général du Théâtre François. Théâtre du second ordre. Tragédies.* Tome i, Paris. Chez Théodore Dabo, 1821. Paris, Bib. Nat., Yf, 5364.

1823. *Venceslas.* In *Répertoire du Théâtre François, Tome I. Chefs-d'œuvre de Scarron et Rotrou.* Paris. Imprimerie de Jules Didot, aîné. 1823. Paris, Bib. Nat., Yf, 5575.

1862. *Venceslas.* In *Chefs-d'Œuvre tragiques.* Vol. i, pp. 55–120.

1875. *Venceslas : Tragédie en cinq actes et en vers. Par Rotrou.* Paris, Michel Lévy Frères, Editeurs, 1875. 8vo, 52 pages. On outside cover: *Bibliothèque Dramatique : Théâtre Moderne.*

1882. *Venceslas.* In Ronchaud, *Théâtre choisi*, etc. Vol. ii, pp. 95–182.

1883. *Venceslas.* In Hémon, *Théâtre choisi*, etc. Pp. 395–454.

TRANSLATIONS

1699. *Il / Vincislao. / Opera Tragicomica / Di / Pietro Cornelio, / Tradotta dal Francese, & / accomodata all' uso / delle Scene / d'Italia. / In Bologna, 1699. / Per il Longhi. Con licenza de' Superiori. /* 12mo, 95 pages. Paris, Bib. Nat., Yf, 6889. A literal prose translation of Rotrou's play curiously enough ascribed to Corneille.

NOTE

The other plays of Rotrou have, since the original editions, been reprinted as follows :

Don Bernarde de Cabrère, in *Théâtre François*, etc., 1705, vol. i; *Théâtre François ou recueil*, etc., 1737, vol. i; Ronchaud, *Théâtre choisi*, 1882, vol. ii; and Hémon, *Théâtre choisi*, 1883.

Hercule mourant, in *Théâtre François*, 1705, vol. i; *Théâtre François*, 1737, vol. i; and Ronchaud, *Théâtre choisi*, vol. i.

Cosroès, in *Théâtre François*, 1737, vol. ii; Ronchaud, vol. ii; and Hémon.

Antigone, in Ronchaud, vol. i.

Laure Persécutée, in *Théâtre François*, 1737, vol. i, and Hémon.

La Sœur, in E. Fournier, *Le Théâtre Français au xvi*[e] *et au xvii*[e] *siècle*, Paris, 1871 ; Hémon ; and T. Martel, *Comédies du xvii*[e] *siècle*, Paris, 1888.

Les Sosies, in *Bibliotheca classica Latina* (Lemaire), vol. liv, Paris, 1830, not complete ; and Hémon.

Les Captifs, in *Bibliotheca classica Latina*, vol. liv, not complete.

Les Ménechmes, in *Bibliotheca classica Latina*, vol. lv, not complete.

The above mentioned plays are of course included in the complete edition of Rotrou's works edited by Viollet-le-Duc, Paris, 1820.

The original editions of Rotrou's plays are now very scarce. The Boston Public Library has a copy of *Les Ménechmes*, Paris, A. de Sommaville, 1636, 4to, and Harvard College Library has an almost complete collection made by the late Professor Bôcher. Only four of the thirty-five plays are lacking: *Célie*, *Clorinde*, *Don Lope de Cardone*, and *Florimonde*.

Since the above Bibliography was prepared I have seen the *Mémoire* of Laurent Mahelot mentioned in note 1 to page 8, printed in the *Mémoires de la Société de l'Histoire de Paris et de l'Île de France*, tome xxviii, 1901, but without the reproduction of the sketches. In the note to page 8 I omitted to say that two additional sketches of Mahelot's scenery are published in the English version of Jusserand's *Shakespeare in France under the Ancien Régime*, New York and London, 1899, pages 71 and 75. These scenes are for Puget de la Serre's *Pandoste ou la Princesse Malheureuse* (*Winter's Tale*) and excellently illustrate the "multiple scene."

INDEX TO INTRODUCTION

INDEX TO NOTES[1]

[1] The references are to lines and to the first occurrence of the word or construction noted. Other instances can usually be found by means of the cross references in the notes.

vapeur = vent, St. G., 1444.

venir à bout de, Venc., 421.

Verb

Absolute use of certain verbs :
commettre, St. G., 1257;
forcer, St. G., 274; obtenir,
Venc., 1860; placer, St. G.,
451; réciter, St. G., 372.

Agreement of singular verb with
several subjects, St. G., 339.

Auxiliary

Être for avoir with périr, St. G.,
765.

Omission or non-repetition of
auxiliary with several compound tenses, St. G., 175.

Compound tenses, position of
object with, St. G., 540.

Construction

After verbs of seeing, etc., indirect object of pronoun for
direct, St. G., 499.

Verb construed with two
complements of a different
nature, St. G., 737.

Forms

Omission of s in first person :
voi for vois, St. G., 1321;
sui for suis, St. G., 1589.

die for dise, St. G., 1127.

puis for peux, St. G., 19.

û for ue : avoûrez, St. G., 303;
désavoûrez, Venc., 973; diminûra, Venc., 816; tûra,
Venc., 1447.

Infinitive

Active with passive sense
after laisser, faire, etc., St.
G., 647.

In exclamatory clauses, St.
G., 597, 1606.

Three infinitives in succession, Venc., 178.

With à, as clause of result,
St. G., 1548; as definition,
Venc., 1365.

Participle, past, absolute use,
Venc., 143.

Participle, present, gerundive
use, St. G., 43; in conditional
sentences, Venc., 1309.

Reflexive verbs, without reflexive pronouns, St. G., 956;
Venc., 204; transferred reflexive, St. G., 436; reflexive
for passive, St. G., 668.

Tenses

Conditional of possibility,
Venc., 667.

Conditional past, Venc., 81.

Future perfect, St. G., 1484.

Imperfect indicative in apodosis of conditional sen-
tences, Venc., 1310.

Present for future, St. G., 1036.

vertu = power, strength, St. G., 656.

vieil, for vieux, Venc., 25.

vif, au, St. G., 581.

vœux = love, affections, St. G., 149.

vouloir de, Venc., 405.